Lecture Notes in Computer Science 6094

Commenced Publication in 1973
Founding and Former Series Editors:
Gerhard Goos, Juris Hartmanis, and Jan van Leeuwen

Editorial Board

David Hutchison
  Lancaster University, UK
Takeo Kanade
  Carnegie Mellon University, Pittsburgh, PA, USA
Josef Kittler
  University of Surrey, Guildford, UK
Jon M. Kleinberg
  Cornell University, Ithaca, NY, USA
Alfred Kobsa
  University of California, Irvine, CA, USA
Friedemann Mattern
  ETH Zurich, Switzerland
John C. Mitchell
  Stanford University, CA, USA
Moni Naor
  Weizmann Institute of Science, Rehovot, Israel
Oscar Nierstrasz
  University of Bern, Switzerland
C. Pandu Rangan
  Indian Institute of Technology, Madras, India
Bernhard Steffen
  TU Dortmund University, Germany
Madhu Sudan
  Microsoft Research, Cambridge, MA, USA
Demetri Terzopoulos
  University of California, Los Angeles, CA, USA
Doug Tygar
  University of California, Berkeley, CA, USA
Gerhard Weikum
  Max-Planck Institute of Computer Science, Saarbruecken, Germany

Vincent Aleven   Judy Kay   Jack Mostow (Eds.)

Intelligent Tutoring Systems

10th International Conference, ITS 2010
Pittsburgh, PA, USA, June 14-18, 2010
Proceedings, Part I

 Springer

Volume Editors

Vincent Aleven
Carnegie Mellon University, Human-Computer Interaction Institute
5000 Forbes Avenue, Pittsburgh, PA 15213, USA
E-mail: aleven@cs.cmu.edu

Judy Kay
University of Sydney, School of Information Technologies
1 Cleveland Street, Sydney 2006, Australia
E-mail: judy.kay@sydney.edu.au

Jack Mostow
Carnegie Mellon University, School of Computer Science
5000 Forbes Avenue, Pittsburgh, PA 15213, USA
E-mail: mostow@cs.cmu.edu

Library of Congress Control Number: 2010927366

CR Subject Classification (1998): I.2.6, J.4, H.1.2, H.5.1, J.5, K.4.2

LNCS Sublibrary: SL 2 – Programming and Software Engineering

ISSN   0302-9743
ISBN-10 3-642-13387-8 Springer Berlin Heidelberg New York
ISBN-13 978-3-642-13387-9 Springer Berlin Heidelberg New York

This work is subject to copyright. All rights are reserved, whether the whole or part of the material is concerned, specifically the rights of translation, reprinting, re-use of illustrations, recitation, broadcasting, reproduction on microfilms or in any other way, and storage in data banks. Duplication of this publication or parts thereof is permitted only under the provisions of the German Copyright Law of September 9, 1965, in its current version, and permission for use must always be obtained from Springer. Violations are liable to prosecution under the German Copyright Law.

springer.com

© Springer-Verlag Berlin Heidelberg 2010
Printed in Germany

Typesetting: Camera-ready by author, data conversion by Scientific Publishing Services, Chennai, India
Printed on acid-free paper   06/3180

Preface

The 10th International Conference on Intelligent Tutoring Systems, ITS 2010, continued the bi-annual series of top-flight international conferences on the use of advanced educational technologies that are adaptive to users or groups of users. These highly interdisciplinary conferences bring together researchers in the learning sciences, computer science, cognitive or educational psychology, cognitive science, artificial intelligence, machine learning, and linguistics. The theme of the ITS 2010 conference was *Bridges to Learning,* a theme that connects the scientific content of the conference and the geography of Pittsburgh, the host city. The conference addressed the use of advanced technologies as bridges for learners and facilitators of robust learning outcomes.

We received a total of 186 submissions from 26 countries on 5 continents: Australia, Brazil, Canada, China, Estonia, France, Georgia, Germany, Greece, India, Italy, Japan, Korea, Mexico, The Netherlands, New Zealand, Pakistan, Philippines, Saudi Arabia, Singapore, Slovakia, Spain, Thailand, Turkey, the UK and USA. We accepted 61 full papers (38%) and 58 short papers. The diversity of the field is reflected in the range of topics represented by the papers submitted, selected by the authors. The most popular topics among the accepted (full and short) papers were: empirical studies of learning with advanced learning technologies (34 accepted papers), educational data mining (EDM) and machine learning (28), evaluation of systems (23), pedagogical agents (21), natural language interaction (20), affect (19), intelligent games (16), pedagogical strategies (15), models of learners, facilitators, groups and communities (15), and domain-specific: mathematics (15). Of course, many papers covered multiple topics.

We are delighted that five outstanding and world-renowned researchers accepted our invitation to give invited talks during the conference. Abstracts of their presentations are included in this set of proceedings. Chee-Kit Looi from the National Institute of Education (Singapore) shared insights into comprehensive initiatives in Singapore's education system, which involve partnerships between researchers and classroom practice. Stacy Marsella from the Institute of Creative Technologies (University of Southern California) spoke about the role of emotion and emotion modeling in systems with virtual characters. Alexander Renkl from the University of Freiburg (Germany) suggested a way of reconciling theoretical views on learning held by proponents of socio-constructivist approaches with cognitively oriented approaches and discussed implications for the design of ITS. Steven Ritter from Carnegie Learning, Inc. (Pittsburgh, USA) spoke about the third wave of ITS, which takes advantage of the large user base of real-world ITS for purposes of data mining and end-user authoring. Finally, Beverly Woolf, from the University of Massachusetts, Amherst, described the emergence of social and caring computer tutors, which respond to both affect and cognition.

The proceedings contain 17 short papers within the important Young Researchers Track (YRT). This track represents the future of our field. It provides a forum in which PhD students present and discuss their work during its early stages, with mentoring from more senior members of the community. All submissions were carefully reviewed by experts. The proceedings also include 18 abstracts of Interactive Events that during the conference showcased an interesting mixture of mature systems and late-breaking developments in ITS and related tools for authoring, assessment, data analysis, etc. Rounding out the scientific program of the conference were six workshops and three tutorials.

All full papers and short papers included in the proceedings were stringently peer-reviewed. Reflecting the strength of the ITS community, we received a large number of submissions of very high quality. The review process rested significantly on the outstanding team of international experts from 24 countries who made up the Program Committee, the Senior Program Committee and the Advisory Board. Reviewers started the process by bidding on abstracts, ensuring that they were reviewing in areas of their particular interest and expertise. Conflicts of interest were identified so that no paper was assigned to a reviewer who is a close collaborator or colleague of any of the paper's authors. Each paper received at least three reviews. One of the reviewers was a member of the Senior Program Committee, who was also responsible for leading an online discussion of the paper and then writing a meta-review. Criteria for reviews of papers were: relevance, originality, significance, evaluation, related work, organization and readability. The final decisions for acceptance were made by the Program Co-chairs who, working in concert, carefully studied the reviews, discussion and meta-reviews, often initiating additional discussion among reviewers. In some cases, we (the Program Co-chairs) sought additional reviewers. For the most difficult decisions, we also read the papers. In making the hard decisions on accepting full papers, we were largely driven by the reviews and meta-reviews. Where the scores were close, we took into account all review criteria, and in our final decision weighed the relative importance of a paper's strengths and weaknesses. We also considered the different classes of contributions: for example, a full paper describing a new system designed to improve learning should include a sound evaluation or at minimum a convincing pilot study. For short papers, the novelty and potential of the work were key requirements. Due to the large number of high-quality submissions, our choices were difficult. This is a very pleasing situation for the ITS community and augurs well for the future as some of the papers we could not accept have the promise to be excellent future publications.

The quality of the reviews was extremely high, which was critical in enabling us to distinguish the highest quality work for acceptance as full papers. In addition, high-quality reviews are critical for researchers as feedback on their research and their papers, regardless of whether they are accepted for publication or not. For example, many reviews pointed to additional relevant literature, identified particular strengths and gave concrete advice on how to address weaknesses. We believe that authors of many of the rejected papers will be able to use this feedback to produce excellent papers in the future. We worked very hard to select the Program Committee, the Senior Program Committee and the Advisory Board so we could meet these goals. We are pleased to announce the following Outstanding Reviewer Awards: Ivon Arroyo,

Kevin Ashley, Ryan Baker, Joseph Beck, Gautam Biswas, Sydney d'Mello, Peter Brusilovsky, Vania Dimitrova, Neil Heffernan, Akihiro Kashihara, Brent Martin, H. Chad Lane, James Lester, Diane Litman, Rose Luckin, Stellan Ohlsson, Niels Pinkwart, Steven Ritter, Ido Roll, Carolyn Rosé, Peter Sloep, John Stamper and Gerhard Weber.

A scientific conference of the size of ITS 2010 can only succeed due to contributions of many people who generously donate their time. Of great significance are the contributions of the large number of people who helped with the review process: the Advisory Board, the Senior Program Committee, the Program Committee, as well as people who volunteered as reviewers. We are extremely grateful to them for the time and effort they put in. Special thanks are due to the people who volunteered to organize workshops and tutorials, which made up a key part of the scientific program of the conference. We also thank the Chairs for Workshops / Tutorials, Young Researcher Track / Doctoral Consortium, Interactive Events, and Panels, all of whom had a major influence on the scientific program. The Local Arrangements Chairs devoted countless hours of preparation to make the conference actually happen successfully "on the ground." The Volunteers / Outings Chairs recruited and organized dozens of students not only to help run the conference but to lead small-group outings tailored to individual interests in the ITS spirit. The Conference Treasurer organized our budget meticulously, the Sponsorship Chair increased it handsomely, and the Publicity Chair got the word out widely. Lynnetta Miller of Carnegie Mellon deserves special recognition for contributing in multiple guises (conference secretary, artist, webmaster). A special word of thanks is due to Carolyn Manley of Carnegie Mellon's Conference and Event Services, who among other things administered (along with programmer Alex Lang) the online registration system. We would like to thank Kevin Ashley, Vania Dimitrova, Ben du Boulay, Claude Frasson, Art Graesser, Alan Lesgold, James Lester, Roger Nkambou, Beverly Woolf, and other past organizers of ITS and AIED conferences for their kind assistance and sage advice. We are very grateful to Jo Bodnar of Carnegie Mellon and student volunteers Matthew Easterday, Richard Gluga, and Michael Lipschultz for the very significant role they played in assembling the proceedings. And we would like to thank our sponsors, listed later, whose support for the conference we gratefully acknowledge.

Our final thanks must be to the authors whose papers appear in these volumes. They have contributed many exciting new ideas and a comprehensive body of carefully validated work that will serve as an advanced technology bridge to improved learning in real educational settings.

April 2010

Vincent Aleven
Judy Kay
Jack Mostow

Organization

Conference Chair: Jack Mostow
Program Chairs: Vincent Aleven, Judy Kay
General Chair: Alan Lesgold
Conference Secretary: Lynnetta Miller
Conference Treasurer: Albert Corbett
Local Arrangements Chairs: Sandra Katz, Bruce McLaren
Workshops and Tutorials Chairs: Joe Beck, Niels Pinkwart
Young Researchers Track Chairs: Ricardo Conejo, Carolyn Penstein Rosé
Interactive Events Chairs: Noboru Matsuda, Tanja Mitrovic
Panels Chairs: Cristina Conati, Chee-Kit Looi
Publicity Chair: Susan Bull
Volunteers Chairs: Collin Lynch, Amy Ogan
Sponsorship Chair: Steve Ritter

Advisory Board

Bert Bredeweg	University of Amsterdam, The Netherlands
Claude Frasson	University of Montreal, Canada
Monique Grandbastien	Université Henri Poincaré, France
Lewis Johnson	University of Southern California, USA
Kenneth Koedinger	Carnegie Mellon University, USA
Gordon McCalla	University of Saskatchewan, Canada
Helen Pain	University of Edinburgh, UK
Beverly Woolf	University of Massachusetts, USA

Senior Program Committee

Esma Aimeur	University of Montreal, Canada
Ivon Arroyo	University of Massachusetts, USA
Kevin Ashley	University of Pittsburgh, USA
Ryan Baker	Worcester Polytechnic Institute, USA
Beatriz Barros	University of Malaga, Spain
Joseph Beck	Worcester Polytechnic Institute, USA
Gautam Biswas	Vanderbilt University, USA
Paul Brna	University of Edinburgh, UK
Peter Brusilovsky	University of Pittsburgh, USA
Tak-Wai Chan	National Central University of Taiwan, Taiwan
Cristina Conati	University of British Columbia, Canada
Ulrike Cress	University of Tübingen, Germany
Vania Dimitrova	University of Leeds, UK

Benedict du Boulay	University of Sussex, UK
Art Graesser	University of Memphis, USA
Jim Greer	University of Saskatchewan, Canada
Peter Hastings	DePaul University, USA
Neil Heffernan	Worcester Polytechnic Institute, USA
Susanne Lajoie	McGill University, Canada
Chad Lane	University of Southern California, USA
James Lester	North Carolina State University, USA
Diane Litman	University of Pittsburgh, USA
Chee-Kit Looi	National Institute of Education, Singapore
Rosemary Luckin	University of Sussex, UK
Jean-Marc Labat	Université Pierre et Marie Curie, France
Brent Martin	University of Canterbury, New Zealand
Tanja Mitrovic	University of Canterbury, New Zealand
Riichiro Mizoguchi	University of Osaka, Japan
Rafael Morales	University of Guadalajara, Mexico
Wolfgang Nejdl	L3S and University of Hannover, Germany
Roger Nkambou	University of Quebec at Montreal, Canada
Niels Pinkwart	Clausthal University of Technology, Germany
Kaska Porayska-Pomsta	London Knowledge Lab, UK
Carolyn Rosé	Carnegie Mellon University, USA
Kurt Van Lehn	Arizona State University, USA
Julita Vassileva	University of Saskatchewan, Canada
Maria Virvou	University of Piraeus, Greece
Vincent Wade	Trinity College Dublin, Ireland
Kalina Yacef	University of Sydney, Australia

Program Committee

Ana Arruarte	University of the Basque Country, Spain
Roger Azevedo	University of Memphis, USA
Tiffany Barnes	University of North Carolina at Charlotte, USA
Mária Bieliková	Slovak University of Technology in Bratislava, Slovakia
Emmanuel Blanchard	McGill University, Canada
Steve Blessing	University of Tampa, USA
Jacqueline Bourdeau	Distance University, University of Quebec at Montreal, Canada
Nicola Capuano	University of Salerno, Italy
Zhi-Hong Chen	National Central University, Taiwan
Chih-Yueh Chou	Yuan Ze University, Taiwan
Scotty Craig	University of Memphis, USA
Alexandra Cristea	University of Warwick, UK
Richard Cox	University of Sussex, UK
Michel Desmarais	Polytechnique Montreal, Canada
Sydney D'Mello	University of Memphis, USA

Peter Dolog	Aalborg University, Denmark
Isabel Fernandez de Castro	University of Basque Country, Spain
Yusuke Hayashi	Osaka University, Japan
Tsukasa Hirashima	Hiroshima University, Japan
Pamela Jordan	University of Pittsburgh, USA
Akihiro Kashihara	The University of Electro-Communications, Japan
Chao-Lin Liu	National Chengchi University, Taiwan
Manolis Mavrikis	London Knowledge Lab, UK
Riccardo Mazza	University of Lugano/University of Applied Sciences of Southern Switzerland, Switzerland
Danielle McNamara	University of Memphis, USA
Erica Melis	German Artificial Intelligence Centre, Germany
Alessandro Micarelli	University of Rome, Italy
Kazuhisa Miwa	Nagoya University, Japan
Chas Murray	Carnegie Learning, Inc., USA
Stellan Ohlsson	University of Illinois at Chicago, USA
Ana Paiva	University of Lisbon, Portugal
Andrew Ravenscroft	London Metropolitan University, UK
Genaro Rebolledo-Mendez	University of Sussex, UK
Steve Ritter	Carnegie Learning, Inc., USA
Didith Rodrigo	Ateneo de Manila University, Philippines
Ido Roll	University of British Columbia, Canada
Sudeshna Sarkar	IIT Kharagpur, India
Yong Se Kim	Sungkyunkwan University, Republic of Korea
Mike Sharples	University of Nottingham, UK
Peter Sloep	Open University, The Netherlands
John Stamper	Carnegie Mellon University, USA
Leen-Kiat Soh	University of Nebraska-Lincoln, USA
Akira Takeuchi	Kyushu Institute of Technology, Japan
Pierre Tchounikine	University du Maine, France
Andre Tricot	University of Toulouse, France
Wouter van Joolingen	University of Twente, The Netherlands
Nicolas Vanlabeke	University of Nottingham, UK
Rosa Vicari	The Federal University of Rio Grande do Sul, Brazil
Gerhard Weber	University of Education Freiburg, Germany
Stephan Weibelzahl	National College of Ireland, Ireland
Lung-Hsiang Wong	Nanyang Technological University, Singapore
Diego Zapata-Rivera	Educational Testing Service, USA

Reviewers

Nilufar Baghaei	CSIRO ICT Centre, Australia
Quincy Brown	University of Maryland, USA
Mingyu Feng	SRI International, USA
Sylvie Girard	Université du Maine, France
Natalie Person	University of Rhodes, USA
Rachel Pilkington	University of Birmingham, UK

Leena Razzaq   University of Massachusetts, USA
Felisa Verdejo   National University of Distance Education, Spain
Ning Wang   University of Southern California, USA
Shumin Wu   IBM, USA

Workshops

Question Generation
Kristy Elizabeth Boyer and Paul Piwek

Culturally Aware Tutoring Systems
Emmanuel G. Blanchard, W. Lewis Johnson, Amy Ogan and Danièle Allard

Supporting the Social Inclusion of Communities with Adaptive Learning Media
Fabio Akhras and Paul Brna

Opportunities for Intelligent and Adaptive Behavior in Collaborative Learning Systems
Ari Bader-Natal, Erin Walker and Carolyn Rosé

Computer-Supported Peer Review in Education: Synergies with Intelligent Tutoring Systems
Ilya Goldin, Peter Brusilovsky, Christian Schunn, Kevin Ashley and I-Han Hsiao

Intelligent Tutoring Technologies for Ill-Defined Problems and Ill-Defined Domains
Collin Lynch, Kevin Ashley, Tanja Mitrovic, Vania Dimitrova, Niels Pinkwart and Vincent Aleven

Tutorials

Using DataShop to Analyze Educational Data
John Stamper

How to Apply Software Architecture and Patterns to Tutoring System Development?
Javier Gonzalez-Sanchez and Maria-Elena Chavez-Echeagaray

Seven Deadly Sins: Avoiding Several Common Statistical Pitfalls
Joseph Beck

Organization   XIII

Sponsors

Apangea Learning
Pittsburgh, PA
www.apangea.com

Carnegie Learning, Inc.
Pittsburgh, PA
www.carnegielearning.com

Edalytics, LLC
Pittsburgh
www.edalytics.com

Grockit
San Francisco, CA
grockit.com

Kaplan, Inc.
New York, NY
www.kaplan.com

Learning Research and Development Center
University of Pittsburgh
www.lrdc.pitt.edu

National Science Foundation
Division of Information and Intelligent Systems
Human-Centered Computing Program
Washington, DC
www.nsf.gov

LearnLab
Pittsburgh Science of Learning Center

Pittsburgh Science of Learning Center
www.learnlab.org

Carnegie Mellon
SCHOOL OF COMPUTER SCIENCE

School of Computer Science
Carnegie Mellon University
www.cs.cmu.edu

UNIVERSITY OF PITTSBURGH
SCHOOL OF EDUCATION

School of Education
University of Pittsburgh
www.education.pitt.edu

Table of Contents – Part I

Invited Talks

Can Research-Based Technology Change School-Based Learning? Perspectives from Singapore 1
Chee-Kit Looi

Modeling Emotion and Its Expression 2
Stacy Marsella

Active Learning in Technology-Enhanced Environments: On Sensible and Less Sensible Conceptions of "Active" and Their Instructional Consequences.. 3
Alexander Renkl

Riding the Third Wave 4
Steven Ritter

Social and Caring Tutors: ITS 2010 Keynote Address 5
Beverly Park Woolf

Educational Data Mining 1

Predicting Correctness of Problem Solving in ITS with a Temporal Collaborative Filtering Approach 15
Suleyman Cetintas, Luo Si, Yan Ping Xin, and Casey Hord

Detecting the Moment of Learning 25
Ryan S.J.d. Baker, Adam B. Goldstein, and Neil T. Heffernan

Comparing Knowledge Tracing and Performance Factor Analysis by Using Multiple Model Fitting Procedures 35
Yue Gong, Joseph E. Beck, and Neil T. Heffernan

Natural Language Interaction 1

Automatic Question Generation for Literature Review Writing Support 45
Ming Liu, Rafael A. Calvo, and Vasile Rus

Characterizing the Effectiveness of Tutorial Dialogue with Hidden Markov Models 55
Kristy Elizabeth Boyer, Robert Phillips, Amy Ingram, Eun Young Ha, Michael Wallis, Mladen Vouk, and James Lester

Exploiting Predictable Response Training to Improve Automatic
Recognition of Children's Spoken Responses......................... 65
  Wei Chen, Jack Mostow, and Gregory Aist

ITS in Ill-Defined Domains

Leveraging a Domain Ontology to Increase the Quality of Feedback in
an Intelligent Tutoring System....................................... 75
  Hameedullah Kazi, Peter Haddawy, and Siriwan Suebnukarn

Modeling Long Term Learning of Generic Skills....................... 85
  Richard Gluga, Judy Kay, and Tim Lever

Eliciting Informative Feedback in Peer Review: Importance of
Problem-Specific Scaffolding.. 95
  Ilya M. Goldin and Kevin D. Ashley

Inquiry Learning

Layered Development and Evaluation for Intelligent Support in
Exploratory Environments: The Case of Microworlds 105
  Sergio Gutierrez-Santos, Manolis Mavrikis, and George Magoulas

The Invention Lab: Using a Hybrid of Model Tracing and
Constraint-Based Modeling to Offer Intelligent Support in Inquiry
Environments 115
  Ido Roll, Vincent Aleven, and Kenneth R. Koedinger

Discovering and Recognizing Student Interaction Patterns in
Exploratory Learning Environments 125
  Andrea Bernardini and Cristina Conati

Collaborative and Group Learning 1

Lesson Study Communities on Web to Support Teacher Collaboration
for Professional Development 135
  Yukari Kato and Masatoshi Ishikawa

Using Problem-Solving Context to Assess Help Quality in
Computer-Mediated Peer Tutoring 145
  *Erin Walker, Sean Walker, Nikol Rummel, and
  Kenneth R. Koedinger*

Socially Capable Conversational Tutors Can Be Effective in
Collaborative Learning Situations 156
  Rohit Kumar, Hua Ai, Jack L. Beuth, and Carolyn P. Rosé

Intelligent Games 1

Facial Expressions and Politeness Effect in Foreign Language Training System 165
  Ning Wang, W. Lewis Johnson, and Jonathan Gratch

Intercultural Negotiation with Virtual Humans: The Effect of Social Goals on Gameplay and Learning 174
  Amy Ogan, Vincent Aleven, Julia Kim, and Christopher Jones

Gaming the System

An Analysis of Gaming Behaviors in an Intelligent Tutoring System 184
  Kasia Muldner, Winslow Burleson, Brett Van de Sande, and Kurt VanLehn

The Fine-Grained Impact of Gaming (?) on Learning 194
  Yue Gong, Joseph E. Beck, Neil T. Heffernan, and Elijah Forbes-Summers

Squeezing Out Gaming Behavior in a Dialog-Based ITS 204
  Peter Hastings, Elizabeth Arnott-Hill, and David Allbritton

Pedagogical Strategies 1

Analogies, Explanations, and Practice: Examining How Task Types Affect Second Language Grammar Learning 214
  Ruth Wylie, Kenneth R. Koedinger, and Teruko Mitamura

Do Micro-Level Tutorial Decisions Matter: Applying Reinforcement Learning to Induce Pedagogical Tutorial Tactics 224
  Min Chi, Kurt VanLehn, and Diane Litman

Examining the Role of Gestures in Expert Tutoring 235
  Betsy Williams, Claire Williams, Nick Volgas, Brian Yuan, and Natalie Person

Affect 1

A Time for Emoting: When Affect-Sensitivity Is and Isn't Effective at Promoting Deep Learning 245
  Sidney D'Mello, Blair Lehman, Jeremiah Sullins, Rosaire Daigle, Rebekah Combs, Kimberly Vogt, Lydia Perkins, and Art Graesser

The Affective and Learning Profiles of Students Using an Intelligent Tutoring System for Algebra 255
  Maria Carminda V. Lagud and Ma. Mercedes T. Rodrigo

The Impact of System Feedback on Learners' Affective and
Physiological States 264
  Payam Aghaei Pour, M. Sazzad Hussain, Omar AlZoubi,
  Sidney D'Mello, and Rafael A. Calvo

Games and Augmented Reality

Investigating the Relationship between Presence and Learning in a
Serious Game 274
  H. Chad Lane, Matthew J. Hays, Daniel Auerbach, and Mark G. Core

Developing Empirically Based Student Personality Profiles for Affective
Feedback Models... 285
  Jennifer Robison, Scott McQuiggan, and James Lester

Evaluating the Usability of an Augmented Reality Based Educational
Application 296
  Jorge Martín-Gutiérrez, Manuel Contero, and Mariano Alcañiz

Pedagogical Agents, Learning Companions, and Teachable Agents

What Do Children Favor as Embodied Pedagogical Agents? 307
  Sylvie Girard and Hilary Johnson

Learning by Teaching SimStudent: Technical Accomplishments and an
Initial Use with Students.. 317
  Noboru Matsuda, Victoria Keiser, Rohan Raizada, Arthur Tu,
  Gabriel Stylianides, William W. Cohen, and Kenneth R. Koedinger

The Effect of Motivational Learning Companions on Low Achieving
Students and Students with Disabilities 327
  Beverly Park Woolf, Ivon Arroyo, Kasia Muldner,
  Winslow Burleson, David G. Cooper, Robert Dolan, and
  Robert M. Christopherson

Intelligent Tutoring and Scaffolding 1

Use of a Medical ITS Improves Reporting Performance among
Community Pathologists.. 338
  Rebecca Crowley, Dana Grzybicki, Elizabeth Legowski,
  Lynn Wagner, Melissa Castine, Olga Medvedeva, Eugene Tseytlin,
  Drazen Jukic, and Stephen Raab

Hints: Is It Better to Give or Wait to Be Asked? 349
  Leena Razzaq and Neil T. Heffernan

Error-Flagging Support for Testing and Its Effect on Adaptation 359
   Amruth N. Kumar

Metacognition

Emotions and Motivation on Performance during Multimedia Learning:
How Do I Feel and Why Do I Care? 369
   Amber Chauncey and Roger Azevedo

Metacognition and Learning in Spoken Dialogue Computer Tutoring . . . 379
   Kate Forbes-Riley and Diane Litman

A Self-regulator for Navigational Learning in Hyperspace 389
   Akihiro Kashihara and Ryoya Kawai

Pedagogical Strategies 2

How Adaptive Is an Expert Human Tutor? 401
   Michelene T.H. Chi and Marguerite Roy

Blocked versus Interleaved Practice with Multiple Representations in
an Intelligent Tutoring System for Fractions 413
   Martina A. Rau, Vincent Aleven, and Nikol Rummel

Improving Math Learning through Intelligent Tutoring and Basic Skills
Training 423
   Ivon Arroyo, Beverly Park Woolf, James M. Royer,
   Minghui Tai, and Sara English

Author Index 433

Table of Contents – Part II

Affect 2

The Intricate Dance between Cognition and Emotion during Expert Tutoring 1
    Blair Lehman, Sidney D'Mello, and Natalie Person

Subliminally Enhancing Self-esteem: Impact on Learner Performance and Affective State 11
    Imène Jraidi and Claude Frasson

Detecting Learner Frustration: Towards Mainstream Use Cases 21
    Judi McCuaig, Mike Pearlstein, and Andrew Judd

Educational Data Mining 2

Enhancing the Automatic Generation of Hints with Expert Seeding 31
    John Stamper, Tiffany Barnes, and Marvin Croy

Learning What Works in ITS from Non-traditional Randomized Controlled Trial Data... 41
    Zachary A. Pardos, Matthew D. Dailey, and Neil T. Heffernan

Natural Language Interaction 2

Persuasive Dialogues in an Intelligent Tutoring System for Medical Diagnosis 51
    Amin Rahati and Froduald Kabanza

Predicting Student Knowledge Level from Domain-Independent Function and Content Words 62
    Claire Williams and Sidney D'Mello

KSC-PaL: A Peer Learning Agent 72
    Cynthia Kersey, Barbara Di Eugenio, Pamela Jordan, and Sandra Katz

Authoring Tools and Theoretical Synthesis

Transforming a Linear Module into an Adaptive One: Tackling the Challenge 82
    Jonathan G.K. Foss and Alexandra I. Cristea

An Authoring Tool to Support the Design and Use of Theory-Based
Collaborative Learning Activities 92
   *Seiji Isotani, Riichiro Mizoguchi, Sadao Isotani, Olimpio M. Capeli,
   Naoko Isotani, and Antonio R.P.L. de Albuquerque*

How to Build Bridges between Intelligent Tutoring System Subfields of
Research 103
   Philip Pavlik Jr. and Joe Toth

Collaborative and Group Learning 2

Recognizing Dialogue Content in Student Collaborative Conversation ... 113
   Toby Dragon, Mark Floryan, Beverly Woolf, and Tom Murray

Supporting Learners' Self-organization: An Exploratory Study 123
   Patrice Moguel, Pierre Tchounikine, and André Tricot

Exploring the Effectiveness of Social Capabilities and Goal Alignment
in Computer Supported Collaborative Learning 134
   *Hua Ai, Rohit Kumar, Dong Nguyen, Amrut Nagasunder, and
   Carolyn P. Rosé*

Intelligent Games 2

Virtual Humans with Secrets: Learning to Detect Verbal Cues to
Deception 144
   *H. Chad Lane, Mike Schneider, Stephen W. Michael,
   Justin S. Albrechtsen, and Christian A. Meissner*

Optimizing Story-Based Learning: An Investigation of Student
Narrative Profiles 155
   Seung Y. Lee, Bradford W. Mott, and James C. Lester

Integrating Learning and Engagement in Narrative-Centered Learning
Environments 166
   *Jonathan P. Rowe, Lucy R. Shores, Bradford W. Mott, and
   James C. Lester*

Intelligent Tutoring and Scaffolding 2

Collaborative Lecturing by Human and Computer Tutors 178
   *Sidney D'Mello, Patrick Hays, Claire Williams, Whitney Cade,
   Jennifer Brown, and Andrew Olney*

Computational Workflows for Assessing Student Learning 188
   Jun Ma, Erin Shaw, and Jihie Kim

Predictors of Transfer of Experimental Design Skills in Elementary and
Middle School Children 198
   *Stephanie Siler, David Klahr, Cressida Magaro, Kevin Willows, and
   Dana Mowery*

Young Researchers Track

Moodle Discussion Forum Analyzer Tool (DFAT) 209
   Palak Baid, Hui Soo Chae, Faisal Anwar, and Gary Natriello

Peer-Based Intelligent Tutoring Systems: A Corpus-Oriented
Approach 212
   John Champaign and Robin Cohen

Intelligent Tutoring Systems, Educational Data Mining, and the Design
and Evaluation of Video Games... 215
   Michael Eagle and Tiffany Barnes

An Intelligent Debater for Teaching Argumentation 218
   Matthew W. Easterday

Multiple Interactive Representations for Fractions Learning 221
   Laurens Feenstra, Vincent Aleven, Nikol Rummel, and Niels Taatgen

An Interactive Educational Diagrammatic System for Assessing and
Remediating the Graph-as-Picture Misconception 224
   Grecia Garcia Garcia and Richard Cox

Long Term Student Learner Modeling and Curriculum Mapping 227
   Richard Gluga

Student Dispositions and Help-Seeking in Collaborative Learning 230
   Iris K. Howley and Carolyn Penstein Rosé

Visualizing Educational Data from Logic Tutors 233
   Matthew Johnson and Tiffany Barnes

An Authoring Language as a Key to Usability in a Problem-Solving
ITS Framework 236
   *Jean-François Lebeau, Luc Paquette, Mikaël Fortin, and
   André Mayers*

Towards the Creation of a Data-Driven Programming Tutor 239
   Behrooz Mostafavi and Tiffany Barnes

Using Expert Models to Provide Feedback on Clinical Reasoning
Skills 242
   Laura Naismith and Susanne P. Lajoie

Algorithms for Robust Knowledge Extraction in Learning
Environments 245
 Ifeyinwa Okoye, Keith Maull, and Tamara Sumner

Integrating Sophisticated Domain-Independent Pedagogical Behaviors
in an ITS Framework... 248
 Luc Paquette, Jean-François Lebeau, and André Mayers

Delivering Tutoring Feedback Using Persuasive Dialogues 251
 Amin Rahati and Froduald Kabanza

Coordinate Geometry Learning Environment with Game-Like
Properties... 254
 Dovan Rai, Joseph E. Beck, and Neil T. Heffernan

Long-Term Benefits of Direct Instruction with Reification for Learning
the Control of Variables Strategy 257
 Michael A. Sao Pedro, Janice D. Gobert, and Juelaila J. Raziuddin

Short Papers

Can Affect Be Detected from Intelligent Tutoring System Interaction
Data? – A Preliminary Study...................................... 260
 Elizabeth A. Anglo and Ma. Mercedes T. Rodrigo

Comparing Disengaged Behavior within a Cognitive Tutor in the USA
and Philippines 263
 *Ma. Mercedes T. Rodrigo, Ryan S.J.d. Baker, Jenilyn Agapito,
 Julieta Nabos, Ma. Concepcion Repalam, and Salvador S. Reyes Jr.*

Adaptive Tutorials for Virtual Microscopy: A Design Paradigm to
Promote Pedagogical Ownership 266
 Dror Ben-Naim, Gary Velan, Nadine Marcus, and Michael Bain

The Online Deteriorating Patient: An Adaptive Simulation to Foster
Expertise in Emergency Decision-Making 269
 *Emmanuel G. Blanchard, Jeffrey Wiseman, Laura Naismith,
 Yuan-Jin Hong, and Susanne P. Lajoie*

DynaLearn: Architecture and Approach for Investigating Conceptual
System Knowledge Acquisition 272
 *Bert Bredeweg, Jochem Liem, Floris Linnebank,
 René Bühling, Michael Wißner, Jorge Gracia del Río, Paulo Salles,
 Wouter Beek, and Asunción Gómez Pérez*

Interfaces for Inspectable Learner Models 275
 *Susan Bull, Andrew Mabbott, Rasyidi Johan, Matthew Johnson,
 Kris Lee-Shim, and Tim Lloyd*

Conceptual Personalization Technology: Promoting Effective
Self-directed, Online Learning 278
  Kirsten R. Butcher, Tamara Sumner, Keith Maull, and
  Ifeyinwa Okoye

Learning to Identify Students' Relevant and Irrelevant Questions in a
Micro-blogging Supported Classroom 281
  Suleyman Cetintas, Luo Si, Sugato Chakravarty, Hans Aagard, and
  Kyle Bowen

Using Emotional Coping Strategies in Intelligent Tutoring Systems 285
  Soumaya Chaffar and Claude Frasson

Showing the Positive Influence of Subliminal Cues on Learner's
Performance and Intuition: An ERP Study 288
  Pierre Chalfoun and Claude Frasson

Exploring the Relationship between Learner EEG Mental Engagement
and Affect 291
  Maher Chaouachi and Claude Frasson

MiBoard: Creating a Virtual Environment from a Physical
Environment 294
  Kyle Dempsey, G. Tanner Jackson, and Danielle S. McNamara

Players' Motivation and EEG Waves Patterns in a Serious Game
Environment 297
  Lotfi Derbali and Claude Frasson

Predicting the Effects of Skill Model Changes on Student Progress 300
  Daniel Dickison, Steven Ritter, Tristan Nixon, Thomas K. Harris,
  Brendon Towle, R. Charles Murray, and Robert G.M. Hausmann

Data Mining to Generate Individualised Feedback 303
  Anna Katrina Dominguez, Kalina Yacef, and James R. Curran

In the Zone: Towards Detecting Student Zoning Out Using Supervised
Machine Learning 306
  Joanna Drummond and Diane Litman

Can We Get Better Assessment from a Tutoring System Compared
to Traditional Paper Testing? Can We Have Our Cake (Better
Assessment) and Eat It too (Student Learning during the Test)? 309
  Mingyu Feng and Neil Heffernan

Using Data Mining Findings to Aid Searching for Better Cognitive
Models 312
  Mingyu Feng, Neil T. Heffernan, and Kenneth Koedinger

Generating Proactive Feedback to Help Students Stay on Track 315
Davide Fossati, Barbara Di Eugenio, Stellan Ohlsson,
Christopher Brown, and Lin Chen

ITS in Ill-Defined Domains: Toward Hybrid Approaches 318
Philippe Fournier-Viger, Roger Nkambou,
Engelbert Mephu Nguifo, and André Mayers

Analyzing Student Gaming with Bayesian Networks 321
Stephen Giguere, Joseph Beck, and Ryan Baker

EdiScenE: A System to Help the Design of Online Learning
Activities 324
Patricia Gounon and Pascal Leroux

Critiquing Media Reports with Flawed Scientific Findings: *Operation*
ARIES! A Game with Animated Agents and Natural Language
Trialogues 327
Art Graesser, Anne Britt, Keith Millis, Patty Wallace,
Diane Halpern, Zhiqiang Cai, Kris Kopp, and Carol Forsyth

A Case-Based Reasoning Approach to Provide Adaptive Feedback in
Microworlds 330
Sergio Gutierrez-Santos, Mihaela Cocea, and George Magoulas

Real-Time Control of a Remote Virtual Tutor Using Minimal
Pen-Gestures 334
Yonca Haciahmetoglu and Francis Quek

Theoretical Model for Interplay between Some Learning Situations and
Brainwaves 337
Alicia Heraz and Claude Frasson

Cultural Adaptation of Pedagogical Resources within Intelligent
Tutorial Systems 340
Franck Hervé Mpondo Eboa, François Courtemanche, and
Esma Aïmeur

An Interactive Learning Environment for Problem-Changing Exercise... 343
Tsukasa Hirashima, Sho Yamamoto, and Hiromi Waki

Towards Intelligent Tutoring with Erroneous Examples: A Taxonomy
of Decimal Misconceptions 346
Seiji Isotani, Bruce M. McLaren, and Max Altman

The Efficacy of iSTART Extended Practice: Low Ability Students
Catch Up 349
G. Tanner Jackson, Chutima Boonthum, and Danielle S. McNamara

Expecting the Unexpected: Warehousing and Analyzing Data from ITS Field Use 352
   W. Lewis Johnson, Naveen Ashish, Stephen Bodnar, and Alicia Sagae

Developing an Intelligent Tutoring System Using Natural Language for Knowledge Representation 355
   Sung-Young Jung and Kurt VanLehn

A Network Analysis of Student Groups in Threaded Discussions 359
   Jeon-Hyung Kang, Jihie Kim, and Erin Shaw

A New Framework of Metacognition with Abstraction/Instantiation Operations 362
   Michiko Kayashima and Riichiro Mizoguchi

Expansion of the xPST Framework to Enable Non-programmers to Create Intelligent Tutoring Systems in 3D Game Environments 365
   Sateesh Kumar Kodavali, Stephen Gilbert, and Stephen B. Blessing

A Computational Model of Accelerated Future Learning through Feature Recognition 368
   Nan Li, William W. Cohen, and Kenneth R. Koedinger

Automated and Flexible Comparison of Course Sequencing Algorithms in the LS-Lab Framework 371
   Carla Limongelli, Filippo Sciarrone, Marco Temperini, and Giulia Vaste

Correcting Scientific Knowledge in a General-Purpose Ontology 374
   Michael Lipschultz and Diane Litman

Learning to Argue Using Computers – A View from Teachers, Researchers, and System Developers 377
   Frank Loll, Oliver Scheuer, Bruce M. McLaren, and Niels Pinkwart

How to Take into Account Different Problem Solving Modalities for Doing a Diagnosis? Experiment and Results 380
   Sandra Michelet, Vanda Luengo, Jean-Michel Adam, and Nadine Madran

Behavior Effect of Hint Selection Penalties and Availability in an Intelligent Tutoring System 384
   Pedro J. Muñoz-Merino, Carlos Delgado Kloos, and Mario Muñoz-Organero

DesignWebs: A Tool for Automatic Construction of Interactive Conceptual Maps from Document Collections 387
   Sharad V. Oberoi, Dong Nguyen, Gahgene Gweon, Susan Finger, and Carolyn Penstein Rosé

Extraction of Concept Maps from Textbooks for Domain Modeling 390
  Andrew M. Olney

Levels of Interaction (LoI): A Model for Scaffolding Learner
Engagement in an Immersive Environment 393
  David Panzoli, Adam Qureshi, Ian Dunwell, Panagiotis Petridis, Sara de Freitas, and Genaro Rebolledo-Mendez

Tools for Acquiring Data about Student Work in Interactive Learning
Environment T-Algebra.. 396
  Rein Prank and Dmitri Lepp

Mily's World: A Coordinate Geometry Learning Environment with
Game-Like Properties 399
  Dovan Rai, Joseph E. Beck, and Neil T. Heffernan

An Intelligent Tutoring System Supporting Metacognition and Sharing
Learners' Experiences 402
  Triomphe Ramandalahy, Philippe Vidal, and Julien Broisin

Are ILEs Ready for the Classroom? Bringing Teachers into the
Feedback Loop 405
  James Segedy, Brian Sulcer, and Gautam Biswas

Comparison of a Computer-Based to Hands-On Lesson in Experimental
Design.. 408
  Stephanie Siler, Dana Mowery, Cressida Magaro, Kevin Willows, and David Klahr

Toward the Development of an Intelligent Tutoring System for
Distributed Team Training through Passive Sensing 411
  Robert A. Sottilare

Open Educational Resource Assessments (OPERA) 414
  Tamara Sumner, Kirsten Butcher, and Philipp Wetzler

Annie: A Tutor That Works in Digital Games 417
  James M. Thomas and R. Michael Young

Learning from Erroneous Examples 420
  Dimitra Tsovaltzi, Bruce M. McLaren, Erica Melis, Ann-Kristin Meyer, Michael Dietrich, and George Goguadze

Feasibility of a Socially Intelligent Tutor 423
  Jozef Tvarožek and Mária Bieliková

Agent Prompts: Scaffolding Students for Productive Reflection in an
Intelligent Learning Environment 426
  Longkai Wu and Chee-Kit Looi

Identifying Problem Localization in Peer-Review Feedback 429
  Wenting Xiong and Diane Litman

AlgoTutor: From Algorithm Design to Coding 432
  Sung Yoo and Jungsoon Yoo

Adaptive, Assessment-Based Educational Games 435
  Diego Zapata-Rivera

Interactive Events

ITS Authoring through Programming-by-Demonstration 438
  Vincent Aleven, Brett Leber, and Jonathan Sewall

A Coordinate Geometry Learning Environment with Game-Like
Properties.. 439
  Dovan Rai, Joseph E. Beck, and Neil T. Heffernan

Adaptive Tutorials and the Adaptive eLearning Platform 440
  Dror Ben-Naim

DomainBuilder – An Authoring System for Visual Classification
Tutoring Systems 441
  Eugene Tseytlin, Melissa Castine, and Rebecca Crowley

AWESOME Computing: Using Corpus Data to Tailor a Community
Environment for Dissertation Writing................................ 443
  Vania Dimitriva, Royce Neagle, Sirisha Bajanki, Lydia Lau, and Roger Boyle

Collaboration and Content Recognition Features in an Inquiry Tutor ... 444
  Mark Floryan, Toby Dragon, Beverly Woolf, and Tom Murray

The Science Assistments Project: Scaffolding Scientific Inquiry Skills ... 445
  *Janice D. Gobert, Orlando Montalvo, Ermal Toto,
  Michael A. Sao Pedro, and Ryan S.J.d. Baker*

Incorporating Interactive Examples into the Cognitive Tutor 446
  *Robert G.M. Hausmann, Steven Ritter, Brendon Towle,
  R. Charles Murray, and John Connelly*

iGeom: Towards an Interactive Geometry Software with Intelligent
Guidance Capabilities 447
  Leônidas O. Brandão, Seiji Isotani, and Danilo L. Dalmon

Acquiring Conceptual Knowledge about How Systems Behave 448
  *Jochem Liem, Bert Bredeweg, Floris Linnebank, René Bühling,
  Michael Wißner, Jorge Gracia del Río, Wouter Beek, and
  Asunción Gómez Pérez*

Learning by Teaching SimStudent 449
  Noboru Matsuda, Victoria Keiser, Rohan Raizada,
  Gabriel Stylianides, William W. Cohen, and Ken Koedinger

Authoring Problem-Solving ITS with ASTUS 450
  Jean-François Lebeau, Luc Paquette, and André Mayers

A Better Reading Tutor That Listens 451
  Jack Mostow, Greg Aist, Juliet Bey, Wei Chen, Al Corbett,
  Weisi Duan, Nell Duke, Minh Duong, Donna Gates,
  José P. González, Octavio Juarez, Martin Kantorzyk, Yuanpeng Li,
  Liu Liu, Margaret McKeown, Christina Trotochaud, Joe Valeri,
  Anders Weinstein, and David Yen

Research-Based Improvements in Cognitive Tutor Geometry 452
  Steven Ritter, Brendon Towle, R. Charles Murray,
  Robert G.M. Hausmann, and John Connelly

A Cognitive Tutor for Geometric Proof 453
  Steven Ritter, Brendon Towle, R. Charles Murray,
  Robert G.M. Hausmann, and John Connelly

Multiplayer Language and Culture Training in ISLET 454
  Kevin Saunders and W. Lewis Johnson

PSLC DataShop: A Data Analysis Service for the Learning Science
Community 455
  John Stamper, Ken Koedinger, Ryan S.J.d. Baker, Alida Skogsholm,
  Brett Leber, Jim Rankin, and Sandy Demi

A DIY Pressure Sensitive Chair for Intelligent Tutoring Systems 456
  Andrew M. Olney and Sidney D'Mello

Author Index 457

Can Research-Based Technology Change School-Based Learning? Perspectives from Singapore

Chee-Kit Looi

National Institute of Education, Nanyang Technological University, Singapore
`cheekit.looi@nie.edu.sg`

We start with the broad realization that despite decades of research work in technology-mediated learning that have produced many exciting systems and studies, we have not seen many pervasive, sustainable and scalable improvements in actual classroom practice. Nonetheless, there are some countries and regions in the world in which such systemic approaches to innovating educational reforms in the classrooms hold the promise of impacting real world practice. In this talk, we would like to present the case of Singapore where such a realistic possibility can be actualized through a coherent program that spans the spectrum of many critical dimensions: from policy imperatives to school ground-up efforts, from research to impacting practice, from one research project in a classroom to sustainability and scaling up, from mere usage to cultural and epistemological shifts of the stakeholders, and from technology experimentation to providing robust technology infrastructures. Addressing these dimensions provide the conditions for technology to have an impact. Situations where technology works include those where students use technology all the time, where technology is truly personal, where the curriculum leverages the affordances of technologies, or where it is easy for teachers or students to add to the repertoire of technology-enabled activities. In Singapore, we have embarked on a journey in the Learning Sciences Lab to conduct school-based research to develop models of how to enact effective innovations and how to sustain their routine use in schools. I will discuss some of the innovations we are working on, and the issues and challenges we still face to achieve adoptability in schools, challenges that the ITS community might well be able to address.

Modeling Emotion and Its Expression

Stacy Marsella

Institute for Creative Technologies, University of Southern California, 13274 Fiji Way,
Marina del Rey, CA 90292, USA
marsella@ict.usc.edu

Emotion and its expression play a powerful role in shaping human behavior. As research has revealed the details of emotion's role, researchers and developers increasingly have sought to exploit these details in a range of applications. Work in human-computer interaction has sought to infer and influence a user's emotional state as a way to improve the interaction. Tutoring systems, health interventions and training applications have sought to regulate or induce specific, often quite different, emotional states in learners in order to improve learning outcomes. A related trend in HCI work is the use of emotions and emotional displays in virtual characters that interact with users in order to motivate, engender empathy, induce trust or simply arouse.

Common to many of these applications is the need for computational models of the causes and consequences of emotions. To the extent that emotion's impact on behavior can be modeled correctly in artificial systems, it can facilitate interactions between computer systems and human users. In this talk, I will give an overview of some of the applications that seek to infer and influence a user's emotions. I will then go into detail on how emotions can be modeled computationally, including the theoretical basis of the models, how we validate models against human data and how human data are also used to inform the animation of virtual characters.

Active Learning in Technology-Enhanced Environments: On Sensible and Less Sensible Conceptions of "Active" and Their Instructional Consequences

Alexander Renkl

Department of Psychology, University of Freiburg, D-79085 Freiburg
renkl@psychologie.uni-freiburg.de

Usually ITSs or, more generally, technology-enhanced learning environments are designed to afford active learning in order to optimize meaningful knowledge construction. However, researchers in learning and instruction hold different conceptions of "active learning." Most socio-constructivist approaches have adopted an *active responding stance*. They regard visible, open learning activities such as solving complex problems, hands-on activities, or argument with peers as necessary for effective learning. This view, however, is challenged by empirical evidence and has theoretical problems. If we assume that learning takes place in the individual learner's mind, then what the mind does, and not overt behavior, is central. Accordingly, the *active processing stance*—the typical stance of most cognitively-oriented educational psychologists—regards effective learning as knowledge construction resulting from actively processing to-be-learned content. Although active processing might be necessary for knowledge construction, it can become unfocused. In hypermedia environments, for example, learners may focus on peripheral information, which may delay or even prevent the acquisition of important content. Against this background, I have recently proposed a modification of the active processing stance. The *focused processing stance* claims that it is crucial that the learners' active processing is related not only to the learning content but to the central concepts and principles to be learned (e.g., mathematical theorems, physics laws).

The *focused processing stance* is of special relevance to technology-enhanced learning environments. Many features of these environments that are meant as supportive might actually induce learning-irrelevant additional demands to the learners (e.g., decisions when to use different help facilities), or these features might be sub-optimally used (e.g., overuse of help). Hence, these "supportive" features can distract from the central concepts and principles to be learned. In this talk I will present instructional procedures and findings from three lines of research that are relevant in helping learners focus on central concepts and principles: (a) Replacing problem-solving demands by worked solutions in the beginning of the learning process in order to reduce unproductive problem-solving attempts; (b) informing the learners of the intended function of a learning environment's "supportive" features in order to optimize their use; (c) prompting by specifically-designed questions in order to focus the learners' attention on the central principles of the learning domain. The findings confirm that it is crucial not only to induce active learner involvement but also to support focused processing in order to optimize learning outcomes.

Riding the Third Wave

Steven Ritter

Carnegie Learning, Inc.
Frick Building, 20th Floor
437 Grant Street
Pittsburgh, PA 15219
USA
sritter@carnegielearning.com

Intelligent tutoring systems work falls into three waves. The first wave involves basic research on technical implementation, including authoring systems and tutoring architectures. Second wave work takes this technological development beyond the laboratory. This work involves deep analysis of domain knowledge and empirical validation of systems. The emerging "third wave" takes advantage of widespread use of systems to refine and improve their effectiveness. Work in this area includes data mining and end-user authoring.

Although many types of systems have followed this evolution, intelligent tutoring systems are uniquely positioned among educational software to take advantage of the third wave. The architecture and authoring work from the first wave and the ability to incorporate domain knowledge and test pedagogical approaches in the second wave make us well positioned to ride this third wave.

In this talk, I will describe Carnegie Learning's experience in riding these waves. We have taken intelligent tutoring systems for mathematics originally developed at Carnegie Mellon to scale with over 500,000 users per year, and are now riding the third wave to leverage this user base and improve the effectiveness and utility of our systems.

Social and Caring Tutors
ITS 2010 Keynote Address

Beverly Park Woolf

Department of Computer Science
University of Massachusetts
bev@cs.umass.edu

Abstract. If computers are to interact naturally with humans, they must express social competencies and recognize human emotion. This talk describes the role of technology in responding to both affect and cognition and examines research to identify student emotions (frustration, boredom and interest) with around 80% accuracy using hardware sensors and student self-reports. We also discuss "caring" computers that use animated learning companions to talk about the malleability of intelligence and importance of effort and perseverance. Gender differences were noted in the impact of these companions on student affect as were differences for students with learning disabilities. In both cases, students who used companions showed improved math attitudes, increased motivation and reduced frustration and anxiety over the long term. We also describe social tutors that scaffold collaborative problem solving in ill-defined domains. These tutors use deep domain understanding of students' dialogue to recognize (with over 85% accuracy) students who are engaged in useful learning activities. Finally, we describe tutors that help online participants engaged in situations involving differing opinions, e.g., in online dispute mediation, bargaining, and civic deliberation processes.

Keywords: Social computing, collaborative problem solving, intelligent tutors, wireless sensors, student emotion, pedagogical agents, affective feedback, gender differences, special needs populations.

1 Introduction

Affect is a central component of human cognition and strongly impacts student learning [1-4]. If computers are to interact naturally with humans, they must recognize affect and express social competencies. Affect has begun to play an important role in intelligent tutors [5-6] and affective tutors seem to increase the effectiveness of tutorial interactions and, ultimately learning. The field of affective tutors investigates techniques for enabling computers to recognize, model, understand and respond effectively to student emotion. One goal of affective computing is to recognize affect or identify the affective state of people from a variety of physical cues that are produced in response to affective changes in the individual [7]. This talk describes the role of technology in automatic recognition of and response to user affect. It provides three examples of social computing in which affective interventions encourage learning, lessen humiliation and provide support and motivation that outweighs or distracts from the unpleasant aspects of failure. Section 2 describes the first example system that includes real-time automatic recognition of emotions exhibited during learning. Section 3 describes automatic generation of appropriate responses to student emotion and Section 4 discusses experiments with affective tutors. Section 5 describes a second example of social computing, support of online collaboration, and Section 6 briefly introduces the third example, a tutor for online social deliberation.

2 Automatic Recognition of Student Affect

The first example of a social tutor is one that embeds affective support into tutoring applications. Prior research has focused on automated detection of affective states as a first step towards this goal [5, 8-10]. Currently there is no gold standard for either labeling a person's emotional state or for responding to it. Our sensor platform of four physiological sensors (Fig. 1), placed on each student's chair, mouse, monitor, and wrist, conveyed information to the tutor about student posture, movement, grip tension, arousal, and facially expressed mental states. The platform is unobtrusive enough to be used by students in a typical setting and resource-conscious enough to run on average computer labs available to students [11]. These sensors collect raw data about physical activity and the state of a student. The challenge remains to map this data into models of emotional states and use this information productively.

Fig. 1. Sensors used in the classroom (clockwise): mental state camera, skin conductance bracelet, pressure sensitive mouse, pressure sensitive chair

Experiments showed that when sensor data supplements a user model based on tutor logs, the model reflects a larger percentage of the students' self-concept than does a user model based on the tutor logs alone [11]. The best classifier of each emotion in terms of accuracy ranges from 78% to 87.5%. By using Stepwise Regression we isolated key features for predicting user emotional responses to four categories of emotion. These results are supported by cross validation, and show improvement using a very basic classifier. We showed that students' self-reports can be automatically inferred from physiological data that is streamed to the tutoring software in real educational settings. Fluctuating student reports were related to longer-term affective variables (e.g., value mathematics and self-concept) and these latter variables, in turn, are known to predict long-term success in mathematics, e.g., students who value math and have a positive self-concept of their math ability perform better in math classes [12].

3 Automatic Response to Student Affect

Once a student's emotion has been recognized, the next issue is to respond to improve student motivation and learning. Providing empathy or support strongly correlates with learning [12, 13] and the presence of someone who cares, or at least appears to care, can be motivating. Various studies have linked interpersonal relationships between teachers and students to motivational outcomes [7, 14]. Can this noted human relationship be reproduced, in part, by apparent empathy from a computer character? Apparently the answer is yes [15]. People seem to relate to computers in the same way they relate to humans and some relationships are identical to real social relationships [16]. For example, students continue to engage in frustrating tasks on a computer significantly longer after an empathetic computational response [17], and have immediately lowered stress level (via skin conduct-ance) after empathy and after apology [18].

Fig. 2. Affective learning companions act out their emotion and talk with students expressing full sentences of cognitive, meta-cognitive and emotional feedback

Pedagogical agents have been developed to improve learning and impact affect [19, 20]. Our gendered learning companions (LC) are *empathetic* in that they visually reflect the last emotion reported by the student (queried within the system every five minutes) [21, 22]; they emphasize the importance of perseverance, express emotions and offer strategies (e.g., "Use the help function"), see Fig. 2 [11, 22]. The characters are highly positive, in the sense that they displayed encouraging gestures (e.g., excitement and confidence). Negative gestures (appearing frustrated or bored) were not effective and were eliminated by the researchers. Mimicking student self-reported emotion is a form of a non-verbal empathetic response (e.g., learning companions appeared excited in response to student excitement, see Fig. 3, right). Companions occasionally expressed non-verbal behaviors of positive valence only (e.g., looking interested), the underlying goal being to make them appear life-like and engaged and to impart some of their enthusiasm to the students.

Companions act out their emotion and talk with students expressing full sentences of metacognitive and emotional feedback. They are non-intrusive—they work on their own computer to solve the problem at hand, and react only after the student has answered the question. Companions respond with some of Carole Dweck's [23] recommendations about disregarding success and valuing effort. This adds a new dimension to the traditional feedback regarding success/no-success generally given to students. Affective companions support students motivationally, by emphasizing the importance of effort and perseverance and the idea that intelligence is malleable instead of a fixed trait [23].

Learning companions delivered approximately 50 different messages emphasizing the malleability of intelligence and the importance of effort and perseverance. The messages also include metacognitive help related to effective strategies for solving math problems and effective use the tutor. The learning companions' interventions are tailored to a given student's needs according and ultimately will be selected based on two models of affect and effort embedded in the tutor. The *effort* model uses interaction features to provide information on the degree of effort a student invests in generating a problem solution. An *affect* model assesses a student's emotional state; based on linear regression, this model is derived from data obtained from a series of studies described in [11, 21]. Ultimately, the interventions will be tailored according to the tutor's affective student model. However, we are currently still validating the models and algorithms for deciding which intervention to provide and when, and thus relied on an effort model only to assign messages.

The characters provided support by responding to the effort exerted by students rather than to the student's emotions. Characters were either unimpressed when effort was not exerted, or simply ignored that the student solved the problem. They also offered praise to students who exerted effort while problem-solving, even if their answers were wrong, highlighting that the goal is to lessen the importance of performance in favor of learning.

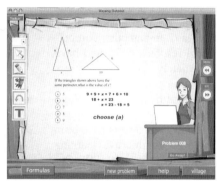

Fig. 3. The Wayang Tutor with the female affective learning companion

4 Experiments with Affective Tutors

Our affect recognition and response software is stand-alone and can provide affective input to any tutor and can generate responses from any tutor. We conducted several empirical evaluations to dynamically identify student emotion during learning, identify emotions through classifiers and then respond to students using companions.

Currently we are using affect systems in tandem with Wayang Outpost, a multimedia tutoring system for high school geometry and algebra [21, 22, 24]. Problems are presented one at a time, each consisting of the problem statement with four or five solution options directly below it. Students select an answer and the tutor provides immediate visual feedback by coloring the answer green or red, for correct or incorrect respectively. Within each topic section, Wayang adjusts the difficulty of problems depending on past student performance.

We conducted several series of experiments involving sensors, learning companions and Wayang Outpost [21, 22]. One study involved 35 students in a public high school in Massachusetts; another involved 29 students in the University of Massachusetts; and the final study involved 29 undergraduates from Arizona State University. Another set of studies quantitatively analyzed the benefit of learning companions on affective and cognitive outcomes. The subjects included one hundred and eight (108) students from two high schools (one low and the other high achieving) in Massachusetts and involved 9th and 10th graders. Two thirds of the students were assigned to a learning companion of a random gender, and one-third to the no learning companion condition. Wayang has been used with thousands of students in the past and has demonstrated improved learning gains in state standard exams [11, 21, 24]

Overall results suggest a general advantage of learning companions (both the female and male ones) for some affective outcomes. Students reported significantly less frustration and more interest (less boredom) when learning companions were used compared to the no learning companion condition. At the same time, students receiving the female learning companion reported significantly higher self-concept and liking of math at posttest time. Students receiving the female companion also reported higher confidence towards problem solving and in post-tutor surveys. While significant results are limited to affective outcomes—learning companions did not impact learning—we are impressed given the short exposure of students to the tutoring system. We carried out Analyses of Covariance (ANCOVA) for each of the affective and behavioral dependent variables (post-tutor and within tutor). Results showed that all students demonstrated math learning after working with Wayang, with low-achieving students learning more than high achieving students across all conditions. Learning companions successfully induced positive student behaviors that have been correlated to learning, specifically, students spent more time on hinted problems [24]. The beneficial effect of learning companions was mainly on affective outcomes, particularly on confidence.

Gender Studies. While learning companions (LC) afford affective advantages for all students, several significant effects in the ANCOVAs indicated a higher benefit of learning companions for female students. In the case of the emotional outcomes just mentioned (confidence and frustration, in particular), the effects are stronger for females than for males. Females' confidence was improved but not confidence for males. It is important to note that these gender effects on emotions (within or after the tutor) are not due to females starting out feeling worse, as our analyses account for that baseline pretest emotion as a covariate. Females especially perceived the learning experience with Wayang significantly better when learning companions were present, while the opposite happened for males, who actually reported worse perceptions of learning when learning companions were present. Female students in the LC condition also had more productive behaviors in the tutor: they spent more time than did males on "helped problems" compared to females in the no-LC condition; they "gamed" less when characters were present (a significant interaction effect revealed that the opposite happens for males).

Studies with Low-achieving Students. Low-achieving students were defined as those who scored lower than median grade on the math pretest [24]. Low-achieving students disliked math more, valued it less, had worse perception of their math ability, and reported feeling worse when solving math problems. Since low achieving students (both with and without disabilities) struggle with math, our conjecture was that *all* low achievers could require additional affective support. Thus, the first goal of the study was to examine the affective needs of both low achieving and learning disability students in our data (15% of subjects).

Low-achieving students who received LCs improved their confidence while using the tutor and more than students with no LCs, while their counterparts in the no-LC condition tended to decrease their confidence. Some differential effects suggest that learning companions are essential for low-achieving students' affect. When LCs are present, low achieving students report positive affect nearly as much as do high-achieving students and it is only when learning companions are absent that a large gap exists between these student groups. This affective gap reduces when learning companions are present. This result is found for several outcome variables: self-concept, perceptions of learning, frustration, and excitement.

5 Supporting Student Collaboration

The second example of social computing comes from a tutor that supports online peer-to-peer collaboration. Social computers should recognize and promote dialogue among groups of people engaged in free-entry text discussion; they should recognize the content of group work, help participants maintain proper focus, provide appropriate feedback and center participants' work as needed.

We developed tools that enable students to work together within Rashi, an inquiry learning system that supports authentic learning experiences by considering real-world inquiry problems. The tutor provides case descriptions for students to investigate, along with information about how to approach each problem [25, 26]. In the Rashi Human Biology Tutor, students evaluate patients and generate hypotheses about their medical condition. Patients' complaints form an initial set of data from which students begin the diagnostic process. Students can interview the virtual patient (Fig. 4, top), perform a physical examination, or run lab tests.

Tools leverage the information provided by students to help the tutor recognize the students' focus.

Fig. 4. Students "interview" the patient in the Rashi system (top) and record their hypotheses for a diagnosis along with evidence supporting and refuting that evidence in the notebook (bottom)

During collaboration, users view each others' notebooks (Fig. 4, bottom), and drag and drop both data and hypotheses from others' notebooks to their own. This supports a variety of collaborative activities ranging from students working in tightly knit groups, where each student takes on a role and contributes in a specific manner, to students working mostly independently but sharing ideas and thoughts when reaching an impasse. The system also provides a chat facility that enables students to discuss issues with members of their group, see Fig. 5. Several features, including text coloring, filtering, and new message notifications increase the usability and quality of the discussion tools. Within the chat feature a group member can click on a chat subject and be quickly taken to related work in a group member's notebook.

In order to recognize the content of group work and help participants maintain proper focus, the system matches student statements to expert knowledge base elements. This is accomplished by using the search engine library, Lucene, to index the individual elements from the knowledge base along with their associated keywords. Rashi uses the expert knowledge base to recognize (with 88% success rate) when students are discussing content relevant to the problem and to correctly link (with 70% success) that content with an actual topic [26]. Subsets of the data indicate that even better results are possible. This research provides solid support for the concept of using a knowledge base to recognize content in free-entry text discussion and to support students engaged in problem-solving activities.

```
Sammy: did you find anything
Anne:   no
Sammy: no brain damage and no alcohol at the time
Anne:   He has no enemies on campus. Chest appears to be normal
Sammy: no spinal damage either
Anne:   5'11" is his height; Knees appear to be normal but there is
        slight swelling in his ankles
Anne:   Normal heart sounds
Sammy: no toxins
Anne:   Normal heart sounds and normal chest exam
Sammy: he claims have no asthma
Anne:   weak heart pulse rate, lungs sound wheezing
Sammy: we found pulmonary problems so something is screwed up with
his lungs and it aint asthma or his phisical or sexual activity
Anne:   its anaphlactic shock
Sammy: we found out he was running before he passed out and he is a
runner so he got tired sat down and leaned against the tree which cant descirbe
the mark on his head.
```

Fig. 5. Actual chat conversation among middle school students (grades 5-6) involved in a Rashi discourse to diagnose a patient. Their discussion is thoughtful and on-task.

The addition of collaboration software also offers unique opportunities to recognize situations where students might be helpful to each other. We hope to allow students to support each other at crucial points in time in the conversation [26]. When attempting to intelligently encourage collaboration, the tutor reasons about all students work at the same time. It supports collaboration by, for example, providing a "Suggested Topics" list adjoining the chat window, populated with items that are related to a group's current work according to the expert knowledge base. Students can then see the connections and gaps in their collective work. The system also detects a specific moment at which an intervention should be given. What opportunities will be recognized as appropriate times for prompting students to discuss the argument with one another? We are taking precautions to avoid interventions that would be disruptive or counter-productive if the tutoring system were to be mistaken about its content recognition abilities.

6 Supporting Online Social Deliberation

The third and final example of social computing is about supporting online social deliberation, especially as it relates to dispute resolution and collaborative inquiry.

This software, which is still in progress, will model and monitor deliberative processes skills while people are either in collaboration or involved in settling disputes. Applications will be for online dispute resolution and collaborative learning, such as seen in Rashi. We intend to improve participants' trust in the quality and legitimacy of these processes and will implement separate tools for facilitators and participants.

An example of one application of this software is to work with participants trying to settle their differences after failing in an eBay transaction. 20% of the eBay disputes require the intervention of human mediators who provide structure for the dispute resolution conversation. The online project will identify the content of the discussion, see Fig. 6, scaffold these situations, add structure to the dialogue and focus attention on social processes.

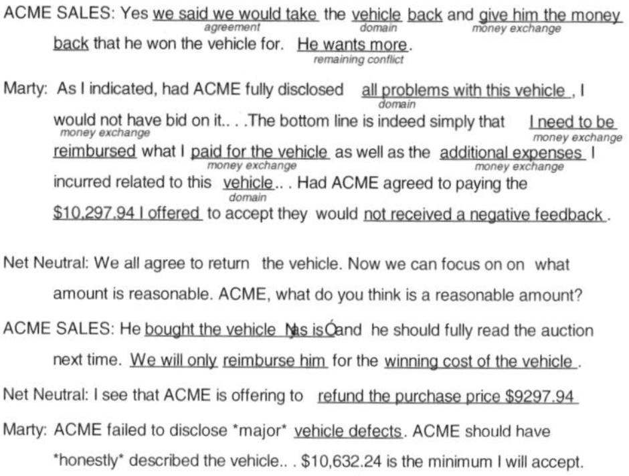

We will test the hypothesis that online users produce more positive results when supported by scaffolding that draws attention to important skills and features of social deliberative processes and by adaptive coaching that provides explicit hints and expert advice. Positive results are defined as helping people to gain both basic and reflective deliberation skills, e.g., the ability to separate facts from opinions and to form logical arguments. The software will integrate artificial intelligence techniques into dialogue environments, prompt or remind people, drawing their attention to important features of the deliberative situation and provide interventions (e.g., visualization tools and process structures).

Fig. 6. Actual conversation among eBay participants after a failed negotiation. A human mediator (NetNeutral) helped frame the discussion and settle the disagreement. Keywords that the software should be able to recognize are underlined.

7 Discussion and Future Work

This talk described three examples of social and caring computer environments and the role of technology in automatic recognition of and response to human affect. The first example described real-time automatic recognition of emotions, automatic generation of responses to student emotion and experiments with affective tutors. The second example described a tutor that supports collaboration among students and the third was software for online social deliberation. These systems contribute to the growing body of work on affective reasoning for computers and represent a first step towards development of social and caring software.

We propose that tutors that can reason about and respond to human affect will ultimately be able to identify desirable (e.g. flow) and non-desirable (e.g., boredom) student states. Different interventions can be tested to keep students in desirable states as long as possible (e.g., a confused student might be invited to slow down, reread the problem and ask for hints). Part of this approach includes user models that provide instructional recommendations and algorithms based on tutor predictions.

There are a number of places for improvement in affective tutors. For example, the impact of specific pedagogical actions on student learning should be investigated and used to quantitatively gauge the influence of competing tutorial strategies on learning. Additionally, summary information of sensor values used in our experiments may be improved by considering the time series of each of these sensors.

Research on affective tutors may ultimately lead to delicate recommendations about the type of support to provide for individual students. Should male students receive affective support at all? Should all females be provided with learning companions? Should students with learning disabilities use learning companions? These are hard questions to answer from initial and limited experiments. While preliminary results suggest that high school females will affectively benefit more than high school males, we cannot conclude that males in general should not receive affective learning companions. Further studies with larger number of students might result in more nuanced recommendations about how to modulate the feedback to individualize instruction in affective tutors.

Acknowledgement

This research was funded by two awards (1) National Science Foundation, #0705554, IIS/HCC *Affective Learning Companions: Modeling and supporting emotion during teaching*, Woolf and Burleson (PIs) with Arroyo, Barto, and Fisher; and (2) U.S. Department of Education to Woolf, B. P. (PI) with Arroyo, Maloy and the Center for Applied Special Technology (CAST), *Teaching Every Student: Using Intelligent Tutoring and Universal Design To Customize The Mathematics Curriculum*. Any opinions, findings, conclusions or recommendations expressed in this material are those of the authors and do not necessarily reflect the views of the funding agencies.

References

1. McQuiggan, S., Mott, B., Lester, J.: Modeling self-efficacy in intelligent tutoring systems: An inductive approach. J. User Modeling and User-Adapted Interaction 18(1), 81–123 (2008)
2. Goleman, D.: Emotional Intelligence. Bantam Books, New York (1995)
3. Efklides, A., Petkakim, C.: Effects of Mood on students' metacogntiive experience. J. Learning and Instruction 15, 415–431 (2005)
4. Brand, S., Reimer, T., Opwis, K.: How do we learn in a negative mood? Effect of a negative mood on transfer and learning. J. Learning and Instruction 17, 1–16 (2007)
5. Conati, C., Mclaren, H.: Evaluating A Probabilistic Model of Student Affect. In: Lester, J.C., Vicari, R.M., Paraguaçu, F. (eds.) ITS 2004. LNCS, vol. 3220, pp. 55–66. Springer, Heidelberg (2004)
6. D'Mello, S.K., Picard, R.W., Graesser, A.C.: Towards an Affect-Sensitive AutoTutor. Special issue on Intelligent Educational Systems, IEEE Intelligent Systems 22(4), 53–61 (2007)
7. Picard, R.W., Papert, S., Bender, W., Blumberg, B., Breazeal, C., Cavallo, D., Machover, T., Resnick, M., Roy, D., Strohecker, C.: Affective Learning–A Manifesto. BT Journal 2(4), 253–269 (2004)

8. D'Mello, S., Graesser, A.: Mind and Body: Dialogue and Posture for Affect Detection in Learning Environments. In: Frontiers in Artificial Intelligence and Applications (2007)
9. McQuiggan, S., Lester, J.: Diagnosing Self-Efficacy in Intelligent Tutoring Systems: An Empirical Study. In: Ikeda, M., Ashley, K., Chan, T.W. (eds.) 8th International Conference on Intelligent Tutoring Systems, Jhongli, Taiwan (2006)
10. Graesser, A.C., Chipman, P., King, B., McDaniel, B., D'Mello, S.: Emotions and Learning with AutoTutor. In: Luckin, R., Koedinger, K., Greer, J. (eds.) 13th International Conference on Artificial Intelligence in Education (AIED 2007), pp. 569–571. IOS Press, Amsterdam (2007)
11. Cooper, D.G., Arroyo, I., Woolf, B.P., Muldner, K., Burleson, W., Christopherson, R.: Sensors Model Student Self Concept in the Classroom. In: International Conference on User Modeling and Adaptive Presentation, June 2009, pp. 30–41 (2009)
12. Zimmerman, B.J.: Self-Efficacy: An Essential Motive to Learn. J. Contemporary Educational Psychology 25, 82–91 (2000)
13. Graham, S., Weiner, B.: Theories and principles of motivation. In: Berliner, D., Calfee, R. (eds.) Handbook of Educational Psychology, pp. 63–84. Macmillan, New York (1996)
14. Wentzel, K., Asher, S.R.: Academic lives of neglected, rejected, popular, and controversial children. J. Child Development 66, 754–763 (1995)
15. Bickmore, T., Picard, R.W.: Establishing and Maintaining Long-Term Human-Computer Relationships. J. Transactions on Computer-Human Interaction 12(2), 293–327 (2004)
16. Reeves, B., Nass, C.: The media equation: How people treat computers, television and new media like real people and places. CSLI, New York (1998)
17. Klein, J., Moon, Y., Picard, R.W.: This Computer Responds to User Frustration: Theory, Design, Results and Implications. J. Interacting with Computers 14(2), 119–140 (2002)
18. Prendinger, H., Ishizuka, M.: The Empathic Companion: A Character-Based Interface that Addresses Users' Affective States. J. Applied Artificial Intelligence 19(3-4), 267–285 (2005)
19. Chan, T.W., Baskin, A.: Learning companion system. In: Frasson, C., Gauthier, G. (eds.) Intelligent Tutoring Systems, pp. 6–33. Ablex Publishing, Norwood (1990)
20. Baylor, A.: The Impact of Pedagogical Agent Image on Affective Outcomes, Workshop on Affective Interactions: Computers in the Affective Loop. In: International Conference on Intelligent User Interfaces, San Diego, CA (2005)
21. Arroyo, I., Woolf, B.P., Royer, J.M., Tai, M.: Affective Gendered Learning Companions. In: 14th International Conference on Artificial Intelligence and Education, pp. 41–48. IOS Press, Amsterdam (2009)
22. Arroyo, I., Cooper, D.G., Burleson, W., Woolf, B.P., Muldner, K., Christopherson, R.: Emotion Sensors Go To School. In: 14th International Conference on Artificial Intelligence and Education, pp. 17–24. IOS Press, Amsterdam (2009)
23. Dweck, C.: Messages that motivate: How praise molds students' beliefs, motivation, and performance (In Surprising Ways). In: Aronson, J. (ed.) Improving academic achievement. Academic Press, New York (2002)
24. Woolf, B., Arroyo, I., Muldner, K., Burleson, W., Cooper, D., Razzaq, L., Dolan, R.: The Effect of Motivational Learning Companions on Low-Achieving Students and Students with Learning Disabilities. In: Aleven, V., Kay, J., Mostow, J. (eds.) ITS 2010, Part I. LNCS, vol. 6094, pp. 327–337. Springer, Heidelberg (2010)
25. Dragon, T., Woolf, B.P., Marshall, D., Murray, T.: Coaching within a domain independent inquiry environment. In: Ikeda, M., Ashley, K.D., Chan, T.-W. (eds.) ITS 2006. LNCS, vol. 4053, pp. 144–153. Springer, Heidelberg (2006)
26. Dragon, T., Floryan, M., Woolf, B.P., Murray, T.: Recognizing Dialogue Content in Student Collaborative Conversation. In: Aleven, V., Kay, J., Mostow, J. (eds.) ITS 2010, Part II. LNCS, vol. 6095, pp. 113–122. Springer, Heidelberg (2010)

Predicting Correctness of Problem Solving in ITS with a Temporal Collaborative Filtering Approach

Suleyman Cetintas[1], Luo Si[1], Yan Ping Xin[2], and Casey Hord[2]

[1] Department of Computer Sciences, Purdue University,
West Lafayette, IN, 47907, USA
{scetinta,lsi}@cs.purdue.edu
[2] Department of Educational Studies, Purdue University,
West Lafayette, IN, 47907, USA
{yxin,thord}@purdue.edu

Abstract. Collaborative filtering (CF) is a technique that utilizes how users are associated with items in a target application and predicts the utility of items for a particular user. Temporal collaborative filtering (temporal CF) is a time-sensitive CF approach that considers the change in user-item interactions over time. Despite its capability to deal with dynamic educational applications with rapidly changing user-item interactions, there is no prior research of temporal CF on educational tasks. This paper proposes a temporal CF approach to automatically predict the correctness of students' problem solving in an intelligent math tutoring system. Unlike traditional user-item interactions, a student may work on the same problem multiple times, and there are usually multiple interactions for a student-problem pair. The proposed temporal CF approach effectively utilizes information coming from multiple interactions and is compared to i) a traditional CF approach, ii) a temporal CF approach that uses a sliding-time-window but ignores old data and multiple interactions and iii) a combined temporal CF approach that uses a sliding-time-window together with multiple interactions. An extensive set of experiment results show that using multiple-interactions significantly improves the prediction accuracy while using sliding-time-windows doesn't make a significant difference.

Keywords: performance prediction, intelligent tutoring systems, temporal collaborative filtering.

1 Introduction

Collaborative information filtering, or collaborative filtering (CF), is an important technology that utilizes how users of a system are associated with items in an application to predict the utility of items for a particular user. Specific type of items and associations differ by target applications (e.g., buying books at Amazon, reading news at Google, and renting CDs at Netflix, etc.). CF techniques have been applied mainly in many e-commerce systems for business purposes. Recently, they have also been used for educational applications such as legal argumentation [10], educational resource recommendation [13], writing skills training [4] and eLearning [8]. An important issue with many applications is that users' behaviors change over time and a

Table 1. Statistics about the number of times each worksheet is repeated

Repetition Statistics	Worksheet Name										
	Equal Group				Multiplicative Compare				Mixed		
	W1	W2	W3	W4	W1	W2	W3	W4	W1	W2	W3
Mean	2.2	4	1.6	1.5	1.3	3.3	1.4	1.2	1.3	1.1	1
Std. Dev.	1.8	2	0.5	0.7	0.5	2.9	0.9	0.6	0.9	0.3	0

static CF approach may not always be optimal to anticipate users' future behaviors. Temporal collaborative filtering (temporal CF) is a CF approach that adapts itself to the constantly changing system dynamics (i.e., user-item associations). Temporal CF has gained substantial interests in business applications such as movie recommendation [5], [6], [7]. However, despite its capability to deal with dynamic educational applications with rapidly changing user-item interactions, temporal CF has not been applied to educational tasks yet.

To the best of our knowledge there is no prior research of temporal CF on the automatic detection of whether a student will be able to correctly answer a question with a high-level student model (i.e., without using any expert knowledge of the domain). Prior research utilized combinations of features such as time, mouse tracking and performance related features [1], [3], [11]; most of which are extracted while a student is solving the problem. However, it is not possible to predict whether a student will be able to solve a problem before the problem is presented to the student (i.e., enough data is collected) which limits the utilization of the student model. For example, related prior research was not able to give an early feedback to the student depending on his likelihood to solve the problem or change the problem with an easier or harder one. Prior work on temporal CF focused on business applications such as movie recommendation [5], [6], [7]. A simple and popular approach in the prior work of temporal CF (to deal with rapidly changing user-item associations) is the utilization of sliding time windows, which uses new data in a current sliding window and discards (or assigns decreasing weights on) old data [5][12]. However, unlike a traditional CF based application (e.g., a user votes for a movie only once), a student has multiple interactions with a task/problem in a problem solving environment and this data is ignored by traditional CF approaches or temporal CF approaches such as sliding window.

This paper proposes a novel temporal CF approach that can automatically predict the correctness of students' problem solving in an intelligent math tutor by utilizing the information coming from multiple interactions. The new approach is compared to i) a traditional CF approach, ii) a temporal CF approach that uses sliding time window but ignores old data and multiple interactions and iii) a novel hybrid temporal CF approach that uses a sliding-time window together with multiple interactions. We show that using multiple interactions significantly improves the prediction accuracy. It is also shown that although using sliding time window has been shown to be effective in prior research [5], [12]; it doesn't make a significant difference in this work. Furthermore, a novel hybrid approach combining the proposed temporal CF together with the temporal CF using sliding time windows is found to be not significantly different than using the proposed temporal CF approach of only utilizing multiple interactions. Finally, the Pearson Correlation Coefficient (PCC) method is found to be not significantly different than the Vector Similarity (VS) while calculating the similarity between two users, although PCC has been shown to be more effective than VS in other applications (e.g., in business domain) [2].

2 Data

Data from a study conducted in fall 2008 and partly in spring 2009 in a nearby elementary school was used in this work. The study was conducted in mathematics classrooms using a math tutoring software (that has been developed by the authors). The tutoring software teaches problem solving skills for Equal Group (EG) and Multiplicative Compare (MC) problems. These two problem types are a subset of the most important mathematical word problem types that represent about 78% of the problems in a fourth grade mathematics textbook [9]. In the tutoring system; first, a conceptual instruction session is studied by a student followed by problem solving sections to test their understanding. Both of conceptual instruction and problem solving parts require students to work one-on-one with the tutoring software and if students fail to pass a problem solving session, they have to repeat the corresponding conceptual instruction and the problem solving session. Details about the number of repetitions of each worksheet (by all students) are given in Table 1. Space limitations preclude discussing in detail but the tutoring software has a total of 4 conceptual instruction sessions and 11 problem solving worksheets that have 12 questions each (4 for Equal Group worksheets, 4 for Multiplicative Compare worksheets, 3 Mixed worksheets each of which include 6 EG & 6 MC problems). The software is supported with animations, audio (with more than 500 audio files), instructional hints, exercises etc.

The study with the tutoring system included 10 students among which 3 students have learning disabilities, 1 student has emotional disorder and 1 student has emotional disorder combined with a mild intellectual disability. Students used the tutor for several class sessions of 30 minutes (on average 18.7 sessions per student with standard deviation of 3.23 sessions) during which their interaction with the tutoring system was logged in a centralized database. A total of 2388 problems (corresponding to a total of 199 worksheets) were solved with 1670 problems correctly solved (with average 167.0 and std. deviation. 23.1) and 718 incorrectly solved (with average 71.8 and std. deviation 32.5). Data from 9 students was used as training data to build the models for making predictions for the remaining 1 student (who is used as the test data) at each configuration. That is, all 10 students are used as the test data alternatively and the data from other 9 students is used as training data. The averages of the results for all configurations are reported.

3 Methods and Modeling Approaches

3.1 Collaborative Filtering Framework

Predicting correctness of problem solving with a high-level student model (i.e., without using any expert knowledge of the domain) can be treated as a collaborative filtering problem, which models students' likelihood to solve problems. The collaborative filtering framework in this work can be defined as follows: assume there are M students and L worksheets in the system, where each of the worksheets has K questions. Note that M is 10, L is 11 and K is 12 in this work. Let w_m^l be the lth worksheet by m^{th} student, $r(w_m^l)$ be the total number of repetitions of lth worksheet by m^{th} student, $w_m^{l,n}$ be the nth repetition of lth worksheet by m^{th} student, $w_m^{l,n}(i)$ be the ith problem in that worksheet and $s(w_m^{l,n}(i))$ be the student's score on the problem (i.e., 1 means the student solved the problem correctly and 0 means the student solved the problem incorrectly). A first step in CF is to calculate the similarities between students. There are two common techniques for this task: Pearson Coefficient Correlation (PCC) and Vector Similarity (VS). PCC can be calculated as follows:

$$Sim(u,u^t) = \frac{\sum_{l=1}^{L}\sum_{k=1}^{K}(s(w_u^l(k)) - \overline{s(w_u)})(s(w_{u^t}^l(k)) - \overline{s(w_{u^t})})}{\sqrt{\sum_{l=1}^{L}\sum_{k=1}^{K}(s(w_u^l(k)) - \overline{s(w_u)})^2}\sqrt{\sum_{l=1}^{L}\sum_{k=1}^{K}(s(w_{u^t}^l(k)) - \overline{s(w_{u^t})})^2}} \quad (1)$$

where $Sim(u, u^t)$ is the similarity score between students u and u^t, $\overline{s(w_u)}$ is the average score of student u on all problems. The vector similarity (VS) can be calculated as follows:

$$Sim(u,u^t) = \frac{\sum_{l=1}^{L}\sum_{k=1}^{K} s(w_u^l(k))\, s(w_{u^t}^l(k))}{\sqrt{\sum_{l=1}^{L}\sum_{k=1}^{K} s(w_u^l(k))^2}\sqrt{\sum_{l=1}^{L}\sum_{k=1}^{K} s(w_{u^t}^l(k))^2}} \quad (2)$$

After the similarity between users are calculated, prediction for a problem can be computed by using the sum of the scores of training users on the problem weighted by the similarity between users as follows:

$$s\widehat{(w_{u^t}^l(k))} = \overline{s(w_{u^t})} + \frac{\sum_{u=1}^{M} Sim(u,u^t)(s(w_u^l(k)) - \overline{s(w_u)})}{\sum_{u=1}^{M}|Sim(u,u^t)|} \quad (3)$$

Note that the above CF approach ignores the multiple interactions (i.e., repetitions of worksheets) and only uses the latest scores of a student on a worksheet (e.g., in the same way it uses the latest rating of a user on a movie). Therefore the repetition index, that should be included as follows $s\left(w_u^{l,r(w_u^l)}(k)\right)$ for a problem $s(w_u^l(k))$, is omitted in the formulas for simplicity.

To predict the correctness of problem solving for a test worksheet of a student, all of the previous worksheets (i.e., the worksheets that are already solved and available for use) of that student are used in this modeling approach.

This modeling approach will serve as a baseline and will be referred as Mod_Baseline_All.

3.2 Temporal Collaborative Filtering with Sliding Time Window

Temporal collaborative filtering is a time-sensitive CF approach that adapts itself to the rapidly changing user-item interactions. The user-item associations in many applications change with time as user's behavior can change over time. One of the simple temporal CF approaches to deal with changing dynamics is to favor newer data than older data for having an up-to-date model of the users' behavior. Sliding time windows (and their variants) that only use the newest data is a popular approach, which has been followed in prior research [5], [12]. To the best of our knowledge, this is the first work utilizing sliding time windows on an application in the education domain. In this work, the sliding time window is defined as using the last x worksheets for $x \in \{1,2,3,4\}$. Sliding time window approach will be referred as Mod_Baseline_Window.

3.3 Temporal Collaborative Filtering with Multiple Interactions and a Hybrid Approach

Unlike traditional user-item interactions, students can work on a problem several times. In most CF based systems, users don't interact with the items multiple times, therefore a CF approach or a temporal CF approach don't take into account the information coming from multiple interactions that happen in educational environments such as tutoring systems with problem solving activities. To predict a student's performance on a problem, the use of the student's past performance on the same problem is a valuable source of data that should not be ignored. By utilizing this data, it becomes possible not only to compare the latest performances of students' on other problems (like in CF or temporal CF approaches) but also to compare the learning curves by comparing their first, second, etc. trials on the same problems. In this work, the temporal CF approach that utilizes multiple interactions can be calculated with the following changes over the VS and prediction formulas as follows: the new vector similarity (VS):

$$Sim(u, u^t) = \frac{\sum_{l=1}^{L} \sum_{n=1}^{r(w_{ut}^l)} \sum_{k=1}^{K} s\left(w_u^{l,n}(k)\right) s\left(w_{u^t}^{l,n}(k)\right)}{\sqrt{\sum_{l=1}^{L} \sum_{n=1}^{r(w_{ut}^l)} \sum_{k=1}^{K} s\left(w_u^{l,n}(k)\right)^2} \sqrt{\sum_{l=1}^{L} \sum_{n=1}^{r(w_{ut}^l)} \sum_{k=1}^{K} s\left(w_{u^t}^{l,n}(k)\right)^2}} \qquad (4)$$

So, if the test student is working on worksheet $w_{u^t}^l$ for the $(r(w_{u^t}^l) + 1)^{th}$ time, her/his 1st trial on the worksheet is compared with other students' first trial on the same worksheet, her/his second trial is compared with others' second trial, and her/his $r(w_{u^t}^l)^{th}$ trial is compared with other students' $r(w_{u^t}^l)^{th}$ trial. In the traditional approach only the latest trials of the test student on previous worksheets (i.e., $l_{prev} < l$ and $w_{u^t}^{l_{prev},r(w_u^{l_{prev}})}$) is compared with only the latest trials of other students on those worksheets (i.e., $w_u^{l_{prev},r(w_u^{l_{prev}})}$). An important thing to note is the dimension mismatch problem that can happen when two students have different number of trials on a worksheet which may cause $r(w_{ut}^l) > r(w_u^l)$ where there is no corresponding trial of worksheet w_u^l from student u to compare with student u^t. In such a case, the approach used in this paper is as follows: $w_u^{l,n}(k) = w_u^{l,r(w_u^l)}(k)$ for $n > r(w_u^l)$. That is, for instance, if the third trial of a test user's worksheet is being compared and a training user has repeated that worksheet only twice, her/his third (or more) trial is assumed to be the same with her/his second (i.e., last) trial. This approach is better than just comparing $r(w_u^l)^{th}$ trials only, for two reasons: i) as the difference $r(w_{ut}^l) - r(w_u^l)$ becomes bigger, the proposed approach punishes the similarity more (and since similar students should have similar repetition behaviors this should be the case) and ii) students solve a worksheet until they master the worksheet and get enough score on the worksheet and therefore their last trial is a good representation of their final status (after their last trial) on that worksheet.

After the new similarity between users is calculated, the new prediction formula becomes:

$$s\left(w_{u^t}^{l,r\left(w_{u^t}^l\right)}(k)\right) = \overline{s(w_{u^t})} + \frac{\sum_{u=1}^{M} Sim(u, u^t)(s\left(w_u^{l,r\left(w_{u^t}^l\right)}(k)\right) - \overline{s(w_u)})}{\sum_{u=1}^{M} |Sim(u, u^t)|} \tag{5}$$

So to predict the $r(w_{u^t}^l)^{th}$ repetition of a worksheet of a test user, only the data from $r(w_{u^t}^l)^{th}$ repetitions of training students are used, rather than using the data from their final (i.e., $r(w_u^l)^{th}$) repetitions. This modeling approach will be referred as Mod_MultInt_All.

To better evaluate the effect of sliding time windows approach, we also propose a novel hybrid approach combining the proposed temporal CF (i.e., Mod_MultInt_All) together with the temporal CF approach that uses sliding time windows. This hybrid temporal CF approach will be referred as Mod_MultInt_Window.

4 Experimental Methodology: Evaluation Metric

Mean Absolute Error (MAE) has been used as a popular evaluation metric in the prior work [2], [5]; and is calculated by looking at the mean absolute deviation of a test student's predicted scores from her/his actual score on the problems. In this work, the MAE of a test worksheet $w_u^{l,n}$ (i.e., the nth repetition of lth worksheet by m^{th} student) can be computed as:

$$MAE(w_u^{l,n}) = \frac{\sum_{k=1}^{K} \left| s\left(w_u^{l,n}(k)\right) - s\left(\widehat{w_u^{l,n}}(k)\right) \right|}{K} \tag{6}$$

where K is the number of problems in a worksheet, $s\left(\widehat{w_u^{l,n}}(k)\right)$ is student's predicted score on the problem (i.e., 1 if predicted to be correctly solved, 0 otherwise) and $s\left(w_u^{l,n}(k)\right)$ is student's actual score (i.e., 1 or 0) on the problem.

Note that while predicting a test worksheet for a user, all of the previous worksheets or part of them (i.e., in the sliding window approach) are used for calculating the similarity between users. For instance, if the 3rd repetition of MC worksheet 2 is the test worksheet; then Mod_Baseline_All will use only the final repetitions of all previous worksheets (i.e., last repetition of EG worksheets 1,2,3,4 and MC worksheet 1). On the other hand Mod_MultInt_All will use the previous repetitions of the test worksheet together with all repetitions of all previous worksheets (i.e., all repetitions of EG worksheets 1,2,3,4 and MC worksheet 1 together with 1st and 2nd repetitions of MC worksheet 2). Sliding window versions of both approaches only utilize the last k of the training worksheets (explained above) depending on the window size. Therefore each worksheet is predicted separately and the MAE is calculated for each

Table 2. Results of the Mod_Baseline_All, Mod_Baseline_Window, Mod_MultInt_All and Mod_MultInt_Window CF approaches in comparison to each other for two similarity configurations: i) Pearson Correlation Coefficient (PCC) and ii) Vector Space (VS) and for four window sizes. The window size is the number of past worksheets used for calculating the similarity between students. The performance is evaluated with the MAE.

Methods			Similarity Metric	
			Pearson Correlation Coefficient (PCC)	Vector Space (VS)
Mod_Baseline_All			0.309	0.308
Mod_Baseline_Window	Window Size	1	0.296	0.306
		2	0.319	0.309
		3	0.296	0.306
		4	0.296	0.306
Mod_MultInt_All			0.268	0.269
Mod_MultInt_Window	Window Size	1	0.265	0.286
		2	0.275	0.285
		3	0.270	0.282
		4	0.275	0.283

predicted worksheet of a student separately. The average of the MAEs for all test worksheets of a student (i.e., all worksheets except the first worksheet, namely EG worksheet 1) is the MAE of that student. The mean of the MAEs of all students is the final MAE; and this final MAE is reported in this work.

5 Experiment Results

This section presents the experimental results of the methods that are proposed in Methods and Models section. All the methods were evaluated on the dataset as described in Data section (i.e., Section 2).

5.1 The Performance of Temporal CF with Sliding Time Window (i.e., Mod_Baseline_Window)

The first set of experiments was conducted to evaluate the effectiveness of the temporal CF approach of using sliding time windows. More specifically, Mod_Baseline_Window and Mod_MultInt_Window CF approaches are compared to Mod_Baseline_All and Mod_MultInt_All CF approaches (details about which are given in Section 3) with each other on the prediction of problem solving task for four different window sizes. Their performance can be seen in Tables 2. It can be seen that the Mod_Baseline_Window approach slightly outperforms Mod_Baseline_All approach for window sizes 1, 3 & 4; and Mod_Baseline_All approach slightly outperforms Mod_Baseline_Window approach for window size 2. Similarly the Mod_MultInt_Window approach slightly outperforms Mod_MultInt_All approach for window size 1 (with PCC) and Mod_MultInt_All approach slightly outperforms Mod_MultInt_Window approach for window sizes more than 2 (and window size 1 with VS). Paired t-tests have been applied for this set of experiments and the improvement gained by using the sliding-time

Table 3. Results of the Mod_MultInt_All and Mod_MultInt_Window CF approaches are shown in comparison to Mod_Baseline_All and Mod_Baseline_Window CF approaches for two similarity configurations: i) Pearson Corrleation Coefficient (PCC) and ii) Vector Space (VS). The performance is evaluated with the MAE.

Methods	Similarity Metric	
	Pearson Correlation Coefficient (PCC)	Vector Space (VS)
Mod_Baseline_All	0.309	0.308
Mod_MultInt_All	0.268	0.269
Mod_Baseline_Window	0.296	0.306
Mod_MultInt_Window	0.266	0.286

window or using different window sizes has been found to be not significant (i.e., p-value is more than 0.01) in most of the configurations (there are some significant differences in favor of and against using time windows at the same time, so it is not possible to see a consistent and significant dominance of either approach over each other). To the best of our knowledge this is the first work using sliding time windows for an educational application (specifically for predicting the correctness of problem solving). Results discussed above show that, sliding time windows (or their variants), despite their positive effect on the applications of temporal CF over business applications [5], [12]; should be carefully considered.

5.2 The Performance of Temporal CF with Multiple Interactions and the Hybrid Approach (i.e., Mod_MultInt_All and Mod_MultInt_Window)

The second set of experiments was conducted to evaluate the effectiveness of the temporal CF approach of using multiple interactions and the hybrid temporal CF approach of using multiple interactions together with the sliding time windows. More specifically, Mod_MultInt_All and Mod_MultInt_Window (with window size 1) CF approaches are compared to Mod_Baseline_All and Mod_Baseline_Window (with window size 1) CF approaches (details about which are given in detail in Section 3) with each other. Their performance can be seen in Table 3. It can be seen that both of Mod_MultInt_All and Mod_MultInt_Window approaches significantly (with p-value less than 0.001) outperform Mod_Baseline_All and Mod_Baseline_Window approaches respectively. This explicitly shows that utilizing the information coming from the multiple interactions (i.e., repetitions of worksheets) is a much better approach than the default CF approach of using the latest user-item interactions for predicting correctness of problem solving.

The hybrid approach of utilizing sliding time window together with multiple interactions (i.e., Mod_MultInt_Window) has not been found to be significantly different than Mod_MultInt_All approach (i.e., p-value is more than 0.01). This is consistent with the results reported in the previous section. To better see the robustness of the Mod_MultInt_All approach, the average of PCC and VS results of the Mod_MultInt_All approach is shown in comparison to Mod_Baseline_All approach in Table 4 for all the test worksheets (i.e., all worksheets except EG worksheet 1). It can be seen that Mod_MultInt_All approach is robust across all worksheets and performs consistently better than the Mod_Baseline_All approach almost for all worksheets. It should also be noted that Mod_MultInt_All achieves comparable

Table 4. Results of the Mod_Baseline_All and Mod_MultInt_All CF approaches in comparison to each other for all test worksheets (i.e., for all worksheets except the 1st worksheet, namely EG Worksheet 1). The performance is evaluated with the MAE and the average of PCC and VS based results are reported.

Methods	Test Worksheets									
	Equal Group			Multiplicative Compare				Mixed		
	W2	W3	W4	W1	W2	W3	W4	W1	W2	W3
Mod_Baseline_All	0.46	0.35	0.38	0.13	0.31	0.28	0.39	0.34	0.18	0.28
Mod_MultInt_All	0.44	0.30	0.34	0.09	0.29	0.24	0.29	0.27	0.21	0.21

performance with prior work on the prediction of problem solving with F_1 scores of 0.780 (for PCC) and 0.778 (for VS) [1], [3].

5.3 The Effect of Using Different Similarity Metrics (i.e., PCC and VS)

The third set of experiments was conducted to evaluate the effectiveness of the two popular similarity metrics: i) Pearson Correlation Coefficient (PCC) and ii) Vector Similarity (VS). It can be seen in Tables 2 and 3 that although the PCC seems to perform slightly better than the VS, the difference in their performance is not found to be significant (i.e., p-value is more than 0.01) for most cases. This is different from the prior work of CF in business domain, where PCC has been shown to perform better than VS [2]. This difference can be explained by the fact that in prior work such as movie recommendation, users' have different voting behaviors (i.e., some users tend to vote higher for all movies and some tend to vote lower). PCC can better deal with this user bias. Yet, in applications where user-item interactions are not user-voluntary such as this work; VS can perform comparable to PCC [2].

6 Conclusion and Future Work

This paper proposes a novel temporal CF approach to predict the correctness of students' problem solving in an intelligent math tutor by utilizing the multiple interactions. Several modeling approaches with different configurations are studied for this application through extensive experiments. Empirical results show that a temporal CF approach utilizing the information coming from multiple interactions between student-problem pairs is much more effective than a CF approach that does not utilize this information. A temporal CF approach that uses a sliding time window is found to be not effective, although it has been shown to be an effective CF approach in business applications such as movie recommendation. Furthermore, a novel hybrid approach combining the proposed temporal CF together with the temporal CF using sliding time windows is found to be not significantly different than using the proposed temporal CF approach of only utilizing multiple interactions. Finally the common Pearson Correlation Coefficient similarity metric is found to be not significantly more effective than the common Vector Similarity, although PCC has been shown to be significantly more effective than VS in business applications such as movie recommendation [2].

There are several possibilities to extend the research. First, it is possible to design sophisticated CF algorithms that model the combination of temporal CF algorithms proposed in this work and some problem features such as irrelevant information and readability intelligently (e.g., via mixture models). Second, data from more students and different applications can be used to assess the robustness of the proposed algorithms. Future work will be conducted mainly in those directions.

Acknowledgements. This research was partially supported by the following grants IIS-0749462, IIS-0746830, DRL-0822296 and STC-0939370. Any opinions, findings, conclusions, or recommendations expressed in this paper are the authors', and do not necessarily reflect those of the sponsor.

References

1. Beck, J.E., Woolf, B.P.: High Level Student Modeling with Machine Learning. In: Gauthier, G., VanLehn, K., Frasson, C. (eds.) ITS 2000. LNCS, vol. 1839, pp. 584–593. Springer, Heidelberg (2000)
2. Breese, J., Heckerman, D., Kadie, C.: Empirical Analysis of Predictive Algorithms for Collaborative Filtering. In: Proceedings of the 14th Conference on Uncertainty in Artificial Intelligence, pp. 43–52. Morgan Kaufmann, San Francisco (1998)
3. Cetintas, S., Si, L., Xin, Y.P., Hord, C.: Predicting Correctness of Problem Solving from Low-level Log Data in Intelligent Tutoring Systems. In: Proceedings of the 2nd International Conference on Educational Data Mining, pp. 230–239 (2009)
4. Cho, K., Schunn, C.C., Wilson, R.W.: Validity and Reliability of Scaffolded Peer Assessment of Writing from Instructor and Student Perspectives. Journal of Educational Psychology 98(4), 891–901 (2006)
5. Ding, Y., Li, X.: Time Weight Collaborative Filtering. In: Proceedings of the 14th ACM International Conference on Information and Knowledge Management, pp. 485–492. ACM, New York (2005)
6. Koren, Y.: Collaborative Filtering with Temporal Dynamics. In: Proceedings of the 15th ACM SIGKDD International Conference on Knowledge Discovery and Data Mining, pp. 447–456. ACM, New York (2009)
7. Lathia, N., Hailes, S., Capra, L.: Temporal Collaborative Filtering with Adaptive Neighborhoods. In: Proceedings of the 32nd International ACM SIGIR Conference on Research and Development in Information Retrieval, pp. 796–797. ACM, New York (2009)
8. Loll, F., Pinkwart, N.: Using Collaborative Filtering Algorithms as eLearning Tools. In: Proceedings of the 42nd Hawaii International Conference on System Sciences, pp. 1–10. IEEE Computer Society, Washington (2009)
9. Maletsky, E.M., Andrews, A.G., Burton, G.M., Johnson, H.C., Luckie, L.A.: Harcourt Math, Indiana edn. Harcourt, Chicago (2004)
10. Pinkwart, N., Aleven, V., Ashley, K., Lynch, C.: Toward Legal Argument Instruction with Graph Grammars and Collaborative Filtering Techniques. In: Ikeda, M., Ashley, K.D., Chan, T.-W. (eds.) ITS 2006. LNCS, vol. 4053, pp. 227–236. Springer, Heidelberg (2006)
11. Robinet, V., Bisson, G., Gordon, M.B., Lemaire, B.: Inducing High-Level Behaviors from Problem-Solving Traces Using Machine-Learning Tools. IEEE Intelligent Systems 22(4), 22–30 (2007)
12. Tsymbal, A.: The Problem of Concept Drift: Definitions and Related Work. Technical report, TCD-CS-2004-15, Comp. Sci. Department, Trinity College Dublin, Ireland (2004)
13. Walker, A., Recker, M., Lawless, K., Wiley, D.: Collaborative Information Filtering: a Review and an Educational Application. International Journal of Artificial Intelligence in Education 14, 1–26 (2004)

Detecting the Moment of Learning

Ryan S.J.d. Baker[1], Adam B. Goldstein[2], and Neil T. Heffernan[2]

[1] Department of Social Science and Policy Studies, Worcester Polytechnic Institute
100 Institute Road, Worcester MA 01609, USA
rsbaker@wpi.edu
[2] Department of Computer Science, Worcester Polytechnic Institute
100 Institute Road, Worcester MA 01609, USA
abgoldstein@gmail.com, nth@wpi.edu

Abstract. Intelligent tutors have become increasingly accurate at detecting whether a student knows a skill at a given time. However, these models do not tell us exactly at which point the skill was learned. In this paper, we present a machine-learned model that can assess the probability that a student learned a skill at a specific problem step (instead of at the next or previous problem step). Implications for knowledge tracing and potential uses in "discovery with models" educational data mining analyses are discussed, including analysis of which skills are learned gradually, and which are learned in "eureka" moments.

Keywords: Educational Data Mining, Bayesian Knowledge Tracing, Student Modeling, Intelligent Tutoring Systems.

1 Introduction

In recent years, educational data mining and knowledge engineering methods have led to increasingly precise models of students' knowledge as they use intelligent tutoring systems. The first stage in this progression was the development of Bayes Nets and Bayesian frameworks that could infer the probability that a student knew a specific skill at a specific time from their pattern of correct responses and non-correct responses (e.g. errors and hint requests) up until that time [cf. 13, 18, 25].

In recent years, a second wave of knowledge modeling has emerged, which attempts to predict student knowledge more precisely based on information beyond just correctness. Beck et al [8] differentiated help requests from errors – however, doing so did not significantly improve predictive power. Baker, Corbett, & Aleven [3, 4] extended Bayesian Knowledge Tracing with contextualized estimation of the probability that the student guessed or slipped, leading to better prediction of future correctness. More recent work has suggested that the exact framework from [3, 4] leads to poorer prediction of post-test scores, but that information on contextual slip can be used in other fashions to predict post-test scores more precisely than existing methods [6]. Other knowledge tracing frameworks have attempted to model performance on problems or problem steps that involve multiple skills at the same time [cf. 21, 22], and have focused on predicting a student's speed of response in addition to just correctness [cf. 20].

Creating more precise models of student learning has several benefits. First of all, to the extent that student practice is assigned based on knowledge assessments [cf. 13], more precise knowledge models will result in better tailoring of practice to individual student needs [cf. 10]. Second, models of student knowledge have become an essential component in the development of models of student behavior within intelligent tutoring systems, forming key components of models of many constructs, including models of appropriate help use [1], gaming the system [5, 27], and off-task behavior [2, 11]. More precise knowledge models can form a more reliable component in these analyses, and reduce the noise in these models.

However, while these extensions to educational data mining have created the potential for more precise assessment of student knowledge at a specific time, these models do not tell us *when* the knowledge was acquired. In this paper, we will introduce a model that can infer the probability that a student learned a skill at a specific step during the problem-solving process. Note that this probability is ***not*** equal to P(T) in standard Bayesian Knowledge Tracing (a full explanation will be given later in this paper). Creating a model that can infer this probability will create the potential for new types of analyses of student learning, as well as making existing types of analyses easier to conduct. For example, this type of approach may allow us to study the differences between gradual learning (such as strengthening of a memory association [cf.20]) and learning given to "eureka" moments, where a skill is suddenly understood [cf. 17]. Do different skills lead to each type of learning?

To give another example, studying which items are most effective (and in which order they are most effective) [cf. 9, 23] will be facilitated with the addition of a concrete numerical measure of immediate learning. Similarly, studying the relationship between behavior and immediate learning is more straightforward with a concrete numerical measure of immediate learning. Prior methods for studying these relationships have required either looking only at the single next performance opportunity [cf. 12], a fairly coarse learning measure, or have required interpreting the difference between model parameters in Bayesian Knowledge Tracing [cf. 8], a non-trivial statistical task. Creating models of the moment of learning may even enable distinctions between behaviors associated with immediate learning and behaviors associated with learning later on, and enable identification of the antecedents of later learning. For example, perhaps some types of help lead to better learning, but the difference is only seen after additional practice has occurred.

In the following sections, we will present an approach for labeling data in terms of student immediate learning, a machine-learned model of student immediate learning (and indicators of goodness of fit), and an example of the type of "discovery with models" analysis that this type of model enables. In that analysis, we will investigate whether learning is differentially "spiky" between different skills, with learning occurring abruptly for some skills, and more gradually for other skills.

2 Data

The analyses discussed in this paper are conducted on data from 232 students' use of a Cognitive Tutor curriculum for middle school mathematics [16], during the 2002-2003 school year. All of the students were enrolled in mathematics classes in one middle school in the Pittsburgh suburbs which used Cognitive Tutors two days a week as part of their regular mathematics curriculum, year round. None of the classes were composed predominantly of gifted or special needs students. The students were in the 6th, 7th, and 8th grades (approximately 12-14 years old), but all used the same curriculum (it was an advanced curriculum for 6th graders, and a remedial curriculum for 8th graders).

Each of these students worked through a subset of 35 different lessons within the Cognitive Tutor curriculum, covering a diverse selection of material from the middle school mathematics curriculum. Middle school mathematics, in the United States, generally consists of a diverse collection of topics, and these students' work was representative of that diversity, including lessons on combinatorics, decimals, diagrams, 3D geometry, fraction division, function generation and solving, graph interpretation, probability, and proportional reasoning. These students made 581,785 transactions (either entering an answer or requesting a hint) on 171,987 problem steps covering 253 skills. 290,698 additional transactions were not included in either these totals or in our analyses, because they were not labeled with skills, information needed to apply Bayesian Knowledge Tracing.

3 Detecting the Moment of Learning

In this paper, we introduce a model that predicts the probability that a student has learned a specific skill at a specific problem step. We refer to this probability as P(*J*), short for "Just Learned". This model is developed using a procedure structurally similar to that in [3, 4], using a two-step process. First, predictions of student knowledge from standard Bayesian Knowledge Tracing are combined with data from future correctness and applications of Bayes' Theorem. This process generates labels of the probability that a student learned a skill at a specific problem step. Then a model is trained, using a broader feature set with absolutely no data from the future, to predict the labeled data.

3.1 Labeling Process

The first step of our process is to label each first student action on a step in the data set with the probability that the student learned the skill at that time, to serve as inputs to a machine learning algorithm. We label each student problem step (*N*) with the probability that the student learned the skill at that step. Specifically, our working definition of "learning at step *N*" is learning the skill between the instant after the student enters their first answer for step *N*, and the instant that the student enters their first answer for step *N+1*.

We label step *N* using information about the probability the student knew the skill before answering on step *N* (from Bayesian Knowledge Tracing) and information on performance on the two following steps (*N+1*, *N+2*). Using data from future actions gives information about the true probability that the student learned the skill during the actions at step *N*. For instance, if the student probably did not know the skill at step *N* (according to Bayesian Knowledge Tracing), but the first attempts at steps *N+1* and *N+2* are correct, it is relatively likely that the student learned the skill at step *N*. Correspondingly, if the first attempts to answer steps *N+1* and *N+2* are incorrect, it is relatively unlikely that the student learned the skill at step *N*.

We assess the probability that the student learned the skill at step N, given information about the actions at steps $N+1$ and $N+2$ (which we term A_{+1+2}), as:

$$P(J) = P(\sim L_n \wedge T \mid A_{+1+2})$$

Note that this probability is assessed as $P(\sim L_n \wedge T)$, the probability that the student did not know the skill and learned it, rather than $P(T)$. Within Bayesian Knowledge Tracing, the semantic meaning of $P(T)$ is actually $P(T \mid \sim L_n)$: $P(T)$ is the probability that the skill will be learned, if it has not yet been learned. $P(T)$'s semantics, while highly relevant for some research questions [cf. 8, 16], are not an indicator of the probability that a skill was learned at a specific moment. This is because the probability that a student learned a skill at a specific step can be no higher than the probability that they do not currently know it. $P(T)$, however, can have any value between 0 and 1 at any time. For low values of $P(L_n)$, $P(T)$ will approximate the probability that the student just learned the skill $P(J)$, but for high values of $P(L_n)$, $P(T)$ can take on extremely high values even though the probability that the skill was learned at that moment is very low.

We can find $P(J)$'s value with a function using Bayes' Rule:

$$P(\sim L_n \wedge T \mid A_{+1+2}) = \frac{P(A_{+1+2} \mid \sim L_n \wedge T) * P(\sim L_n \wedge T)}{P(A_{+1+2})}$$

The base probability $P(\sim L_n \wedge T)$ can be computed fairly simply, using the student's current value for $P(\sim L_n)$ from Bayesian Knowledge Tracing, and the Bayesian Knowledge Tracing model's value of $P(T)$ for the current skill:

$$P(\sim L_n \wedge T) = P(\sim L_n) P(T)$$

The probability of the actions at time $N+1$ and $N+2$, $P(A_{+1+2})$, is computed as a function of the probability of the actions given each possible case (the skill was already known, the skill was unknown but was just learned, or the skill was unknown and was not learned), and the contingent probabilities of each of these cases.

$$P(A_{+1+2}) = P(A_{+1+2} \mid L_n) P(L_n) + P(A_{+1+2} \mid \sim L_n \wedge T) P(\sim L_n \wedge T) \\ + P(A_{+1+2} \mid \sim L_n \wedge \sim T) P(\sim L_n \wedge \sim T)$$

The probability of the actions at time $N+1$ and $N+2$, in each of these three cases, is a function of the Bayesian Knowledge Tracing model's probabilities for guessing (G), slipping (S), and learning the skill (T). Correct answers are notated with a **C** and non-correct answers (e.g. errors or help requests) are notated with a **~C**.

$P(A_{+1+2} = C, C \mid L_n) = P(\sim S)^2$ $P(A_{+1+2} = C, \sim C \mid L_n) = P(S) P(\sim S)$
$P(A_{+1+2} = \sim C, C \mid L_n) = P(S) P(\sim S)$ $P(A_{+1+2} = \sim C, \sim C \mid L_n) = P(S)^2$
$P(A_{+1+2} = C, C \mid \sim L_n \wedge T) = P(\sim S)^2$ $P(A_{+1+2} = C, \sim C \mid \sim L_n \wedge T) = P(S) P(\sim S)$
$P(A_{+1+2} = \sim C, C \mid \sim L_n \wedge T) = P(S) P(\sim S)$ $P(A_{+1+2} = \sim C, \sim C \mid \sim L_n \wedge T) = P(S)^2$

$P(A_{+1+2} = C, C | \sim L_n \wedge \sim T) = P(G)P(\sim T)P(G) + P(G)P(T)P(\sim S)$
$P(A_{+1+2} = C, \sim C | \sim L_n \wedge \sim T) = P(G)P(\sim T)P(\sim G) + P(G)P(T)P(S)$
$P(A_{+1+2} = \sim C, C | \sim L_n \wedge \sim T) = P(\sim G)P(\sim T)P(G) + P(\sim G)P(T)P(\sim S)$
$P(A_{+1+2} = \sim C, \sim C | \sim L_n \wedge \sim T) = P(\sim G)P(\sim T)P(\sim G) + P(\sim G)P(T)P(S)$

Once each action is labeled with estimates of the probability P(J) that the student learned the skill at that time, we use these labels to create machine-learned models that can accurately predict P(J) at run-time. The original labels of P(J) were developed using future knowledge, but the machine-learned models predict P(J) using only data about the action itself (no future data).

3.2 Features

For each problem step, we used a set of 25 features describing the first action on problem step N. The features used in the final model are shown in Table 1. 23 of those features were previously distilled to use in the development of contextual models of guessing and slipping [cf. 3, 4]. These features had in turn been used in prior work to develop automated detectors of off-task behavior [2] and gaming the system [5].

The 24th and 25th features were used in prior models of gaming the system and off-task behavior, but not in prior contextual models of guessing and slipping. These features are the probability that the student knew the skill before the first attempt on action N, P(L_{n-1}), and the probability that the student knew the skill after the first attempt on action N, P(L_n). There are some arguments against including these features, as P($\sim L_n$) is part of the construct being predicted, P($\sim L_n \wedge T$). However, the goal of this model is to determine the probability of learning, moment-by-moment, and the students' current and previous knowledge levels, as assessed by Bayesian Knowledge Tracing, are useful information towards this goal. In addition, other parameters in the model will be more interpretable if these terms are included. Without these terms, it would be difficult to determine if a parameter was predicting T or $\sim L_n$. With these terms, we can have greater confidence that parameters are predictive of learning (not just whether the skill was previously unknown), because L_n is already accounted for in the model. However, in accordance with potential validity concerns stemming from including P(L_{n-1}) and P(L_n) in the model, we will also present goodness-of-fit statistics from a model not including these features.

While it is possible that features tailored to researchers' intuitions of what sorts of behaviors ought to predict moment-to-moment learning might perform better than these re-used features, the repeated utility of these features in model after model suggests that these features capture constructs of general applicability. Nonetheless, it will be valuable to consider additional features in future models of P(J). An additional aspect to consider with regards to the features is which actions the features are distilled for. As these features involve the first action at problem step N, they represent the student's behavior at the moment right before learning, more than the student's behavior exactly at the moment of learning (which takes place in our model after the first action of problem step N and before the first action of problem step N+1, as previously discussed). As such, the model's features should perhaps be interpreted as representing immediate antecedents of the moment of learning, as opposed to the exact characteristics of the moment of learning itself. Despite this limitation of our feature set, the model is still accurate at identifying the moment of learning (as discussed below). However, extending the model with a new set of features relevant to subsequent actions on problem step N (e.g. the second action to the last action) may improve model accuracy and interpretability.

3.3 Machine Learning

Given the labels and the model features for each student action within the tutor, two machine-learned models of P(J) were developed. As discussed above, one model used all 25 features, the other model only used the 23 features from [3, 4]. Linear regression was conducted within RapidMiner [19]. All reported validation is batch 6-fold cross-validation, at the student level (e.g. detectors are trained on five groups of students and tested on a sixth group of students). By cross-validating at this level, we increase confidence that detectors will be accurate for new groups of students. Linear Regression was tried both on the original feature sets and on interaction terms of the features; slightly better cross-validated performance was obtained for the original feature sets, and therefore we will focus on the models obtained from this approach.

3.4 Results

The model with 25 features, shown in Table 1, achieved a correlation of 0.446 to the labels, within 6-fold student-level cross-validation. The model with only 23 features achieved a weaker correlation of 0.301.

We can compute the statistical significance of the difference in correlation in a way that accounts for the non-independence between students, by computing a test of the significance of the difference between two correlation coefficients for correlated

Table 1. The machine learned model of the probability of learning at a specific moment. In the unusual case where output values fall outside the range {0,1}, they are bounded to 0 or 1.

Feature	P(J) =
Answer is correct	- 0.0023
Answer is incorrect	+ 0.0023
Action is a help request	- 0.00391
Response is a string	+ 0.01213
Response is a number	+ 0.01139
Time taken (SD faster (-) / slower (+) than avg across all students)	+ 0.00018
Time taken in last 3 actions (SD off avg across all students)	+ 0.000077
Total number of times student has gotten this skill wrong total	- 0.000073
Number of times student requested help on this skill, divided by number of problems	- 0.00711
Number of times student made errors on this skill, divided by number of problems	+ 0.0013
Total time taken on this skill so far (across all problems), in seconds	+ 0.0000047
Number of last 5 actions which involved same interface element	- 0.00081
Number of last 8 actions that involved a help request	+ 0.00137
Number of last 5 actions that were wrong	+ 0.00080
At least 3 of last 5 actions involved same interface element & were wrong	- 0.037
Number of opportunities student has already had to use current skill	- 0.0000075
F24: The probability the student knew the skill, after the current action (L_n)	- 0.053
F25: The probability the student knew the skill, before the current action (L_{n-1})	+ 0.00424
Constant Term	+ 0.039

samples [cf. 14] for each student, and then aggregating across students using Stouffer's Z [23]. According to this test, the difference between the two models is highly statistically significant, Z=116.51, p<0.0001.

Although correlation was acceptable, one limitation of this model is that it tended to underestimate values of P(*J*) that were relatively high in the original labels. While these values remained higher than the rest of the data (hence the model's reasonable correlation to the labels), they were lower, in absolute terms, than the original labels. This problem could be addressed by weighting the (rarer) high values more heavily during model-fitting, although this approach would likely reduce overall correlation.

As with any multiple-parameter linear regression model (and most other model frameworks as well), interpretability of the meaning of any parameter in specific is not entirely straightforward. This is because every parameter must be considered in the context of all of the other parameters – often a feature's sign can flip based on the other parameters in the model. Hence, significant caution should be taken before attempting to interpret specific parameters as-is. It is worth noting that approaches that attempt to isolate specific single features [cf. 8] are significantly more interpretable than the internal aspects of a multiple parameter regression model such as this one. It is also worth remembering that these features apply to the first action of problem step *N* whereas the labels pertain to the student's learning between the first action of problem step *N* and the first action of problem step *N+1*. Hence, the features of this model can be interpreted more as representing the antecedents of the moment of learning than as representing the moment of learning itself – though they do accurately predict the moment of learning.

One interesting aspect of this model (and the original labels) is that the overall chance of learning a skill on any single step is relatively low within this tutor. However, there are specific circumstances where learning is higher. Many of these circumstances correlate to time spent, and the student's degree of persistence in attempting to respond. Larger numbers of past errors appear to predict more current learning than larger numbers of past help requests, for instance. This result appears at a surface level to be in contrast to the findings from [8], but is potentially explained by the difference between learning from requesting help once – the grain-size studied in [8] – and learning from requesting the same help sequence many times. It may be that learning from errors [cf. 26] is facilitated by making more errors, but that learning from help does not benefit from reading the same help multiple times.

4 Studying the Spikiness of Student Learning

A key way that the model presented here can be scientifically useful is through its predictions, as components in other analyses. Machine-learned models of gaming the system, off-task behavior, and contextual slip have proven useful as components in many other analyses [cf. 2, 12, 27]. Models of the moment of student learning may turn out to be equally useful.

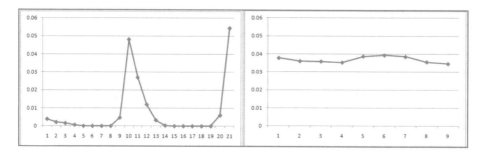

Fig. 1. A relatively "spiky" graph of a student's performance on a specific skill, indicating eureka learning (left), and a relatively smooth graph, indicating more gradual learning (right). The X axis shows how many problem steps have involved the current skill, and the Y axis shows values of P(*J*).

One research area that models of the moment of student learning may shed light on is the differences between gradual learning (such as strengthening of a memory association [cf. 20]) and learning given to "eureka" moments, where a skill is understood suddenly [cf. 17]. Predictions of momentary learning for a specific student and skill can be plotted, and graphs which are "spiky" (e.g. which have sudden peaks of learning) can be distinguished from flatter graphs, which indicate more gradual learning. Examples of students experiencing gradual learning and eureka learning are shown in Figure 1. Note that the graph on the left in Figure 1 shows two spikes, rather than just one spike, a fairly common pattern in our data. Understanding why some spiky graphs have two spikes, and others have just one, will be an important area for future investigation. The degree to which learning involves a eureka moment can be quantified through a measure of "spikiness", defined as the maximum value of P(*J*) for a student/skill pair, divided by the average value of P(*J*) for that same student/skill pair. This measure of spikiness is bounded between 1 (minimum spikiness) and positive infinity (maximum spikiness).

Spikiness may be influenced by the number of opportunities to practice a skill, as more opportunities may (by random variation) increase the potential maximum value of P(*J*). Therefore, to compare spikiness between skills, we only consider skills practiced at least 6 times, and only consider the first 20 steps relevant to that skill. Spikiness values range for skills between {1.12, 113.52}, M=8.55, SD=14.62. A valuable area of future work would be to study what characterizes the skills that have high spikiness and low spikiness. Spikiness values range for students between {2.22, 21.81}, M=6.81, SD=3.09, considerably less spikiness (on the whole) than the differences in spikiness seen between skills. Interestingly, however, a student's spikiness is a good predictor of their final knowledge; the correlation between a student's average final P(L_n) and their average spikiness is a very high 0.71, which is statistically significantly different than chance, F(1,228)=230.19, p<0.0001. This result suggests that learning spikes may be an early predictor of whether a student is going to achieve good learning of specific material.

5 Discussion and Conclusions

In this paper, we have presented a first model of P(J), the probability that a student learned a specific skill on a specific opportunity to practice and learn that skill. Though this model builds off of past attempts to contextualize student modeling [e.g. 3, 4] and to study the impact of different events on learning [e.g. 8, 23], this model is distinct from prior models of student learning, focusing on assessing the likelihood of learning on individual problem steps. We show that the model achieves acceptable correlation to the labels of this construct; there is still considerable room for improvement, potentially achievable through broadening the feature set.

We also show that the model's assessments of P(J) can be used to distill a secondary measure, the "spikiness" of learning, defined as the maximum momentary learning, divided by the average momentary learning. We find that a student's spikiness is an excellent predictor of their final knowledge, and that skills have greater variance in spikiness than students. Studying which aspects of skills predicts spikiness may be a valuable tool for further research into what types of skills are learned gradually or through "eureka" experiences. In addition, given the correlation between spikiness and final knowledge, models of P(J) are likely to prove useful for student knowledge modeling, as contextual guess and slip have been [e.g. 3, 4], and in the long term may lead to more effective adaptation by Intelligent Tutoring Systems.

Acknowledgements. This research was supported via NSF grant award number DGE0742503, by the Pittsburgh Science of Learning Center, NSF award number SBE-0836012, and by U.S. Department of Education program grant #R305A070440.

References

1. Aleven, V., McLaren, B., Roll, I., Koedinger, K.: Toward meta-cognitive tutoring: A model of help seeking with a Cognitive Tutor. International Journal of Artificial Intelligence and Education 16, 101–128 (2006)
2. Baker, R.S.J.d.: Modeling and Understanding Students' Off-Task Behavior in Intelligent Tutoring Systems. In: Proc. ACM CHI: Computer-Human Interaction, pp. 1059–1068 (2007)
3. Baker, R.S.J.d., Corbett, A.T., Aleven, V.: More Accurate Student Modeling Through Contextual Estimation of Slip and Guess Probabilities in Bayesian Knowledge Tracing. In: Woolf, B.P., Aïmeur, E., Nkambou, R., Lajoie, S. (eds.) ITS 2008. LNCS, vol. 5091, pp. 406–415. Springer, Heidelberg (2008)
4. Baker, R.S.J.d., Corbett, A.T., Aleven, V.: Improving Contextual Models of Guessing and Slipping with a Truncated Training Set. In: Proceedings of the 1st International Conference on Educational Data Mining, pp. 67–76 (2008)
5. Baker, R.S.J.d., Corbett, A.T., Roll, I., Koedinger, K.R.: Developing a Generalizable Detector of When Students Game the System. User Modeling and User-Adapted Interaction 18(3), 287–314 (2008)
6. Baker, R.S.J.d., Corbett, A.T., et al.: Contextual Slip and Prediction of Student Performance After Use of an Intelligent Tutor. Article under review
7. Baker, R., Walonoski, J., Heffernan, N., Roll, I., Corbett, A., Koedinger, K.: Why Students Engage in "Gaming the System" Behavior in Interactive Learning Environments. Journal of Interactive Learning Research 19(2), 185–224 (2008)
8. Beck, J.E., Chang, K.-m., Mostow, J., Corbett, A.T.: Does Help Help? Introducing the Bayesian Evaluation and Assessment Methodology. In: Woolf, B.P., Aïmeur, E., Nkambou, R., Lajoie, S. (eds.) ITS 2008. LNCS, vol. 5091, pp. 383–394. Springer, Heidelberg (2008)

9. Beck, J.E., Mostow, J.: How who should practice: using learning decomposition to evaluate the efficacy of different types of practice for different types of students. In: Woolf, B.P., Aïmeur, E., Nkambou, R., Lajoie, S. (eds.) ITS 2008. LNCS, vol. 5091, pp. 353–362. Springer, Heidelberg (2008)
10. Cen, H., Koedinger, K.R., Junker, B.: Is Over Practice Necessary? Improving Learning Efficiency with the Cognitive Tutor. In: Proceedings of the 13th International Conference on Artificial Intelligence and Education
11. Cetintas, S., Si, L., Xin, Y.P., Hord, C., Zhang, D.: Learning to Identify Students' Off-Task Behavior in Intelligent Tutoring Systems. In: Proceedings of the 14th International Conference on Artificial Intelligence in Education, pp. 701–703 (2009)
12. Cocea, M., Hershkovitz, A., Baker, R.S.J.d.: The Impact of Off-task and Gaming Behaviors on Learning: Immediate or Aggregate? In: Proceedings of the 14th International Conference on Artificial Intelligence in Education, pp. 507–514 (2009)
13. Corbett, A.T., Anderson, J.R.: Knowledge Tracing: Modeling the Acquisition of Procedural Knowledge. User Modeling and User-Adapted Interaction 4, 253–278 (1995)
14. Ferguson, G.A.: Statistical Analysis in Psychology and Education. McGraw-Hill, New York (1971)
15. Gong, Y., Rai, D., Beck, J., Heffernan, N.: Does Self-Discipline Impact Students' Knowledge and Learning? In: Proc. of the 2nd International Conference on Educational Data Mining, pp. 61–70 (2009)
16. Koedinger, K.R.: Toward evidence for instructional principles: Examples from Cognitive Tutor Math 6. In: Proceedings of PME-NA XXXIII (the North American Chapter of the International Group for the Psychology of Mathematics Education) (2002)
17. Lindstrom, P., Gulz, A.: Catching Eureka on the Fly. In: Proceedings of the AAAI 2008 Spring Symposium (2008)
18. Martin, J., Van Lehn, K.: Student Assessment Using Bayesian Nets International. International Journal of Human-Computer Studies 42, 575–591 (1995)
19. Mierswa, I., Wurst, M., Klinkenberg, R., Scholz, M., Euler, T.: YALE: Rapid Prototyping for Complex Data Mining Tasks. In: Proc. of the 12th ACM SIGKDD International Conference on Knowledge Discovery and Data Mining (KDD 2006), pp. 935–940 (2006)
20. Pavlik, P.I., Anderson, J.R.: Using a Model to Compute the Optimal Schedule of Practice. Journal of Experimental Psychology: Applied 14(2), 101–117 (2008)
21. Pavlik, P.I., Cen, H., Koedinger, K.R.: Performance Factors Analysis – A New Alternative to Knowledge Tracing. In: Proceedings of the 14th International Conference on Artificial Intelligence in Education, pp. 531–538 (2009)
22. Pardos, Z., Beck, J.E., Ruiz, C., Heffernan, N.T.: The Composition Effect: Conjunctive or Compensatory? An Analysis of Multi-Skill Math Questions in ITS. In: Proceedings of the 1st International Conference on Educational Data Mining, pp. 147–156 (2008)
23. Pardos, Z., Heffernan, N.: Determining the Significance of Item Order in Randomized Problem Sets. In: Proc. of the 1st Int'l. Conf. on Educational Data Mining, pp. 111–120 (2009)
24. Rosenthal, R., Rosnow, R.L.: Essentials of Behavioral Research: Methods and Data Analysis, 2nd edn. McGraw-Hill, Boston (1991)
25. Shute, V.J.: SMART: Student modeling approach for responsive tutoring. User Modeling and User-Adapted Interaction 5(1), 1–44 (1995)
26. VanLehn, K., Siler, S., Murray, C., et al.: Why Do Only Some Events Cause Learning During Human Tutoring. Cognition and Instruction 21(3), 209–249 (2003)
27. Walonoski, J.A., Heffernan, N.T.: Detection and analysis of off-task gaming behavior in intelligent tutoring systems. In: Ikeda, M., Ashley, K.D., Chan, T.-W. (eds.) ITS 2006. LNCS, vol. 4053, pp. 382–391. Springer, Heidelberg (2006)

Comparing Knowledge Tracing and Performance Factor Analysis by Using Multiple Model Fitting Procedures

Yue Gong, Joseph E. Beck, and Neil T. Heffernan

Computer Science Department, Worcester Polytechnic Institute
100 Institute Road, Worcester, MA, 01609, USA
{ygong,josephbeck,nth}@wpi.edu

Abstract. Student modeling is very important for ITS due to its ability to make inferences about latent student attributes. Although knowledge tracing (KT) is a well-established technique, the approach used to fit the model is still a major issue as different model-fitting approaches lead to different parameter estimates. Performance Factor Analysis, a competing approach, predicts student performance based on the item difficulty and student historical performances. In this study, we compared these two models in terms of their predictive accuracy and parameter plausibility. For the knowledge tracing model, we also examined different model fitting algorithms: Expectation Maximization (EM) and Brute Force (BF). Our results showed that KT+EM is better than KT+BF and comparable with PFA in predictive accuracy. We also examined whether the models' estimated parameter values were plausible. We found that by tweaking PFA, we were able to obtain more plausible parameters than with KT.

Keywords: Student modeling, Knowledge tracing, Performance Factors Analysis, Expectation Maximization, Machine learning, Model fitting approaches.

1 Introduction

Student modeling is one of the major issues for Intelligent Tutoring System as it has been widely used for making inferences about the student's latent attributes. Its working mechanism is to take observations of a student's performance (e.g. the correctness of the student response in a practice opportunity) or a student's actions (e.g. the time he stayed for a question), and then use those to estimate the student's underlying hidden attributes, such as knowledge, goals, preferences, and motivational state, etc. Those attributes are unable to be determined directly, thus student modeling techniques have always attracted a great deal of attention.

In ITS, student modeling has two common usages. The first, and most frequently used one, is to predict student behaviors, such as student performance in the next practice opportunity. The second one is to obtain plausible and explainable parameter estimates, where plausibility concerns how believable the parameters are, often tested by comparing them to some external gold standards. Being explainable indicates the parameter estimates produced by the model have practical meanings, which can help researchers know more about learning. Consequently, student models are evaluated by how well they predict student's behaviors, as well as by parameter plausibility [1].

1.1 Knowledge Tracing Model

There are a variety of student models. The knowledge tracing model [2] shown in Fig. 1, has been broadly used. It is based on a 2-state dynamic Bayesian network where student performance is the observed variable and student knowledge is the latent. The model takes student performances and uses them to estimate the student's level of knowledge. There are two performance parameters: slip and guess, which mediate student knowledge and student performance. The guess parameter represents the fact that the student may sometimes generate a correct response in spite of not knowing the correct skill. The slip parameter acknowledges that even students who understand a skill can make an occasional careless mistake. There are also two learning parameters. The first is initial knowledge (K0), the likelihood the student knows the skill when he first uses the tutor. The second is the learning rate, the probability a student will acquire a skill as a result of an opportunity to practice it.

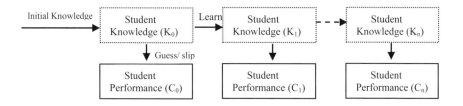

Fig. 1. Knowledge tracing model

As pointed out in [3, 4], KT suffers two major problems with trying to estimate parameters: local maxima and multiple global maxima. The first one is common to many error surfaces and has known solutions such as multiple restart. The second difficulty is known as identifiability and means that for the same model structure, given the same data, there are multiple (differing) sets of parameter values that fit the data equally well. Based on statistical methods, there is no way to differentiate which set of parameters is preferable to the others. Consequently, for the KT model, different model fitting approaches lead to different parameter estimation outcomes.

1.2 Performance Factor Analysis

Recently, a new alternative student modeling approach was presented by Pavlik et al. [5], Performance Factor Analysis (PFA). PFA is a variant of learning decomposition [6], and is based on reconfiguring Learning Factor Analysis (LFA) [7]. Briefly speaking, it takes the form of standard logistic regression model with the student performance as dependent variable. It reconfigures LFA on its independent variables, by dropping the student variable and replacing the skill variable with the question identity (i.e. one parameter per question). The model estimates a parameter for each item representing the item's difficulty, and also two parameters for each skill reflecting the effects of the prior successes and prior failures achieved for that skill.

Previous work compared KT and PFA models, and found PFA to be superior. In this study, we ran replication study, but also focusing on the impacts when using different model fitting approaches for KT. In addition, we attempted and tested different methods of handling multiple-skill problems. We present our comparison results based on both predictive accuracy and parameter plausibility.

2 Methodology

2.1 Model Fitting Approaches for Knowledge Tracing Model

Aside from student models, there are also a variety of model fitting approaches. Different approaches have various criteria to fit the data, and thus produce different parameter estimates and further lead to different predictive abilities. Therefore, we explored the impact of modeling fitting approach on model accuracy and plausibility.

The Expectation Maximization (EM) algorithm is a model fitting approach for KT. It finds a set of parameters that maximize the data likelihood (i.e. the probability of observing the student performance data). EM processes student performance as a piece of evidence with time order, and uses this evidence for the expectation step where the expected likelihood is calculated. The model then computes the parameters which maximize that expected likelihood. The algorithm, by accessing more evidence, iteratively runs these two steps until it finds the final best fitting parameters. There is no guarantee of finding a global, rather than a local, maxima.

Recently, the brute force approach has been proposed for estimating parameters for KT. The algorithm uses exhaustive search for finding the best set of parameters over a reasonable sampling of the entire parameter space. Contrary to EM that maximizes the data likelihood, it attempts to minimize the sum of squared error (SSE). Originally, KT's parameters are continuous, so that there is no way to compose a finite search space, which, however, is a must for an exhaustive search. We used source code provided by Ryan Baker, which resolves the issue by only considering two decimal places of precision. In this way, the parameter space is reduced from infinity to 99^4 possible parameter sets for each skill (i.e. there are four parameters for each skill and each of them has 99 possible values ranging from 0.01 to 0.99). Initially, every parameter starts from the value of 0.01 and is incremented by 0.01 on every iteration. Ultimately, for each skill, it finds the lowest SSE, and the corresponding set of parameters for that skill. The major drawback is that the method suffers from a severe computational cost problem due to the large search space, so most of the time the search space is cut down even smaller by setting searching boundaries. In order to make a careful comparison, we followed the same protocol as Pavlik et al. followed [5]. Specifically, we used the same set of bounded ceiling values for the four parameters, so that the maximum probabilities of initial knowledge, guess, slip and learning are 0.85, 0.3, 0.1 and 0.3, respectively.

Conjugate Gradient Descent, an optimization method used to solve systems of equations, is used to estimate parameters in the CMU cognitive tutors. Chang et al. [8]

found that EM produces models with higher predictive accuracy than Conjugate Gradient Descent.

Unlike the KT model, the family of learning decomposition models is based on the form of standard logistic regression, so that the model fitting procedure is ensured to reach global maxima; thus resulting in unique best fitting parameters. Consequently, for PFA, the model fitting approach is not an issue.

2.2 Problem with Multiple Skill Questions in KT Model

The KT framework has a major problem: when there is more than one skill involved in a question, the model lacks the ability to handle all the skills simultaneously, because KT works by looking at historical observations on *a* skill. However, in some tutors, a question is usually designed to require multiple skills to achieve a correct answer. If a student model cannot take this common phenomenon well, its ability of making plausible parameter estimates and accurate prediction is likely to be weakened.

A common solution is to attach performance on the problem with all skills needed to solve it, by listing the performance in all of those skills' historical observations [e.g., 10]. Thus, a multiple skill question is split into multiple single skill questions. This strategy enables parameter estimation to proceed, but increases the probability of over fitting and also results in an accompanying problem: multiple predicted performances. Each split performance is associated with a particular skill that has its own set of parameters. We then are able to use those parameters to calculate the predicted performance. However, those calculated values are probably not equivalent across all of the skills, which means for the same student, on the same practice opportunity, our models make different claims about how likely he is to produce a correct response. Given the conflicting predictions, some means of making a prediction is needed.

In this study, we attempted two approaches to address the problem. The first is similar to [9] and inspired by the joint probability in Probability Theory. The probability a student generates a correct answer in a multi-skill question is dependent on his ability to achieve correctness in all required skills. Therefore, we multiplied each skill's predicted performance together and assign the product as the new predicted performance for all corresponding observations. Yet, the reasonableness of this method relies on an assumption, which is how likely a student can answer correctly for one skill must be independent of the probability that he responds correctly in another skill. Although this independence assumption sounds strong, most student modeling approaches adopt it for simplicity (e.g. Knowledge Tracing).

The second approach, on the other hand, takes the minimum probability of the predicted performances as the final value. The intuition behind this strategy is the likelihood a student gets a correct answer is dominated by his knowledge of his weakest skill.

The above strategies are necessary options for KT due to its lack of ability to handle multi-skill performances. However, it is not the case for PFA, which does have the ability to handle with multi-skill performances. Therefore in this study, in addition to repeating multiple skill questions like we do for KT, we also examined PFA using the data that still keeps the original multi-skill performances.

2.3 Data Set

For this study, we used data from ASSISTment, a web-based math tutoring system. The data are from 343 twelve- through fourteen- year old 8th grade students in urban school districts of the Northeast United States. They were from four classes. These data consisted of 193,259 problems completes in ASSISTment during Nov. 2008 to Feb. 2009. Performance records of each student were logged across time slices for 104 skills (e.g. area of polygons, Venn diagram, division, etc).

3 Results

We used Bayesian Network Toolkit for Student Modeling (BNT-SM) [8] to perform the EM algorithm for the knowledge tracing model to estimate the model parameters. We used Ryan Baker's unpublished java code to accomplish the brute force model fitting method. We also replicated the PFA model using the same model settings as in [5], except where noted below. We fit the three models with the data that contains split performances (i.e. problems that require multiple skills). For PFA, we also examined it by fitting the original data which keeps multi-skill questions as a single unit. We referred the PFA model handling multi-skill performances as PFA_M and the other as PFA_S. We did 4-fold crossvalidation and tested our models on the unseen students, which is different from what Pavlik, et al. did. They conducted 7-fold crossvalidation and tested their models on seen students' unseen performances. We prefer to hold out at the student level since that results in a more independent test set. Another aspect in which our approach differed from Pavlik's is that we did not restrict the impact of a correct response to be non-negative, that is, skill could have negative "learning rates."

3.1 Main Model Comparisons: Predictive Accuracy

Predictive accuracy is the measure of how well the instantiated model fits the data. We used three metrics to examine the model predictive performance on the unseen test set: Mean Squared Error (MSE), R^2 and AUC (Area Under Curve) of ROC curve. We also reported the number of parameters produced by each model.

Table 1. Crossvalidated predictive accuracy comparison among three main models

	MSE	R^2	AUC	# of parameters
KT + EM	0.215	0.072	0.661	416
KT + BF	0.223	0.036	0.656	416
PFA_S	0.220	0.048	0.673	1013

Table 1 shows the results of the comparison for the three metrics. The values are calculated by averaging corresponding numbers obtained in the 4-fold crossvalidation. R^2 values seem considerably low, however, typically models that predict performance on individual trials achieve low R^2 values [10, e.g. 6]. If instead we model aggregate trials we have an R^2 of 0.88; so our skill model is reasonably accurate and our data register student learning.

Although most numbers seem very close, KT+EM outperforms KT+BF in all three metrics, and PFA_S seems to beat KT+BF as well. To examine whether the differences are statistically reliable, for every two models, we did a 2 tailed paired t-test based on the results from the crossvalidation. Only between KT+BF and KT+EM, we found the differences are significant in all three metrics (p<0.01 in MSE and R^2; p=0.02 in AUC). We failed to find any reliable differences between PFA_S and KT+BF, even though the mean values appear a trend suggesting PFA_S is probably better than KT+BF. Compared to PFA_S, KT+EM wins in the first two metrics, but does worse on the third one. Besides, none of the statistical test results suggests there are any significant differences between these two models. We noticed that PFA produced more parameters than KT, which seems inconsistent with the results reported in [5].But, given that the number of parameters in PFA = 2*# of skills + # of items, while the number of parameters in KT is 4*# of skills. Consequently having fewer items favors PFA, while fewer skills benefits KT.

One reason for the lack of reliable difference could be the relatively low statistical power of the t-tests. Four independent observations (one for each fold of the cross validation) provide low power to differentiate samples. Although further research needs to perform the comparisons based on larger samples, for now we maintain a conservative view of KT+EM is comparable with PFA_S.

KT+EM provides more accurate predictions than KT+BF. We think this consequence is caused by the range restrictions used on the search space. In contrast, EM derives its estimations without such range restrictions, so it is more likely for EM to produce more plausible parameter estimates which further are used to yield more accurate prediction.

One aspect hindering the performance of PFA_S is that the PFA model is designed to handle problems that require multiple skills. Hence, it is more reasonable to inspect PFA's performance when it works in its natural way. To make a fair comparison, we trained and tested PFA using the same data sets as we used for the other models, but without splitting multi-skill performances.

Table 2. Crossvalidated comparisons among PFA with different model settings

	R^2	AUC
PFA_S (base line)	0.048	0.673
PFA_M	0.047	0.680
PFA_S_bounded	0.066	0.681
PFA_M_bounded	0.074	0.690

As seen in the first two rows of Table 2, generally PFA_M results in comparable performances, although the difference in AUC is statistically reliable at p<0.01. This implies that PFA works better when used in its original spirit for handling multiple skill questions. However, compared to KT+EM, shown in Table 1, we only found little evidence to support it is good at multi-skill questions (its AUC value is higher, but not reliably so). Therefore, again we failed to be able to show that the true PFA can reliably outperform this version of KT+EM that also attempts to deal with multi-skill questions. We do not present MSE in Table 2 since PFA_S and PFA_M use slightly different datasets, it is not appropriate to compare MSE.

One drawback of PFA models is they could produce negative learning rates due to over fitting, so in the original work [3], the researchers set 0 as the lower bound. We were unable to get our model fitting software (SPSS 17.0) to replicate this procedure[1]. Since PFA's lack of better predictive performance could result from loosing this constraint, we next manually checked which skills had negative learning rates, substituted 0 in, and then re-ran the model predicting procedure on the test data using the altered parameters. We found almost half of the skills had negative learning rates. The results shown in the last two rows of Table 2 indicate both two bounded models indeed achieved higher predictive accuracy ($p<0.01$ in all two metrics, compared to PFA_S), suggesting that the negative learning rates were not accurate and the result of overfitting. Considering the number of negative learning rates produced at first, it seems that setting bounded value is necessary for PFA.

3.2 Comparing Approaches to the Problem of Multi-skill Questions

Given the problem of multi-skill questions in KT, we compared the two proposed approaches for predicting performance (multiplication and min()) with the default model (making multiple, different predictions, on student performance on a problem, one for each skill).

Table 3. Crossvalidated comparisons of the min models and the default models

	MSE	R^2	AUC
KT_BF	0.223	0.036	0.656
KT_BF_min	0.220	0.046	0.670
KT_EM	0.215	0.072	0.661
KT_EM_min	0.214	0.073	0.676

We found the approach of calculating the product results in worse predictive accuracy in all attempted models, and do not report it here. However, taking the minimum value of the predicted performances provides more accurate models. As shown in Table 3, the min models are generally better than the default models, with the AUC values are reliably different in every pair of the comparisons.

The problem of multi-predicted performances also influences PFA, when it takes the data with manually split performances. Therefore, we applied the two approaches on PFA_S and PFA_S_bounded as well. We found that min model didn't consistently work well for PFA.

3.3 Parameter Plausibility

Predictive accuracy is a desired property, but ITS researchers are also interested in interpreting models to make scientific claims. Therefore, we prefer models with more

---

[1] If any readers know how to coerce SPSS's logistic regression function to do so, they are invited to contact us.

plausible parameters when we want to use those for scientific study. We followed the technique in [4]: using external measurement to evaluate parameter plausibility.

The students in our study had taken a 33-item algebra pre-test before using ASSISTment. Taking the pre-test as external measure of incoming knowledge, we calculated the correlation between the students' initial knowledge estimated by the models and their pretest scores.

In other to acquire student's initial knowledge parameter, we used KT to model the students instead of skills (see [4] for details). Since PFA has no student parameter by default, we tweaked it to include student as an additional independent variable. In Table 4, we see that the PFA model that fit by the data keeping multi-skill performances produces the strongest correlation. Even, PFA_S, modified to behave like KT with respect to multiple skill questions, the number still remains the largest (0.886) compared to the rest. KT+BF surprisingly shows a higher ability to estimate plausible parameters than KT+EM. One thing to notice is this correlation is produced by KT+BF with bounded parameter values, thus if the search space is enlarged, it might be able to derive potentially better parameter estimates. The KT+EM is reliably different ($P<0.05$) from PFA_S and PFA_M; none of the other differences is reliable.

Table 4. Comparison of parameter plausibility

	KT+BF	KT+EM	PFA_S	PFA_M
Correlation	0.865	0.827	0.886	0.906

4 Contributions and Future Work

This paper examines and compares the different model fitting approaches of estimating parameters for the knowledge tracing model. We are able to extend the result that EM produces more predictive models than conjugate gradient descent [3]; we are now able to say, at least for our dataset, that EM also has better predictive accuracy than the brute force algorithm. Others [11] have found brute force outperforms EM, so more work is needed here. Furthermore, we inspect the parameter plausibility produced by the models with these two fitting methods and found brute force estimates more plausible parameters.

This work also replicates the comparison between PFA and KT [5]. This replication is non-trivial, as there are concerns that a research finding is less likely to be true than its statistical test results suggest [12]. It suggests that independent replication should be given great importance as it extends the original work by changing the researchers' biases in terms of what is important to measure and how to measure it. In this case, our replication differed somewhat as we found that PFA is comparable to KT. We also examine the PFA's predictive performances given different model settings. PFA with bounded learning rates that directly models multi-skill questions outperforms the other models. In addition, by tweaking PFA to endow it with a powerful ability to capture individual differences, the model produces highly plausible student parameters.

We also attempt two methods to solve the problem of multi-skill questions. Since regular KT has no ability to deal with such questions, we compared using the skill with the lowest knowledge vs. the product for predicting performances on multiple skill questions. We found some evidence to support that using the knowledge of the least known skill (the "weakest link" in solving the problem) is somewhat better than the default models in both KT+EM and KT+BF.

There are several interesting unresolved questions. First, brute force is a new, and thus relatively unexplored, model fitting approach for KT. Therefore, there are several open issues. Setting bounded values for parameter estimation is important and somewhat necessary, as removing bounds can seriously reduce the algorithm's performance (due to over fitting, observed in some preliminary experiments). How to select reasonable ceiling values is a difficult issue, especially when the approach is applied to a new tutor environment. Second, it might be possible to speed up the algorithm by first performing coarse-grained search with BF, and after locating the promising regions use a fine-grained search. In some ways this process is similar to beam search in that both maintain a list of promising regions to explore further.

Although this study failed to find PFA outperforms KT, one of our hypotheses is that perhaps PFA works better in the circumstance where questions for a particular skill vary greatly in difficulty. In this case, the question difficulty parameters in PFA might be able to differentiate student performance better and further achieve high predictive accuracy. One line of research is to consider integrating this concept with KT. Since it makes sense to be aware of the question difficulty when using a model to fit student performances, it potentially helps the KT model capture more variance in the data, leading to more plausible parameters and more accurate predictions.

5 Conclusions

PFA is an alternative approach to KT. In this study, we failed to show there are any real differences in predictive accuracy between PFA and a version of KT that attempts to deal with multi-skill questions. We were able to show that for fitting KT, EM achieves significantly higher predictive accuracy than brute force. We also found that, for multi-skill problems, considering the skill with the lowest proficiency was the superior approach for predictive accuracy.

Parameter plausibility is another comparison object in this study. We showed that PFA is the best method for estimating student knowledge parameters, as PFA without any bounded values resulted in negative learning rates in half of the skills in our dataset. For KT, brute force found more plausible parameters than EM, and has the potential ability to achieve even higher plausibility as the current results were obtained based on the limited search space.

In conclusion, researchers can use either PFA or KT. PFA works well with the provision that restricting learning rates to be non-negative. However, the use of KT requires a careful consideration of model fitting approaches for parameter estimation and the methods for the handling of multi-skill problems, as performance varies.

Acknowledgments. This research was made possible by the US Dept. of Education, Institute of Education Science, "Effective Mathematics Education Research" program grant #R305A070440, NSF CAREER award to Neil Heffernan, the Spencer Foundation, and a Weidenmeyer Fellowship from WPI.

References

1. Beck, J.E.: Difficulties in inferring student knowledge from observations (and why you should care). In: Proceedings of the AIED 2007 Workshop on Educational Data Mining, Marina del Rey, CA, pp. 21–30 (2007)
2. Corbett, A., Anderson, J.: Knowledge tracing: Modeling the acquisition of procedural knowledge. User modeling and user-adapted interaction 4, 253–278 (1995)
3. Beck, J.E., Chang, K.-m.: Identifiability: A Fundamental Problem of Student Modeling. In: Conati, C., McCoy, K., Paliouras, G. (eds.) UM 2007. LNCS (LNAI), vol. 4511, pp. 137–146. Springer, Heidelberg (2007)
4. Rai, D., Gong, Y., Beck, J.E.: Using Dirichlet priors to improve model parameter plausibility. In: Proceedings of the 2nd International Conference on Educational Data Mining, Cordoba, Spain, pp. 141–148 (2009)
5. Pavlik, P.I., Cen, H., Koedinger, K.: Performance Factors Analysis - A New Alternative to Knowledge. In: Proceedings the 14th International Conference on Artificial Intelligence in Education, Brighton, UK, pp. 531–538 (2009)
6. Beck, J.E., Mostow, J.: How who should practice: Using learning decomposition to evaluate the efficacy of different types of practice for different types of students. In: Woolf, B.P., Aïmeur, E., Nkambou, R., Lajoie, S. (eds.) ITS 2008. LNCS, vol. 5091, pp. 353–362. Springer, Heidelberg (2008)
7. Cen, H., Koedinger, K., Junker, B.: Learning Factors Analysis - A General Method for Cognitive Model Evaluation and Improvement. In: Ikeda, M., Ashley, K.D., Chan, T.-W. (eds.) ITS 2006. LNCS, vol. 4053, pp. 164–175. Springer, Heidelberg (2006)
8. Chang, K.-m., Beck, J., Mostow, J., Corbett, A.: A Bayes Net Toolkit for Student Modeling in Intelligent Tutoring Systems. In: Ikeda, M., Ashley, K.D., Chan, T.-W. (eds.) ITS 2006. LNCS, vol. 4053, pp. 104–113. Springer, Heidelberg (2006)
9. Pardos, Z.A., Beck, J., Ruiz, C., Heffernan, N.T.: The Composition Effect: Conjunctive or Compensatory? An Analysis of Multi-Skill Math Questions in ITS. In: Baker, Beck (eds.) Proceedings of the First International Conference on Educational Data Mining, Montreal, Canada, pp. 147–156 (2008)
10. Heathcote, A., Brown, S., Mewhort, D.J.K.: The Power Law repealed: The case for an Exponential Law of Practice. Psychonomic Bulletin & Review (2002)
11. Baker, R.: Personal communication (2010)
12. Ioannidis, J.P.A.: Why Most Published Research Findings Are False. PLoS Med. 2(8), e124 (2005)

Automatic Question Generation for Literature Review Writing Support

Ming Liu[1], Rafael A. Calvo[1], and Vasile Rus[2]

[1] University of Sydney, Sydney NSW 2006, Australia
[2] University of Memphis, Memphis TN 38152, USA

Abstract. This paper presents a novel Automatic Question Generation (AQG) approach that generates trigger questions as a form of support for students' learning through writing. The approach first automatically extracts citations from students' compositions together with key content elements. Next, the citations are classified using a rule-based approach and questions are generated based on a set of templates and the content elements. A pilot study using the Bystander Turing Test investigated differences in writers' perception between questions generated by our AQG system and humans (Human Tutor, Lecturer, or Generic Question). It is found that the human evaluators have moderate difficulties distinguishing questions generated by the proposed system from those produced by human (F-score=0.43). Moreover, further results show that our system significantly outscores Generic Question on overall quality measures.

Keywords: Automatic Question Generation, Natural Language Processing, Academic Writing Support.

1 Introduction

Many studies have shown that most learners have problems recognizing their own knowledge deficits and ask very few questions [1]. Questions are useful to recognize learners's knowledge deficits and improve their learning. When students are asked to prepare a literature review or write an essay, it is often not only to develop disciplinary communication skills but to learn and reason from multiple documents, a skill often called *sourcing* (i.e., citing sources as evidences to support their arguments) and *information integration* (i.e., presenting the evidences in a cohesive and persuasive way).

Simple generic questions are often provided for students to trigger reflection, for example:

- *Have you clearly identified the contributions of the literature reviewed?*
- *Have you identified the research methods used in the literature reviewed?*

Reynolds and Bonk [2] showed that a group of students given generic trigger questions performs better than those students who receive no trigger questions in a writing activity. However, such questions are too general and not likely to provide strong support in the process of writing on a specific topic. More content-related questions need to be asked and most academics would ask such questions in the process of providing feedback to students.

In the field of Automatic Question Generation (AQG), most of AQG systems [3,4,5] focus on the text-to-question task, where a set of content-related questions are generated based on a given text. Usually, the answers to the generated questions are contained in the text. For example, Heilman and Smith [4] presented an AQG system to generate factual questions with an 'overgenerating and ranking' strategy based on natural language processing techniques, such as Name Entity Recognizer and Wh-movement Rules, and a statistical ranking component for scoring questions based on features. The target applications of such systems are reading comprehension and vocabulary assessment which may not be suitable for academic writing.

The aim of this study is to scaffold students' reflection on their academic writing with content-related trigger questions which are automatically generated from citations using Natural Language Processing techniques. Table 1 shows examples of generated questions according to the citation category.

Table 1. An Example of Content-Related Trigger Questions produced by AQG system

Category	Question
Opinion	Why did Cannon challenge this view mentioning that physiological changes were not sufficient to discriminate emotions? (What evidence is provided by Cannon to prove the opinion?) Does any other scholar agree or disagree with Cannon?
Result	Does Davis objectively show that this classification accuracy gets higher from about 70 % up to 98 % while actors express emotions and computers perform the...? (How accurate and valid are the measurements?) How does it relate to your research question?
System	In the study of Macdonald, why does workbench tool provide feedback on spelling, style and diction by analyzing English prose and suggesting possible improvements? What are the strength and limitations of the system? Does it relate to your research question?

The remainder of the paper is organized as follows: section 2 provides a brief review of the literature focusing on writing support systems and several AQG systems relevant to our approach. Section 3 describes the system design and architecture while section 4 details a pilot study we conducted to assess the quality of the generated questions. Section 5 discusses the results we obtained and gives suggestions on future work.

2 Related Area

Research into ways of supporting academic writing includes Sourcer's Apprentice Intelligent Feedback mechanism (SAIF) [6], a computer assisted essay writing tool used to detect plagiarism, uncited quotations, lack of citations, and limited content integration problems using a rule-based approach and Latent Semantic Analysis (LSA).

Glosser [7], an automated feedback system for students' writing, provides feedback on four aspects of the writing: structure, coherence, topics, and concept visualization. Glosser uses text mining and computational linguistics algorithms that quantify features of the text (supportive content) and a set of trigger questions. The set of trigger questions in Glosser is limited as they must be predefined for each course and they are too general.

AUTOQUEST [3], one of the earliest automatic question generation systems, uses pure syntactic pattern-matching approach to generate content-related questions in order to improve the independent study of any textual material. Recent advances in Natural Language Processing made it possible for more advanced computational question generation models to be proposed: multi-choice question generation [8], factual question generator [9,4], and medical concept question generator [5]. One of the most relevant works to ours is by Kunichika et. al. [10] who proposed an AQG approach based on both the syntactic and semantic information extracted from the original text. Their approach is based on DCG (Definite Clause Grammar) for grammar and reading comprehension assessment about a story. The extracted syntactic features include subject, predicate verb, modal verb, auxiliary verb, object, voice, tense which were used to transform declarative sentences into interrogative sentences (subject-auxiliary-Inversion). They used three predefined grammatical categories: noun, verb, and preposition to determine the interrogative pronoun for the question. Their empirical results showed that 80% of questions were considered as appropriate for novices to learn English and 93% questions are semantically correct.

3 System Design and Architecture

In this section we provide an overview of the system's pipeline architecture shown in Figure 1 and describe each step in detail. The input to the system is a literature review paper and the output is a set of generated questions. The question generation process follows 3 steps shown in Figure 1:

Step 1. Pre-processing. The aim of Step 1 is to extract citations from papers. Powley and Dale [11] define 5 types of citation styles: Textual Syntactic, Textual Parenthetical, Prosaic, Pronominal, and Numbered.

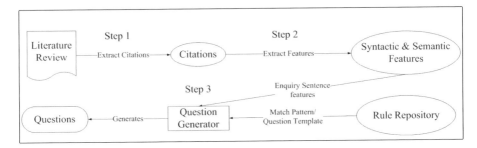

Fig. 1. System Architecture

A pattern matching technique was used to extract Textual Syntactic and Textual Parenthetical citation style. The regular expression code is shown below.

```
\([a-zA-Z]*\s*\d{4}\)|\([p.]+\s*\d{1,4}\)|\([a-zA-Z]+\s*[a-zA-Z]*
\s*[a-zA-Z]*\W*\d{4}|\([^)]*\d{4}\s?\)
```

A state of art Named Entity Tagger (NER), LBJ [12], was used to identify citations with Prosaic style and a simple Pronoun Resolver, finding the nearest Name Entity appearing before the pronoun, was used to identify citations with Pronominal style. In the current implementation the Numbered citation style (as in this paper) is not recognized.

Step 2. Extracting Syntactic and Semantic features. Syntactic features include subject, predicate verb, auxiliary verb (e.g. be, am, will, have and can) and predicate, voice and tense which are essential to perform subject-auxiliary inversion. We use Tregex on the Phrase Structure Tree derived from the original citation to extract syntactic features. The Stanford Parser is used to parse a sentence into a Phrase Structure Tree. Tregex is a powerful pattern matching technique which can match an individual word, regular expression, a POS tag or group of POS tags such as a Noun Phrase (NP) or Verb Phrase (VP). The following Tregex expressions are used to extract simple Subject, Predicate Verb, and Predicate from a sentence.

```
Subject: NP > (S > ROOT)    Predicate Verb: /^VB/ > ( VP > ( S >ROOT))
Predicate : VP > (S > ROOT)
```

According to the predicate verb or auxiliary verb we can determine the tense of the sentence and get the verb lemma by using WordNet. We also use the Stanford Parser to derive the Type Dependency relations from a sentence in order to detect the voice of sentences. For example, the nsubjpass dependency between the governor (predicate verb) and dependency (subject) indicates passive voice.

The semantic features include the name of the author and the citation category (one of 'Opinion', 'Result', 'Aim of Study', 'System' or 'Method'), based on a taxonomy of conceptual citation categories proposed by Lehnert et al [13]. For example, Result: a result is claimed in the referenced paper; e.g. *"In [Cohen 87], it is shown that PAs are Turing-equivalent..."*

We use the LBJ NER Tagger to detect authors' names and a rule-based approach to classify the citations. There are many learning materials for academic writing [14] which define three categories of reporting verbs: opinion, aim of study and result. Such reporting verb lists are used in our system to determine the corresponding citation category by matching the predicate verb in a citation with a verb in one of the categories. The matching verb category provides the citation category. If they are no match, a sentiment analysis step is used to detect whether the citation may fall in the Opinion citation category. SENTIWORDNET [15] is used to determine whether the citation contains sentiment words. Tregex expression patterns were developed to detect citations in the System and Method categories. Examples of two Tregex expression patterns are shown below:

```
Method: VP>(S>ROOT)<<,(use|apply)<<(NP<<-(method|approach|))
System: NP > (S > ROOT) << (system|tool)
```

Table 2. The Rule Definition for Patterns and Templates

Rule	Pattern	Category	Question Template
1	Reporting Verb	Opinion	Why +subject_auxiliary_inversion()? What evidence is provided by +subject+ to prove the opinion? Does any other scholar agree or disagree with +subject+ ?
2	Reporting Verb	Aim	Why does +subject+ conduct this study to +predicate+? What is the research question formulated by +subject+? What is +subject+s contribution to our understanding of the problem?
3	Reporting Verb	Result	subject_auxiliary_inversion()? Is the analysis of the data accurate and relevant to the research question? How does it relate to your research question?
4	Tregex Rules	Method	In the study of +subject+, why +subject_auxiliary_inversion()? Which dataset does +subject+ use for this experiment? Could the problem have been approached more effectively from another perspective?
5	Tregex Rules	System	In the study of +subject+, why +subject_auxiliary_inversion()? What are the strength and limitations of the system? Does it relate to your research question?

According to Hyland's citation study [16], there are three main grammatical ways to refer to sources: using reporting verbs, using nouns, and using passive constructions. Sometimes, syntactic structure transformations were needed in order to perform the subject-auxiliary inversion in our final stage. For example, *Wallraff's opinion is that there is a rate of growth...* The citer use the noun:*opinion* to refer to the resource as the citee's opinion. This sentence will be transformed into: *Wallraff states that there is a rate of growth...*

Step 3. Generation. This is the final step in generating questions with our template-based approach. Once the semantic and syntactic features extracted from a citation match the predefined patterns in our repository of templates the corresponding questions are generated. Table 2 shows the five rules defined in our Rule Repository. Rules 1, 2, or 3, are fired when a citation contains a reporting verb and and fall in one of the following citation categories: Opinion, Result, or Aim of Study, respectively. Rules 4 or 5 are fired when a citation is of type System or Method. We also defined two addition rules, 6 and 7. Rule 6 is fired when a citation does not contain a reporting verb but contains sentiment words. Rule 7 is similar to Rule 6 except the citation does not contain a sentiment word. For example, a citation is extracted in Step 1: *Cannon (Cannon 1927) challenged this view mentioning that, physiological changes were not sufficient to discriminate emotions.* Step 2 identifies the citation category as Opinion by matching the predicate verb (*challenge*) with an entry in our reporting verb database. Step 3 applies Rule 1 to generate a question by matching the pattern that requires the citation contain a reporting verb and of of type Opinion. Table 1 shows the generated questions.

4 Pilot Study

We explored the ability of our AQG system to generate quality questions by comparing automatically generated questions to those produced by humans. Like the Bystander Turing Test conducted by Person and Graesser [17], our judges were asked to rate each question along several dimesions of quality. Also, we conducted an evaluation in which judges were asked to ascertain whether the question was generated by a human (lecturer, tutor, generic) or a system. The major difference between the test carried out by Person and Graesser and our evaluation is the application context: we focus on questions for academic writing while they used a snippets of tutorial dialog. Also, our judges were the writers of the source content based on which the questions were generated while their judges did not know the content before the experiment. This is an advantage of our methodology because our judges were experts on the content the questions asked about. Section 4.1 describes the participants and procedure we used in the pilot study. Section 4.2 reports the AQG system performance in terms of the semantic correctness of the generated question as well as the accuracy relative to the citation extraction step. Section 4.3 shows the results along 5 dimensions of quality and of the Bystander Turing test. Section 5 discusses these results.

4.1 Participants and Procedure

A pilot study was conducted on six participants (postgraduate students) from the Faculty of Engineering from whom six literature reviews were collected. The reviews were used the source content for generating the questions. A total of twenty questions (5 each) were generated by the tutor, by a lecturer with expertise in the topic, by our system, and also using generic questions. Each student-author acted as an evaluator in our experiments.

Students were asked to rate the quality of questions generated from his/her literature review paper. Five quality measures inspired by Heilman and Noah [4] were used to evaluate each question: *This question is correctly written (QM1); This question is clear (QM2); This question is appropriate to the context (QM3); This question makes me reflect about what I have written (QM4); This is a useful question (QM5)*. The agreement with each of these statements was marked by the evaluators using a Likert scale were 1 was 'strongly disagree' and 5 'strongly agree'.

4.2 System Performance Evaluation and Result

We first assess our system's ability to extract citations from the source content. The dataset contains 1,088 sentences including 221 citations. Table 3 shows that 145 citations have been extracted and the recall is 0.66 in average.

Table 3. Citation Extraction Result

	Rule 1	Rule 2	Rule 3	Rule 4	Rule 5	Rule 6	Rule 7	Total
Number of Citations	18	22	12	50	16	29	74	221
Number of Retrieved Citations	10	12	7	27	10	17	62	145
Recall	0.56	0.55	0.58	0.54	0.63	0.59	0.84	0.66

Table 4 illustrates 161 questions generated and the average semantic correctness: 60%. Two human annotators reached substantial agreement as measured by Cohen's kappa coefficient (0.61).

Table 4. Question Generation Result

	Rule 1	Rule 2	Rule 3	Rule 4	Rule 5	Rule 6	Rule 7	Total
Number of Generated Questions	10	9	14	7	6	17	98	161
Number of Correct Questions	6	9	9	4	4	10	56	97
Precision	0.6	1	0.64	0.57	0.67	0.59	0.57	0.60

4.3 Question Quality Evaluation and Result

Each of the 20 questions, randomly selected, was evaluated by the student-authors. Because we have six authors, 120 questions were evaluated. A one-way ANOVA setting the confidence interval at 95% was conducted to examine whether there are statistical difference in Overall, QM1, QM2, QM3, QM4 or QM5 among questions generated by the lecturer, Tutor, AQG system and Generic. The ANOVA yielded a significant difference in Overall (F(3,596)=2.63, P<0.05), QM3(F(3, 116)=4.085, P<0.05), QM4(F(3, 116)=8.65, P<0.05, QM5(F(3, 116)=5.305, P<0.05) and no significant difference in QM1(F(3,116)= 2.69, P>0.05) and QM2 (F(3,116)= 2.335, P>0.05). Follow-up Fishers least significant difference (LSD) tests with 95% confidence interval were performed to determine whether significant differences occurred between the mean scores for each pair of treatments. Figure 2 illustrates the comparisons of mean scores and Table 5 shows that the questions from AQG system significantly outscored Generic Questions in Overall (0.346>LSD=0.283) and QM5 (0.733>LSD=0.633), while questions from the tutor significantly outscored AQG system in QM3 (0.667>LSD=0.593), QM4 (1>LSD=0.648) and Overall (0.6>LSD=0.283). There are no statistically significant differences between questions generated by the lecturer and AQG system. Also, we did not observe any significant differences between the Tutor and AQG system in QM 5 (0.533<LSD=0.633).

The quality of each rule was also evaluated. Fig. 3 shows the average scores. Rule 5 got the highest score (4.3), Rule 4 and Rule 6 took the second place (3.9) and Rule 7 reached the lowest score (3.0). It was also found that Rules 1, 2, 3, 4 and 7 decreased from Quality Measure 4, 5 to Quality Measure 1,2,3 while Rule 5 was stable in along all five quality measures.

Each evaluator was asked to ascertain who wrote this question: Lecturer, Tutor, System or other. In order to clearly evaluate the participants' classification

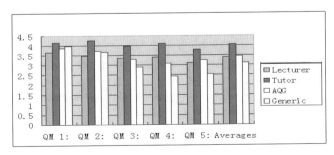

Fig. 2. Comparisons of normalized mean scores

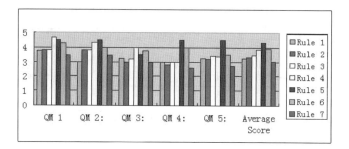

Fig. 3. Comparisons of scores for each rule

Table 5. Fisher's least significant difference (LSD) tests with 95% confidence interval

	Lecturer v. AQG	Tutor v. AQG	AQG v.GQ
QM3(LSD=0.593)	0.067	0.667	0.367
QM4(LSD=0.648)	0.333	1	0.633
QM5(LSD=0.633)	0.133	0.533	0.733
Overall(LSD=0.283)	0.047	0.6	0.346

Table 6. Confusion Matrix (Average)

Real \ Response	Tutor	Lecturer	AQG System
Tutor	0.7	2.7	1.6
Lecturer	0.8	1.2	3
AQG	1.4	1.0	2.6

ability between a Human and a System, we did not take the Generic Question into consideration. Therefore, only 15 questions evaluated by a participant were considered. We use the balanced F-score to evaluate the classification result and F-score is defined as follows: F-score=2*Precision*Recall/(Precision+Recall). Table 6 shows the participants' average performance on the classification, which found that they achieved F-score of 0.43 on AQG system, F-score of 0.24 on Lecturer and F-score of 0.18 on Tutor category.

5 Discussion

This paper presents a novel Automatic Question Generation approach to support literature review writing and also describes a pilot study evaluating the system performance along several dimensions—the Citation Extraction Ability and Semantic Correctness of the generated questions and Question Quality—and comparing it with humans and generic questions.

The study has a few limitations including a relatively small number of subjects (6) and questions (120). Furthermore, it only evaluates a set of very specific types of questions that refer to only one aspect (citations) out of the many involved in literature review. In a real teaching scenario, the human assessors (tutor and lecturer) would prepare questions on other issues besides the citations. For the future, we plan on having pedagogical experts involved to help with the question formulation as well as with the evaluation. Despite these shortcomings, we believe that the dataset is large enough and the evaluation meaningful because we use real academic writings, i.e. student-written literature review papers, as our dataset and the evaluators have higher education background and are very familiar with the source content, as being the authors of the review papers used, and thus being in a better position than others to judge quality of questions.

Within these limitations, this pilot study suggests that the AQG system can produce questions that are as helpful to promote students' reflection on their academic writing as those by human tutors. The most significant finding from this pilot study was that writers found it moderately difficult to distinguish between questions generated by humans and automatically generated questions. This claim is supported by the fact that students perceive approximately as much value in automatically generated questions as in those written by the lecturer.

As we had expected, the AQG system outscored Generic Questions because the content-related questions were more helpful than the generic questions. Surprisingly, we found that our AQG system slightly outperformed the Lecturer, which may be explained by some factors. First, students may intend to give higher scores to a Lecturer. Second, it took a lot of effort for a lecturer to create 30 questions in total for six literature review papers across different topics. This might affect the lecturer's performance on creating pertinent questions. Finally, the length of template-questions, longer on average than questions generated by the lecturer, may affect the evaluation.

There are two main reasons for generating incorrect semantic questions(40% inaccuracy):1 The NER component and 2: Citation Category Classifier. Because the LBJ NER tagger was primarily trained on News Text Corpora it might affect its performance on academic articles. Our current Citation Category Classifier is based on a rule-based approach which is simple but not scalable. As we can see from Figure 3 and Table 4, we may need to add extra patterns to Rule 5 to generate more questions while also improving the question templates in Rules 1, 2, 3 and 4 in order to achieve higher scores on Quality Measures 4 and 5. In addition, more citation categories might be explored which could improve the performance for Rule 6 and Rule 7.

Future work will focus on ranking the generated questions, combining a Machine Learning approach with a rule-based approach to improve the citation category classification, training the LBJ NER tagger on a large collection of academic papers, and upgrading the taxonomy of citation category in our system. It is also planned to integrate the AQG system into our peer review system which will be used for students in Research Method course next semester.

Acknowledgements

The authors would like to thank Jorge Villalon and Setphen O'Rourke for the development of TML and Glosser. Ming is partially supported by a N.I. Price scholarship. This project was partially supported by a University of Sydney TIES grant and Australian Research Council Discovery Project DP0986873.

References

1. Graesser, A.C., Person, N.K.: Question asking during tutoring. American Educational Research Journal 31, 104–137 (1994)
2. Reynolds, T., Bonk, C.: Computerized prompting partners and keystroke recording devices: Two macro driven writing tools. Educational Technology Research and Development 44(3), 83–97 (1996)
3. Wolfe, J.H.: Automatic question generation from text - an aid to independent study. SIGCUE Outlook 10(SI), 104–112 (1976)
4. Heilman, M., Noah, S.A.: Question generation via overgenerating transformations and ranking. In: The 14th Annual Conference on Artificial Intelligence in Education Workshop on Question Generation (2009)
5. Wang, W.M., Hao, T.Y., Liu, W.Y.: Automatic question generation for learning evaluation in medicine. In: Leung, H., Li, F., Lau, R., Li, Q. (eds.) ICWL 2007. LNCS, vol. 4823, pp. 242–251. Springer, Heidelberg (2008)
6. Britt, M.A., Wiemer-Hastings, P., Larson, A.A., Perfetti, C.A.: Using intelligent feedback to improve sourcing and integration in students' essays. Int. J. Artif. Intell. Ed. 14(3,4), 359–374 (2004)
7. Villalon, J., Kearney, P., Calvo, R.A., Reimann, P.: Glosser: Enhanced feedback for student writing tasks. In: Proc. Eighth IEEE International Conference on Advanced Learning Technologies ICALT 2008, July 1-5, pp. 454–458 (2008)
8. Mitkov, R., Ha, L.A.: Computer-aided generation of multiple-choice tests. In: Proceedings of the HLT-NAACL 2003 workshop on Building educational applications using natural language processing, Association for Computational Linguistics, Morristown, NJ, USA, pp. 17–22 (2003)
9. Rus, V., Cai, Z.Q., Graesser, A.C.: Experiments on generating questions about facts. In: Gelbukh, A. (ed.) CICLing 2007. LNCS, vol. 4394, pp. 444–455. Springer, Heidelberg (2007)
10. Kunichika, H., Katayama, T., Hirashima, T., Takeuchi, A.: Automated question generation methods for intelligent english learning systems and its evaluation. In: Proc. of ICCE 2001 (2001)
11. Powley, B., Dale, R.: Evidence-based information extraction for high-accuracy citation extraction and author name recognition. In: Proceedings of the 8th RIAO International Conference, Pittsburgh, PA (2007)
12. Ratinov, L., Roth, D.: Design challenges and misconceptions in named entity recognition. In: CoNLL 2009 (2009)
13. Lehnert, W., Cardie, C., Riloff, E.: Analyzing research papers using citation sentences. In: Proceedings of the Twelfth Annual Conference of the Cognitive Science Society, pp. 511–518 (1990)
14. University of Glasgow: Writing an assignment: reporting verbs. Technical report, University of Glasgow (2009)
15. Esuli, A., Sebastiani, F.: Sentiwordnet: A publicly available lexical resource for opinion mining. In: Proceedings of the 5th Conference on Language Resources and Evaluation (LREC 2006), pp. 417–422 (2006)
16. Hyland, K.: Academic attribution: citation and the construction of disciplinary knowledge. Applied Linguistics 20, 341–367 (1994)
17. Person, N.K., Graesser, A.C.: Human or computer? autotutor in a bystander turing test. In: Cerri, S.A., Gouardéres, G., Paraguaçu, F. (eds.) ITS 2002. LNCS, vol. 2363, pp. 821–830. Springer, Heidelberg (2002)

Characterizing the Effectiveness of Tutorial Dialogue with Hidden Markov Models

Kristy Elizabeth Boyer[1,*], Robert Phillips[1,2], Amy Ingram[3], Eun Young Ha[1], Michael Wallis[1,2], Mladen Vouk[1], and James Lester[1]

[1] Department of Computer Science, North Carolina State University
[2] Applied Research Associates, Inc.
[3] Department of Mathematics and Computer Science, Meredith College
Raleigh, North Carolina, USA
keboyer@ncsu.edu

Abstract. Identifying effective tutorial dialogue strategies is a key issue for intelligent tutoring systems research. Human-human tutoring offers a valuable model for identifying effective tutorial strategies, but extracting them is a challenge because of the richness of human dialogue. This paper addresses that challenge through a machine learning approach that 1) learns tutorial strategies from a corpus of human tutoring, and 2) identifies the statistical relationships between student outcomes and the learned strategies. We have applied hidden Markov modeling to a corpus of annotated task-oriented tutorial dialogue to learn one model for each of two effective human tutors. We have identified significant correlations between the automatically extracted tutoring modes and student learning outcomes. This work has direct applications in authoring data-driven tutorial dialogue system behavior and in investigating the effectiveness of human tutoring.

Keywords: Tutorial dialogue, natural language, tutoring strategies.

1 Introduction

A key issue in intelligent tutoring systems research is identifying effective tutoring strategies to support student learning. It has been long recognized that human tutoring offers a valuable model of effective tutorial strategies, and a rich history of tutorial dialogue research has identified some components of these strategies [1-4]. An important research direction is to use dialogue corpora to create models that can assess strategies' differential effectiveness [5, 6]. There is growing evidence that tutorial dialogue structure can be automatically extracted from corpora of human tutoring, and that the resulting models can illuminate relationships between tutorial dialogue structure and student outcomes such as learning and motivation [7-11]. This paper takes a step beyond the previous work by identifying relationships between student learning and automatically extracted tutoring strategies, or *modes*. This modeling framework for extracting tutoring strategies and analyzing their differential effectiveness has

---

[*] Corresponding author.

direct applications in authoring data-driven tutorial dialogue system behavior and in research regarding the effectiveness of human tutors.

2 Related Work

Identifying effective tutoring strategies has long been a research focus of the intelligent tutoring systems community. Empirical studies of human and computer tutoring have revealed characteristics of novice and expert tutors [12, 13], Socratic and didactic strategies [14], collaborative dialogue patterns in tutoring [15], and interrelationships between affect, motivation, and learning [1, 16]. As a rich form of communication, tutorial dialogue is not fully understood: recent work suggests that the interactivity facilitated by human tutoring is key to its effectiveness [6], and other research indicates that students can learn effectively by watching playbacks of past tutoring sessions [17]. Such findings contribute to our understanding of tutoring phenomena, but also raise questions about the relative effectiveness of different tutoring approaches.

To shed further light on this issue, an important line of research involves modeling the specific relationships between different types of tutoring interactions and learning [5]. Some studies have investigated how shallow measures, such as average student turn length, correlate with learning in typed dialogue [18-20]. Analysis at the dialogue act and bigram levels has uncovered significant relationships with learning in spoken dialogue [7]. Recently, we have seen a growing emphasis on applying automatic techniques to investigate learning correlations across domains and modalities [21] and for devising optimal local strategies [9, 22]. Our work contributes to this line of investigation by applying hidden Markov models (HMMs) in a novel way to characterize the effectiveness of tutorial dialogue. HMMs have been applied successfully to such tasks as modeling student activity patterns [23, 24], characterizing the success of collaborative peer dialogues [25], and learning human-interpretable models of tutoring modes [8]. For tutorial dialogue, the doubly stochastic structure of HMMs (Section 5.1) is well suited to capturing local dependencies and to extracting structures whose components are distributed across entire tutoring sessions.

3 Tutoring Study

The corpus that serves as the basis for this work was collected during a human-human tutoring study. The goal of this study was to produce a sizeable corpus of effective tutoring from which data-driven models of task-oriented tutorial dialogue could be learned. In keeping with this goal, the study features two paid tutors who had achieved the highest average student learning gains in two prior studies [10, 26]. Tutor A was a male computer science student in his final semester of undergraduate studies. Tutor B was a female third-year computer science graduate student. An initial analysis of the corpus suggested that the tutors took different approaches; for example, Tutor A was less proactive than Tutor B [27]. As we describe below, the two tutors achieved similar learning gains.

Students were drawn from four separate sections, or modules, of the same university computer science course titled "Introduction to Programming – Java". They participated on a voluntary basis in exchange for a small amount of course credit. A total of 61 students completed tutoring sessions, constituting a participation rate of 64%. Ten of these sessions were omitted due to inconsistencies (e.g., network problems, students performing task actions outside the workspace sharing software). The first three sessions were also omitted because they featured a pilot version of the task that was modified for subsequent sessions. The remaining 48 sessions were utilized in the modeling and analysis presented here.

In order to ensure that all interactions between tutor and student were captured, participants reported to separate rooms at a scheduled time. Students were shown an instructional video that featured an orientation to the software and a brief introduction to the learning task. This video was also shown to the tutors at the start of the study. After each student completed the instructional video, the tutoring session commenced. The students and tutors interacted using software with a textual dialogue interface and a shared task workspace that provided tutors with read-only access. Students completed a learning task comprised of a programming exercise that involved applying concepts from recent class lectures including for loops, arrays, and parameter passing. The tutoring sessions ended when the student had completed the three-part programming task or one hour had elapsed.

Students completed an identical paper-based pretest and posttest designed to gauge learning over the course of the tutoring session. These free-response instruments were written by the research team and revised according to feedback from an independent panel of three computer science educators, with between three and twenty years of classroom experience. This panel assessed the difficulty of each question and the degree to which it addressed the targeted learning concepts.

According to a paired sample t-test, the tutoring sessions resulted in a statistically significant average learning gain as measured by posttest minus pretest (*mean=7%*; $p<0.0001$). There was no significant difference between the mean learning gains by tutor (*mean$_A$=6.9%*, *mean$_B$=8.6%*; $p=0.569$). Analysis of the pretest scores indicates that the two groups of students were equally prepared for the task: Tutor A's students averaged 79.5% on the pretest, and Tutor B's students averaged 78.9% (t-test *p=0.764*).

4 Corpus Annotation

The raw corpus contains 102,315 events. 4,806 of these events are dialogue messages. The 1,468 student utterances and 3,338 tutor utterances were all subsequently annotated with dialogue act tags (Section 4.1). The remaining events in the raw corpus consist of student problem-solving traces that include typing, opening and closing files, and executing the student's program. The entries in this problem-solving data stream were manually aggregated into significant student work events (Section 4.2), resulting in 3,793 tagged task actions.

4.1 Dialogue Act Annotation

One human tagger applied the dialogue act annotation scheme (Table 1) to the entire corpus. A second tagger annotated a randomly selected subset containing 10% of the utterances. The resulting Kappa was 0.80, indicating *substantial* agreement.[1]

Table 1. Dialogue act annotation scheme

Dialogue Act	Tutor Example	Student Example
Statement	Arrays in java are indexed starting at 0.	I'm going to do this method first.
Question	Which one do you want to start with?	What index do arrays in java start at?
Assessing Question	Do you know how to declare an array?	Does my loop look right?
Positive Feedback	Right.	Yes.
Positive Content Feedback	Yep, your array is the right size.	Yes, I know how to declare an array.
Negative Feedback	No.	No.
Negative Content Feedback	No, that variable needs to be an integer.	No, I've learned about objects but not arrays.
Lukewarm Feedback	Almost.	Sort of.
Lukewarm Content Feedback	It's almost right, but your loop will go out of bounds.	I'm not sure how to declare an array.
Extra-Domain	Somebody will be there soon.	Can I take off these headphones?
Grounding	Ok.	Thanks.

4.2 Task Annotation

Student task actions were recorded at a low level (i.e., individual keystrokes). A human judge aggregated these events into problem-solving chunks that occurred between each pair of dialogue utterances and annotated the student work for subtasks and correctness. The task annotation protocol was hierarchically structured and, at its leaves, included more than fifty low-level subtasks. After tagging the subtask, the judge tagged the chunk for correctness. The correctness categories were *Correct* (fully conforming to the requirements of the learning task), *Buggy* (violating the requirements of the learning task), *Incomplete* (on track but not yet complete), and *Dispreferred* (functional but not conforming to the pedagogical goals of the task).

One human judge applied this protocol to the entire corpus, with a second judge tagging 20% of the data that had been selected via random sampling stratified by tutor in order to establish reliability of the tagging scheme. Because each judge independently played back the events and aggregated them into problem-solving chunks, the two taggers often identified a different number of events in a given window. Any unmatched subtask tags were treated as disagreements. The simple Kappa statistic for subtask tagging was 0.58, indicating *moderate* agreement. However, because there is a sense of ordering within the subtask tags (i.e., the 'distance' between subtasks *1a* and *1b* is smaller than the 'distance' between subtasks *1a* and *3b*), it is also meaningful to consider the weighted Kappa statistic, which was 0.86, indicating *almost perfect* agreement. To calculate agreement on the task correctness tag, we considered all task actions for which the two judges agreed on the subtask tag. The resulting Kappa

---

[1] Throughout this paper we employ a set of widely used agreement categories for interpreting Kappa values: *fair, moderate, substantial,* and *almost perfect* [29].

statistic was 0.80, indicating *substantial* agreement. At the current stage of work, only the task correctness tags have been included as input to the HMMs; incorporating subtask labels is left to future work.

5 Hidden Markov Models

The annotated corpus consists of sequences of dialogue and problem-solving actions, with one sequence for each tutoring session. Our modeling goal was to extract tutoring modes from these sequences in an unsupervised fashion (i.e., without labeling the modes manually), and to identify relationships between these modes and student learning. Findings from an earlier analysis [27] suggested that the two tutors employed different strategies than each other; therefore, we disaggregated the data by tutor and learned two models. In prior work we found that identifying dependent pairs of dialogue acts and joining them into a single bigram observation during preprocessing resulted in models that were more interpretable [28]. In the current work we found that this preprocessing step produced a better model fit in terms of HMM log likelihood; the resulting hybrid sequences of unigrams and bigrams were used for training the models reported here.

5.1 Modeling Framework

In our application of HMMs to tutorial dialogue, we treat the hidden states as tutorial strategies, or modes, whose structure is learned during model training.[2] These states are characterized by *emission probability distributions*, which map each hidden state onto the observable symbols. The *transition probability distribution* determines transitions between hidden states, and the *initial probability distribution* determines the starting state [30]. Model training is an iterative process that terminates when the model parameters have converged or when a pre-specified number of iterations have been completed. Our training algorithm varied the number of hidden states from two to twenty and selected the model size that achieved the best average log-likelihood fit across ten stratified subsets of the data.

5.2 Best-Fit HMMs

The best-fit HMM for Tutor A's dialogues features eight hidden states. Figure 1 depicts a subset of the transition probability diagram with nodes representing hidden states (tutoring modes). Inside each node is a histogram of its emission probability distribution. For simplicity, only five of the eight states are displayed in this diagram; each state that was omitted mapped to less than 5% of the observed data sequences and was not significant in the correlational analysis. We have interpreted and named each tutoring mode based on its structure. For example, State 4 is dominated by correct task actions; therefore, we name this state *Correct Student Work*. State 6 is comprised of student acknowledgements, pairs of tutor statements, some correct task

---

[2] The notion that tutorial dialogue strategies, or modes, constitute a portion of the underlying structure of tutorial dialogue is widely accepted. However, describing these hidden states as *tutoring modes* is an interpretive choice because the HMMs were learned in an unsupervised fashion.

actions, and assessing questions by both tutor and student; we label this state *Student Acting on Tutor Help*. The best-fit model for Tutor B's dialogues features ten hidden states. A portion of this model, consisting of all states that mapped to more than 5% of observations, is displayed in Figure 2.

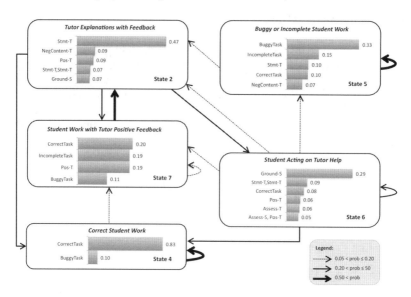

Fig. 1. Subset of HMM transition diagram for Tutor A. Histograms represent emission probability distributions. (Emission and transition probabilities < 0.05 are not displayed.).

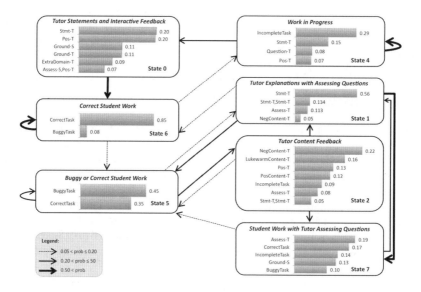

Fig. 2. Subset of HMM transition diagram for Tutor B. Histograms represent emission probability distributions. (Emission and transition probabilities < 0.05 are not displayed).

5.3 Model Interpretation

Some tutoring modes with similar structures were identified by both models. Both models feature a *Correct Student Work* mode characterized by the student's successful completion of a subtask. This state maps to 38% of observations with Tutor A and 29% of observations with Tutor B. In both cases the *Correct Student Work* mode occurs more frequently than any other mode. Each of the next three most frequently occurring modes maps onto 10-15% of the observations. For Tutor A, one such mode is *Tutor Explanations with Feedback*, while for Tutor B a corresponding mode is *Tutor Explanations with Assessing Questions*. In both cases, the mode involves tutors explaining concepts or task elements. A key difference is that with Tutor A, the explanation mode includes frequent negative content feedback or positive content-free feedback, while for Tutor B the explanation mode features questions in which the tutor aims to gauge the student's knowledge. A similar pattern emerges with each tutor's next most frequent mode: for Tutor A, this mode is *Student Work with Tutor Positive Feedback*; for Tutor B, the mode is *Student Work with Tutor Assessing Questions*. These corresponding modes illuminate a tendency for Tutor A to provide feedback in situations where Tutor B chooses to ask the student a question. For Tutor A, the only mode that featured assessing questions was *Student Acting on Tutor Help*, which as we will discuss, was positively correlated with student learning.

5.4 Correlations with Student Outcomes

With the learned models in hand, the next goal was to identify statistical relationships between student learning and the automatically extracted tutoring modes. The models presented above were used to map each sequence of observed dialogue acts and task actions onto the set of hidden states (i.e., tutoring modes) in a maximum likelihood fashion. The transformed sequences were used to calculate the frequency distribution of the modes that occurred in each tutoring session (e.g., State 0 = 32%, State 1 = 15%...State 8 = 3%). For each HMM, correlations were generated between the learning gain of each student session and the relative frequency vector of tutoring modes for that session to determine whether significant relationships existed between student learning and the proportion of discrete events (dialogue and problem solving) that were accounted for by each tutoring mode. For Tutor A, the *Student Acting on Tutor Help* mode was positively correlated with learning ($r=0.51$; $p<0.0001$). For Tutor B, the *Tutor Content Feedback* mode was positively correlated with learning ($r=0.55$; $p=0.01$) and the *Work in Progress* mode was negatively correlated with learning ($r=-0.57$; $p=0.0077$).

6 Discussion

We have identified significant correlations between student learning gains and the automatically extracted tutoring modes modeled in the HMMs as hidden states. While students who worked with either tutor achieved significant learning on average, each group of students displayed a substantial range of learning gains. The correlational analysis leveraged this data spread to gain insight into which aspects of the tutorial interaction were related to higher or lower learning gains.

For Tutor A, the relative frequency of the *Student Acting on Tutor Help* mode was positively correlated with student learning. This mode was characterized primarily by student acknowledgments and also featured tutor explanations, correct student work, positive tutor feedback, and assessing questions from both tutor and student. The composition of this tutoring mode suggests that these observed events possess a synergy that, in context, contributed to student learning. In a learning scenario with novices, it is plausible that only a small subset of tutor explanations were grasped by the students and put to use in the learning task. The *Student Acting on Tutor Help* mode may correspond to those instances, in contrast to the *Correct Student Work* mode in which students may have been applying prior knowledge.

For Tutor B, the *Tutor Content Feedback* mode was positively correlated with student learning. This mode was relatively infrequent, mapping to only 7% of tutoring events. However, as noted in Section 5.3, providing direct feedback represents a departure from this tutor's more frequent approach of asking assessing questions of the student. Given the nature of the learning task and the corresponding structure of the learning instrument, students may have identified errors in their work and grasped new knowledge most readily through this tutor's direct feedback.

For Tutor B, the *Work in Progress* mode was negatively correlated with learning. This finding is consistent with observations that in this tutoring study, students did not easily seem to operationalize new knowledge that came through tutor hints, but rather, often needed explicit constructive feedback. The *Work in Progress* mode features no direct tutor content feedback. Tutor questions and explanations (which are at a more abstract level than the student's solution) in the face of incomplete student work may not have been an effective tutoring approach in this study.

7 Conclusion and Future Work

We have collected a corpus of human-human tutorial dialogue, manually annotated it with dialogue acts and task actions, and utilized HMMs to extract the tutoring modes present in the corpus in an unsupervised fashion. We have examined two by-tutor HMMs and identified correlations between these models and student learning. This work extends findings that have correlated learning with highly localized structures such as unigrams and bigrams of dialogue acts [7, 10]. Using HMMs, we have correlated student learning with automatically extracted tutoring modes whose structure was learned from tutoring sessions. This work takes a step toward fully automatic extraction of tutorial strategies from corpora, a contribution that has direct application in human tutoring research. The approach also has application in tutorial dialogue system development, for example, by producing a data-driven library of system strategies.

A promising direction for future work involves learning models that more fully capture the tutorial phenomena that influence learning. There seems to be significant room for improvement in this regard, as evidenced by the fact that relatively few of the automatically extracted tutorial dialogue modes were correlated with learning. Continuing work on rich dialogue act and task annotation and deep linguistic analysis of dialogue utterances are important directions. Additionally, future work should leverage details of the task structure to a greater extent by considering regularities within tasks and subtasks as part of an augmented model structure in order to more fully capture details of the tutorial interaction.

Acknowledgments. The authors wish to thank Tiffany Barnes for insightful discussions. Thanks to Chris Eason, Lauren Hayward, and Dan Longo for expert review of the learning instruments. This work is supported in part by the NCSU Department of Computer Science along with the National Science Foundation through a Graduate Research Fellowship and Grants CNS-0540523, REC-0632450 and IIS-0812291. Any opinions, findings, conclusions, or recommendations expressed in this report are those of the participants, and do not necessarily represent the official views, opinions, or policy of the National Science Foundation.

References

1. Lepper, M.R., Woolverton, M., Mumme, D.L., et al.: Motivational Techniques of Expert Human Tutors: Lessons for the Design of Computer-Based Tutors. In: Lajoie, S.P., Derry, S.J. (eds.) Computers as Cognitive Tools. Lawrence Erlbaum Associates, Hillsdale (1993)
2. Fox, B.A.: The Human Tutorial Dialogue Project. Lawrence Erlbaum Associates, Hillsdale (1993)
3. Graesser, A.C., Person, N., Magliano, J.: Collaborative Dialogue Patterns in Naturalistic One-to-One Tutoring. Jl. of Applied Cog. Psych. 9, 269–306 (2004)
4. Chi, M.T.H., Siler, S.A., Jeong, H., et al.: Learning from Human Tutoring. Cog. Sci. 25, 471–533 (2001)
5. Ohlsson, S., Di Eugenio, B., Chow, B., Fossati, D., Lu, X., Kershaw, T.C.: Beyond the Code-and-Count Analysis of Tutoring Dialogues. In: 13th International Conference on AI in Education, pp. 349–356 (2007)
6. Chi, M., Jordan, P., VanLehn, K., Litman, D.: To Elicit Or to Tell: Does it Matter? In: 14th International Conference on AI in Education, pp. 197–204 (2009)
7. Litman, D., Forbes-Riley, K.: Correlations between Dialogue Acts and Learning in Spoken Tutoring Dialogues. Nat. Lang. Eng. 12, 161–176 (2006)
8. Boyer, K.E., Ha, E.Y., Wallis, M.D., Phillips, R., Vouk, M.A., Lester, J.C.: Discovering Tutorial Dialogue Strategies with Hidden Markov Models. In: 14th International Conference on AI in Education, pp. 141–148 (2009)
9. Chi, M., Jordan, P., VanLehn, K., Hall, M.: Reinforcement Learning-Based Feature Selection for Developing Pedagogically Effective Tutorial Dialogue Tactics. In: 1st International Conference on Educational Data Mining, pp. 258–265 (2008)
10. Boyer, K.E., Phillips, R., Wallis, M.D., Vouk, M.A., Lester, J.C.: Balancing Cognitive and Motivational Scaffolding in Tutorial Dialogue. In: Woolf, B.P., Aïmeur, E., Nkambou, R., Lajoie, S. (eds.) ITS 2008. LNCS, vol. 5091, pp. 239–249. Springer, Heidelberg (2008)
11. Forbes-Riley, K., Litman, D.: Adapting to Student Uncertainty Improves Tutoring Dialogues. In: 14th International Conference on AI and Education, pp. 33–40 (2009)
12. Evens, M., Michael, J.: One-on-One Tutoring by Humans and Computers. Lawrence Erlbaum Associates, Mahwah (2006)
13. Cade, W., Copeland, J., Person, N., D'Mello, S.: Dialog Modes in Expert Tutoring. In: Woolf, B.P., Aïmeur, E., Nkambou, R., Lajoie, S. (eds.) ITS 2008. LNCS, vol. 5091, pp. 470–479. Springer, Heidelberg (2008)
14. Rosé, C.P., Moore, J.D., VanLehn, K., et al.: A Comparative Evaluation of Socratic Versus Didactic Tutoring. #LRDC-BEE-1 (2000)

15. Graesser, A.C., Person, N.K., Magliano, J.P.: Collaborative Dialogue Patterns in Naturalistic One-to-One Tutoring. Applied Cog. Psych. 9, 495–522 (1995)
16. D'Mello, S., Taylor, R.S., Graesser, A.: Monitoring Affective Trajectories during Complex Learning. In: 29th Annual Cognitive Science Society, pp. 203–208 (2007)
17. Chi, M.T.H., Roy, M., Hausmann, R.G.M.: Observing Tutorial Dialogues Collaboratively: Insights about Human Tutoring Effectiveness from Vicarious Learning. Cog. Sci. 32, 301–341 (2008)
18. Core, M.G., Moore, J.D., Zinn, C.: The Role of Initiative in Tutorial Dialogue. In: 10th Conference of the European Chapter of the Association for Computational Linguistics, pp. 67–74 (2003)
19. Katz, S., Allbritton, D., Connelly, J.: Going Beyond the Problem Given: How Human Tutors use Post-Solution Discussions to Support Transfer. International Journal of Artificial Intelligence in Education 13, 79–116 (2003)
20. Rosé, C., Bhembe, D., Siler, S., Srivastava, R., VanLehn, K.: The Role of Why Questions in Effective Human Tutoring. In: International Conference on AI in Education, pp. 55–62 (2003)
21. Litman, D., Moore, J., Dzikovska, M., Farrow, E.: Using Natural Language Processing to Analyze Tutorial Dialogue Corpora Across Domains and Modalities. In: 14th International Conference on AI in Education, pp. 149–156 (2009)
22. Tetreault, J.R., Litman, D.J.: A Reinforcement Learning Approach to Evaluating State Representations in Spoken Dialogue Systems. Speech Comm. 50, 683–696 (2008)
23. Beal, C., Mitra, S., Cohen, P.R.: Modeling Learning Patterns of Students with a Tutoring System using Hidden Markov Models. In: 13th International Conference on AI in Education, pp. 238–245 (2007)
24. Jeong, H., Gupta, A., Roscoe, R., Wagster, J., Biswas, G., Schwartz, D.: Using Hidden Markov Models to Characterize Student Behaviors in Learning-by-Teaching Environments. In: Woolf, B.P., Aïmeur, E., Nkambou, R., Lajoie, S. (eds.) ITS 2008. LNCS, vol. 5091, pp. 614–625. Springer, Heidelberg (2008)
25. Soller, A., Stevens, R.: Applications of Stochastic Analyses for Collaborative Learning and Cognitive Assessment. In: Hancock, G.R., Samuelsen, K.M. (eds.) Advances in Latent Variable Mixture Models, pp. 217–253. Information Age Publishing (2007)
26. Boyer, K.E., Vouk, M.A., Lester, J.C.: The Influence of Learner Characteristics on Task-Oriented Tutorial Dialogue. In: Proceedings of the 13th International Conference on AI in Education, pp. 365–372 (2007)
27. Boyer, K.E., Phillips, R., Wallis, M.D., Vouk, M.A., Lester, J.C.: The Impact of Instructor Initiative on Student Learning through Assisted Problem Solving. In: 40th Tech. Symposium on Computer Science Education, pp. 14–18 (2009)
28. Boyer, K.E., Phillips, R., Ha, E.Y., Wallis, M.D., Vouk, M.A., Lester, J.C.: Modeling Dialogue Structure with Adjacency Pair Analysis and Hidden Markov Models. In: NAACL HLT, Short Papers, pp. 49–52 (2009)
29. Landis, J.R., Koch, G.: The Measurement of Observer Agreement for Categorical Data. Biometrics 33, 159–174 (1977)
30. Rabiner, L.R.: A Tutorial on Hidden Markov Models and Selected Applications in Speech Recognition. Proceedings of the IEEE 77, 257–286 (1989)

Exploiting Predictable Response Training to Improve Automatic Recognition of Children's Spoken Responses[*]

Wei Chen[1], Jack Mostow[1], and Gregory Aist[1,2]

[1] Project LISTEN, School of Computer Science, Carnegie Mellon University,
Pittsburgh, PA 15213, USA
[2] Applied Linguistics and Communication Studies, Iowa State University,
Ames, IA 50011, USA
{weichen,mostow}@cs.cmu.edu, gregory.aist@alumni.cmu.edu

Abstract. The unpredictability of spoken responses by young children (6-7 years old) makes them problematic for automatic speech recognizers. Aist and Mostow proposed predictable response training to improve automatic recognition of children's free-form spoken responses. We apply this approach in the context of Project LISTEN's Reading Tutor to the task of teaching children an important reading comprehension strategy, namely to make up their own questions about text while reading it. We show how to use knowledge about strategy instruction and the story text to generate a language model that predicts questions spoken by children during comprehension instruction. We evaluated this model on a previously unseen test set of 18 utterances totaling 137 words spoken by 11 second grade children in response to prompts the Reading Tutor inserted as they read. Compared to using a baseline trigram language model that does not incorporate this knowledge, speech recognition using the generated language model achieved concept recall 5 times higher – so much that the difference was statistically significant despite small sample size.

Keywords: children's free-form spoken responses, predictable response training, automatic speech recognition, language model, self-questioning strategy for reading comprehension, Project LISTEN's Reading Tutor.

1 Introduction

Speech is a natural way for humans to communicate. Intelligent tutoring system developers have started to treat automatic speech recognition (ASR) as a desirable way to enhance human-computer interaction [1-3]. Compared to typing [4], verbal input is especially convenient for children in the early years of elementary schools (i.e., first and second grades, roughly ages 6-7). Unlike older students, young children have

---

[*] The research reported here was supported by the Institute of Education Sciences, U.S. Department of Education, through Grant R305B070458. The opinions expressed are those of the authors and do not necessarily represent the views of the Institute and the U.S. Department of Education. We also thank the educators, students, and LISTENers who helped generate and analyze our data.

trouble typing accurately or quickly. Compared to multiple choice interfaces, a speech interface is less distracting, and it allows a broader range of input.

However, recognizing children's free-form speech is a tricky problem [5, 6]. Acoustic parameters of children's speech, such as formants, are harder to capture and more variable than those of adult speech [7]. Besides, children are creative in syntactic-lexical use of language, and their speech can be ungrammatical [8], which increases the unpredictability of the speech.

To reduce this unpredictability, we apply predictable response training [9]. We then exploit knowledge of predictable responses in the language model of a speech recognizer. We develop this approach in a Reading Tutor that teaches young children to generate questions about story texts (also known as "self-questioning"). Teaching this strategy has been shown to improve children's reading comprehension [10, 11].

The rest of this paper is organized as follows. Section 2 introduces predictable response training for self-questioning. Section 3 and 4 respectively describe how to generate and improve a language model that exploits such training. Section 5 reports results. Section 6 summarizes contributions, limitations, and future work.

2 Predictable Response Training in Self-questioning Instruction

Our self-questioning instruction [12] attempts to teach a young child to wonder about text while reading it aloud to Project LISTEN's Reading Tutor [13]. In a self-questioning activity, the Reading Tutor prompts the child now and then to ask a question out loud about the text, and records the free-form spoken responses.

Unpublished data from a previous study [14] found considerable variation in children's responses to self-questioning prompts such as *What else are you wondering about rainbows? Ask a question out loud*. Out of 23 recorded responses, only one response was a grammatical question relevant to the text (*Does a rainbow come out when it snows?*). The rest contained only classroom background noise, did not take a question form (e.g. *Nothing, Thank god I could make a promise about rainbow*), were ungrammatical (e.g., *How they get the colors where they come from yada yada I'm done*), or were irrelevant to the text (*Why do you ask so many questions*).

To reduce the unpredictability of children's responses in self-questioning, we built predictable response training into the instruction. We train three types of questions, namely *Why*, *How*, and *What*. Our instruction guides students to compose questions in multiple steps, so as to elicit predictable segments. We decompose a question about a fictional text into a question stem (e.g., *Why was*), a character to ask about (e.g., *the country mouse*), and a question completer (e.g., *surprised*). We follow an instructional model that gradually transfers responsibility from tutor to student [15]:

(1) <u>Describe the strategy</u>: the tutor introduces the strategy of self-questioning and explains an important component of a question, namely the question stem:
Tutor[1]: *I'm going to tell you about a reading strategy called QUESTIONING.*
 QUESTIONING means you ask YOURSELF questions WHILE you read.

---

[1] Tutor prompts: *italics* = spoken; **boldface** = displayed; ***bold italics*** = both; * = elicits speech.

Asking yourself questions while you read can help you understand better. A good way to start a question is with a question word. These are some good question words: why, who, where, when, what, and how.

(2) Model the strategy: the tutor models the strategy with an example question.
Tutor: *This part of the story makes me think of this question:*
  "Why was the country mouse surprised?"

[Student reads more text]

(3) Scaffold the strategy: To help the child make a question, the tutor provides multiple choices for all or some question segments.

Tutor: *Let's make a question about ___ (the town mouse; the country mouse; the man of the house; the cat).*

Student: [In the on-screen menu of 4 choices, the student clicks on **the country mouse**.]

Tutor: *Let's ask a ___ (what; why; how) question.*

Student: [The student chooses **why**.]

Tutor: *Let's complete your question: Why did the country mouse___ (decide to send the cat; try to taste everything before his tummy was full; run)?*

Student: [The student chooses **decide to send the cat**.]

* Tutor: *Ok, now I want you to read your question out loud before you continue the story.*

Student reads aloud: **Why did the country mouse decide to send the cat?**

[Student reads more text]

After the child chooses a character to ask about and a question type, the tutor asks him or her to complete the question by saying the whole question out loud.

Student: [The student chooses **the cat** and **how**.]

* Tutor: *Now finish your question by saying the whole thing out loud, and completing the rest.*

Student: **How did the cat** *see the mice?*

[Student reads more text]

(4) Prompt the use of the strategy: the tutor prompts the child to ask a question without assistance.

* Tutor: *Think of a question to ask about the story, and say it out loud.*

Student: *Why did the two mice come out?*

The inserted tutor prompts typically total around 1 minute of instruction.

3 Core Language Model

Speech recognition uses an acoustic model of how sounds represent words, and a language model of how words are combined into utterances. Generally, the better the acoustic model captures how users pronounce words, and the better the language model captures how users construct utterances out of words, the better the recognition. Thus, researchers seeking to improve speech recognition performance typically focus on improving the acoustic model, the language model, or both. Researchers also seek to improve audio quality and reduce the range of likely ways to say things within the user's task. This paper focuses on language modeling approaches that exploit knowledge of a constrained range of likely utterances.

To exploit predictable response training, we build into the language model questions generated automatically from the text. Our question generator [12] combines a question stem with two other segments it extracts from the text – a character to ask about, and a question completer. Our language model generator then compiles the resulting questions into a finite state grammar (FSG). Fig. 1 shows an example language model that incorporates the questions from step (3) in Section 2.

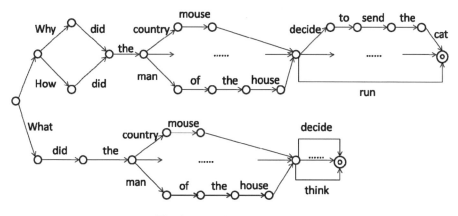

Fig. 1. Example language model

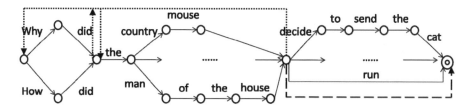

Fig. 2. A fragment of core language model with disfluency modeling. Dotted arrows represent repetition; dashed arrows represent early termination.

Modeling disfluency. Disfluency, a common phenomenon in children's speech [6], includes hesitations, filled pauses (e.g., *uh, um*), repetition (e.g., *How did how did the cat see the mice?*), and early termination (e.g., *Why did the cat*). To model hesitations and filled pauses, we exploit the recognizer's ability to insert silences and noises between words, using a noise dictionary including every phoneme. To model repetition, we add transition arcs from segment boundaries to previous segment boundaries.

To model early termination, we add transition arcs from segment junctions to the end state. Fig. 2 shows part of the resulting "core language model."

4 Enhancing Robustness of the Language Model

For guidance to help us improve the core language model, we used a 168-word corpus from a spring 2009 pilot test of self-questioning instruction generated for Aesop's fable "The Country Mouse and the Town Mouse." This corpus consists of 12 responses by 7 second graders to self-questioning prompts starred with * in Section 2.

In principle, we could train a language model directly from questions spoken by trained students, but practically speaking we'd need a substantially larger corpus. For the related task of recognizing children's spontaneous summarization, Hagen et al. [1] trained language models from 10 stories and different numbers of students' summaries. They reported needing at least 40 summaries to achieve better recognition than the initial language model trained from 10 stories.

The language model predicts both the content of the questions and their form. Predictable response training mainly elicits the form of children's questions, with limited possibilities for the question stem and character, but the question completer segment is more open-ended both in the words it can use and the order they can occur.

Expanding the vocabulary with story words and common words. There is a tradeoff between the coverage and precision of the language model. As ASR vocabulary grows, coverage of children's speech increases, but so does the risk of misrecognition. Hence we want only words likely to appear in children's responses. Children's questions can reach beyond vocabulary output by our question generator: the core language model vocabulary covers only 38% of the 60 word types in our 168-word pilot corpus. To improve coverage, we add the Dolch list [16] of 220 words common in children's books. We expect children's questions to be about story text, so we add all the story words. We further expand the resulting vocabulary by using a morphology generator to add all inflections of each verb.

Interpolating the language model with more general language models. To boost robustness, we tried interpolating the core language model with broader models: a unigram model, a part of speech (POS) bigram model, and a trigram model.

We trained the unigram model on 158,079 words in 673 children's stories from Project LISTEN. We incorporated it by inserting a self-looping state in the core FSG to allow any sequence of words after the character segment, using the unigram probability for each word. We give the transition into this state a low weight (.0001) as a penalty so as to give such sequences lower probabilities than generated questions.

Our POS-bigram language model approximates bigram probability $P(w_2 | w_1)$ as $P(POS(w_2) | POS(w_1))$, e.g. P(*mice* | *the*) as P(NNS | DT), where NNS means a plural noun, and DT means a determiner. We tagged all 673 stories using the Stanford POS tagger, and trained a bigram model on the resulting POS sequences using the SRILM language modeling toolkit [17]. To incorporate this model in the FSG, we added a state for each POS tag. We assigned the transition from the character segment to the VB (verb) state the probability .0001, and transitions between POS states their POS bigram probabilities. We tagged each word with its most frequent POS. Thus this model approximates P(*find the mice*) as .0001 * P(DT | VB) * P(NNS | DT).

To construct a trigram language model, we first extracted from the 976,992,639 Google 3-grams [18] the 727,348 consisting solely of the 477 words in predicted questions, the story, and the Dolch list. Next, we approximated our FSG in trigram form by enumerating predicted questions and a subset of their disfluent forms (restricting repetition to 2 times) and collecting their trigram counts. We multiplied them by 1000 to weight them more heavily, added them to the Google n-gram counts, and used the combined counts to train our interpolated trigram language model.

5 Evaluation and Results

We conducted ASR experiments to evaluate predictable response training by comparing language models that exploit such training against a baseline that does not.

5.1 Evaluation Metrics

To evaluate how many words our model correctly recognizes, we report word accuracy (WA), measured as the number of correctly recognized words divided by the total number of words in the human transcript. WA penalizes substitutions and deletions by the ASR; word error rate (WER) additionally penalizes insertions.

Concept coverage. From an application point of view, WA is not the ultimate objective function. The more important goal is to extract spoken meaning, not to transcribe the exact words spoken, especially function words such as *the* and *of*. We therefore ignore function words, and measure precision and recall of *concepts*, which we operationalize as word classes defined by word stems – i.e., two words denote the same concept if they share the same stem. If a child says the same thing twice and the speech recognizer hears it only once, concept precision and recall are unaffected.

Upper bound of a language model. Given the acoustic model, how well can a language model possibly do in terms of ASR accuracy? To obtain a rough upper bound on ASR accuracy, we did a "cheating experiment" using a FSG language model consisting of just the 12 transcribed word sequences from our pilot set.

5.2 Evaluation Results on Pilot Data

Table 1 shows results for the various language models described in Sections 3 and 4. As a baseline, we trained a trigram language model on the same 673 stories, but restricted its vocabulary to the words from "The Country Mouse and the Town Mouse." Exploiting predictable response training increased WA from 8.9% (WER 118%) for the baseline model to as high as 73.2% (WER 57.1%) for the core language model interpolated with a POS bigram model. To evaluate how well the speech recognizer performs with different vocabularies, we report recall of concepts from the core language model, from the story, and from all transcribed responses. The core LM + POS-bigram model achieved the highest all-concept recall – significantly higher (despite the small sample size) than the baseline model that did not exploit this training (n = 12 responses, $p < 0.001$ on a paired T-test, Cohen's d = 1.362). To our surprise, it actually beat the cheating model on 2 of the 3 recall measures, presumably due to greater flexibility in recognizing speech atypical of the acoustic models.

Table 1. ASR results on pilot data (168 words). The baseline model is a trigram LM trained on children's stories. The Core LM covers automatically generated questions and disfluency. The next three models interpolate it with n-gram models to cover question completers better. This and subsequent tables show the highest non-cheating value(s) in each column in **boldface**.

Language Model	Word Accuracy	Recall Core LM concepts	Recall Story concepts	Recall All concepts	Precision
Baseline (3-gram)	8.9%	16.7%	17.6%	11.7%	**81.8%**
Core Language Model	67.9%	**92.6%**	80.4%	64.9%	65.8%
Core LM + unigram	68.5%	**92.6%**	80.4%	64.9%	69.4%
Core LM + POS-bigram	**73.2%**	88.9%	**88.2%**	**68.9%**	57.0%
Core LM + Google 3gram	42.3%	59.3%	56.9%	42.9%	57.9%
Cheating Experiment	89.3%	87.0%	86.3%	84.4%	87.8%

5.3 Improving Precision by Reducing Insertions

Most ASR errors were insertions caused by background speech and noise. To improve precision, we tried two approaches: (1) post-processing ASR output to filter out low-confidence words; (2) tightening search by lexicalizing question segments. Table 2 shows their effects on the output of the Core LM+POS-bigram model.

Table 2. Improving precision on pilot data (168 words)

Configuration	Word Accuracy	Recall Core LM concepts	Recall Story concepts	Recall All concepts	Precision
Core LM+POS-bigram	**73.2%**	88.9%	**88.2%**	**68.9%**	57.0%
Confidence thresholding	64.3%	79.6%	82.3%	62.3%	72.7%
HMM filter	57.2%	74.1%	70.6%	57.1%	75.9%
Lexicalized model	47.5%	**94.4%**	78.4%	66.2%	**76.1%**

Confidence thresholding. The speech recognizer we used assigns each hypothesized word a confidence score between 0 and 1 to indicate how likely it was recognized correctly. To separate correctly recognized words from misrecognized words with maximum accuracy, we chose a threshold on the confidence score that minimized the sum of false positive rate plus false negative rate.

Training an HMM sequential model for filtering. The confidence score rates each hypothesis word independent of its context. However, misrecognized words tend to appear in a row, and so do correctly recognized words. A sequential model, such as a Hidden Markov Model (HMM), can capture this characteristic.

Our HMM filter combines the confidence score with an intensity threshold to filter out background speech and noise, which typically have a lower intensity than student speech into a close-talking headset microphone. Since the speech recognizer may have trouble distinguishing background speech or noise from user speech, a threshold on intensity can help indicate which regions of the signal to ignore. Most of our recordings start with silence and speech by the Reading Tutor. Thus, to set an intensity threshold, the first 0.5 seconds of speech is assumed to be a silence or noise region.

Then the threshold is set to be the average intensity of this noise region plus 20 times its standard deviation. We classify regions that exceed the intensity threshold as foreground speech. We used this classification and the confidence score for each hypothesis word as feature vectors to train an HMM with two states (each with a 2-dimensional Gaussian emission distribution and diagonal covariance matrix). We expect these two states to represent correct and incorrect recognition.

Lexicalizing the language model. User-testing showed that children often paused between question segments and within question completers, but not within question stem and character segments, as in *Why did ... the man of the house ... try to hurt things, um, the mice?* These pauses suggest a high cognitive load [19] when starting a new segment or thinking up a question completer.

To exclude unlikely pauses from the language model, we lexicalized question stems and character segments. Thus the stem *Why did* mapped to a single lexical item *why-did*, and the character segment *the man of the house* to *the-man-of-the-house*.

5.4 Results on Unseen Test Data

Table 3 shows results on 18 self-questioning responses by 11 students, collected after the analyses reported above. Even with so little data, the difference between all-concept recall for Core LM+POS-bigram and the baseline was again sufficiently dramatic (5x) to be statistically significant (n = 18, p < 0.0001, Cohen's d = 1.364). The baseline and POS-bigram models had WER 93.4% and 64.2%, respectively.

Table 3. Results on unseen test data (137 words)

Configuration	Word Accuracy	Recall Core LM concepts	Recall Story concepts	Recall All concepts	Precision
Baseline	6.6%	14.0%	17.5%	10.3%	46.7%
Core LM	**60.6%**	**80.0%**	**77.5%**	**58.8%**	50.6%
Core LM+POS-bigram	40.9%	68.0%	65.0%	50.0%	54.8%
Confidence filter	38.5%	64.0%	57.5%	49.7%	**84.4%**
HMM filter	31.2%	50.0%	50.0%	43.4%	75.6%
Lexicalized model	54.7%	78.0%	75.0%	57.4%	73.6%

Both overall and story-concept recall on unseen data were encouraging, but lower than on the pilot data we used to tune the language model weight, repetition weight, vocabulary, filler word penalty, silence penalty, and filter model parameters. This tuning likely overfit the small amount of pilot data we used for development.

6 Contributions, Limitations, and Future Work

This paper describes a 2-part approach to improve ASR of children's free-form spoken responses. One part trains children to make more predictable responses. Ideally we could evaluate this part by comparing speech with versus without predictable response training as the only manipulation, but the training is inextricably interwoven with the strategy instruction itself, and ASR performance reported earlier on free-form responses elicited by different instruction [14] was very low.

The other part generates language models to exploit this predictability by integrating constraints on expected content and form, not just interpolating n-gram models from different sources [20]. We constrain content by limiting vocabulary to the story, questions generated from it, common words, and verb inflections. We constrain form based on the instruction and on word order in the story and other text.

We demonstrated ASR accuracy 5-fold higher than for a baseline language model, tested various methods to improve precision and recall, and compared their effects. Future work includes generalizing to other text, and to tasks besides self-questioning.

As a reviewer of this paper pointed out, predictable response training may itself have educational benefits. A direct benefit to the student comes from the schema that gives rise to the predictability: the same scaffold that makes responses predictable also makes them easier for the student to generate, and hence to learn. An indirect benefit is to facilitate assessment: predictable responses are easier to score. This paper has shown how to exploit predictable response training in ASR, paving the way to realize this benefit in intelligent tutors that listen to children not just read but talk.

References (LISTEN publications are at www.cs.cmu.edu/~listen)

1. Hagen, A., Pellom, B., Vuuren, S.v., Cole, R.: Advances in Children's Speech Recognition within an Interactive Literacy Tutor. In: HLT-NAACL, Association for Computational Linguistics, Boston, pp. 25–28 (2004)
2. Litman, D.J., Silliman, S.: ITSPOKE: an intelligent tutoring spoken dialogue system. In: Demonstration Papers at HLT-NAACL, Association for Computational Linguistics, Boston, pp. 5–8 (2004)
3. Meron, J., Valente, A., Johnson., W.L.: Improving the Authoring of Foreign Language Interactive Lessons in the Tactical Language Training System. In: SLaTE, Farmington, PA (2007)
4. Wijekumar, K., Meyer, B.J.F.: Design and pilot of a web-based intelligent tutoring system to improve reading comprehension in middle school students. International Journal of Technology in Teaching and Learning 2(1), 36–49 (2006)
5. Russell, M., D'Arcy, S.: Challenges for computer recognition of children's speech. In: SLaTE, Pittsburgh, PA, pp. 108–111 (2007)
6. Potamianos, A., Narayanan, S.: A Review of the Acoustic and Linguistic Properties of Children's Speech. In: Proceedings of IEEE Multimedia Signal Processing Workshop, Chania, Crete, Greece, pp. 22–25. IEEE, Los Alamitos (2007)
7. Eguchi, S., Hirsh, I.J.: Development of speech sounds in children. Acta Oto-Laryngologica Supplementum 257, 1–51 (1969)
8. Gerosa, M., Giuliani, D., Narayanan, S.: Acoustic analysis and automatic recognition of spontaneous children's speech. In: Interspeech, Pittsburgh, PA, pp. 1886–1889 (2006)
9. Aist, G., Mostow, J.: Designing Spoken Tutorial Dialogue with Children to Elicit Predictable but Educationally Valuable Responses. In: Interspeech, Brighton, UK (2009)
10. Rosenshine, B., Meister, C., Chapman, S.: Teaching students to generate questions: A review of the intervention studies. Review of Educational Research 66(2), 181–221 (1996)

11. NRP: Report of the National Reading Panel. Teaching children to read: An evidence-based assessment of the scientific research literature on reading and its implications for reading instruction, Washington, DC (2000),
    http://www.nichd.nih.gov/publications/nrppubskey.cfm
12. Mostow, J., Chen, W.: Generating Instruction Automatically for the Reading Strategy of Self-Questioning. In: 14th International Conference on Artificial Intelligence in Education, pp. 465–472. IOS Press, Brighton (2009)
13. Mostow, J., Beck, J.: When the Rubber Meets the Road: Lessons from the In-School Adventures of an Automated Reading Tutor that Listens. In: Schneider, B., McDonald, S.-K. (eds.) Scale-Up in Education, vol. 2, pp. 183–200. Rowman & Littlefield Publishers, Lanham (2007)
14. Zhang, X., Mostow, J., Duke, N.K., Trotochaud, C., Valeri, J., Corbett, A.: Mining Free-form Spoken Responses to Tutor Prompts. In: Proceedings of the First International Conference on Educational Data Mining, Montreal, pp. 234–241 (2008)
15. Duke, N.K., Pearson, P.D.: Effective Practices for Developing Reading Comprehension. In: Farstrup, A.E., Samuels, S.J. (eds.) What Research Has To Say about Reading Instruction, International Reading Association, Newark, DE, pp. 205–242 (2002)
16. Dolch, E.W.: A Basic Sight Vocabulary. The Elementary School Journal (1936)
17. Stolcke, A.: SRILM – An Extensible Language Modeling Toolkit. Proc. Intl. Conf. on Spoken Language Processing 2, 901–904 (2002)
18. Brants, T., Franz, A.: Web 1T 5-gram Version 1. Linguistic Data Consortium (2006)
19. Berthold, A., Jameson, A.: Interpreting Symptoms of Cognitive Load in Speech Input. In: Proceedings of the Seventh International Conference on User Modeling, Banff, Canada, pp. 235–244 (1999)
20. Jang, P.J., Hauptmann, A.G.: Improving Acoustic Models with Captioned Multimedia Speech. ICMCS 2, 767–771 (1999)

Leveraging a Domain Ontology to Increase the Quality of Feedback in an Intelligent Tutoring System

Hameedullah Kazi[1,3], Peter Haddawy[1], and Siriwan Suebnukarn[2]

[1] Computer Science & Information Management Program,
Asian Institute of Technology, Thailand
[2] School of Dentistry, Thammasat University, Thailand
[3] Department of Computer Science, Isra University, Pakistan
{hameedullah.kazi,haddawy}@ait.ac.th, ssiriwan@tu.ac.th,
hkazi@isra.edu.pk

Abstract. Tutoring systems typically contain or generate a set of approved solutions to problems presented to students. Student solutions that don't match the approved ones, but are otherwise partially correct, receive little acknowledgment as feedback, stifling broader reasoning. Additionally, feedback mechanisms rely on having the student model, which requires extensive effort to build. This paper provides an alternative to the traditional ITS architecture by using a hint generation strategy that bypasses the student model and instead leverages off of the domain ontology. Concept hierarchy and co-occurrence between concepts in the domain ontology are drawn upon to ascertain partial correctness of a solution and guide student reasoning towards the correct solution. We describe the strategy incorporated in a tutoring system for medical PBL, wherein the widely available UMLS is deployed as the domain ontology. Evaluation of expert agreement with system generated hints on a 5-point likert scale resulted in an average score of 4.44 ($r = 0.9018$, $p < 0.05$). Hints containing partial correctness feedback scored significantly higher than those without it (Wilcoxon Rank Sum, $p < 0.001$).

Keywords: Ontology, hint generation, student model, intelligent tutoring systems, medical PBL, UMLS, knowledge acquisition bottleneck.

1 Introduction

Tutoring systems normally contain either a set of approved solutions or, a mechanism that generates approved solutions to problems presented to the students. Evaluation of the student solution and feedback returned is tailored to be effective only within the knowledge confines of the approved solutions. Tutoring systems are typically unable to assess the partial correctness of student solutions when they fall outside the scope of the approved ones. Moreover, for the purpose of solution representation, students are restricted to the choice of domain concepts from a custom built repository which is often quite narrow. Such characteristics lend themselves to a tutoring approach that is fairly brittle and quite opposed to how a human tutor would behave. A human tutor on the other hand, allows a diverse choice of domain concepts, assesses where the student solution lies in the broad knowledge space, acknowledges the partially correct aspects of the solution and guides the students back to the correct solution. Thus in order for a tutoring system to exhibit robust tutoring, it needs a broad knowledge base to allow students to explore a large space of novel solutions and work creatively, while still being able to steer them towards a correct solution if they get off track.

An ontology presents great potential for reuse and as a knowledge base that could be exploited for reasoning purposes. Several tutoring systems have employed ontologies [1, 2, 3], but they require extensive effort in encoding the relevant knowledge into the ontology. The Constraint Acquisition System [4] uses a more feasible method of encoding the ontology constraints by learning from examples, but its initial design still needs to be defined manually.

The construction of a tutoring system typically requires knowledge acquisition in the three areas of domain model, student model and pedagogical model. Acquiring and encoding the relevant knowledge can lead to a large overhead in the development time of a tutoring system [5, 6]. Attempts to expand the system and reuse the existing domain model for the rapid addition of new problems or cases are often hindered by the daunting task of acquiring the burdensome student model.

While the importance of the student model has been advocated [7], the design of some tutoring systems has excluded the student model based on the needs of the tutoring task [8]. Similar to Andes [8], our system too, does not use assessment to select the next task to be offered to the student. Because of the extensive effort required in designing, tutoring systems often excel in one or two of the three models mentioned above and maintain a more simplified form of the remaining ones [9].

The development time for a tutoring system has also come under scrutiny in the comparison between Model Tracing (MT) and Constraint Based Modeling (CBM) [10, 11]. Kodaganallur et al., [10] and Mitrovic et al., [11] have acknowledged the tradeoff between the reduction in development time and the quality of hints generated. The development time required to add a case is expected to vary based on the nature of the task domain. For the domain of statistical hypothesis testing, Kodaganallur et al., [10] report the development time of 5 person-days for problem modeling and 18 person-days for encoding the relevant knowledge in the case of CBM, whereas the development time was greater for MT. CBM simplifies the creation of new cases and has a reduced development time; however, its hints are not as effective and specialized as those in MT [10, 11].

In order to ease the knowledge acquisition bottleneck, Martin & Mitrovic [12] adopt a CBM approach, where the student model is an overlay of the domain model constraints. Their student model simply contains a score of the times a constraint has been satisfied or violated during problem solving. However, defining and encoding the constraints is still a burdensome task. Defining the constraints would be even a greater burden and challenge for an ill-defined domain such as medical PBL [13].

In the ill-defined domain of medical PBL, students may arrive at a solution from a variety of reasoning paths [14], making it a daunting task to build the student model. Based on our previous experience with the COMET system for medical PBL [15], it takes about one person-month to build the cognitive student model for each problem scenario. Modeling the diverse set of reasoning paths would be even more challenging if the system is expected to be robust in its tutoring approach by allowing students to explore a much broader solution space as mentioned above.

We extend our work on expanding the plausible solution space by deploying the widely available knowledge source, the Unified Medical Language System (UMLS) [16], as the domain ontology in a tutoring system for medical PBL [17]. In this paper we present a strategy for alleviating the overhead required to expand the tutoring system in adding new cases, by sidestepping the student model. We exploit the structure of the domain ontology to assess the partial correctness of student solutions and generate hints that are relevant to the student activity during problem solving. Furthermore, the time and effort required to add a new problem scenario to the tutoring system is reduced to 4-5 person-hours.

2 Related Work

The concept of partial correctness has been discussed in the context of tutoring systems [3, 18], wherein a part of the solution is explicitly recognized as correct. Our notion of partial correctness is different and is assessed through knowledge inference rather than explicitly encoded knowledge. Fiedler & Tsovaltzi [18] employ a domain ontology for tutoring mathematics theorem proving. The domain ontology of concepts contains some objects and relations defined as anchoring points, which serve as the basis for the content of the generated hints. Our hint generation strategy is different and draws inferences from the structure of the existing domain ontology at run-time without recourse to explicit encoding of knowledge into the ontology.

The design of medical tutoring systems built to date, have typically been based on customized knowledge bases that offer students a limited set of medical terms and concepts, to form their solution. The CIRCSIM-Tutor [3] teaches cardiovascular physiology by describing a perturbation of a cardiovascular condition, and initiating a question answer dialog with the student. The scope of hypothesis (solution) representation is narrow, as students are confined to assigning values to a small set of variables for forming their hypothesis. The SlideTutor [1] teaches dermatopathology by presenting a visual slide as a problem scenario and asks students to classify the diseases. Solutions accepted by the tutoring system are based on the ontology customized for the system. Thus students are not allowed to present alternative plausible hypotheses that may lie beyond the scope of this customized ontology.

The ReportTutor [19] teaches students diagnostic report writing by presenting a virtual slide and asking the students to write their report using a natural language interface. The pedagogical module refers to the expert model to see the list of goals that need to be accomplished and provides feedback based on the goals on the stack. The system does not make use of an explicit student model. Their work is similar to ours in generating hints without differentiating between two students having different knowledge levels performing the same exercise.

3 Medical PBL and System Prototype

In a typical PBL session in the medical domain, a problem scenario is presented to a group of 6-8 students, who form their hypothesis in the form of a causal graph, where graph nodes represent hypothesis concepts and directed edges (causal links) represent cause effect relationships between respective concepts. The hypothesis graph is based on the Illness Script, where hypothesis nodes may represent enabling conditions, faults or consequences [20]. Enabling conditions are factors that trigger the onset of a medical condition, e.g., aging, smoking, etc.; faults are the bodily malfunctions that result in various signs and symptoms, e.g., pneumonia, diabetes, etc.; consequences are the signs and symptoms that occur as a result of the diseases or disorders, e.g., fatigue, coughing, etc.

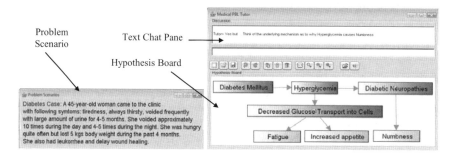

Fig. 1. System Prototype Interface

Our work is based on the extension of the COMET system [15] designed to cover medical PBL for various domains. In the COMET system, each problem scenario is first referred to human domain experts who provide an expert solution that is eventually encoded into the system. Student solutions are compared against this expert solution for evaluation. Thus a plausible student solution that does not match the expert solution is not entertained. The system allows students to form their hypothesis by choosing medical concepts from a repository manually encoded into the system. Students are given feedback based on the current state of their knowledge, which is assessed against a cognitive student model [15].

In our new system METEOR (Medical Tutor Employing Ontology for Robustness), problem solutions collected from experts are combined with UMLS tables to form the domain model. The pedagogical module of the system comprises a hint generation mechanism that leverages off of the UMLS concept hierarchy and provides students a measure of partial correctness of their hypotheses. Assessment of student solutions is not used to select the next step or task to be offered to the students. Furthermore, the hint generation employs the rich domain knowledge of the UMLS in lieu of a student model. Thus the design of our tutoring system does not include a student model.

The problem representation in METEOR is the same as that in COMET of a directed acyclic graph for forming the hypothesis. The student user is provided with a workspace as a hypothesis board to form the hypothesis, along with a text chat pane that returns hints to guide the student in clinical reasoning, as shown in Figure 1. The student chooses concepts from the UMLS Metathesaurus [16] as hypothesis nodes and draws edges between nodes, using a mouse. The problem solving activity begins as the student is presented a problem scenario, such as the one shown in Figure 1.

After studying the above problem scenario related to diabetes, the student hypothesizes that *Diabetes Mellitus* is a cause of *Hyperglycemia*, which is shown to be a cause of *Diabetic Neuropathy*, as shown in Figure 1.

4 System Domain Model

The UMLS [16] is a widely available medical knowledge source and is essentially a collation of various medical ontologies and terminologies (MeSH, SNOMED-CT, Gene Ontology, etc). The broad and diverse UMLS contains about two million medical concepts covering various medical domains [16].

The system domain model comprises UMLS tables and an additional table that is henceforth referred to as the *expert knowledge base*. The *expert knowledge base* is encoded with the help of human domain experts, and it contains causal relationship between various medical concepts, such as:

Hyperglycemia → *Decreased Glucose Transport into Cells*
Diabetic Neuropathies → *Numbness*
Decreased Glucose Transport into Cells → *Fatigue*

The *expert knowledge base* is formed through the collation of expert solutions to various problem scenarios. On average each expert solution leads to the addition of about 70-80 causal links to the *expert knowledge base*. The construction of an expert solution requires about 3-4 hours. Since each solution is in the form of a hypothesis graph, the collation of different solutions implies the incremental addition of the causal links in each solution, to the *expert knowledge base*.

5 Pedagogy of Assessment and Feedback

The hints generated by the system are composed of two elements: assessment of the partial correctness of the student solution and guidance towards a correct solution. Each hypothesis causal link drawn by the student is evaluated by the system through a strategy that accepts plausible solutions beyond the scope of the explicitly encoded ones [17]. If the link is found to be acceptable, the system allows the directed edge (causal link) to be drawn; otherwise the system disallows the edge to be drawn and returns an appropriate hint as feedback to the student. If the causal relationship drawn by the student is essentially correct but requires additional intermediate nodes in between, then the system disallows the edge to be drawn and encourages the student to describe the underlying mechanism. For example, considering the diabetes case described above, if the student draws the link: *hyperglycemia*→ *numbness*, the system would respond with the hint: **"Yes, but…Think of the underlying mechanism as to why *hyperglycemia* causes *numbness*."** On the other hand, if the student were to draw the reverse link: *numbness*→*hyperglycemia*, the system would respond with the hint: **"On the contrary, think of hyperglycemia as a cause of numbness."**

If the student link does not fall into any of the cases described above, the system makes use of a heuristic method to assess its partial correctness and deliver a hint to guide the student towards the correct link. The purpose of partial correctness feedback is to inform the student how close his/her solution is to be accepted. The hint pre-amble containing the partial correctness feedback is phrased as one of the following: 1. "You are very close", 2. "You are somewhat close", 3. "You are a little far off", 4. "You are quite far off", 5. "Hmm... Not sure. They may be a causal relation between the two", and 6. "Hmm... Can't say about the relation between the two."

5.1 Example 1: Partial Correctness through Semantic Distance

Imagine a situation related to the diabetes case mentioned above, where a student tries to draw a causal link: *hyperlipidemia* → *diabetic neuropathy*. Suppose the *expert knowledge base* does not recognize this link, however it recognizes that there is an expert link: *hyperglycemia* → *diabetic neuropathy*. In other words, what should have been *hyperglycemia* has been hypothesized by the student to be *hyperlipidemia*.

In order to assess the partial correctness of the student link, the system tries to find the semantic distance between *hyperlipidemia* and *hyperglycemia*. The semantic distance is measured by employing a modified version of the method described by Al-Mubaid & Nguyen [21]. Parent-child relationships from the UMLS Metathesaurus are used to construct the isa hierarchy of both nodes between which semantic distance is to be measured, as shown in Figure 2(a). Based on the value of the semantic distance, the system judges whether the nodes are *very close, somewhat close, little far,* or *quite far.* In this case, the system finds the two nodes to be *somewhat close.*

5.1.1 Guidance towards the Correct Solution

In order to guide the student towards the correct solution, the system examines the parent-child hierarchy to judge the commonality between the student link and the correct expert link. The system tries to find the lowest node in the hierarchy that is a common ancestor to both concepts in question: *hyperlipidemia* and *hyperglycemia*. The system finds that *metabolic diseases* is a common ancestor to both the concepts, as shown in Figure 2(a). Thus the system infers that the student knows that a kind of *metabolic disease* leads to *diabetic neuropathy*, however the student is not clear which kind. The hint content is framed to guide the student reasoning from its current position to the correct solution. This reasoning path of the hint content is shown in the dotted arrow in Figure 2(a), which leads from *hyperlipidemia* round the common ancestor towards *hyperglycemia*. Based on the assessment of partial correctness and the reasoning path en route the correct solution, the system responds with the hint: **"You are somewhat close. For causes of *diabetic neuropathy* ... Instead of *hyperlipidemia*, think about other kinds of *metabolic diseases*. Think of *A heterogeneous group of disorders characterized by glucose intolerance*".**

Here, 'A heterogeneous group of disorders characterized by glucose intolerance' is the definition in UMLS for the concept: *glucose metabolism disorder*. In other words the system gives the hint template: "Instead of <student node>, think about other kinds of <common ancestor> and <definition of next child in line from the common ancestor towards the expert node>".

If the student draws the link, *renal glomerular disease* → *diabetic neuropathy*, the system measures the semantic distance between *hyperglycemia* and *renal glomerular disease* and finds the two nodes to be *a little far off*. The hint is framed: **"You are a little far off. For causes of *diabetic neuropathy* ... Instead of *renal glomerular*** *disease*, think more specifically about other kinds of *Disorder of body system*. Think of *Abnormally high BLOOD GLUCOSE level, beyond the normal range*."

If the student draws the link *glucose metabolism disorder* → *diabetic neuropathy*, the system measures the semantic distance between *hyperglycemia* and *glucose metabolism disorder* and finds the two nodes to be *very close* and accepts the student link by giving the hint: **"You are very close. I was thinking of *hyperglycemia* → *diabetic neuropathy*, but *glucose metabolism disorder* is also acceptable. Good."**

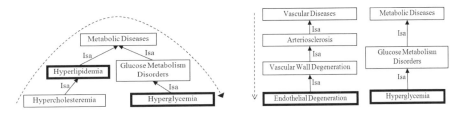

Fig. 2. (a) Concept Hierarchy: Example 1   (b) Concept Hierarchy: Example 2

5.2 Example 2: Partial Correctness through Co-occurrence Frequency

Imagine a situation related to a heart attack case, where a student tries to draw a causal link: *hyperlipidemia* → *hyperglycemia*. The system does not find this link to be acceptable, however, it finds an expert causal link: *hyperlipidemia* → *endothelial degeneration*. In other words what should have been *endothelial degeneration* has been hypothesized by the student to be *hyperglycemia*.

The system tries to find a common ancestor to both *hyperglycemia* and *endothelial degeneration*, but is unable to find one. In this situation, the system cannot assess the partial correctness through the semantic distance measure. As a weaker measure, it checks to see if the UMLS has any information regarding the co-occurrence of *hyperlipidemia* and *hyperglycemia* in medline citations. If the normalized co-occurrence frequency is found to be greater than zero, the system forms the hint pre-amble: **"Hmm... There may be a causal relation between *hyperlipidemia* and *hyperglycemia*."** Otherwise the following hint pre-amble is formed: **"Hmm... Can't say about the causal relation between *hyperglycemia* and *hyperlipidemia*."**

5.2.1 Guidance towards the Correct Solution

In order to guide the student towards the correct solution, the system adopts an approach similar to the one described for Example 1. Since there is no common ancestor in this case, the system tries to direct the student towards *endothelial degeneration* by starting from a few ancestors above, as shown in Figure 2(b). The hint is framed as: **"For effect of *hyperlipidemia* ... Instead of *hyperglycemia*, think of kinds of *vascular diseases* and *thickening and loss of elasticity of arterial walls*."**

Here, 'Thickening and loss of elasticity of arterial walls' is the definition in UMLS for the concept *arteriosclerosis*. In other words the system gives the hint template: "Instead of <student node>, think about kinds of <great grandfather of expert node> and <definition of grandfather of expert node>".

6 Results

We classified the different kinds of hints and randomly selected 30 system generated hints from student log files, which were evenly distributed across the hint classes. Five faculty members from Thammasat University having more than five years of experience in using PBL in teaching medicine, were asked to rate the sample of hints on a 5-point likert scale: 1 (strongly disagree) to 5 (strongly agree). For each sample, experts were shown the causal link drawn by the student and the corresponding expert link as the correct solution, along with the hint generated by the system, as shown in Figure 3 (a). In order to evaluate the utility of the partial correctness feedback, experts were presented two versions of the same hint. As shown in Figure 3 (a), hint from Tutor A contains the pre-amble of partial correctness feedback, for example 'You are somewhat close', whereas the Tutor B hint is without this feedback pre-amble.

Hints containing partial correctness led to an average score of 4.44 ($r = 0.9018$, $p < 0.05$), whereas those without it led to an average score of 3.58 ($r = 0.8463$, $p < 0.05$). Hints with partial correctness scored significantly higher than those without it (Wilcoxon Rank Sum, $p < 0.001$). In order to measure the percentage of expert agreement with hints, we collapsed the rating scale to Agree (4 or 5) and Disagree (1, 2 or 3); results of agreement with each of the five experts are shown in Figure 3 (b).

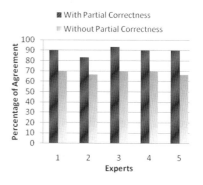

Fig. 3. (a) Sample of Hint for Evaluation   (b) Percentage of Agreement

7 Discussion

The overall average score of 4.44 and high percentages of agreement indicate strong expert acceptance of the system generated hints. The expert, who agreed with the system hints the most, agreed 93% of the time, whereas the expert with least agreement agreed 83% of the time. Furthermore, the hints including the element of partial correctness scored significantly higher than those without it, which shows that the experts found the partial correctness feedback to be very useful.

According to one PBL expert, some of the content in the sample of hints was even better than what an average PBL tutor would be able to conceive of. This is because not all PBL tutors are experts in all of the PBL cases. Their knowledge about concepts is sometimes lacking in certain areas and they are not always able to conceive of the right description for a particular concept. In fact, this is also possible in the case of

UMLS, where the definition text is missing for some concepts. It is worth noting that hints that contained the concept definition text scored higher than those where this text was missing in UMLS. Thus in domain areas where UMLS had knowledge gaps, the generated hints were not as good. This reflects some similarity between the hint leveraging off of UMLS and the hints produced by a human expert.

8 Conclusions

In this paper we have described how to ease the bottleneck of expanding a tutoring system. We have described how an existing broad knowledge source such as the UMLS, can be deployed as the domain ontology and its structure leveraged to assess the partial correctness of the student solution and generate hints based on the context of the student activity. Compared to the previous version of COMET, the time for the development and encoding of a new problem scenario has been drastically reduced from one person-month to 4-5 person-hours.

We have described the system implementation in the context of medical PBL, but the techniques could easily be applied to other domains where the task involves causal relationships and the domain ontology also contains a textual definition of the concepts. The techniques could be particularly relevant for other ill-defined domains, which require greater flexibility in assessment and feedback.

In interpreting the results of the proposed techniques, it is worth noting that the domain ontology has not been crafted specially for the task of medical PBL. A purpose built domain ontology is likely to yield better results, especially when its utility for hint generation is considered at the time of design.

Inference techniques applied to a large knowledge source such as UMLS, can be quite taxing on the processing power and result in delayed system response. Furthermore, our hint generation strategy leveraging off an existing knowledge source does not take into account the possibility of students having misconceptions at the ontology level, which could be addressed in a future study.

We intend to evaluate the impact of hints containing partial correctness on the student learning outcomes and have students evaluate the generated hints too. Finally we would like to compare and examine the tradeoffs between the clinical reasoning gains acquired through METEOR and through COMET, especially in light of the fact that as previous studies have shown, a feedback strategy such as the one proposed in this paper, may not be as effective as those that stem from a carefully captured cognitive student model. Nonetheless the tradeoff may be worth it, if one considers the long term ramifications in adding new cases for the large scale deployment of tutoring systems for instructional purposes.

References

1. Crowley, R., Medvedeva, O.: An Intelligent Tutoring System for Visual Classification Problem Solving. Artificial Intelligence in Medicine 36(1), 85–117 (2006)
2. Day, M.Y., Lu, C., Yang, J.D., Chiou, G., Ong, C.S., Hsu, W.: Designing an Ontology-Based Intelligent Tutoring Agent with Instant Messaging. In: Fifth IEEE International Conference on Advanced Learning Technologies, pp. 318–320 (2005)

3. Mills, B., Evens, M., Freedman, R.: Implementing directed lines of reasoning in an intelligent tutoring system using the atlas planning environment. In: International Conference on Information Technology, pp. 729–733 (2004)
4. Suraweera, P., Mitrovic, A., Martin, B.: A Knowledge Acquisition System for Constraint Based Intelligent Tutoring Systems. In: Conference on AI in Education, pp. 638–645 (2005)
5. Anderson, J.R., Corbett, A., Koedinger, K., Pelletier, R.: Cognitive tutors: Lessons learned. Journal of the Learning Sciences 4(2), 167–207 (1996)
6. Mitrovic, A.: Experiences in implementing constraint-based modelling in SQL-Tutor. In: Goettl, B.P., Halff, H.M., Redfield, C.L., Shute, V.J. (eds.) ITS 1998. LNCS, vol. 1452, pp. 414–423. Springer, Heidelberg (1998)
7. Self, J.A.: Bypassing, the Intractable Problem of Student Modelling. In: Proceedings of ITS 1988, Montreal, pp. 18–24 (1988)
8. VanLehn, K., Lynch, C., Schulze, K., Shapiro, J.A., Shelby, R., Taylor, L., Treacy, D., Weinstein, A., Wintersgill, M.: The Andes Physics Tutoring System: Lessons Learned. International Journal of Artificial Intelligence in Education 15, 147–204 (2005)
9. Murray, T.: Expanding the knowledge acquisition bottleneck for intelligent tutoring systems. International Journal of Artificial Intelligence in Education 8, 222–232 (1997)
10. Kodaganallur, V., Weitz, R.R., Rosenthal, D.: A Comparison of Model-Tracing and Constraint-Based Intelligent Tutoring Paradigms. International Journal of Artificial Intelligence in Education 152, 117–144 (2005)
11. Mitrovic, A., Koedinger, K.R., Martin, B.: A Comparative Analysis of Cognitive Tutoring and Constraint-Based Modeling. In: Brusilovsky, P., Corbett, A.T., de Rosis, F. (eds.) UM 2003. LNCS, vol. 2702, pp. 313–322. Springer, Heidelberg (2003)
12. Martin, B., Mitrovic, A.: Easing the ITS Bottleneck with Constraint-Based Modelling. New Zealand Journal of Computing 8(3), 38–47 (2001)
13. Pople Jr., H.E.: Heuristic Methods for Imposing Structure on Ill-Structured Problems: The Structuring of Medical Diagnostics. In: Szolovits, P. (ed.) Artificial Intelligence in Medicine, ch. 5. Westview Press, Boulder (1982)
14. Kazi, H., Haddawy, P., Suebnukarn, S.: Expanding the Space of Plausible Solutions in a Medical Tutoring System for Problem Based Learning. International Journal of Artificial Intelligence in Education (in Press)
15. Suebnukarn, S., Haddawy, P.: Modeling Individual and Collaborative Problem-Solving in Medical Problem-Based Learning. User Modeling and User-Adapted Interaction 16(3-4), 211–248 (2006)
16. U.S. National Library of Medicine, http://www.nlm.nih.gov/research/umls/
17. Kazi, H., Haddawy, P., Suebnukarn, S.: Expanding the Space of Plausible Solutions For Robustness in an Intelligent Tutoring System. In: Woolf, B.P., Aïmeur, E., Nkambou, R., Lajoie, S. (eds.) ITS 2008. LNCS, vol. 5091, pp. 583–592. Springer, Heidelberg (2008)
18. Fiedler, A., Tsovaltzi, D.: Domain-Knowledge Manipulation for Dialogue-Adaptive Hinting. In: Proceedings of the 12th International Conference on Artificial Intelligence in Education (AIED 2005), pp. 801–803 (2005)
19. Crowley, R.S., Tseytlin, E., Jukic, D.: ReportTutor - an intelligent tutoring system that uses a natural language interface. In: Proc. AMIA Symp. 2005, pp. 171–175 (2005)
20. Feltovich, P.J., Barrows, H.S.: Issues of generality in medical problem solving. In: Schmidt, H.G., De Volder, M.L. (eds.) Tutorials in problem-based learning: A new direction in teaching the health professions. Van Gorcum, The Netherlands (1984)
21. Al-Mubaid, H., Nguyen, H.A.: A Cluster Based Approach for Semantic Similarity in the Biomedical Domain. In: Proceedings of the 28th IEEE EMBS Annual International Conference, New York, USA, August 30-September 3 (2006)

Modeling Long Term Learning of Generic Skills

Richard Gluga, Judy Kay, and Tim Lever

University of Sydney, Sydney NSW 2006, Australia

Abstract. Many of the most important learning goals can only be achieved over several years. Our CUSP system helps achieve this over the 3-to-5 years of a university degree: it enables each teacher to map their own subject design to institutional learning goals; it creates both subject and degree-level models. It tackles the semantic mapping challenges using a highly flexible lightweight approach. We report its validation for 102 degrees and 1237 subject sessions. CUSP makes a contribution to understanding how to model long term learning of generic skills, using a lightweight semantic mapping based on multiple sets of externally defined learning goals. The work contributes to understanding of how to create comprehensive models of long term learning within degrees that are practical in real environments.

Keywords: Curriculum Mapping, Graduate Attributes, Accreditation Competencies, Learner Model.

1 Introduction

University degrees typically aim to build learners generic skills, such as written and spoken communication, team work and design and problem solving. These are highly valued both within learning institutions and by outside groups, notably employers. Learners need to develop these skills progressively, over several years, aided by a suitable sequence of learning experiences.

To ensure such long term learning over a whole degree, designers of each subject must appreciate how their subject fits into the full curriculum. Also, those responsible for each degree must ensure that generic skills are developed via a series of learning activities across subjects. This is quite complex, especially where students have flexibility to select elective subjects that match their background, interests and goals.

Despite the importance of learning generic skills, it is difficult to rigorously classify the skills learned in each subject. For this, we need to define two aspects: the generic skill; and the level of that skill. ITS research has typically dealt with fine grained ontological models for learning design, such as [10]. This is not adequate for our goals to model long term learning of generic skills.

A central problem is that the semantic model describing the learning progression must be agreed upon and used by several groups of people. Firstly, the lecturer responsible for teaching a particular subject must understand just what is required from their subject; otherwise they may fail to keep it true to the curriculum. Secondly, people at the faculty level must understand the curriculum design well enough to assess if it does develop the faculty's required generic attributes. Outside the university, accreditation bodies must be convinced that their stated learning requirements are met. Importantly, universities and accreditation bodies each define their own descriptions of generic skills.

For example, our Bachelor of Software Engineering (BSE) degree, must meet curriculum requirements defined in:

1. Engineering Australia (EA) Stage 1 Accreditation competencies,
2. Association of Computing Machinery learning objective recommendations,
3. Australian Computer Society skill recommendations and
4. University of Sydney Faculty of Engineering Graduate Attributes.

Note the different terms: skills, competencies, learning objectives, attributes. For the rest of the paper, we refer to these as *attributes*.

Another challenge comes from subject choice. Any allowed elective subjects must enable the student to achieve required attributes. Students must do them in the correct sequence, for progressive learning. So, curriculum designer must identify the attributes learned in each subject in designing a degree.

So far we have considered a single degree. A university can offer many. For example, in 2010, our university will offer over 600 degrees and over 13,000 subject sessions. Many must meet external accreditation, vocational and institutional attributes like those of the BSE.

We now describe how we have tackled this problem of modeling subjects and degrees. The next section describes related work, followed by our approach and the user view of our CUSP system. We then report its validation. We conclude with lessons learned and future work.

2 Related Work

The need for better support for designing and maintaining university degrees is recognized: as described by Mulder et. al. [8] for European standards-based design of university curricula. They report on various projects from England, Germany, France and Netherlands, noting the need for quality control, the lack of support tools for this and the challenge of multiple descriptions of the learning goals as we discussed above. McKenney et. al. [7] describe the multi-phased nature of this process and they reiterate the need for better tools to support curriculum designers.

Koper [6] explored approaches to modeling curriculum elements via a meta-model, in EML (Educational Modeling Language)[1]. With an e-Learning focus, subjects were represented as collections of reusable learning objects (LOs). It is unclear how this can scale to the degree level. While various other modeling standards (e.g. IEEE LOM, IMS LIP, SCORM, HR-XML, IMS-RDCEO) deal with parts of a whole degree, they do not help with the degree design complexity problems or multiple attribute framework semantic mapping challenges.

---

[1] Educational modeling Language, http://www.learningnetworks.org/?q=EML

Ontological approaches to such mappings have been attempted in various forms by Mizoguchi [10] (also using EML and IMS-LD), Van Assche [1], Paquette et. al. in the LORNET TELOS project [9] and others. These are promising, but cannot meet our goals. Paquette et. al. express this concern: *"what is yet to be proven is that the general approach presented here can be used at different levels by average design practitioners and learners"*. Kalz et. al. [5] also share this view: *"the design and implementation of competence ontologies is still a very complex and time-consuming task"*.

Bittencourt et. al. [2] explore use of semantic web technologies to improve curriculum quality and support the design process. They conclude, however, that *"a large-scale use of SW for education is still a futuristic vision rather than a concrete scenario"* and the implementation of ontologies is sometimes *"more an art rather than technology"*. Winter et. al. [11] also realize the strengths and limitations of traditional ITS systems with *"carefully crafted"* content and ontologies vs. e-Learning systems that are typically standards based but have *"content crafter by normal authors"*. To support lifelong learning, domain-specific ontologies will need to be mapped to each other but *"in a realistic setting...this may be difficult to do"* [11].

A limited implementation of attribute-to-subject mapping was employed by Calvo and Carroll [4] in their Curriculum Central (CC) system. It had a single attribute framework, to map a large set of subjects to these attributes. However, it could not deal with the critical external accreditation or vocational attributes, nor the complexity of elective subject choices.

Bull & Gardner [3] mapped multiple choice questions, in several subjects, to UK SPEC Standards for Professional Engineering attributes (UK-SpecIAL). As students complete online questions, the system builds open learner models, enabling students to see their learning progress, and which subjects could provide the missing attributes. This gave students a valuable big-picture view. However, the system lacks the generality we need, i.e. mapping across all forms of learning activities and assessments and supporting multiple sets of learning attributes.

3 Approach

Our approach is to create lightweight, two part models, based on *attribute definitions* and *level definitions*. These support models with the semantic relationships between any sets of attributes. We took this approach for modeling generic skills, due to the generality of their *attribute definitions* with the *level definitions* being sub-concepts that are also broad. This approach seemed promising for our multiple goals, notably the pragmatics of meeting the needs of teaching staff, institutions and accreditation.

Taking the institutional goals as the *base model*, we establish a set of *attribute definitions* from the established set of graduate attributes. This is an important decision: we consider the foundation should come from the institution's own goals. In our case, this has just 7 top-level attributes, most covering generic skills. For example, *Design and Problem Solving Skills*, one of the 7 top-level attributes, is defined as the *Ability to work both creatively and systematically in developing effective, sustainable solutions to complex practical problems.*

To model progression in learning, we assigned 4 or 5 *level definitions* for each attribute. This gives a coarse set of levels for key stakeholders to agree on, both for the levels and for classifying learning activities. This granularity is meaningful to model progression over the 3 to 5 years of a degree.

To incorporate other attribute frameworks into the *base model*, the curriculum designer maps their attributes against the *base model attribute definitions* and *level definitions*. So, for example, the EA Accreditation Competency statement *"experience in personally conducting a major design exercise to achieve a substantial engineering outcome to professional standards'* maps to our faculty *Design and Problem Solving Skills* attribute at *Level 3*. Additional frameworks can be systematically incorporated into the model by repeating this process. This means that *subject lecturers* map their subject assessments and learning activities to the institutional *base model*. They can ignore other attributes sets, minimizing demands on them. A big-picture view of a degree can be extracted from the model for any of the attribute frameworks, simply by resolving the semantic relationships.

4 CUSP User View

CUSP[2] implements this approach, with interfaces to manage the modeling processes. Figure 1 illustrates part of the *base model*, with the two level hierarchy of *attribute definitions* such as *Fundamentals of Science and Engineering* and an associated *level definition*, expanded in the figure. It aims to avoid restrictions on the structure of an attribute set. Attributes can be arbitrarily nested, or flat. Each attribute can be given a code, a label and a description and it can have any number of levels, each with their own descriptions. Clicking the yellow 'E' control next to an attribute or level brings up the floating Equivalence editor (bottom-right of Figure 1). This enables *curriculum designers* to define many-to-many semantic relationships between attributes or levels from different sets. The mappings are accessible and editable from either side.

We now describe the lecturer view for individual subjects. A lecturer can define a high level subject outline with information such as a handbook description, prerequisite/prohibition subject requirements, teaching methods & activities, learning outcomes, assessment tasks, resources and scheduling information. The fields are on the tabs for easy navigation as shown in Figure 2.

This shows a set of 5 attributes from our Faculty of Engineering Graduate Attribute Framework. Each maps to a specific level (clicking the attribute brings up full textual descriptions). The lecturer provides a free-form description stating how the attribute is supported by the subject. The subject attributes are further mapped (by lecturers) to learning outcomes and indirectly to assessments (each assessment can be mapped to one or more weighted learning outcomes).

On the degree side, a degree coordinator links a degree to any number of attribute frameworks. Our Bachelor of Software Engineering degree links to the

---

[2] Course & Unit of Study Portal - *course* being a degree and *unit of study* a subject.

Modeling Long Term Learning of Generic Skills 89

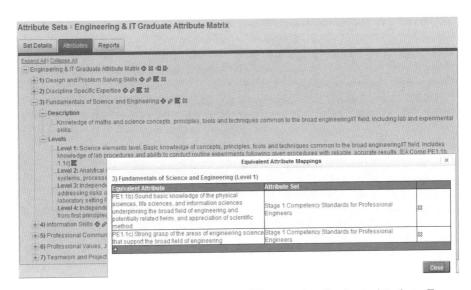

Fig. 1. Example of attributes from Faculty of Engineering Graduate Attribute Framework, with floating equivalent editor bottom-right

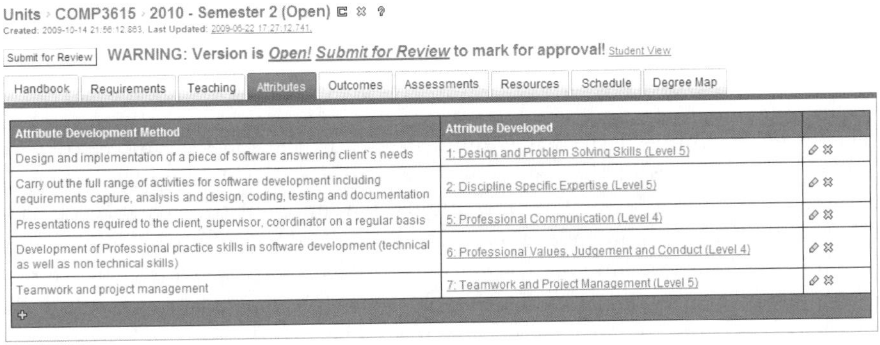

Fig. 2. Attributes linked to a subject and described by lecturers via development methods

Faculty of Engineering Attribute Framework and the EA Accreditation Stage 1 Competency Standards. The degree structure is then defined in terms of core and elective subjects, streams and recommended elective blocks.

We now have multiple attribute frameworks captured in the system, as well as the semantic relationships between attributes and levels, the mappings of attributes to subjects, learning activities and assessments, and the degree core/elective subject structures. These are all the pieces we need to start building our big-picture view of full 3-to-5 year degrees.

Figure 3 shows our Bachelor of Software Engineering degree in terms of the Faculty of Engineering Attribute Framework. The left column of the matrix has 7 top-level attributes and along the top are columns for each level defined.

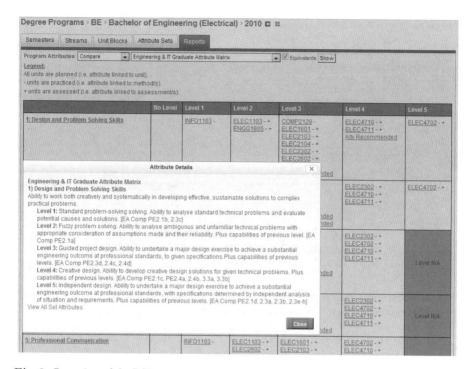

Fig. 3. Overview of the BSE degree in terms of planned, practiced and assessed attributes

Clicking an attribute in the left column brings up the full descriptive text for reference. In the cells of the matrix lists of subjects that develop the attribute at the corresponding level. The plus/minus markers next to each subject code differentiate between planned, practiced and assessed[3] attributes. The red *Adv. Recommended* subject label in *Design and Problem Solving Skills, Level 4* represents a subject recommended elective block (the placement of this block in the matrix is based on a CP threshold formula). The two drop-down boxes at the top allow the selection between different report types and, importantly, between the different attribute frameworks linked to the degree.

Switching to the EA Accreditation attribute framework regenerates the report as shown Figure 4. We now see the EA Accreditation competencies along the left column and the relevant subject codes in the right column. The EA attributes do not have any levels and hence no additional cells to the right. The list is easily scrollable however and an accreditation review panel could easily look at this to see which subjects support each attribute and if there are any knowledge gaps. Clicking on the subject takes the user to the full outline describing the precise attribute mappings. Notice that this report is generated by exercising our semantic equivalence mappings. We could easily map additional attribute frameworks to our BSE degree and generate similar reports.

---

[3] Here planned means material is in the curriculum but there are no linked learning activities or assessments, practiced means there are activities but no assessments.

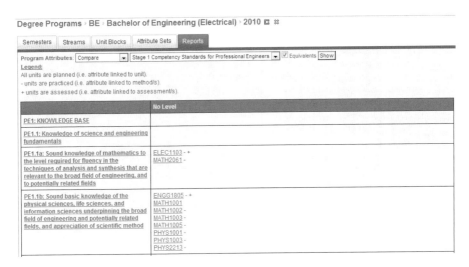

Fig. 4. Switch to the EA Stage 1 Accreditation Competency Framework

The chart visualization in Figure 5 is another big-picture view of our BSE degree. Along the x-axis we have the 7 faculty attributes. Along the y-axis we have the percentage distribution of each attribute in terms of assessments. That is, the BSE degree devotes roughly 22% of all assessment tasks to *Design and Problem Solving Skills*. Each column is further broken down into the corresponding attribute levels, which are color-coded. A mouse-over reveals the precise percentage distribution of each level.

5 Validation

The CUSP system has been deployed to three Faculties, namely Engineering, Architecture, Design and Planning, and Health Sciences. It has been populated with 8 generic attribute sets, 278 individual attributes, 102 degrees, 886 subjects, 1237 subject sessions, 3849 learning outcomes and 2418 assessment items. Altogether 2189 of the 2418 assessment items have been mapped to specific subject learning outcomes which were in turn aligned to the relevant generic attributes for the subject. The capture of outcomes, assessments and graduate attribute relationships has relied upon a combination of lecturer and administrative staff input. Outcome and assessment mappings have been reviewed and adjusted by degree coordinators or other experienced staff wherever possible. Quality of mappings varies widely from subject to subject and degree to degree but the data has been sufficient to begin generating some quality review reports through the system itself.

We conducted a test to validate the equivalence mapping approach as described in Section 4. To make this test more effective we performed it on two very different professionally accredited degrees: a 2-year Masters degree and a 4-year Bachelor degree; each in a different faculty. Subjects for each degree were

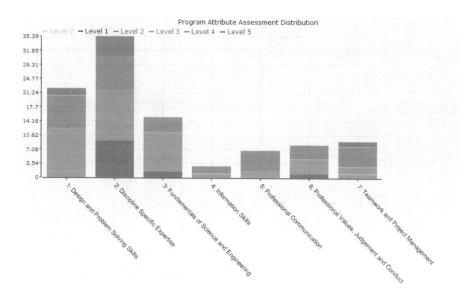

Fig. 5. A stacked column chart showing percentage distribution of assessed faculty attributes

mapped against the relevant faculty's primary attribute framework, which was in turn mapped, via equivalence relationships, to a second framework comprised of competency standards required for accreditation.

A report compiling subject learning outcomes under accreditation competency headings was generated for each degree. A recent graduate of each degree was asked to examine each outcome and determine in each case whether it represented a meaningful contribution to the competency descriptor under which it appeared. In cases where the match was not confirmed, the learning outcome mapping to the faculty graduate attribute framework was checked, by a curriculum expert, to determine whether the failure came from original data entry (learning outcome mapped to incorrect generic attribute/level), or from an equivalence mapping error (learning outcome mapped to correct generic attribute/level, but accreditation competency equivalence mapped to incorrect generic attribute level), or an attribute translation error (learning outcome mapped to correct generic attribute/level with correct equivalence mapping, but mismatch with learning outcome). All three failure types were found, as shown in Table 1 below.

The Masters degree had a high match ratio between learning outcomes and equivalence attribute mappings (92.28%), with only 4.56% of mismatches due to attribute translation errors (i.e. loss of context in cross-mapping more granular accreditation competencies to more generic faculty attributes, which are then mapped to more granular subject learning outcomes). The Bachelor degree did not fair as well with only a 49.63% match ratio between learning outcomes and accreditation attributes. The primary cause of this low ratio was due to incorrect

Table 1. Learning Outcomes matching accreditation competency descriptors as resolved via attribute equivalence mappings for two professional degrees

	Masters	%	Bachelor	%
Learning outcome mapping relationships	285		544	
Relationships confirmed	263	92.28	270	49.63
Relationships not confirmed	22	7.72	274	50.37
Failure at learning outcome source	8	2.82	208	38.24
Error in equivalence settings	1	0.35	27	4.96
Attribute grouping hard to translate	13	4.56	38	6.99

mappings between learning outcomes and the core faculty attribute framework. The attribute translation failure rate was only 6.99%. This degree, related subjects and core faculty attribute mappings were imported from an earlier system which had no accreditation competency equivalences defined, whereas the Masters was a newly created degree and hence had more accurate data.

This validation exercise shows our light-weight approach does not provide perfect mappings between degree subjects and multiple attribute frameworks. Equivalence translation errors sometimes appear due to the multi-level mapping of attributes at different granularities. The mappings are, however, valid to a large extent when data is correctly entered. High mismatches can be identified via the reporting tools which signal the need for further evaluation to determine the source of failure, which is valuable for long term degree quality control.

6 Conclusions and Future Work

We have described our approach to support design of flexible degrees that are accountable in terms of ensuring that important generic skills and accreditation requirements are met over the full 3-to-5 year duration. We have implemented this in CUSP and reported its use to map multiple attribute frameworks to individual degrees, and map attributes to each core or elective subject that is part of a degree. The CUSP reporting tools give lecturers and degree coordinators a big picture view of entire degrees. This helps identify knowledge gaps, accreditation requirement gaps, and progressive learning inconsistencies.

We have validated our approach by deploying the system on a large scale in a live university environment with real data. The system is in active use with 102 degrees, 1237 subject sessions and 8 different attribute frameworks. From the evidence of Table 1, the equivalence mapping tool is certainly not a mechanism for eliminating all errors or weakness in curriculum design and documentation but rather tends to amplify the impact of any errors present. In doing so, it provides a sensitive test of quality in all the elements concerned.

While CUSP has demonstrated the value of our approach for curriculum designers, at the level of the subject and the degree, we plan to extend our approach to incorporate available assessment data within each subject to create detailed individual student models. To do this, we will move beyond our current mapping of attributes to assessments via learning outcomes. This will allow us to explore the value of personalized attribute progress matrices for students in terms of making more informed subject enrollment decisions, personal reflection and gaining a better understanding of the governing factors influencing their degree. It will also provide a basis for longitudinal data mining of the learner models to improve understanding of the causes of student difficulties.

Acknowledgments. The CUSP Project is supported by the University of Sydney's Teaching Improvement and Equipment Scheme (TIES).

References

[1] Assche, F.V.: Linking learning resources to curricula by using competencies. In: First International Workshop on LO Discovery & Exchange (2007)
[2] Bittencourt, I., Isotani, S., Costa, E., Mizoguchi, R.: Research directions on Semantic Web and education. Journal of Scientia-Interdisciplinary Studies in Computer Science 19(1), 59–66 (2008)
[3] Bull, S., Gardner, P.: Highlighting learning across a degree within an independent open learner model. AIED 200, 275–282 (2009)
[4] Calvo, R., Carroll, N., Ellis, R.: Curriculum central: A portal system for the academic enterprise. IJCEELL 17(1), 43–56 (2007)
[5] Kalz, M., van Bruggen, J., Rusman, E., Giesbers, B., Koper, R.: Positioning of learners in learning networks with content, metadata and ontologies. Interactive Learning Environments 15(2), 191–200 (2007)
[6] Koper, R.: Modeling units of study from a pedagogical perspective: the pedagogical meta-model behind EML. In: OTEC (2001)
[7] McKenney, S., Nieveen, N., van den Akker, J.: Computer support for curriculum developers: CASCADE. JETRD 50(4), 25–35 (2002)
[8] Mulder, M., Weigel, T., Collins, K., Bibb, B.: The concept of competence in the development of vocational education and training in selected EU member statesa critical analysis. JVET 59(1), 67–78 (2007)
[9] Paquette, G., Rosca, I., Mihaila, S., Masmoudi, A.: TELOS, a Service-Oriented framework to support learning and knowledge management. In: E-Learning Networked Environments and Architectures: A Knowledge Processing Perspective, p. 434 (2007)
[10] Psych, V., Bourdeau, J., Mizoguchi, R.: Ontology development at the conceptual level for Theory-Aware ITS authoring systems. In: AIED, pp. 491–493 (2003)
[11] Winter, M., Brooks, C., Greer, J.: Towards best practices for semantic Web student modelling. In: Proceedings: 12th ICAIED, pp. 694–701. IOS Press, Amsterdam (2005) (Citeseer)

Eliciting Informative Feedback in Peer Review: Importance of Problem-Specific Scaffolding

Ilya M. Goldin[1,2] and Kevin D. Ashley[1,2,3]

[1] Intelligent Systems Program
[2] Learning Research & Development Center
[3] School of Law
University of Pittsburgh
Pittsburgh, PA
{goldin,ashley}@pitt.edu

Abstract. In a controlled experiment using Comrade, a computer-supported peer review system, student reviewers offered feedback to student authors on their written analyses of a problem scenario. In each condition, reviewers received a different type of rating prompt: domain-related writing composition prompts or problem/issue specific prompts. We found that the reviewers were sensitive to the type of rating prompts they saw and that their ratings of authors' work were less discriminating with respect to writing composition than to problem-specific issues. In other words, when students gave each other feedback regarding domain-relevant writing criteria, their ratings correlated to a much greater extent, suggesting that such ratings are redundant.

Keywords: computer-supported peer review, ill-defined problem-solving.

1 Introduction

Computer-supported peer review deserves the attention of ITS researchers as an instructional activity that seems to bring many benefits to both students and educators. [1] For instance, students benefit in that receiving feedback from multiple peers' on the first draft of an assignment can lead them to improve the quality of their second drafts even more than receiving feedback from an expert. [2] Student authors receive an extra channel of feedback in addition to and distinct from assessment by the instructor or self-assessment [3], and, in playing both roles of author and reviewer, students may learn from engaging in an authentic activity in the many professional domains that institutionalize peer review. One advantage to educators is that when students give each other feedback, they free the educator to focus on other tasks (such as providing struggling students with individual attention).

When augmented with AI techniques, computer-supported peer review may provide ITS research with methods for addressing ill-defined problems even in writing-intensive courses. Ill-defined problem-solving presents a test case for Intelligent Tutoring System technology. [4] ITS have been used for problem-solving when a student's answer or solution procedure can be compared against a gold standard, in domains such as geometry and physics. [5, 6] In contrast, ill-defined problems may have no correct answer, or multiple defensible answers, or no way to define *a priori* what constitutes an acceptable response. So long as an ITS cannot assess a student's answer, it cannot update its representation of what the student does and does not know, the so-called student model. This precludes it from tutoring the student through guidance, feedback and selection of new problems. Writing-intensive courses often focus on problems that are ill-defined. These problems are usually distinguished by a goal that can be perceived only through analysis and refinement, and by allowing multiple acceptable solution paths. Solvers may frame ill-defined problems differently according to their knowledge, beliefs, and attitudes, thereby yielding different representations for the problem in terms of relevant facts and applicable operators. [7] Analyses of ill-defined problems are often in free-form text since they require arguments and justifications for one solution over others. They exist in many domains, and they are central to domains such as law, where practitioners must map statutes and precedents to the facts of new cases, as the law students had to in the peer-reviewed exercise in the experiment described below.

Free-form student answers to ill-defined problems may be difficult for a computer to interpret, but not for a student's peers. In our computer-supported peer-review system, called Comrade, AI techniques are used to aggregate the feedback that peer reviewers give each other into a student model that estimates attainment of learning objectives. Comrade asks reviewers to provide written feedback as well as numeric ratings of peer work. In this paper, we examine an important aspect of the feasibility of Comrade's design, namely the extent to which student peer reviewers are sensitive to different types of rating prompts. As students evaluate each other's written work, these prompts serve as a scaffold, focusing the reviewers on different aspects of the work. In addition, as Comrade compiles a student model based on the students' feedback, it needs to know whether the reviewers' ratings provide useful information.

A variety of peer review systems has been developed in support of teaching in many domains and according to different instructional strategies and demands. [2, 8-13] Some systems, including SWoRD [2], CPR [8], and Comrade, allow the instructor to specify the rubric according to which reviewers evaluate the peer author's work. The designers of SWoRD purposefully focused prompts on three criteria (insight, logic, and style) that could be applied to writing in any domain. For example, a domain-independent rating point from a SWoRD rubric on the logic of the argument was "All but one argument strongly supported or one relatively minor logical flaw in the argument." [1] It is also possible for a rubric to be highly specific to the assignment. In one deployment of CPR, the rubric contained the question "Does the summary state that the study subject was the great tit (*Parus major*) or the Wytham population of birds? AND does the summary further state that the sample size was 1,104 (egg) clutches, 654 female moms, or 863 identified clutches?" [15]

Given the variety of possible strategies that can be employed in creating prompts for peer review, and given the fact that prompts influence the experience of both reviewers and authors, it is important to determine whether some kinds of prompts are more valuable than others. For example, it is desirable to avoid prompts that yield redundant information. It is also possible that some prompts can scaffold reviewers in acquiring domain knowledge better than others. In the work described here, we compared the effects of two types of rating prompts: prompts that focus on

---

[1] For an example of a full SWoRD rubric, see the appendix to [14].

domain-relevant aspects of writing composition versus prompts that focus on issues directly pertaining to the problem and to the substantive issues under analysis. We considered that when an instructor gives a student a rubric to assess another's paper, interacting with this rubric can cause the student to focus on those issues that are made prominent in the rubric. For example, if the rubric looks at domain-independent issues of writing composition, that communicates to the reviewer that the instructor sees various discourse features as important. We then articulated two kinds of prompts which may be particularly useful to the reviewer. Prompts that focus on writing in the domain can communicate to the reviewer the importance of various domain-specific discourse features, while prompts that relate to the subject of the essay under review can emphasize critical elements of the assignment.

In section 2 of this paper, we describe the Comrade system and the two kinds of prompts (domain writing versus problem/issue specific) it delivered to students in a controlled experiment involving peer-review of a take-home midterm examination essay. In section 3, we present empirical evidence that student peer reviewers are sensitive to the two types of rating prompts and that their ratings of each other's work are less discriminating with respect to writing composition than problem-specific issues. As discussed in section 4, this is pedagogically important. When students give each other feedback regarding domain-relevant writing criteria, their ratings correlated to a much greater extent, suggesting that the ratings are redundant. We discuss the significance of these results for the design, implementation, and evaluation of intelligent tutoring systems that employ peer review as a mechanism for teaching skills of ill-defined problem-solving.

2 Methods

Hypotheses. Our first hypothesis is that peer reviewers are sensitive to the difference between prompts that focus them on writing in the domain (from now, "domain-writing prompts") vs. prompts that focus them on details of the assignment (from now, "problem-specific prompts"). This hypothesis is operationally defined in our study as a between-subjects manipulation with two conditions: domain-writing prompts and problem-specific prompts. To test this hypothesis, we first introduce a definition:

Consider that peer review can be seen as a directed graph. Let every student be viewed as a node. When the student acts as a reviewer, there are outbound edges from this student to the peer authors whose work she is reviewing. When the student acts as an author, there are inbound edges to this student from the other students reviewing her work. Thus, the ratings received by a student are that student's inbound ratings, and the ratings given by a student are that student's outbound ratings.

If peer reviewers are not sensitive to variations in rating prompts, then peer authors' inbound ratings according to different prompts will be highly correlated; if reviewers are sensitive, peer authors' inbound ratings will not be highly correlated.

Our second hypothesis is that when a rubric supports a reviewer in evaluating another student's work, the rubric may act as a scaffold in focusing the reviewer on key domain concepts, thus making it more likely that the reviewer will understand these concepts. We compared student understanding of key domain concepts before and after reviewing in terms of performance on an objective test, as described below.

Participants. All 58 participants were second or third year students at a major US law school, enrolled in a course on Intellectual Property law. Students were required to take a midterm examination and to participate in the subsequent peer-review exercise. For purposes of ensuring comparability of conditions and interpreting results, the participants' Law School Admission Test (LSAT) scores, and instructor-assigned scores on the midterm were collected (48 of 58 students opted to allow their LSAT scores to be used). The participants were randomly assigned to one of the two conditions in a manner balanced with respect to their LSAT scores. For simplicity of analysis, an author could only receive reviews from reviewers in the same condition.

Participants were asked to perform a good-faith job of reviewing. The syllabus indicated, "a lack of good-faith participation in the peer-reviewing process as evidenced by a failure to provide thoughtful and constructive peer reviews may result in a lower grade on the mid-term."

Apparatus. As noted, we hypothesize that different kinds of ratings prompts focus reviewers on different aspects of the author's work. In this paper, we only examine reviewer responses to rating prompts, although reviewers also gave written evaluations of the same dimensions of peer work that they rated numerically. We collected

Table 1. Domain-writing rating prompts. Reviewers rated peer work on four criteria pertaining to legal writing.

Issue Identification ("issue")	1 - fails to identify any relevant IP issues; raises only irrelevant issues 3 - identifies few relevant IP issues, and does not explain them clearly; raises irrelevant issues 5 - identifies and explains most (but not all) relevant IP issues; does not raise irrelevant issues 7 - identifies and clearly explains all relevant IP issues; does not raise irrelevant issues
Argument Development ("argument")	1 - fails to develop any strong arguments for any important IP issues 3 - develops few strong, non-conclusory arguments, and neglects counterarguments 5 - for most IP issues, applies principles, doctrines, and precedents; considers counterarguments 7 - for all IP issues, applies principles, doctrines, and precedents; considers counterarguments
Justified Overall Conclusion ("conclusion")	1 - does not assess strengths and weaknesses of parties' legal positions; fails to propose or justify an overall conclusion 3 - neglects important strengths and weaknesses of parties' legal position; proposes but does not justify an overall conclusion 5 - assesses some strengths and weaknesses of the parties' legal positions; proposes an overall conclusion 7 - assesses strengths and weaknesses of parties' legal positions in detail; recommends and justifies an overall conclusion
Writing Quality ("writing")	1 - lacks a message and structure, with overwhelming grammatical problems 3 - makes some topical observations but most arguments are unsound 5 - makes mostly clear, sound arguments, but organization can be difficult to follow 7 - makes insightful, clear arguments in a well-organized manner

Table 2. Problem-specific rating prompts. Reviewers rated peer work on five problem-specific writing criteria (the claims), which all used the same scale.

Claims:	Smith v. Barry for breach of the nondisclosure/noncompetition agreement ("nda")
	Smith v. Barry and VG for trade-secret misappropriation ("tsm")
	Jack v. Smith for misappropriating Jack's idea for the I-phone-based instrument-controller interface ("idea1")
	Barry v. Smith for misappropriating Barry's idea for the design of a Jimi-Hydrox-related look with flames for winning ("idea2")
	Estate of Jimi Hydrox v. Smith for violating right-of-publicity ("rop")
Rating scale:	1 - does not identify this claim
	3 - identifies claim, but neglects arguments pro/con and supporting facts; some irrelevant facts or arguments
	5 - analyzes claim, some arguments pro/con and supporting facts; cites some relevant legal standards, statutes, or precedents
	7 - analyzes claim, all arguments pro/con and supporting facts; cites relevant legal standards, statutes, or precedents

ratings according to Likert scales (7 points, grounded at 1,3,5,7). Each condition received a different set of rating prompts, either domain-writing (Table 1), or problem-specific (Table 2).

The researchers conducted the study via Comrade, a web-based application for peer review. For purposes of this study, Comrade was configured to conduct peer review in a manner that approximates the formal procedures of academic publication. In the tradition of the SWoRD and CPR systems, peer review in the classroom usually involves the following sequence of activities:

1. Students write essays.
2. Essays are distributed to a group of N student peers for review.
3. The peer reviewers submit their feedback to the essay authors.
4. The authors give "back reviews" to the peer reviewers.
5. The authors write new drafts of their essays.

Steps 2-5 can be repeated for multiple drafts of the same essay. In SWoRD, reviewers generate feedback (step 3) according to instructor-specified criteria, and authors evaluate the feedback they receive (step 4). Papers are chosen using an algorithm that ensures that the reviewing workload is distributed fairly, and that all authors receive a fair number of reviews. Conventionally, all students act as both authors and reviewers. As authors, they may write in response to the same domain problem or different problems. As reviewers, they may formulate their feedback in different formats, including written comments and numeric ratings.

For this study, we followed phases 1 through 4, and omitted phase 5. In addition, students took a pretest (described below) between phases 1 and 2, and a posttest between phases 2 and 3. After authors gave back-reviews in phase 4 and before back-reviews were delivered to reviewers, all students were invited to fill out a survey.

Procedure. As stated, the participants' activities in our study proceeded in five phases, with a pretest and posttest before and after the reviewing.

Just prior to the peer-review exercise, participants completed writing a mid-term, open-book, take-home examination. It comprised one essay-type question, and students were limited to writing no more than four double-spaced or 1.5-spaced typed pages. Students had 3 days to answer the exam question.

As is typical of law school essay exams, the question presented a fairly complex (2-page, 1.5-spaced) factual scenario and asked students "to provide advice concerning [a particular party's] rights and liabilities given the above developments." The instructor designed the facts of the problem to raise issues involving many of the legal claims and concepts (e.g., trade secret law, shop rights to inventions, right of publicity, passing off) that were discussed in the first part of the course. Each claim involves different legal interests and requirements and presents a different framework for viewing the problem. Students were expected to analyze the facts, identify the claims and issues raised, make arguments pro and con resolution of the issue in terms of the concepts, rules, and cases discussed in class, and make recommendations accordingly. Since the instructor was careful to include factual weaknesses as well as strengths for each claim, the problem was ill-defined; strong arguments could be made for and against each party's claims.

Based roughly on the legal claims, concepts, and issues addressed in the exam question, the instructor also designed a multiple choice test in two equivalent forms (A and B), each with 15 questions. The test was intended to assess whether student reviewers learned from the peer-reviewing experience. The questions addressed roughly the same legal claims and concepts as the exam, but not in the same way as the exam, involving completely different facts, and in a multiple choice format rather than in essay form. After preparing the tests, the instructor invited several particularly strong students who had taken the same course in prior years to take the test. The instructor then revised the test based on these students' answers to multiple choice questions and other feedback.

On Day 1, students uploaded their anonymized midterm exam answers to Comrade from wherever they had an Internet connection. From Day 3 to 7, students logged in to review the papers of the other students. Each student received four papers to review, and each review was predicted to take about 2 hours. Before a student began reviewing, and again before he received his reviews from other students, each student completed a multiple choice test as the pretest and posttest. To control for differences between the test forms, half of the students in each condition received form A as the pretest and form B as the posttest; the other half received them in the opposite order. On Day 8, students logged in to receive reviews from their classmates. On Day 10, students provided the reviewers with back-reviews explaining whether the feedback was helpful. Students also took a brief survey on their peer review experience.

3 Results

Sensitivity to Prompts. We computed every peer author's mean inbound peer rating for each rating prompt across the reviewers. For example, for a student in the domain-writing condition, we took four means across reviewers, namely for the prompts "issue", "argument", "writing", and "conclusion" (see Table 1). We examined the distribution of mean inbound peer ratings for each rating prompt to determine the extent to which these different rating prompts yielded non-redundant information from reviewers. Mean inbound peer ratings ranged from a low of 1.86 (problem-specific condition, "idea2" prompt) to a high of 5.54 (domain-writing condition, "writing" prompt) on a 7-point Likert scale (Table 3), showing that peer reviewers do respond to different prompts with different answers.

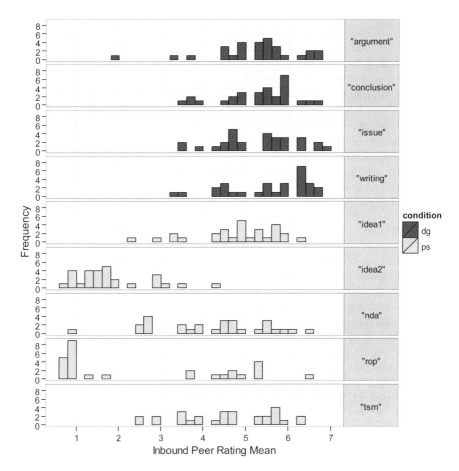

Fig. 1. Frequency of inbound ratings per dimension. *dg* = domain-writing dimensions, *ps* = problem-specific.

In particular, they distinguish less among various aspects of writing composition than they do among problem-specific issues. This becomes apparent by visualizing the frequency of the inbound ratings, as in Figure 1. All the ratings in response to domain-writing prompts tend to the right on the X axis, while the problem-specific ratings have no consistent distribution. Within each condition, we computed pairwise correlations of the mean inbound peer ratings for the prompts in that condition. The mean pairwise correlation among domain-writing ratings is 0.68, while the mean pairwise correlation among ratings in response to problem-specific prompts is 0.15.

Table 3. Mean inbound peer ratings for each rating dimension

Dimension (Domain-Writing)	argument	conclusion	issue	writing	
Mean (SD)	5.23 (1.02)	5.34 (0.838)	5.33 (0.93)	5.54 (0.98)	
Dimension (Problem-Specific)	idea1	idea2	nda	rop	tsm
Mean (SD)	4.83 (0.995)	1.86 (0.878)	4.26 (1.34)	2.65 (2.02)	4.59 (1.12)

Learning Outcomes. We measured student comprehension of some aspects of domain knowledge before and after students gave feedback to each other. Neither the ratings that authors received with respect to domain writing skills nor those related to problem-specific issues were predictive of their performance on pre-test or post-test. For each kind of rating prompt, we used a linear regression to model pre-/post-test performance as a function of mean inbound peer ratings. In each case, the linear models predicted less than 1% of the variance in test performance.

4 Discussion

Our aim is to understand how peer review can bring value to the classroom, and to emphasize those elements of peer review that benefit learners the most. We have presented evidence that student peer reviewers are sensitive to the difference between two types of rating prompts, domain-writing and problem-specific, and that their ratings of each other's work are less discriminating with respect to the former than to the latter. This is likely to be pedagogically important. Since peer reviewers' ratings of different aspects of domain-specific writing composition are highly correlated, they are likely to communicate redundant information to authors, and soliciting these ratings is not an effective use of the reviewers' time. On the other hand, if problem-specific support to reviewers leads to ratings that do not correlate with each other, such ratings are not redundant, and more likely to be informative. In particular, the problem-specific support relates to legal claims, each of which provides a different framework for analyzing the ill-defined problem. The different problem-specific reviews may thus lead authors to frame the problem in different ways, and the exercise of reading and making sense of the somewhat divergent problem-specific suggestions is likely to be pedagogically fruitful. [16, 17] One direction for future research is to examine whether peer authors respond differently to feedback on writing versus on problem-specific aspects by looking at back-reviews (the authors' responses to reviewers) and subsequent drafts, and by surveying students. If problem-specific support is indeed valuable, this suggests that intelligent and adaptive support for peer review may also benefit students.

Our study complements the research of Wooley [18], which showed that students' subsequent writing improves when they give ratings and written comments, and not only numeric ratings. Subsequent writing quality was operationally defined as expert-assigned scores of student essays. In both conditions of our experiment, reviewers gave feedback as ratings and as written comments. Having thus controlled for the effect identified by Wooley, we found that giving feedback did not contribute to student understanding of key domain concepts, as measured by an objective test. It is possible that our objective test was not sensitive to what students were learning from the act of giving feedback, and it remains for future work to examine in detail the written comments that students give each other, and to look for signs that the prompts seen by students have an effect in the reviewers' and authors' subsequent writing. Author understanding of domain-independent feedback is a critical mediating factor in what feedback authors actually implement in a subsequent draft. [14] Our study suggests that feedback regarding problem-specific aspects may be more useful to authors than feedback on writing composition; making feedback more useful may lead to greater implementation as well.

Although we found that giving feedback in response to either kind of prompt did not contribute to student understanding of key domain concepts, many others have found that prompts can indeed support learning. Renkl and colleagues found positive learning outcomes for students who received metacognitive scaffolding through prompts rather than the support of "cognitive" task-oriented prompts. [19, 20] We explore metacognitive support for peer review in another study. In related work, King describes several discourse patterns that can benefit learning outcomes in settings such as problem solving and peer tutoring. [21] Another way to encourage learning in peer reviewers could be to ensure that all students review low-quality work. [22]

These results have significance for the design, implementation, and evaluation of intelligent tutoring systems that employ peer review as a mechanism for teaching skills of ill-defined problem-solving. For instance, we expect the problem-specific ratings to be especially useful for Comrade; as it compiles a student model based on the students' feedback, it needs to know whether the reviewers' ratings provide useful information. We plan to investigate its impact on reviewers and authors in future work.

References

1. Topping, K.: Peer assessment between students in colleges and universities. Review of Educational Research 68, 249–276 (1998)
2. Cho, K., Schunn, C.D.: Scaffolded writing and rewriting in the discipline: A web-based reciprocal peer review system. Computers and Education 48 (2007)
3. Sluijsmans, D.: The use of self-, peer- and co-assessment in higher education: a review of literature. Educational Technology Expertise Centre Open University of the Netherlands, Heerlen (1998)
4. Goldin, I.M., Ashley, K.D., Pinkus, R.L.: Teaching Case Analysis through Framing: Prospects for an ITS in an Ill-defined Domain. In: Workshop on Intelligent Tutoring Systems for Ill-Defined Domains, 8th International Conference on Intelligent Tutoring Systems, Jhongli, Taiwan (2006)
5. VanLehn, K., Lynch, C., Schulze, K., Shapiro, J., Shelby, R., Taylor, L., Treacy, D., Weinstein, A., Wintersgill, M.: The Andes Physics Tutoring System: Lessons Learned. International Journal of Artificial Intelligence and Education 15 (2005)
6. Koedinger, K., Anderson, J., Hadley, W., Mark, M.: Intelligent tutoring goes to school in the big city. International Journal of Artificial Intelligence in Education 8, 30–43 (1997)

7. Voss, J.: Toulmin's Model and the Solving of Ill-Structured Problems. In: Arguing on the Toulmin Model: New Essays in Argument Analysis and Evaluation. Springer, Heidelberg (2006)
8. Russell, A.: Calibrated Peer Review: A writing and critical thinking instructional tool. In: Invention and Impact: Building Excellence in Undergraduate Science, Technology, Engineering and Mathematics (STEM) Education. American Association for the Advancement of Science (2004)
9. Gehringer, E.: Strategies and mechanisms for electronic peer review. In: 30th Annual Frontiers in Education Conference, vol. 1, pp. F1B/2–F1B/7 (2000)
10. Zhi-Feng Liu, E., Lin, S., Chiu, C., Yuan, S.: Web-based peer review: the learner as both adapter and reviewer. IEEE Transactions on Education 44, 246–251 (2001)
11. Masters, J., Madhyastha, T., Shakouri, A.: ExplaNet: A collaborative learning tool and hybrid recommender system for student-authored explanations. Journal of Interactive Learning Research 19, 51–74 (2008)
12. Hsiao, I., Brusilovsky, P.: Modeling peer review in example annotation. In: 16th International Conference on Computers in Education, Taipei, Taiwan, pp. 357–362 (2008)
13. Gouli, E., Gogoulou, A., Grigoriadou, M.: Supporting self-, peer-, and collaborative- assessment in e-learning: the case of the PEer and Collaborative ASSessment Environment (PECASSE). Journal of Interactive Learning Research 19, 615 (2008)
14. Nelson, M., Schunn, C.D.: The nature of feedback: how different types of peer feedback affect writing performance (2008)
15. Walvoord, M.E., Hoefnagels, M.H., Gaffin, D.D., Chumchal, M.M., Long, D.A.: An analysis of Calibrated Peer Review (CPR) in a science lecture classroom. Journal of College Science Teaching 37, 66–73 (2008)
16. Pinkus, R., Gloeckner, C., Fortunato, A.: Professional knowledge and applied ethics: a cognitive science approach (under review)
17. McNamara, D., Kintsch, E., Songer, N., Kintsch, W.: Are good texts always better? interactions of text coherence, background knowledge, and levels of understanding in learning from text. Cognition and Instruction 14, 1–43 (1996)
18. Wooley, R., Was, C.A., Schunn, C.D., Dalton, D.W.: The effects of feedback elaboration on the giver of feedback. In: Love, B.C., McRae, K., Sloutsky, V.M. (eds.) Proceedings of the 30th Annual Conference of the Cognitive Science Society, pp. 2375–2380. Cognitive Science Society, Washington (2008)
19. Hübner, S., Nückles, M., Renkl, A.: Prompting cognitive and metacognitive processing in writing-to-learn enhances learning outcomes. In: 28th Annual Conference of the Cognitive Science Society (2006)
20. Nückles, M., Hübner, S., Renkl, A.: Enhancing self-regulated learning by writing learning protocols. Learning and Instruction 19, 259–271 (2009)
21. King, A.: ASK to THINK-TEL WHY: A model of transactive peer tutoring for scaffolding higher level complex learning. Educational Psychologist. 32, 221–235 (1997)
22. Cho, K., Cho, Y.H.: Learning from ill-structured cases. In: 29th Annual Cognitive Science Society Conference, p. 1722. Cognitive Science Society, Austin (2007)

Layered Development and Evaluation for Intelligent Support in Exploratory Environments: The Case of Microworlds

Sergio Gutierrez-Santos[1], Manolis Mavrikis[2], and George Magoulas[1,*]

[1] Birkbeck College
[2] Institute of Education
London Knowledge Lab
23-29 Emerald Str,
WC1N 3QS, London, UK

Abstract. This paper focuses on microworlds, a special type of Exploratory Learning Environment, where students freely interact with the system to create their own models and constructions. Most microworlds developed so far provide integrated scaffolds to help students' learning process, but the nature of the interaction makes it difficult to design, develop and evaluate *explicit* adaptive support according to students' needs. Building on previous work in the field, this paper proposes a layered approach that simplifies the development and allows both formative and summative evaluation of the different components of the system. As a case study, we present the development of intelligent support for a microworld in the MiGen project, and discuss its evaluation that includes both technical and pedagogical experts of the team.

Keywords: exploratory environments, architecture, evaluation.

1 Introduction

Microworlds (or model-building systems [1]) are a special type of Exploratory Learning Environments (ELEs), in which students undertake tasks by constructing and exploring models. This has several benefits to the learning process: e.g. students usually get more engaged with the activity, and they have a sense of ownership over their learning [2]. Research in the learning sciences (e.g. [3]) suggests that freedom of exploration without a proper degree of support can be problematic. Moreover, taking into account that teachers have a limited capacity to support students introduces a clear need for computer-based support.

However, the nature of the students' interactions in microworlds, and the constructivist intentions behind their design, make the already challenging and costly problems of ITS design, development, and evaluation (c.f. [4]) even more

---

[*] The authors would like to acknowledge the rest of the members of the MiGen team and financial support from the TLRP (e-Learning Phase-II, RES-139-25-0381).

difficult. In this paper, we present our approach which is driven by the following challenges: (i) the need to break down into tractable problems the complex process of monitoring and reacting to students' interactions in such an unconstrained environment, (ii) the high cost of communication between several kinds of experts (e.g. computer and learning scientists) which are required to tackle this problem, (iii) the difficulty to evaluate the different components and the system overall. Building on former work in the field (see Section 2), and inspired from successful methodologies in robotics [5] and adaptive systems [6], we propose a layered approach to development and evaluation. This is presented in Section 3. Such a layered approach separates the different conceptual scopes in the design process. Additionally, as discussed in Section 4, it eases the evaluation process which needs to include members of the design team with different backgrounds. A separated, focused, and early evaluation of the different components of the system facilitates the detection of problems at a stage where the system components can be modified and tuned.

2 Related Work

Our layered module-based approach has been influenced by the subsumption architecture used in robotics [5], where complicated intelligent behaviour is organised into layers of simple behaviour modules. The problem presents several similarities: unstructured input data, difficulty of representation, and real-time action requirements. In the field of ITS, one of the few attempts to provide intelligent support in microworlds is presented in [7]. In contrast to our approach, the separation of the intelligent feedback components in layers is not explicit in that paper. However, the authors make an attempt to separate analysis and aggregation employing pedagogical agents and a voting mechanism. Regarding encapsulation of the feedback layer a particularly relevant example is [8]. Their 'bar codes', that encapsulate pedagogical situations, are conceptually similar to the classes of feedback strategies that we employ as inputs to our feedback layer.

In relation to evaluation, our approach recognises that it is a difficult problem (c.f. [9]). The case of microworlds, with the unstructured interaction and their complex relationship to learning, makes the problem even more challenging. Therefore, we believe that the appropriate evaluation in such a case needs to borrow ideas from several fields, including software engineering [10,11], artificial intelligence [5], AI in Education [12,13], adaptive systems [14,6,15], and HCI [16]. In particular, as discussed in more detail in Section 4, layered evaluation methodologies [6,15] fit perfectly with our approach.

Architectural approaches [17,18] and design patterns(e.g. [19]) for ITS that have focused on reusability are also relevant to our work. However, to the best of our knowledge, none of these approaches employs a conceptual separation of concerns to facilitate early evaluation of the system or to ease the communication between technical and non-technical members of the research team. It is these concerns that guide the approach we present in the next section.

3 Layered Approach for Development of ISEE

Examining both the architectural and evaluation approaches mentioned in Section 2, we consider four conceptual layers in the development and evaluation of intelligent support in microworlds. This conceptualisation is general enough, as it does not make any assumptions about the microworlds or the exact computational techniques used in the different layers, while, at the same time, provides a useful guide for the development and evaluation of Intelligent Support in Exploratory Environments (ISEE). The details of the four layers are presented below. Fig. 1 depicts the information flow from the lower to upper layers. The loop through the user represents how the learning feedback influences the actions of the students as they interact with the microworld.

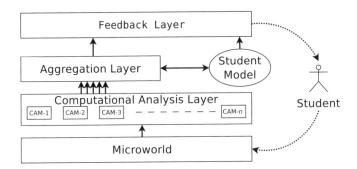

Fig. 1. Layered design and evaluation of intelligent support

3.1 Microworld Layer: The Expresser

The lower layer represents the microworld or the exploratory environment itself. The students interact freely with the environment, usually trying to perform some kind of task given in advance. The exploratory nature of the environment provides a high number of possible courses of action. Some of these courses of action will lead to the completion of the task, some will make some partial progress in that direction, and some of them will be off-task (e.g. playful behaviour). As a case study, Figure 2 shows the eXpresser microworld developed in the context of the MiGen project. eXpresser encourages students to build patterns out of square tiles and to find general algebraic expressions underpinning them.

Figure 2 illustrates some of the core aspects of the eXpresser. In order to represent the generalities they perceive, students can use numbers that can be 'unlocked' to become variables. Locked and unlocked numbers can be used in expressions. This microworld gives a lot of freedom to students to construct their patterns in a multitude of different but equivalent ways. For a detailed description of the eXpresser the interested reader is referred to [20].

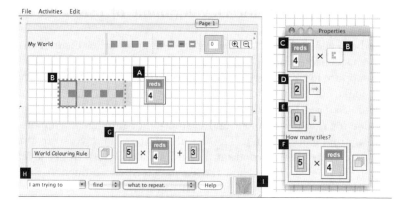

Fig. 2. Constructing a pattern in eXpresser and describing it with a rule. Main features: (A) An 'unlocked' number that acts like a variable is given the name 'reds' and signifies the number of red (dark grey) tiles in the pattern. (B) Building block to be repeated to make a pattern. (C) Number of repetitions (i.e. the value of the variable 'reds'). (D,E) Number of grid squares to translate B to the right and down after each repetition. (F) Local rule: units of colour needed. (G) General rule: gives the total number of units of colour required to paint the whole pattern (if correct, solves the task). (H) Help-seeking area with drop down menus and (I) suggestion box for feedback provision.

3.2 Computational Analysis

On top of the microworld layer, there is a layer composed of several computational analysis modules (CAM). Every module concentrates on a particular aspect of the actions of the student, and tries to solve a different well-defined problem. Therefore, every module filters the data provided by the environment to use only those that are needed, and uses different AI techniques adapted to the particular problem that it solves. Given the unstructured nature of the data provided by most microworlds, the specificity of the computational analysis modules eases their development. As an example, the computational analysis modules used in MiGen are summarised in Table 1.

This focus on small, specific problems also facilitates the reuse of modules among systems based on different microworlds. Although there is always a certain level of coupling between the analysis module and the microworld, modules that tackle well-defined and general problems can be used across different systems. For example, the construction evaluation module has been reused from previous work on a microworld called ShapeBuilder (c.f. [21]).

3.3 Aggregation Layer

The output of the different modules on the computational analysis layer is fragmented and unsuitable of being used directly for providing feedback. There is a need for an additional layer that interprets the combination of the output of the different modules.

Table 1. Computational analysis modules in MiGen

Name	Function
Apparent Solution Detector	Returns true if the construction on the screen has the same appearance as a solution.
Construction Evaluator	Given a set of expected solutions and common mistakes, returns a similarity measurement to each of them
Rhythm Detector	Detects rhythm in the actions of the student, because rhythmic repetition of patterns can give an understanding of implicit structures in the students' minds [20]
Clutter Detector	Detects spurious elements in the construction of the students, that may distract them in their thinking
Generality Verifier	Verifies whether the solution given by the student is able to generate all possible expected patterns. If yes, returns true; if not, returns a counterexample.
General Rule Verifier	Returns true if the rule (i.e. formula) provided is always valid
Inactivity Detector	Detects students' inactivity
Unlock Detector	Detects whether students are using at least one variable (i.e. unlocked number)

This aggregation of information happens on the third layer. There can be more than one aggregation components, each of them using the output of modules from the lower layer and/or the information of the student model, each of them dealing with different aspects of the feedback.

In MiGen the aggregation requirements have been derived by a knowledge elicitation process, more details of which are provided in [22]. In our case, the aggregation layer is implemented using a rule-based approach because, it fits our requisites and it is easier to maintain and scrutinise. The layer takes the output of the modules in the layer underneath and follows a series of rules to produce a feedback class that can be sent to the feedback layer.

An example of such a rule takes the output of four different modules: Apparent Solution Detector, Construction Evaluator, Unlock Detector, and General Rule Verifier. The output of the first three is combined to check that the student has built a construction that looks like a solution, that the construction is very similar (maybe equal) to one of the expected solutions to the task, and that they have already unlocked some numbers (so that the eXpresser can show several instances of the construction). Then, if in spite of all this, the final expression is not correct, a feedback strategy StrategyGeneralRuleFromLocalRule is called. In its abstract form, this strategy aims to help students develop a simple heuristic: that the general expression can be found by adding all the local expressions that are on the canvas. Other examples of feedback strategies appear in [22].

Input to the rules comes from the analysis modules and from the user model. Rules can either produce calls for an abstract feedback strategy (to be instantiated at the upper layer) or update the student model. When several rules fire simultaneously, there must be a policy of priorities between them. The interested reader is referred to [23] for an example of a a multi criteria decision making process to generate priorities depending on the context.

3.4 Feedback Layer

The last layer of the architecture is the feedback layer. This layer is responsible of producing the actual feedback that will be presented to the student based on the output of the other three layers plus the student model. The feedback layer combines the output from the aggregation layer (i.e., the feedback strategy to be followed) and the information in the student model (i.e., characteristics and other historical information with regard to their short-term interaction) to create an adequate instance of the feedback to be presented.

In MiGen, this layer takes care of presentational aspects (e.g. appropriate location of feedback and use of figures) and student adaptation (e.g. not presenting recent feedback, co-locating images and text with current constructions). In particular, inspired by the typical approaches in the field, the feedback layer is responsible for scaffolding consistent with the principles discussed in [24]. Accordingly, the feedback layer adapts the feedback provided in order to provide gradually more specific help but not more than the system's belief about the minimal help required to ensure progress.

In our implementation this is achieved first by grading the feedback according to the following three types: 'nudge' questions, comments and suggestions and subsequently the degree of intervention on the students' construction. In particular, 'nudge' questions are rhetorical questions designed to draw students' attention to a specific aspect of their construction or a recent action that might have introduced a problem (e.g., 'Did you notice how this [↓] changed when you unlocked the number'?). Comments provide a factual remark on the current state of the microworld or of the students' problem solving process towards a specific task (e.g. 'The pattern cannot be animated, there are no unlocked numbers'). Suggestions provide a direct hint towards a plan or an idea proposed for the students' consideration (e.g., 'It seems you are repeating this building block [image]. Try to make the pattern using this [image].'). Finally, the last level, usually consists of a direct action in students' canvas, designed either to help them improve their construction or to change something that might help them think what to do further. Again, these were co-designed by the research team with teachers. More examples and specific details of strategies appear in [22]. We intend that in the future it will be possible for teachers (or appropriate task designers) to define their own adaptive scaffolds for the tasks they develop.

4 Evaluating Intelligent Support

Evaluating intelligent support in microworlds entails particular challenges that arise from the fact that a complete interaction with the microworld requires a significant amount of time. Students need to be introduced to the system through tutorial sessions, and subsequently interact with a variety of tasks. This introduces a series of issues which are difficult to control or factor out. These and other general problems have been discussed in detail (e.g. [9]). Our concern lies both in a 'cause attribution' problem (that is, the difficulty to identify what to regard as the cause behind unexpected results) and the need for early detection

Layered Development and Evaluation for ISEE: The Case of Microworlds

Table 2. Evaluation of intelligent support on every layer

Layer	Responsibilities	Experts involved	Evaluation	Dependencies
Microworld	Direct interaction with the student, providing a certain level of freedom. Provision of integrated feedback. Output: log of actions	Pedagogical in design, technical in implementation.	Pedagogical validity, usability, and HCI	Does not use the output of other layers. Can be tested independently.
Computational Analysis	Analysis of student's actions Output: variable, depending on ITS module	Technical	Whitebox and blackbox evaluation. For some modules, gold-standard.	Uses the output of the microworld. Depending on the module, gold-standard validation can be performed independently or needs to be tested along with microworld.
Aggregation	Aggregation of the output of the computational analysis modules to generate feedback strategy classes. Output: feedback strategy classes	Technical	Sensitivity analysis. Gold-standard.	Uses the output of the two former layers and the user model. Can be tested independently.
Feedback	Generation of expressions of feedback based on feedback classes and information from the user model. Output: all expressions of explicit feedback for the student.	Pedagogical in design, technical in implementation	Gold-standard validation using wizard-of-oz techniques	Uses the output of the other layers and the user model. Can be tested independently.

of errors. For example, students' interpretation of feedback, particularly in such a complex environment, is full of confounding factors varying from interface (e.g., the look and feel of the messages) to technical issues (e.g., a wrong weight in an algorithm), and from cognitive (e.g., their perception) to educational (e.g., the design of the pedagogical strategy of the system). Waiting until the whole system is assembled to detect these problems are extremely costly: detecting the causes of problems is difficult, and their resolution may need at that stage an amount of resources that is not available. Early and focused detection of problems is crucial.

This requires following a layered evaluation methodology (c.f. [14]), which closely matches our development approach and compartmentalises the scope of the evaluation. The layered separation of scopes means that components of each layer can be tested individually, before they are integrated in the holistic evaluation scheme for the whole system. This is summarised on Table 2. In MiGen in particular, our approach to evaluating the system is driven by replicated data from students' interactions and an adaptation of traditional *wizard-of-oz* techniques, as explained in [22].

The first layer refers to the evaluation of the microworld itself. In our approach we assume that this has been conducted in advance, ensuring that it achieves an appropriate level of usability. Otherwise, it might compromise the purpose of the whole system. Accordingly, it must be checked that the microworld is adequate for its pedagogical purpose; that is, that the metaphors used clearly express the concepts involved and do not favour misconceptions in the student's mind.

The computational analysis modules need to be tested in two steps. The first step involves only technical skills, and consists of white-box and black-box tests that check that the functionality of the modules agrees with their specification. A series of scenarios has to be generated by the development team to test the modules. These scenarios can be gathered directly from real studies, but some situations (e.g. if the microworld is being developed in parallel) may require the use of scenarios based on artificial data. The second step involves additional elicitation of knowledge from pedagogical experts through a process of gold-standard validation: several scenarios are shown to experts, asking them for a diagnosis; their answers are then checked against the answers given by the modules, testing their accuracy (see an example related to the Construction Evaluator module on Figure 3). Depending of the nature of the analysis modules, gold-standard validation is not always needed, e.g. there is no subjective decision in the output of the Generality Detector.

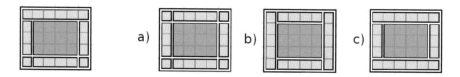

Fig. 3. Gold standard evaluation of the Construction Evaluator. Pedagogical experts are asked which figures are the most and less similar to the first one. Results are compared with the output of the Construction Evaluator module.

The aggregation layer is important to produce adequate feedback, and it is paramount to check that the aggregation mechanism is robust. The effect of varying the inputs of the underlying layers on the output of the aggregation layer must be ascertained by following a form of sensitivity analysis. In MiGen we are particularly concerned in the effect that different values stored in the student model have on the feedback strategy proposed by the rule based system. This demonstrates to us whether the layer lacks some pedagogical expertise. Additionally, we need to evaluate its output given the likely educational outcomes according to pedagogical experts.

The feedback layer is responsible of directly interacting with the student. Therefore, it involves a lot of subjective aspects regarding feedback, that need to be evaluated with the help of pedagogical experts. There is an important obstacle at this stage: it is difficult for experts to accommodate their expertise in different contexts, e.g. a tutor may be expert in providing feedback to students face-to-face, but the communication capacity of a computer-based system is much lower than that. We have developed a process to gradually accommodate the feedback techniques that human experts follow into a computer interface; a detailed explanation of our Communication Capacity Tapering methodology is provided in [22]. As a result of this process, a series of scenarios is produced where the feedback provided by human tutors can be compared to that provided by the system in the same situation (defined by a feedback strategy and the information in the user model), thus detecting differences.

Once this formative evaluation process of the different layers has been completed, the different components can be assembled together. This enables a summative evaluation, which assesses the pedagogical validity of the whole system.

5 Conclusions and Future Work

This paper presents an approach to designing and evaluating intelligent support for microworlds in particular and exploratory or other environments in general. The approach increases the tractability of the solution by defining four conceptual layers that can help compartmentalise the design and evaluation. This separation of concerns has three advantages. First, it allows parallel development of different aspects of the intelligent support. Second, it facilitates the communication between researchers in interdisciplinary teams. In MiGen, this allowed the different researchers to concentrate in a problem of their expertise at a time. Finally, and most important, early evaluation of separated components results in a more robust and useful system before evaluating the whole system with students in classrooms. At that point, detecting and correcting problems in such a complex system can be difficult at best and too costly at worst. As an added benefit, a layered approach facilitates the reuse of components between systems. Modules tackle very well-defined and general problems, so they can be useful for different systems. Nevertheless, we plan to study the possibility of using our modules in other systems. Reuse of intelligent components in microworlds is a process that is not well understood and demands further investigation.

References

1. Lynch, C.F., Ashley, K.D., Aleven, V., Pinkwart, N.: Defining ill-defined domains; a literature survey. In: Intelligent Tutoring Systems (ITS 2006): Workshop on Intelligent Tutoring Systems for Ill-Defined Domains (2006)
2. Joolingen, W.R., Zacharia, Z.C.: Developments in inquiry learning. In: Balacheff, N., Ludvigsen, S., de Jong, T., Lazonder, A., Barnes, S. (eds.) TEL, pp. 21–37 (2009)
3. Mayer, R.E.: Should there be a three-strikes rule against pure discovery learning? - the case for guided methods of instruction. American Psychologist, 14–19 (2004)
4. Murray, T.: Authoring intelligent tutoring systems: An analysis of the state of the art. International journal of artificial intelligence in education 10, 98–129 (1999)
5. Brooks, R.A.: Intelligence without representation. Artificial Intelligence 47, 139–159 (1991)
6. Paramythis, A., Weibelzahl, S.: A decomposition model for the layered evaluation of interactive adaptive systems. In: Ardissono, L., Brna, P., Mitrović, A. (eds.) UM 2005. LNCS (LNAI), vol. 3538, pp. 438–442. Springer, Heidelberg (2005)

7. Webber, C., Pesty, S., Balacheff, N.: A multi-agent and emergent approach to learner modelling. In: Eur. Conf. on Artifical Intelligence, pp. 98–102 (2002)
8. Duquesnoy, L., Berger, J.-L., Prévôt, P., Sandoz-Guermond, F.: SIMPA: A training platform in work station including computing tutors. In: Cerri, S.A., Gouardéres, G., Paraguaçu, F. (eds.) ITS 2002. LNCS, vol. 2363, pp. 507–520. Springer, Heidelberg (2002)
9. Tintarev, N., Masthoff, J.: Evaluating recommender explanations: Problems experienced and lessons learned for the evaluation of adaptive systems. In: 6th Workshop on User-Centred Design and Evaluation of Adaptive Systems, UMAP (2009)
10. Sharples, M., Jeffery, N., du Boulay, B., Teather, D., Teather, B.: Socio-cognitive engineering. In: European Conference on Human Centred Processes (1999)
11. Boehm, B.: A spiral model of software development and enhancement. SIGSOFT Softw. Eng. Notes 11(4), 14–24 (1986)
12. Johnson, L.W., Beal, C.: Iterative evaluation of a large-scale, intelligent game for language learning. In: Proceedings of the International Conference on Artificial Intelligence in Education, pp. 290–297 (2005)
13. Conlon, T., Pain, H.: Persistent collaboration: a methodology for applied AIED. International Journal of Artificial Intelligence in Education 7, 219–252 (1996)
14. Weibelzahl, S., Weber, G.: Evaluating the inference mechanism of adaptive learning systems. In: Brusilovsky, P., Corbett, A.T., de Rosis, F. (eds.) UM 2003. LNCS (LNAI), vol. 2702, pp. 154–168. Springer, Heidelberg (2003)
15. Magoulas, G.D., Chen, S.Y., Papanikolaou, K.A.: Integrating layered and heuristic evaluation for adaptive learning environments. In: Workshop on Empirical Evaluation of Adaptive Systems, Int. Conf. on User Modeling (2003)
16. Beyer, H., Holtzblatt, K.: Contextual Design: Defining Customer-Centered Systems (Interactive Technologies), 1st edn., September 1997. Morgan Kaufmann, San Francisco (1997)
17. El-Sheikh, E., Sticklen, J.: Generating intelligent tutoring systems from reusable components and knowledge-based systems. In: Cerri, S.A., Gouardéres, G., Paraguaçu, F. (eds.) ITS 2002. LNCS, vol. 2363, pp. 199–207. Springer, Heidelberg (2002)
18. Linn, J.G., Segedy, J., Jeong, H., Podgursky, B., Biswas, G.: A reconfigurable architecture for building intelligent learning environments. In: Dimitrova, V., Mizoguchi, R., du Boulay, B., Graesser, A.C. (eds.) Proceedings of the 14th International Conference on Artificial Intelligence in Education, AIED 2009, pp. 115–122 (2009)
19. Debedzic, V.: Applying patterns to its architectures. In: Gauthier, G., VanLehn, K., Frasson, C. (eds.) ITS 2000. LNCS, vol. 1839, pp. 123–132. Springer, Heidelberg (2000)
20. Noss, R., Hoyles, C., Mavrikis, M., Geraniou, E., Gutierrez-Santos, S., Pearce, D.: Broadening the sense of 'dynamic': a microworld to support students' mathematical generalisation. Int. Journal on Mathematics Education 41(4), 493–503 (2009)
21. Cocea, M., Gutierrez-Santos, S., Magoulas, G.: The challenge of intelligent support in exploratory learning environments: A study of the scenarios. In: Workshop in Intelligent Support for Exploratory Environments, ECTEL 2008 (2008)
22. Mavrikis, M., Gutierrez-Santos, S.: Not all wizards are from Oz: Iterative design of intelligent learning environments by communication capacity tapering. Computers & Education (in press)
23. Cocea, M., Magoulas, G.: Context-dependent personalised feedback prioritisation in exploratory learning for mathematical generalisation. In: Houben, G.-J., McCalla, G., Pianesi, F., Zancanaro, M. (eds.) UMAP 2009. LNCS, vol. 5535, pp. 271–282. Springer, Heidelberg (2009)
24. Wood, H.: Help seeking, learning and contingent tutoring. Computers & Education 33(2-3) (1999)

The Invention Lab: Using a Hybrid of Model Tracing and Constraint-Based Modeling to Offer Intelligent Support in Inquiry Environments

Ido Roll[1], Vincent Aleven[2], and Kenneth R. Koedinger[2]

[1] Carl Wieman Science Education Initiative, University of British Columbia, Vancouver, BC
[2] Human-Computer interaction Insititute, Carnegie Mellon University, Pittsburgh, PA
ido@phas.ubc.ca, aleven@cs.cmu.edu, koedinger@cmu.edu

Abstract. Exploratory Learning Environments (ELE) facilitate scientific inquiry tasks in which learners attempt to develop or uncover underlying scientific or mathematical models. Unlike step-based Intelligent Tutoring Systems (ITS), and due to task characteristics and pedagogical philosophy, ELE offer little support at the domain level. Lacking adequate support, ELE often fail to deliver on their promise. We describe the Invention Lab, a system that combines the benefits of ELE and ITS by offering adaptive support in a relatively unconstrained environment. The Invention Lab combines modeling techniques to assess students' knowledge at the domain and inquiry levels. The system uses this information to design new tasks in real time, thus adapting to students' needs while maintaining critical features of the inquiry process. Data from an in-class evaluation study illustrates how the Invention Lab helps students develop sophisticated mathematical models and improve their scientific inquiry behavior. Implications for intelligent support in ELE are discussed.

Keywords: intelligent tutoring systems; exploratory learning environments; invention as preparation for learning; model tracing; constraint-based modeling.

1 Introduction

Exploratory Learning Environments (ELE) facilitate inquiry tasks in which students are instructed to develop or uncover an underlying scientific or mathematical model [1]. Adhering to constructivist instructional principles [2], ELE give the learners more responsibility over controlling the learning process, compared with step-based problem-solving environments [3]. For example, students in ELE are expected to analyze data, raise hypotheses, monitor their progress, and in general, behave the way scientists do [1,2]. This is hypothesized to enhance transfer [4], facilitate acquisition of meta-cognitive and self-regulation skills [5], and increase motivation [6]. However, classroom evaluations have repeatedly demonstrated that students often exhibit unproductive inquiry behaviors, subsequently failing to acquire the desired learning goals [1]. These disappointing outcomes have led to an increased interest in supporting students while working with ELE [6,7].

In order to support students at the domain-independent inquiry level, many ELE scaffold the inquiry process using *cognitive tools* [8]. For example, *Rashi*, *Smithtown*, and *SimQuest* include inquiry notebooks with templates in which students raise hypotheses, document observations, make conjectures, etc. [5,6,9]. Using cognitive tools to scaffold the inquiry process decreases the rate of unproductive behaviors and makes the inquiry process visible, thus helping students internalize the desired inquiry skills [10]. Cognitive tools can also be used to label students' inputs and linearize the inquiry process, making it easier for the ELE to trace students' progress in the task. Consequently, a number of ELE give students feedback on their domain-independent inquiry behavior. For example, Rashi gives feedback to students who make circular arguments [9], the *Science Learning Spaces* gives feedback on experimental designs that do not use the control of variables strategy [11], and *ACE* prompts students who have not explored the interaction space sufficiently [12].

While domain-independent support of the general inquiry cycle is important, evidence suggests that students are also in need for support at the domain level [7]. To do that, ELE should evaluate the content of students' actions. Many Intelligent Tutoring Systems (ITS) evaluate students' responses by tracing their actions using a comprehensive set of rules that outlines common correct or buggy solution paths (termed *model tracing*, [3,13]). However, applying a similar mechanism to ELE faces a two-fold challenge. First, ELE should evaluate answers that vary a lot in content and complexity, compared with most step-based ITS. For example, Figure 1 shows an inquiry task in which students are asked to invent a method for calculating variability. Every algebraic procedure is a potential response to this task, and thus should be evaluated by the system. For instance, one common error that students often make is to use the range function as a measure of variability (using "range" implies that variability is determined only by the extreme values). However, students may use different morphs of range, such as "range+1" or "2*range" (all example methods in this paper are taken from students' inventions during the classroom studies). While simplifying students' methods algebraically may simplify the modeling task, it often fails to capture students' misconceptions. For example, several students added up the distances between all subsequent pairs of numbers, which is mathematically equivalent to range: $(a_1-a_2)+(a_2-a_3)+\ldots+(a_{n-1}-a_n)=a_1-a_n$. However, this method reveals a different conceptual error compared with range, since the more complex (yet mathematically equivalent) method uses all data points (and not merely the extreme values) to determine range.

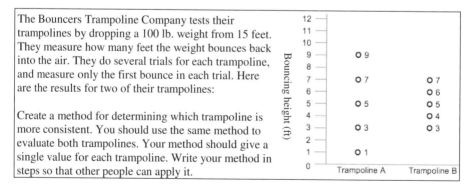

Fig. 1. An example of an invention task. Data is presented in the form of contrasting cases that direct students' attention to deep features of the domain.

In addition to the virtually intractable interaction space, ELE should also deal with an under-defined solution space. This means that not all classes of solutions (whether correct or not) can be defined in advance. While most step-based ITS assume that a solution that is not part of the cognitive model is incorrect [13], this assumption cannot be made with inquiry tasks, in which students may develop methods that do not correspond to classes of solutions identified in advance by the expert modeler.

Due to these challenges, most ELE do not assess students' knowledge at the domain level. Those who do often limit the vocabulary students can use and map the entire solution space. For example, SimQuest evaluates the complete subset of potential experiments that can support or refute each stated hypothesis [6]. Similarly, *Eco-Lab* and Smithtown map all possible nodes in the interaction space [5,14]. Naturally, this approach is not scalable for ELE that facilitate complex tasks or that allow for a large variety of inputs.

In addition to the challenge of analyzing students' errors, ELE designers face the challenge of responding to these errors, that is, designing effective domain-level support that does not undermine the exploratory nature of the inquiry task [6]. While ITS often set sub-goals for students and give them immediate feedback on errors [3,13], the pedagogical philosophy behind ELE suggests that students, and not external agents, should have responsibility over these tasks [2]. Therefore, many ELE offer no support at the domain level [7]. Other ELE give students immediate feedback, thus potentially hindering the benefits of inquiry learning [5]. A better solution would be to support students by adapting the task to their demonstrated proficiencies. For example, EcoLab directs students to one of three canned sets of directions and hints [14]. While this approach adheres to the pedagogical principles of ELE, having canned versions of the tasks is not a scalable solution. Adapting the task to a wide range of knowledge deficits, as students demonstrate in a wide range of situations, remains to be solved.

This paper addresses the two research questions outlined above. First, we describe a novel approach for evaluating students' knowledge at the domain level in ELE. We demonstrate this approach using the Invention Lab, an ELE for invention tasks. Second, we describe how the Invention Lab adapts the task to students' demonstrated proficiencies, thus supporting students while maintaining the exploratory nature of the task. Last, we illustrate how intelligent support can aid learning at the domain and scientific reasoning levels using log-files from a classroom evaluation of the lab.

2 The Invention Lab

The Invention Lab facilitates a type of inquiry activities called invention tasks. In invention tasks students are asked to invent novel methods for calculating target properties of data [4,15]. Figure 2 shows the Trampoline problem (from Figure 1) as it appears in the lab. In this example students are asked to invent a method for comparing the variability of two datasets. Invention tasks use contrasting cases to direct students' attention to deep features of the domain [4]. For example, the contrasting cases in Figure 2 (region (2c)) share the same average and sample size, but differ in their range. Following the invention attempt, students receive direct instruction on the canonical solutions for the same problem, and practice applying these solutions to

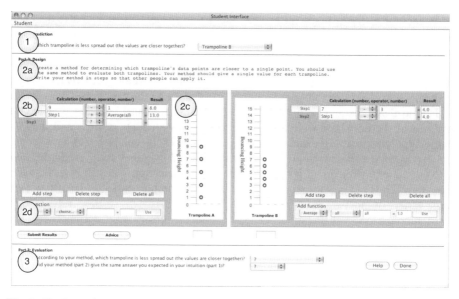

Fig. 2. The Invention Lab interface. Students are first asked to rank the contrasting cases (1). Upon successful ranking, the system asks the students to invent a method that will reflect their ranking (2a). The students express their method in steps (2b), using points from the contrasting cases (2c), and using basic functions (2d). Last, students evaluate their method (3) and revise it as needed. Students repeat the cycle using different contrasting cases.

different problems. The instruction and practice are done outside the lab. For example, the invention task from Figure 2 is followed by direct instruction on mean absolute deviation (the average distance from the mean). Multiple classroom studies have shown that invention tasks followed by direct instruction and practice lead to more robust learning compared with direct instruction and practice alone [4,15]. This effect was also termed "productive failure" [16], since the benefits of invention tasks were found even though most students failed to invent valid methods.

The Invention Lab facilitates invention tasks at the middle- and high-school levels. We first describe the interaction flow in the Invention lab from the students' point of view. We then describe the intelligent components of the system.

Students begin their invention activity by ranking two given contrasting cases according to the target concept (e.g., the data for Trampoline B is less spread out; region (1) in Figure 2). This qualitative ranking serves as the baseline against which students can later evaluate their inventions [4].

Upon successful ranking students move on to the design phase (region (2a)). In this phase students design a method for calculating the spread of the data. In previous studies we found that students prefer to express their methods as a sequence of steps (rather than a unified formula, see Figure 3). The lab retains this characteristic by supporting design in steps (region (2b) in Figure 2). Each step has the simple form of number - operator - number. While students need to invent a general method, they need not express it as such. Instead, in order to reduce cognitive load, students

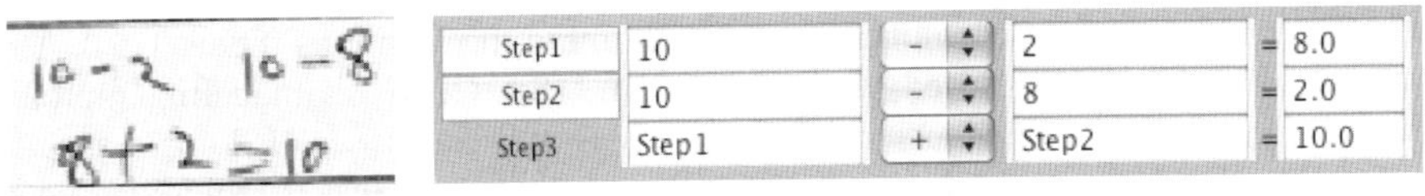

Fig. 3. A method designed by a student on paper (left) and the same method in the lab (right)

demonstrate their method by instantiating it using the given contrasting cases. For example, in order to "design" range, students enter "9-1" in the left graph by clicking on the "9" data-point (region (2c)), choosing the minus sign, and clicking on the "1" data-point. Students can also add basic functions to their methods (sum, average, median, and count; region (2d)). Last, students can add and delete steps, and use the results from previous steps in a current step.

Students apply their method to both contrasting cases and then submit it. No feedback is given during the design phase with the single exception of checking upon submission whether the same method was applied to both contrasting cases.

The evaluation phase (region (3) in Figure 2) asks students to compare the outcomes of their methods to their initial ranking. Feedback on evaluation incorporates an intelligent novice model, in that students are given the opportunity to notice the limitations of their method and revise it prior to receiving feedback [17]. When the invented method fails to generate the correct ranking (as established in the qualitative analysis), the system points that out and prompts the students to revise their method. When the method generates the correct ranking the system analyzes the method and identifies conceptual errors (for example, using range does not take into account other data points). The system uses this information to generate new contrasting cases that target the identified knowledge gaps. The number of ranking > design > evaluation cycles is not limited, and tasks are designed to engage students for 30 minutes. Students usually use the lab in pairs, though no explicit support for collaboration was implemented.

2.1 Intelligent Support in the Invention Lab

Support at the inquiry level. The Invention Lab scaffolds the inquiry process using cognitive tools (such as the step-based formula builder). The explicit scaffold of the inquiry process (i.e., *ranking -> design -> evaluation*) makes it a good candidate for applying a model-tracing approach. By tracing students' actions using a cognitive model of the inquiry process, the Invention Lab can give students adaptive and domain-independent feedback on their progress in the inquiry process. For example, when students fail to notice that predictions derived from their methods do not match their initial ranking, the tutor responds by explicitly pointing out that "your answer to the last question is not the same as your initial prediction."

Identifying errors at the domain level. As described above, evaluating students' methods at the domain level is particularly challenging. The virtually intractable interaction space makes it hard to trace students' actions, and the under-defined solution space makes it hard to evaluate complete solutions as a whole. Therefore, instead of pre-defining the complete set of solution classes, we chose to define the set of requirements from a valid solution (without defining the solutions themselves). This is done using Constraint-Based Modeling (CBM, [18]). CBM is a modeling approach that evaluates whether students' answers satisfy (or violate) a set of domain-specific constraints. Each constraint is associated with a characteristic that is required from all correct solutions. Therefore, all methods that violate a specific constraint reflect a similar knowledge gap. This quality of CBM makes it suitable for ill-defined domains and tasks [19]. The Invention Lab uses CBM to test whether the invented methods capture the deep features of the domain. For example, valid solutions should use all data points to calculate variability. However, many of the methods described above use only the extreme data points (e.g., range). The Invention Lab need not represent all the possible ways of demonstrating this knowledge gap. Rather, it can identify when the only arguments used by a method are the extreme values. Therefore, one of the constraints in the Invention Lab specifies that students should not use only the extreme values. A comprehensive list of 6 target features with 14 common errors (i.e., violated constraints) was compiled based on students' inventions in a previous paper-and-pencil study [4]. Table 1 shows a subset of these features. Notice that each solution can violate more than one constraint. Additional constraints help the lab give feedback on general mathematical errors, such as inconclusive methods.

To the extent that every algebraic method (at the middle school level) can be expressed using the Invention Lab interface and every invention can be analyzed according to the features described above, the cognitive model of the lab can analyze any method. Both components of the cognitive model (model tracing and CBM) were implemented with 59 production rules written in Jess using the Cognitive Tutor Authoring Tools [20]. The entire cognitive model could have also been implemented using a CBM approach.

Table 1. Analyzing methods using constraints. The four bottom rows show methods invented by students during the classroom studies, when applied to sample data ({2,4,4,7,8}).

Target feature (constraint):	Variability is determined by all data points	Variability depends on sample size	Variability depends on distances
Common conceptual errors (violations):	Method uses only extreme values	Method uses a sequential subset of points	Method does not control for sample size	Method does not calculate distances
Range * 2 $(8-2)*2 = 16$	X		X	
Largest gap $(7-4) = 3$		X	X	
# of close points $N(\{2,4,4\}) = 3$		X	X	X
(Min+max) / # of points $(2+8)/5 = 2$	X			X

Designing domain level support. Like many other ITS, the Invention Lab uses its evaluation of students' knowledge to adapt the task to students' demonstrated proficiencies. The Invention Lab does so by giving students contrasting cases that direct students' attention to the limitations of their previous methods and help them encode the deep structure of the domain. However, using canned contrasting cases may not be the right way to go. Students in the Invention Lab reveal their conceptual errors in different ways, when analyzing different data. Canned contrasting cases may lead students to create a collection of ad-hoc methods, resulting in scattered bits of knowledge. Instead, the Invention Lab designs in real time new contrasting cases to match students' needs. Each common conceptual error has an associated method for generating new contrasting cases that target that error. The process is designed to ensure that new sets of cases are easy to compare with regard to the target concept (so ranking will be simple), and that the most recent lacking method would fail on them. For example, if the student uses only extreme values, the system will generate two new cases that share the same range but have distinctive variability. Last, the process uses the recent set of cases, to help students build upon their prior experiences and create more cohesive knowledge. Table 2 demonstrates this process.

Table 2. An example for the contrasting-cases generation algorythm. Steps 1 and 2 are generic. Step 3 changes based on the target conceptual error. The given example targets the use of only extreme values to determine variability.

	Case A	Case B	Comments
Original task			
Original cases:	1 3 5 7 9	3 4 5 6 7	
Invented method: range	9 - 1 = 8	7 - 3 = 4	
New task			
1. Keep the case with the higher variability from the previous cycle	1 3 5 7 9		This encourages students to transfer from previous experiences
2. Copy the values that were used by the student in her previous method to the other case	1 3 5 7 9	1 9	This ensures that the pervious method fails to distinguish between the cases in the new set.
3. Populate the other case with values that are halfway between the original case and the average	1 3 5 7 9	1 4 5 6 9	This ensures that the two sets have distinct variability, the same average, and are easy to judge perceptually. (Halfway between 3 and average is 4; Halfway between 5 and average is 5; Halfway between 7 and average is 6)

2.2 Evaluating the Invention Lab

The Invention Lab was evaluated with 92 students in a public middle school in the Pittsburgh area. While the outcomes of the study are outside the scope of this paper, log files from the study offer us a window into students' learning with the lab[1]. The following example spans the first 20 minutes of one pair of students trying to invent a method for calculating variability.

First, the students receive the contrasting cases shown in Figure 2: *(Trampoline A: 1,3,5,7,9; Trampoline B: 3,4,5,6,7)*. The students rank the cases correctly *("Trampoline B has lower variability")*, and "invent" range *(Trampoline A: "9-1=9"; Trampoline B: "7-3=4")*.

The lab analyzes the method and chooses what feature to focus on next. In this case, the highest priority is to help the students understand that variability is determined by more than merely the extreme values. The lab generates new contrasting cases that fix range and keep one of the previous cases intact *(Trampoline A: 1,3,5,7,9; Trampoline B: 1,4,5,6,9; see Table 2)*.

The students rank the cases correctly *("Trampoline B has lower variability")*, and begin their design by applying the previously successful method, range. *(Trampoline A: "9-1=8"; Trampoline B: "9-1=8")*. The students fail to notice that range gives the same result for both contrasting cases, which does not match their initial ranking. Therefore, the students receive detailed feedback from the system (*"your answer to the last question is not the same as your initial prediction. Please check your method"*).

The students then attempt several central tendency measures (such as mean and median), however, these methods fail to generate correct ranking (since the contrasting cases share the same mean and median). This time around the students notice the failure of their methods and do not submit them for evaluation.

The students then try range again, and scrap the method before submitting it.

At this point, the log-files reveal a mini a-ha moment, when the students realize that they can extrapolate range to the second-furthest pair of points in each graph. They first list the two distances without relating them to one another *(Trampoline A, step 1: "9-1=8", step 2: "7-3=4"; Trampoline B, step 1: "9-1=8", step 2: "6-4=2")*. They submit this method, at which point the system prompts them that their method is inconclusive, since it does not assign a single value for each graph. The students, possibly encouraged by their success to extrapolate distance to other numbers, apply the concept of distance to the distances themselves. In other words, they subtract step 2 from step 1: *(Trampoline A, step 1: "9-1=8", step 2: "7-3=4", step 3: "step1-step2=4"; Trampoline B, step 1: "9-1=8", step 2: "6-4=2", step 3: "step1-step2=6")*. The students submit this method, but then realize its shortcoming – the method predicts that Trampoline A has lower variability, which is different from their initial ranking. They delete the method before approving it and resume the drawing board.

The students invent few additional methods before trying to add up the distances: *(Trampoline A, step 1: "9-1=8", step 2: "7-3=4", step 3: "step1+step2=12"; Trampoline B, step 1: "9-1=8", step 2: "6-4=2", step 3: "step1+step2=10")*. This method produces the desired ranking, thus concluding the current cycle.

This snippet of interaction reveals an interesting learning trajectory. First, we can see that the cognitive model of the lab identifies valid features, and its contrasting

---

[1] Results, to be detailed elsewhere, show that students who designed methods in the Invention Lab acquired more robust learning compared with students who were not instructed to design new methods. These results echo the findings of an earlier paper-and-pencil study [23].

cases generator creates contrasting cases that achieve their goal. Second, we can see how students' thinking unfolds, and how their mental models of spread evolve (including the a-ha moment before extrapolating range). Last, in addition to students' progression at the domain level, the students came across rich experiences at the scientific inquiry level. The students improved their tendency and ability to evaluate their methods. They also encountered the limitations of inconclusive methods that do not give a single number, and found that the same method always gives the same result when applied to the same data. Other log files demonstrate the ability of the Invention Lab to interpret novel methods. For example, several students have continued the line of reasoning demonstrated above, and designed a method that averages all "recursive ranges" (i.e., distances between highest and lowest, second highest and second lowest, etc.) We did not anticipate this solution, which is not a common measure of spread. However, upon closer examination, we concluded that recursive-range is a valid measure of spread. Indeed, when encountered by the Invention Lab, the lab concluded that this method satisfies all required constraints[2].

3 Summary and Contributions

We describe the Invention Lab, an ELE for facilitating invention tasks. The lab uses a hybrid of modeling techniques: it applies a model tracing approach to trace students' inquiry behavior, and applies a CBM approach to evaluate domain-level inputs. The Invention Lab also creates contrasting cases in real time. This allows the system to adapt its tasks to individual students without reducing critical features of the inquiry process. Last, we demonstrate how the combination of scaffold and feedback at the inquiry and domain levels helps students develop sophisticated mathematical models and improves their understanding of scientific reasoning. While the lab supports one type of inquiry tasks, invention activities, it demonstrates the feasibility of adding intelligent support at the domain and inquiry levels to ELE, thus bridging two schools of thought in the field of educational technologies.

Acknowledgement. This work was supported in part by a Graduate Training Grant awarded to Carnegie Mellon University by the Department of Education (#R305B040063) and by the Pittsburgh Science of Learning Center, which is funded by the National Science Foundation (award #SBE-0354420).

References

1. de Jong, T., van Joolingen, W.R.: Scientific discovery learning with computer simulations of conceptual domains. Rev. of Ed. Res. 68, 179–201 (1998)
2. Duffy, T.M., Cunningham, D.J.: Constructivism: Implications for the design and delivery of instruction. In: Jonassen, D.H. (ed.) Handbook of research for educational communications and technology, pp. 170–198. Macmillan, New York (1996)

---

[2] To be exact, "averaged recursive range" works well only for data with an even number of points. No student was successful at extending this method to data with an odd number of points. A more complete (and conventional) solution is to use mean absolute deviation (the averaged distance from the mean).

3. VanLehn, K.: The Behavior of Tutoring Systems. Int. J. Artif. Intell. Educ. 16(3), 227–265 (2006)
4. Roll, I., Aleven, V., Koedinger, K.R.: Helping students know 'further' - increasing the flexibility of students' knowledge using symbolic invention tasks. In: The 31st Annual Conference of the Cognitive Science Society, pp. 1169–1174. Cognitive Science Society, Austin (2009)
5. Shute, V.J., Glaser, R.: A Large-Scale Evaluation of an Intelligent Discovery World: Smithtown. Interactive Learning Environments 1, 51–77 (1990)
6. Veermans, K., de Jong, T., van Joolingen, W.R.: Promoting Self-Directed Learning in Simulation-Based Discovery Learning Environments Through Intelligent Support. Interact. Learn. Envir. 8(3), 229–255 (2000)
7. Mulder, Y.G., Lazonder, A.W., de Jong, T.: Finding out how they find it Oout: An empirical analysis of inquiry learners' need for support. Int. J. Sci. Educ., 1–21 (2009)
8. Jonassen, D.: Designing constructivist learning environments. In: Reigeluth, C.M. (ed.) Instructional-design theories and models, pp. 215–239. Routledge, Hillsdale (1999)
9. Woolf, B.P., Marshall, D., Mattingly, M., Lewis, J., Wright, S., et al.: Tracking student propositions in an inquiry system. In: The 11th International Conference on Artificial Intelligence in Education, pp. 21–28. IOS Press, Sydney (2003)
10. Roll, I., Aleven, V., McLaren, B.M., Koedinger, K.R.: Designing for metacognition - applying cognitive tutor principles to the tutoring of help seeking. Metacognition and Learning 2(2), 125–140 (2007)
11. Koedinger, K.R., Suthers, D.D., Forbus, K.D.: Component-Based construction of a science learning space. Int. J. Artif. Intell. Educ. 10, 292–313 (1999)
12. Bunt, A., Conati, C.: Probabilistic student modelling to improve exploratory behaviour. User Model. User-Adap. 13(3), 269–309 (2003)
13. Koedinger, K.R., Corbett, A.T.: Cognitive tutors: Technology bringing learning science to the classroom. In: Sawyer, K. (ed.) The Cambridge Handbook of the Learning Sciences, pp. 61–78. Cambridge University Press, New York (2006)
14. Luckin, R., du Boulay, B.: Ecolab: The development and evaluation of a vygotskian design framework. Int. J. Artif. Intell. Educ. 10(2), 198–220 (1999)
15. Schwartz, D.L., Martin, T.: Inventing to prepare for future learning: The hidden efficiency of encouraging original student production in statistics instruction. Cognition Instruct. 22(2), 129–184 (2004)
16. Kapur, M.: Productive failure. Cognition Instruct. 26(3), 379–424 (2008)
17. Mathan, S.A., Koedinger, K.R.: Fostering the intelligent novice: Learning from errors with metacognitive tutoring. Educ. Psychol. 40(4), 257–265 (2005)
18. Mitrovic, A., Koedinger, K.R., Martin, B.: A comparative analysis of cognitive tutoring and constraint-based modeling. In: Brusilovsky, P., Corbett, A.T., de Rosis, F. (eds.) UM 2003. LNCS (LNAI), vol. 2702, pp. 313–322. Springer, Heidelberg (2003)
19. Mitrovic, A., Weerasinghe, A.: Revisiting ill-definedness and the consequences for ITSs. In: The 14th Conference on Artificial Intelligence in Education, pp. 375–382. IOS Press, Marina Del Ray (2009)
20. Aleven, V., McLaren, B.M., Sewall, J., Koedinger, K.R.: The Cognitive Tutor Authoring Tools (CTAT): Preliminary evaluation of efficiency gains. In: Ikeda, M., Ashley, K.D., Chan, T.-W. (eds.) ITS 2006. LNCS, vol. 4053, pp. 61–70. Springer, Heidelberg (2006)

Discovering and Recognizing Student Interaction Patterns in Exploratory Learning Environments

Andrea Bernardini[1] and Cristina Conati[2]

[1] Fondazione Ugo Bordoni, Via B. Castiglione 5900142, Roma, Italy
bernardini.andrea@gmail.com
[2] University of British Columbia, 2366 Main Mall, Vancouver, BC, V6T1Z4, Canada
conati@cs.ubc.ca

Abstract. In a Exploratory Learning Environment users acquire knowledge while freely experiencing the environment. In this setting, it is often hard to identify actions or behaviors as correct or faulty, making it hard to provide adaptive support to students who do not learn well with these environments. In this paper we discuss an approach that uses Class Association Rule mining and a Class Association Rule Classifier to identify relevant interaction patterns and build student models for online classification.

We apply the approach to generate a student model for an ELE for AI algorithms and present preliminary results on its effectiveness.

Keywords: Educational Data Mining, Student Modeling, Exploratory Learning Environments.

1 Introduction

Exploratory learning environments (ELEs) provide functionalities such as interactive simulations and visualizations for student-led exploration of a target domain. The idea is to promote active discovery of knowledge, which in turns triggers deeper understanding of the target domain than more controlled instruction. Research however, has suggested that the pedagogical effectiveness of an ELE is highly dependent on the student who uses it: while some students appreciate the independence afforded by of this learning activity, others suffer from the lack of structure and would benefit from more guidance during interaction [1]. Such findings highlight the need for ELEs to provide adaptive support for students with diverse abilities or learning styles.

One of the challenges of providing this support is the difficulty in identifying student behaviors that warrant interventions vs. behaviors that indicate an effective learner. Traditional approaches based on creating datasets of human-labeled patterns [2][3] that can be used to classify new users are often unfeasible, because they need a priori definitions of relevant behaviors when there is limited knowledge of what these behaviors may be.

In this paper, we explore an alternative approach that relies on mining Class Association Rules to automatically identify common interaction behaviors and then uses these rules to build a user model based on a Class Association Rule Classifier. In previous work, we presented a version of the approach that used clustering algorithms to first identify learner types based on the potential effectiveness of their interaction behaviors, and then to classify new students in real time based on these clusters [11]. While the approach showed good classification accuracy in terms of the student's learning outcomes, it does not allow the system to isolate the specific behaviors that cause a given student to learn effectively or not from the environment. The approach based on association rules and a class association rule classifier that we present in this paper has a finer classification granularity, and thus it is better suited at guiding adaptive interventions to improve interaction effectiveness. We test the approach on AISpace[4], an ELE that uses interactive visualizations to help students understand Artificial Intelligence (AI) algorithms.

Several other researchers have looked at using association rules in ITS. To our knowledge, however, ours is the first attempt at using this approach for on-line student modeling with an ELE. In [5], logged data from students interaction with an ITS for the SQL database were mined using association rules to discover error patterns that can help teachers improve their presentation of this topics. In [6], the authors use association rules to discover similarities among exercises in terms of solution difficulty by mining logs of student solutions in an ITS. [7] uses association rules for the off-line analysis of students usage of a web based educational system spanning a complete university course, once the course is complete. Further off-line processing of the rules generates recommendations for teachers as to which usage patterns are more relevant for course revision.

The paper is structure has follows. We first describe our general approach to detect and recognize relevant interaction patterns in ELEs. We then introduce the ELE we used in this research. Next, we describe association rules and how they are used in our approach, and we presents results on their effectiveness in identifying effective and ineffective learners in AISpace. We conclude with a discussion of future work.

2 General Student Modeling Approach

Our student modeling approach for ELEs divides the modeling process into two major phases: offline identification and online recognition.

In the offline phase, raw, unlabelled data from student interaction with the target environment is first collected and then preprocessed. The result of preprocessing is a set of feature vectors representing individual students in terms of their interaction behavior. These vectors are then used as input to an unsupervised clustering algorithm that groups them according to their similarity. The resulting groups, or 'clusters', represent students who interact similarly with the environment. These clusters are then analyzed to determine which interaction behaviors are effective or ineffective for learning. The analysis consists of first identifying how the different clusters relate to learning outcomes, and then isolating in each cluster those behaviors that are responsible for the learning effects. Understanding the effectiveness of students' interaction behaviors with an ELE is useful in itself to increase educator awareness of the pedagogical benefits of these environments, as well as to reveal to developers how the ELE can be improved [8][9][10]. However, our long-term goal is to use the interaction behaviors to guide automatic ELE adaptations while a student is interacting with the system. Thus, in the online recognition phase, the clusters identified in the offline phase are used directly in a classifier user model. The user model's classifications and the learning behaviors identified by cluster analysis can eventually be used to inform an adaptive ELE component to encourage effective learning behaviors and prevent detrimental ones.

In our previous investigations of this approach [11], the identification of behaviors that influence learning outcomes in each cluster was done by hand, using formal statistical tests to evaluate cluster similarities and dissimilarities along each of the feature dimensions. The outcome of this step is useful to help educators and developers gain insights on the different learning behaviors and design appropriate adaptive interventions targeting them. It was not, however, directly used during on-line learner recognition. For this phase, we devised an online k-means classifier, trained on the clusters identified in the offline phase. This classifier incrementally updates the classification of a new student into one of the clusters from the offline phase, as the student interacts with the target ELE. While this classifier showed very good performance in predicting student learning outcomes with two different ELEs, it can't identify which behaviors caused the classification at any given time. For instance, when applied to the ELE that we describe later in this paper, this approach identifies two clusters, one of high learners and one of low learners. Each cluster includes a variety of behaviors that can impact learning but the classifier can't tell which behaviors are responsible for the student's classification as student actions come in. This limits the ability of the approach to support adaptive interventions that target the relevant behaviors (e.g. discourage superficial browsing of functionalities). To address this limitation, we have introduced the use of Class Association Rules, described in the next section.

3 Using Class Association Rules for Learner Classification in ELEs

Association rules were originally devised for finding the hidden connections between items in a transaction database[12], and are generally used to find co-occurrence patterns in data. The connections are expressed as rules $X \rightarrow Y$, indicating that when X occurs, Y occurs with a given probability greater than zero. This probability is called the *confidence* of the rule $conf(R)$, which essentially represents the strength of the correlation between X and Y. Algorithms for generating association rules use this measure, along with a measure of the relevance of a rule in a dataset, to select a set of appropriate rules among a usually very large pool of candidates. The measure of relevance is commonly known as *support* of the rule $sup(R)$, computed as the percentage of datapoints satisfying both X and Y in the dataset.

The use of association rules to construct a classifier is called Associative classification mining or Associative Classification [13]. Algorithms for Associative Classification usually operate by first generating a complete set of class association rules (CARs) from training data, and then by pruning this initial set to obtain a subset of rules that constitute the classifier. When a new unknown object (a student in our case) is presented to the classifier, it is compared to a number of CARs and its class is predicted. The selection of the representative subset of CARs is one of the crucial steps in Associative Classification, entailing understanding what is the best number of CARs needed for classification, as well as which measures to use to select them.

We use Associative classification to increase the grain size of the on-line classification in the student modeling approach we described in Section 2. The overall approach is modified as follows. We still rely on an off-line clustering algorithm for generating the clusters that form the basis for the classifier, and each cluster is labeled with the overall learning performance of the corresponding student group. The off-line phase is then augmented by performing Associative Classification within each cluster, thus obtaining a set of CARs that, for each cluster, link specific interaction behaviors with learning outcomes. During on-line classification, user interaction behaviors are tracked and updated after each action, as before. This time, however, they are matched against all available CARs and a classification is selected based on the cluster that has the highest percentage of matched rules. Thus, at any given point of the interaction, our student models generates a prediction of both the current student's learning success, as well as the behaviors that influence it.

In the rest of the paper, we provide details on the approach and its effectiveness in the context of its usage for modeling students as they interact with the ELE known as AIspace CSP applet, described in the next section.

4 The AISpace CSP Applet

The ELE we use as a testbed for our approach is the Constraint Satisfaction Problem (CSP) Applet, one of a collection of interactive tools for learning common Artificial Intelligence algorithms, called AIspace [4]. Algorithm dynamics are demonstrated via interactive visualizations on graphs by the use of color and highlighting, and graphical state changes are reinforced through textual messages (see Figure 1 for an example).

A CSP consists of a set of variables, variable domains and a set of constraints on legal variable-value assignments. The goal is to find an assignment that satisfies all constraints. The CSP applet illustrates the Arc Consistency 3 (AC-3) algorithm for solving CSPs represented as networks of variable nodes and constraint arcs. AC-3 iteratively makes individual arcs consistent by removing variable domain values inconsistent with a given constraint until all arcs have been considered and the network is consistent. Then, if there remains a variable with more than one domain value, a procedure called domain splitting can be applied to that variable to split the CSP into disjoint cases so that AC-3 can recursively solve each case or sub-network.

The CSP applet provides several mechanisms for interactive execution of the AC-3 algorithm, accessible through the toolbar shown at the top of Figure 1 or through direct manipulation of graph elements. Here we provide a brief description of these mechanisms necessary to understand the results of applying our student modeling approach to this environment:

- *Fine Stepping.* Cycles through three detailed algorithm steps: selecting an arc, testing it for consistency, and removing variable domain values when necessary.
- *Direct Arc Clicking.* Allows the user to decide which arc to test, and then performs three *Fine Steps* on that arc to make it consistent.
- *Auto Arc Consistency (Auto AC).* Automatically *Fine Steps* through the network.

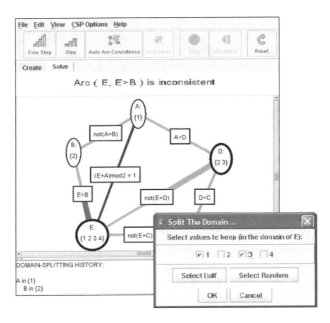

Fig. 1. CSP applet with example CSP

- *Stop.* Stops *Auto AC.*
- *Domain Splitting (DS).* Allows the user to select a variable domain to split, and specify a sub-network for further application of AC-3.
- *Backtracking.* Recovers the alternative sub-network set aside by *DS*.
- *Resetting.* Resets the CSP network to its initial state.

Currently, AI space does not provide any explicit support on how to use the available mechanisms to learn at best from the interactive visualizations delivered by its applets. Research, however, shows that students may benefit from this support, since unaided exploration of interactive visualizations often fails to help students learn[11]. In the following sections, we describe the application of the modeling approach described in Section 3 to create a classifier user model that can detect suboptimal student interactions with the CSP applet and guide adaptive interventions aimed at improving them.

5 Modeling Student Interaction with the CSP Applet

The data we use for this research was obtained from a previous experiment investigating the effects of studying sample problems with the CSP applet. We use the following data collected from 24 students who participated in the study: time-stamped logs of user interactions with the applet, and learning gains computed from pre and post tests administered to the study participants. From the logged data we obtained 1931 actions of users over 205.3 minutes. In the off-line phase, in order to find clusters of students who interact with the CSP Applet in similar ways, each student must be represented by a multidimensional data point or 'feature vector'. From the logged user study data, we computed 24 feature vectors corresponding to the 24 study participants. The feature vectors had 21 dimensions, resulting from deriving three features for each of the seven actions described in the previous section: (1) action frequency, (2) the average latency after an action (reported as *avg* in tables), and (3) the standard deviation of the latency after an action (reported as *STD* in tables). The latency dimensions are intended to measure if and how a student is reflecting on action results. Specifically, the second dimension is an indicator of student reflection, and the third dimension is an indicator of reflection selectiveness since varied latency may indicate planned rather than impulsive or inattentive behavior (e.g., consistently rushing through actions vs. selectively attending to the results of actions).

After forming the feature vector representation of the data, the next step in the off-line phase is to perform clustering on the feature vectors to discover patterns in the students' interaction behaviors. After experimenting with various clustering algorithms (including EM and hierarchical clustering) we chose k-means[14] for this dataset. K-means converges to different local optima depending on the selection of the initial cluster centroids and so in this research we execute 25 trials (with randomly selected initial cluster centroids) and use the highest quality clusters (based on Fisher's criterion [15]) as the final cluster set. We also experimented with k set to 2, 3 and 4, and obtained the best results for $k = 2$. More details on cluster generation can be found in [11].

When we compared average learning gains between the two clusters found by k-means, we found that one cluster (4 students) had statistically significantly higher learning gains (7 points) than the other cluster (20 students, 3.08 points gain). Hereafter, we will refer to these clusters as 'HL' (high learning) cluster, and 'LL' (low learning) cluster respectively.

5.1 CARs and Multiple Class Association Rule Classifier

The next step in the student modeling process is to generate CARs to identify, for each cluster, the interaction behaviors that best characterize its students. In this work, we used the Hotspot algorithm in Weka [16], which inspects the training data and generates the association rules corresponding to a class label in the form of a tree. Table 1 shows the CARs generated for the HL and LL clusters, where we report the preconditions for each rule but leave out the consequence (Label HL for the high learners cluster and LL for the low learners cluster). Table 1 also shows, for each rule, its level of confidence (*conf*), and support within its cluster (*supp*).

It should be noted that the attribute values mentioned in the rules in table 1 are discrete, while our original dimensions are continuous. Although CAR algorithms work with both discrete and continuous values, using continuous values in our dataset would produce a large number of very fine-grained rules, unsuitable for classification. We thus discretized our attributes using the equal-width method proposed in [17], which consists of dividing the range of observed values into k equally bins. For the time being we selected k=2, thus discretizing each attribute into HIGH and LOW values, although we plan to experiment with a higher number of bins to see how that affects the accuracy of the classifier.

Table 1. CARs for HL and LL clusters (*STD* refers to standard deviation, *Avg* referes to average)

Rules for HL cluster

Rule 1: *Stop Pause STD = HIGH; conf=100%; supp =50%*
Rule 2: *Fine Step Pause STD = HIGH; conf=80% supp =100%*
|Rule 3 *Fine Step Pause STD = HIGH & Fine Step frequency = LOW*
  conf=100% supp=100%
|Rule 4 *Fine Step Pause STD = HIGH & Domain Split Pause STD = LOW*
  conf=100% supp =100%

Rules for LL cluster

Rule 1 *Fine Step Pause STD = LOW; conf=100%; supp =100%*
Rule 2 *Stop frequency = LOW; conf= 95% ; supp =95%*
*| **Rule 3** Stop frequency = LOW & Fine Step Pause Avg = 'LOW*
  conf=100% supp=100%
*| **Rule 4** Stop frequency = LOW & Reset Pause Avg = 'LOW*
  conf=100% supp=100%

The Hotspot algorithm has three parameters that influence the type and number of rules generated: the minimum level of support requested for a rule to be considered relevant; the branching factor of the tree, influencing how many new rules can be generated from an existing one by adding a new condition to its current set; the minimum improvement in confidence requested for creating a new branch in the tree.

We kept the default values for minimum improvement (0.01) and branching factor (2), while we used the minimum level of support within each cluster as a criterion to filter the number of rules generated [18]. Essentially, for each cluster we need to find a few rules that characterize as many elements in the cluster as possible and provide an easily understandable explanation of students' behaviors for each learning outcome. After experimenting with various levels of support, we selected 50% for both the HL and the LL cluster, i.e., a rule has to involve at least half of the students in the cluster to be generated.

The CARs produced are shown in Table 1. They indicate that, for instance, high learners show more selective attention when observing the workings on the CSP algorithm in the applet (see high values for standard deviation in latency after stopping a running of Autosolve in Rule 1, and in latency during fine stepping in Rules 2-4). Low learners, on the other hand, are characterized by non-selective attention during fine stepping (see low standard deviation for pausing times during stepping in rule 1). Rule 2 represents a different detrimental behavior, i.e. short latency during stepping and limited usage of stopping during autosolving, indicating that the student is not taking the time to analyze the workings of the algorithm.

After producing the CARs for each cluster, the CARs were used as input to a classifier based on multiple class association rules. This classifier can generate a prediction in terms of high or low learning for a new user after each user action in the CSP applet. For each new action, all the related feature dimensions are recomputed (e.g., action frequency and the various latency dimensions), and the updated feature vector is matched against all existing CARs. The final classification is generated by selecting the cluster with the highest percentage of matched rules.

5.2 Evaluation

To evaluate our approach, we used the same methodology followed in [11] and based on a 24-fold leave-one-out cross validation (LOOCV). In each fold, we removed one student's data from the set of *N* available feature vectors, used *k*-means to re-cluster the reduced feature vector set and generated CARs for each newly generated cluster. Next, the removed student's data (the test data) was fed into the CAR Classifier trained on the reduced set, and online predictions were made for the incoming actions as described above. Model accuracy is evaluated by checking after every action whether the current student is correctly classified into the cluster to which he/she was assigned in the offline phase. The percentage of correct classifications is shown in Figure 2 as a function of the percentage of student actions seen by the model (solid line labeled 'Overall' in the figure's legend). The figure also shows the model's performance in classifying HL students into the HL cluster (dotted line), LL students into the LL cluster (dashed line), and the performance of a base-line most-likely classifier.

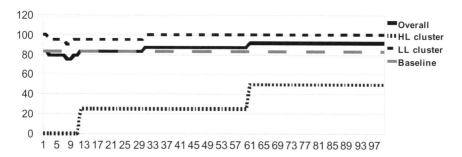

Fig. 2. Classifier accuracy (y axis) as a function of observed actions (x-axis)

The classifier performs very well in identifying LL learners (100% accuracy after seeing about 30 actions), while it performs poorly with the HL learners. This is not surprising, since the HL cluster used to derive the CARs rule for this group contains on average only 3 data points during LOOCV. The high performance on the LL cluster, on the other hand, is very encouraging, because this cluster, although much larger than HL, still includes a relatively limited number of datapoints (20 on average). Still, we managed to learn from this dataset a CAR classifier that is very good at detecting students with suboptimal learning behaviors, indicating that overall performance can be significantly improved by collecting a richer dataset for model training.

It is interesting to compare the performance of our CAR Classifier with the performance of the previous k-means classifier [11]. That classifier had slightly lower accuracy on LL (constantly above 90% but never reaching100%) but scored much better than the CAR classifier in classifying HL, converging to about 75% accuracy after seeing about 40% of the available actions. These results suggests that the k-mean classifier learns more reliably from small datasets that the CAR classifier, but the price to pay is no information on which behaviors are responsible for a user's classification at any given point of the interaction. The CAR classifier, on the other hand, can help identify these behaviors after every user action by providing the rules that were matched to generate the classification. This information can be used to provide adaptive hints to correct behaviors that can be detrimental for learning. For instance, if Rule 3 below fires to classify a student as low learner (see Table 1)

Rule 3 *Stop frequency = LOW and Fine Step Pause Avg = 'LOW*

the ELE can try to make the learner stop more often when running the CSP algorithm in autosolve mode, and pause more in between stepping actions to reflect on the outcome of each step of the algorithm

6 Conclusions and Future Work

We presented a student modeling approach that uses Class Association Rules and a Class Association Rule Classifier to discover and monitor student behaviors that can impact learning during interaction with an ELE. Modeling student interactions with ELEs is important to provide adaptive support for those students who do not learn well in absence of more structured instruction. It is also challenging, because in these environments it can be hard to identify a priory actions or behaviors as correct or faulty. We have provided initial results showing that our approach can identify these behaviors, and have discussed implications for providing adaptive support in ELE. One line of future work, thus, is to implement this adaptive support. In parallel, we want to refine our student modeling approach by experimenting with alternative techniques for selecting the set of relevant association rules (e.g. based on a variety of functions of support and confidence). We also want to see how our approach performs on larger datasets and how it transfers to different ELEs, for instance the ELE for mathematical functions that we used to test transfer of the first version of our approach without association rules [11].

References

1. Shute, V.J.: A comparison of learning environments: All that glitters.. In: Computers as Cognitive Tools, pp. 47–73. Lawrence Erlbaum Associates, Hillsdale (1993)
2. Merten, C., Conati, C.: Eye-Tracking to Model and Adapt to User Meta-Cognition in Intelligent Learning Environments. In: Proceedings of Intelligent User Interfaces (2006)
3. Baker, R.S.J.d., et al.: Adapting to when students game an intelligent tutoring system. In: Ikeda, M., Ashley, K.D., Chan, T.-W. (eds.) ITS 2006. LNCS, vol. 4053, pp. 392–401. Springer, Heidelberg (2006)
4. Amershi, S., Carenini, G., Conati, C., Mackworth, A., Poole, D.: Pedagogy and Usability in Interactive Algorithm Visualisations: Designing and Evaluating CIspace. Interacting with Computers 20(1), 64–96 (2008)
5. Merceron, A., Yacef, K.: A web-based tutoring tool with mining facilities to Improve Teaching and Learning. In: AIED 2003, pp. 201–208 (2003)

6. Freyberger, J., Heffernan, N., Ruiz, C.: Using association rules to guide a search for best fitting transfer models of student learning. In: Workshop on analyzing student-tutor interactions logs to improve educational outcomes at ITS conference, pp. 1–4 (2004)
7. García, E., Romero, C., Ventura, S., Castro, C.D.: An architecture for making recommendations to courseware authors using association rule mining and collaborative filtering. UMUAI 19, 99–132 (2009)
8. Hunt, E., Madhyastha, T.: Data Mining Patterns of Thought. In: Proceedings of the AAAI Workshop on Educational Data Mining (2005)
9. Merceron, A., Yacef, K.: TADA-Ed for Educational Data Mining. Interactive Mulitmedia Electronic Journal of Computer-Enhanced Learning (2005)
10. Talavare, L., Gaudioso, E.: Mining Student Data to Characterize Similar Behavior Groups in Unstructured Collaboration Spaces. In: Proceedings of the European Conference on AI Workshop on AI in CSCL (2004)
11. Amershi, S., Conati, C.: Combining Unsupervised and Supervised Machine Learning to Build User Models for Exploratory Learning Environments. The Journal of Educational Data Mining 1(1), 18–71 (2009)
12. Agrawal, R., Srikant, R.: Fast Algorithms for Mining Association Rules in large Databases. In: VLDB 1994, pp. 487–499 (1994)
13. Thabtah, F.A.: A review of associative classification mining. Knowl. Eng. Rev. 22(1), 37–65 (2007)
14. Duda, R.O., Hart, P.E., Stork, D.: Pattern Classification. Wiley- Interscience, New York (2001)
15. Fisher, R.A.: The Use of Multiple Measurements in Taxonomic Problems. Annals of Eugenics 7, 179–188 (1936)
16. Weka project, http://www.cs.waikato.ac.nz/~ml/weka/
17. Dougherty, J., Kohavi, R., Sahami, M.: Supervised and unsupervised discretization of continuous features. In: Proceedings of the 12th International Conference on Machine Learning, pp. 194–202 (1995)
18. Liu, B., Hsu, W., Ma, Y.: Mining association rules with multiple minimum supports. In: Proceedings of the Fifth ACM SIGKDD international Conference on Knowledge Discovery and Data Mining, KDD 1999, pp. 337–341. ACM, New York (1999)

Lesson Study Communities on Web to Support Teacher Collaboration for Professional Development

Yukari Kato[1] and Masatoshi Ishikawa[2]

[1] Tokyo University of Agriculture and Technology
3-5-8 Saiwaicho, Fuchu, Tokyo, Japan, 183-8509
[2] Tokyo Seitoku University
1-7-13 Jyujyo dai, Kita-ku, Tokyo, Japan, 114-0033
kathy@cc.tuat.ac.jp, ishikawa@tsu.ac.jp

Abstract. This paper addresses how the peer review system (FD Commons on WEB) was used as an analytical tool to identify key principles and criteria for assessing teaching and learning in higher education. The focus of this study was to understand various reviewers' viewpoints of educational events during "lesson study" by examining type of knowledge shared by reviewers. We present the overview of our Peer Review Process Project and report on five pilot studies conducted during spring term 2009. The successive trials revealed the following three points: (1) the lecture summary content differed between reviewers depending on specialty and teaching experience, (2) reviewers wrote more comments concerning lecture quality than basic teaching skills, (3) as keywords for self-reflection, lecturers used content information rather than pedagogical points.

Keywords: Lesson Study, e-Teaching Portfolio, the Quality of Teaching and Students' Learning, Japanese Higher Education.

1   Community Practice for Common Assessment

Several recent projects involving peer review of teaching might be classified as communities of practice in professional settings [1]. For example, the Peer Review of Teaching Project headquartered at the University of Nebraska, the Visible Knowledge Project of Georgetown University, and the Carnegie Foundation's Knowledge Media Laboratory (KML) have all explored alternative genres to enable scholars of teaching and learning to document their work online in ways not possible in regular print. The KML encourages viewers of their galleries to view online portfolios to snapshots for ideas to improve their teaching, and to use the portfolios as "launching points for discussions and reflections, peer review of teaching and learning, collaborative inquiries, and further investigations" [2].

Researches have found that collaborative professional communities of teachers support ongoing professional reform and student achievement [3]-[4]. In particular, collaborative professional communities enhance teachers' ability to meet the increasingly diverse learning needs of students [2], [4]-[6]. In Japan and the U.S. several national and local projects involving peer review of teaching might be classified as "community of practice." These activities are based on some consensus about what constitutes teaching excellence and on providing those conducting the reviews with good evidence on which to base their judgment.

Hatch [7] notes that as more faculty make presentations of their teaching publicly available via the web, there are increased opportunities to view the experiences of many different teachers working in many different disciplines and contexts. Through this process, educators will provide opportunities for others to generalize from those experiences, and to develop, explore, and challenge new ideas and theories about teaching and learning. Such rich representations by new media and network support to build the "Teaching Commons," which are communities of educators committed to pedagogical inquiry and innovation who come together to exchange ideas about teaching and learning, and use those ideas to meet the challenges of educating students for personal, professionals, and civic life in the twenty-first century [6]. All who are committed to this teaching mission need ways to make new pedagogical practices, tool, and understandings broadly available, not only by building their teaching but also by ensuring access thorough new media and network. Another trend, called "electronic teaching portfolios," can enhance the ability of teaching portfolios to provide rich presentations of college teaching and learning. A teaching portfolio is a collection of materials that document teaching performance [8]. It brings together information about a professor's most significant teaching accomplishments. If any teaching portfolio is stored on and accessed through electronic media, it qualifies as an electronic teaching portfolio. Most importantly, by placing a teaching portfolio on the web, a faculty member takes a crucial step toward making his or her teaching public and available for others to comment on and learn from [9].

2 Lesson Study in Japanese Primary and Secondary Education

Unfortunately, in the context of university education, it is difficult for lecturers to learn from each other and to break the pervasive isolation of professionals. Recently, higher education institutions have provided various institutional programs for educating and developing academic staff members: development of teaching philosophies, campaigns to raise awareness of certain key components, strategic use of experts such as educational developers and teaching fellows, and funding for projects aimed at specific issues. This traditional faculty development approach, however, is sometimes problematic. One reason is that faculty members have few incentives and little time to pursue these professional development efforts; even when faculty members recognize the scholarship of teaching and its difficulties, they often are pulled in other directions because, at many academic institutions, research and publishing are valued more highly than teaching [10]. Another reason is that workshops and seminars tend to be isolated, generic, and decontextualized. Therefore, the models of instruction used for many faculty development efforts are not conducive to helping faculty members change their approach to brushing up on teaching skills.

Because of inherent problems with 'top-down' models of faculty development, more effective strategies should be utilized, based upon individual contacts between staff at all levels, a mentor/developer, and students at the faculty's institution. In other words, a more bottom-up approach is needed in order to organize a faculty learning community and effect real change in teaching strategies for a greater number of academic staff members. The most effective way to improve teaching/learning activities is the rooted in the real-world context of practice [11]. Engagement in professional development requires teachers to examine their own practice, promotes reflection, and provides opportunities for socializing.

"Lesson study (Jyugyo kenkyu)," however, is a popular professional development approach in Japan whereby school teachers collaborate in order to improve instruction and learning by studying content, instruction, and how students solve problems and reach for understanding [4] From engaging in "lesson study," teachers feel connected to each other and to a body of knowledge that they generate, share, and continuously refine. In other words, it is a highly justified activity, which allows teachers to come together to develop their pedagogical knowledge and skills.

In this paper, we report on the ongoing effects of Tokyo University of Agriculture and Technology's Center for Higher Education to conduct "lesson study" by use of a peer review system (FD Commons on WEB). This system development realizes ubiquitous peer reviewing and reuse of comments of reviewers for assessment of teaching/learning in higher education. Moreover, the database of reviewer annotation has capability of reusing collected comments in order to suggest weak and strong points of class lectures and to design the rubric to evaluate lectures as e-teaching portfolio. This paper will also present an overview of our peer review project and five pilot studies conducted in 2009. By presenting results of our trials, we hope to gain new insights regarding best practices for learning and teaching in higher education.

3 Overview of the Peer Review System Development

The main objectives of this project are to support the peer review process and to restore and retrieve key concepts with multimedia information for the purpose of constructing e-teaching portfolio. We developed a class lecture recording application (FD Commons: http://www.tuat.ac.jp/~fd_tools) for reviewers allowing them to multicast to streaming video, images, and text from tablet PCs and PDAs [12],[13]. This project aims to provide teachers with online and offline peer review opportunities that are necessary to and relevant to their teaching/learning improvement as shown in Fig.1. Moreover, the database of reviewer comments is capable of reusing collected comments in order to suggest weak and strong points in class lectures and to design a rubric to evaluate lectures for assessment of teaching/learning in higher education.

138   Y. Kato and M. Ishikawa

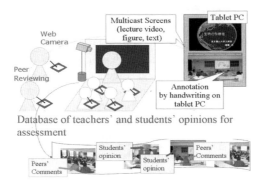

Fig. 1. Project Overview

3.1 Knowledge Sharing System for Peer Review Process

The project have designed and developed the system (FD Commons Ver. 3) can assist the peer-reviewers and students monitors to review the class rlectures and to record and retrieve the reviews comments on video lactures. The following fuctions are realised by use of InkML technology and multmedia networking technology (DirectShow) [13].

1) Collecting comments effectively from peer reviewers outside and students in class by tablets PC over networks. Both peer reviewers and student monitors can check the multi screens and write comments and annotation on the video lectures and ppt slides by use of tablet PCs.
2) Develop application for viewing reviewers' annotations to streaming class lecture as time sequence data of pen-tip coordinates.

The collected annotations are used to suggest weak and strong points of class lectures for teaching/learning evaluation. Moreover, they are used to make the rubric to evaluate the quality of teaching/learning for self-reflection and lesson study [14]-[15].

Fig. 2. Screenshot of FD Commons (Ver. 3)

In the next phase, we have designed and developed the "FD Commons on WEB" to promote knowledge sharing between reviewers and teachers. The system developed using a Web server with PHP and JavaScript, which realized integrated video streaming, snapshots with annotations for review lectures as shown in Fig.3. The data of class lectures were originally recorded and stored as part of FD Commons ver.3, however, they are currently distributed as part of the next FD Commons on WEB. The system architecture consists of three servers; a www server, a database server, and a streaming server. The streaming server delivers the class lecture movies linked to the annotations and comments by the request of its browser client, which are controlled and identified by the meta data on the database server.

Fig. 3. Screenshots FD Commons on WEB

Such convenient representations by networking will support the building of "Teaching Commons," which are communities of educators committed to pedagogical inquiry and innovation who come together to exchange ideas about teaching and learning. By placing a knowledge sharing system on the web, a faculty member takes a crucial step toward making his or her teaching public and available for others to comment on and learn from each other [9].

3.2 Pilot Studies for Evaluating the Peer Review Process

This evaluation study continued our inquiry on how to best implement lesson study in using FD Commons on WEB. This evaluation was based on data collected in a qualitative and quantitative studies conducted with three reviewers at Tokyo University of Agriculture and Technology during spring term 2009.

In order to determine any differences in identifying educational events in use of FD Commons, the novice teachers and faculty developer comments are compared on three main "perspectives" in Version 3 and one perspective including basic teaching skill factors, which are usually recorded and checked in end-of-term questionnaire. The following two research questions were investigated in this pilot studies.

1) By using a pen-based device, do reviewers write more comments and mark more points on class lecture videos, in comparison with the usual end-of-term questionnaire?
2) Are there any differences in comments made by novice teachers and the faculty developer when using FD Commons?

3.3 Participants

In the pilot studies, we investigated the effects and operability of the peer review system on three reviewers. All were faculty members at Tokyo University of Agriculture and Technology. One teacher (Reviewer A) was an instructional designer from our Educational Development Center (faculty developer) and has experienced "lesson study" at another university. The other two teachers were academic staff specializing in Biology (Reviewer B) and Physics (Reviewer C). Both reviewers were in charge of conducting a Good Practice Project (GP) supported by Japanese Ministry of Education, Culture, Sports, Science and Technology. In each trial, two reviewers took note of the contextual focus on the lesson and recorded the sequence of activities during lesson study in use of FD Commons.

In total, five trials were conducted from April to June 2009, as shown in Table 1. Regarding research the second question, Reviewer B and C were assigned to novice teachers group with respect to their teaching experience.

Table 1. Pilot Study of FD Commons

	Date	Class	Class Size (level)	Reviewer A (Teaching Experience)	Reviewer B&C (Teaching Experience)
1	April 28, 2009	Plant Physiology	80 students (Undergraduate)	Instructional Design (15 Yrs)	Biology (1 Yr)
2	May 18, 2009	Vegetation Management	90 students (Undergraduate)	Instructional Design (15 Yrs)	Physics (3 Yrs)
3	May 20, 2009	Plant Physiology	70 students (Undergraduate)	Instructional Design (15 Yrs)	Biology (1 Yr)
4	May 25, 2009	Vegetation Management	90 students (Undergraduate)	Instructional Design (15 Yrs)	Biology (1 Yr)
5	June 10, 2009	Plant Physiology	70 students (Undergraduate)	Instructional Design (15 Yrs)	Biology (1 Yr)

3.4 Data Source and Analysis

To answer the research questions, "by using a pen-based device, do reviewers write more comments and mark more points on class lecture videos, in comparison with the usual end-of-term questionnaire? " and "are there any differences in comments made by novice teachers and the faculty developer when using FD Commons? ", we used the content analysis approach. To measure the differences between evaluation instruments or reviewers' use of FD Commons, "Snap Shots" data from different sessions of the same class (Plant Physiology) were collected on April 28, May 20, and June 10. Based on the types of comments, each "Snap Shot" was classified into one of four categories: interaction, content, methodology, and basic teaching skills as shown in Table 2.

The first three categories were designed as stamps of previous FD Commons [12]-[15]. These three "perspectives", interaction, content, and methodology, need to be drawn on to record the properties of educational events adequately and clearly during the review of class lectures [16]. According to Hirayama's categories for qualitative class analysis, these three perspectives (interaction, content, and methodology) are called as "high inference items" because of the reviewer's insights and experiences. One additional category was used to check basic teaching skills, including oral presentation, writing on the blackboard, and lecture pace added in Version 3. These perspectives on basic teaching skills were used to collect student feedback on the effectiveness of the course and teachers as part of the usual end-of-term questionnaire. Hirayama [16] called it "low inference item", because it is transparent and easily identified by reviewers.

Table 2. Observation Guideline: Categories of Leaning Events

Categories	
Interaction (High Inference Items)	Students' and teacher social behavior, student participation etc.
Content (High Inference Items)	Students' understanding of content, levels, validation, and variation of content
Methodology (High Inference Items)	Levels, validation, and variation of methodology, student motivation
Basic Skills (Low Inference Items)	Basic lecture skills (oral presentation, writing on the blackboard, and lecture pace)

To address the first research question, we used content analysis approach to investigate the difference between reviewers' comments and student survey results. The total number of "Snap Shots" was 255. As shown in Table 3, 37.6% of the recorded comments on "Snap Shots" were related to lecture content and 29.0% related to the interaction between teacher and students during class activities. Only 12.2% mentioned basic teaching skills, which are usually covered by end-of-term questionnaires. The results indicated that use of FD Commons promoted more variation of comments than student evaluation survey.

Table 3. Comments on Class Lectures by Four Categories

	Interaction between teacher and students (%)	Lecture content (%)	Methodology (%)	Basic teaching skills (Voice, Writing, Pace) (%)	Total (%)
All reviewers	74 (29.0)	96 (37.6)	54 (21.2)	31 (12.2)	255 (100.0)

Regarding the second research question, the data were analyzed using Chi-square contingency table tests. There was a significant difference between the faculty developer and novice teachers in how they evaluated class lectures ($\chi^2 = 14.13$, d.f. =3, p< .01). As shown in Table 4, residual analysis showed a significant difference with respect to the categories of "Lecture content" and "Methodology" (p< .01). No significant difference was found for the "Interaction" and "Basic teaching skills" categories.

The results indicated that a faculty developer (Reviewer A) is more likely than novice teachers to report comments regarding methodology. Novice teachers (Reviewers B & C) are more likely to focus on lecture content.

Table 4. Comments on Class Review by Category

	Interaction between teacher and students (%)	Lecture content (%)	Methodology (%)	Basic teaching skills (Voice, Writing, Pace) (%)	Total (%)
FD	45 (40.3)	39** (52.3)	38** (29.5)	17 (16.9)	139 (100.0)
Novice	29 (33.7)	57** (43.7)	16** (24.5)	14 (14.1)	116 (100.0)
	74	96	54	31	255

**p<. 01, Expected value (in parentheses).

3.5 Lecturers' Self-reflection toward Reviewers' Comments

With respect to reviewers' comment on FD Commons, we got the following comments form the lecturers during the lesson study following class observation:

1) Reviewer B, recommended on the weak and strong points of my lecture. Especially, as keywords for my self-reflection in preparing my next class lecture, I used his comments on content rather than pedagogical issues. He likely has the similar viewpoint as students because he just finished his Ph.D. course and knows the content well. (Professor, Plant Physiology as lecturer)

2) Unintentionally, I checked green stamps (for positive points) for class observation. One of the reviewers used stamps with regard to basic skills many times during the class reviewing. I think the faculty developer made comments from the viewpoints of students' understanding. (Professor, Vegetation Management as lecturer).

4 Conclusions

In this study, we reported on ongoing system development and five evaluation studies for investigating the usability and effects of FD Commons. We endeavored to determine whether FD Commons can record and restore the useful comments for educational improvement. Specifically, we examined differences between student survey and FD Commons in identification of educational events. The results indicate that greater variation in comments was found when FD Commons was used. More importantly, this finding also suggested that the use of FD Commons might promote more variation in comments than student evaluation surveys.

Second, we examined the differences between novice teachers and faculty developer in identifying educational events when using of FD Commons. The content analysis of "Snap Shots" suggested a significant difference in the "Property of lecture content" and "Methodology" categories. The results indicate that FD Commons is capable of suggesting weak and strong points in class lectures as qualitative feedback from different reviewers' perspectives. When using FD Commons, more details of class lecture may be analyzed and discussed by peer faculty and student monitors, which contributes to an understanding of teacher performance, best practice, and student learning in higher education.

As with any other research, the limitation of our work should be noted. The first limitation of the study was the small quantity of data being analyzed. This is due to the fact that we discontinued the FD Commons (Version 3) based on evaluation studies. Now we have developed FD Commons on WEB, and plan to conduct new evaluation studies. Further studies with lager sizes would be useful to verify our findings.

In future studies, we will develop a database of reviewer annotations as teaching portfolios capable of reusing collected comments to design a rubric to evaluate lectures as an e-teaching portfolio. The collected annotations are used to suggest weak and strong points of class lectures for teaching/learning evaluation. When using FD Commons in our institution, we hope to construct "Teaching Commons," a community of educators and student mentors committed to pedagogical inquiry and innovation.

Acknowledgments. This work has been partly supported by Microsoft Research Asia (MSRA) under Mobile Computing in Education Theme, Innovation Based on Recognition Research Platform. I wish to thank the following individuals: Mr. Soutaro Houri, Dr. Hironori Egi, Dr. Wataru Tsukahara, and Prof. Masaki Nakagawa. The next evaluation step will be supported by the CASIO Science Promotion Foundation and GP project (SEED Program) at TUAT. More information about this project can be found online at: http://www.tuat.ac.jp/~fd_tools. Information about the GP project can be found online at: http://www.tuat.ac.jp/~seed/index.html

References

1. Wenger, E.: Community of practice: Learning, meaning, and identity. Cambridge University Press, Cambridge (1999)
2. Huber, M.T., Hutchings, P.: The Advancement of Leaning. Jossey-Bass, San Francisco (2005)
3. Shank, M.J.: Teacher storytelling: A means for creating and learning within a collaborative space. Teaching and Teacher Education 22, 711–721 (2006)
4. Fernandez, C., Yoshida, M.: Lesson Study. In: Cambridge, B.L. (ed.) Campus Progress. Washington DC, AAHE. Lawrence, New Jersey (2004)
5. Lieberman, A., Miller, L.: Professional development of teachers. In: Alkin, M. (ed.) Encyclopedia of educational research, 6th edn., vol. 3, pp. 1045–1053. Macmillan, New York (1992)
6. Cambridge, B.L. (ed.): Campus Progress. AAHE, Washington (2004)
7. Hatch, T.: A fantasy in teaching and learning: Imaging a future for on-line teaching portfolio. Presented at the American Educational Research Association, New Orleans, LA (2000), http://gallery.carnegiefoundation.org/collections/castl_he/thatch/fantasyintchandlearn.pdf (2010.1.16)
8. Seldin, P.: The Teaching portfolio (3rd). Anker Publishing Company, Boston (2004)
9. Kahn, S.: Making good work public through electronic teaching portfolio. In: Seldin, P. (ed.) The Teaching portfolio (3rd), pp. 36–50. Anker Publishing Company, Boston (2004)

10. Boyer, E.: Scholarship Reconsidered, Princeton, NJ (1990)
11. Fishman, B.J., Davis, E.A.: Teacher learning research and the learning sciences. In: Sawyer, R.K. (ed.) The Cambridge Handbook of the Learning Sciences, pp. 535–550. Cambridge University Press, New York (2006)
12. Kato, Y., Egi, H., Tsukahara, W., Nakagawa, M.: E-Teaching portfolio for ubiquitous peer reviewing to improve the quality of class lectures. In: Proc. of the 33rd Annual Conference of Japanese Society for Information and System in Education, pp. 398–399 (2008)
13. Houri, S., Terada, T., Kato, Y., Egi, H., Tsukahara, W., Nakagawa, M.: A peer review system on lecture with handwritten annotation, Technical Report of IECE, pp. 17–22 (2008)
14. Kato, Y., Houri, S., Tsukahara, W., Egi, H., Nakagawa, M.: E-Teaching Portfolio to Enable an Ubiquitous Peer Reviewing Process. In: Proc. of ICALT, pp. 334–336 (2009a)
15. Kato, Y., Houri, S., Egi, H., Tsukahara, W., Nakagawa, M.: E-Teaching Portfolio to Realize Ubiquitous Peer Reviewing Process in Higher Education. International Journal for Educational Media and Technology 3, 81–91 (2009b)
16. Hirayama, M.: Lesson Study by Qualitative Method, Kitaoji Shobo, Kyoto (1997)

Using Problem-Solving Context to Assess Help Quality in Computer-Mediated Peer Tutoring

Erin Walker[1], Sean Walker[1], Nikol Rummel[2], and Kenneth R. Koedinger[1]

[1] Human-Computer Interaction Institute, Carnegie Mellon University, USA
[2] Institute of Psychology, University of Freiburg, Germany
erinwalk@andrew.cmu.edu, walker.sean.m@gmail.com,
rummel@psychologie.uni-freiburg.de, koedinger@cmu.edu

Abstract. Collaborative activities, like peer tutoring, can be beneficial for student learning, but only when students are supported in interacting effectively. Constructing intelligent tutors for collaborating students may be an improvement over fixed forms of support that do not adapt to student behaviors. We have developed an intelligent tutor to improve the help that peer tutors give to peer tutees by encouraging them to explain tutee errors and to provide more conceptual help. The intelligent tutor must be able to classify the type of peer tutor utterance (is it next step help, error feedback, both, or neither?) and the quality (does it contain conceptual content?). We use two techniques to improve automated classification of student utterances: incorporating domain context, and incorporating students' self-classifications of their chat actions. The domain context and self-classifications together significantly improve classification of student dialogue over a baseline classifier for help type. Using domain features alone significantly improves classification over baseline for conceptual content.

Keywords: intelligent tutoring, computer-supported collaborative learning, adaptive collaborative learning systems, peer tutoring.

1 Introduction

Student participation in online collaborative classroom activities can increase both group performance and individual learning outcomes. However, these positive effects are not always found [1], in part because when left to their own devices students may not interact in ways that lead them to benefit from collaboration. One common technique for improving computer-mediated collaborative interaction is *scripting*, where the collaboration is structured so that students take on particular roles and go through designated phases in order to increase the effectiveness of their collaboration [see 2 for review]. Although scripts have been shown to be effective, they have been criticized for over-structuring the collaboration for some students, decreasing these students' motivation, while under-structuring the collaboration for others, failing to provide them with sufficient support [3]. It has been theorized that an intelligent tutor for collaboration that is responsive to student needs and to the current interaction state might be more effective [4], and, in fact, adaptive support for collaboration has been demonstrated to be an improvement over no support and fixed support at increasing learning [5, 6]. Despite these potential advantages, intelligent tutoring for collaborative learning is still at an early phase, and few classroom-ready systems have been developed and evaluated.

A key component of improving collaborative interactions is supporting students in conducting productive dialogues. Thus, developing mechanisms for assessing student dialogues has been a focus of research in this area. One way of assessing student dialogue is through *self-classification*, where students are asked to indicate the type of statement that they are making before or after they compose it. For example, students may select a sentence starter like "We need to work together on this..." to begin their utterance. Based on the starters that students select, the system can make inferences about what students are saying, and use these inferences to provide feedback [e.g., 7]. However, students do not consistently select sentence starters or classifiers that match the content of their utterances, and therefore the inferences that the system makes based on those labels can be inaccurate [8]. Consequently, researchers have been moving towards using *machine classification* to assess student dialogue as it occurs in order to provide students with assistance. So far this technology has been used in limited ways in intelligent tutoring for collaborative learning; for instance, for classifying the topic of conversation [6], or for assessing student accuracy when they use sentence starters [8]. As the quality of student dialogue contributes to how students benefit from collaboration, improving our ability to automatically classify student utterances would increase our ability to target support to those utterances.

We have developed an intelligent tutor for collaborative learning by extending the Cognitive Tutor Algebra, an existing successful intelligent tutoring system, to support two students of similar abilities in tutoring each other in algebra. Within the context of providing intelligent support for peer tutoring, we explore two different approaches for improving the accuracy of dialogue classification: incorporating information about the domain context, and incorporating student self-classifications. Firstly, we use information about the domain context of the interaction as additional features for a machine learning classifier. This context includes information directly taken from the students' problem-solving behavior (e.g., a student has just taken a incorrect step in the problem), information about how student dialogue relates to the problem-solving context (e.g., a student has referred to another student's incorrect step), and information about the history of the interaction (e.g., a student has referred to another student's incorrect steps 10 times over the course of the whole interaction). There is a precedent for this approach: The few adaptive collaborative learning systems that have used domain information have shown gains both in the variety of support that those systems provide and in the effects of support [e.g., 9], but they have not applied these models to the classification of collaborative dialogue. However, this approach has been applied successfully in asynchronous collaborative contexts [10], and domain features have been successfully used to enhance the ability of automatic classifiers in other fields [e.g., 11]. Secondly, we use student self-classifications of their own chat dialogue as a potential feature for improving the accuracy of the machine classifier. As described above, it is common in adaptive collaborative learning systems to ask students to classify their own utterances. While these classifications are not always accurate, they may still be relevant for assisting the machine classifier in labeling the utterance.

In this paper, we explore how incorporating information on the domain context and self-classification features might improve the classification of peer tutor dialogue. We describe the details of our collaborative learning system, the model of peer tutoring that we are trying to support, and our data collection procedure. We then describe the classification approaches we compare: baseline classification of student dialogue based solely on text features (*B*), baseline classification with additional domain features (*B+D*), baseline classification with additional self-classification features (*B+SC*), and baseline with problem-solving and self-classification features (*B+D+SC*). We discuss the results of comparing the classifiers and their implications.

2 Context

We attempt to automatically classify student dialogue within the context of an intelligent tutoring system for reciprocal peer tutoring, called APTA (the Adaptive Peer Tutoring Assistant). APTA provides an interface for one student to tutor another student on algebra problems, and then provides the peer tutor with assistance on how to be a better tutor. To do so, APTA maintains a model of good peer tutoring and compares student actions to the model. Accurately assessing the quality of student chat actions enables this comparison to be made and effective assistance to be given. In the following section, we describe the functionality of APTA in more detail, to make it clear which aspects of student dialogue we are trying to assess and why.

2.1 APTA: Adaptive Peer Tutoring Assistant

Reciprocal peer tutoring is a collaborative learning activity where two students of similar abilities take turns tutoring each other. It has been shown to improve student learning over unscripted collaboration and individual learning [12], and is an effective intervention even for low-ability students [13]. We have constructed a peer tutoring addition to the Cognitive Tutor Algebra (CTA), a successful intelligent tutoring system for high school mathematics [14]. In our peer tutoring script, students are given a task like "Solve for x," for an equation like "ax + by = c." Students go through two phases: a preparation phase and a collaboration phase. In the *preparation phase*, peer tutors solve problems using the CTA, receiving hints and error feedback when necessary. During the *collaboration phase*, students are grouped into pairs and collaborate at different computers, taking turns being peer tutors and peer tutees. Peer tutees solve the same problems as their tutor solved in the preparation phase, using the same equation solver interface. Peer tutors can see their peer tutee's actions, but cannot solve the problem themselves. Instead, they can mark the peer tutee's actions right or wrong, and interact with the tutee in a chat tool, where they can give help and feedback. We augmented the chat tool with sentence classifiers, asking peer tutors to label their utterances as a prompt ("asks for explanation"), error feedback ("explains why wrong"), a hint ("gives hint"), or an explanation ("explains next step"). Peer tutors had to select a classifier before they typed in an utterance, but they could also choose to click a neutral classifier ("comments").

As most students are novice tutors and need support to collaborate effectively, they receive two different types of assistance from the system as part of the script (see Figure 1). First, we have augmented the script with adaptive *domain support* for the peer tutor. If the peer tutor marks a correct tutee action wrong in the interface, or an incorrect action right, the cognitive tutor will intervene by indicating that the step was marked incorrectly, and providing feedback on what to do next. The peer tutor can also request a domain hint from the cognitive tutor at any time. Second, we augmented the script with adaptive *interaction support* for the peer tutor. This support primarily takes the form of reflective prompts delivered to both students in the chat window such as, "Tutor, you might want to explain that further", and "Tutee, did you understand what the tutor just said?" For these prompts to be effective, they must contain relevant information and be presented at moments when the peer tutor can apply them to the interaction. Therefore, we maintain both a model of good peer tutoring and a running assessment of the actual quality of the students' tutoring.

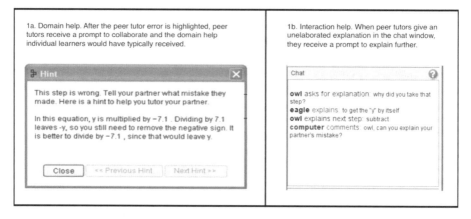

Fig. 1. Two forms of assistance in the Adaptive Peer Tutoring Assistant (APTA). Peer tutors are provided with domain support and interaction support.

2.2 Modeling Reciprocal Peer Tutoring

To provide support for the peer tutor role in reciprocal peer tutoring, we have constructed a production-rule model for peer tutor help-giving. Our production rule model focuses on three help-giving skills, derived from the following research. Tutors have been found to benefit from the tutoring activity by reflecting on their existing knowledge as they observe tutee problem-solving steps and errors, and then constructing new knowledge as they compose explanations [15]. In order for tutees to benefit from the activity, peer tutor help should be given at impasses, should target tutee level of understanding, should explain errors, should provide assistance for the next-step, and should be conceptual & elaborated [16]. The first skill in our model prescribes that the peer tutor should give help when needed, which we operationalize as giving help after tutee help requests and errors, but not after correct steps (*S1: Help When Needed*). The second skill prescribes that the peer tutor should give relevant help for the tutee's specific needs. For example, after a tutee error, the peer tutor should respond by prompting tutees to self-explain and then, if necessary, explaining the tutee mistake (*S2: Appropriate Help*). Finally, the peer tutor should explain the rationale behind problem-solving steps, rather than simply saying what to do. In particular, when peer tutors give help on the next step, they are expected to use hints and explanations that reference relevant domain concepts (*S3: Conceptual Help*).

We assess these collaboration skills using Bayesian knowledge tracing, and provide feedback based on the assessment [17]. In order to determine whether peer tutors are displaying the above three skills, we need to classify two aspects of the help peer tutors give in their dialogue with tutees:

1. *Help type.* Are peer tutors giving next-step help, error feedback, both, or no help at all? Using the classified help type in conjunction with the problem-solving context (e.g., knowing whether the tutee has just made a correct step, incorrect step, or help request) can help us decide whether tutors are giving the appropriate kind of help (*S2*) when it is needed (*S1*).
2. *Conceptual content.* Are peer tutors giving help that explains concepts rather than simply stating what to do next? Being able to identify this aspect lets us know whether tutors are providing enough conceptual help (*S3*).

By accurately classifying these aspects of student dialogue, we can develop intelligent support for peer tutoring that enables us to improve peer tutor performance on the above three help-giving skills.

2.3 Corpus and Data Coding

We used a corpus drawn from a classroom study we conducted comparing adaptive support for peer tutoring to fixed support for peer tutoring. As part of the study, students participated in two supported peer tutoring sessions; one in which they acted as the tutor, and one in which they acted as the tutee. We have a total of 84 tutoring sessions from both conditions, consisting of an average of 21.77 tutor lines of dialogue per session (SD = 10.25). Two raters coded tutor utterances for help type and conceptual content. We computed interrater reliability on 20% of the data, and the remainder of the data was coded by one rater and checked by the second. All disagreements were resolved through discussion. We segmented the dialog by chat messages, creating a new segment every time students hit enter. First, each help segment was coded for help type by determining whether it consisted of *previous-step help* relating to an action tutees had already taken (e.g., "no need to factor because there is only one g"; kappa = 0.83), and whether it consisted of *next-step help* relating to a future action in the problem (e.g., "how would you get rid of $2h$?"; kappa = 0.83). If the help segment contained both categories, its help type was labeled "both", and if it contained neither category (e.g., "on to the next problem"), its help type was labeled "none". Second, each help segment was coded for whether it contained a concept (e.g., "add ax" was purely instrumental help, while "add ax to cancel out the $-ax$" was conceptual). Kappa for conceptual help was 0.72. In our dataset, 935 tutor instances were coded as "none", 764 were coded as "next-step help", 83 were coded as "previous-step help", and 47 were coded as "both"; 1654 instances were coded as non-conceptual help, and 165 were coded as conceptual help.

3 Method

3.1 Baseline Classification

We generated baseline machine classifiers for *help type* and *conceptual content* using Taghelper Tools, state of the art text-classification technology designed for coding collaborative dialogue [18]. Taghelper automatically extracts several dialogue features for use in machine classification, including unigrams, bigrams, line length, and punctuation. In our dataset, Taghelper generated 641 features. We used a chi-squared feature selection algorithm to rank the most predictive features, and selected 150 features for help type and 125 features for conceptual content. We used 10-fold cross validation to train a support vector machine classifier for each dimension.

3.2 Incorporating Domain Features

We augmented the dialogue features generated by Taghelper with domain context features. After assembling the problem-solving context, text substitution, and history features described below, we again used a chi-squared feature selection algorithm to rank the most predictive features. We used 10-fold cross validation to train a support vector machine classifier for help type and conceptual content.

Problem-Solving Context. In general, features describing the tutee's problem-solving progress may provide information about the type and quality of the help peer tutors tend to give (e.g., peer tutors may be more likely to give error feedback after the tutee has made an error). Thus, we added a total of 10 features for the classifier, created using information from the CTA models of student problem-solving. This information included whether the last step taken on the problem was correct or incorrect, the student's progress in the problem (i.e. the number of correct, incorrect, and total steps taken), and the student's problem-solving momentum (e.g. the number of incorrect steps the student had made in a row).

Text Substitutions. We then added features representing whether peer tutors *referred* to problem-solving elements in their utterances (e.g., "subtract x" refers to a specific problem-solving action). By treating different references to the problem as members of a higher-level category, we can compensate for a lack of training data and enable the classifier to transfer between different units of the problem. More specifically, we extracted a list of problem-related actions from the CTA menu options that tutees were able to select in the unit (e.g., {factor, distribute, add, subtract}), and a list of problem-related variables from the problem-statement (e.g., $x = a + b$ would return $\{x,a,b\}$). We then substituted specific occurrences of a problem-related action or term in the text with general terms (see the "Substituted Text" column in Table 1), and used the new text as input into Taghelper. We also added a feature that indicated that a substitution had been made ("Action Present" and "Term Present" in Table 1).

Further, by tracking which specific aspects of the problem tutee utterances referred to, we hoped to be able to better identify the target of the help given by the peer tutor. Thus, we added a feature representing whether the substituted terms referred to the tutee's last correct step or last incorrect step (e.g., in the second row of Table 1, "add x to the left side" sets the Term Present feature to "last-correct", indicating that there is a term in the problem which refers to the last correct step). We also made substitutions based on whether peer tutors referenced terms that appeared in the problem-solving hints generated by the cognitive tutor. We created a list of verbs and nouns found in the hints, and then substituted a generic "concept" word for these words (as in the third row of Table 1). We added an additional feature representing whether a concept term had been substituted. Finally, we created substitution features to indicate whether multiple substitutions of the different types had occurred. The presence of multiple substitutions in an utterance makes it more likely that a reference to the problem actually occurred. This approach emphasized those utterances where multiple substitutions were done, while deemphasizing utterances where only a single substitution took place. Overall, we added 7 text substitution features.

Table 1. Selected features created from particular tutor utterances. If the tutee's last action was "factor x", and this action was correct, the following are the substitutions that would be made.

Chat Text	Substituted Text	Action Present	Term Present	Term-Concept Present	Action-Term Present
now factor	now action	last-correct	no	no	no
add x to the left side	action term to the left side	yes	last-correct	no	yes
isolate the p	concept the term	no	yes	yes	no

Substitution History. Finally, we added 6 history features in an attempt to provide holistic information about the overall quality of the interaction. The history features were based on the numbers of each type of substitution made; features were created for what percent of the peer tutor's total number of utterances referred to a concept, what percent referred to a correct or incorrect action, and what percent referred to a correct or incorrect term. We also included a simple yes/no feature as to whether or not a substitution of a specific type was made at any point, under the rationale that somebody who has given a certain kind of help in the past would be more likely to give that kind of help in the future. All history features were updated with each tutor utterance; that is, history features were only computed based on all utterances that had occurred *prior* to the current utterance, so that the algorithm could be applied to a learning situation as it unfolds. We based the history features on the substitutions rather than on the machine classifications to avoid being stuck in a state where, for example, because the machine has not yet classified an utterance as conceptual help, it is likely to never classify an utterance as conceptual help.

3.4 Adding Self-classification

In addition to creating domain features, we also added two features that involved students' self-classification of their actions. As described in Section 2, before composing an utterance peer tutors were asked to label their utterance as a prompt, error feedback, a hint, an explanation, or a comment. The label selected by the peer tutor, as well as their overall use of sentence classifiers, may be predictive of the type of help the peer tutor gave in a particular utterance. We added the self-classification specified by the tutor and the number of non-comment sentence classifiers used by the tutor in total as features in the machine classification.

4 Results

We hypothesized that both the domain features (B+D) and the self-classification (B+SC) would lead to an improvement over the baseline classification (B), with a classifier containing all three sets of features being the most effective (B+D+SC). We compared Cohen's kappa for all classifiers in the Weka Experimenter using 10 repetitions of 10-fold cross-validation (see Table 2) [19]. We use kappa instead of percent accuracy due to the imbalanced frequency distribution between categories (for example, there was over 10 times more non-conceptual help utterances than conceptual help utterances). Weka uses paired t-tests corrected for dependence between samples to compare classifiers. For help type, B+D+SC was significantly better than the B classifiers ($p < .05$). For conceptual help, only B+D was significantly better than baseline ($p < .05$). It is encouraging that the help type kappa for BS+D+SC approached the kappa we achieved for human interrater reliability, and that the conceptual help kappa improved substantially between the B and B+D.

Table 2. Kappas for the baseline (B), baseline plus self-classification (B+SC), baseline plus domain (B+D), and baseline plus self-classification plus domain feature sets (B+D+SC). Kappas are reported for both the help type and conceptual help classifications.

Classifier	Help Type Kappa M	SD	Conceptual Help Kappa M	SD
B	.78	.04	.59	.10
B + SC	.78	.04	.60	.10
B + D	.80	.04	.66*	.10
B + D + SC	.81*	.04	.65	.11

Examining which features were ranked highly by the chi-squared feature selection algorithm for the B+D+SC feature set, we can see that our domain context features consisted of 7 of the top 10 features for the help type classification, and 7 of the top 10 features for the conceptual help classification (see Table 3). In addition, one highly ranked feature for help type was the sentence classifier used, part of the SC feature set. Overall, for the help type classifier, only 3 of the domain context features created were not selected to be part of the machine classifier, and 2 of these features related to the number of correct steps that had recently been taken by the tutee. It is interesting that while incorrect problem-solving actions appeared somewhat predictive of the type of help given, correct problem-solving actions did not. This result makes sense, as it is more likely that tutors would refer to a previous incorrect step than to a previous correct step. For the conceptual help classifier, 14 of the 25 conceptual help features were not selected, suggesting that conceptual help classification is less dependent on domain context.

Table 3. The top ten ranked features in chi-squared feature selection for help type and conceptual help for the baseline plus problem-solving plus self-classification feature set

Rank	Help Type Kappa	Conceptual Help Kappa
1	action present	concept present
2	"action"	"concept"
3	term present	concept & term present
4	"term"	"concept_term"
5	"BOL_action"	line length
6	action & term present	"you_concept"
7	classifier used	percent concepts used
8	"term_EOL"	"how_do"
9	"BOL_undo"	"you"
10	"undo"	"term_by"

5 Conclusion

The focus of this paper was to increase the accuracy of automated classification of peer tutor utterances in order to improve the ability of an intelligent tutoring system for peer tutoring to provide appropriate support. To do so, we explored the use of domain context features, extracted from individual domain models found in the Cognitive Tutor Algebra, as input into dialogue classifiers to augment automatically extracted text features. We also examined whether student self-classifications of their own utterances might improve the machine classification. We found that domain context features in combination with self-classifications significantly improved the accuracy of an automated classifier with respect to help type, but only domain context improved the accuracy of conceptual content classification.

We incorporated three different types of domain context features into the machine classifier: problem-solving context, text substitutions, and substitution history. Of those features, relevant text substitution and substitution history features were highly related to the machine classification for each dimension; for example, substitutions of references to tutee actions were highly predictive of help type, while substitutions of references to concepts were highly predictive of conceptual help. In contrast, self-classifications were less effective; they appeared to augment the results of the help-type classifications, but inhibit the results of the conceptual help classification. This result is not unexpected, as the self-classifications that students made were far more relevant to the help type dimension than to the conceptual help dimension. Perhaps student self-classifications that were more related to whether the utterance included conceptual help would have a positive effect on a conceptual help classifier.

These results make the argument for an emphasis on designing adaptive support for collaboration that is rooted in problem-solving context. If domain context information can improve the accuracy of automated collaborative dialogue classification, it would make sense for intelligent tutoring systems for collaborative learning to incorporate domain models. While domain models are difficult to build from scratch, integrating adaptive collaborative learning systems with existing individual intelligent tutoring systems may be a way to leverage sophisticated domain information in order to improve the effectiveness of intelligent tutoring for collaborative learning.

Acknowledgments. This research is supported by the Pittsburgh Science of Learning Center, NSF Grant #SBE-0836012. Thanks to Carolyn Rose, Ruth Wylie, & Amy Ogan.

References

1. Lou, Y., Abrami, P.C., d'Apollonia, S.: Small group and individual learning with technology: A meta-analysis. R. of Ed. Res. 71(3), 449–521 (2001)
2. Kollar, I., Fischer, F., Hesse, F.W.: Computer-supported collaboration scripts – a conceptual analysis. Ed. Psych. Review 18(2), 159–185 (2006)
3. Dillenbourg, P.: Over-scripting CSCL: The risks of blending collaborative learning with instructional design. In: Kirschner, P.A. (ed.) Three worlds of CSCL. Can we support CSCL, pp. 61–91. Open Univeriteit Nederland, Heerlen (2002)
4. Rummel, N., Weinberger, A.: New challenges in CSCL: Towards adaptive script support. In: Kanselaar, G., Jonker, V., Kirschner, P.A., Prins, F. (eds.) International perspectives of the learning sciences: Cre8ing a learning world. Proceedings of the Eighth International Conference of the Learning Sciences (ICLS 2008). ISLS, vol. 3, pp. 338–345 (2008)
5. Gweon, G., Rosé, C., Carey, R., Zaiss, Z.: Providing support for adaptive scripting in an on-line collaborative learning environment. In: Proc. of SIGCHI Conference on Human Factors in Computing Systems, pp. 251–260. ACM Press, New York (2006)
6. Kumar, R., Rosé, C.P., Wang, Y.C., Joshi, M., Robinson, A.: Tutorial dialogue as adaptive collaborative learning support. In: Luckin, R., Koedinger, K.R., Greer, J. (eds.) Proceedings of AIED 2007, pp. 383–390. IOS Press, Amsterdam (2007)
7. Tedesco, P.: MArCo: Building an artificial conflict mediator to support group planning interactions. IJAIED 13(1), 117–155 (2003)
8. Israel, J., Aiken, R.: Supporting collaborative learning with an intelligent web-based system. IJAIED 17(1), 3–40 (2007)
9. Baghaei, N., Mitrovic, T., Irwin, W.: Supporting Collaborative Learning and Problem Solving in a Constraint-based CSCL Environment for UML Class Diagrams. IJCSCL 2(2-3), 159–190 (2007)
10. Wang, Y.C., Joshi, M., Rosé, C.P., Fischer, F., Weinberger, A., Stegmann, K.: Context Based Classification for Automatic Collaborative Learning Process Analysis. In: Poster in AIED 2007 (2007)
11. Dybowski, R., Laskey, K.B., Myers, J.W., Parsons, S.: Introduction to the Special Issue on the Fusion of Domain Knowledge and Data for Decision Support. J. of Machine Learning Research 4, 293–294 (2003)
12. Fantuzzo, J.W., Riggio, R.E., Connelly, S., Dimeff, L.A.: Effects of reciprocal peer tutoring on academic achievement and psychological adjustment: A component analysis. Journal of Educational Psychology 81(2), 173–177 (1989)
13. Robinson, D.R., Schofield, J.W., Steers-Wentzell, K.L.: Peer and Cross-age Tutoring in Math: Outcomes and Their Design Implications. Educational Psychology 17, 327–361 (2005)

14. Koedinger, K., Anderson, J., Hadley, W., Mark, M.: Intelligent tutoring goes to school in the big city. IJAIED 8, 30–43 (1997)
15. Roscoe, R.D., Chi, M.: Understanding tutor learning: Knowledge-building and knowledge-telling in peer tutors' explanations and questions. R. of Ed. Res. 77(4), 534–574 (2007)
16. Webb, N.M.: Peer interaction and learning in small groups. I. J. of Ed. Res. 13, 21–39 (1989)
17. Beck, J., Sison, J.: Using Knowledge Tracing in a Noisy Environment to Measure Student Reading Proficiencies. IJAIED 16(2), 129–143 (2006)
18. Rosé, C.P., Wang, Y.C., Cui, Y., Arguello, J., Fischer, F., Weinberger, A., Stegmann, K.: Analyzing Collaborative Learning Processes Automatically: Exploiting the Advances of Computational Linguistics in Computer-Supported Collaborative Learning. IJCSCL (to appear)
19. Hall, M., Frank, E., Holmes, G., Pfahringer, B., Reutemann, P., Witten, I.H.: The WEKA Data Mining Software: An Update. SIGKDD Explorations 11(1) (2009)

Socially Capable Conversational Tutors Can Be Effective in Collaborative Learning Situations

Rohit Kumar[1], Hua Ai[1], Jack L. Beuth[2], and Carolyn P. Rosé[1]

[1] Language Technologies Institute, [2] Department of Mechanical Engineering,
Carnegie Mellon University
5000 Forbes Avenue, Pittsburgh, Pennsylvania 15213
{rohitk,huaai,beuth,cp3a}@andrew.cmu.edu

Abstract. Tutorial Dialog has been shown to be effective in supporting both individual as well as group learners. However, unlike the case with individual learners, teams of learners often ignore and abuse the automated tutors. Both theory and empirical work in the area of small group communication argue that group participants display both task as well as socio-emotional behaviors during interactions. However, in connection with automated conversational agents, the effects of socio-emotional behaviors are much less well understood, especially in the case of multi-party interactions. In this paper, we will describe an evaluation of a socially capable conversational tutor that supports teams of three (or more) learners in a design task. This tutor is evaluated in comparison with a socially neutral baseline agent and human capability "gold standard" tutors demonstrating that the socially capable tutor achieves significantly higher learning gains than the neutral, purely task focused tutor and learning gains not significantly different from the human capability "gold standard" tutors.

Keywords: social interaction, tutorial dialog, conversational agents, collaborative learning, small group communication.

1 Introduction

Conversational Tutors are autonomous agents that interact with users via spoken or written conversation. Automated tutoring is a widely studied application of language technologies to education. Conversational tutors have been developed for a variety of educational domains including algebra, calculus, computer literacy, engineering, foreign languages, geometry, physics, reading and research methods. Numerous evaluations show that these tutors can be effective support for learners [1][2][3].

While most of the work on conversational tutors has focused on one-on-one tutoring involving only one learner, use of such tutors in collaborative learning situations involving two or more human students has been investigated. Our previous work [2] has shown that tutors in a collaborative learning situations can lead to over one letter grade improvement. Other work [4][5][6][7] has explored a variety of interaction patterns / tactics that can be used in multi-party educational situations.

However, despite the effective support that automated tutors offer to students learning in groups, it has been reported that groups of students often ignore and abuse the tutor, unlike the case where students are individually tutored [2][8]. We reason that the presence of other students in collaborative learning scenarios causes the tutors to compete for the attention of the students. Since the tutors do not participate in social interaction that makes up the bulk of formative interaction in the group, they are pushed to the periphery of the learning group.

Research in the area of small group communication has shown that humans employ both task related strategies as well as social interaction strategies while interacting in groups. However, research on conversational tutors has focused on presenting only task related information, i.e., lessons and instructions in case of tutors. In this paper we report the first study in our investigation on the effects that conversational agents in general can achieve if they are equipped with social conversational skills.

The rest of the paper is organized as follows: In the next section, we motivate social interaction strategies for agents based on relevant literature from small group communication research. Section 3 describes our flexible architecture and implementation details for a tutor with social conversational skills. Results from the evaluation of the tutor against a baseline as well as human tutors are presented in section 4, and then we conclude with a discussion of current directions.

2 Small Group Communication

Theoretical and empirical study of group interaction processes has been of interest in sociology and communications research communities since the 1950's. McGrath [9] reviews various theories that address the functions of group interaction processes. Of particular interest among these are the theories proposed by Robert F. Bales [10] and Wilfred R. Bion [11]. Both of these theories propose that two fundamental processes operate within groups, i.e., instrumental (task related) vs. expressive (socio-emotional) in the case of Bales and work vs. emotion in the case of Bion. Over attention on one of these processes causes lapses on the other. Hence, interaction shifts between these two in order to keep the group functional.

In the case of conversational tutors, the task (or work) related interactions include aspects like instructing students about the task, delivering appropriate interventions in suitable form (e.g. socratic dialog, hints), providing feedback and other such tactics [12]. Some studies [13] [14] have evaluated the effect of these task related conversational behaviors in tutorial dialog scenarios. Work in the area of affective computing and its application to tutorial dialog has focused on identification of students' emotional states [15] and using those to improve choice of task related behavior by tutors. However, there has been only limited study of expressive (socio-emotional) aspects of the tutor's conversations with learning groups. Besides focusing on the expressive behavior of the tutor, the novelty of this work lies in the use of small group communication as a context for designing tutor behavior.

2.1 Social Behavior for Conversational Tutors

As discussed earlier, current state-of-the-art conversational tutors do not perform the socio-emotional function of interaction that is known to be a fundamental aspect of group interaction. Hence, we hypothesize that socially capable tutors will be able to perform better in collaborative learning scenarios. In order to further specify social capability, we use the interaction process analysis (IPA) schema developed by Bales [19]. Besides the influence and popularity of IPA over the last five decades, our choice is based on the unit of analysis on which IPA is applied, i.e., individual utterances compared to Bion's units of analysis (sessions) that are typically much larger (10-50 utterances).

IPA identifies three positive socio-emotional interaction categories: showing solidarity, precipitating tension release, and agreeing. We have mapped these categories to practically implementable conversational strategies, which are distinguishable from each other and are relevant to interactive situation employed in our experiment. This mapping is shown in Table 1 below.

Table 1. Social Interaction Strategies based on three of Bales' Socio-Emotional Interaction Categories

---
1. Showing Solidarity: *Raises other's status, gives help, reward*
1a. Do Introductions: *Introduce and ask names of all participants*
1b. Be Protective & Nurturing: *Discourage teasing*
1c. Give Reassurance: *When student is discontent, asking for help*
1d. Complement / Praise: *To acknowledge student contributions*
1e. Encourage: *When group or members are inactive*
1f. Conclude Socially

2. Precipitating Tension Release: *Jokes, laughs, shows satisfaction*
2a. Expression of feeling better: *After periods of tension, work pressure*
2b. Be cheerful
2c. Express enthusiasm, elation, satisfaction: *On completing significant task steps*

3. Agreeing: *Shows passive acceptance, understands, concurs, complies*
3a. Show attention: *To student ideas as encouragement*
3b. Show comprehension / approval: *To student opinions and orientations*

Each strategy is implemented as an instantiation of a conversational behavior. Most of these strategies are realized as prompts, triggered by rules based on agent plan, discourse and context features. For example, strategy 1e is triggered when one or more students in the group are found to be inactive for over 5 minutes. In this event, the tutor chooses to raise the status of the inactive students by eliciting contributions from them through a prompt like: *Do you have any suggestions Mike?* We did a pilot evaluation with 6 subjects to ensure that the strategies were perceived as we expected.

3 Overview of Socially Capable Tutors

The interaction between the students and tutor in the experiment presented in this paper is situated in a freshmen engineering course. In this course college students learn about basic mechanical engineering concepts like force, moment, stress, etc. The students interact with the tutor as part of a computer-aided design competition where the students are asked to design a better wrench with consideration to ease of use, safety and material cost. Students could interact with each other and the tutor using a text-based chat room that includes a shared whiteboard [16].

Table 2. Excerpt of a tutor providing a lesson to a team of four students

	Speaker	Contribution
64	Tutor	Intuitively, if you wanted to make the wrench easier to use, would you make it longer or shorter?
67	S5	Longer
70	Tutor	That's right. A longer wrench is better.
72	Tutor	Why is a longer wrench easier to use though! Let's look at the concept of Moment.
73	Tutor	When you use a wrench to turn a bolt, do you want a higher or lower moment?
74	S16	Higher

The task of the tutor is to provide lessons on the underlying theoretical concepts while the students work through a worksheet to explore various design choices. An excerpt of a lesson on the concept about the relationship between the length of a wrench and its ease of use is shown in Table 2 above. Besides performing its task related functions, the tutor also employs the social interaction strategies listed in the previous section. We have implemented this tutor using the Basilica architecture [17].

Using the Basilica architecture, conversational agents are modeled as a network of behavioral components. Each component implements a behavior that could be a combination of perception, thought and action. The Basilica architecture allows a developer to build agents by adding behavioral components incrementally. Since each component is not tightly coupled to all others, it provides the flexibility to easily change a single behavior. Also, it allows components to be reused between agent/tutor implementations for different tasks. Further, each component is fully programmable and not restricted to a small set of acts and operators, as is the case with most other dialog/conversational system architectures. This makes Basilica a suitable choice for an architecture to build agents with novel rich behavior like the social behavior we investigate here. The technical details of the implementation of the Avis agent are discussed in a separate publication [19].

Table 3 shows an excerpt of an actual conversation between a team of three students and our tutor agent Avis. Names are changed to preserve anonymity. Turn 142 concludes a lesson about the relationship of stress and ease of use of a wrench. As that plan step is completed, Avis decides to compliment (strategy 1d) one of the students in turn 144 for participating in the discussion. Following that turn, Avis is able to proceed to the next step as we see from turn 150 onwards. Also note that one of the students exhibits enthusiasm about their team's designs in turns 143 and 146. The tutor exhibits cheerfulness (strategy 2b) in turn 145 and 147 to reciprocate the student's enthusiasm.

Table 3. Excerpt of an conversation between three students and Avis (Tutor)

	Speaker	Contribution
139	Tutor	One last thing on this topic, Does more (or less) stress in a wrench make it easier to use?
140	S95	no change?
141	Tutor	You are correct about that.. Stress doesn't determine ease of use.
142	Tutor	It's the moment achieved by the wrench that determines the ease of use.
143	S89	yay!
144	Tutor	It's good to have your contributions in the discussion Jackie :-)
145	Tutor	Go team :-)
146	S89	Go team yay
147	Tutor	I am happy to be working with our team
148	S89	Me too
150	Tutor	Unfortunately maximum stress (12800) in our design1 is ...

As mentioned earlier, the amount of social behavior the tutor can perform is regulated using a social ratio parameter that is set at 20% for our social tutors. This is based on the percentage of positive socio-emotional turns reported in Bales' empirical experiments with small groups. Note that the social ratio parameter is only the upper limit of the percentage of social turn.

4 Evaluation

The rest of the paper describes the procedures and results from a controlled experiment we conducted to validate our hypothesis mentioned in section 2.1.

4.1 Design

We designed a study with three conditions. In the experimental condition (*Social*), students interacted with a tutor that was equipped with the eleven social interaction strategies, unlike the control condition (*Task*) which is our lower baseline condition. In a third (gold standard) condition, a human tutor was allowed to perform social interaction while the students interacted with a tutor similar to the *Task* condition. The human tutors were instructed to not give any task related information/instructions. They were asked to trigger appropriate social prompts (from the same list the automated tutor uses) when they thought it was appropriate. Human tutors were allowed to make modifications to the prompts before triggering them. They were also allowed to type in new prompts.

In all three conditions, students would receive the same task related information (instructions / lessons / feedback) through the automated tutor. Based on the examples in Table 2, we notice that in the task condition, the tutor has features (like asking questions and giving feedback) that most common tutors do. The time allotted for the interaction is the same for each group. The only manipulation in this design is the amount of social interaction that varies from minimal (*Task*) to computationalizable (*Social*) to ideal (*Human*). According to our hypothesis, socially capable tutors used in the *Social* and the *Human* conditions will perform better than the *Task* condition.

4.2 Procedure and Outcome Measures

We conducted a between-subjects experiment during a college freshmen computer-aided engineering lab project. 98 mechanical engineering students enrolled in the lab participated in the experiment, which was held over six sessions spread evenly between two days. The two days of the experiment were separated by two weeks. Students were grouped into teams of three to four individuals. Each group communicated using a private chatroom [8]. No two members of the same group sat next to each other during the lab. The groups were evenly distributed between the three conditions in each session.

Table 4. Items about Tutor and Learning Task rated by students on a 7-point Likert Scale

Q1	I liked the tutor very much.
Q2	The tutor was very cordial and friendly during the discussion
Q3	The tutor was providing very good ideas for the discussion
Q4	The tutor kept the discussion at a very comfortable level socially
Q5	The tutor was part of my team
Q6	The tutor received the ideas and suggestions I contributed to the discussion positively
Q7	I am happy with the discussion we had during the design challenge
Q8	My group was successful at meeting the goals of the design challenge
Q9	The design challenge was exciting and I did my best to come up with good designs

Each session started with a follow along tutorial of computer-aided analysis where the students analyzed a wrench they had designed in a previous lab. A pre-test with 11 questions (7 multiple choice questions and 4 brief explanation questions) was administered after the analysis tutorial. The experimental manipulation happened during the Collaborative Design Competition after the pre-test. Students were asked to work as a team to design a better wrench taking three aspects into consideration: ease of use, material cost, and safety. Students were instructed to make three new designs and calculate success measures for each of the three aspects under consideration. They were also told that a tutor will help them with the first and the second designs so that they are well prepared to do the final design. No additional details about the tutor were given. Besides receiving lab credit, students were told that every member of the team that learns the most will receive a $10 gift card as prize.

After the students spent 35 minutes on the design competition, a post-test was administered. Following the test, student filled out a perception survey. The survey comprised of eighteen items to be rated on a seven point Likert-scale ranging from Strongly Disagree (1) to Strongly Agree (7). Six of the items were based on Burke's survey [18] rephrased to elicit ratings about the tutor's behavior. Three questions were designed to elicit ratings of task satisfaction, satisfaction with group discussion and perceived task legitimacy. These questions are shown in Table 4. The other questions were about group climate and perceptions of other group members.

4.3 Results and Analysis

Learning Outcomes. Using an ANOVA, we saw that there was no significant differences (p = 0.680) between pre-test scores for the three conditions (*Task, Social, Human*). To evaluate the effect of the tutor's social capability on the post-test achievement, we used an ANCOVA model with day of the experiment and the condition as independent variables. Pre-test score was used as a covariate. We found a significant main effect of the condition variable $F(2, 93) = 10.56$, $p < 0.001$. A pairwise Tukey test post-hoc analysis revealed that both the *Human* and *Social* conditions were significantly better than *Task* condition. This is consistent with our hypothesis. The *Social* and *Human* conditions were not significantly different on this measure. The relative effect sizes with respect to the *Task* condition was 0.93 standard deviations (σ) for the *Human* condition and 0.71σ for the *Social* condition. There was no main effect of day of experiment on this outcome.

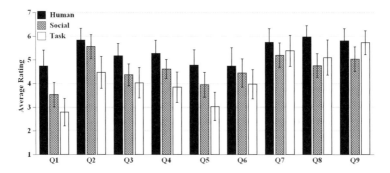

Fig. 1. Average ratings for the Tutor (Q1-Q6) and the Learning Task (Q7-Q9)

Perception Ratings. Figure 1 shows the average ratings by the students for the survey items. Using condition and day of the experiment as independent variables in an ANOVA, we modeled the ratings for the items. There was a significant main effect of condition ($p < 0.05$) on the first five items. There was no significant difference on the item about tutor agreeing with the students (Q6). Also, there was no main effect of day of experiment on these outcomes. Pairwise Tukey test post-hoc analysis showed the only tutors in the *Human* condition were significantly ($p < 0.05$) better than *Task* condition for the first five questions (Q1-Q5). The tutor in *Social* condition was rated significantly ($p < 0.05$) better only for Q2 (being friendly) and marginally better ($p < 0.08$) for Q5 (being part of the team). The social tutors were not significantly better than our lower baseline (*Task*) on the other four items (Q1, Q3, Q4, Q6).

On the task satisfaction item (Q8) there was significant main effect of both condition $F(2,92) = 4.91$, $p < 0.01$ as well as day of experiment $F(1, 92) = 11.57$, $p < 0.001$. The *Social* condition was the worst of the three conditions on this measure. However, only the difference between *Human* and *Social* conditions was significant. There were no main effects on Q7 and Q9.

4.4 Analysis and Discussion

In order to compare our implementation of the social tutors and human tutors, we counted the instances of actual display of social behaviors by those tutors. The turns were classified as one of seven behaviors listed in Table 5 based on the social prompt closest to the turn. Table 5 also shows the average turn counts for the seven types of social behavior for the two types of tutors. All the differences between the tutors shown in Table 5 are significant. We note that except the number of turns related to tension release strategies (2a, 2b, 2c), the human tutors performed significantly more social turns. Also, we note that the human tutors performed additional social behaviors that were not part of the social strategies implemented in our social tutors on some occasions. Both the Pushing and Being Antagonist behavior classify as negative socio-emotional interaction categories in Bales' IPA scheme [10].

Table 5. Average number of social behavior turns displayed by tutor

Behavior	Strategy	Social	Human
Doing Introductions	1a	2.67	3.80
Being Friendly	1b-1e	5.61	8.10
Doing Conclusions	1f	0.97	1.80
Trying to Release Tension	2a-2c	5.81	1.77
Agreeing	3a-3b	1.78	4.90
Pushing			0.57
Being Antagonist			1.23

5 Conclusion

First and foremost, the study presented in this paper shows that conversational tutors used in collaborative learning scenarios can be improved significantly by making them socially capable while keeping the task (tutoring) related behavior the same. Specifically, we have shown that a tutor with human-level social capability can achieve a 0.93σ of learning effect compared to a tutor without any social interaction capability. We also see that our upper baseline (*Human*) tutors are perceived significantly better on five out of six items on a survey.

Furthermore, we have described an approach to bridge research in small group communication and conversational tutors using the flexibility provided by the Basilica architecture for developing such interactive agents. The first implementation of a tutor with social interaction capabilities using this approach showed a significant learning effect of 0.71σ compared to the baseline. However, on perception metrics, this implementation of the tutor did not perform significantly better than the baseline.

Overall, the results presented here show a promise in further pursuing this line of investigation. Several improvements need to be made to our current set of social interaction strategies and their implementation to match human performance both on the performance as well as perception measures to ensure the observed effects can be consistently manifested in deployable conversational tutors. Our next step in that direction is guided by the observation that tutors in the *Human* condition performed many more social interaction turns than our implementation of the social tutors. This suggests that insufficient amount of social behavior performed by our social tutors could be a reason for their inferior perception compared to the human tutors.

Acknowledgments. The research was supported by NSF grant number DUE 0837661.

References

1. Arnott, E., Hastings, P., Allbritton, D.: Research Methods Tutor: Evaluation of a dialog based tutoring system in the classroom. Behavior Research Methods 40, 694–698 (2008)
2. Kumar, R., Rosé, C.P., Wang, Y.C., Joshi, M., Robinson, A.: Tutorial Dialogue as Adaptive Collaborative Learning Support. In: Proc. of AI in Education (2007)
3. Graesser, A.C., Chipman, P., Haynes, B.C., Olney, A.: AutoTutor: An Intelligent Tutoring System with Mixed-initiative Dialog. IEEE Trans. in Education 48, 612–618 (2005)
4. Liu, Y., Chee, Y.S.: Designing Interaction Models in a Multiparty 3D learning environment. In: Proc. of Intl. Conf. on Computers in Education (2004)
5. Kumar, R., Gweon, G., Joshi, M., Cui, Y., Rosé, C.P.: Supporting students working together on Math with Social Dialogue. In: Proceedings of Speech and Language Technology in Education (2007)
6. Chaudhuri, S., Kumar, R., Joshi, M., Terrell, E., Higgs, F., Aleven, V., Rosé, C.P.: It's Not Easy Being Green: Supporting Collaborative Green Design Learning. In: Woolf, B.P., Aïmeur, E., Nkambou, R., Lajoie, S. (eds.) ITS 2008. LNCS, vol. 5091, pp. 807–809. Springer, Heidelberg (2008)
7. Chaudhuri, S., Kumar, R., Howley, I., Rosé, C.P.: Engaging Collaborative Learners with Helping Agents. In: Proc of AI in Education (2009)
8. Bhatt, K., Evens, M., Argamon, S.: Hedged responses and expressions of affect in human/human and human/computer tutorial interactions. In: Proc. of the Cognitive Science Society (2004)
9. McGrath, J.E.: Groups: Interaction and Performance. Prentice-Hall, New Jersey (1984)
10. Bales, R.F.: Interaction process analysis: A method for the study of small groups. Addison-Wesley, Cambridge (1950)
11. Bion, W.R.: Experiences in groups: And other papers. Basic Books, New York (1961)
12. Graesser, A.C., Person, N., Harter, D.: TRG: Teaching tactics and dialog in AutoTutor. Intl. Journal of AI in Education 12(3), 257–279 (2001)
13. Wang, N., Johnson, L.W.: The Politeness Effect in an intelligent foreign language tutoring system. In: Proc. of Intelligent Tutoring Systems (2008)
14. Rosé, C.P., Moore, J.D., VanLehn, K., Allbritton, D.: A Comparative Evaluation of Socratic versus Didactic Tutoring. In: Proc. of Cognitive Sciences Society (2001)
15. D'Mello, S.K., Craig, S.D., Gholson, B., Frankin, S., Picard, R., Graesser, A.C.: Integrating Affect Sensors in an Intelligent Tutoring System. In: Proc. of Workshop on Affective Interactions: The Computer in the Affective Loop at IUI (2005)
16. ConcertChat, http://www.ipsi.fraunhofer.de/concert/index_en.shtml?projects/chat
17. Kumar, R., Rosé, C.P.: Basilica: An architecture for building conversational agents. In: Proc. of NAACL-HLT, Boulder, CO (2009)
18. Burke, P.T.: The development of Task and Social-Emotional Role Differentiation. Sociometry 30(4), 379–392 (1967)

Facial Expressions and Politeness Effect in Foreign Language Training System

Ning Wang[1], W. Lewis Johnson[2], and Jonathan Gratch[1]

[1] USC Institute for Creative Technologies
13274 Fiji Way, Marina del Rey, CA 90202 USA
{nwang,gratch}@ict.usc.edu
[2] Alelo Inc.
12910 Culver Boulevard Suite J, Los Angeles, California 90066 USA
ljohnson@alelo.com

Abstract. Previous studies on the Politeness Effect show that using politeness strategies in tutorial feedback can have a positive impact on learning (McLaren et al. 2010; Wang and Johnson 2008; Wang et al. 2005). While prior research efforts tried to uncover the mechanism through which the politeness strategies impact the learner, the results were inconclusive. Further, it is unclear how the politeness strategies should adapt over time. In this paper, we analyze the video tapes of participants' facial expression while interacting with a polite or direct tutor in a foreign language training system. The Facial Action Coding System was then used to analyze the facial expressions. Results show that as social distance decreases over time, polite feedback is received less favorably while the preference for direct feedback increases.

Keywords: politeness effect, facial expression, facial action coding system, second language acquisition.

1 Introduction

In recent years, there has been rigorous research on pedagogical agents' ability to facilitate learning (Atkinson, 2002; Johnson et al. 1998; Lester et al. 2000; Moreno, 2005). While some research focused on the agent's appearance and voice (Baylor, 2005; Baylor et al. 2003; Graesser et al. 2003; Moreno and Mayer, 2000; Moreno et al. 2001), we focused instead on the way agent's feedback is delivered. We conducted a series of studies on the use of politeness strategies in tutorial feedback and showed that the pedagogical agent's use of politeness strategies can promote better learning results (Wang et al. 2005; Wang and Johnson, 2008). This *politeness effect* was later tested in real classroom settings (McLaren et al. 2007). The latest study shows that individual differences, such as level of domain knowledge, can impact the *politeness effect* (McLaren et al. 2010). While the *politeness effect* was well studied in terms of its impact on learning, it was unclear what may be the mediating factors. In our earlier analysis, we hypothesized that motivation, in particular self-efficacy and sense of autonomy, are the factors through which politeness operate upon (Wang and Johnson 2008; Wang et al. 2005). However, results from the analysis were inconclusive.

Brown and Levinson (1987) argue that people in all cultures have face wants. The notion of face wants refers of two specific kinds of desires: the desire to be unimpeded in one's action (negative face), and the desire to be approved of (positive face). The use of politeness strategies is to mitigate the threat to face wants and facilitate harmonious interaction. An alternative explanation for the *politeness effect* could simply be that the use of politeness strategies puts the learner in an affective state that is more suitable for learning. Research on emotion and emotional expression shows that people categorize facial expressions of emotions in a similar way across cultures, and that people produce simulations of facial expressions that are characteristic of each specific emotion (Ekman, 1993). In our study of the politeness effect in a foreign language culture training system, we recorded participants' facial expressions while they interacted with the system. In this paper, we present our investigation of learners' affective states through analysis of learners' facial expressions.

Another question left unanswered is how adaptive the politeness strategies are over time, when used in tutorial feedback. The proper level of politeness depends on the potential threat of a communicative act. In the Brown and Levinson model (1987), evaluation of face threat depends upon several factors. First, the relative weight of different face threats is culturally dependent. This culture dependency is defined as the ranking of impositions by the degree to which they are considered to be interfering with one's want of autonomy and approval. Second, the weight of a face-threatening act also depends upon the relative power between the speaker and the listener. Tutors generally have power relative to learners, so we would generally expect tutors to make use of weaker politeness strategies when speaking to learners than the learners use in reverse. Finally, the weightiness of a face threat depends upon the social distance between the two parties. As two people interact over time, their social distance often decreases, reducing the severity of face threatening acts and increasing the likelihood of actions such as direct requests that lack face-saving features. In tutoring sessions, the first two factors, culture and relative power, do not change much over time. However, the social distance between the learner and the tutor could decrease. If the politeness strategies do not adjust to the change of social distance over time, would the learner react to the feedback differently?

In this paper, we investigate the following research hypotheses:

H1. Learner affect is a mediating factor between politeness and learning.

H2. The use of politeness strategies in tutorial feedback needs to adapt to the change in social distance between the learner and pedagogical agent over time.

2 Facial Action Coding System

To analyze the facial expressions, we used the Facial Action Coding System (FACS) (Ekman and Friesen, 1978). The FACS is arguably the most widely used method for coding facial expressions in the behavioral sciences. The system describes facial expressions in terms of 46 component movements, which roughly correspond to the individual facial muscle movements. FACS provides an objective and comprehensive way to analyze expressions into elementary components. Because it is comprehensive, FACS has proven useful for discovering facial movements that are indicative of cognitive and affective states (Ekman and Rosenberg, 2005).

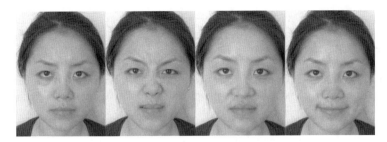

Fig. 1. From left to right, pictures of facial display of AU 4 (Brow Lower), AU 9 (Nose Wrinkle), AU 10 (Upper Lip Raise) and AU 12 (Lip Corner Puller)

3 CERT

The primary limitation to the widespread use of FACS (Ekman and Friesen, 1978) is the time required to code. FACS was developed for coding by hand, using human experts. It takes over 100 hours of training to become proficient in FACS, and it takes approximately 2 hours for human experts to code each minute of video.

Table 1. Action Units automatically coded by CERT

Action Unit	Description	Action Unit	Description
1	Inner Brow Raise	15	Lip Corner Depressor
2	Outer Brow Raise	17	Chin Raiser
4	Brow Lowerer	18	Lip Pucker
5	Upper Lid Raise	20	Lip Stretch
6	Cheek Raise	23	Lip Tightener
7	Lids Tight	24	Lip Presser
9	Nose Wrinkle	25	Lips Part
10	Upper Lip Raiser	26	Jaw Drop
12	Lip Corner Puller	27	Mouth Stretch
14	Dimpler	28	Lips Suck

To analyze the facial expressions more efficiently, we processed our video data through the Computer Expression Recognition Toolbox (CERT) developed by the University of California at San Diego (Bartlett et al. 2004). CERT is a user independent fully automatic system for real time recognition of facial actions from the Facial Action Coding System (FACS). The current version of CERT produces a 20 channel output stream. Each output stream channel consists of one real valued number for an Action Unit (AU), for each frame of the video. The real valued number indicates the distance to the separating hyper-plane for each classifier Support Vector Machine classifier. Previous work showed that the distance to the separating hyper-plane (the margin) contained information about Action Unit intensity (Bartlett et al. 2006). The 20 Action Units CERT output are shown in Table 1. Previous work (Susskind et al. 2007) shows that CERT performs comparably to human observers in the discrimination of distinct basic emotion classes and judgments of the similarity between distinct basic emotions.

In the investigator's guide to FACS, Ekman and Friesen (1978) describe the Action Units that are generally associated with facial expressions of different emotions. For example, facial expressions of joy typically include the activation of AU 12 (Lip Corner Puller) and AU 6 (Cheek Raise). AU 9 (Nose Wrinkle) or AU 10 (Upper Lip Raise) is often seen in facial expressions of disgust. Following the investigator's guide, we used AU 6 and AU 12 as indications of positive emotional facial expressions and AU 4, AU 9 and AU 10 as indications of negative emotional facial expressions (Figure 1). Positive and negative emotional facial expressions can certainly include other Action Units. However, from the actions units that can be automatically detected by CERT so far, these are the most commonly associated with positive and negative emotional facial expression.

In the analysis of learner facial expressions when interacting with the AutoTutor, McDaniel et al. (2007) correlated the learner reported affective states and FACS coding from two independent coders. The analysis identified eight Action Units (AU1, AU4, AU7, AU12, AU25, AU26, AU43 Eye Closure and AU45 Blink) that significantly correlated with five affective states (Boredom, Confusion, Delight, Frustration and Neutral). In this paper, we focus on analyzing facial expressions indicated by six of these eight Action Units (excluding AU 43 AND 45 since CERT does not output these two at the moment) and the ones generally associated with positive and negative emotions as described above.

4 Data Description

Tactical Iraqi is one of several game-based courses developed by Alelo Inc. It is a training system that supports individualized language learning and helps military service members quickly acquire functional communication skills. Tactical Iraqi includes three modules: the Skill Builder, the Mission Game and the Arcade Game. The Skill Builder consists of interactive lessons and exercises, and interactive game experiences. Learners use headset microphones to interact with the software, along with a keyboard and mouse. Lessons, exercises, and game experiences all involve speaking in the target language; speech recognition software is used to interpret the learner's speech. The current study focuses on Skill Builder only. More information on the Arcade Game and Mission Game can be found in Johnson (2007).

To investigate the effect of politeness strategies in tutorial feedback, we created two types of feedbacks: polite feedback which is phrased using various politeness strategies and direct feedback which is phrased without any politeness strategies. An example of direct feedback is "No, that means 'This is a sergeant.' Try again." An example of polite feedback is "It's usually hard to get answers to this question right, but that means 'This is a sergeant.' How about we try it again?" Details about the politeness strategy can be found in Wang and Johnson (2008).

Sixty-one volunteers (59% women, 41% men) from the greater Los Angeles area participated in the study. They were recruited by responding to recruitment posters on Craigslist.com and were compensated $40 for three hours of their participation. On average, the participants were 38.4 years old (min=21, max=63, std=11.5). The study design was a between-subjects experiment with two conditions: Polite (n=31) and Direct (n=30), to which participants were randomly assigned.

Participants filled out the pre-questionnaire packet and started training in the Skill Builder in Tactical Iraqi. Participants in the Polite condition received polite feedback while participants in the Direct condition received direct feedback. Participants completed one hour training in day 1, returned to the lab next day and completed another hour of training. At the end of their training in day 2, participants were asked to write down the name of the lessons they took in Skill Builder. Then participants filled out the post-questionnaire packets and took the quizzes from the lessons they took in Skill Builder. The quizzes were constructed by our research team.

Learning Gains were measured using quizzes at the end of each lesson in the Skill Builder. The quizzes contain three types of questions. First type of question is Utterance-Formation questions, where participants answer questions by recording their own speech. The second type is Multiple-Choice questions. The third type is Match-Item questions, where participants match phrases in Iraqi Arabic to translations in English. Each correct answer gets 1 point. Participants took quizzes from all the lessons that they took during the 2 hour training.

Two indexes of motivation were measured: self-efficacy and perceived autonomy. Self-efficacy was measured both in the pre-training questionnaire ($\alpha=.829$) and the post-training questionnaire ($\alpha=.713$). Items from the self-efficacy scale are modified from the scales published in Boekaerts (2002). The difference between pre and post training results allows interpretation of how self-efficacy changes due to the training. Sense of autonomy ($\alpha=.885$) was measured only in the post-training questionnaire. The measure was designed by our research team. Example items from the autonomy measure include "I feel the system was deciding what I should do next for me."

5 Results

Data from eleven sessions were excluded. Two sessions were excluded because a computer crash and a speech recognizer malfunction. One session was excluded because a participant's hearing and speech impairment. Four sessions were excluded because the participants "cheated" on the post-test. Four other sessions were excluded because CERT failed to locate the participant's face in the video, which is a pre-step to facial expression coding. As a result, data from 46 sessions ($N_{Polite} = 22$, $N_{Direct} = 24$) were included in the analysis. In this paper, we focus on the analysis of facial expressions. Results on learning and motivation are in Wang and Johnson (2008).

To process the CERT output, we adopted the statistical method Littlewort and her colleagues used to differentiate posed and genuine pain (Littlewort et al. 2007). This method strips out the individual variance in CERT output, e.g. different individuals have different baselines. It also sums up the overall activity of the Action Unit. We calculated the mean of the Z-scores for each participant (speaker only) and each AU detector as $Z=(x-\mu)/\sigma$, where (μ,σ) are the mean and variance for the output of the parts of each participant's video where the face was relatively neutral. Duration of the neutral face range from 3 seconds to 37 seconds (100 frames to 1114 frames).

Overall, we did not find any significant difference on individual Action Units between the Polite and Direct group. Correlation analyses showed that there was no significant correlation between the quiz score, self-efficacy and autonomy with any facial Action Units we tested. Previous analysis showed that politeness did not impact the overall quiz score but did help the learner perform better on more difficult and complex problems – the Utterance Formation quiz questions (Wang and Johnson, 2008). Further correlation analysis shows that AU 7 (Lids tight) is positively correlated with the Utterance Formation quiz score ($r=.315$, $p=.033$). We followed up with a stepwise linear regression using the Utterance Formation quiz score as the dependent variable, the experiment condition and the Action Units as independent variables. The model kept AU 7 and excluded the experiment condition and other Action Units. The resulting model with AU 7 is statistically significant ($F=4.835$, $p=.033$). Since previous study showed that age can significantly impact performance on the recall test (Wang and Gratch, 2009), we added age as an independent variable to this model. The resulting model with AU 7 and age is statistically significant ($F=5.193$, $p=.01$). This means that the learner's age and AU 7 activity are significant predictors of his/her performance on difficult and complex problems.

To investigate whether the learner perceived the politeness strategies of the same politeness level differently over time, we conducted a General Linear Model Repeated Measure analysis using activation of facial Action Units in the first session and second session (day 1 and day 2) as the dependent variable and the experiment condition as the independent variable. Results show that there is a significant interaction of AU 12 activity over time and experiment condition. ($p_{Time}=.743$, $p_{Time*Condition}=.041$). Figure 2 shows that activation of AU 12 decreases over time for learners in the Polite group. But for learners in the Direct group, their AU 12 activity increases from day 1

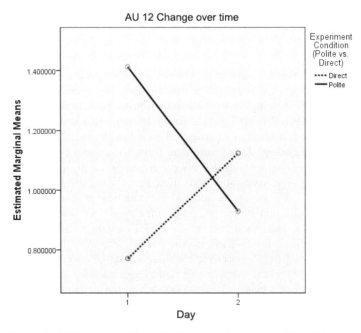

Fig. 2. Activity of AU12 changes differently from the first session (day 1) to second session (day 2) for learners in the Polite and Direct group

to day 2. AU 12 is strongly correlated with joy and delight (Ekman and Friesen, 1978, McDaniel 2007). This means that learners in the Polite condition initially enjoyed the polite feedback but found the feedback less enjoyable over time. On the other hand, learners in the Direct condition grew increasingly accustomed to the direct feedback and perceived it more favorably over time. We did not find any significant interaction of AU 6 activity over time and experiment condition. However, the overall level of AU 6 activity is significantly correlated with AU 12 activity ($p=.003$, $r=.423$).

6 Discussion

In this paper, we seek to test two hypotheses regarding the *politeness effect*. First, we hypothesize that learner affect could be a mediating factor between politeness and learning. This hypothesis was not supported. Results show that there was no significant difference on any facial Action Units between the polite and direct conditions. However, correlation analysis shows that AU 7 is significantly correlated with performance on difficult and complex problems. AU 7 is more predictive of learner performance than experiment manipulation. Previous studies showed that AU 7 is positively correlated with confusion and delight, and negatively correlated with boredom and the neutral affective state (McDaniel et al. 2007). This suggests that being in the affective states of confusion and delight may be related to learning difficult and complex issues.

The second hypothesis we tested was that the use of politeness strategies in tutorial feedback needs to adapt to the change of the social distance between the learner and pedagogical agent over time. Results show that, over time, activity of AU 12 decreases in learners who received polite feedback but increases in learners who received direct feedback. The interaction between feedback politeness levels and AU 6 activity over time was not statistically significant. There is, however, a significant correlation between overall activity of AU 6 and AU 12. AU 12 is associated with facial expressions of joy and delight (Ekman and Friesen, 1978; McDaniel 2007). And AU 6, in addition to AU 12, is the key to the Duchenne smile, which is considered by many researchers as an indication of genuine spontaneous emotions (Ekman, Davidson and Friesen, 1990). These results suggest that the second hypothesis was only partially supported. Future analysis of student's self-report of affective states and subjective evaluation of the tutorial feedback could help clarify the influence of politeness feedback on student's affective states.

The decision to use politeness strategies is mainly based on the need to mitigate face threat and the need for efficiency. As the learner becomes more familiar with the tutor, the need to mitigate face threat decreases and the need for efficiency increases. For learners in the polite group, the use of politeness strategies may become excessive over time. For learners in the direct group, the appreciation for efficiency in the feedback may increase. This suggests that the design of politeness strategies should adapt to the change of relationship between learner and pedagogical agent. Once the social distance decreases, the lower politeness level becomes more appropriate and more efficient. One possible improvement to this study is to check how the learner's perception of social distance with the pedagogical agent changes over time.

Future work could focus on more fine-grained analysis of facial expressions, e.g. analysis of instances where AU 6 and AU 12 coincide, instead of correlating gross activities throughout the study. In the current study, we have only two data points to show how perception of politeness, through facial expressions, in tutorial feedback changes over time. Future studies that expand over weeks or months could demonstrate whether this change is linear or nonlinear, or when would be the optimal time to adjust the politeness level. As facial expression recognition and other affect recognition techniques became available and more accurate (D'Mello et al. 2007; Zeng et al. 2009), it would help informing the pedagogical agents how the feedback was received and when the politeness level needs to be updated. Future research on the politeness effect could use these technologies to dynamically adjust politeness levels and make the pedagogical agent more socially intelligent.

References

1. McLaren, B.M., DeLeeuw, K.E., Mayer, R.E.: A Politeness Effect in Learning with Web-Based Intelligent Tutors. To be Presented at the 2010 American Educational Research Association (AERA) Annual Meeting, Denver, Colorado, April 30 - May 4 (2010)
2. Wang, N., Johnson, W.L.: The Politeness Effect in Intelligent Foreign Language Tutoring System. In: Woolf, B.P., Aïmeur, E., Nkambou, R., Lajoie, S. (eds.) ITS 2008. LNCS, vol. 5091, pp. 270–280. Springer, Heidelberg (2008)
3. Wang, N., Johnson, W.L., Mayer, R.E., Rizzo, R., Shaw, E., Collins, H.: The politeness effect: Pedagogical agents and learning gains. In: The 12th International Conference on Artificial Intelligence in Education (2005)
4. Atkinson, R.K.: Optimizing learning from examples using animated pedagogical agents. Journal of Educational Psychology 94, 416–427 (2002)
5. Johnson, W.L., Rickel, J., Stiles, R., Munro, A.: Integrating pedagogical agents into virtual environments. Presence 7(5) (1998)
6. Lester, J., Towns, S.G., Callaway, C.B., Voerman, J.L., FitzGerald, P.J.: Deictic and Emotive Communication in Animated Pedagogical Agents. In: Cassell, J., Prevost, S., Sullivan, J., Churchill, E. (eds.) Embodied Conversational Agents, pp. 123–154. MIT Press, Cambridge (2000)
7. Moreno, R.: Multimedia Learning with Pedagogical Agents. In: Mayer, R.E. (Hrsg.) The Cambride Handbook of multimedia learning, pp. 507–523. Cambridge University Press, New York (2005)
8. Baylor, A.L.: The impact of pedagogical agents image on affective outcomes. In: Proc. of the International Conference on Intelligent User Interfaces (2005)
9. Baylor, A.L., Ryu, J.: Does the presence of image and animation enhance pedagogical agent persona? Journal of Educational Computing Research 28 (2003)
10. Graesser, A.C., Moreno, K., Marineau, J., Adcock, A., Olney, A., Person, N.: AutoTutor improves deep learning of computer literacy: Is it the dialog or the talking head? In: Hoppe, U., Verdejo, F., Kay, J. (eds.) Proceedings of Artificial Intelligence in Education, pp. 47–54. IOS Press, Amsterdam (2003)
11. Moreno, R., Mayer, R.E.: Meaningful design for meaningful learning: Applying cognitive theory to multimedia explanations. In: ED-MEDIA 2000 Proceedings, pp. 747–752. AACE Press, Charlottesville (2000)

12. Moreno, R., Mayer, R.E., Spires, H., Lester, J.: The case for social agency in computer-based teaching: Do students learn more deeply when they interact with animated pedagogical agents? Cognition and Instruction 19, 177–213 (2001)
13. McLaren, B.M., Lim, S., Yaron, D., Koedinger, K.R.: Can a Polite Intelligent Tutoring System Lead to Improved Learning Outside of the Lab? In: Luckin, R., Koedinger, K.R., Greer, J. (eds.) Proceedings of the 13th International Conference on Artificial Intelligence in Education, pp. 433–440. IOS Press, Amsterdam (2007)
14. Brown, P., Levinson, S.C.: Politeness: Some universals in language use. Cambridge University Press, New York (1987)
15. Ekman, P.: Facial expression of emotion. American Psychologist 48, 384–392 (1993)
16. Ekman, P., Friesen, W.: Facial Action Coding System: A Technique for the Measurement of Facial Movement. Consulting Psychologists Press, Palo Alto (1978)
17. Ekman, P., Rosenberg, E.L. (eds.): What the face reveals: Basic and applied studies of spontaneous expression using the FACS. Oxford University Press, Oxford (2005)
18. Bartlett, M., Littlewort, G., Lainscsek, C., Fasel, I., Movellan, J.: Machine learning methods for fully automatic recognition of facial expressions and facial actions. In: IEEE International Conference on Systems, Man & Cybernetics, The Hague, Netherlands, pp. 592–597 (2004)
19. Bartlett, M.S., Littlewort, G.C., Frank, M.G., Lainscsek, C., Fasel, I., Movellan, J.R.: Automatic recognition of facial actions in spontaneous expressions. Journal of Multimedia 1(6), 22–35 (2006)
20. Susskind, J.M., Littlewort, G.C., Bartlett, M.S., Movellan, J.R., Anderson, A.K.: Human and Computer Recognition of Facial Expressions of Emotion. Neuropsychologia 45(1), 152–162 (2007)
21. McDaniel, B.T., D'Mello, S.K., King, B.G., Chipman, P., Tapp, K., Graesser, A.C.: Facial Features for Affective State Detection in Learning Environments. In: McNamara, D.S., Trafton, J.G. (eds.) Proceedings of the 29th Annual Meeting of the Cognitive Science Society, pp. 467–472. Cognitive Science Society, Austin (2007)
22. Johnson, W.L.: Serious use of a serious game for language learning. In: Luckin, R., et al. (eds.) Artificial Intelligence in Education, pp. 67–74. IOS Press, Amsterdam (2007)
23. Boekaerts, M.: The On-Line Motivation Questionnaire: A self-report instrument to assess students' context sensitivity. In: Pintrich, P.R., Maehr, M.L. (eds.) New Directions in Measures and Methods, Series in Advances in Motivation and Achievement, vol. 12, pp. 77–120 (2002)
24. Littlewort, G., Bartlett, M.S., Lee, K.: Automated measurement of spontaneous facial expressions of genuine and posed pain. In: Proc. International Conference on Multimodal Interfaces (2007)
25. Wang, N., Gratch, J.: Can Virtual Human Build Rapport and Promote Learning? In: Proc. of The 14th International Conference on Artificial Intelligence in Education (2009)
26. Ekman, P., Davidson, R.J., Friesen, W.V.: The Duchenne smile: Emotional expression and brain psysiology II. Journal of Personality and Social Psychology 58, 342–353 (1990)
27. D'Mello, S.K., Picard, R., Graesser, A.C.: Toward an affect-sensitive AutoTutor. IEEE Intelligent Systems 22(4), 53–61 (2007)
28. Zeng, Z., Pantic, M., Roisman, G.I., Huang, T.S.: A Survey of Affect Recognition Methods: Audio, Visual, and Spontaneous Expressions. IEEE Transactions on Pattern Analysis and Machine Intelligence 31(1), 39–58 (2009)

Intercultural Negotiation with Virtual Humans: The Effect of Social Goals on Gameplay and Learning

Amy Ogan[1], Vincent Aleven[1], Julia Kim[2], and Christopher Jones[1]

[1] Human-Computer Interaction Institute, Carnegie Mellon University, USA
[2] Institute for Creative Technologies, University of Southern California, USA
{aeo,aleven,cjones}@andrew.cmu.edu, kim@ict.usc.edu

Abstract. One innovative use of digital games is to facilitate learning skills with social components by simulating human behavior with virtual humans. We investigate learners' social goals to understand how they help learners learn intercultural skills from virtual humans in BiLAT, a virtual world that teaches cross-cultural negotiation. We hypothesize that students learn more when they approach the simulation as a social interaction rather than taking a trial-and-error approach perhaps characteristic of video gaming. In a randomized controlled experiment with 59 participants, we found that participants improved cross-cultural negotiation skills through game play. Our hypothesis that participants given an explicit social goal would learn more than those given task-related goals was not confirmed. We did, however, find a positive relation between students' self-reported social goals, regardless of condition, and their learning results. This relation was confirmed through analysis of log data. Although it is still an open question how best to promote students' approaching a simulation with a social orientation, the results underline the importance of such goals.

Keywords: social motivation, virtual environments, intelligent agents.

1 Introduction

Virtual humans are increasingly being used as pedagogical agents [2], and one of their most intriguing roles may be in facilitating the learning of social or interpersonal skills, such as conflict resolution, in game-based instructional systems [14]. These skills are traditionally taught in environments like business training or foreign language classes, using methods like role playing, or lecture and discussion. Unfortunately, these methods are either highly resource-intensive or lack an experiential component where learners practice these skills [10]. Computer-based simulations, which are growing more realistic, offer a major advantage for social learning by providing a cheaper solution to a much larger number of learners. Social learning systems have leveraged video game and learning technologies to create immersive environments with virtual human characters that simulate interpersonal interactions with complex behavioral models (see [11] for a review of intercultural systems). Recent advances in artificial intelligence and cognitive modeling now permit rich modeling of affect, culture, and more in virtual humans [e.g., 18]. The virtual humans' models drive the interaction that theoretically leads to learning. BiLAT, the game-based system in which we situate this work, is a virtual environment that supports learners in developing cross-cultural skills in the context of a negotiation task [8]. In this game, virtual humans take on a role that would typically be played by a human from another culture, in which they gesture, speak, and behave in ways that would be appropriate in that culture. Such games allow us to study the effects of virtual humans on social learning.

Unlike many pedagogical agents in the role of teacher, these virtual humans do not provide support for problem solving. Rather, learners benefit from the practice they receive through interacting with them, as they would from role-playing practice with a human. If we are to make optimal use of virtual humans as agents for social learning, it is helpful to understand our interactions with them. Related work supports the hypothesis that humans interact socially with computers. According to a wide-ranging series of studies by Reeves and Nass [15], people have an inherent bias that leads them to react to media like computers in fundamentally social ways. For example, people rate more highly computers that are endowed with a similar "personality" to their own. Recently, others have shown similar results investigating virtual humans, who can evoke responses that follow social psychology theory in automated processes such as proxemics (differences in physical distances between people) [1].

However, there are contradictory findings when more conscious, cognitive functions are involved [16]. Bailenson, Blascovich, Beall, and Loomis propose that social responses to virtual humans are forthcoming in *low-level* responses such as proxemics, while *high-level* responses such as having a meaningful conversation are governed by the human participants' belief in the agency of the virtual human [1]. Learning may very well be one such high-level area that requires attention and processing [3]. Okita, Bailenson, and Schwartz [12] found that learners who believed there was a human behind an avatar in a virtual environment exhibited better learning, more attention, and higher arousal than learners who believed they were interacting with a machine. One explanation for this result is that learners believe they are taking a socially relevant action when they interact with a human, and thus pay more attention and feel more accountable. It is clear that our social responses to technology are not the same in all cases. If learners are to benefit from these interactions it may be necessary for them to perceive the agents as social beings.

Even if learners do not produce social responses naturally, it may be possible to introduce social orientations into human-agent interactions. A significant area of research involves learners' motivational orientations towards learning environments [5]. In a domain like culture that focuses on social interactions, social motivation can have a great influence on learning [20]. Motivation is a *goal*-directed process that instigates or sustains behavior [17]. When cultural differences arise, people with different cultural identities are often categorized as members of an "outgroup" [13], which can exacerbate biases and lead to social goals like the desire to be seen as superior to the outgroup [19]. These motives may be detrimental to learning about a new culture. On the other hand, if the learner possesses social goals such as a need for affiliation or the desire to conform to social rules, learning may increase. It is an open question whether such goals can be explicitly manipulated in a way that improves learning in environments like BiLAT, in which learners interact with virtual characters from a different culture.

Social goals have been studied in human-human contexts that do not focus on learning, in a way that might lead to successful interventions for learning purposes. Negotiation researchers have shown that having a sense of a shared group identity, as indicated by holding social goals such as the desire for affiliation, can lead towards a win-win perspective and even increase negotiation outcomes for both parties [e.g., 21]. Social goals have also been manipulated to reduce outgroup bias in cross-cultural contact with successful results [6]. To study goal orientations, researchers give brief instructions that encourage specific goals for the task, which has been shown to have a significant impact on students' goals [5]. In the same way, we can give learners social goals to influence their orientation towards virtual humans. It is still an open question whether providing a social goal to students working with a social simulation results in interactions that can be viewed as more social and to better learning.

In this paper we describe an empirical study that investigates the effects of manipulating learners' social goals on their learning and gameplay. This research explores whether students learn intercultural competence skills from BiLAT, whether learners with a social orientation towards virtual humans show increased learning, and whether giving learners social goals for interacting with virtual humans increases their social orientation. This paper presents a randomized controlled study in which learners played the game with or without the addition of an explicit social goal introduced into the interface of BiLAT.

2 Game Context

The environment we use for our investigation is BiLAT [8], a game-based simulation for practicing bilateral meetings in a cross-cultural context. BiLAT integrates research technologies such as virtual human characters and intelligent tutoring support. Scenarios derived from real-world events drive the game experience. The learner is put into the role of a U.S. Army officer tasked with meeting with Iraqi townspeople to accomplish peace-keeping and rebuilding missions. The learner is given concrete, negotiation task-related goals for each meeting.

BiLAT was designed to address learning objectives related to negotiation generally as well as the specific cultural knowledge and skills that support more effective negotiations in the Iraqi culture. A primary learning objective is considering the meeting counterpart's interests in order to achieve "win-win" results. To play, learners begin by preparing for a meeting in the "prep room." Here, they learn about the character from a variety of sources of varying degrees of trustworthiness, similar to gathering such information in a real world situation. Learners then move into the meeting (see Fig 1). They communicate with each BiLAT character by selecting from a menu of communicative actions that includes greetings, smalltalk, task-related dialog, and more. The character responds to players' actions in both text and synthesized speech as well as culturally-appropriate non-verbal behaviors. Guiding each virtual character's responses is an underlying social simulation that contains a model of culture and personality. Once the meeting objectives have been obtained, the meeting is complete and the player will receive the next set of objectives for the scenario and new characters who might help them achieve those objectives. It is also possible to have an unsuccessful meeting (e.g. by offending the host), in which case the character asks the learner to leave and return for another meeting to try again.

Intercultural Negotiation with Virtual Humans 177

Fig. 1. A meeting in BiLAT with police captain Farid, with the goal of solving a problem with a market in an Iraqi town

3 Experimental Study

In the BiLAT environment, we ran a between-subjects randomized controlled study to investigate student interactions and learning results with different goals. Participants were randomly assigned to either the task condition in which they viewed only task-related goals, or the social goal group with an additional social goal. The social goal learners received was, "Come to understand Farid's point of view," where Farid was replaced with the name of the current meeting partner. BiLAT displayed this goal as a single sentence which learners had to select each time they started a meeting, and which was also available in the list of goals throughout the meeting (see Fig 1). This social goal was chosen by reflecting on the main focus of both the negotiation and cultural learning objectives, which has been found to improve learning: perspective taking. Our hypotheses for this study were:

H1: Students show learning of culture from the system.
H2: Students in the social goal condition have more social goals for interaction with the virtual characters.
H3: Students with social goals perform better on overall learning measures.
H4: Students with social goals have more social patterns of interaction with the virtual characters.

Participants were 59 learners (32 males, 27 females, mean age = 20.8, SD = 2.71) from two universities who were all U.S. citizens. In a demographics questionnaire we asked about participants' formal negotiation training (M=1.20, SD=0.58) and knowledge of Arab cultures (M=1.98, SD=1.22), each using a scale of 1 (none) to 7 (extensive).

3.1 Measures

Intercultural negotiation is an ill-defined domain and assessment is therefore challenging. We used two different measures. First, we developed an assessment to test a learner's ability to develop an accurate model of the virtual characters and the tasks in the scenario. Specifically, we asked participants to rate the truth of various items relating to the task and to the character (e.g., "Farid could be described as a family-oriented man"). These items were taken from the information participants received in the "prep room," information which they knew might be accurate or misleading. Participants evaluated the items as true, false, or unknown. Throughout the course of a meeting with a character, successful participants should be able to revise their understanding of the character and the task through their interactions, and make more appropriate judgments about the accuracy of the information from the sources in the prep room. We called this measure *Information Integration*.

For our second measure we used a selection of questions from a validated instrument called the Cultural Assimilator [4]. In this assessment, participants read a scenario about people experiencing a foreign culture and chose the best of four possible cultural explanations for the events that occurred. The Cultural Assimilator deals with scenarios from both Iraqi and other cultures therefore testing whether students can transfer their knowledge to novel situations. We used two versions of the assessment. Each contained six items, and in the study pretests and posttests were counter-balanced with isomorphic items.

Finally, we wanted to determine whether our manipulation had the desired effect on participants' goals in the game. We therefore asked them to list their goals in free text after meeting with a character.

3.2 Procedure

Participants began by taking a demographics questionnaire and then watching a video about the concepts and skills related to the learning objectives. This video gave participants an introduction to the material they then practiced in BiLAT, as well as an introduction to using the system. All participants were told in the introductory video that interpersonal aspects of the interaction are an important consideration for successful negotiations. Participants then took the Culture Assimilator pretest assessment.

Next, they entered the game. They explored the "prep room" to learn about the scenario and the first character they were going to meet. Also, the goals for the meeting were introduced, including the social goal for those participants in the social goal condition. After leaving the "prep room," the Information Integration items for that character were administered. Participants then saw the meeting goals again and met with the first character until an agreement on the negotiation was reached. If the participant did not come to an agreement within forty-five minutes, the experimenter moved the participant along to the next step. At this point, participants were asked to list their goals for the meeting in free text and then took the Information Integration items for that character again as a posttest. Following this posttest, participants repeated this procedure with a second character who was part of the same scenario. Finally, participants took the Culture Assimilator posttest.

4 Results

While 59 participants completed the study, we dropped 5 participants due to computer error or complete lack of engagement. In our final analyses, we compared 25 participants in the social goal group to 29 participants playing with the standard task-related game objectives.

H1 stated that we would observe learning gains from playing the game. To analyze the data, we conducted a paired t-test to compare pretest scores to posttest scores across all students. On the Information Integration items, participants were given a point for each item that matched a subject matter expert's rating of the information. Students showed significant overall learning from pre to post ($t(49) = 9.213$, $p=.004$). On the Culture Assimilator, participants were given a point for each item that matched the most appropriate response from the validated measure. On this measure as well there was significant overall learning from pre to post ($t(47) = 4.582$, $p=.038$).

H2 stated that the social goals group would have more social goals for interacting with the virtual characters. To investigate, we coded participants' answers to their free-response goals for the meeting. As mentioned above, students in the task condition saw two task goals. Students in the social condition saw the same two task goals and a third (social) goal, "Come to understand Farid's point of view". Interestingly, although it was not presented to them, a number of participants in the task condition reported a similar or related social goal. Because the main focus of our experiment was to investigate the effects of playing the game while holding social goals, we categorized participants as "no reported social goals" and "reported social goals", regardless of their condition. Two independent coders rated anything that focused on social interaction with the virtual character in the "reported social goals" category. Table 1 has examples of reported social goals from both conditions.

Table 1. Reported social goals from each condition

Social goals in task goals condition	Social goals in social goal condition
Establish a good relationship	To establish a positive personal relationship with Farid
Build trust	Maintaining a strong personal rapport with Farid.
Establish a trustworthy relationship between Farid in myself. I wanted to get support and unity with the Iraqi police but I also wanted to attend to Farid's needs in order to keep the relationship open and favorable.	Building the foundations for a long term relationship with Farid.

Reporting a social goal was not significantly related to the demographic characteristics we measured: age, negotiating experience, knowledge of Arab cultures, or frequency of playing games. Neither did the reported social goal participants have higher pretest scores on the Information Integration items or the Culture Assimilator (all $p > .2$). The number of participants with reported social goals was significantly influenced

Table 2. Number of participants by condition and reported goals

Given Condition	Reported goals No social	Social	Total
Task	20	9	29
Social	9	16	25
Total	29	25	54

by condition according to a chi square test ($\chi^2(1, N = 54) = 5.868, p=.015$). Table 2 shows the participants with social goals by condition.

H3 stated that students with social goals would perform better on overall measures of learning. We examined all of the learning results with respect to the learner's *given goals* (social vs. task). To analyze the data we conducted repeated measures analysis of variance (ANOVAs) with condition as the between-subjects factor and test time (pretest and posttest) as the within-subject factor. Here, our hypothesis was not confirmed. However, because almost a third of all participants did not report their goals as we expected based on the condition they were given, we examined all the learning results again with respect to the learner's *reported goals* from the manipulation check ("reported social goals" vs. "no reported social goals"). We added "reported social goals" as a between-subjects variable to repeated measures ANOVAs with test time (pretest and posttest) as the within-subject factor. On the Information Integration items, the ANOVA showed that reported social goals significantly influenced learning ($F(1,49) = 3.979, p=.052$). An ANCOVA model of the Culture Assimilator test also showed that reported social goals significantly influenced learning ($F(1,47) = 8.314, p=.006$). On both assessments, learners who reported social goals outperformed learners who did not report social goals.

H4 stated that students with social goals would have more social patterns of play in the game. To examine this hypothesis, we did an investigation into participants' actions taken in the game and compared them across reported goals. Game actions were classified by the developers into business, social, opening (e.g., greetings), and closing (e.g., leave-taking) categories. Participants who *reported social goals* took significantly fewer total actions in the game than participants who did not report social goals (see Table 3 for all statistics). Broken down by action type, these participants took significantly fewer business actions, while taking a statistically similar number

Table 3. Gameplay differences between "reported social goals" groups; * indicates statistically significant difference

	t(52)	p	M_{social}	SD_{social}	$M_{no-social}$	$SD_{no-social}$
Total actions	2.45	.018*	79.0	27.0	107.0	49.0
Business actions	2.60	.012*	40.0	16.1	29.6	12.6
Social actions	1.82	.073	50.1	21.3	67.1	42.2
Unique actions	2.24	.029*	37.0	7.1	43	8.6
Meetings	2.04	.046*	2.8	1.6	3.9	2.3
Time played	0.23	.8	46.2	10.3	47.0	13.6

of social actions. They also held fewer meetings before they achieved their objectives. Participants with reported social goals also took significantly fewer unique communication actions. However, although time on task was not strictly controlled by the experimenters, there were no significant differences between groups in the amount of time the game was played.

5 Discussion

Our four hypotheses were confirmed, although not in the way that we expected. First, we found that overall, participants did learn from interacting with the virtual humans in BiLAT. Showing that such a system can produce increases on a validated assessment is a win given the current state of evaluation in the field [11]. The results of the explicit goals manipulation in the study require closer consideration. Relevant to *H2*, a significantly higher percentage of participants who were explicitly given a social goal in the game interface did report having a social goal as a meeting objective than those who were not given such a goal. Therefore, some students in the social goal condition did appear to be influenced to consider such goals as important. However, a third of the students in that condition did not seem to heed the manipulation. These students may not have understood how to achieve the social goal they were given, or may not have wanted to achieve it. Additionally, unlike other similar learning orientation manipulations (e.g., [5]), simply attempting to manipulate students' social goals was not beneficial to learning.

What we saw instead, confirming *H3*, was that learners with *self-reported social goals* for the interaction had increased learning over learners without such goals. The results of this study extend two sets of seemingly conflicting evidence. Okita et al. suggest that students need to believe that virtual characters are real to benefit from interacting with them [12, 16]. However, the Media Equation [15] suggests that social responses to virtual characters are automatic. We saw that participants with self-reported social goals, regardless of condition, learned more about the scenario and characters and were better able to transfer their knowledge to novel situations. Thus, it appeared that while learners did not need to be told that the virtual humans were real humans to learn, having social goals for the interaction was beneficial.

Additionally, we saw that students who reported a social goal played the game in a qualitatively different way (confirming *H4*). In an identical amount of time in the game, they took fewer actions, which may indicate that they spent more time reflecting on each action to consider their partners' perspective. They took fewer total actions relating to business and a higher percentage of social actions than students who did not report social goals. Additionally, they took fewer unique actions, signifying less exploration of the conversation space (seemingly avoiding dialog actions that could potentially be seen as offensive). Together, these patterns seem to present a social orientation towards gameplay, where participants hold some theory of mind about their virtual partner. This outlook is in contrast to a prominent view of learning from gameplay, which involves exploring a risk-free, task-oriented environment for discovery (as suggested by the PsychoSocial Moratorium principle and other theories of game-based learning) [7, 9]. This principle states that games are a place where learners take risks they would not normally be comfortable taking in the real world. In

BiLAT, learners might manifest this principle by intentionally offending the virtual character, or experimenting with all available actions in an attempt to understand the boundaries of acceptable behavior. This type of gameplay would be at odds with a social perspective, in which learners would carefully consider their partner's perspective, attempt to avoid giving offense, and avoid exploration that would take them into unknown territory of culturally acceptable behaviors.

Our results show that a social orientation towards interaction with virtual humans in learning intercultural negotiation and perhaps similarly complex social skills may not always happen, but when it does, it is associated with increased learning. Although these results may not apply to domains such as algebra where social skills are not critical, the trend in these domains towards social methods of instruction such as virtual peer tutoring may make them relevant. The results can guide us towards designing improved ways to support social learning through virtual environments. It appears that learning social skills in virtual environments can be more effective if we can promote a social orientation. However, presenting explicit social goals is not the most effective way of doing so. Instead, our search continues for ways to promote a social orientation more implicitly. A second avenue for future research is to investigate those students who arrive at a learning environment already holding social goals. Reporting a social goal was not tied to any of the demographics that we measured (e.g., prior negotiation training, knowledge of Arab cultures), nor did these participants appear to be of higher ability based on their pretest scores. It may be that other measures such as social intelligence or personality traits can provide a better characterization of these learners. We intend to build a model of how social goals are influenced by and interact with these learner characteristics. Then, we will investigate how social goals can be promoted for those students who do not already hold them.

Acknowledgments. Thanks to Eric Forbell for his great effort at support and implementation. Part of this work has been sponsored by the U.S. Army Research, Development, and Engineering Command (RDECOM). Statements and opinions expressed do not necessarily reflect the position or the policy of the United States Government, and no official endorsement should be inferred. The research was supported by the Institute of Education Sciences, U.S. Department of Education, through Grant R305B040063 to CMU.

References

1. Bailenson, J., Blascovitch, J., Beall, A., Loomis, J.: Interpersonal Distance in Immersive Virtual Environments. Personality and Social Psych. Bulletin 29(7), 819–833 (2003)
2. Chou, C.-Y., Chan, T.-W., Lin, C.-J.: Redefining the learning companion: the past, present, and future of educational agents. Computers & Education 40, 255–269 (2003)
3. Cohen, A., Ivry, R.I., Keele, S.W.: Attention and structure in sequence learning. J. Exp. Psych. Learning, memory, and cognition 16(1) (1992)
4. Cushner, K., Brislin, R.: Intercultural Interactions: A Practical Guide, 2nd edn. Sage Publications, Inc., Thousands Oaks (1995)
5. Dweck, C.S., Leggett, E.L.: A social-cognitive approach to motivation and personality. Psychological Review 95, 256–273 (1988)

6. Gaertner, S.L., Dovidio, J.F., Anastasio, P.A., Bachman, B.A., Rust, M.C.: The common ingroup identity model: Recategorization and the reduction of intergroup bias. European Review of Social Psych. 4, 1–26 (1993)
7. Gee, J.P.: What video games have to teach us about learning and literacy. Palgrave/Macmillan, New York (2003)
8. Hill, R.W., Belanich, J., Lane, H.C., Core, M.G., Dixon, M., Forbell, E., Kim, J., Hart, J.: Pedagogically Structured Game-based Training: Development of the ELECT BiLAT Simulation. In: Proc. 25th Army Science Conf. (2006)
9. Johnson, S.: Everything bad is good for you: How today's popular culture is actually making us smarter. Riverhead Books, New York (2006)
10. Landis, D., Bennett, J., Bennett, M.J.: Handbook of Intercultural Training, 3rd edn. Sage Publications, Inc., Thousand Oaks (2003)
11. Ogan, A., Lane, H.C.: Virtual Learning Environments for Culture and Intercultural Competence. In: Handbook of Intercultural Training (in press)
12. Okita, S.Y., Bailenson, J., Schwartz, D.L.: Mere Belief of Social Action Improves Complex Learning. In: Barab, S., Hay, K., Hickey, D. (eds.) Proc. of the 8th Int. Conf. for the Learning Sciences (2008)
13. Prentice, D.A., Miller, D.T.: The psychology of cultural contact. In: Prentice, D.A., Miller, D.T. (eds.) Cultural divides: Understanding and overcoming group conflict, pp. 1–19 (1999)
14. Raybourn, E.M., Waern, A.: Social Learning Through Gaming. Extended Abstracts of CHI Proceedings 2004. ACM Press, New York (2004)
15. Reeves, B., Nass, C.: The Media Equation: How People Treat Computers, Television, and New Media like Real People and Places. Cambridge University Press, Cambridge (1996)
16. Rosé, C.P., Torrey, C.: Interactivity versus Expectation: Eliciting Learning Oriented Behavior with Tutorial Dialogue Systems. In: Costabile, M.F., Paternó, F. (eds.) INTERACT 2005. LNCS, vol. 3585, pp. 323–336. Springer, Heidelberg (2005)
17. Schunk, D.H., Pintrich, P.R., Meece, J.: Motivation in Education: Theory, Research, and Applications, 3rd edn. Prentice Hall, Englewood Cliffs (2007)
18. Swartout, W., Gratch, J., Hill, R., Hovy, E., Marsella, S., Rickel, J., Traum, D.: Toward virtual humans. AI Magazine 27(2), 96–108 (2006)
19. Taylor, D.M., Moghaddam, F.M.: Theories of intergroup relations: International social psychological perspectives, 2nd edn. Praeger, New York (1994)
20. Urdan, T., Maehr, M.: Beyond a Two-Goal Theory of Motivation and Achievement: A Case for Social Goals. Review of Educational Research 65(3), 213–243 (1995)
21. Weingart, L.R., Bennett, R.J., Brett, J.M.: The impact of consideration of issues and motivational orientation on group negotiation process and outcome. J. Applied Psych. 78(3), 504–517 (1993)

An Analysis of Gaming Behaviors in an Intelligent Tutoring System

Kasia Muldner, Winslow Burleson, Brett Van de Sande, and Kurt VanLehn

Arizona State University
{katarzyna.muldner,winslow.burleson,bvds,kurt.vanlehn}@asu.edu

Abstract. We present results from an analysis of students' shallow behaviors, i.e., *gaming*, during their interaction with an Intelligent Tutoring System (ITS). The analysis is based on six college classes using the Andes ITS for homework and test preparation. Our findings show that student features are a better predictor of gaming than problem features, and that individual differences between students impact where and how students game.

1 Introduction

Students have long found ways to avoid reasoning about instructional materials, e.g., by copying from examples to generate problem solutions [1] or by avoiding effective study strategies such as self explaining domain principles [2]. In human tutoring contexts, students often passively listen to tutors' didactic explanations, without providing substantial follow ups even though more active participation is needed for effective learning [3]. These behaviors also occur in students' interactions with *intelligent tutoring systems* (ITSs). A name given to shallow reasoning in the context of an ITS is gaming, "*attempting to succeed in a learning environment by exploiting properties of the system rather than by learning the material*" [4]. Not surprisingly, gaming can be detrimental to learning [5], and so there have been efforts in detecting [6, 7], understanding [4, 8, 9] and preventing [10, 11] gaming.

We add to this research by presenting an in-depth analysis of log data corresponding to several years worth of students interacting with Andes, a tutoring system for Newtonian physics [12]. To identify gaming episodes in this data, we applied a computational gaming detector that we calibrated with a hand-analysis of the data. Contrary to some prior findings (e.g., [4]), we found that gaming is best predicted by student features, rather than instructional aspects. This lead us to perform a descriptive analysis of students' gaming behaviors that focused in part on understanding which tutor actions lead students to game. While we found individual differences between low and high gamers, high-level hints were one of the most gamed features. However, in contrast to other work [4], our analysis suggests that poor hint usability may not be the culprit, and so that other factors such as student motivation (or lack of) are at play.

We begin with a survey of related work, and then present our gaming detector, the log data analysis and results, and finally a discussion of our findings and future work.

2 Related Work

Several approaches for detecting gaming have been used. Some research has relied on human observers for real-time gaming identification [5]. This approach is challenging as observers may miss nuances in a fast-paced classroom environment and so others have turned to post hoc hand labeling of log data [4]. The latter approach affords the human coder time to consider all student actions but is costly, since copious amounts of data must be hand labeled. A potential issue with using human coders is that they may be inconsistent in identifying gaming episodes, something that machine algorithms for gaming identification address [6, 7, 13, 14].

A key challenge is understanding what causes gaming. Some researchers propose that gaming is due to features of the instructional materials, including (poor) ITS design. For instance, Baker et al. [4] found that ITS features, such as unhelpful hints and non-intuitive toolbar icons, explained more of the variance in the data than prior approaches using student features; a similar result was obtained in [15]. Other work focuses on identifying student characteristics that drive gaming. For instance, since students game on steps that they do not know [13], it has been proposed that item difficulty leads to gaming. Another student characteristic influencing gaming is affect, with boredom being the most frequent emotion to precede gaming [8]. There has also been research on how performance goal orientation impacts gaming [16]; this work failed to find the anticipated link between gaming and performance goals.

As far as gaming prevention is concerned, a number of strategies have been developed, including the use of animated agents that show disapproval when gaming occurs [17], software design via a mandatory delay before a student can ask for a hint [10, 18], and/or by letting students choose the hint level [19].

3 The Data and Gaming Detector

The Data. Our data, obtained from the Pittsburgh Learning Center DataShop, corresponds to logs of students using the Andes ITS [12] for assigned class homework and test preparation (from six different physics classes over the span of about three years). Andes tutors Newtonian physics and is described in detail elsewhere (e.g., [12]); here we provide a very brief overview. Students solve problems in the Andes interface by drawing diagrams and typing equations. Such a user interface action will be called an *entry*. Andes provides immediate feedback for correctness on students' entries, by coloring the entry red (incorrect) or green (correct). As students solve problems, they can ask Andes for a hint; the Andes hint sequence starts out general and ends with a bottom-out hint that indicates precisely the step to enter (e.g., *"Why don't you continue with the solution by working on setting the pressure at a point open to the atmosphere "* ... *"Write the equation Pa = Pr0"*). To discourage students from always going to the bottom-out hint, Andes assigns a score to each problem, which is decremented slightly every time a bottom-out hint is requested.

The Gaming Detector. After irrelevant actions are removed from the log data, a log consists of a time-stamped sequence of *tutor-student turn* pairs (e.g., tutor indicates an entry is incorrect, student responds by asking for a hint). To address our research questions, we needed to know which of these turn pairs corresponded to gaming.

Table 1. *Tutor-Student* turn pairs (gamed cells shaded)

	(a) Student: hint request		(b) Student: Entry	
	fast	slow	fast	slow
(1) Tutor: bottom-out hint	Skip hint (S)	-	Copy hint (C)	-
(2) Tutor: High-level hint	Skip hint (S)	-	-	-
(3) Tutor: Incorrect (Red)	-	-	Guess (G)	-
(4) Tutor: Correct (Green)	No planning (P)	-	-	-

Given that our data comprised over 900,000 pairs, manual analysis was not feasible. Thus, we first hand-analyzed a fragment of the log data to identify rules to detect gamed turn pairs, which we then encoded into a computational gaming detector that could automatically label the data. We then applied the detector, hand-checking its output on a new data fragment, revising as necessary.

For purposes of this analysis, we considered the following *tutor* turns: (1) coloring an entry red (incorrect), (2) coloring an entry green (correct), (3) giving a bottom-out hint, or (4) giving a high-level hint (we did not further subdivide the *high-level* hints since the number and characteristics of such hints varied considerably). We classified a *student's* turn as either (a) asking for a hint or (b) generating an entry. Thus, there are 4*2=8 types of turn pairs (see Table 1). Each turn pair has a time duration associated with it, which is how long the student paused between seeing the tutor's turn and starting to take action. We assume that turn pairs with long durations are *not* gaming. Of the eight possible turn pairs with short durations (see Table 1), we consider the following five to be gaming: (1-2) *Skipping a hint:* the tutor presents a hint and the student skips the hint by quickly asking for another hint (see 'S' cells in Table 1); (3) *Copying a hint:* the tutor presents a bottom-out hint and the student quickly generates a solution entry, suggesting a shallow copy of the hint instead of learning of the underlying domain principle[1] (see 'C' cell, Table 1); (4) *Guessing:* after the tutor signals an incorrect entry, the student quickly generates another *incorrect*[2] entry, suggesting s/he is guessing instead of reasoning about why the entry is incorrect (see 'G' cell in Table 1); (5) *Lack of planning:* after the tutor signals a correct entry, the student quickly asks for a hint, suggesting reliance on hints for planning the solution (see 'P' cell, Table 1). Note that item 1, *skipping hints*, does not take into account the possibility that a student may copy the hint and *then* reason about it. This was explored in [20], by analyzing time after a hint was copied. Time alone, however, does not necessarily indicate that the student is reasoning about the hint, since they may be, for instance, thinking about the next step. Thus, for the time being, we decided to only consider time before an entry is generated, as we felt this was more likely to correspond to reasoning about the entry.

Accurate gaming detection relies on having reasonable time thresholds, one for each of the five gamed turn pairs. To set the threshold, we obtained a value for each

---

[1] A high-level hint followed by a fast entry is not gaming since you can't copy high-level hints.
[2] This is the only student entry where we take into account correctness of the student entry, as not doing so might incorrectly classify fixing slips as gaming.

pair based on our review of the log file data. As a final check, we obtained a frequency distribution graph for each of the gamed pairs. The graph allowed us to ensure that the threshold we chose was not unrealistic (e.g., so high that all students would be considered gaming). Note that we were conservative when setting our thresholds: for instance, we set the *skipping* hint threshold $T = < 3$sec. While this threshold may not afford enough time to read all of a hint, it captures instances when students are skipping most of the hint.

4 Results

Our analysis is based on applying the above-described gaming detector to data from a set of 318 unique problems and 286 students. We now describe our results.

4.1 What Is a Better Predictor of Gaming: Student or Problem?

As we mentioned above, a central question pertains to what causes gaming, and in particular, whether student or problem features better predict gaming. To address this question, we obtained the following measures:

$$PerGaming_{sp} \qquad \text{percentage of gaming by a student } s \text{ on a problem } p \qquad (1)$$

$$\sum_{p=0}^{p=N} PerGaming_{sp} / N \qquad \text{i.e., average gaming by a student } s \text{ across all } N \text{ problems } p \text{ solved by that student} \qquad (2)$$

$$\sum_{s=0}^{s=M} PerGaming_{sp} / M \qquad \text{i.e., average gaming on a problem } p \text{ across all } M \text{ students } s \qquad (3)$$

We used *problem* as the unit of analysis (see equation 1; equations 2 and 3 rely on it). Some research has used lesson as the primary unit of analysis [4]. In fact, the ideal unit would correspond to tutor-student turn pairs, as these are when student makes a game vs. no-game decision. However, we need a unit of analysis that can be compared across students, so that we can determine whether all students tend to game at "the same" place. It would be difficult to determine if turn-pair from one student are "the same" as a turn-pair from another student. The smallest unit of analysis that allows simple equivalence across students is the problem. Thus, we chose problems as the unit of analysis instead of lesson (too large) or tutor-student turn pairs (not equatable; too small). We used percentage of gaming (see equation 1) instead of raw values to avoid biasing the analysis towards, for instance, short problems.

To investigate predictors of gaming we conducted a linear regression analysis, with $PerGaming_{sp}$ (equation 1 above) as the dependent variable, and two independent variables: (1) *student*, the average gaming by a student s across all N problems p solved by that student (equation 2 above), and (2) *problem*, the average gaming on a problem p across all M students s who solved that problem (equation 3 above). The model is significant (F=16915, $p < 0.001$), and accounts for 60.7% of the variance ($R^2 = .607$). In this model, both *student* and *problem* yield a significant correlation with the dependent variable (*student*: standardized coefficient=.658, t=152.7, p<0.001; *problem*: standardized coefficient=.325, t=74.23, p<0.001). If we enter the independent variables separately to analyze the variance explained by each, (1) the *student* variable accounts for 49.6% of the variance, while (2) the *problem* variable accounts for 18.6% of the variance.

To identify the impact of a particular data set (i.e., class/semester), we re-ran the regression analysis with a third independent variable, namely *data set id*. This variable explained only an additional 1% of the variance, showing that data set had at best a weak effect on gaming, and so we did not consider it in subsequent analysis.

Another way to verify whether students are more consistently gaming across problems or if instead problems are more consistent across students is to randomly subdivide students (or problems) into buckets and then check for correlation between the buckets. To this end, we created two buckets by randomly assigning students to a given bucket. For each bucket, we obtained the average percentage of gaming for each problem in that bucket (equation 3 above), and then performed correlation analysis between buckets A and B. We found a high degree of association between the two data sets (R^2=.89 p < 0.001). That is, if a problem was often gamed by students in bucket A, then it was also often gamed by students in bucket B. We used an analogous technique to verify that problems were consistently gamed on between students (i.e., obtained two bucket by randomly assigning problems to a given bucket, and applied equation 2 above to obtain the average percentage of gaming by a student); the analysis yielded a high degree of association (R^2=.963, p<0.001). That is, if a student tended to game the problems in the A bucket, then that student also tended to game problems in the B bucket. Jointly, these analyses show that *students* are more consistent than *problems*: if a student is a high gamer on one half of the problem, then the student is also a high gamer on the other half; in contrast, if a problem is a high-gaming problem for half the students, then it is less likely to be a high-gaming problem for the other half. Thus, these analyses support the above regression results.

Yet another way to test our hypotheses is to examine histograms of gaming frequency. That is, we can look at how many students are high frequency gamers vs. middle vs. low frequency gamers. If individual differences among students are completely unimportant, and all students tend to solve roughly the same set of problems, then gaming frequency should be normally distributed. In fact, the distribution is significantly different from the normal (Shapiro-Wilks test of normality W=.8, p<0.01), and appears bimodal (see Figure 1, left). There seems to be one group of students who are frequent gamers, and another group who seldom game. This again suggests that individual differences play an important role in gaming frequency.

On the other hand, if the characteristics of problems are completely unimportant, then a histogram of the number of problems (y-axis) gamed at a certain range of frequencies (x-axis) should be normally distributed (Figure 1, right). This is in fact the case: the Shapiro-Wilks test of normality showed that the problem distribution is not significantly different from normal (W=.9, p>0.05). Thus, it appears once again that characteristics of students are more important than characteristics of problems in determining the frequency of gaming.

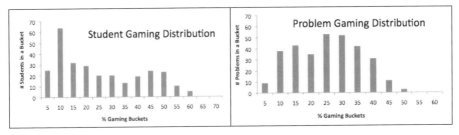

Fig. 1. Student (left) and problem (right) gaming distributions. Each bucket contains students (or problems) with a gaming range (e.g., bucket 10 has 5% < gaming < 10%).

4.2 Gaming Profiles: How Much and Where Are Student Gaming?

This section presents a descriptive analysis of the data, starting with how much students are gaming overall. On average, 22.5% of the tutor-student turn pairs were gamed. While this is higher than reported in [5], in that study students were in the presence of observers. This may have provided social deterrents for gaming, while in our study students were using Andes in private. We then analyzed where the gaming was occurring; Table 2 shows the results (the shaded cells indicate gamed turn pairs). In general, students most frequently took advantage of the opportunity to game when the tutor presented a high-level hint: on average, 18.4% of all actions corresponded to gaming on these hints; when given such a hint, students gamed 58.5% of the time.

In order to compare the gaming patterns of students who frequently gamed with those who infrequently gamed, we divided students into low gamers and high gamers based on a median split. On average, low gamers were significantly more likely than high gamers to game by guessing (46% vs. 13.2%; $F(1,283)=126$, $p<.01$). On the other hand, in contrast to low gamers, high gamers had a significantly higher proportion of skipped high-level hints (61.6% vs. 43.4%; $F(1, 283)=64$, $p<.01$), lack of planning (18.5% vs. 8.9%; $F(1,283)=159$, $p<.01$) and bottom-out hint copying (6.5% vs. 1.7% ; $F(1,283)=215$, $p<.01$).

4.3 Are Hints the Culprit or Is It the Students?

Over all students' gaming opportunities (see Table 2), as well as proportion of gaming for high gamers, high-level hints elicited the most gaming. Thus, we wanted to explore how students used hints and if hints were helpful during problem solving.

Hint Viewing. The most basic analysis is to calculate time students spent on hints. To do so, we obtained the latency between the provision of a hint and the next student action. On average, students spent 9.2 sec. vs. 5.7 sec. on bottom-out vs. high-level hints. High gamers spent significantly less time on hints than low gamers, both on bottom-out hints (7.5sec vs. 10.9sec.; $F(1, 277)=71$, $p<.01$) and high-level hints (3.2sec vs. 8.1sec; $F(1,286)=246$, $p<.01$). Since the bottom-out viewing is well above the gaming threshold, on average, neither low or high gamers skipped bottom-out hints. In contrast, high gamers average viewing time for high-level hints is just above the gaming threshold of 3 seconds, showing that in contrast to low gamers, these students did not pay much attention to high-level hints.

Table 2. Gaming opportunities for each *Tutor–Student* turn pair. Shown in each cell: (1) the mean % of a student response given a tutor action over all 16 possible combinations, (2) (*mean % of a student response for that row's tutor action*).

	(a) Student: Hint Request		(b) Student: Entry	
	fast	slow	fast	slow
(1) Tutor: B-O Hint	0.02 (.3)%	.2 (2)%	1.8 (23.6)%	5.7 (74)%
(2) Tutor: H-L Hint	**18.4 (58.5)%**	5.8 (18.3)%	.7 (2.3)%	6.4 (20.6)%
(3) Tutor: Incorrect	2.5 (10.1)%	3 (12.4) %	5.4 (21.9) %	13.6 (55.5)%
(4) Tutor: Correct	5.2 (15.6) %	3.7 (10.2)%	14.1 (38.2)%	13.3 (36)%

Legend: *fast: student action < gaming threshold; slow: student action >gaming threshold;* B-O: Bottom-out, H-L: High-level.

Are Hints Helpful? Prior work suggests that a factor related to gaming is *reading hints does not influence solution entry success* [4]. Sophisticated techniques exist for analyzing the utility of help by looking at its impact on future student performance [21]. It is not clear, however, how these methods account for gaming, which can make it difficult to interpret results (e.g., if a student skips a hint repeatedly, is the hint not helpful or is the student unmotivated to use it?). Thus, for the time being, we analyze hint impact on short-term performance, i.e., can the student generate an entry after seeing a hint. Specifically, for each student, we obtained the percentage of time s/he was successful at generating a *correct* entry after receiving each type of hint (bottom out, high level). Note that (1) students may require several attempts to generate a correct entry and (2) if hint *B* is requested after hint *A* but prior to generating a correct entry, then hint *A* is not counted as "successful" for helping the student.

If for a moment we don't consider entry correctness, high gamers tried to generate an entry only 18% of the time after receiving a high-level hint, immediately asking for another hint the other 82% of the time. Low gamers, on the other hand, responded to a high-level hint with an entry 43% of the time. This is in contrast to bottom-out hints, when *both* low and high gamers responded to the hint with an entry about 97% of the time. When students did generate an entry after seeing a bottom-out hint, on average, they were successful in 90% of instances (i.e., obtained a correct entry). There was little difference between low and high gamers for this analysis (89% vs. 92%, respectively, NS difference). After high-level hints, students generated a correct entry 73% of the time. Again, there was little difference between low and high gamers (72% vs. 73%, respectively, NS difference). This suggests that high-level hints helped students generate the solution in about three out of four instances.

Now let's look at time and number of attempts needed to produce a correct entry. After bottom-out hints, on average students required 1.1 attempts (1.23 for low gamers vs. 1.19 for high gamers, NS), and took 29 sec. to do so (34sec. for low gamers vs. 23sec. for high gamers, $F(284,1)=4$, $p = .052$). After high-level hints, on average students required 1.83 attempts; here low gamers needed significantly fewer attempts than high gamers (1.66 vs. 2.01, $F(1,284)= 17$, $p<0.001$), suggesting that perhaps the low gamers were more diligent about applying high-level hints. This conjecture is supported by the fact that low-gamers spent significantly longer than high-gamers to generate a correct entry after seeing a high-level hint (37 sec vs. 28 sec; $F(1,286)=9$, $p<0.01$).

5 Discussion and Future Work

A prerequisite for the design of effective interventions to discourage gaming is understanding its causes. Past research has shown that both student and instructional aspects influence gaming, but to date there does not exist agreement as to which is the stronger predictor. Baker et al. [4] argue that it is the latter, i.e., instructional aspects, that drive gaming. In contrast, our findings suggest that student features, namely the average percentage of gaming by a student over all the problems s/he solved, was a stronger predictor of gaming. There are a number of possibilities as to the cause of the difference between our findings and those in [4]. First, the Andes system might have less instructional variability than the one in [4]. Second, [4] used *lesson* as the grain-size, while we used *problem*, a smaller grain size. We did not use *lesson* since as already described in Section 2 we felt such a large grain size may obscure the results. Third, we used data from college students working at home while data in [4] came from high school students working in classrooms. When we recently did a preliminary analysis on a set of high school honours students using Andes mostly in their classroom, we found that their gaming levels were lower than those of college students; thus it is possible that gaming behaviors differ between these two populations and contexts, something that warrants further analysis and validation. A fourth possibility pertains to the way the analysis was done. Baker et al. [4] considered lesson features (e.g., does a lesson have many problems that use the same number for different quantities), and determined how much gaming variance was associated with each feature. Similarly, Baker et al. [15] determined the variance explained by features of students. Our analysis did not use problem features or student features, but rather individual problems and individual students. Our logic was that if there was something "wrong" with a problem, then almost all students should game on that problem; similarly, if there was something "wrong" with a student, then that student should game on almost all problems. In general, this discrepancy in findings in terms of whether problem or student features best predict gaming highlights the need for more work and validation of the factors influencing gaming.

In addition to exploring predictors of gaming, we also analyzed the impact of individual differences on how students were gaming. We found that when we looked at gaming opportunities over the tutor-student turn pairs, students tended to seize the opportunity to game after the tutor presented them with a high level hint. However, when we analyzed the *proportion* of each type of gaming over the total gaming events for each class of gamers, in contrast to high-gamers (who primarily skipped hints), the low gamers had a higher incidence of guessing on entries. One possible explanation for this difference, supported by literature on individual differences in help seeking behaviors [22], is that the low gamers preferred to obtain the solution on their own, without the tutor's help. Another possibility relates to Andes' scoring system. Recall that students were penalized for asking for a bottom out hint but were not penalized for guessing, and so perhaps the low gamers were simply more concerned about their Andes score than high gamers. Our analysis also showed, however, that low gamers spent more time with hints and took longer to generate a solution entry after seeing a hint. Since no points were awarded for taking time, this suggests that obtaining a higher score was not the only incentive for the high-gamers, indicating that perhaps these students were motivated and/or diligent in the problem-solving process. Jointly, these findings point to the need to tailor gaming interventions to student characteristics in ITS design.

Prior research suggests that poor hint usability leads to gaming [4]. To see if this was the case in our data, we analyzed how students used hints. We found that when the tutor presented a high-level hint, high gamers were quite unlikely to even *try* generating a corresponding solution entry, as compared to low gamers. If students did try to generate a solution entry, both low and high gamers were moderately successful when given a high-level hints. This provides some indication for the utility of these hints, suggesting that their abuse may be driven by other factors. It is possible, however, that students didn't bother to use the high-level hint at all, and were successful because they generated the solution on their own. To have a better understanding of hint utility, one could obtain students' base-rate performance. However, Andes makes hints available on demand, and students sometimes abuse these. This makes it less clear how to determine this base performance, and is something we leave for future work. We also plan to analyze deeper the student (and problem) features that predict gaming frequency, as well as analyze how gaming influences learning outcomes – although preliminary steps have been taken (e.g., [5]), more work is needed.

Acknowledgements. The authors thank the anonymous reviewers for their helpful suggestions. This research was funded the National Science Foundation, including the following grants: (1) IIS/HCC *Affective Learning Companions: Modeling and supporting emotion during learning* (#0705883); (2) *Deeper Modeling via Affective Meta-tutoring* (DRL-0910221) and (3) *Pittsburgh Science of Learning Center* (SBE-0836012).

References

1. VanLehn, K.: Analogy Events: How Examples Are Used During Problem Solving. Cognitive Science 22(3), 347–388 (1998)
2. Renkl, A.: Learning from Worked-Examples: A Study on Individual Differences. Cognitive Science 21(1), 1–30 (1997)
3. Chi, M., Siler, S.A., Jeong, H., Yamauchi, T., Hausmann, R.G.: Learning from Human Tutoring. Cognitive Science 25, 471–533 (2001)
4. Baker, d.C., Raspat, J., Aleven, V., Corbett, A.T., Koedinger, K.R.: Educational Software Features That Encourage and Discourage "Gaming the System". In: 14th International Conference on Artificial Intelligence in Education, pp. 475–482 (2009)
5. Baker, R.S., Corbett, A., Koedinger, K., Wagner, A.Z.: Off-Task Behavior in the Cognitive Tutor Classroom: When Students "Game the System". In: ACM CHI 2004: Computer-Human Interaction, pp. 383–390 (2004)
6. Baker, R., Corbett, A., Roll, I., Koedinger, K.: Developing a Generalizable Detector of When Students Game the System. User Modeling and User-Adapted Interaction 18(3), 287–314 (2008)
7. Baker, R., Corbett, A., Koedinger, K., Roll, I.: Generalizing Detection of Gaming the System across a Tutoring Curriculum. In: 11'th International Conference on Intelligent Tutoring Systems, pp. 402–411 (2006)

8. Rodrigo, M., Baker, R., d'Mello, S., Gonzalez, M., Lagud, M., Lim, S., Macapanpan, A., Pascua, S., Santillano, J., Sugay, J., Tep, S., Viehland, N.: Comparing Learners' Affect While Using an Intelligent Tutoring Systems and a Simulation Problem Solving Game. In: Woolf, B.P., Aïmeur, E., Nkambou, R., Lajoie, S. (eds.) ITS 2008. LNCS, vol. 5091, pp. 40–49. Springer, Heidelberg (2008)
9. Baker, R., Walonoski, J., Heffernan, N., Roll, I., Corbett, A., Koedinger, K.: Why Students Engage in "Gaming the System". Journal of Interactive Learning Research 19(2), 185–224 (2008)
10. Murray, R.C., VanLehn, K.: Effects of Dissuading Unnecessary Help Requests While Providing Proactive Help. In: Artificial Intelligence in Education, pp. 887–889 (2005)
11. Walonoski, J., Heffernan, N.: Prevention of Off-Task Gaming Behavior in Intelligent Tutoring Systems. In: Ikeda, M., Ashley, K.D., Chan, T.-W. (eds.) ITS 2006. LNCS, vol. 4053, pp. 722–724. Springer, Heidelberg (2006)
12. VanLehn, K., Lynch, C., Schulze, K., Shapiro, J., Shelby, R., Taylor, L., Treacy, D., Weinstein, A., Wintersgill, M.: The Andes Physics Tutoring System: Lessons Learned. International Journal of Artificial Intelligence and Education 15(3), 1–47 (2005)
13. Baker, R., Corbett, A., Koedinger, K.: Detecting Student Misuse of Intelligent Tutoring Systems. In: Lester, J.C., Vicari, R.M., Paraguaçu, F. (eds.) ITS 2004. LNCS, vol. 3220, pp. 531–540. Springer, Heidelberg (2004)
14. Walonoski, J., Heffernan, N.: Detection and Analysis of Off-Task Gaming Behavior in Intelligent Tutoring Systems. In: Ikeda, M., Ashley, K.D., Chan, T.-W. (eds.) ITS 2006. LNCS, vol. 4053, pp. 382–391. Springer, Heidelberg (2006)
15. Baker, R.: Is Gaming the System State-or-Trait? Educational Data Mining through the Multi-Contextual Application of a Validated Behavioral Model. In: Workshop on Data Mining for User Modeling, pp. 76–80 (2007)
16. Baker, R.S., Roll, I., Corbett, A., Koedinger, K.: Do Performance Goals Lead Students to Game the System. In: International Conference on Artificial Intelligence and Education (AIED 2005), pp. 57–64 (2005)
17. Baker, R., Corbett, A., Koedinger, K., Evenson, E., Roll, I., Wagner, A., Naim, M., Raspat, J., Baker, D., Beck, J.: Adapting to When Students Game an Intelligent Tutoring System. In: Ikeda, M., Ashley, K.D., Chan, T.-W. (eds.) ITS 2006. LNCS, vol. 4053, pp. 392–401. Springer, Heidelberg (2006)
18. Aleven, V.: Helping Students to Become Better Help Seekers: Towards Supporting Metacognition in a Cognitive Tutor. Paper Presented at German-USA Early Career Research Exchange Program: Research on Learning Technologies and Technology-Supported Education (2001)
19. Harris, A., Bonnett, V., Luckin, R., Yuill, N., Avramides, K.: Scaffolding Effective Help-Seeking Behaviour in Mastery and Performance Oriented Learners. In: Artificial Intelligence in Education, pp. 425–432 (2009)
20. Shih, B., Koedinger, K., Scheines, R.: A Response Time Model for Bottom-out Hints as Worked Examples. In: International Conference on Educational Data Mining, pp. 117–126 (2008)
21. Beck, J., Chang, K., Mostow, J., Corbett, A.: Does Help Help? Introducing the Bayesian Evaluation and Assessment Methodology. In: Woolf, B.P., Aïmeur, E., Nkambou, R., Lajoie, S. (eds.) ITS 2008. LNCS, vol. 5091, pp. 383–394. Springer, Heidelberg (2008)
22. Gall, S.N.-L.: Help-Seeking Behavior in Learning Review of Research in Education 12, 55–90 (1985)

The Fine-Grained Impact of Gaming (?) on Learning

Yue Gong, Joseph E. Beck, Neil T. Heffernan, and Elijah Forbes-Summers

Computer Science Department, Worcester Polytechnic Institute
100 Institute Road, Worcester, MA, 01609, USA
{ygong,josephbeck,nth,flveggie}@wpi.edu

Abstract. One of the common expectations of ITS designers is that students efficiently learn from every practice opportunity. However, when students are using an Intelligent Tutoring System, they can exhibit a variety of behaviors, such as "gaming," which can strongly reduce learning. In this paper, we present a new approach to infer the impact of gaming on learning at the fine-grained level. We integrated a knowledge tracing model of the student's knowledge with the student's gaming state (as identified by our gaming detector). We found that when gaming, students learn almost nothing (on the order of one-twelfth to one-fiftieth as efficiently). A student's gaming amount is associated with aggregate effects on his knowledge and learning, leading to less learning even in the practice opportunities where no gaming occurs. In addition, we found that students tend to game in those skills on which they have relatively low knowledge. Furthermore, we found that knowing the identity of the student is more important than knowing the skill for predicting whether gaming will occur.

Keywords: Gaming, Knowledge tracing, Influences on learning.

1 Introduction

With more and more students using Intelligent Tutoring Systems (ITS) in their daily study activities, their strategies for how to use ITS are becoming an important issue. Although ITS have been shown to have positive effects on helping student learning, different strategies of using ITS can lead to different learning outcomes [1, 2, 3, 4]. There are a variety of strategies exhibited by students, including "gaming," receiving a great deal of attention. A student is gaming if he is attempting to systematically use the tutors' feedback and help methods as a means to obtain a correct answer with little or no work [5].

There have been many prior works showing that gaming behavior is generally associated with a reduced learning rate. Baker, et al. [3] used a traditional analysis method, applying a pretest and a posttest, to show that student gaming results in a poorer learning gain. A similar trend has been found by Walonoski, et al. [5] in a different computer tutor environment (ASSISTment) and using a different analysis method: longitudinal data analysis. However, those previous works explored the impact of gaming on learning by focusing on the long-term effects, thus their conclusions are based on the aggregated data. In other words, during a period of time, the researchers tracked a sequence of student's performances, and also the conditions of whether and how much gaming occurred during that time. They then came to the conclusion based on examining the relation between aggregate gaming occurrences and student performance. Perhaps the students who game happen to be the ones who don't learn, but gaming is not the direct cause of the poor learning. Recent work by Corea, et al. [6] showed gaming has both immediate and aggregate effects on learning. They assessed whether gaming behavior is associated with immediate poorer learning, by applying learning decomposition method [7], where performance on a given skill at a given time is predicted based on the number times where the student previously engaged in gaming behavior on this skill. They found that the number of previous gaming behaviors is associated with less learning. Therefore, lower performance is predictable in the next problem after the student engages in gaming actions. They also pointed out that the apparent immediate impact of gaming, at the step level, appears to be due to a lack of learning at that very step where the gaming occurred; in other words, by gaming, an opportunity to learn is wasted.

One of the objectives of this study is to give a closer look at gaming's impact on learning at the fine-grained level, namely, rather than examining the cumulative effects of gaming on learning during an amount of time, or the immediate effects contributed by the number of gaming behaviors that occurred previously, we aimed to track gaming's quantitative impact on learning at the problem-solving level. We used student modeling as our conceptual framework, as it matches our requirements by taking observations of a student's performance and gaming state, and then using those to estimate the student's latent attributes. We chose the knowledge tracing model (KT) [8], which is one of the most broadly used student modeling approach. It takes student performances as observations and uses those to estimate the student's level of knowledge. Our motivation for using the knowledge tracing model is that we assume if a student games on a problem, it negatively impacts the amount of learning from that problem. In addition, gaming is a state that varies across time, similarly to student knowledge in KT model. Therefore the knowledge tracing model is a good technique for our goal of exploring gaming's impact on learning at the fine-grained level.

2 Methodology

2.1 Detection of Gaming

Student gaming is a kind of behaviors that cannot be determined as precisely as other student attributes, such as the correctness of a student's response. In order to build the model for exploring the impact of gaming on learning, we first must have some way of informing the model that gaming occurred. For simplicity, rather than treating gaming as a latent variable, we used a knowledge-engineering approach and tagged it using human-made heuristics.

In ASSISTment (the computer tutor environment we used), a main question consists of an initial question and a number of helps. There are two approaches for assisting students: hints give information on how to solve the initial question, and scaffolds break the initial question into a series of component problems. A particular problem will either offer hints or provide scaffolding.

Only the initial question's correctness is recorded as the student's performance of the current practice opportunity. Usually, students perform multiple actions when solving a main question. Specifically, if the student generates an incorrect response in his first attempt, the system would record this question wrong. Furthermore, the system allows the student to do three main kinds of actions:

1) **Answer**. A student's response to the question.

2) **Hint**. A student can request a hint. After seeing a hint message it is optional whether the student makes more attempts on the question or asks for additional hints. The student could run though all hints until the bottom-out hint where the answer to the question is provided. The student must submit the correct answer to proceed.

3) **Scaffold**. This event occurs when ASSISTment's strategy is to scaffold and the student submits an incorrect response. Once scaffolding begins, a student must proceed through all of the scaffolding steps. A scaffolding question is similar to a main question except it doesn't have its own scaffolding questions. Therefore, in a scaffolding question, the student could do *answer* and *hint* actions as well.

Based on analyzing the patterns of those actions, we constructed a gaming detector that contains three criteria.

- Rapid Guessing: in a question (initial or scaffolding), submit two attempted answers less than 2 seconds apart in two successive questions (initial or scaffolding).
- Rapid Response: perform any action after a hint or starting a problem before a reasonable amount of time has passed (where "reasonable" is a fast reading speed for the content of the hint or problem body. We chose a reading rate of 400 words per minute).
- Repeatedly Bottom-out Hinting: reach a bottom out hint on three consecutive questions (initial or scaffolding).

Note: according to these criteria, the majority of actions coded as gaming are associated with incorrect answers. However, in the knowledge tracing model, the probability of learning is independent of the correctness of the response, so the impact of gaming behaviors on learning won't be confounded.

For each action in a main question, our gaming detector assigned a gaming score that ranges between 0 and 1 (0 is not-gaming and 1 is gaming). If there are no previous records of a student, we assume the student starts with a gaming score of 0. If the student does some action (matching at least one of the three gaming criteria is required) that we think is gaming, the gaming score's value goes straight to 1. The student later can "recover" from a gaming state by performing any non-gaming actions (any other actions where none of the criteria is satisfied). With a non-gaming action detected, 0.5 is subtracted from the gaming score. Therefore, each main question might be associated with multiple gaming scores representing how well the student performed in every sub-step of that main question. We then tagged that main question using the score calculated by averaging across the gaming scores for all the actions of that student within that main question.

Since we chose the knowledge tracing model as our framework, and since discrete variables are more commonly used in Bayesian Networks, we further converted the continuous gaming score into a discrete value by selecting 0.5 as the cut-off point. In other words, if a main question is tagged with the average gaming score as greater than or equal to 0.5, the gaming state is labeled by 1; otherwise, 0 is assigned.

Although initially we were interested in gaming behaviors, our gaming detector seems to capture broader actions. We realized that's probably a good thing (see Results), and probably captures a larger set of actions than just gaming, but we don't (yet) have a good vocabulary for "non-productive behavior," so stuck with "gaming."

2.2 Student Modeling Framework

Knowledge tracing model
Knowledge tracing [2], shown in Fig. 1, is an approach for taking student observations and using those to estimate the student's level of knowledge.

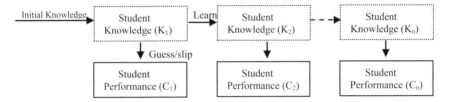

Fig. 1. Knowledge tracing model

There are two learning parameters. The first is initial knowledge (K_0), the likelihood the student knows the skill when he first uses the tutor. The second learning parameter is the learning rate, the probability a student will acquire a skill as a result of an opportunity to practice it. In addition to the two learning parameters, there are two performance parameters: guess and slip, which mediate student knowledge and student performance. In this paper we focus on the learning rather than the performance parameters.

Modified Knowledge tracing model
In order to explore the impact of gaming on learning at the problem-solving level, we first need to include student gaming state in the student model. We integrated it with knowledge tracing by putting in an additional node in the model structure, which indicates the gaming variable, shown in Fig. 2.

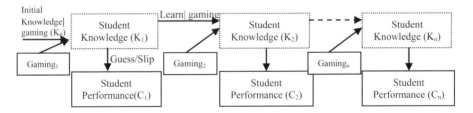

Fig. 2. Modified knowledge tracing model

The two performance parameters remain invariant after the modification, while the two learning parameters are changed. Initial knowledge is transformed from a prior probability to a conditional probability, thus there are two initial knowledge rates corresponding to the two given conditions: gaming and not-gaming. They indicate the likelihoods the student knows the skill when he first used the tutor, given whether he gamed on his first attempt or not. Similarly, the learning rate becomes two numbers after conditioning on the gaming state. The two learning rates are our major interests in this study. They indicate how much a student learns from a practice opportunity when he engages, or does not engage in gaming behaviors in that practice. The difference between these two, if there is any, should be viewed as the immediate impact of gaming behaviors on learning.

To train the model, we used *smoothing* [14] to infer the values of the knowledge tracing parameters that maximize likelihood of the observed data. Specifically, smoothing uses all of the data, even data occurring after a particular time slice, to estimate the model parameters. We can use smoothing since our experiments are conducted off line. In addition to estimating model parameters, smoothing also provides an estimate of the student's knowledge at each time step. This estimate is more accurate than a student modeling system used in an online manner, since the online system can only use past observations to evaluate the student (i.e. it does not have access to what will happen in the future).

2.3 Data Set

For this study, we used data from ASSISTment, a web-based math tutoring system. The data are from 343 twelve- through fourteen- year old 8th grade students in urban school districts of the Northeast United States. They were from four classes. These data consisted of 193,259 main problems of ASSISTment usage during Nov. 2008 to Feb. 2009. Performance records of each student were logged across time slices for 106 skills (e.g. area of polygons, Venn diagram, division, etc).

For each student performance, we applied our gaming detector to identify the gaming state, and then fit the data to the modified knowledge tracing model. We used the Bayesian Network Toolkit for Student Modeling (BNT-SM) [9] and the expectation maximization (EM) algorithm to optimize data likelihood (i.e. the probability of observing our student performance data) in order to estimate the model's parameters. We used the smoothing inference method [14] for using future data to estimate more plausible parameters. To address the problem of identifiability [10], we set Dirichlet priors [11] to initialize the EM algorithm.

3 Results

3.1 The Impact of Gaming

We trained a modified knowledge tracing model for each skill, i.e. observe all the data across all students for each skill and derive a set of 6 parameters (initial knowledge | gaming, initial knowledge | no-gaming, learning | gaming, learning | no-gaming, and guess and slip) for that particular skill. Thus, for 106 skills, we estimated 106 sets of parameters. Then, we calculated the mean values across all the skills (see Table 1). We also reported median to minimize the effect of outliers.

Table 1. Extended knowledge tracing model's estimates of the learning parameters

Across Skills	Percent of gaming	Initial knowledge| no gaming (K_0|~G)	Initial knowledge| gaming (K_0|G)	Learning| no gaming (L|~G)	Learning| gaming (L|G)
median	0.139	0.527	0.149	0.158	0.003
mean	0.148	0.540	0.171	0.207	0.017
SD	0.06	0.137	0.098	0.150	0.042

From Table 1, we see that median and mean values suggest the similar trend that when students game in their first attempt with a skill, it is associated with lower initial knowledge. Meanwhile, when a gaming behavior occurs, it immediately results in *much* less learning. The median value of L|G is 0.003, which is nearly 0, indicating essentially no learning. Although the corresponding mean is higher than the median, still, 0.017 is a very small number, especially compared to the counterpart 0.207, suggesting students learn approximately 12 times (0.207/0.017) faster when they are not gaming.

Another interesting observation is that, across 106 skills, our detector found that students gamed approximately 14% of the time. This number is much higher than what Baker reported in [12]. Given the vast difference in learning rates shown in Table 1 for gaming vs. non-gaming behaviors (0.158 vs. 0.003 using median, and 0.207 vs. 0.017 using mean), it is plausible that our gaming detector successfully captured certain kinds of non-productive behaviors. Since this behavior happens 14% of the time and is associated with almost no learning, it is certainly a behavior of note and one that we should focus on. If the goal of ITS research is to promote student learning, we should care about all behaviors that negatively impact learning. Our view is that it would be a better goal for researchers to focus on the question of "what types of behaviors result in little or no learning," rather than specific, named, behaviors.

3.2 The Impact of Gaming Amount

After examining the immediate impact of gaming at the level of individual problems, we now inspect its aggregate impact at the student level. In other words, are there any differences between the students who appeared to game more and the students who behaved more seriously?

In order to make claims about students, we trained one model for each student by observing his responses in all questions across all skills. For each student, the model estimated a set of learning parameters corresponding to his individual initial knowledge and his learning rate, given whether he was gaming.

Based on how much a student gamed overall, we divided students into three equal sized groups having relatively high, medium and low gaming level. To avoid the potential impact of outliers, for each group, we employed the more robust measure of central tendency, the median (reported in Table 2). Also, the mean value and standard deviation and range of the amount of gaming of each group are listed.

Table 2. Knowledge tracing parameters disaggregated by amount of overall gaming

Overall amount of gaming	Initial knowledge| no gaming (K_0|~G)	Initial knowledge| gaming (K_0|G)	Learning| no gaming (L|~G)	Learning| gaming (L|G)	Amount of gaming		
					mean	SD	range
High	0.337	0.235	0.114	0.021	33.2%	0.11	19.7% - 85.3%
Medium	0.538	0.345	0.151	0.049	13.3%	0.03	8.4% -19.6%
Low	0.705	**0.358**	0.219	0.089	4.1%	0.03	0 - 8.3%

As shown in the in Table 2 (first two columns), students who don't game much start with more initial knowledge, or conversely, students behave thoughtlessly on skills with low initial knowledge. One question is whether "low" is defined in absolute or relative terms? As can be seen in Table 2, low gaming students game with an average initial knowledge of 0.358, but when high gaming students are *not* gaming their average initial knowledge is 0.337 (bolded values). Therefore, it appears an absolute threshold does not exist, and the low knowledge that determines whether a student games is relative. In other words, students are inclined to game on their relatively weaker skills.

For learning rate, there is a consistent trend that students who game less learn more quickly both when gaming and when not. We noticed for those frequently gaming students, even for those skills they don't appear to game, their initial knowledge is still fairly low and the learning rates remain the lowest among the three groups. We think those students who are found to game here probably also game in other contexts, including before our study. Therefore, they are estimated with lower initial knowledge due to the possibility that a lot of practice opportunities were wasted. Another possibility for their lower initial knowledge is their learning rate is not as high as the serious students'.

3.3 Which Is More Useful for Predicting Gaming: Student or Skill?

Prior work inspected lesson vs. student [13], finding that for determining gaming, knowing the students has much less predictive power than knowing the tutor lessons. Our objective is to compare between student and skill. Is this just the fact that some students game more than others? Or are some skills just too hard to solve, so the students game on those problems? In order to resolve this problem, we did two ANOVAs. For each student, for each skill he attempted, we calculated the percent of gaming that occurred across all the questions he solved for that skill. E.g. one row of the well-prepared data is "Tom, Venn Diagram, 15%".

We assigned percent of gaming as the dependent variable in two models, and student as the independent variable in one ANOVA, and skill as the independent in the other one. We compared the two models to see which one accounts for more variance of the dependent. We found that the R^2 from the student ANOVA is 0.61, which is more than 5 times greater than the R^2 from the skill ANOVA, 0.11. Thus, student is more closely related to, and more predictive of gaming than, skill.

4 Contributions and Future Work

This paper makes contributions to our knowledge of gaming/non-productive learning behaviors, to how we build classifiers to detect problematic learner behaviors, and to student modeling.

For our knowledge of gaming, we found that students do not learn when they are gaming. Although this statement sounds trivial, it has not been demonstrated at the fine-grained level (e.g. [6]). Our temporal linkage of gaming behaviors to near-zero student learning makes a causal connection between the two much more plausible than simple correlational evidence that students who game more tend to have lower knowledge. We also found, contrary to [13], the student identity was very predictive of whether students chose to game. Such contrary empirical results are to be expected, since the result is really about how much variability there is in the student population relative to the construct in question. Similarly, our "gaming" detector fired much more frequently (about 14% of actions) than is typical [5,13]. This result suggests that we were measuring a construct that perhaps included gaming, but also some other behaviors that led to almost no learning.

Scientifically, we have constructed a detector that appears to measure something other than gaming. We don't have a good name for what we're measuring but, whatever it is, it is a powerful predictor of whether a student learns or not. We argue that, if what we care about is student learning, then this is the type of research we should be pursuing: rather than attempting to build classifiers for various "named" student behaviors, instead we should focus when students don't learn, and focus on naming various behavior clusters later.

Within student modeling, rather than having a detector that operates independently of the student model (e.g. [3,5]), we have integrated them into one framework. Conceptually, this unification is sensible as both knowledge as well as poor behaviors should be viewed of as part of the student model. Pragmatically, this unification enables better tracking of student knowledge since we found that students learn considerably less in some practice opportunities than in others. In addition, we have introduced to the ITS community the concept of using smoothing to achieve more accurate student knowledge estimates. This approach does not work for online tutors since they do not have future student performance data available, but is a powerful technique for post hoc offline analyses. The use of smoothing is a powerful argument for using Bayesian networks as an analytic framework, since they provide such inference "for free" as a standard reasoning approach.

There are several interesting, unresolved issues. First, we found that gaming was slightly more likely on skills where the student's knowledge was relatively, rather than absolutely, weak. This result contradicted our expectations. One issue is whether there is a deeper meaning behind the result. One possible interpretation is students perceive some skills as being their "weak ones", thus are unwilling to expend effort on them. Even good students appear to have such a list, although they had fewer non-productive behaviors. Better understanding this result and the metacognitive implications is an interesting piece of research. To our knowledge, no one has investigated this issue before. Will this result replicate across student populations and in different tutoring systems?

Improving the integration of the detector with standard student modeling approaches would enhance the technique. For example, we could treat gaming as a latent variable, the same as we do for knowledge, and model both of them as latent nodes in our graphical model. Estimating two latents from one observable variable, correctness, will not work. Therefore, some means of transforming the inputs to our detector relating to speeded responses, bottom out hinting, etc. into a stream used by the combined student model is needed.

The graphical model that we used has somewhat troubling semantics. It states that gaming on the current problem impacts how much students learn from the prior problem. Although this statement sounds nonsensical, empirically the support is strong. However, a logical next experiment would be to consider models that examine how gaming on a problem impacts how much students learn from that problem. Conceptually, this can be thought of as having an arrow from gaming point to knowledge in the *next* time slice, rather than the current one. An alternate way of thinking about the problem is to redefine the gaming node to refer to how much the student gamed on the prior, rather than the current, problem. Determining exactly where gaming negatively impacts knowledge would be a useful contribution.

5 Conclusions

This paper has presented a novel approach for estimating the impact of gaming at the fine-grained level. We integrated student gaming state with the knowledge tracing model and used smoothing to take advantage of future data, without any human-made heuristics, in order to produce plausible parameter estimates.

We found that gaming has strong negative impact on learning. When gaming occurs, students basically don't learn. The amount of gaming has aggregate impact on student knowledge and learning as well. In addition, we found that students tend to game on those skills on which they have relatively lower incoming knowledge. Thus even for those well-behaved students, they may engage in gaming if they are required to solve the questions beyond their knowledge. Furthermore, with respecting to gaming behavior, we compared the predictive power from knowing the student vs. knowing the skill. We have shown that being aware of the student is more helpful for predicting whether gaming will occur. Finally it's worth pointing out that it's important to consider any type of non-productive behavior, and not to focus on known ones, as we found 14% of actions are associated with no learning—and that is almost certainly an underestimate.

Acknowledgments. This research was made possible by the US Dept. of Education, Institute of Education Science, "Effective Mathematics Education Research" program grant #R305A070440, NSF CAREER award to Neil Heffernan, the Spencer Foundation, and a Weidenmeyer Fellowship from WPI.

References

1. Aleven, V., McLaren, B.M., Roll, I., Koedinger, K.R.: Toward tutoring help seeking: Applying cognitive modeling to meta-cognitive skills. In: Lester, J.C., Vicari, R.M., Paraguaçu, F. (eds.) ITS 2004. LNCS, vol. 3220, pp. 227–239. Springer, Heidelberg (2004)
2. Arroyo, I., Woolf, B.: Inferring learning and attitudes from a Bayesian Network of log file data. In: Proceedings of the 12th International Conference on Artificial Intelligence in Education, pp. 33–40 (2005)
3. Baker, R.S., Corbett, A.T., Koedinger, K.R., Wagner, A.Z.: Off-Task Behavior in the Cognitive Tutor Classroom: When Students "Game The System". In: Proceedings of ACM CHI 2004: Computer-Human Interaction, pp. 383–390 (2004)
4. Stevens, R., Soller, A., Cooper, M., Sprang, M.: Modeling the Development of Problem-Solving Skills in Chemistry with a Web-Based Tutor. In: Lester, J.C., Vicari, R.M., Paraguaçu, F. (eds.) ITS 2004. LNCS, vol. 3220, pp. 580–591. Springer, Heidelberg (2004)
5. Walonoski, J., Heffernan, N.: Detection and analysis of off-task gaming behavior in intelligent tutoring systems. In: Ikeda, M., Ashley, K.D., Chan, T.-W. (eds.) ITS 2006. LNCS, vol. 4053, pp. 382–391. Springer, Heidelberg (2006)
6. Cocea, M., Hershkovitz, A., Baker, R.S.J.d.: The Impact of Off-task and Gaming Behaviors on Learning: Immediate or Aggregate? In: Proceedings of the 14th International Conference on Artificial Intelligence in Education, pp. 507–514 (2009)
7. Beck, J.E., Mostow, J.: How who should practice: Using learning decomposition to evaluate the efficacy of different types of practice for different types of students. In: Woolf, B.P., Aïmeur, E., Nkambou, R., Lajoie, S. (eds.) ITS 2008. LNCS, vol. 5091, pp. 353–362. Springer, Heidelberg (2008)
8. Corbett, A., Anderson, J.: Knowledge tracing: Modeling the acquisition of procedural knowledge. In: User Modeling and User-Adapted Interaction, pp. 253–278 (1995)
9. Chang, K.-m., Beck, J., Mostow, J., Corbett, A.: A Bayes Net Toolkit for Student Modeling in Intelligent Tutoring Systems. In: Ikeda, M., Ashley, K.D., Chan, T.-W. (eds.) ITS 2006. LNCS, vol. 4053, pp. 104–113. Springer, Heidelberg (2006)
10. Beck, J.E., Chang, K.-m.: Identifiability: A Fundamental Problem of Student Modeling. In: Conati, C., McCoy, K., Paliouras, G. (eds.) UM 2007. LNCS (LNAI), vol. 4511, pp. 137–146. Springer, Heidelberg (2007)
11. Rai, D., Gong, Y., Beck, J.E.: Using Dirichlet priors to improve model parameter plausibility. In: Proceedings of the 2nd International Conference on Educational Data Mining, Cordoba, Spain, pp. 141–148 (2009)
12. Baker, R.S.J.d., de Carvalho, A.M.J.A.: Labeling Student Behavior Faster and More Precisely with Text Replays. In: Proceedings of the 1st International Conference on Educational Data Mining, pp. 38–47 (2008)
13. Baker, R.S.J.d.: Differences between Intelligent Tutor Lessons, and the Choice to Go Off-Task. In: Proceedings of the 2nd International Conference on Educational Data Mining, pp. 11–20 (2009)
14. Russell, S., Norvig, P.: Artificial Intelligence: A Modern Approach, 2nd edn. (2003)

Squeezing Out Gaming Behavior in a Dialog-Based ITS

Peter Hastings[1], Elizabeth Arnott-Hill[2], and David Allbritton[1]

[1] DePaul University
[2] Chicago State University

Abstract. Research Methods Tutor (RMT) is a dialog-based intelligent tutoring system which has been used by students in Research Methods in Psychology classes since 2003. Students interact with RMT to reinforce what they learn in class in five different topics. In this paper, we evaluate a different population of students and replicate our prior research: despite the relatively small amount of exposure during the term to RMT compared to other course-related activities, students learn significantly more on topics covered with RMT [1]. However, we did not find the same advantage for the dialog-based tutoring mode of RMT over the CAI mode. When transcript analyses indicated that a small but significant number of students were gaming the system by entering empty or nonsense responses, we modified the tutor to require reasonable attempts. This did lead some students to reform their gaming ways. In other cases, however, it resulted in disengagement from tutoring at least temporarily because reasonable answers were not recognized.

Keywords: Dialog-based ITS, Gaming behaviors, Motivation.

1 Introduction

Most collegiate Psychology programs require one or more classes in Research Methods [2]. Unfortunately, Psychology students find these classes to be especially difficult. The material is abstract and is normally learned by studying many specific cases of psychological research and then inferring general principles which will apply to their own experiments. We developed Research Methods Tutor (RMT), a dialog-based ITS, to help reinforce the concepts that students learn in research methods courses by engaging them in conversations about those topics. In previous research, we showed that RMT is effective. In this paper, we present data that replicates our previous results with a very different set of students. In related research, we identified a small, but significant number of students who were engaging in "gaming the system" behaviors. We also describe what happened when we modified RMT to encourage these students to re-engage with the tutor.

2 RMT in the Field

2.1 The Tutor

RMT was modeled after the AutoTutor system [3] which was designed to follow the behavior of (non-expert) human tutors [4]. Some basic assumptions of this approach are:

- The tutor tends to control the dialog, using a variety of dialog moves to induce the student to provide particular information, and providing it when the student cannot.
- The tutor has a relatively shallow evaluation of the student's answers, and simply compares the student's response to the expected response to the current question.
- The tutor seldom gives direct negative feedback, instead preferring to simply give the expected answer or move to a related question.
- The tutor does not try to create an overall model of the student's knowledge, but comes to the tutoring session with a script of topics to cover.

These assumptions allow RMT to engage the student in extended conversations on the tutoring topics using relatively simple Natural Language Understanding techniques including LSA and keyword matching [5].

Research with AutoTutor has shown that it can produce remarkable learning effect sizes of up to 1σ [6]. However, most of this research has been done in a laboratory setting where research pool participants take a pretest, use the tutor intensively for some hours, and come back a week later for a second session of tutoring and the posttest. RMT was created first and foremost with the goal of providing additional support to our research methods students, and thus, our evaluations have differed significantly from the lab-based model.

Our participants take the pretest at the beginning of the term when they start their research methods class. In the first week of class, they are asked to login to RMT via the web to introduce themselves to the software, and install extensions for the agent-based version of the system if they can. (If they can't, they automatically use the text-only version of the system which provides the same information but doesn't use the talking head.) RMT includes five conceptual modules: Variables, Reliability, Validity, Experimental Design, and Ethics.[1] During the course of the term, the students are assigned to use RMT during the five weeks in which these topics are covered in class.

We have used two different types of control groups to assess the impacts of RMT. One control group is students in another section of Research Methods which is taught by the same instructor but without the use of RMT. Although students are (obviously) not randomly assigned to sections, we adopted this approach to minimize whatever carryover effects between conditions that might occur for students in the same sections. The other control condition (besides

---

[1] Additional modules are currently being developed, including statistics and graph interpretation.

no-tutoring) is a computer-aided instruction (CAI) condition in which students read (or are "read to" by the talking head) short passages of text and then take a few multiple choice questions. The text in the CAI condition was derived from the tutoring topics to ensure equivalent conceptual content. For each question answered in the CAI condition, the student is told whether the answer was right or wrong, but they are not told what their overall score was and are not required to achieve any particular level of performance in order to get credit for completing that CAI module. Students in the RMT classes are randomly split into two groups. One group gets tutoring for the first, third, and fifth modules, and CAI for the second and fourth, and the situation is reversed for the other group. At the end of the term, the students take a post-test which covers the original topics plus a transfer component.

2.2 Summary of Prior Results

In 2007, RMT was tested with almost 160 students from 5 sections of research methods classes at DePaul University. We compared the learning gains of tutored and non-tutored students, and performed a within-subjects comparison of tutoring versus CAI. The details were published in [7,1] and are summarized here.

Using an ANCOVA with pretest score as covariate, and posttest score as the dependent variable, we found found that students in RMT classes scored significantly higher than students in control classes $[F(1, 155) = 23.21, p < .01]$. Using the learning effect size formula from the National Reading Panel [8], we calculated that the students in RMT classes learned 0.76σ more than control students. We were, frankly, astonished to see such a large effect size given the realities of our evaluation:

- The students only used the system for a combined total of 2–4 hours over the course of a ten-week term.
- They were interacting with the system primarily from their own homes or dorm rooms, often late at night, with (presumably) a range of distractions present.
- All the other class activities (lectures, tests, projects) may well have masked and/or interfered with whatever was learned from the tutor.

We concluded that RMT was very effective in *reinforcing* what the students were learning in the class, by having students engage in dialogs about those concepts.

In our within-subjects comparison of CAI versus tutoring, we found that students learned significantly more on topics on which they were tutored than on those on which they used CAI $[F(1, 71) = 4.627, p = .035]$. The NRP learning effect size was 0.34σ. We also checked if there were differences between students who used the agent-based mode of the system compared to the text-only mode. There was a marginally significant advantage of the agent-based mode $[F(1, 74) = 3.701, p = .058]$. This result must be interpreted with caution, however, since students essentially self-selected into this condition; if they couldn't follow the installation instructions or didn't have their own computer, they were put into the text-only condition.

2.3 New Learning Evaluations

In 2008, one of us took a faculty position at Chicago State University. This allowed us to attempt to replicate our evaluations of RMT with a very different group of students. Although both Chicago State and DePaul are located within Chicago, the student populations differ significantly. Table 1 summarizes a few differences.

Table 1. Comparison of student populations

DePaul University	Chicago State University
– 40% students of color – 77% of UG students are under 24 – 99% of incoming freshmen are under 21 – 75% of freshman live on campus	– 98% students of color – 60% have full-time jobs – 80% are parents – Average age of UG student = 26 – 95% of students live off-campus

Before evaluating the CSU students, we created a more concise version of the pre- and posttest. At 106 questions, our original test was rather onerous to the students, and we were concerned that they might not be trying their best on it — especially at the end of the term. The new version of the pretest had 50 questions, 10 per topic. The new posttest had the same questions plus five additional questions per topic as a transfer task. These questions presented experimental scenarios requiring more analytical than conceptual knowledge [9].

Students in the RMT condition ($n = 56$) took the tests and used the tutor or CAI as described above, with the exception that, as CSU runs on a semester schedule, the testing and tutoring took place over the course of 15 weeks instead of the 10 in DePaul's quarters. Students in the other section ($n = 31$) did not use RMT and served as the non-equivalent control group.

Again, we raised the same primary research question: Do students who use the tutor show higher learning gains from pretest to posttest than controls? We used an ANCOVA with the pretest score as the covariate, the condition (RMT, control) as independent variable, and posttest score as dependent variable. The results are shown in Table 2. The table gives the mean scores, standard deviations, and effect sizes for the RMT and control conditions on the first 50 questions of the posttest (identical to the pretest), the 25 transfer questions, and on the complete test.

Thus, for overall learning gains, we replicated our prior results showing that students learn significantly more when they use tutoring and CAI than when they do not, and achieved impressive effect sizes of 1.4σ, 0.7σ, 1.2σ on the basic test, transfer test, and complete test respectively.

Table 2. Evaluation results, 2008, CSU students

Test questions	Control	RMT	$F(1, 84)$	Effect
First 50	19.8 (11.3)	32.5**(7.0)	54.78	1.39
Transfer (25)	9.1 (5.8)	12.9**(4.8)	14.05	0.71
Complete (75)	28.9 (16.7)	45.4**(10.5)	42.99	1.21

Significance level: $** \ p \leq .01$.

We also addressed the question, does the dialog-based tutor result in higher learning gains on the posttest than the CAI version? Using a repeated measures ANOVA, we compared the scores for each student on tutor modules vs. CAI modules. Contrary to our prior results, there was no significant difference between the tutoring and CAI conditions $[F(1, 27) = 3.202, p = 0.085]$. Tutor modules produced an average gain per module of 2.5. The average gain for CAI modules was 2.46.

Our third research question was: Does the agent result in greater learning gains on the posttest than text-only? Here, too, we found no significant differences between conditions with the CSU student population $[F(1, 26) = 2.247, p = 0.146]$. There was a significantly smaller number of students using the agent condition at CSU (31% compared to 79% of the DePaul students). Two major factors could explain this: Microsoft has discontinued support for Microsoft Agents, and it doesn't work with the newer version of Internet Explorer. Fewer students had their own computers and were not allowed to install the software on lab computers.

Overall, we showed that use of RMT for tutoring and CAI does provide significant learning gains to students at Chicago State University. However, we did not find the advantage that we had found earlier for tutoring over CAI. One possible explanation that we wanted to explore was that these students were more adept in finding ways to "game the system". This topic is addressed in the next section.

3 Gaming Behaviors

Identifying and counteracting gaming behaviors has become somewhat of a hot topic within the ITS community in recent years. When students "game the system," they typically focus their energies on finding ways to circumvent whatever pedagogical support the system was intended to provide. In this section, we describe some of the recent research in identifying and correcting gaming behaviors. Then we describe our analyses of gaming in RMT, and the steps that we took to counteract it.

3.1 Related Work

Previous research in off-task or gaming behaviors in interactive learning environments has focused on five areas. Examples of the research findings follow:

1. Analyzing the effects of off-task or gaming behaviors on learning outcomes: Gaming was the only off-task behavior significantly correlated with learning gains [10]. Gaming has negative effects on learning both immediately, and in the aggregate [11].
2. Creating methods for automatically identifying off-task behaviors: Based on very fast actions, very slow actions, requests for help, and/or errors [12].
3. Determining features of individual learning problems that are correlated with gaming: [13] found only one of 79 features of cognitive tutor algebra problems that was significantly correlated with off task behaviors. Students went off-task much less when they were doing equation-solving. Other factors: abstract, ambiguous, or unclear problems [14].
4. Determining affective antecedents of gaming in participants: Students tend to game the system when they dislike the subject matter, have little educational self-drive, and are frustrated [15].
5. Trying to ascertain effective strategies for counteracting off-task behaviors. Better understanding of gaming *should* help reduce it [10,11,12,13,14,15,16], though there seems to be less empirical evidence supporting such claims.

While much of the recent research on off-task and gaming behaviors has been done within the context of cognitive tutors and the like, a notable exception is [16]. The authors call Crystal Island a Narrative-centered learning environment. It could also be called a serious game. Interestingly, gaming or off-task behavior within this type of game parallels that in the real world. Students may choose not to engage in goal-oriented behavior (according to the goal set in the game scenario), but instead to wander about, exploring the environment. This study used path analysis to differentiate goal-oriented and non-goal-oriented movements within Crystal Island.

3.2 Identifying Gaming Behaviors in RMT

In a dialog-based ITS, the student's actions are closer in some ways to those in a narrative-centered learning environment than in a traditional ITS. The student can enter absolutely any text in response to the tutor's questions or prompts. A cognitive tutor interface provides a limited number of actions. RMT's interface is exceedingly simple: besides the talking head or the text which present tutor utterances, there is only a text input box. What the student types into that box is only constrained by their educational motivation, their adoption of Gricean dialog maxims, and, of course, their understanding of the tutor's intentions and the intended answer.

While collecting materials for a large corpus analysis study, we noticed a small, but significant number of student transcript segments which indicated that the student was making a less-than-valiant attempt to answer the tutor. Some examples of such utterances are: "asdf,", "j", "hello" 60 times in a row, "help" 10 times in a row, "dude you voice is creepy," "this is boring," and "".

RMT was designed to handle a range of different responses. In addition to student answers to its questions, RMT recognizes many different ways of asking it to repeat the question like (e.g. "what", "come again"), statements about the student's own comprehension (e.g. "dont know", "do I need to know this?"), and questions about terminology. Capitalization and punctuation are ignored by the tutor and usually by the students. RMT includes an automatic spellchecker that attempts to map unrecognized words into those in its vocabulary. Because student spelling and word choice are so creative and because natural language processing in general is intractable, RMT attempts to "understand" student utterances that don't fall into one of the categories above by comparing them to a small set of expected answers using LSA and keyword matching. This makes RMT fairly good at detecting *good* answers, but not so good at recognizing different types of (unexpected) bad answers.[2] In particular, RMT can not distinguish plain old bad answers from creative / unexpected good answers, other requests than those above, or random character strings. And because RMT is a helpful interlocutor, bad (non-good) answers prompt the tutor to provide the expected answer, and then ask a related question. Eventually, when the topic material has been covered by the tutor or the student, the tutor will provide a summary, and move on to the next problem.

We looked for evidence of gaming in transcripts of 234 students who used RMT between 2005 and 2009. Students were identified as extensive gamers if more than half of their utterances were blank, random strings, or non-responsive in some other way. Although our initial scan of transcripts indicated substantial gaming in about 10% of transcripts, only 15 out of 234 (6.4%) were labeled as extensive gamers. Seven more students showed significant but sub-threshold levels of gaming.

To examine the effects of gaming behavior on learning, we compared the learning outcomes of gamers and non-gamers. In marked contrast to previous research our data showed no significant effects of gaming on learning gains. One possible explanation is the great difference in the size of the two sets. Furthermore, students who gamed the tutor did not necessarily game the CAI modules. Module-by-module analyses showed no significant differences, but here the number of gamed tutor modules was even smaller than the number of gamers overall. If we combine the gamers with people who did not finish their modules we find that — although there aren't significant differences, gamers and non-finishers together scored lower overall on all outcome measures. They scored significantly lower on the variables topic.

3.3 Manipulating Gaming

Although the overall extent of gaming was relatively small, it seemed both unnecessary and easily remedied (potentially). If RMT simply rejected answers with a similarity score of 0 to expected answers, then it could eliminate both empty and random responses and maintain its generous behavior for "nice tries". We added a third level (:ZERO) of evaluation for student answers, and altered the transition network which controls the tutors behavior. If a student answer got a :ZERO evaluation, the tutor would said something like, "I didn't get that"

---

[2] RMT will trigger a remedial dialog for an expected bad answer.

or "huh?", and repeat the previous question. We tested the system's behavior on a wide range of answers, and found that it was working as planned, so we included the modification in the online version of RMT approximately halfway through the Fall 2009 semester.

At the end of the semester, we examined the transcripts to see if we were successful in eliminating gaming. To our surprise (and embarrassment) the first thing we noticed was that a number of students required 2-3 times more turns to finish some of the topics. There were two culprits. One question had an obscure expected answer that LSA did not recognize as having any similarity with most student responses. Two questions expected numerical answers. Because LSA was trained to ignore numbers, our text pre-processor removed numbers along with punctuation before strings were spellchecked and compared to expected answers. When students reached this question, no answer they could give was accepted by RMT, and it continually repeated the same question. Thus, when we created one manipulation to attempt to reduce gaming behavior, we inadvertently created another that could frustrate students and increase gaming behavior.

3.4 Results

This section describes our analyses of the results of this dual manipulation of gaming behavior. As with the overall comparison of gamers and non-gamers across the different terms, the students in Fall 2009 showed no significant effects of gaming on learning gains. Again a relatively small number of students (4 of 39) provided a significant number of non-responsive answers. For two of these students, the modification of the tutor's behavior appeared effective in eliminating gaming behavior. On the topics completed before the modification, both students entered primarily blank or random answers. After the modification, they answered the questions.

For the problematic questions where the tutor accepted few or no answers, we coded the students as "frustrated" if after a number of attempts, they began to enter blank or random responses. Although 6 students appeared to engage in gaming behavior when frustrated in this way, 4 of them subsequently completed other tutor modules without gaming. Furthermore, students who were "frustrated" did not score differently on any of the subtopics or the posttest overall.

Although there were no significant differences in learning gains between CAI and tutoring conditions for the CSU students as a whole, in Fall 2009, with the anti-gaming manipulation, students learned significantly more from the CAI modules than they did from the tutoring modules. A repeated measures ANOVA comparing each participant's scores for the tutor modules to that same participant's score for the CAI modules showed that the scores on the CAI modules were significantly higher, $[F(1,21) = 7.299, p = 0.013]$, tutoring mean gain = 2.4 $(SE = .34)$, CAI mean gain = 4.2 $(SE = .91)$.

Although fewer students completed the tutoring topics covered later in the Fall 2009 semester, this pattern was noted in other terms as well. There was no significant difference in the rates of topic completion between the terms.

4 Conclusions and Future Work

In this paper, we described learning results for RMT in two different student populations. Significantly, these learning gains were recorded in everyday use of the system, not in a laboratory context. We also described our analyses of gaming behavior in RMT and our (somewhat unfortunate) attempts to deter gaming. Analyses of the student transcripts showed that the change did, in fact, lead to reduction in gaming behavior in some, but not all students who had previously started gaming the system.

We also had the opportunity to analyze the effects of increased frustration on users of a dialog-based tutor. Although some students did disengage, for most it was only temporary. When they went on to other topics, they went back to interacting with the tutor as they had before.

Although it was too late to help the Fall 2009 students, the "number problem" was easily fixed, and RMT now accepts numerical answers. The tutor's behavior now makes it easier to identify obscure expected answers as well. Previously, the tutor's behavior wasn't markedly different for problematic errors. Now, we can integrate triggers into RMT that identify when students get stuck on a particular question, allowing the student to continue on, and alerting us that the expected answers may need to be changed.

In future work, we would also like to explore the possibility of giving the student some indicator of the cummulative quality of their responses. We hope that this could make it more clear to the students the relationship between the effort they put into answering the questions, and the efficiency with which they move through the tutoring topics. We would also like to develop a test harness for the system. This is will be a challenge, however, due to the natural language input to the system, and the dynamic determination of response and dialog direction.

References

1. Arnott, E., Hastings, P., Allbritton, D.: Research Methods Tutor: Evaluation of a dialogue-based tutoring system in the classroom. Behavior Research Methods 40(3), 672–694 (2008)
2. Perlman, B., McCann, L.I.: The structure of the psychology undergraduate curriculum. Teaching of Psychology 26, 171–176 (1999)
3. Graesser, A., Person, N., Harter, D.: The TRG: Teaching tactics and dialog in AutoTutor. International Journal of Artificial Intelligence in Education 12, 23–39 (2001)
4. Person, N.K.: An analysis of the examples that tutors generate during naturalistic one-to-one tutoring sessions. PhD thesis, University of Memphis, Memphis, TN (1994)
5. Wiemer-Hastings, P., Allbritton, D., Efron, J., Arnott, E.: Research methods tutoring in the classroom. In: AIED 2003 - Supplementary Proceedings of the 11th International Conference on Artificial Intelligence in Education, pp. 388–392. University of Sydney, Sydney (2003)

6. Graesser, A., Jackson, G., Mathews, E., Mitchell, H., Olney, A., Ventura, M., Chipman, P., Franceschetti, D., Hu, X., Louwerse, M., Person, N.: TRG: Why/AutoTutor: A test of learning gains from a physics tutor with natural language dialog. In: Proceedings of the 25th Annual Conference of the Cognitive Science Society. Erlbaum, Mahwah (2003)
7. Arnott, E., Hastings, P., Allbritton, D.: RMT in the classroom. In: Proceedings of the Midwest Artificial Intelligence and Cognitive Science Conference (2007)
8. National Reading Panel: Teaching children to read: An evidence-based assessment of the scientific research literature on reading and its implications for reading instruction. Technical Report NIH 00-4754, National Institute of Child Health & Human Development, Washington, DC (2008)
9. Bloom, B. (ed.): Taxonomy of educational objectives: The classification of educational goals: Handbook I, cognitive domain. Longmans, New York (1956)
10. Baker, R.S., Corbett, A.T., Koedinger, K.R., Wagner, A.Z.: Off-task behavior in the cognitive tutor classroom: When students "game the system". In: ACM CHI 2004: Computer-Human Interaction, pp. 383–390 (2004)
11. Cocea, M., Hershkovitz, A., Baker, R.: The impact of off-task and gaming behaviors on learning: Immediate or aggregate? In: Dimitrova, V., Mizoguchi, R., du Boulay, B. (eds.) Proceedings of the 14th International Conference on Artificial Intelligence in Education, pp. 507–514. IOS Press, Amsterdam (2009)
12. Baker, R.S.: Modeling and understanding students' off-task behavior in intelligent tutoring systems. In: CHI 2007: Proceedings of the SIGCHI Conference on Human Factors in Computing Systems, pp. 1059–1068. ACM, New York (2007)
13. Baker, R.: Differences between intelligent tutor lessons, and the choice to go off-task. In: Proceedings of the 2nd International Conference on Educational Data Mining, pp. 11–20 (2009)
14. Baker, R.S., de Carvalho, A.M., Raspat, J., Aleven, V., Corbett, A.T., Koedinger, K.R.: Educational software features that encourage and discourage "gaming the system". In: Dimitrova, V., Mizoguchi, R., du Boulay, B. (eds.) Proceedings of the 14th International Conference on Artificial Intelligence in Education, pp. 507–514. IOS Press, Amsterdam (2009)
15. Baker, R., Walonoski, J., Heffernan, N., Roll, I., Corbett, A., Koedinger, K.: Why students engage in "gaming the system" behavior in interactive learning environments. Journal of Interactive Learning Research 19(2), 185–224 (2008)
16. Rowe, J.P., McQuiggan, S.W., Robison, J.L.: Off-task behavior in narrative-centered learning environments. In: Dimitrova, V., Mizoguchi, R., du Boulay, B. (eds.) Proceedings of the 14th International Conference on Artificial Intelligence in Education, pp. 99–106. IOS Press, Amsterdam (2009)

Analogies, Explanations, and Practice: Examining How Task Types Affect Second Language Grammar Learning

Ruth Wylie[1], Kenneth Koedinger[1], and Teruko Mitamura[2]

[1] Human-Computer Interaction Institute, [2] Language Technologies Institute
Carnegie Mellon University, 5000 Forbes Avenue
Pittsburgh, Pennsylvania 15213 USA
{rwylie,krk,teruko}@cs.cmu.edu

Abstract. Self-explanation is an effective instructional strategy for improving problem solving in math and science domains. However, our previous studies, within the domain of second language grammar learning, show self-explanation to be no more effective than simple practice; perhaps the metalinguistic challenges involved in explaining using one's non-native language are hampering the potential benefits. An alternative strategy is tutoring using analogical comparisons, which reduces language difficulties while continuing to encourage feature focusing and deep processing. In this paper, we investigate adult English language learners learning the English article system (e.g. the difference between "*a* dog" and "*the* dog"). We present the results of a classroom-based study (N=99) that compares practice-only to two conditions that facilitate deep processing: self-explanation with practice and analogy with practice. Results show that students in all conditions benefit from the instruction. However, students in the practice-only condition complete the instruction in significantly less time leading to greater learning efficiency. Possible explanations regarding the differences between language and science learning are discussed.

Keywords: Intelligent Tutoring Systems, Self-Explanation, Analogical Comparisons, Second Language Learning.

1 Introduction

Many studies have shown self-explanation to be an effective instructional strategy [1, 2, 3]. Early work by Chi and colleagues [4] showed that students who spontaneously self-explain more, learn more. Later studies showed that students who are prompted to self-explain learn more than those who are not prompted [1], and finally, Aleven and Koedinger's work reveals that the advantages of self-explanation prompts persist even when students do not generate the self-explanation on their own but instead are asked to select the general principle from a menu [2]. Roy and Chi [5] propose that the benefits of self-explanation are due to increased involvement in the learning process, and that as a result of self-explaining, students focus on the meaningful aspects of the material.

While self-explanation shows great promise in increasing learning, most studies have dealt with math and science domains and relatively little work has been done in areas like second language learning. In a previous study, we investigated the effects of adding self-explanation prompts to an English as a Second Language (ESL) grammar tutor used to teach the English article system (i.e. teaching students when to use "a", "an", "the", or no article). Results showed that while prompting for self-explanations lead to significant learning gains, there was not a clear advantage for self-explaining over simple practice where students did fill-in-the-blank tasks (choosing the best article to complete the sentence) without prompts to self-explain [6]. One reason could lie in the metalinguistic challenges that students face when doing self-explanation in their non-native language. For example, many of the article rules contain challenging and domain-specific vocabulary that may be difficult for a non-native speaker (e.g. "Use 'a' when the noun is general, singular, and begins with a consonant sound.") Thus, we began to look for other instructional strategies that encourage deep processing without the extraneous, metalinguistic challenges.

One candidate is analogical comparison. In a typical analogical comparison problem, students are presented with two worked examples and asked to compare the similarities and differences between them. Analogical comparisons reduce the metalinguistic demands compared to prompted self-explanation (i.e. in the analogy problems, students don't have to tackle domain-specific vocabulary words like "consonant"), and multiple comparisons provide the added advantage of presenting students with more examples of correct article use, which alone may be beneficial for language learning [10]. The assumption behind analogical comparisons is that by comparing the examples, students will be able to extrapolate the underlying schema of the two problems [7]. Like self-explanation, analogy training has proven to be successful for a variety of domains and learners. In a study investigating business negotiation training, Gentner, et al. [8] found students who were instructed using analogical encoding produced better written solutions on posttest items and were able to transfer their skills to the more challenging modality of face-to-face negotiation. While much of the existing work has looked at students' mapping schemas from a well-understood example to a novel one, there is also evidence that students benefit when the two examples are only partially understood [9].

In this work, we explore the effects of using strategies that encourage deep processing of the material on students' learning in the challenging domain of the English article system. We begin by describing three problem types (practice, self-explanation, and analogical comparison). Using these activities, we created three computer-based tutoring conditions (practice-only, self-explanation with practice, and analogical comparison with practice) and evaluated their effects on knowledge acquisition and learning efficiency in a controlled classroom study.

2 Problem Types

This study employed three types of tutored problems: practice, self-explanation, and analogical comparison. For the *practice* problems (Figure 1), students were given a sentence and chose the article (*a, an, the*, or no article) that best completed the sentence. For the *self-explanation* problems (Figure 2), students were presented with a sentence with the target article highlighted and chose the rule or reason driving the article decision (e.g. "the noun has already been mentioned" or "the noun is general and non-count"). For each self-explanation problem, students chose from a menu of six rules, always presented in the same order. The order was kept constant to reduce the search time students needed to select their answers. In order to align the tutors with previous classroom instruction, we used the same vocabulary that was used in the students' textbooks [11]. Similarly, for the *analogical comparison* problems (Figure 3), students were given a sentence with the target article highlighted and chose the analogous sentence that used the same article rule as the given sentence. For example, given the sentence, *Last week, I bought a car. Today, **the** car broke*, students should choose the sentence *Sally found a dog, and **the** dog is small and black* since both the given and analogous sentences use the rule that if a noun has already been mentioned then "the" is used. There was one analogous sentence for each of the six article rules covered in the material. In an attempt to prevent students from developing spurious associations, all the analogous sentences were approximately equal in length and used similar vocabulary. In addition, the analogous sentences used simple vocabulary and were easy to read (Flesch-Kincaid Grade Level = 2.0). The same six analogous sentences were presented in the same order for each of the analogy problems.

During the instruction phase, students received immediate feedback on their selections (the answer turned green if it was right, red if it was wrong) and had access to on-demand hints. The tutors were developed in Flash using the Cognitive Tutor Authoring Tools [12] and deployed via the web. All student actions were logged and time-stamped.

2.1 Tutoring Conditions

Three corresponding experimental conditions were created using the above task types: practice-only, self-explanation with practice, and analogy with practice. Students in all conditions received 30 identical practice problems. In addition, students in each condition received 30 condition-dependent items: students in the self-explanation with practice condition received 30 self-explanation problems, students in the analogy with practice condition received 30 analogy problems, and students in the practice-only condition received 30 additional practice problems.

Previous research has shown the benefits of interleaving examples with problem-solving practice [13] and that learning from examples is more beneficial during early rather than later stages of skill acquisition [14]; therefore, we had students in the self-explanation with practice and analogy with practice conditions do more condition dependent items in the beginning and then move to interleaved blocks of matched practice and condition dependent problems, and finally, end with practice problems. More specifically, in the self-explanation with practice condition, the first ten problems were self-explanation problems; the next forty problems consisted of alternating blocks of five practice problems and five explanation problems, and finally, students completed ten practice problems. The analogy and practice condition used the same structure but students did analogy problems in place of the self-explanation items (Table 1).

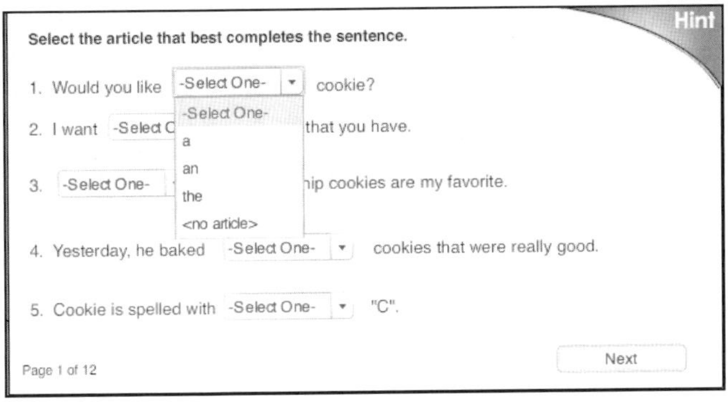

Analogies, Explanations, and Practice   217

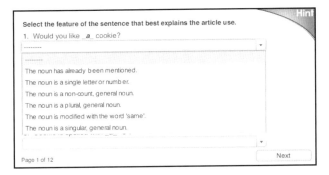

Fig. 1. Example practice problems. In the practice problems, students select the article that best completes the sentence.

Fig. 2. Example Self-Explanation Problems. In the explanation problems, students select the rule or feature of the sentence that best explains the article use.

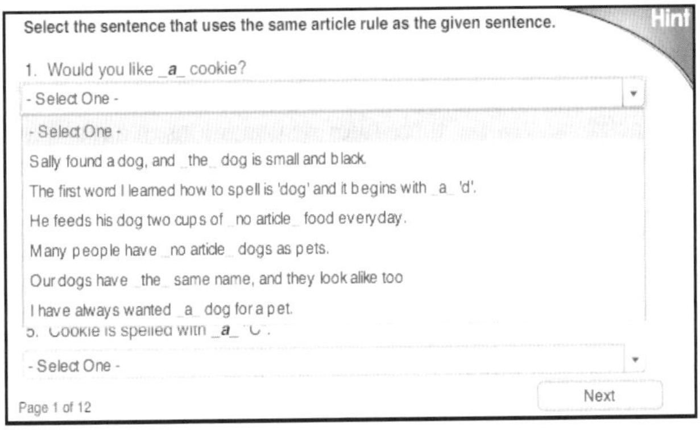

Fig. 3. Example Analogy Problems. In the analogy problems, students select the example sentence that uses the same rule as the given sentence.

Table 1. Sequence of problem type by condition. Students in the practice-only condition completed sixty practice items, while students in the analogy and practice and explanation and practice conditions also completed sixty items, alternating between blocks of practice and analogy or explanation items.

Item #	Practice-only	Analogy and Practice	Explanation and Practice
1-5		Analogy	Explanation
6-10		Analogy	Explanation
11-15		Practice	Practice
16-20		Analogy	Explanation
21-25		Practice	Practice
26-30	Practice	Analogy	Explanation
31-35		Practice	Practice
36-40		Analogy	Explanation
41-45		Practice	Practice
46-50		Analogy	Explanation
51-55		Practice	Practice
56-60		Practice	Practice

We controlled for several factors in the design of the three conditions: all condition used the same sixty target sentences, presented in the same order, and the hints presented the same information, although in slightly different forms. For the practice problems, the features of the sentence important for choosing which article to use were presented in the first hint; next, students were given the complete rule, and finally, students were told which article to select. When completing the explanation problems, students were first presented with the important features of the sentence, and then told which explanation to choose. Finally, for the analogy problems, students first saw the important features; second, they were given the example sentence that contained the same feature; and, finally, told which example sentence to select.

3 Classroom Evaluation

To evaluate the effectiveness of the three tutoring conditions in a real-life setting, a classroom study was conducted at the University of Pittsburgh's English Language Institute. Students (N=99) were adult English language learners (mean age = 27.9, SD=6.6) and participated as part of their regular grammar class. Data collection was completed within one 50-minute class period. Genders were equally represented, and students came from a variety of first language backgrounds, which were equally distributed across conditions ($\chi^2(2, N=99) = 27.2, p = 0.71$). After a brief introduction to the tutoring systems, students completed a computer-based pretest and were randomly assigned to a tutoring condition: practice-only (n=33), analogy with practice (n=34), or self-explanation with practice (n=32). Students completed the posttest, which was isomorphic to the pretest, immediately after finishing the tutoring. Pre and posttest items were identical in form to the practice problems students saw during tutoring (i.e. students chose the article that best completed the sentence). However, while taking the tests, students did not receive feedback on their selections and did not have access to hints.

3.1 Hypotheses

In our study, we were primarily concerned with two metrics: learning gains and instructional time. We hypothesize that students in the analogical comparison with practice condition will demonstrate greater learning gains than those in the practice-only condition due to increased engagement and deeper processing of the material. In addition, we expect students in the analogy with practice condition to show greater gains than those in the self-explanation condition due to the reduced linguistic demands of analogies compared to self-explanations *(H1)*. Namely, we believe that the concepts governing ESL article usage will be acquired more easily implicitly (i.e. through analogies) than explicitly (i.e. through rules and self-explanation).

While our main goal is to increase student performance, given the limited amount of classroom time available, it is also important that the instruction be efficient. We hypothesize that students in the practice-only condition will complete the instruction faster than those in the other conditions *(H2)*. When making article selections (versus choosing explanations or analogies), students only have four options from which to choose (*a, an, the*, or no article), fewer words to read, and practice alone may be less cognitively challenging than explaining or choosing analogies.

3.2 Results

In *H1*, we hypothesized that the analogy with practice condition would lead to greater learning gains compared to the other conditions. Results of a repeated measures analysis of variance (ANOVA) with test score as the dependent measure, test time (pretest and posttest) as a within-subject factor, and tutoring condition as a between-subject factor reveals a significant main effect for test time ($F(1,96) = 63.6$, $p < 0.001$) but no interaction of test time by condition ($F(2, 96)=1.30$, $p = 0.28$). Students, regardless of condition, demonstrate significant learning gains (Figure 4).

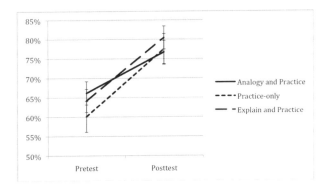

Fig. 4. Students in all three conditions show significant pre to posttest learning gains

H2 stated that students in the practice-only condition would complete the instruction faster than those in the analogy with practice and self-explanation with practice conditions, and timing results support this hypothesis. An ANOVA with total time spent using the tutor as the dependent variable reveals a significant effect of condition ($F(2, 96) = 6.44$, $p = 0.002$). Post-hoc Tukey HSD tests reveal that students in the practice-only condition complete the instruction the fastest (M=13.4 minutes, SD=4.3) and significantly faster than those in the analogy with practice condition (p=0.045, M=17.0 minutes, SD=7.5) and the self-explanation with practice condition (p=0.002, M=18.6, SD=6.0). No significant difference was found between the time-on-task of students in the two deep-processing conditions. However, a closer analysis of the timing data reveals a more nuanced result. We used a MANOVA with condition as the independent variable and time to complete the identical practice problems and condition dependent problems as the dependent variables. These results revealed that students in the practice-only and analogy with practice conditions completed the identical practice problems in the same amount of time (practice-only M=6.14, SD=18.8, analogy M=6.18, SD=2.06, p=0.99) and significantly faster than students in the self-explanation with practice condition (M=7.87, SD=2.29, Tukey HSD p=0.003). For the condition-dependent items, students in the practice-only condition completed their items the fastest (M=7.21, SD=2.58) and significantly faster than the analogy with practice (M=10.78, SD=5.89, p = 0.004) and self-explanation with practice conditions (M=10.78, SD=4.08, p = 0.004) (Figure 5).

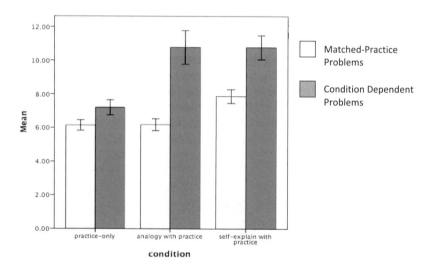

Fig. 5. Breakdown of tutor time by problem type. Students in both the practice-only and analogy with practice conditions completed the identical practice problems faster than students in the self-explain with practice condition. In addition, students in the practice-only condition completed the condition dependent items significantly faster than students in both the analogy with practice and self-explanation with practice conditions.

We also looked at how much instructional support (e.g. hint requests, incorrect steps, etc.) students used while completing the instruction. Hypothetically, students in one condition might request more hints or make more incorrect selections, actions that would increase the amount of time it takes for the task to be completed. Similarly, some tasks may be more prone to gaming (e.g. systematically going through the menu choices in order to get the correct answer [15]), resulting in smaller learning gains. To address these issues, we looked at the frequency of hint requests and incorrect answer choices. On average students requested hints on only 6.7% of the problems (SD=10.5), and an ANOVA showed no significant differences between conditions (F (2,96)=0.560, p = 0.573). With respect to errors, overall, students made an incorrect selection on 26.1% of the problems (SD=16.3), and again there were no differences between conditions (F (2,96) = 1.32, p = 0.27).

4 Discussion

This study addressed the issue of which instructional strategy (practice-only, analogy with practice, or self-explanation with practice) is best for learning the English article system. The results show that students in all conditions make significant learning gains but that practice-only is more efficient than self-explanation and analogical comparisons. Students in the practice-only condition learned as much as those in the other conditions but required significantly less time to complete the instruction. Furthermore, since there were no differences among conditions with respect to instructional support (e.g. number of hints requested, amount of incorrect feedback received), the greater efficiency is not due to students in one condition spending more time reading hints or gaming the system. These results suggest that the extra time it takes students to choose the explanation or analogous sentence is not beneficial.

One way to explain these results is to examine the knowledge type (explicit vs. implicit) and instructional approach (deep processing vs. no deep processing) for each of the tutoring conditions (Table 2). First, it is important to note that all conditions were equally beneficial when looking at learning gains alone, suggesting that both types of knowledge and instructional strategies are beneficial for learning. However, the differences between the conditions become more prevalent when looking at the timing data. Table 2 suggests an explanation for the timing difference between the condition-dependent problems. Again, the condition dependent problems used the same sentence stimuli but differed in the task students performed. Results show that deep processing of the material (e.g. self-explanation or analogy selection) requires more time than simple problem solving. Further, since learning gains are constant across conditions, it does not seem that the added time required to deeply process the material is beneficial for the students. In addition, timing data from the identical practice problems (problems that all students, regardless of condition, completed) show that students in the analogy with practice and practice-only conditions complete these problems significantly faster than students in the self-explanation with practice condition. Again, Table 2 suggests why this difference occurs; namely, while students in the analogy with practice and practice-only conditions are using implicit knowledge; students in the self-explanation with practice condition are relying on explicit knowledge to make their article selections. The process of retrieving explicit knowledge is more time consuming using implicit knowledge to complete the problems.

Table 2. Classification of tutoring condition by knowledge type and instructional approach

	Deep Processing	No Deep Processing
Implicit Knowledge	Analogy	Practice
Explicit Knowledge	Self-Explanation	

One open question is why do these results differ from the many studies that show an advantage for self-explanation and analogical comparisons; what makes second language grammar learning different? We propose that it is not the domains that are driving these differences but the number of mental steps required to solve the problem. For example, a typical geometry problem may include a diagram and ask students to calculate the value of an unknown angle. To successfully solve this problem, students need to develop and execute a rather complicated plan (Figure 6). However, a typical English article problem (e.g. *Yesterday, I bought new shoes. ___ shoes are red.*) requires fewer steps: (1) Set goal to choose the article. (2) Select (either implicitly or explicitly) the correct rule (*If a noun has already been mentioned, use the*), and (3) apply it (*Yesterday, I bought new shoes. The shoes are red*). We believe that the understanding acquired through deep processing scaffolds the generation of a correct knowledge application plan. When this plan involves many mental steps, as in often the case in math and science, this scaffolding is necessary and helpful. However, when the knowledge application plan is short, the benefits of deep processing decrease. Future research should empirically investigate this argument by conducting a 2x2 experiment which examines the effects of deep processing instructional manipulations on math and language problems with both short and long solution plans.

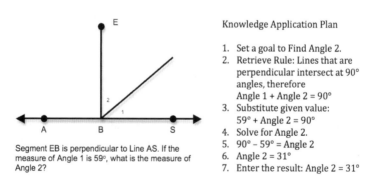

Fig. 6. Example of a typical geometry problem that requires several mental steps to solve

In conclusion, this work suggests that repeated practice is more efficient for learning the English article domain than self-explanation with practice or analogical comparisons with practice. It provides a possible explanation for why these findings differ from much of the previous work. Future work plans to further investigate these differences in an attempt to establish boundary conditions for instructional strategies that foster effective processing of the material.

Acknowledgments. Special thanks to our partner teachers and the PSLC CTAT and DataShop teams, and the three anonymous reviewers for their suggestions and feedback. This work was supported in part by the PSLC which is funded by the National Science Foundation award number SBE-0354420 and by the Institute of Education Sciences, U.S. Department of Education, through Grant R305B040063 to Carnegie Mellon University.

References

1. Chi, M.T.H., de Leeuw, N., Chiu, M.H., LaVancher, C.: Eliciting self-explanations improves understanding. Cognitive Science 18, 439–477 (1994)
2. Aleven, V., Koedinger, K.: An effective metacognitive strategy: Learning by doing and explaining with a computer-based cognitive tutor. Cognitive Science 26, 147–179 (2002)
3. McNamara, D.: SERT: Self-Explanation Reading Training. Discourse Processes 38(1), 1–30 (2004)
4. Chi, M.T.H., Bassok, M., Lewis, M.W., Reimann, P., Glaser, R.: Self-explanations: How students study and use examples in learning to solve problems. Cognitive Science 13, 145–182 (1989)
5. Roy, M., Chi, M.: The self-explanation principle in multimedia learning. In: Mayer, R.E. (ed.) The Cambridge handbook of multimedia learning, pp. 271–286. Cambridge University Press, Cambridge (2005)
6. Wylie, R., Koedinger, K., Mitamura, M.: Is Self-Explanation Always Better? The Effects of Adding Self-Explanation Prompts to an English Grammar Tutor. In: Proceedings of the 31st Annual Conference of the Cognitive Science Society, pp. 1300–1305. Cognitive Science Society, Austin (2009)
7. Gentner, D.: Structure-mapping: A theoretical framework for analogy. Cognitive Science 7(2), 155–170 (1983)
8. Gentner, D., Loewenstein, J., Thompson, L.: Learning and transfer: A general role for analogical encoding. Journal of Educational Psychology 95(2), 393–408 (2003)
9. Kurtz, K.J., Miao, C., Gentner, D.: Learning by analogical bootstrapping. Journal of the Learning Sciences 10(4), 417–446 (2001)
10. Mitchell, R., Myles, F.: Second language learning theories, 2nd edn. Edward Arnold, London (2004)
11. Fuchs, M., Bonner, M., Westheimer, M.: Focus on Grammar 3: An Integrated Skills Approach, 3rd edn. Pearson Education, Inc., White Plains (2006)
12. Aleven, V., McLaren, B.M., Sewall, J., Koedinger, K.R.: Example-tracing tutors: A new paradigm for intelligent tutoring systems. International Journal of Artificial Intelligence in Education (in press)
13. Pashler, H., Bain, P., Bottge, B., Graesser, A., Koedinger, K., McDaniel, M., Metcalfe, J.: Organizing Instruction and Study to Improve Student Learning (NCER 2007-2004). In: National Center for Education Research, Institute of Education Sciences, U.S. Department of Education, Washington DC (2007)
14. Atkinson, R.K., Derry, S.J., Renkel, A., Wortham, D.W.: Learning from examples: Instructional principles of the worked examples research. Review of Educational Research 70, 181–214 (2000)
15. Baker, R.S., Corbett, A.T., Koedinger, K.R., Wagner, A.Z.: Off-task behavior in the cognitive tutor classroom: when students "game the system". In: Proceedings of the SIGCHI conference on Human factors in computer systems, Vienna, Austria, pp. 383–390 (2004)

Do Micro-Level Tutorial Decisions Matter: Applying Reinforcement Learning to Induce Pedagogical Tutorial Tactics

Min Chi[1], Kurt VanLehn[2], and Diane Litman[3]

[1] Machine Learning Department, Carnegie Mellon University, PA, 15213 USA
minchi@cs.cmu.edu
[2] School of Computing and Informatics, Arizona State University, AZ, 85287 USA
Kurt.Vanlehn@asu.edu
[3] Department of Computer Science & Learning Research Development Center, University of Pittsburgh, PA, 15260 USA
litman@cs.pitt.edu

Abstract. Pedagogical tutorial tactics are policies for a tutor to decide the next action when there are multiple actions available. When the contents were controlled so as to be the same, little evidence has shown that tutorial decisions would impact students' learning. In this paper, we applied Reinforcement Learning (RL) to induce two sets of tutorial tactics from pre-existing human interaction data. The NormGain set was derived with the goal of enhancing tutorial decisions that contribute to learning while the InvNormGain set was derived with the goal of enhancing those decisions that contribute less or even nothing to learning. The two sets were then compared with human students. Our results showed that when the contents were controlled so as to be the same, different pedagogical tutorial tactics would make a difference in learning and more specifically, the NormGain students outperformed their peers.

Keywords: Reinforcement Learning, Human Learning, Intelligent Tutoring Systems, Pedagogical Strategy.

1 Introduction

Human one-on-one tutoring is one of the most effective educational interventions in that tutored students often perform significantly better than students in classroom settings[4]. One hypothesis as to the effectiveness of human one-on-one tutoring comes from the detailed management of "micro-steps" in tutorial dialogue[12, 13]. A typical Intelligent Tutoring System (ITS) is step-based[20]. Once a student enters a step, then the tutor gives feedback and/or hints. For example, in order to solve a physics problem, the student need to apply several domain principles, some of which may need to be applied multiple times. Each principle application can be seen as a step in the ITS. In a physics tutor, for example, applying the definition of Kinetic Energy ($KE = \frac{1}{2}mv^2$) to solve for the kinetic energy of a falling rock at T_0 is a step. Human tutors, by contrast,

1. **T:** So let's start with determining the value of KE_0.
2. **T:** Which principle will help you calculate the rock's kinetic energy at T0? Please provide the name of the principle, not an equation. **{ELICIT}**
3. **S:** Definition of kinetic energy
4. **T:** Yes, I agree. Now I will write the equation for applying the definition of kinetic energy to the rock at T0: KE0 = 1/2*m*v0^2 **{TELL}**

Fig. 1. An example Dialog

often scaffold students via a series of micro-steps leading to the full step. In the step mentioned above, for instance, a human tutor can take the following **micro-level** steps: selecting the principle to apply; writing the corresponding equation; solving the equation; and engaging in some qualitative discussion about the principle.

Fig. 1 shows a sample dialog for two micro-steps. In Fig. 1, each numbered line represents a dialog turn. The labels **T** and **S** designate tutor and student turns respectively. In this example, the tutor and the student first select a principle (lines 2 & 3) and then write the corresponding equation (line 4). Some of the tutor turns in Fig. 1 are labeled **{ELICIT}** or **{TELL}**. This label designates a *tutorial decision step* wherein the tutor has to make a tutorial decision deciding whether to elicit the requisite information with a question or to tell the student the information. For example, in line 2, the tutor chooses to *elicit* the answer from the student by asking the question, "Which principle will help you calculate the rock's kinetic energy at T0? Please provide the name of the principle, not an equation." If the tutor elected to tell the students, however, then he or she would have stated, "To calculate the rock's kinetic energy at T0, let's apply the definition of Kinetic Energy." Both actions cover the same target knowledge.

If the effectiveness of human one-on-one tutoring lies in tutors' ability to scaffold a series of micro-steps leading to a step entry, then we would expect human tutors to be more effective than step-based tutors as both require students to enter the same major steps. In several tests of this hypothesis, neither human tutors nor Natural Language (NL) tutoring systems designed to mimic human tutors, outperformed step-based systems[10, 22]. All three types of tutors, however, were more effective than no instruction (e.g., students reading material and/or solving problems without feedback or hints). One possible conclusion is that tutoring is effective, but that the micro-steps of human tutors and NL tutoring systems provide no additional value beyond conventional step-based tutors[21].

On the other hand, such a conclusion would be premature. It could simply be that neither human tutors nor their computer mimics are good at making micro-step decisions. That is, the use of micro-steps is good, but human tutors (and their mimics) lack the effective pedagogical skills to select appropriately. Indeed, although it is commonly assumed that human expert tutors have effective pedagogical skills, little evidence has been presented to date demonstrating that. In order to execute pedagogical skills effectively, it is assumed that tutors should adapt their behaviors to students' needs based upon students' current knowledge level, general aptitude, emotional state and other salient features. However, previous research has cast doubt on the assumption. Chi, Roy, and Hausman[8] found that human tutors do not seem to maintain an accurate model of student's knowledge level during the tutoring process. Similarly, Putnam[17] found that experienced tutors did not attempt to form detailed models of the students' knowledge before attempting remedial instruction. Rather, each teacher appeared to move through a general curricular script irrespective of the student's state. For the purposes of this paper the term *"pedagogical tutorial tactics"* will be used to refer to the policies for selecting the tutorial action at each micro-step level when there are multiple actions available.

In this study, our primary research question is whether pedagogical tutorial tactics would impact students' learning. We focus on two types of tutorial decisions, Elicit vs.Tell (ET) and Justify vs. Skip-Justify (JS). When making ET decisions the tutor decides whether to *elicit* the next step from the student or to *tell* them the step directly. The JS decisions address points where the tutor may optionally ask students to *justify* a step they have taken or entry they have made. Neither decision is well-understood. There are many theories, but no widespread consensus on how or when an action should be taken[1, 7, 9, 14].

In order to investigate our research question, we applied a general data-driven methodology, Reinforcement Learning (RL), to induce pedagogical tutorial tactics directly from pre-existing interactivity data. We used an NL Tutoring System called Cordillera[23]. In order to avoid confounds due to imperfect NL understanding, we replaced the NL understanding module with a human wizard. During tutoring, the wizard's sole task was to match students' answers to one of the available responses. The wizard made no tutorial decisions.

Previously we investigated whether the RL-induced pedagogical tutorial tactics would improve students' learning[6]. This was done by first collecting an Exploratory dataset in 2007. 64 college students, the Exploratory group, were trained on a version of Cordillera, called random-Cordillera, where both ET and JS decisions were made randomly. From the Exploratory corpus, we applied RL to induce a set of policies, named DichGain policies. They were named after the fact that when applying RL, we dichotomized the reward function so that there were only two levels of reward. The induced DichGain policies were implemented back to Cordillera and the new version of Cordillera was named DichGain-Cordillera. Apart from following the policies (random vs. DichGain), the remaining components of Cordillera, including the GUI interface, the same training problems, and the tutorial scripts, were left untouched. DichGain-Cordillera's effectiveness was tested by training a new group of 37 college students in 2008. It was shown that no significant overall difference was found between the two groups on the pretest, posttest, or the NLGs[6, 5]. There were at least two potential reasons for such lack of difference. First, it might be caused by limitations in our RL approach;

for example, in order to induce the DichGain policies, we defined only 18 features and used a greedy-like procedure to search for a small subset of it as the state representation[6]. Second, rather than randomly assigning students into the two groups, the Exploratory data was collected in 2007 while the DichGain data was collected in 2008.

Therefore, in this study we included multiple training datasets, a larger feature set and more feature selection approaches in our RL approach and run a full comparison by random assignment of students to two comparable groups. More specifically, we induced two sets of tutorial tactics: the Normalized Gain (NormGain) tactics were derived with the goal of making tutorial decisions that contribute to students' learning, while the Inverse Normalized Gain (InvNormGain) tactics were induced with the goal of making less beneficial, or possibly useless, decisions. The two sets were then compared by making all students studying the same materials and training on the Cordillera that covered the same subject matter and training problems, and used the same tutorial scripts and user interface. If our application of RL to induce pedagogical tutorial tactics is effective, then we expect that the NormGain students will outperform their InvNormGain peers. This would occur if the micro-level decisions on ET and JS impact learning. In the following, we will briefly describe how we applied RL to induce the pedagogical tutorial tactics and then describe our study and finally present our results.

2 Applying RL to Induce Pedagogical Tutorial Tactics

Previous research on using RL has typically used Markov Decision Processes (MDPs)[18]. MDP is a formal state model, commonly used to model dialogue data. Formally, an MDP is a 4-tuple (S, A, T, R), where: $S = \{S_1, \cdots, S_n\}$ is a state space; $A = \{A_1, \cdots, A_m\}$ is an action space represented by a set of action variables; $T : S \times A \times S \rightarrow [0, 1]$ is a set of transition probabilities between states describing the dynamics of the modeled system (e.g. $P(S_j|S_i, A_k)$ is the probability that the model will transition from state S_i to state S_j by taking action A_k); $R : S \times A \times S \rightarrow R$ is a reward model that assigns reward values to state transitions and models payoffs associated with the transitions. Finally, $\pi : S \rightarrow A$ is a policy.

The central idea behind this approach is to transform the problem of inducing effective pedagogical tactics into computing an optimal policy for choosing actions in an MDP. Inducing pedagogical tutorial tactics can be easily represented using an MDP: the states are vector representations composed of relevant student-tutor interaction characteristics; $A = \{Elicit, Tell\}$ for inducing ET policies and $\{Justify, Skip - Justify\}$ for inducing JS policies, and the reward function is calculated from the system's success measures and we used learning gains. Given that a student's learning gain will not be available until the entire tutorial dialogue is completed, only terminal dialogue state has non-zero reward. Once the S, A, R has been defined, the transition probabilities T are estimated from the training corpus, which is the collection of dialogues, as:

$T = \{p(S_j|S_i, A_k)\}_{i,j=1,\cdots,n}^{k=1,\cdots,m}$. More specifically, $p(S_j|S_i, A_k)$ is calculated by taking the number of times that the dialogue is in state S_i, the tutor took action A_k, and the dialogue was next in state S_j divided by the number of times the dialogue was in S_i and the tutor took A_k. The reliability of these estimates clearly depends upon the size and structure of the training data. Once a complete MDP is constructed, a dynamic programming approach can be used to learn the optimal control policy π^* and here we used the toolkit developed by Tetreault and Litman[19]. The rest of this section presents a few critical details of the process, but many others must be omitted to save space.

In this study, the reward functions for inducing both the NormGain and the InvNormGain sets were based on Normalized Learning Gain (NLG). This is because NLG measures a student's gain *irrespective of his/her incoming competence* and we have: $NLG = \frac{posttest-pretest}{1-pretest}$. Here *posttest* and *pretest* refer to the students' test scores before and after the training respectively; and 1 is the maximum score. More specifically, the NormGain tutorial tactics induced by using the student's $NLG \times 100$ as the final reward while the InvNormGain ones was induced by using the student's $(1 - NLG) \times 100$ as the final reward. Apart from the reward functions, they were induced using the same general procedure.

2.1 Knowledge Component (KC) Based Pedagogical Strategies

In the learning literature, it is commonly assumed that relevant knowledge in domains such as math and science is structured as a set of independent but co-occurring Knowledge Components (KCs) and that these KCs are learned independently. A KC is "a generalization of everyday terms like concept, principle, fact, or skill, and cognitive science terms like schema, production rule, misconception, or facet"[23]. For the purpose of ITSs, these are the atomic units of knowledge. It is assumed that a tutorial dialogue about one KC will have no impact on the student's understanding of any other KCs. This is an idealization, but it has served ITS developers well for many decades, and is a fundamental assumption of many cognitive models[2, 16]. When dealing with a specific KC, the expectation is that the tutor's best policy for teaching that KC (e.g., to Elicit vs. to Tell) would be based upon the student's mastery of the KC in question, its intrinsic difficulty, and other relevant, but not necessarily known, factors specific to that KC. In other words, an optimal policy for one KC might not be optimal for another. Therefore, one assumption made in this paper is that inducing pedagogical policies specific to each KC would be more effective than inducing an overall KC-general policy.

The domain selected for this project is a subset of the physics work-energy domain, which is characterized by eight primary KCs. Given these independence assumptions, the problem of inducing a policy for ET decisions and a policy for JS decisions may be decomposed into 8 sub-problems of each type, one per KC. More specifically, in order to learn a policy for each KC, we annotated our tutoring dialogues and action decisions with the KCs covered by each action. For each KC, the final kappa was ≥ 0.77, fairly high given the complexity of the task. A domain expert also mapped the pre- and post-test problems to relevant

KCs. This resulted in a KC-specific NLG score for each student. KC_1 does not arise in any JS decisions and thus only an ET policy was induced for it. For the remaining seven KCs, a pair of policies, one ET policy and one JS policy, were induced. So we induced 15 KC-based NormGain and 15 KC-based InvNormGain policies. There were some decision steps that did not involve any of the eight primary KCs. For them, two KC-general policies, an ET policy and a JS policy, were induced. To sum, a total of 17 NormGain and 17 InvNormGain policies were induced.

2.2 Inducing NormGain and InvNormGain Policies

In order to apply RL to induce pedagogical tutorial tactics, a training corpus is needed. In this study, we have three training corpora available from the previous study[6]: the Exploratory corpus collected in 2007, the DichGain corpus collected in 2008, and a Combined training corpus. In order to examine a range of possible tactics, we included 50 features based upon six categories of features considered by previous research[15, 3, 11] to be relevant. We also used a different method of searching the power set of the 50 features and directly used the $NLG \times 100$ for inducing NormGain policies and $(1-NLG) \times 100$ for inducing InvNormGain ones instead of dichotomizing the NLGs when inducing DichGain policies previously.

Fig. 2 shows an example of a learned NormGain policy on KC_{20}, "Definition of Kinetic Enegy", for ET decisions. The policy involves three features:

[StepDifficulty:] encodes a step's difficulty level. Its value is estimated from the Combined Corpus based on the percentage of correct answers given on the step.
[TutorConceptsToWords:] which represents the ratio of the physics concepts to words in the tutor's dialogue. This feature also reflects how often the tutor has mentioned physics concepts overall.
[TutorAverageWordsSession:] The average number of words in the tutor's turn in this session. This feature reflects how verbose the tutor is in the current session.

[Feature:]
   StepDifficulty: $[0, 0.38) \to 0; [0.38, 1] \to 1$
   TutorConceptsToWords: $[0, 0.074) \to 0; [0.074, 1] \to 1$
   TutorAverageWordsSession: $[0, 22.58) \to 0; [22.58, \infty) \to 1$
[Policy:]
  Elicit: 0:0:0 0:0:1 1:0:1 1:1:0 1:1:1
  Tell: 0:1:0
  Else: 0:1:1 1:0:0

Fig. 2. A NormGain Policy on KC_{20} For ET Decisions

MDP generally requires discrete features and thus all the continuous features need to be discretized. Fig. 2 listed how each of the three features was discretized. For example, For StepDifficulty, if its value is above 0.38, it is 1 otherwise, it is 0. There were 8 rules learned: in 5 situations the tutor should elicit, in one situation it should tell; in the remaining 2 cases either will do. For example, when all three features are zero (which means when the current step's difficulty level is low, the tutor ratio of physics concepts to words is low, and the tutor is not very wordy in the current session), then the tutor should elicit as 0:0:0 is listed next to the [elicit]. As you can see, three features already provide relatively complex tutorial tactics and the induced policies were not like most of the tutorial tactics derived from analyzing human tutorial dialogues.

The resulting NormGain and InvNormGain policies were then implemented back into Cordillera yielding two new versions of the system, named NormGain-Cordillera and InvNormGain-Cordillera respectively. The induced tutorial tactics were evaluated on real human subjects to see whether the NormGain students would out-perform the InvNormGain peers.

3 Methods

3.1 Participants

Data was collected over a period of two months during the summer of 2009. Participants were 64 college students who received payment for their participation. They were required to have a basic understanding of high-school algebra. However, they could not have taken any college-level physics courses. Students were randomly assigned to the two conditions. Each took from one to two weeks to complete the study over multiple sessions. In total, 57 students completed the study (29 in the NormGain group and 28 in the InvNormGain group).

3.2 Domain and Procedure

Our work used the Physics work-energy domain as covered in the first-year college physics course. The eight primary KCs were: the weight law (KC1), definition of work (KC14), Definition of Kinetic Energy (KC20), Gravitational Potential Energy (KC21), Spring Potential Energy (KC22), Total Mechanical Energy (KC24), Conservation of Total Mechanical Energy (KC27), and Change of Total Mechanical Energy (KC28).

All participants experienced the identical procedure and materials. More specifically, participants all completed 1) a background survey; 2) read a textbook covering the target domain knowledge; 3) took a pretest; 4) solved the same seven training problems in the same order on Cordillera; and 5) finally took a posttest. The pretest and posttest were identical. Except following the policies (NormGain vs. InvNormGain), the remaining components of Cordillera, including the GUI interface, the same training problems, and the tutorial scripts, were identical for all students.

3.3 Grading

All tests were graded in a double-blind manner by a single experienced grader. In a double-blind manner, neither the students nor the grader know who belongs to which group. For all identified relevant KCs in a test question, a KC-based score for each KC application was given. We evaluated the student's competence in the following sections based on the sum of these KC-based scores. This is because the KC-based pre- and post-test scores were used to define the reward functions when applying RL to induce policies. Later analysis showed that the same findings stand for other scoring rubrics. The tests contained 33 test items which covered 168 KC occurrences. For comparison purposes all test scores were normalized to fall in the range of [0,1].

4 Results

Random assignment appears to have balanced the incoming student competence across conditions. There were no statistically significant differences between the two conditions in the pre-test scores $t(55) = 0.71, p = .484$. Additionally, no significant differences were found between the two conditions on the mathSAT scores and the total training time spent on Cordillera: $t(39) = 0.536, p = 0.595$ and $t(55) = -.272, p = .787$ respectively.

A one-way ANOVA was used to test for learning performance differences between the pre- and posttests. Both conditions made significant gains from pre-test to post-test: $F(1, 56) = 31.34, p = .000$ for the NormGain condition and $F(1, 54) = 6.62, p = .013$ for the InvNormGain condition. Table 1 compares the pre-test, post-test, adjusted-post-test, and NLG scores between the two conditions. In Table 1, the Adjusted Post-test scores were compared between the two conditions by running an ANCOVA using the corresponding pre-test score as the covariate. The second and third columns in Table 1 list the means and SDs σ of the NormGain and InvNormGain groups' corresponding scores. The fourth column lists the corresponding statistical comparison and the fifth column lists the effect size of the comparison and we used Cohen's d. This is defined as the mean learning gain of the experimental group minus the mean learning gain of the control group, divided by the groups' pooled standard deviation. Table 1 shows that there was no significant difference between the two groups on pre-test scores. However, there were significant differences between the two groups on

Table 1. NormGain vs. InvNormGain on Various Test Scores

	NormGain	InvNormGain	Stat	cohen d
Pretest	0.42 (0.16)	0.39 (0.23)	$t(55) = 0.71, p = .484$	0.15
Posttest	0.65 (0.15)	0.54 (0.20)	$t(55) = 2.32, p = 0.024$	0.65 **
Adjusted Posttest	0.63 (.095)	0.55 (.095)	$F(1, 54) = 10.689, p = .002$	0.86 **
NLG	0.41 (0.19)	0.25 (0.21)	$t(55) = 3.058, p = 0.003$	0.81 **

the post-test, adjusted-post-test, and NLG scores. Across all measurements, the NormGain group performed significantly better than the InvNormGain peers. The effect size, Cohen's d, was large.

To summarize, our results showed that both groups had significant learning gains after training on Cordillera. More importantly, although no significant difference was found in time on task and in the pre-test scores, the NormGain group out-performed the InvNormGain group on the post-test, adjusted post-test, and NLG scores regardless of the grading criteria. Therefore, the overall results show that the micro-level pedagogical tutorial decisions made a significant difference in the students' learning.

Later a post-hoc comparison was done across the NormGain, Exploratory and DichGain groups because the NormGain policies were induced from the Exploratory and DichGain corpora. Despite the lack of random assignments, no significant difference was found among the three groups in the pretest. However, the NormGain group significantly outperformed both groups in the posttest, adjusted posttest scores, and NLGs[5]. Similarly, a post-hoc comparison was done across the InvNormGain, Exploratory and DichGain groups but no difference was found among the three groups on pretest, posttest, adjusted posttest scores or NLGs. The lack of a significant difference among the InvNormGain, DichGain, and Exploratory groups seemingly contradicts the initial predictions since the InvNormGain strategies were specifically induced to enhance those decisions that contribute less or even none to the students' learning. Therefore, a lower performance on the students' part there than in at least the DichGain group, which sought to enhance the tutorial decisions that contribute to the students' learning, was expected. One possible explanation for the lack of difference among the three groups is that the tutorial tactics employed by the DichGain- and Random-Cordillera systems were ineffective and thus presented a minimum bar. By 'ineffective' it does not mean that they prevented the students from learning but rather that they were not able to make a positive impact on their learning above and beyond the baseline provided by Cordillera itself. Here the basic practices and problems, domain exposure, and interactivity of Cordillera set a minimum bar of students' learning that the tactics, however poor, cannot prevent. This is only a post-hoc explanation not a tested hypothesis, however it merits further investigation.

5 Conclusion

In this study, students were randomly assigned to balanced conditions and received identical training materials and procedures apart from the tutoring tactics employed. After spending the same amount of time on training, the NormGain group outperformed the InvNormGain group in terms of posttest scores, the adjusted post-test scores and the normalized learning gains. This results support the hypothesis that micro-step interactive tutorial decisions such as the Elicit vs. Tell and Justify vs. Skip-justify decisions do affect students' learning. Therefore, future work is needed to investigate the induced NormGain and InvNormGain tutorial tactics and find out what actually caused these learning differences.

Moreover, this study also suggests that RL is a feasible approach for inducing pedagogical policies by using a relatively small human interaction corpus. However, it is not trivial. The DichGain tutorial tactics, for example, did not seem to be more effective than the random decisions in Random-Cordillera. As future work, we would like to explore the use of richer POMDP models, and do additional empirical evaluation of the RL approach.

Finally, this study suggests that the fine-grained interaction (micro-steps) of human tutoring are a potential source of pedagogical power, but human tutors may not be particularly skilled at choosing the right micro-steps. Given how much computation we had to perform in order to learn which micro-steps were best, it is hardly surprising that human tutors have not (yet) acquired similar skill. This raises an interesting question: Can a NL tutoring system that is extensively trained be significantly more effective than expert human tutors? This would be an excellent question for future research.

Acknowledgments. NSF (#0325054) supported this work and NSF (#SBE-0836012) supported its publication. We thank Learning Research Development Center for providing all the facilities for this work. We also thank Collin Lynch and the reviewers for helpful comments.

References

[1] Aleven, V., Ogan, A., et al.: Evaluating the effectiveness of a tutorial dialogue system for self-explanation. In: Lester, J.C., Vicari, R.M., Paraguaçu, F. (eds.) ITS 2004. LNCS, vol. 3220, pp. 443–454. Springer, Heidelberg (2004)

[2] Anderson, J.R.: The architecture of cognition. Harvard University Press, Cambridge (1983)

[3] Beck, J., Woolf, B.P., et al.: Advisor: A machine learning architecture for intelligent tutor construction. In: AAAI, pp. 552–557. AAAI Press, Menlo Park (2000)

[4] Bloom, B.S.: The 2 sigma problem: The search for methods of group instruction as effective as one-to-one tutoring. Educational Researcher 13, 4–16 (1984)

[5] Chi, M.: Do Micro-Level Tutorial Decisions Matter: Applying Reinforcement Learning To Induce Pedagogical Tutorial Tactics. Ph.D. thesis, School of Art & Science University of Pittsburgh (December 2009)

[6] Chi, M., Jordan, P.W., et al.: To elicit or to tell: Does it matter? In: Dimitrova, V., Mizoguchi, R., et al. (eds.) AIED, pp. 197–204. IOS Press, Amsterdam (2009)

[7] Chi, M.T.H., de Leeuw, N., et al.: Eliciting self-explanations improves understanding. Cognitive Science 18(3), 439–477 (1994)

[8] Chi, M.T.H., Siler, S., et al.: Can tutors monitor students' understanding accurately? Cognition and Instruction 22(3), 363–387 (2004)

[9] Collins, A., Brown, J.S., et al.: Cognitive apprenticeship: Teaching the craft of reading, writing and mathematics. In: Resnick, L.B. (ed.) Knowing, learning and instruction: Essays in honor of Robert Glaser, ch. 14, pp. 453–494 (1989)

[10] Evens, M., Michael, J.: One-on-one Tutoring By Humans and Machines. Erlbaum, Mahwah (2006)

11. Forbes-Riley, K., Litman, D.J., et al.: Comparing linguistic features for modeling learning in computer tutoring. In: AIED, vol. 158, pp. 270–277. IOS Press, Amsterdam (2007)
12. Graesser, A.C., Person, N., et al.: Collaborative dialog patterns in naturalistic one-on-one tutoring. Applied Cognitive Psychology 9, 359–387 (1995)
13. Graesser, A.C., VanLehn, K., et al.: Intelligent tutoring systems with conversational dialogue. AI Magazine 22(4), 39–52 (2001)
14. Katz, S., O'Donnell, G., et al.: An approach to analyzing the role and structure of reflective dialogue. International Journal of AI and Education 11, 320–343 (2000)
15. Moore, J.D., Porayska-Pomsta, K., et al.: Generating tutorial feedback with affect. In: Barr, V., Markov, Z. (eds.) FLAIRS Conference. AAAI Press, Menlo Park (2004)
16. Newell, A. (ed.): Unified Theories of Cognition. Harvard University Press, Cambridge (1994) (reprint edition)
17. Putnam, R.T.: Structuring and adjusting content for students: A study of live and simulated tutoring of addition. American Educational Research Journal 24(1), 13–48 (1987)
18. Sutton, R.S., Barto, A.G.: Reinforcement Learning. MIT Press/Bradford Books (1998)
19. Tetreault, J.R., Litman, D.J.: A reinforcement learning approach to evaluating state representations in spoken dialogue systems. Speech Communication 50(8-9), 683–696 (2008)
20. VanLehn, K.: The behavior of tutoring systems. International Journal AI in Education 16(3), 227–265 (2006)
21. VanLehn, K.: The interaction plateau: Answer-based tutoring < step-based tutoring = natural tutoring. In: Woolf, B.P., Aïmeur, E., Nkambou, R., Lajoie, S. (eds.) ITS 2008. LNCS, vol. 5091, p. 7. Springer, Heidelberg (2008)
22. VanLehn, K., Graesser, A.C., et al.: When are tutorial dialogues more effective than reading? Cognitive Science 31(1), 3–62 (2007)
23. VanLehn, K., Jordan, P., et al.: Developing pedagogically effective tutorial dialogue tactics: Experiments and a testbed. In: Proc. of SLaTE Workshop on Speech and Language Technology in Education ISCA Tutorial and Research Workshop (2007)

Examining the Role of Gestures in Expert Tutoring

Betsy Williams[1], Claire Williams[2], Nick Volgas[1],
Brian Yuan[1], and Natalie Person[3]

[1] Department of Computer Science, Rhodes College, Memphis, TN, USA
[2] Institute for Intelligent Systems, University of Memphis, Memphis, TN, USA
[3] Department of Psychology, Rhodes College, Memphis, TN, USA
williamsb@rhodes.edu, mcwllams@memphis.edu, volna@rhodes.edu,
yuabl@rhodes.edu, person@rhodes.edu

Abstract. It is well established that expert human tutors are significantly more effective than novice tutors [6]. Moreover, the dialogue moves of one–to–one expert tutoring sessions can be systematically analyzed and used to build a computational model that incorporates effective pedagogical strategies. Such a model can be successfully integrated into a computerized tutoring system [24]. The present work examines the role of gestures and body movements of tutors in one–to–one expert tutoring sessions. Specifically, we closely examine and characterize the gestures and movements of expert tutors at the dialogue move level. The goal of this work is to provide insight into the pedagogical gestures of expert human tutors so that a computerized animated agent can be employed to mimic the body language of an expert tutor.

Keywords: gestures, expert tutors, tutoring.

1 Introduction

Human gestures play an important role in communication [20]. Moreover, researchers, [10], have shown that the same areas of the brain are involved in the production of oral language and expressive gestures. The simultaneous formation of language and gesture in the human mind to convey a particular thought further indicates the integral role of gestures in conveying human ideas [20].

Many Intelligent Tutoring Systems (ITSs) rely on animated pedagogical agents to facilitate learning [12]. The motivation behind using such a character in a computer–generated learning environment is derived from natural human–human interaction. As Atkinson [2] points out, an animated pedagogical agent allows the developer to control where a learner's attention is focused, provide feedback through gazing and gestures, and convey emotion. However, empirical studies involving animated pedagogical agents report mixed results regarding their benefits. For example, it has been shown that an animated agent provides greater learning gains and/or better attitudes toward the content [21,22,26] in contrast to other studies, [1,4,11,19], that report no increase in motivation or learning. Clark and Choi [9] explain that these mixed results are largely due to the design of the studies. We believe that the specific gestures of the pedagogical agents used in these studies along with the dialogue context of these gestures may further explain the ambiguity of the agents' effectiveness. Specifically, animated agents might give distracting gestures that detract from learning. Thus, the goal of the present work is to help identify natural gestures that are used in tutoring pedagogy. Specifically, we are interested in characterizing the gestures and gaze patterns that an expert tutor employs as a function of the context of the tutoring dialogue.

This research examines the gestures and movements used in specified tutorial dialogue *moves* (speech acts) [23]. It is widely accepted that accomplished human tutors are more effective in terms of learning gains and motivational engagement than novice tutors. Recent research has focused much attention on investigating the pedagogical dialogue strategies of these expert tutors [7,23]. Person et al. [24] have shown that the pedagogical dialogue moves of tutors can be characterized and incorporated into a computer generated tutoring system, AutoTutor. This work is a natural extension of Person et al. [24], and seeks to uncover the gestures and body movements involved in expert tutoring so that they may be used to animate a pedagogical agent in a computerized tutoring system. The system envisioned would be different than others, [8,17], in that appropriate agent gestures, movements, and gazes would be generated at the fine–grain dialogue *move* level.

In this work we use the term "gesture" loosely to refer to a variety of movements, including movements of arms and hands, gaze direction, self–touching (e.g., scratching an itch), adjustment of posture, and nervous ticks. However, Roth [25] defines gestures as hand movements that have the following four characteristics: beginning from a rest position, having a peak phase, having a recovery and preparation phase, and having a tendency to be symmetrical. The ultimate goal of this work is to develop a compelling, naturalistic animated computer tutor. Thus, we felt it necessary to capture as many movements of the human tutors as possible. We group our gestures into different categories so that we can formally analyze Roth's "gestures." It is important to note that some researchers, [16], have shown that arm motions are the only important gestures used in communication and that all other movements can be treated as background. Thus, much of the gesture analysis research, [3,25], is limited to hand motions. We come back to this issue in Section 3. Other researchers, however, have found that gazing is an important part of human communication [5].

Researchers have proposed different taxonomies of gestures [20,25]. Most education researchers seem to focus on the gesture framework outlined by McNeill [20]. In this framework, gestures, as defined by Roth [25], can be grouped into one of four categories, deictic, iconic, metamorphic, and beats. Deitic gestures are used in pointing. Iconic gestures are representational and have a perceptual relationship with concrete entities. Metamorphic gestures are similar to ionic, yet they refer to entities in an imagined scene. Beats are the up and down movement of the hand to emphasize points. Research,[18], has shown that deictic gestures do play a role in communication. However, the value of ionic gestures and metamorphic gestures remains contested [25].

2 Method

2.1 The Expert Tutoring Corpus

Our expert tutoring corpus was comprised of 50 one-to-one tutoring sessions between an accomplished tutor and a student having difficulty in a particular math or science course. There were ten different expert tutors in this dataset in the following areas: algebra, geometry, physics, chemistry, and biology. The students in our corpus were either recommended by school personnel or voluntarily sought professional help. The expert tutors were recruited from public and private schools in a large urban school district and were recommended by academic support personnel who have long histories with these tutors and often refer them to parents and students. Our expert tutors had a minimum of five years experience of one-to-one tutoring, a secondary teaching license, a degree in the subject that they tutor, an outstanding reputation as a private tutor, and an effective track record (i.e., students who work with these tutors show marked improvement in the subject areas for which they receive tutoring). Videos of the tutoring sessions were recorded and later transcribed. During the tutoring sessions, the tutors and students sat together at a desk or table and shared a common workspace or frame of reference. Thus, relevant books and notebooks are considered part of the workspace. The dialogue of the transcribed sessions were coded in two ways: by the detailed tutor and student dialogue *moves* [23] and by the broader pedagogically distinct phases known as *modes* [7].

The 47,256 dialogue *moves* in the corpus corresponded were classified into 43 different pedagogical categories inspired by previous tutoring research, [13,14]. Of the 43 categories of dialogue *moves*, there were 27 distinct dialogue *moves* associated with the tutors and 16 associated with the student. The tutor dialogue *moves* consisted of various forms of information delivery (e.g., direct instruction, explanation, example), questions and cues to get the student to do the talking (e.g., hints, prompts, pumps, forced choices), feedback (positive, negative, neutral), motivational moves (general motivation statement, solidarity statement), humor, and off-topic conversation. The student dialogue *moves* could be related to the quality of their answer (e.g., correct answer, partially-correct answer, error-ridden answer) or to unique actions (e.g., reading aloud or solving a problem). More detailed descriptions of the dialogue *move* coding scheme can be found in [23]. Next, the dialogue of the tutoring sessions were classified according its pedagogically distinct phase or dialogue *mode*. There are eight distinct *modes* (Introduction, Lecture, Highlighting, Modeling, Scaffolding, Fading, Off Topic, Conclusion) that usually endured for several minutes and encompassed multiple dialogue *moves* [7]. In particular, we examine the gestures in the Lecture and Scaffolding *modes*. The Lecture *mode* is defined as a phase in which the tutor explicitly dispenses information. In the Scaffolding *mode*, the tutor and the student work together on a specified problem and the tutor helps the student arrive at the correct answer. The Scaffolding and Lecture *modes* appeared the most frequently in our dataset, representing 27.8% and 22.1% of the dialogue *moves*, respectively, and 46.4% and 30.2% of turns, respectively. A turn is defined as a dialogue shift from tutor to student or vice-versa.

2.2 Coding Tutor Gestures

Coding the entire expert tutoring corpus for tutor gestures was not feasible, therefore we coded a subset of the corpus. We choose 200 turns from each of the different tutors in the expert tutoring corpus. Of those 200 turns, 100 of the turns were associated with Lecture *mode* while the other 100 turns were associated with the Scaffolding *mode*. Each set of 100 turns appeared consecutively in the tutoring dialogue. We counter-balanced the turns across subjects so that some of the turns were extracted near the beginning of the tutoring session, some near the the middle, and others toward the end. Thus, our gesture corpus consisted of 2,000 turns which corresponded to 2,874 dialogue *moves*. Our coding scheme consisted of 35 different gestures that fully captured the range of gestures of the tutors in the expert tutoring corpus. The gestures were coded by *move*. Thus, the coder examined the corresponding video sequence of each *move* and observed the tutor's gestures. A *move* often had more than one gesture associated with it. The coding scheme was finalized prior to coding all 2,874 *moves*. These *moves* were coded by two of our co–authors and the inter-judge reliability of the coding system showed a Cohen's kappa ranging from 0.93–1.0 for each of the 35 different gesture categories.

We classify each of the 35 gestures or movements into one of seven categories described below. A sample dialogue coded with our scheme is provided in Table 1.

1. **Deictic** (*point at workspace, hold up workspace*). The deictic gestures refer to pointing gestures.
2. **Iconic** (*animate the subject matter*). The iconic gestures illustrate what is being said and have concrete semantic meaning.
3. **Beat**(*count on fingers, point upwards, fist pump, open hands when explaining*). Beat gestures are rhythmic in nature and used to emphasize a certain aspect of the dialogue.
4. **Personal** (*cross arms across chest, scratch itch, play with pen, cross hands on desktop, adjust glasses, cough, put hand on face, lean back in chair, tap fingers, check time on watch, adjust scarf, pet animal, fidget in chair, scratch head in thought, talk on phone*). Personal movements involve self–touching, nervous ticks, etc.
5. **Gaze** (*look at student, look at workspace, look up to think, look off at a distance*). The gaze is used to indicate where the tutor is looking.
6. **Paralinguistic** (*gesture for student to take notes, shrug shoulders, shake head no, what do you think (palms up), hand prompt for answer, nod*). Paralinguistic movements communicate an idea without language.
7. **Action** (*write on workspace, thumb through pages, use computer*). This category describes movements associated with specific actions that tutors might often carry out and were not well described by the other categories.

Table 1. This table provides a sample of Scaffolding dialogue. The columns represent the transcribed dialogue from the tutoring session, the related dialogue *move*, and the tutor's corresponding gesture, respectively. The speaker is denoted in the first column with a "T" for Tutor and an "S" for student.

T: What's going on? What's the process?	new problem	point at workspace, look at student, what do you think
S: They're con-	vague answer	cross arms, look at student
T: <repeatedly puts hands together>	hint	animate subject matter, look at student
S: They're binding.	error ridden answer	animate subject matter, look at student
S: [I don't know how to say it.]	metacomment	animate subject matter, look at student
T: [<laughs>.]	other	cross arms, fidget in chair, look at student
S: They're-	vague answer	cross arms, fidget in chair, look at student
T: Crossing over.	provide correct answer	nod, cross arms, fidget in chair, look at student
S: Oh.	acknowledgment	cross arms, fidget in chair, look at student
T: Right?	comprehension engaging question	nod, cross arms, look at workspace, look at student
T: This is crossing over. See what it looks like? Doesn't it look like theyre crossing over?	direct instruction	point at workspace, animate subject matter, look at student
S: Mm hmm.	acknowledgment	animate the subject matter, look at student
T: Yup.	positive feedback	animate subject matter, nod, look at workspace, look at student
T: That's when mom and dad have a have a leg over each other.	example	point at the workspace, look at workspace
T: Crossing over. Theyre exchanging DNA. Ok? And this is prophase 1. Ok. So, this is the first round of meiosis and the second round of meiosis. Ok? First round - second round, [ok.]	direct instruction	point at workspace, animation subject matter, look at workspace, look at student
S: [Mm hmm.]	acknowledgment	point at workspace, look at workspace
T: So, we started with 4 chromosomes and 2 pairs.	direct instruction	look at workspace, point at workspace
T: How many would we need to have at the end of the first round?	new problem	point at workspace, what do you think, look at workspace, look at student
S: 1. 1 and-	error ridden answer	cross arms, look at student
T: How many chromosomes?	simplify problem	point at workspace, what do you think, look at student
S: 2.	correct answer	point at workspace, look at student
T: 2 chromosomes.	repetition	point at workspace, look at student
T: How many pairs?	simplify problem	what do you think, look at workspace, look at student
S: 1.	correct answer	point at workspace, look at student
T: 1.	repetition	point at workspace, nod, look at student
T: So, what did we do during the first round?	simplify problem	what do you think, point at workspace, look at workspace
T: What did we split?	hint	animate subject matter, what do you think, point at workspace, look at workspace
S: We split the pairs.	correct answer	animate subject matter, look at student

2.3 Results

In Table 2, we outline the most frequently used dialogue *moves* and the most frequently used gestures within that *move*. The most frequently used gestures broken down by *mode* can be seen in Table 3. We performed a multivariate analysis of variance (MANOVA) on our data with the 35 different gestures as the dependent variables and tutor, *mode*, and *move* as the independent variables. The multivariate results revealed a main effect of tutor ($F(270) = 7.3, p < .01$), *mode* ($F(30) = 1.7, p < .01$), and *move* ($F(1260) = 2.9, p < .01$). These results, respectively, indicate that each tutor can be uniquely identified by their gestures, that tutors use different gestures in the two different *modes*, and that the tutors use certain gestures during a specific dialogue *move*. The tutor by *mode*, tutor by *move*, and *mode* by *move* interactions were also significant ($F(270) = 4.1, p < .01$; $F(7050) = 1.3, p < .01$, $F(1050) = 1.1, p < .01$). Thus, different tutors systematically use certain gestures in certain *modes* and these gestures differ across tutor. The same is true for the dialogue *moves*. Additionally, specific gestures are used for *moves* in a certain *mode*. The three-way interaction was also significant, $F(4200) = 1.2, p < .01$.

We analyzed the gestures according to their categories:

Table 2. This table shows the most common dialogue *moves* in our dataset. The percentage of their appearance is indicated to the right of each moves. The speaker of the dialogue move is indicated by an *T* for tutor and *S* for student. Underneath each *move*, the corresponding means (or percent used) and standard deviations of gestures that appear above a threshold of 10% are reported.

T: Direct Instruction/Explanation (18.8%), Example: *so that's your lateral area*			
look at workspace	.84 (.37)	point at workspace	.49 (.50)
look at student	.38 (.49)	write on workspace	.27 (.42)
animate subject matter	.16 (.37)		
S: Acknowledgment (12.6%), Example: *yeah ok*			
look at workspace	.56 (.50)	look at student	.48 (.50)
point at workspace	.24 (.43)		
T Positive Feedback (8.2%), Example: *very good alright*			
nod	.26 (.44)	look at student	.27 (.45)
put hand on face	.12 (.32)	point at workspace	.11 (.32)
cross arms	.11 (.31)	write on workspace	.11 (.32)
S: Correct Answer (6.4%), Example: *2 so v equals 4 squared*			
look at workspace	.65 (.48)	look at student	.43 (.50)
point at workspace	.19 (.39)	write on workspace	.14 (.35)
cross arms	.13 (.34)		
T: Conversational Ok (5.5%), Example: *alrighty*			
look at workspace	.76 (.43)	look at student	.29 (.45)
point at workspace	.12 (.33)		
T: Simplified Problem (5.0%), Example: *what inside the cell would have an electrical charge*			
look at workspace	.76 (.43)	what do you think	.48 (.50)
point at workspace	.40 (.49)	look at student	.34 (.48)
write on workspace	.16 (.36)	cross arms	.13 (.34)
T: Other (4.4%), Example: *does he give you a time limit*			
look at workspace	.74 (.44)	look at student	.38 (.49)
thumb through pages	.16 (.37)	point at workspace	.20 (.40)
write on workspace	.14 (.35)		
S: Other (3.4%), Example: *yes ma'am*			
look at workspace	.60 (.49)	look at student	.45 (.50)
point at workspace	.14 (.34)		
T: Comprehension Gauging Question (3.1%), Example: *you see what I'm saying*			
look at student	.72 (.45)	look at workspace	.33 (.47)
point at workspace	.21 (.41)		
S: Partially Correct Answer (3.1%), Example: *so so that would be 2nd strong or 2nd weakest*			
look at workspace	.85 (.36)	look at student	.28 (.45)
write on workspace	.18 (.39)	point at workspace	.17 (.38)
cross arms	.16 (.37)	nod	.10 (.31)

1. **Deictic.** A MANOVA on the deictic gestures with the same independent measures, tutor, *mode*, *move* revealed a significant effect of tutor, $F(18) = 5.2, p < .01$, and *move*, $F(84) = 3.4, p < .01$. Different tutors show different patterns of pointing to the common workspace. However, pointing was more likely to occur in specific dialogue *moves*. There was a significant interaction of tutor and *mode* ($F(18) = 3.0, p < .01$) tutor and *move* ($F(470) = 1.1$,

Table 3. This table shows the most common gestures in our dataset broken down by gesture. For the purposes of space, we left out uncommon gestures. The percentage used and standard deviations appear beside each *mode*.

Gestures	Lecture (std)	Scaffolding (std)
look at workspace	.67 (.02)	.73 (.02)
look at student	.38 (.02)	.36 (.02)
point at workspace	.21 (.02)	.29 (.02)
write on workspace	.14 (.01)	.13 (.01)
nod	.11 (.01)	.10 (.01)
cross arms	.10 (.01)	.08 (.01)
animate subject matter	.07 (.01)	.05 (.01)
what do you think	.07 (.01)	.05 (.01)
thumb through pages	.05 (.01)	.06 (.01)
cross hands	.04 (.01)	.06 (.01)
put hand on face	.03 (.01)	.09 (.01)
lean back in chair	.03 (.01)	.08 (.01)

$p = .04$), and *mode* and *move*, $F(70) = 1.9, p < .01$. Mode and the three–way interaction were not significant.

2. **Iconic.** The analysis of variance on iconic gestures for effects of tutor, *mode*, and *move* also revealed interesting effects. Tutor, *move*, and the two–way interaction of tutor and *mode* were significant ($F(54) = 4.0, p < .01$, $F(252) = 2.1, p < .01$, $F(54) = 2.2, p < .01$, respectively). Certain tutors "animated the subject matter" more than others. Interestingly, using gestures to animate the current topic is dependent on the move. There were no other effects or interactions.

3. **Beats.** A multivariate analysis on beat gestures involving tutor, *mode*, and *move* conditions showed only a main effect of tutor, $F(27) = 2.4, p < .01$. The beats that tutors use seem to uniquely identify the tutor.

4. **Personal.** A MANOVA on personal gestures found a significant of effect of tutor, $F(117) = 6.8, p < .01$, and move, $F(546) = 1.3, p < .01$. All three 2–way interactions were significant, tutor×mode ($F(117) = 1.3, p < .01$), tutor×move ($F(3055) = 1.2, p < .01$) and mode×move ($F(455) = 1.2, p < .01$). The three–way interaction was also significant, $F(1820) = 1.2, p < .01$. Tutors use unique personal gestures in certain *moves* and *modes*.

5. **Gaze.** A multivariate analysis on gaze gestures revealed a main effect of tutor, *mode*, and *move*, ($F(27) = 12.1, p < .01$, $F(3) = 7.7, p < .01$, $F(126) = 2.3, p < .01$, respectively). The 2–way interactions of tutor and mode ($F(27) = 5.3, p < .01$), and tutor and move ($F(705) = 1.2, p < .01$).

6. **Paralinguistic.** A MANOVA with the paralinguistic gestures showed a main effect of tutor, $F(54) = 7.5, p < .01$, and move, $F(252) = 8.2, p < .01$. The 2–way interactions of tutor and *mode*, $F(54) = 3.7, p < .01$, and tutor and *move*, $F(1410) = 2.2, p < .01$ had a significant effect on gesture. The three-way interaction was also significant, $F(840) = 1.2, p < .01$.

7. **Action.** A MANOVA revealed a significant effect of tutor, $F(18) = 8.7, p < .01$, and *move*, $F(84) = 2.0, p < .01$. All of the interactions were also signficant: tutor×*mode* ($F(18) = 8.1, p < .01$), tutor×*move* ($F(470) = 1.2, p < .01$), *mode*×*move* ($F(70) = 1.6, p < .0$), and tutor×*mode*×*move*, $F(280) = 1.3, p < .01$.

In particular, we were interested in examining the gestures as outlined by McNeill [20]. Thus, we used a multivariate analysis looking at beat, deictic, and iconic gestures. We found a main effect of tutor, $F(54) = 4.0, p < .01$, *move*, $F(252) = 2.1, p < .01$, and the interaction of tutor and *mode*, $F(54) = 2.2, p < .01$. There were no other effects or interactions. The tutors in our dataset can be uniquely defined by the combination of beat, deictic, and iconic gestures that they use. Furthermore, these gestures are related to the pedagogical dialogue *moves*. Interestingly, each tutor also had certain gesture patterns depending on the *mode*.

We reasoned that tutors could be uniquely identified by their personal gestures. Thus, we ran an additional analysis without these gestures. The MANOVA revealed a significant effect of tutor, $F(153) = 7.2, p < .01$, *mode*, $F(17) = 2.2, p < .01$, and *move*, $F(714) = .2, p < .01$. The interactions of tutor×*mode* and tutor×*move* were significant ($F(153) = 4.2, p < .01$, $F(3995) = 1.5, p < .01$, respectively). The three–way interaction was significant, $F(2380) = 1.1, p = .05$.

3 Discussion

Our results suggest that expert tutors rely on pedagogical gestures as part of their tutoring strategy. Interestingly, every gesture category has a significant effect of dialogue *move*, except beats. We believe that this provides counter–support to the claim that only deictic gestures are important. As shown in Table 2, expert tutors spend the most of their time providing direct instruction, [7], or dispensing information. In this particular *move*, it seems natural that tutors often look at the workspace (84%) and the student (38%), point at the workspace (49%), write on the workspace (27%), and use their hands to "act–out" what they are currently discussing (16%). Inspection of our data seems to suggests that biology tutors might "animate the subject matter" more than math tutors. However, we do not have enough tutors in our corpus to substantiate this effect. The most popular student dialogue *move* is acknowledgment. When students give the tutor acknowledgment (*yeah*, *ok*), tutors are likely to be looking at the student, looking at the workspace, and/or pointing at the workspace. It also seems natural that when tutors give positive feedback, they might nod. Tutors also frequently look at the student when the student provides a correct answer. Interestingly, an expert tutor often accompanies a "simplify problem" dialogue *move* with a "what do you think gestures" (elbows bent, palms up).

Examining Table 3 reveals that tutors spend most of their time either looking at the student or looking at the workspace (Table 3). This suggests the importance of incorporating gaze into an animated pedagogical agent. This supports the theory of Cassell [8] and Johnson et al.[15] that an effective animated conversational agent should use gaze in communication. Expert tutors often use deictic gestures as they are the third most common movement found in our dataset. Furthermore, we expected that tutors would frequently write on the workspace. However, we were surprised to see that tutors often "nod." It is also important to note that our expert tutors also seem likely to "animate the subject matter" or give the paralinguistic "what do you think" gesture.

We reasoned that personal movements would be individualized by tutor and were surprised every group of gestures showed a significant effect of tutor. The gestures of expert tutors were more individually stylized than we hypothesized. The results presented here indicate that expert tutors have a certain style or employ a certain set of gestures that uniquely identifies them.

This work provides insight into the gestures that an expert tutor employs in one–to–one tutoring. We hope to incorporate these findings into an animated agent. One of the important lessons of this work is that although tutors are stylized, they do appear to use certain gestures systematically. In particular, using gazing, deictic and ionic gestures appropriately and in reference to certain dialogue *moves* may increase the effectiveness of these pedagogical agents.

Acknowledgments. This research was supported by the by the Institute of Education Sciences, U.S. Department of Education, through Grant R305A080594. The opinions expressed are those of the authors and do not represent views of the funding agencies.

References

1. André, E., Rist, T., Müller, J.: Employing ai methods to control the behavior of animated interface agents. Applied Artificial Intelligence 13(4), 415–448 (1999)
2. Atkinson, R.K.: Optimizing learning from examples using animated pedagogical agents. Journal of Educational Psychology 94(2), 416–427 (2002)
3. Baveles, J., Chovin, N.: Visible acts of meaning: An integrated message model of language in face-to-face dialogue. Journal of Language and Social Psychology 19, 163–194 (2000)
4. Baylor, A.: Expanding preservice teachers metacognitive awareness of instructional planning through pedagogical agents. Educational Technology Research & Development 2(50), 5–22 (2002)
5. Beattie, G.: A further investigation of the cognitive interference hypothesis of gaze patterns. British Journal of Social Psychology 20(4), 243–248 (1981)
6. Bloom, B.: The 2 sigma problem: The search for methods of group instruction as effective as one-to-one tutoring. Educational Researcher (13), 4–16 (1984)
7. Cade, W., Copeland, J., Person, N., D'Mello, S.: Evaluating an animated pedagogical agent. In: ITS 2008 (2008)
8. Cassell, J., Pelachaud, C., Badler, N., Steedman, M., Achorn, B., Bechet, T., Douville, B., Prevost, S., Stone, M.: Animated conversation: Rule-based generation of facial expression gesture and spoken intonation for multiple conversataional agents. In: Proceedings of SIGGRAPH 1994, July 1994, pp. 413–420 (1994)

9. Clark, R.E., Choi, S.: Five design principles for experiments on the effects of animated pedagogical agents. Journal of Educational Computing Research 32(3), 209–225 (2005)
10. Corballis, M.C.: From Hand to Mouth: The Origins of Language, September 2003. Princeton University Press, Princeton (2003)
11. Craig, S.D., Driscoll, D.M., Gholson, B.: Constructing knowledge from dialog in an intelligent tutoring system: Interactive learning, vicarious learning, and pedagogical agents. Journal of Ed. Multimedia and Hypermedia 12(13), 163–183 (2004)
12. Craig, S.D., Gholson, B., Driscoll, D.M.: Animated pedagogical agents in multimedia educational environments: Effects of agent properties, picture features, and redundancy. Journal of Educational Psychology 94(2), 428–434 (2002)
13. Cromley, J., Azevedo, R.: What do reading tutors do? A naturalistic study of more and less experienced tutors in reading. Discourse Processes 40(2), 83–113 (2003)
14. Graesser, A., Person, N., Magliano, J.: Collaborative dialogue patterns in naturalistic one-to-one tutoring. Applied Cognitive Psychology 9(6), 495–522 (1995)
15. Johnson, W.L., Rickel, J., Lester, J.C.: Animated pedagogical agents: Face-to-face interaction in interactive learning environments. International Journal of Artificial Intelligence in Education 11, 47–78 (2000)
16. Kendon, A.: Conducting Interaction: Patterns of Behavior in Focused Encounters. Cambridge University Press, Cambridge (1990)
17. Levine, S., Theobalt, C., Koltun, V.: Real-time prosody-driven synthesis of body language. In: SIGGRAPH Asia 2009: ACM SIGGRAPH Asia 2009 papers, pp. 1–10. ACM, New York (2009)
18. Levinson, S.: Language and cognition: The cognitive consequences of spatialdescription in guugu yimithirr. Journal of Linguistic Anthropology 7, 98–131 (1981)
19. Mayer, R.E., Dow, G.T., Mayer, S.: Multimedia learning in an interactive self-explaining environment: What works in the design of agent-based microworlds? Journal of Education Psychology 95(4), 806–812 (2003)
20. McNeill, D.: Hand and Mind: What Gestures Reveal about Thought. The University of Chicago Press, Chicago (1992)
21. Mitrovic, A., Suraweera, P.: Evaluating an animated pedagogical agent. In: Gauthier, G., VanLehn, K., Frasson, C. (eds.) ITS 2000. LNCS, vol. 1839, p. 73. Springer, Heidelberg (2000)
22. Moundridou, M., Virvou, M.: Evaluating the persona effect of an interface agent in a tutoring system. Journal of Computer Assisted Learning 18(3), 253–261 (2002)
23. Person, N., Lehman, B., Ozbun, R.: Pedagogical and motivational dialogue moves used by expert tutors. In: 17th Annual Meeting of the Society for Text and Discourse (2007)
24. Person, N.K., Graesser, A.C., Kreuz, R., Pomeroy, V., Group, T.R.: Simulating human tutor dialog moves in autotutor. International Journal of Artificial Intelligence in Education 12, 23–39 (2003)
25. Roth, W.M.: Gestures: their role in teaching and learning. In: Review of Educational Research, pp. 365–392 (2001)
26. Ryokai, K., Vaucelle, C., Cassell, J.: Virtual peers as partners in storytelling and literacy learning. Journal of Computer Assisted Learning 19, 195–208 (2003)

A Time for Emoting: When Affect-Sensitivity Is and Isn't Effective at Promoting Deep Learning

Sidney D'Mello, Blair Lehman, Jeremiah Sullins, Rosaire Daigle, Rebekah Combs, Kimberly Vogt, Lydia Perkins, and Art Graesser

Institute for Intelligent Systems, University of Memphis, USA
{sdmello,balehman,jsullins,rpdaigle,rcombs,kvogt,lrperkin, a-graesser}@memphis.edu

Abstract. We have developed and evaluated an affect-sensitive version of AutoTutor, a dialogue based ITS that simulates human tutors. While the original AutoTutor is sensitive to learners' cognitive states, the affect-sensitive tutor is responsive to their affective states as well. This affective tutor automatically detects learners' boredom, confusion, and frustration by monitoring conversational cues, gross body language, and facial features. The sensed affective states guide the tutor's responses in a manner that helps students regulate their negative emotions. The tutor also synthesizes affect via the verbal content of its responses and the facial expressions and speech of an embodied pedagogical agent. An experiment comparing the affect-sensitive and non-affective tutors indicated that the affective tutor improved learning for low-domain knowledge students, particularly at deeper levels of comprehension. We conclude by discussing the conditions upon which affect-sensitivity is effective, and the conditions when it is not.

Keywords: affect-sensitive, AutoTutor, supportive, confusion, frustration.

1 Introduction

Intelligent tutoring systems (ITSs) such as AutoTutor, Andes physics tutor, and Cognitive Tutor, have come a long way towards modeling and responding to learners' cognitive states. This allows ITSs to implement some of the ideal tutoring strategies such as error identification and correction, building on prerequisites, frontier learning (expanding on what the learner already knows), student modeling (inferring what the student knows and having that information guide tutoring), and building coherent explanations [1-7].

However, ITSs can be more than mere cognitive machines, and the link between emotions and learning suggests that they should be affective processors as well [8, 9]. Affect-sensitivity is important for ITSs that aspire to model human tutors because it has been claimed that expert teachers are able to recognize a student's emotional state and respond in an appropriate manner that has a positive impact on the learning process [10, 11]. An affect-sensitive ITS would incorporate assessments of the students' cognitive and affective states into its pedagogical and motivational strategies in order to keep students engaged, boost self-confidence, heighten interest, and presumably maximize learning.

The idea of having a tutoring system detect, respond to, and synthesize affect was once a seductive vision [9]. This vision is now a reality as affect-sensitive learning environments are coming online [7, 12-18]. However, to our knowledge, there has not yet been any evidence demonstrating that, compared to their non-affective counterparts, affect-sensitive ITSs yield impressive learning gains, particularly at deeper levels of comprehension.

We have recently developed an affect-sensitive version of AutoTutor, an ITS with conversational dialogues [19]. The original AutoTutor has a set of fuzzy production rules that are sensitive to the cognitive, but not to the affective states of the learner. The affect-sensitive AutoTutor has a set of production rules that map dynamic assessments of learners' cognitive and affective states with tutor actions to address the presence of boredom, confusion, and frustration. The obvious prediction is that compared to the non-affective tutor, learning gains should be superior for the affect-sensitive version of AutoTutor.

This hypothesis was tested in the current paper where 84 students completed a 60-minute training session with either the regular (non-affective) or the affect-sensitive AutoTutor. Scores from knowledge tests administered before and after each tutorial session were used to determine if the affect-sensitivity yielded enhanced learning.

We begin with a brief description of the affect-sensitive AutoTutor. Since the system is quite complex and a detailed description is beyond the scope of this paper, we focus on a high-level description of the major components of the system. More detailed descriptions can be obtained from previous publications [18, 20-22].

2 The Affect-Sensitive AutoTutor

AutoTutor is a dialogue based ITS for Newtonian physics, computer literacy, and critical thinking. AutoTutor's dialogues are organized around difficult questions and problems (called main questions) that require reasoning and explanations in the answers. When presented with these questions, students typically respond with answers that are only one word to two sentences in length. In order to guide students in their construction of an improved answer, AutoTutor actively monitors learners' knowledge states and engages them in a turn-based dialogue. AutoTutor adaptively manages the tutorial dialogue by providing feedback on the learner's answers (e.g. "good job", "not quite"), pumping the learner for more information (e.g. "What else"), giving hints (e.g. "What about X"), prompts (e.g. "X is a type of what "), correcting misconceptions, answering questions, and summarizing topics.

AutoTutor can keep the dialogue on track because it is always comparing what the student says to anticipated input (i.e., the expectations and misconceptions in the curriculum script). This constitutes AutoTutor's model of the student's knowledge and cognitive states. Pattern matching operations and pattern completion mechanisms drive the comparison. These matching and completion operations are based on symbolic interpretation algorithms [23] and statistical semantic matching algorithms [24].

Boredom, confusion, and frustration are the major negative states that students experience during interactions with AutoTutor and other learning environments [21, 25].

These are states that, if addressed appropriately, can have a positive impact on learning outcomes. Therefore, the current version of the affect-sensitive focuses on detecting and responding to boredom, frustration, and confusion. The tutor is called the *Supportive* tutor because it responds to learners' affective states via empathetic and motivational responses that always attribute the source of the negative affect to itself or the material, instead of the learners' themselves.

2.1 Detecting Affect

The affect detection system monitors conversational cues, gross body language, and facial features to detect boredom, confusion, frustration, and neutral (no affect) (see Figure 1). Automated systems that detect these emotions have been integrated into AutoTutor and have been extensively described and evaluated in previous publications [20-22, 25]. Each channel independently provides its own diagnosis of the student's affective state. These individual diagnoses are combined with a decision-level fusion algorithm that selects a single affective state and a confidence value of the detection. The algorithm relies on a voting rule enhanced with a few simple heuristics.

Fig. 1. Monitoring affective states during interactions with AutoTutor

2.2 Responding to Affect

An examination of the literature provided some guidance on how best to respond to the states of boredom, confusion, and frustration. We considered some major theoretical perspectives that address the presence of these negative emotions. These included attribution theory [26-28], cognitive disequilibrium during learning [29-32], politeness [33, 34], and empathy [35, 36]. In addition to theoretical considerations, the assistance of experts in tutoring was enlisted to help create the set of tutor responses.

We created a set of production rules that addressed the presence of these negative affective states by incorporating perspectives from the psychological theories and from the expert's recommendations. When there was no guidance from theory or expertise, the research group added production rules that were intuitively plausible. So in a nutshell, the production rules were determined by theory, experts, and intuition.

The production rules were designed to map dynamic assessments of the students' cognitive and affective states with appropriate tutor actions. There were five parameters in the student model and five parameters in the tutor model. The parameters in the student model included: (a) the current affective state detected, (b) the confidence level of that affect classification, (c) the previous state detected, (d) a global measure of student ability (dynamically updated throughout the session), and (e) the conceptual quality of the student's immediate response. AutoTutor incorporated this five-dimensional assessment of the student and responded with: (a) feedback for the current answer, (b) an affective statement, (c) the next dialogue move, (d) an emotional display on the face of the tutor agent, and (e) an emotional modulation of the voice produced by AutoTutor's text-to-speech engine.

Fig. 2. Affective AutoTutor Interface

As an example, consider a student that has been performing well overall (high global ability), but the most recent contribution was not very good (low current contribution quality). If the current state was classified as boredom, with a high probability, and the previous state was classified as frustration, then AutoTutor might say the following: "Maybe this *topic* is getting old. I'll help you finish so we can try something new." This would be a randomly selected phrase from a list that was designed to indirectly address the student's boredom and to try to shift the topic a bit before the student became disengaged from the learning experience. In this sense, the rules were context sensitive and were dynamically adaptive to each individual learner.

A screenshot of the affective AutoTutor is shown in Figure 2. Here the tutor is displaying a skeptical face because it detected that the student was hedging. Alternate facial expressions include approval, disapproval, enthusiasm, surprise, empathy, and neutral.

3 Method

3.1 Participants and Design

84 participants from a mid south university in the US participated for course credit. The experiment had a between-subjects design where participants were randomly assigned to either the Regular or the Supportive AutoTutor. Participants in each condition completed two training sessions with the *same* version of AutoTutor but on two *different* computer literacy topics (hardware, operating systems, the Internet). Participants did not receive tutoring for the third computer literacy topic; learning gains for this topic were used to assess knowledge transfer. The order in which topics were covered was counterbalanced across participants with a Latin Square.

3.2 Content Covered in AutoTutor Sessions

Participants completed three challenging computer literacy questions in each tutoring session. Hence, each participant received training for six questions over both sessions. Each problem required approximately three to seven sentences of information for a correct answer. The questions required answers that involved inferences and deep reasoning, such as *why, how, what-if, what if not,* and *how is X similar to Y?* Examples of these questions are, "How can John's computer have a virus but still boot to the point where the operating system starts?" (hardware question), "How would you design an operating system that can manage memory demands from multiple concurrent jobs?" (operating systems), and "How will you design a network that will continue to function, even if some connections are destroyed? (Internet)".

3.3 Knowledge Tests

Participants were tested on their knowledge of computer literacy topics both before and after the tutorial session (pretest and posttest, respectively). The testing materials were adapted from computer literacy tests used in previous experiments involving AutoTutor [19]. The items were designed to assess deep levels of knowledge (e.g., "How does the computer assure that other stored information is not overwritten when a save command is given?") rather than recall of shallow facts (e.g. "What does RAM stand for?").

Each test had 8 questions on each topic, yielding 24 questions in all. Participants completed alternate test versions for pretest and posttest. The two test versions, composed of different questions, tested learners on the same subject matter and content. The assignment of test versions to pretest versus posttest was counterbalanced across participants.

3.4 Procedure

Participants were tested individually during a 1.5 to 2 hour session. First, participants completed an informed consent and then the pretest. Participants were instructed to take a seat at the computer console and to put on a pair of headphones. Next, the general features of AutoTutor's dialogue and pedagogical strategies were described to the participant. On the basis of random assignment, participants interacted with either the Supportive or the Regular AutoTutor. They were tutored on one computer literacy topic until three main questions were successfully answered or the 30-minute training period had elapsed (Session 1). They then interacted with the *same* version of AutoTutor on *another* computer literacy topic until three main questions were successfully answered or the 30-minute training period had elapsed (Session 2). Finally, participants completed the posttest and were debriefed.

4 Results and Discussion

Pretest and posttest scores were computed as the proportion of questions answered correctly. Proportional learning gains were computed as (posttest–pretest)/(1-pretest). Separate proportional scores were computed for Session 1 and Session 2. We also computed proportional learning gains for the topic for which participants received no tutoring to assess knowledge transfer.

There was no significant difference in prior knowledge across conditions (M_{REG} = .188, SD_{REG} = .090; M_{SUP} = .177, SD_{SUP} = .080; p = .557). Participants were assigned to either a low or a high prior-knowledge group based on a median split on their pretest scores (median = .17). The analyses consisted of 2 (tutor: regular vs. supportive) × 2 (prior knowledge: low vs. high) between-subjects ANOVAs for learning gains in each session and for knowledge transfer.

Table 1 shows descriptive statistics on proportional learning gains. The main effect for tutor was significant for Session 1, $F(1, 80) = 2.53$, $p = .043$. There was a low to medium sized effect ($d = .375$) in favor of the regular AutoTutor. The tutor × prior-knowledge interaction was also significant, $F(1, 80) = 3.91$, $p = .051$ (see Figure 3). There was no difference in learning gains across tutors for the low prior-knowledge participants ($d = .017$). However, there was a significant ($p = .022$) and substantial effect ($d = .824$) in favor of the regular tutor for students with high prior-knowledge.

There was a different pattern in learning gains for participants' second AutoTutor session. The main effect for tutor was not significant ($p = .973$), but there was a significant tutor × prior-knowledge interaction, $F(1, 80) = 5.07$, $p = .027$ (see Figure 3). Low prior-knowledge participants learned significantly more from the supportive AutoTutor than the regular tutor ($d = .713$). There was no significant difference in learning gains across tutors for the high prior knowledge students.

Table 1. Descriptive statistics on proportional learning gains

Session	Version	Tutor [Main Effect] M	SD	Tutor × Prior Knowledge [Interaction] Low M	SD	High M	SD
Session 1	Regular	.389	.320	.346	.343	.441	.289
	Supportive	.249	.420	.340	.353	.114	.481
Session 2	Regular	.377	.328	.382	.247	.370	.413
	Supportive	.407	.386	.549	.221	.198	.480
Transfer	Regular	.001	.439	.095	.267	-.113	.572
	Supportive	.092	.387	.244	.244	-.130	.454

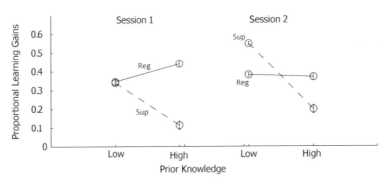

Fig. 3. Interactions between prior knowledge and tutor type

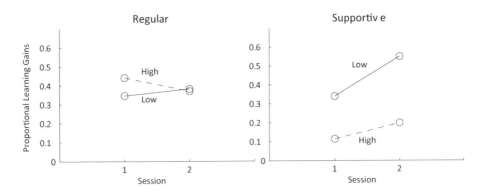

Fig. 4. Trends in learning gains across sessions

There was no significant effect for tutor ($p = .448$), nor a significant tutor × prior-knowledge interaction ($p = .338$) for topics for which participants received no tutoring (transfer topic). However, there was a medium sized effect ($d = .583$) in favor of the supportive tutor for the low prior-knowledge students; this effect might be significant with a larger sample.

Figure 4 portrays the same data in a slightly different way. Low prior-knowledge students show a dramatic improvement ($p < .05$; $d = .71$) in learning gains from Session 1 to Session 2 when interacting with the supportive versus the regular AutoTutor. Learning gains between sessions remained approximately consistent for high prior-knowledge students ($p > .05$).

5 General Discussion

The results of this experiment support a number of conclusions regarding the effectiveness of affect-sensitivity in promoting deep learning gains. First, the supportive AutoTutor was more effective than the regular tutor for low-domain knowledge students in the second session, but not the first session. These results suggest that it is inappropriate for the tutor to be supportive to these students before there has been enough context to show there are problems. Simply put, don't be supportive until the students need support. Second, the students with more knowledge never benefited from the supportive AutoTutor. These students don't need the emotional support, but rather they need to go directly to the content. Third, there are conditions when emotional support is detrimental, if not irritating to the learner. There appears to be a liability to quick support and empathy compared to no affect-sensitivity.

The central message is that there is an appropriate time for affect-sensitivity in the form of supportive dialogues. Just as there is a "time for telling"; there is a "time for emoting." We could imagine a trajectory where low-knowledge students start out with a non-emotional regular tutor until they see there are problems. Then after that they need support, as manifested in Session 2 of our study. Regarding high-knowledge students, they are perfectly fine working on content for an hour or more and may get irritated with an AutoTutor showing compassion, empathy, and care. But later on there may be a time when they want a shake-up AutoTutor for stimulation, challenge, and a playful exchange. Or maybe even a supportive AutoTutor. These are all questions to explore for future research.

Acknowledgements. We thank our research colleagues in the Emotive Computing Group at the University of Memphis the Affective Computing group at MIT.

This research was supported by the National Science Foundation (REC 0106965, ITR0325428, HCC0834847). Any opinions, findings and conclusions, or recommendations expressed in this paper are those of the authors and not the NSF.

References

1. Aleven, V., Koedinger, K.: An Effective Metacognitive Strategy: Learning by Doing and Explaining with a Computer-Based Cognitive Tutor. Cognitive Science 26(2), 147–179 (2002)

2. Anderson, J., Douglass, S., Qin, Y.: How Should a Theory of Learning and Cognition Inform Instruction? In: Healy, A. (ed.) Experimental cognitive psychology and it's applications, pp. 47–58. American Psychological Association, Washington (2005)
3. Gertner, A., VanLehn, K.: Andes: A Coached Problem Solving Environment for Physics. In: Gauthier, G., VanLehn, K., Frasson, C. (eds.) ITS 2000. LNCS, vol. 1839, pp. 133–142. Springer, Heidelberg (2000)
4. Koedinger, K., Anderson, J., Hadley, W., Mark, M.: Intelligent Tutoring Goes to School in the Big City. International Journal of Artificial Intelligence in Education 8, 30–43 (1997)
5. Lesgold, A., Lajoie, S., Bunzo, M., Eggan, G.: SHERLOCK: A Coached Practice Environment for an Electronics Troubleshooting Job. In: Larkin, J.H., Chabay, R.W. (eds.) Computer-assisted instruction and intelligent tutoring systems, pp. 201–238. Erlbaum, Hillsdale (1992)
6. Sleeman, D., Brown, J. (eds.): Intelligent Tutoring Systems. Academic Press, New York (1982)
7. Woolf, B.: Building Intelligent Interactive Tutors. Morgan Kaufmann Publishers, Burlington (2009)
8. Issroff, K., del Soldato, T.: Incorporating Motivation into Computer-Supported Collaborative Learning. In: Proceedings of European Conference on Artificial Intelligence in Education, Ficha Tecnica, Lisbon (1996)
9. Picard, R.: Affective Computing. MIT Press, Cambridge (1997)
10. Lepper, M., Woolverton, M.: The wisdom of practice: Lessons Learned from the Study of Highly Effective Tutors. In: Aronson, J. (ed.) Improving academic achievement: Impact of psychological factors on education, pp. 135–158. Academic Press, Orlando (2002)
11. Goleman, D.: Emotional Intelligence. Bantam Books, New York (1995)
12. Arroyo, I., Woolf, B., Cooper, D., Burleson, W., Muldner, K., Christopherson, R.: Emotion Sensors Go To School. In: Dimitrova, V., Mizoguchi, R., Du Boulay, B., Graesser, A. (eds.) Proceedings of 14th International Conference on Artificial Intelligence in Education, pp. 17–24. IOS Press, Amsterdam (2009)
13. Burleson, W., Picard, R.: Evidence for Gender Specific Approaches to the Development of Emotionally Intelligent Learning Companions. IEEE Intelligent Systems 22(4), 62–69 (2007)
14. Conati, C., Maclaren, H.: Empirically Building and Evaluating a Probabilistic Model of User Affect. User Modeling and User-Adapted Interaction 19(3), 267–303 (2009)
15. Forbes-Riley, K., Litman, D.: Adapting to Student Uncertainty Improves Tutoring Dialogues. In: Dimitrova, V., Mizoguchi, R., Du Boulay, B. (eds.) Proceedings of the 14th International Conference on Artificial Intelligence in Education, pp. 33–40. IOS Press, Amsterdam (2009)
16. Chaffar, S., Derbali, L., Frasson, C.: Inducing Positive Emotional State in Intelligent Tutoring Systems. In: Dimitrova, V., Mizoguchi, R., Du Boulay, B., Graesser, A. (eds.) Proceedings of 14th International Conference on Artificial Intelligence in Education, pp. 716–718. IOS Press, Amsterdam (2009)
17. Robison, J., McQuiggan, S., Lester, J.: Evaluating the Consequences of Affective Feedback in Intelligent Tutoring Systems. In: Proceedings of International Conference on Affective Computing & Intelligent Interaction, pp. 37–42 (2009)
18. D'Mello, S., Craig, S., Fike, K., Graesser, A.: Responding to Learners' Cognitive-Affective States with Supportive and Shakeup Dialogues. In: Jacko, J. (ed.) Human-Computer Interaction. Ambient, Ubiquitous and Intelligent Interaction, pp. 595–604. Springer, Heidelberg (2009)

19. Graesser, A., Lu, S.L., Jackson, G., Mitchell, H., Ventura, M., Olney, A., Louwerse, M.: AutoTutor: A Tutor with Dialogue in Natural Language. Behavioral Research Methods, Instruments, and Computers 36, 180–193 (2004)
20. D'Mello, S., Graesser, A.: Automatic Detection of Learners' Affect from Gross Body Language 23(2), 123–150 (2009)
21. D'Mello, S., Picard, R., Graesser, A.: Towards an Affect-Sensitive AutoTutor. IEEE Intelligent Systems 22(4), 53–61 (2007)
22. D'Mello, S., Craig, S., Witherspoon, A., McDaniel, B., Graesser, A.: Automatic Detection of Learner's Affect from Conversational Cues. User Modeling and User-Adapted Interaction 18(1-2), 45–80 (2008)
23. Rus, V., Graesser, A.: Lexico-Syntactic Subsumption for Textual Entailment. In: Nicolov, N., Bontcheva, K., Angelova, G., Mitkov, R. (eds.) Recent Advances in Natural Language Processing IV: Selected Papers from RANLP 2005, pp. 187–196. John Benjamins Publishing Company, Amsterdam (2007)
24. Landauer, T., McNamara, D., Dennis, S., Kintsch, W. (eds.): Handbook of Latent Semantic Analysis. Erlbaum, Mahwah (2007)
25. Baker, R., D'Mello, S., Rodrigo, M., Graesser, A.: Better to be Frustrated than Bored: The Incidence and Persistence of Affect During Interactions with Three Different Computer-Based Learning Environments. International Journal of Human-Computer Studies 68(4), 223–241 (2010)
26. Batson, C., Turk, C., Shaw, L., Klein, T.: Information Function of Empathic Emotion - Learning That We Value the Others Welfare. Journal of Personality and Social Psychology 68(2), 300–313 (1995)
27. Heider, F.: The Psychology of Interpersonal Relations. John Wiley & Sons, New York (1958)
28. Weiner, B.: An Attributional Theory of Motivation and Emotion. Springer, New York (1986)
29. Piaget, J.: The Origins of Intelligence. International University Press, New York (1952)
30. Craig, S.D., Graesser, A.C., Sullins, J., Gholson, J.: Affect and Learning: An Exploratory Look into the Role of Affect in Learning. Journal of Educational Media 29, 241–250 (2004)
31. Festinger, L.: A Theory of Cognitive Dissonance. Stanford University Press, Stanford (1957)
32. Graesser, A., Olde, B.: How Does One Know Whether a Person Understands a Device? The Quality of the Questions the Person Asks When the Device Breaks Down. Journal of Educational Psychology 95(3), 524–536 (2003)
33. Wang, N., Johnson, W.L., Mayer, R.E., Rizzo, P., Shaw, E., Collins, H.: The Politeness Effect: Pedagogical Agents and Learning Outcomes. International Journal of Human-Computer Studies 66(2), 98–112 (2008)
34. Brown, P., Levinson, S.: Politeness: Some Universals in Language Usage. Cambridge University Press, Cambridge (1987)
35. Lepper, M., Chabay, R.: Socializing the Intelligent Tutor: Bringing Empathy to Computer Tutors. In: Mandl, H., Lesgold, A. (eds.) Learning Issues for Intelligent Tutoring Systems, pp. 242–257. Erlbaum, Hillsdale (1988)
36. Dweck, C.: Messages that Motivate: How Praise Molds Students' Beliefs, Motivation, and Performance (In Surprising Ways). In: Aronson, J. (ed.) Improving academic achievement: Impact of psychological factors on education, pp. 61–87. Academic Press, Orlando (2002)

The Affective and Learning Profiles of Students Using an Intelligent Tutoring System for Algebra

Maria Carminda V. Lagud[1] and Ma. Mercedes T. Rodrigo[2]

[1] Education Department, Ateneo de Manila University
[2] Department of Information Systems and Computer Science,
Ateneo de Manila University
minminvl@gmail.com, mrodrigo@ateneo.edu

Abstract. We investigate whether high-performing students' experience of affect (boredom, confusion, delight, flow, frustration, neutrality and surprise) is different from that of low-performing students while using Aplusix, an ITS for Algebra. We found that students with the highest number of correct answers experienced flow the most while students with the lowest number of correct answers experienced confusion and boredom the most. Students who attempted the most difficult problems experienced flow the most while students who tried the lowest levels experienced more boredom and confusion. Students who took the longest time in solving the algebra problems experienced confusion the most while students who took the shortest time experienced confusion the least. Students who used the most number of steps to solve a problem experienced confusion and boredom the most. Students who used the least number of steps experienced more flow.

Keywords: affect, Aplusix, affective profile, learning profile.

1 Introduction

Aplusix II: Algebra Learning Assistant is an intelligent tutoring system (ITS) for algebra. The system allows a student to solve an algebraic equation on a step-by-step basis. At each step, Aplusix provides the student with feedback indicating whether indeed a prior step and a current step were mathematically equivalent. Errors are immediately visible, prompting the student to make corrections early in the solution process. Prior research on Aplusix has shown that it has the capability to increase learning by 70% to 250% [2].

As with many other ITSs, Aplusix tends to track student performance, using this as basis for its subsequent interactions with the student. However, learning is not just a cognitive process. Learning also involves affect. Piaget (1989, in [8]) wrote that there is no cognitive mechanism without the affective element since affectivity motivates the intellectual activity. Thus, in recent years, more and more researchers and educators have been studying affect and its relationship with learning.

Affect pertains to a broad class of mental processes, including feelings, emotions, moods, and temperament (Dictionary of Psychology, Second Revised Edition., s. v. "affect"). Affect is related to motivation in that learners have feelings, emotions, and moods that they bring to bear on a task. "Students are more motivated when they feel optimistic about their goals and the chances of meeting them and when students are more excited after success, they are more willing to engage in the behavior again" [10]. Affect is also related to learning and cognition. The more emotional students feel about a piece of material, the more likely they are to remember it [10].

We aim to describe the relationship between the affective and learning profiles of students while interacting with Aplusix. We use the term "affective state" to refer to one emotion, feeling, or mood that a student displays during an observation, while term "affective profile" is the percentage of time a student displays each affective state during an observation period. For the purposes of this study, focus will be given to the affective states boredom, frustration, confusion, flow and delight, following the research of Craig et al. [3] and Rodrigo et al [13, 14, 15]. We use the term "learning profile" to refer to the number of correct items the student solved, the highest difficulty level he or she attempted, his or her average time to solve an item, and his or her average number of steps taken to solve an item.

2 Methods

2.1 Research Subjects and Setting

The participants for the study were first and second year high school students from four schools within Metro Manila and one school in Cavite. The students' age ranged from 12 to 15 with an average age of 13.5 and a modal age of 14. One hundred and forty students participated in the Aplusix study (83 female, 57 male). They were all computer-literate but none of them had previously used Aplusix. In groups of 10, participants were asked to use Aplusix for 42 minutes.

2.2 Aplusix

Aplusix covers six topics or categories of algebra: numerical calculation, expansion and simplification, factorization, solving equations, solving inequalities and solving systems of equations or inequalities. Each of these categories is again broken down into four to nine levels of difficulty. At the start of an Aplusix tutorial session, the student firsts select a problem set. The ITS presents a problem that the student must solve. Using an advanced editor of algebraic expressions (See Figure 1), the student then makes step-by-step calculations towards the solution. Two black parallel bars between two steps mean that the two steps are equivalent. Two red parallel bars with an X mean that the two steps are not equivalent. Aplusix also gives reports on the student's progress on the resolution of the problem. The report may include existence of errors or of an expression not yet in its simplest form. At any time, the student can end the exercise, ask for a hint or for the final answer or solution to be shown [9].

2.3 Quantitative Field Observations

We collected data regarding student affective states using the quantitative field observation methods discussed in Baker, et al [1]. The observations were carried out by a team of six observers, working in pairs. The observers were Masters students in Education or Computer Science, and all but one had prior teaching experience. The observers trained for the task through a series of pre-observation discussions on the meaning of the affective categories. Observations were conducted according to a guide that gave examples of actions, utterances, facial expressions, or body language that would imply an affective state, and practiced the coding categories during an unrelated observation prior to this study.

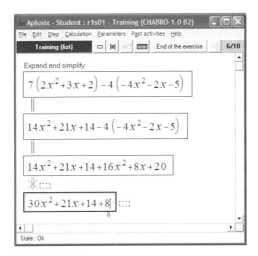

Fig. 1. A screen shot of Aplusix

Each observation lasted twenty seconds. Observers stood diagonally behind or in front of the student being observed and avoided looking at the student directly, in order to make it less clear exactly when an observation was occurring. If two distinct affective states were seen during an observation, only the first was coded, and any behavior by a student other than the student currently being observed was not coded. Since each observation lasted twenty seconds, each student was observed once per 180 seconds. The affective categories coded used were those from Rodrigo, et al.'s [15] study and were boredom, confusion, delight, surprise, frustration, flow [5] and the neutral state. "Flow" refers to full immersion in an activity; the participant is focused on a task to the point that he or she is unaware of the passage of time [5]. The utterances, postures, and facial expressions that were used to identify each state were discussed in [15].

Some of these affective categories may not be mutually exclusive (such as frustration and confusion), though others clearly are (delight and frustration). For tractability, however, the observers only coded one affective state per observation. Thirteen pairs of observations were collected per student. Inter-rater reliability was acceptably high: Cohen's κ=0.63.

2.4 Aplusix Log Files

As the student uses Aplusix, the software logs all user interactions. Each exercise is recorded in one log.

Figure 2 shows how a raw log file looks like. The raw log files were processed, combined and summarized into a more comprehensible master table of log files, a part of which is shown in Table 1.

```
;FeuilleDeCalculs;2;actions;□{[Type FeuilleDeCalculs] [Activite Entrainement] [expression <<{[{[5*4*2]_etape_ □["Calculate"]_etape_
["40"]_etape_ ["TpbCalculer"]}]_donne_ [{[40]_etape_ [""]_etape_ □["Solved"]_etape_ [""]}]}>>] [score 1.000000000] [ExpressionGlobale
<<{[5*4*2]_etape_ □["Calculate"]_etape_ [""]_etape_ ["TpbCalculer"]}>>] [CreditsIndications -1]}□□
%;FICHIER-ACTIONS;#VersionProtocoles=1;#Appli=APLUSIX II1.01b□□%;ELEVE□#identifiant="r1s01"□#passe="0F/D2F-C0C"□#nom=""□
#prenom=""□#NumeroAnonyme=1□#Role=Eleve□#SousRole=()□#Email=""□#Langue=()□#premierlancement="false"□#RepSaveAs="C:"□
#laclasse="AHS Run 1"□#CheminRepertoireActivite="C:\PROGRAM FILES\APLUSIX II\APLUSIXSYSTEM\..\..\..\WINDOWS\All Users\Application
Data\Aplusix\Classes\AHS Run 1\r1s01\D-2007-03-01\A-15-46-17-Entrainement"□#Activite=Entrainement□#DureeDuTest=1800□
#SorteListeExercice=ListeExercices□#ListeExercices=((<<5*4*2>> PatronCalculCE22) (<<-5-9+8>> PatronCalculCE12) (<<3(2-3)>>
PatronCalculCE31) □(<<4*2*5>> PatronCalculCE22) (<<6+7-5>> PatronCalculCE12) (<<3(2-3)>> PatronCalculCE31) □(<<5(3-5)+2(2-4)>>
PatronCalculCE32) (<<15-(-6-3)>> PatronCalculCE12) (<<-14*9>> □PatronCalculCE21) (<<15+7>> PatronCalculCE11))□#NumeroExercice=
#TempsTestRestant=0□#FichierListeExercices=""□#InfoListeEngendree=("CHABRO-1.0" "A1")□#ExerciceHorsListe=()□#FichierPointAlg=""□
#FeuilleCalculTerminee=vrai□#DocumentModifie=()□#verification=permanente□#LeScoreMax=20□□%;PARAMETRES□
#VerificationCalculs=ChoixEleve□#PorteeVerification=tout□#RaisonnementCorrect=non□#SansMalFormee=oui□#SansErronee=oui□
#CommandeCalculsNumeriques=decimal□#CommandeDevelopperReduire=non□#CommandeFactoriser=rien□#CommandeResoudreEquation=ri
#OrdreExerciceAleatoire=oui□#IncitationCommentaire=non□#PresentationSolution=oui□#RetourEnArriere=oui□#DureeTest=@30□
#petiteFleche=ChoixEleve□#EtapeInterneModifiable=oui□#AvecSelection=oui□#FrappeParentheses=texte□#FrappeFraction=infixee□
#CreationEleve=oui□#ScoreMaxi=@20□#PositionIncitationCommentaire=Partout□#VerificationResolu=vrai□□%;CHAMPS□
No;duree;action;erreur;etape;expression;etat;curseur;selection;equivalence;resolu;□□
%;ACTIONS;#Date=3/1/07#Heure=15:46:17;#TypeProbleme=TpbCalculer□0;0.0;structure;();0;();();();();();□1;0.0;enonce;();0;5*4*2
devant);rien;;N1;□2;6.7;placerCurseur;();0;5*4*2;();(2 0 derriere);rien;;N1;□3;6.8;commentaireetape : 40;();0;5*4*2;();(2 0
derriere);rien;;N1;□4;11.8;dupliquer;();1;5*4*2;();(2 0 derriere);rien;V1;N1;□5;1.6;BackSpace;();1;5*4*?;();(2 dedans);rien;V-;N-;□
6;0.2;BackSpace;();1;5*4;();(1 derriere);rien;V0;N0;□7;0.2;BackSpace;();1;5*?;();(1 dedans);rien;V-;N-;□8;0.2;BackSpace;();1;5;();
```

Fig. 2. Sample Raw Log File

Table 1. Sample Data from the Master Table of the Log Files

Column No.	1	2	3	4	5	6	7	8	9	10
Heading	School	Run	Student No.	Set No.	Problem No. within the set	Absolute Problem No.	Date	Time Started	Level	Step No.
Rows of Data	Alphonsus	1	07	1	01	1	1/22/07	00:33:29	B1	0
	Alphonsus	1	07	1	01	1	1/22/07	00:33:29	B1	0
	Alphonsus	1	07	1	01	1	1/22/07	00:33:29	B1	0

continuation

Column No.	11	12	13	14	15	16	17	18	19	20
Heading	Duration	Action	Error	Etape	Expression	Etat	Cursor	Selection	Equivalence	Resolution
Rows of Data	0	structure	()	0	()	()	()	()	()	()
	0	enonce	()	0	-8x(-8x-4)	()	(devant)	rien	()	N1
	0	termine	()	0	-8x(-8x-4)	()	(devant)	rien	()	N1

The columns in the table are as follows:
1. School – the name of the participating school
2. Run – the student's run or batch number. Three to four batches of 10 students each were observed per school. The run number ranges from 1 to 4.
3. Student No. – the identification number of the student within the run taking the exercise. The student number ranges from 1 to 10.
4. Set No. – the set number of the current exercise. A set is composed of a group of items under a specific exercise category
5. Problem No. Within Set – the item number within the set number chosen

6. Absolute Problem No. – the item no. relative to all the problems answered by the student
7. Date – the date when the exercise was done.
8. Time Started – the time when the student started with the specific problem (identified by column 5 or 6)
9. Level – the degree of difficulty of the topic.
10. Step No. – the number of the current step
11. Duration – the number of seconds describing how long each step was done
12. Action – the action performed by the student. Terms used are expressed in French (Fr.).
13. Error – the error committed by the student while solving the problem
14. Etape (Fr.) – the stage or phase of the solution
15. Expression – the state of the mathematical expression
16. Etat (Fr.) – the current state or condition of the solution
17. Cursor – location of the cursor. Examples for Cursor values are: devant (Fr.)- in front of/ outside, dedans (Fr.) – inside
18. Selection – selected values in the solution.
19. Equivalence – indicates whether the equation is correct or not.
20. Resolution – indicates if the problem has been solved or not.

Only column numbers 1, 2, 3, 4, 5, 6, 7, 8, 9, 10, 11, 20 were used for this research to help identify the learning profile of the students.

2.5 Affective Profile

The affective profile of each student was derived based on the quantitative field observations.

Table 2. Affective Profile of a Student ABC

Time	Rater 1	Rater 2	BOR	CON	DEL	FLO	FRU	SUR	NEU	Total
1	NEU	FLO				0.5			0.5	
2	FLO	FLO				1				
3	FLO	FLO				1				
4	FLO	FLO				1				
5	FLO	FLO				1				
6	FLO	CON		0.5		0.5				
7	FLO	FLO				1				
8	CON	CON		1						
9	FLO	FLO				1				
10	FLO	FLO				1				
11	FLO	FLO				1				
12	FLO	FLO				1				
13	FLO	FLO				1				
Total			0 or 0%	1.5 or 11.54%	0 or 0%	11 or 84.62%	0 or 0%	0 or 0%	0.5 or 3.85%	13 or 100%

To generate the affective profile from the data collection instrument, points were given to affective states observed. An affective state noted by both observers will be given 1 point for the particular time slice. If the two observers did not agree, 0.5 point will be given for each of the observed affective state. The number of times when each of the affective states was observed will be divided by 13 (for the 13 time slices) to get the percentage of time an affective state has been observed from a student. Table 2 shows the point system used. From the table, Student ABC can now be described as being in the state of flow 84.62% of the time, confused 11.54% of the time and showed neutrality 3.85% of the time.

2.6 Learning Profile

Using the Aplusix logs, we determined each student's learning profile, defined as the number of problems correctly solved, the highest difficulty level attempted, the average time to solve a problem, and the average number of steps used to solve the problem.

The means and standard deviations of each of the four variables were computed. For each of the four variables, we grouped the students into three: those within one standard deviation (average group), those above one standard deviation (above average group) and those below one standard deviation (below average group). We found, though, that the above average and below average groups were very small, e.g. less than 10 people, as opposed to over 95 people in the average group. We therefore decided to group the students terciles or by dividing the sample into three groups (average, above average, below average) centered on the median.

2.7 Comparison

We then computed for the affective profile of each tercile by taking the average incidence of each affective state of each student within the group. The affective profiles of the terciles were then compared with one another using a One-Way Analysis of Variance (ANOVA) with Statistical Package for Social Sciences (SPSS). Table 3 shows the tercile where the same Student ABC used in Table 2 belongs.

Table 3. Sample Tercile Group

Student	BOR	CON	DEL	FLO	FRU	SUR	NEU	Total
AAA	0.00%	23.08%	7.69%	69.23%	0.00%	0.00%	0.00%	100.00%
AAB	0.00%	7.69%	0.00%	92.31%	0.00%	0.00%	0.00%	100.00%
ABB	0.00%	3.85%	0.00%	96.15%	0.00%	0.00%	0.00%	100.00%
ABC	0.00%	11.54%	0.00%	84.62%	0.00%	0.00%	3.85%	100.01%
BBC	7.69%	3.85%	3.85%	76.92%	3.85%	0.00%	3.85%	100.01%
:	:	:	:	:	:	:	:	:
:	:	:	:	:	:	:	:	:
YYZ	0.00%	7.69%	0.00%	61.54%	30.77%	0.00%	0.00%	100.00%
XYZ	0.00%	3.85%	11.54%	84.62%	0.00%	0.00%	0.00%	100.01%
47 students	4.75%	16.53%	5.89%	68.49%	2.70%	0.33%	0.00%	99.67%

3   Results and Discussion

The following ANOVA results were obtained. Scheffe posthoc tests were also done to identify which particular groups showed significant differences.

In terms of correct items solved, the group that scored the highest (above average) experienced flow the most (F=3.948; p=0.022) with a mean difference of ± .106014 between the above and below average groups from the Scheffe posthoc tests. The group that scored the lowest experienced (below average) the most boredom (F=3.995; p=0.021) with a mean difference of ± .040057 between the above and below average groups. The group that scored the lowest experienced the most confusion (F=5.163; p=0.007) with a mean difference of ± .070853 between the above and below average groups..

In terms of highest difficulty level attempted, the group that tried the most difficult levels (above average) experienced flow the most (F=5.994; p=0.003) with a mean difference of ± .125430 between the above and below average groups. The group that tried the lowest levels experienced significantly more boredom (F=5.495; p=0.005) with a mean difference of ± .045826 between the below average and average groups and a mean difference of ± .042088 between the above and below average groups. Same with boredom, the group that tried the lowest levels experienced significantly more confusion (F=6.006; p=0.003) with a mean difference of ± .073079 between the above and below average groups.

The group that took the longest time in solving (below average) experienced confusion the most while the group that took the shortest time in solving (above average) experienced confusion the least (F=4.726; p=0.010) with a mean difference of ± .064378 between the above and below average groups.

Finally, the group that used the most number of steps (below average) experienced confusion (F=4.082; p=0.019) with a mean difference of ± .057691 between the above and below average groups. The below average group also experienced boredom the most (F=3.617; p=0.029) with a mean difference of ± .040382 between the average and below average groups. The average group and the group that used the least number of steps experienced flow more than the group that used the most number of steps (F=3.476; p=0.034).

All learning groups in all categories experienced flow to a great extent. The significant differences lie in the degree to which the groups experienced flow. The groups that scored the highest based on the number of correct items solved, those who tried the most difficult levels and those who took fewer number of steps in solving an item experienced significantly more flow than those in other groups. These findings support findings from other studies that indicate that flow is experienced more by people who are more motivated, those who are willing to go further, those willing reach for higher levels of challenge and are achievers or experts [4, 5, 12]. There are also significant differences in the degree to which the learning groups experienced confusion. The group that scored the lowest, the group that answered items in the lowest levels, the group that took the most number of steps in solving an item and the group that used the most time in answering an item experienced significantly more confusion than other groups. These are aligned findings from definitions of confusion: a feeling of perceptual disorientation and lack of clear thinking [6] or a feeling of not knowing, when information is not present in memory [7]. On the other hand, confusion can also be equated with a constructive form of cognitive dissonance, which is positively related to optimum learning gains [3]. This may account for the fact that groups with higher levels achievement experienced confusion as well.

In terms of boredom, the group that scored the lowest, the group that used the most number of steps and those who stayed in the lowest difficulty level experienced significantly more boredom the other groups. The students may have used repetitive steps that contributed to the high quantity of steps used. For one, based from the logs, the student who used the highest average of steps (i.e. 403 steps) only tried answering three items. This student tended to type numbers and erase them repeatedly—as if he was thrashing. According to English & English [6] boredom is felt when doing uninteresting activities. Perkins and Hill [11] also discussed the association of boredom with subjective monotony.

4 Conclusion

The results of this study are consistent with intuition: Good students tend to experience more flow, less boredom and less confusion than students who are struggling. What makes this study interesting, though, is that it attempts to quantify levels of achievement and their associated affective states. In the design of affective interventions, findings such as these might give ITS designers clues as to how students who are performing poorly are feeling. Designers might therefore arrive at appropriate intervention strategies that address not just the students' cognitive problems but their affect-related issues as well.

Acknowledgements. We thank Dr. Ryan Baker for his continuing support and guidance. We thank Jean-Francois Nicaud of the Laboratoire d'Informatique de Grenoble for the use of Aplusix. We thank Sheryl Ann Lim, Alexis Macapanpan, Sheila Pascua, Jerry Santillano, Jessica Sugay, Sinath Tep, and Norma Jean Viehland, and Dr. Ma. Celeste T. Gonzalez for their assistance in organizing and conducting the studies reported here. We also thank the Ateneo de Manila High School, Kostka School of Quezon City, School of the Holy Spirit of Quezon City, St. Alphonsus Liguori Integrated School and St. Paul's College Pasig for their participation in the studies conducted. This research undertaking was made possible by the Philippines Department of Science and Technology Engineering Research and Development for Technology Consortium under the project "Multidimensional Analysis of User-Machine Interactions Towards the Development of Models of Affect".

References

1. Baker, R.S., Corbett, A.T., Koedinger, K.R., Wagner, A.Z.: Off-Task Behavior in the Cognitive Tutor Classroom: When Students "Game the System". In: Proceedings of ACM CHI 2004: Computer-Human Interaction, pp. 383–390 (2004)
2. Bouhineau, D., Nicaud, J.F., Chaachoua, H., Huguet, T., Bittar, M., Bronner, A.: Two years of use of the Aplusix System. In: Proceeding of the 8th IFIP World Conference on Computer in Education, p. 23. University of Stellenbosch, Cape Town South Africa (2005)

3. Craig, S.D., Graesser, A.C., Sullins, J., Gholson, B.: Affect and Learning: An Exploratory Look into the Role of Affect in Learning with AutoTutor. Journal of Educational Media 29(3), 241–250 (2004)
4. Csikszentmihalyi, M., Rathunde, K., Whalen, S.: Talented Teenagers: The Roots of Success and Failure. Cambridge University Press, New York (1993)
5. Csikszentmihalyi, M.: Flow: The Psychology of Optimal Experience. Harper & Row, New York (1990)
6. English and English: A comprehensive dictionary of psychological and psychoanalytic terms. New York: Longmans, Green and Co. (1958)
7. Hess, U.: Now You See It, Now You Don't - The Confusing Case of Confusion as an Emotion: Commentary on Rozin and Cohen. Emotion 3(1), 76–80 (2003)
8. Jaques, P.A., Bocca, E., Vicari, R.M.: Considering Student's Emotions in Computational Educational Systems. In: Simposio Brasileiro de Informatica na Educacao, pp. 543–552, UFRJ: Rio de Janeiro (2003)
9. Nicaud, J.F., Bouhineau, D., Chaachoua, H., Huguet, T., Bronner, A.: A computer program for the learning of algebra: description and first experiment. In: Proceedings of PEG 2003, Saint Petersburg (2003)
10. Ormrod, J.: Educational Psychology: Developing Learners, 6th edn. Pearson Merril Prentice Hall, New Jersey (2008)
11. Perkins, R.E., Hill, A.B.: Cognitive and affective aspects of boredom. British Journal of Psychology 76, 221–234 (1985)
12. Rathunde, K., Csikszentmihalyi, M.: Middle School Students' Motivation and Quality of Experience: A Comparison of Montessori and Traditional School Environments. American Journal of Education 111(3), 341–371 (2005)
13. Rodrigo, M.M.T., Anglo, E.A., Sugay, J.O., Baker, R.S.J.d.: Use of Unsupervised Clustering to Characterize Learner Behaviors and Affective States while Using an Intelligent Tutoring System. In: Chan, T.-W., Biswas, G., Chen, F.-C., Chen, S., Chou, C., Jacobson, M., Kinshuk, K.F., Looi, C.-K., Mitrovic, T., Mizoguchi, R., Nakabayashi, K., Reimann, P., Suthers, D., Yang, S., Yang, J.-C. (eds.) International Conference on Computers in Education 2008, pp. 57–64. Asia Pacific Society for Computers in Education (2008)
14. Rodrigo, M. M.T., Baker, R.S.J.d., D'Mello, S.K., Gonzalez, M. C.T., Lagud, M.C.V., Lim, S.A.L., Macapanpan, A.F., Pascua, S.A.M.S., Santillano, J.Q., Sugay, J.O., Tep, S., Viehland, N.J.B.: Comparing Learners' Affect While Using an Intelligent Tutoring System and a Simulation Problem Solving Game. In: Woolf, B.P., Aïmeur, E., Nkambou, R., Lajoie, S. (eds.) ITS 2008. LNCS, vol. 5091, pp. 40–49. Springer, Heidelberg (2008)
15. Rodrigo, M.M.T., Baker, R.S.J.d., Lagud, M.C.V., Lim, S.A.L., Macapanpan, A.F., Pascua, S.A.M.S., Santillano, J.Q., Sevilla, L.R.S., Sugay, J.O., Tep, S., Viehland, N.J.B.: Affect and Usage Choices in Simulation Problem-solving Environments. In: Luckin, R., Koedinger, K.R., Greer, J. (eds.) Artificial Intelligence in Education: Building Technology Rich Learning Contexts that Work, pp. 145–152. IOS Press, Amsterdam (2007)

The Impact of System Feedback on Learners' Affective and Physiological States

Payam Aghaei Pour[1], M. Sazzad Hussain[1], Omar AlZoubi[1], Sidney D'Mello[2], and Rafael A. Calvo[1]

[1] School of Electrical and Information Engineering, University of Sydney, Australia
[2] Institute for Intelligent Systems, University of Memphis, Memphis, USA
{payama,sazzzad,oalzoubi,rafa}@ee.usyd.edu.au,
sdmello@memphis.edu

Abstract. We investigate how positive, neutral and negative feedback responses from an Intelligent Tutoring System (ITS) influences learners' affect and physiology. AutoTutor, an ITS with conversational dialogues, was used by learners (n=16) while their physiological signals (heart signal, facial muscle signal and skin conductivity) were recorded. Learners were asked to self-report the cognitive-affective states they experienced during their interactions with AutoTutor via a retrospective judgment protocol immediately after the tutorial session. Statistical analysis (Chi-square) indicated that tutor feedback and learner affect were related. The results revealed that after receiving positive feedback from AutoTutor, learners mostly experienced 'delight' while surprise was experienced after negative feedback. We also classified physiological signals based on the tutor's feedback (Negative vs. Non-Negative) with a support vector machine (SVM) classifier. The classification accuracy, ranged from 42% to 84%, and was above the baseline for 10 learners.

Keywords: feedback, emotion, affective computing, multimodal interfaces, AutoTutor.

1 Introduction

The connection between emotions and deep learning has recently received increased attention in the interdisciplinary arena that spans psychology, education [1, 2], neuroscience, and computer science [3-5]. Although several important questions pertaining to the affect-cognitive relationship during the learning process still remain unanswered [6], there is some evidence that the more typically studied six basic emotions [7] (happiness, sadness, surprise, disgust, anger and fear) are not the emotions most pertinent to learning, at least not for short learning sessions that last under 2 hours. Instead, affective states such as confusion, boredom, flow, curiosity, interest, surprise, delight, and frustration have emerged as highly relevant and influential to the learning experience; many of these states are frequently experienced during tutorial sessions with both Intelligent Tutoring Systems as well as human tutors [4, 8-11].

Inspired by the inextricable link between affect and learning, some researchers have worked to endow ITS with the ability to detect learners' affective states (e.g. confusion, frustration, etc.), respond to these states, and generate appropriate emotional expressions by embodied pedagogical agents. These affect-sensitive ITSs aspire to narrow the interaction bandwidth between computer tutors and human tutors with the hope that this will lead to an improved user experience and enhanced learning gains [12-14].

Accurate affect-detection is clearly an essential challenge to be overcome before functional affect-sensitive ITSs can become a reality. Although a number of studies have attempted to recognize learners' affect from facial expressions and speech [15-17], studies using physiological signals especially in educational contexts are relatively scarce. This is because, physiological sensors are often considered invasive and not suitable for learning environments as the sensors might interfere with the primary task of learning or problem solving. Fortunately, concerns pertaining to intrusiveness of the sensors, are somewhat less problematic with the recent advent of wearable physiological sensors [18]. Therefore, a re-investigation of the possibility of inferring a learner's affective state by monitoring physiological sensors is warranted. It should also be noted that although physiological responses to affective events has been a century long endeavor, most of the investigations traditionally studied the basic emotions, and little is known about the physiological manifestations of the learning-centered cognitive-affective states such as confusion and frustration.

Toward more real-world environment for physiological data collection, and the imperative to better understand the role of emotion in learning, we describe a study that collected physiological data to investigate the viability of detecting learning-centered affective states from physiology. We begin with a discussion of relevant affective computing research using physiological signals.

2 Recognizing Affective States through Physiology

Some important questions need to be addressed before functional physiological-based affect detectors for learning environments can be developed. Perhaps the most vital is whether distinct physiological patterns can be associated with particular emotions. Although the common answer is an enthusiastic "yes", the scientific research is much more controversial [19]. What is clear, however, is that some physiological correlations of the "basic" emotions can be identified more reliably than others. For example, fear has been related to an increase of heart rate, skin conductance level and systolic blood pressure [20], while anger has been related to an increase of heart rate, and both systolic and diastolic blood pressure [21]. In contrast, the physiology of sadness has proven to be difficult to pin-point physiologically, and has been associated with both an increase [22] and a decrease [20] in heart rate. Whether the more learning-centered emotions would prove to be as physiologically elusive as sadness or more consistent like anger awaits further research.

In addition to these challenges, the situation is more complicated because several of the studies investigating the physiology of emotion have adopted experimental protocols that have little relevance for ITSs, which have to operate in the real world. Pioneering work studying physiological states during ITS interactions by Conati was not conclusive on how these studies could be best performed [23]. More recently, recordings with one physiological sensor in naturalistic scenarios have been reported, so important progress is being made [24].

The current paper reports on a study that investigated the physiological embodiment in response to tutor feedback during learning sessions with AutoTutor, an ITS that provides conversational dialogues (described below). In addition to investigating the physiological correlates of the affective states we also focus on the feedback that the tutor provides to the learners. Focusing on feedback is critical because, in addition to being *directive* (i.e. tells students what needs to be fixed) and *facilitative* (i.e. helps students conceptualize information), feedback can also influence learners' affective and motivational processes [25].

The present study monitored learners' cognitive-affective states, their physiological signals, and the tutor's feedback during a 45 minute session with AutoTutor on topics in Computer Literacy [26]. AutoTutor is a validated ITS that helps students learn topics in Newtonian physics, computer literacy, and critical thinking via a mixed-initiative natural language dialogue. AutoTutor's dialogues are organized around difficult questions and problems (called main questions) that require reasoning and explanations in the answers. When presented with these questions, students typically respond with answers that are only one word to two sentences in length. In order to guide students in their construction of an improved answer, AutoTutor actively monitors learners' knowledge states and engages them in a turn-based dialogue. AutoTutor adaptively manages the tutorial dialogue by providing feedback on their answers (e.g. "good job", "not quite"), probing the learner for more information (e.g. "What else"), giving hints (e.g. "What about X"), prompts (e.g. "X is a type of what "),correcting misconceptions, answering questions, and summarizing topics.

Although affect and learning connections have been explored in previous studies with AutoTutor [27], the current study focuses specifically on the physiological states of the learners. This topic has not been explored in previous studies with AutoTutor. In particular, the specific research questions that motivated the current study include: (a) What is the relationship between the tutor's feedback and the learner's self-reported affective states?, (b) What are the physiological correlates of these cognitive-affective states, and (c) How does the tutor's feedback influence the learners' physiological signals?

3 Data and Methods

The participants in this study consisted of 16 paid volunteers, most of whom were engineering students, from The University of Sydney. All participants signed an informed consent form approved by a Human Research Ethics Committee. The study typically lasted 2.5 hours for each participant.

Participants completed a 45 minute AutoTutor training session on one out of three randomly assigned topics in computer literacy (hardware, Internet, or operating systems). During this interactive session, a video of the learner's face and a video of his or her computer screen were recorded. In addition, three physiological sensors measured heart activity (electrocardiogram - ECG), face muscle activity (electromyogram - EMG), and galvanic skin response recorded from the tip of the fingers (GSR). The physiological signals were acquired using a BIOPAC MP150 system with

AcqKnowledge software at a sampling rate of 1,000 Hz for all channels. ECG was collected with two electrodes from the wrists and a ground on the left ankle. Only one channel of EMG was recorded from a corrugator muscle with two electrodes each 2 cm apart. GSR was recorded from the index and middle finger (left hand).

Learners retrospectively provided self-report affect judgments immediately after their AutoTutor session. The collection of these self-reported judgments proceeded in the following way. A learner would view a video of himself/herself during the interaction simultaneously with a video capture of his/her screen interaction with AutoTutor. The videos automatically paused every 20 seconds at which point learners were asked to select one o r more affective states from a list of eight states, in addition to an "other" category. These states were: confusion, frustration, boredom, flow/engagement, curiosity, surprise, delight, and frustration. Fig. 1 reflects the proportional values and 95% confidence interval for the affective states reported by all learners. Where more than one state was selected, the learner was then asked to indicate the most pronounced state. The current analysis only considers the more pronounced affective state for each 20-second block.

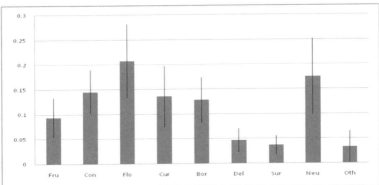

Notes. Fru = Frustration, Con = Confusion, Flo = Flow/engagement, Cur = Curiosity, Bor = Boredom, Del = Delight, Sur = Surprise, Neu = Neutral, Oth = Other.

Fig. 1. Proportional values with 95% confidence interval for affective states reported by all learners

4 Results and Discussion

AutoTutor's short feedback (positive, neutral, negative) is manifested in its verbal content, intonation, and a host of other non-verbal conversational cues. . Positive feedback accompanies correct answers, negative feedback incorrect answers, while the tutor provides neutral feedback when the student's answer lies between these two extremes. Although the feedback selection mechanism is more sophisticated that this simple description suggests, of greatest relevance is the fact that the feedback evokes strong emotional responses from participants [6, 8]; this emotional-elicitation quality of the tutor's feedback is very relevant for the present paper.

Our analyses are organized around three questions: (a) how tutor feedback impacts the affective state of the student (based on the self-report)?, (b) how tutor feedback influences the physiological state of the students?, and (c) how the self-reported affective states correlate with physiology. These three questions were addressed by constructing supervised classifiers. The assumption is that if a classification model with accuracy higher than a baseline can be built, then the affective response to a stimulus is not random.

Self-report annotations were synchronized with AutoTutor's feedback type (mined from AutoTutor's logs) and with corresponding physiological signals. Then, 20-second blocks for the affect annotations and 10-second blocks after the feedback were extracted from the physiological signals.

The Waikato Environment for Knowledge Analysis (Weka), a data mining package [28], was used for the classification of the three pairs of data described here, all based on a 10-fold cross validation. The default parameter values were used for classification in this study. The ZeroR classifier represents the baseline for classification accuracy; differences in baseline accuracy are based on differences in the class distributions of individual learners. Support vector machine (SVM) classifier with a linear kernel was utilized for training classification models which is based on John Platt's sequential minimal optimization algorithm for training a support vector machines classifier [29]. A feature selection algorithm was used to reduce the dimensionality of the physiological data. A chi-square (X^2) feature selection as implemented in Weka was used for selecting the ten most relevant features. The X^2 feature selection evaluates attributes by computing the value of the chi-squared statistic with respect to the class label either feedback or self-report emotion [30].

4.1 Feedback and Affect

Affective states of all learners are significantly dependent with AutoTutor feedback. A 5 x 9 Chi-square (X^2) analysis revealed this dependency. A chi square value of approximately 165.0 with 32 degrees of freedom ($\alpha = 0.05$) was obtained. Table 1 shows the contingency table of all feedback types and self-reported affective states for all learners.

Table 1. A contingency table of 16 learners for all feedback types and affective states (self-report)

Feedback	Fru	Con	Flow	Cur	Bor	Del	Sur	Neu	Oth
Positive	7	7	24	12	19	39	2	27	5
Neutral Positive	2	12	5	7	2	1	1	7	1
Neutral	12	22	29	25	30	22	3	34	1
Neutral Negative	8	5	7	3	6	0	4	3	0
Negative	57	65	60	41	45	4	29	50	16

Notes. Fru = Frustration, Con = Confusion, Flow = Flow/engagement, Cur = Curiosity, Bor = Boredom, Del = Delight, Sur = Surprise, Neu = Neutral, Oth = Other.

Using the data for all learners, the five different feedback types produced by AutoTutor were used to classify the self-reported affective states. The frequency of each cognitive-affective state varied: Boredom (102), confusion (111), Delight (66), Frustration (86), Neutral (121), Curiosity (88), Frustration (86), Flow (125), Surprise (39). Table 2 gives the classification results for affective states that had accuracy above the ZeroR baseline. As a result the study looked at pairs of cognitive-affective states that can best be separated, or in other words, determining the effect of system feedback on the cognitive-affective state of the learner using only pairs of cognitive-affective states. The results showed that the pair Delight and Surprise could best be separated with a recognition rate of 86.67% and kappa 0.7 where, Delight was related to a positive feedback and Surprise to a negative feedback. Delight in general was best separated from other affective states, whereas, the Delight and Frustration pair had a high separation of 82.89 %; frustration is related to a negative feedback as well. Flow, Neutral, and Curiosity could not be separated effectively from other classes. Boredom, Frustration, and Confusion showed weak separation among others.

Table 2. Classification results for discriminating affect-pairs from feedback

Affect Pair	ZeroR (baseline) (% Correct))	SVM (%Correct)
Boredom -Confusion	52.1	56.8
Boredom -Delight	60.7	69.0
Boredom-Frustration	54.2	57.98
Confusion-Delight	62.71	73.45
Confusion-Neutral	52.16	58.62
Curiosity-Delight	57.14	70.13
Curiosity-Frustration	50.57	60.34
Delight - Flow	65.45	69.63
Delight-Frustration	56.58	82.89
Delight-Neutral	64.71	67.91
Delight-Surprise	62.86	86.67
Flow-Neutral	50.81	53.25
Frustration -Neutral	58.45	56.04

4.2 Feedback and Physiology

The results of SVM classification from the physiological data based on feedback for all features and selected features are given in Table 3. For some learners, there were data sparseness problems with tutor feedback, which made automatic classification unfeasible. In order to alleviate this problem, we grouped AutoTutor's feedback types into two classes; the majority feedback (negative) in a 'Negative' class and the rest in the 'Other' class.

Table 3. Physiological data classification based on Feedback, Negative Class Vs. Other Class

Learner	Negative Count	Other Count	ZeroR (Baseline) (% Correct)	SVM (All features) (% Correct)	SVM (10 features)) (% Correct)
1	24	23	42.55	72.34	63.83
2	18	18	44.44	47.22	63.89
3	32	17	65.31	69.39	67.35
4	26	20	56.52	41.30	50
5	31	26	54.39	47.37	50.88
6	19	27	58.70	39.13	56.52
7	28	35	55.56	57.14	71.43
8	18	24	57.14	78.57	76.19
9	20	18	52.63	73.68	84.21
10	29	35	54.69	50	42.19
11	23	30	56.60	60.38	66.04
12	20	21	51.22	60.98	58.54
13	22	22	45.45	65.91	72.73
14	18	27	60	53.33	60
15	25	27	51.92	59.62	61.54
16	14	24	63.16	57.89	65.79
Total	367	394	51.77	49.67	52.56

The counts column in Table 3 shows the number of instances for each class. Results emphasize differences among learners; 12 learners had classification accuracy above the baseline. This suggests that there are physiological patterns that can be identified from feedback. It was also noticeable that the learners with higher classification accuracy had a mix of ECG, EMG, and SC as selected features, while those with low accuracies had only ECG features selected. This implies that multimodal features can increase the classification accuracy in automatic affect recognition. The Chi square feature selection improved the classification accuracy in most cases, by selecting the most informative features, and discarding those features that are redundant or irrelevant to the classification task; however for some cases it degraded the classification accuracy due to the loss of some informative features, and this is subject dependent as our results suggest. Further investigations are needed to find more efficient feature selection methods. The classification for the combined data considering all learners was no better than the baseline, which indicates that physiological patterns in response to feedback are different among individuals.

4.3 Self-report and Physiology

The second part of the project is to study how physiological patterns could be mapped into self-reported cognitive-affective states, in the sense that students during interaction with Autotutor system would experience some emotions that affect their physiology. If we were able to build models that can map these physiological changes into affective states, we would be able to adapt the tutoring system to students' current emotional state; we hypothesize that such an adaptation will enhance the learning experience of students in future development of tutoring systems. For this paper we evaluated only standard techniques but results were not significantly above the baseline so they are not discussed in detail. Hence, a more detailed investigation is required. Meanwhile it is interesting to consider the issues that would arise when attempts to identify the cognitive-affective states from the physiological signals.

- The differences between subjects make it unlikely that a classifier trained with data from all subjects would be accurate [31].
- The cognitive-affective state categories have very skewed distributions and training a classifier with highly unbalanced data is more difficult.

5 Conclusion

We investigated the impact of an Intelligent Tutoring System's feedback on learners' self-reported affective states and their physiological states. The results indicated that there was a relationship between tutor feedback and self-reported affective states, as well as between feedback and physiology. Automatic classifiers achieved accuracies above the baseline showing that both affective states and physiology can be predicted from the tutor feedback. These results are significant since different feedback types (negative or positive) from AutoTutor indicate possible influence in learners' emotional and physiological states. This suggests that here is some coherence in the way that learners physiologically respond to tutor feedback.

A preliminary study of possible relationships between the affective states and physiology did not show significant relationships. A more thorough study of these relationships was planned as the second part of this project. The effect of specific stimulus (e.g. a photograph) on subjects' physiology can provide information to create models [32] that can predict learners' affective states in learning scenarios. As for future work, 'normative databases' can help to create such models suitable for learning scenarios.

References

1. Lepper, M., Henderlong, J.: Turning 'play' into 'work' and 'work' into 'play': 25 years of research on intrinsic versus extrinsic motivation. In: Intrinsic and extrinsic motivation: The search for optimal motivation and performance, pp. 257–307 (2000)
2. Linnenbrink, E., Pintrich, P.: The role of motivational beliefs in conceptual change. Practice 115, 135 (2002)

3. Kort, B., Reilly, R., Picard, R.: An affective model of interplay between emotions and learning. In: Reengineering educational pedagogy-building a learning companion, pp. 43–48 (2001)
4. Craig, S., Graesser, A., Sullins, J., Gholson, B.: Affect and learning: an exploratory look into the role of affect in learning with AutoTutor. Journal of Educational Media 29 (2004)
5. Picard, R.: Affective Computing. The MIT Press, Cambridge (1997)
6. D'Mello, S., Graesser, A., Picard, R.: Toward an affect-sensitive AutoTutor. IEEE Intelligent Systems 22, 53–61 (2007)
7. Ekman, P., Levenson, R., Friesen, W.: Autonomic nervous system activity distinguishes among emotions. Science 221, 1208–1210 (1983)
8. D'Mello, S., Craig, S., Witherspoon, A., Mcdaniel, B., Graesser, A.: Automatic detection of learner's affect from conversational cues. User Modeling and User-Adapted Interaction 18, 45–80 (2008)
9. Burleson, W., Picard, R.: Affective agents: Sustaining motivation to learn through failure and a state of stuck. Citeseer (2004)
10. Csikszentmihalyi, M.: Flow: The psychology of optimal experience, New York (1990)
11. Graesser, A., McDaniel, B., Chipman, P., Witherspoon, A., D'Mello, S., Gholson, B.: Detection of emotions during learning with AutoTutor. In: Proceedings of the 28 th Annual Meetings of the Cognitive Science Society, pp. 285–290 (2006)
12. Klein, J., Moon, Y., Picard, R.: This computer responds to user frustration: Theory, design, and results. Interacting with computers 14, 119–140 (2002)
13. Prendinger, H., Ishizuka, M.: The Empathic Companion: A Character-Based Interface That Addresses Users' Affective States. Applied Artificial Intelligence 19, 267–286 (2005)
14. Picard, R.W., Vyzas, E., Healey, J.: Toward machine emotional intelligence: analysis of affective physiological state. IEEE transactions on Pattern Analysis and Machine Intelligence 23, 1175–1191 (2001)
15. Cowie, R., Douglas-Cowie, E., Tsapatsoulis, N., Votsis, G., Kollias, S., Fellenz, W., Taylor, J.: Emotion recognition in human-computer interaction. IEEE Signal Processing Magazine 18, 32–80 (2001)
16. Polzin, T.: Detecting Verbal and Non-verbal cues in the communication of emotion. Unpublished Doctoral Dissertation, School of Computer Science, Carnegie Mellon University (2000)
17. Yacoob, Y., Davis, L.: Recognizing human facial expressions from long image sequences using optical flow (1996)
18. Picard, R., Vyzas, E., Healey, J.: Toward machine emotional intelligence: Analysis of affective physiological state. IEEE transactions on Pattern Analysis and Machine Intelligence, 1175–1191 (2001)
19. Barrett, L.: Are Emotions Natural Kinds? vol. 1 58 (2006)
20. Christie, I.C.: Multivariate discrimination of emotion-specific autonomic nervous system activity (2002)
21. Fredrickson, B.L., Mancuso, R.A., Branigan, C., Tugade, M.M.: The undoing effect of positive emotions. Motivation and Emotion 24, 237–258 (2000)
22. Levenson, R.W., Ekman, P., Friesen, W.V.: Voluntary facial action generates emotion-specific autonomic nervous system activity. Psychophysiology 27, 363–384 (1990)
23. Conati, C., Chabbal, R., Maclaren, H.: A study on using biometric sensors for monitoring user emotions in educational games. In: Workshop on Assessing and Adapting to User Attitudes and Affect: Why, When and How (2003)
24. Arroyo, I., Cooper, D., Burleson, W., Woolf, B., Muldner, K., Christopherson, R.: Emotion Sensors go to School (2009)

25. Narciss, S.: Motivational Effects of the Informativeness of Feedback (1999)
26. Graesser, A., Chipman, P., Haynes, B., Olney, A.: AutoTutor: An intelligent tutoring system with mixed-initiative dialogue. IEEE Transactions on Education 48, 612–618 (2005)
27. D'Mello, S., Picard, R., Graesser, A.: Toward an Affect-Sensitive AutoTutor. IEEE Intelligent Systems 22, 53–61 (2007)
28. Witten, I.H., Frank, E.: Data Mining: Practical Machine Learning Tools and Techniques, 2nd edn. Morgan Kaufmann Series in Data Management Systems. Morgan Kaufmann, San Francisco (2005)
29. Platt, J.: Machines using Sequential Minimal Optimization. In: Schoelkopf, B., Burges, C., Smola, A. (eds.) Advances in Kernel Methods - Support Vector Learning (1998)
30. Duda, R.O., Hart, P.E., Stork, D.G.: Pattern Classification. John Wiley & Sons, New York (2001)
31. Calvo, R.A., Brown, I., Scheding, S.: Effect of Experimental Factors on the Recognition of Affective Mental States Through Physiological Measures. In: Nicholson, A., Li, X. (eds.) AI 2009. LNCS, vol. 5866. Springer, Heidelberg (2009)
32. Lang, P.J., Greenwald, M., Bradley, M.M., Hamm, A.O.: Looking at pictures: Evaluative, facial, visceral, and behavioral responses, vol. 30, pp. 261–274 (1993)

Investigating the Relationship between Presence and Learning in a Serious Game

H. Chad Lane, Matthew J. Hays, Daniel Auerbach, and Mark G. Core

Institute for Creative Technologies
University of Southern California

Abstract. We investigate the role of presence in a serious game for intercultural communication and negotiation skills by comparing two interfaces: a 3D version with animated virtual humans and sound against a 2D version using text-only interactions with static images and no sound. Both versions provide identical communicative action choices and are driven by the same underlying simulation engine. In a study, the 3D interface led to a significantly greater self-reported sense of presence, but produced significant, but equivalent learning on immediate posttests for declarative and conceptual knowledge related to intercultural communication. Log data reveals that 3D learners needed fewer interactions with the system than those in the 2D environment, suggesting they benefited equally with less practice and may have treated the experience as more authentic.

Keywords: presence, serious games, intercultural competence, virtual humans.

1 Introduction

After the release of *Avatar*, more than 1000 posts appeared on a website from fans who wanted to share ideas for how to "cope with the depression of the dream of Pandora being intangible" [1]. The use of high-fidelity 3D animation and sound apparently left some viewers in a state of deep sadness upon realization that Pandora, the fictional world depicted in the film, was not their reality. Interestingly, some of the more common suggestions on the forum for coping included playing the Avatar video game and exploring recreations of Pandora in virtual worlds.

Examples like this have driven researchers to dig deeper into the psychology of immersive experiences and how they relate to entertainment, learning, and addiction.[1] Whether reading a book, watching a movie, or playing a game, people seem capable of changing their frame of reference such that narrative or virtual experiences are temporarily experienced as reality [2]. This phenomenon has generated enthusiasm from many education theorists (e.g., [3]) and researchers (e.g., [4]) who perceive it to have potential to enhance learner engagement, motivation to learn, and time-on-task. In this paper, we consider the question of whether sense of presence matters in a serious game for learning intercultural communication skills and how it affects learner behaviors within that game.

---

[1] http://mediagrid.org/groups/technology/PIE.TWG/

2 Games, Motivation, Presence, and Learning

There is a growing body of evidence that educational games, when built on sound pedagogical design principles, are effective at promoting learning [5-6]. However, it has been suggested that these learning gains are often due to instructional design features (e.g., availability of feedback) rather than any unique properties of games [7]. Of course, advocates quickly point out that there is more to learning than just cognitive gain. A good example comes from Malone and Lepper [8] who focused on nurturing *intrinsic motivation*—the "will to learn" for its own sake, without extrinsic reward. They analyzed opinions of elementary school students on a variety of games (circa 1980) in order to identify which properties were most appealing. A key finding was that the children displayed a preference for *fantasy* contexts that could evoke "mental images of physical or social situations not actually present" (p. 240). Further, for educational games, they assert that fantasies should be made *endogenous*, which means mastery of the learning content should lead to success in the game. Fantasy, something that is not typically considered important in instructional design, has been shown to enhance learning and dramatically increase learner motivation [9-10].

Fantasy therefore seems like an important element for educational game design, but how can we determine whether a learner has chosen to engage the fantasy? Answering this question requires a closer look at the learning experience from the learner's point of view. One potential indicator is whether the learner experiences a greater *sense of presence* while using the game. We adopt Lombard and Ditton's definition of presence as "the illusion of non-mediation" in which "a person responds as if the medium were not there" [11]. For the purposes of our task domain, intercultural communication, we are specifically interested in *social presence*—the degree to which a learner feels that an interaction with a virtual character is real.

Most studies examining the role of presence in immersive learning environments have not shown a direct link. Crystal Island, a 3D game for teaching microbiology and genetics, has been shown to enhance presence, involvement, and motivation, but not learning when compared to a comparable non-game-based control [12]. An immersive version of Design-a-Plant [13] was compared with a less immersive counterpart, but produced no differences in learning. However, *personalization* did lead to a greater sense of social presence with a pedagogical agent, and this positively influenced learning. In a study of the virtual Puget Sound, presence also lead to better conceptual understanding of water movement and salinity [14]. The authors hypothesize that higher presence may pay off only when the targeted domain knowledge directly involves it (e.g., understanding of a physical space in this case).

3 BiLAT: A Serious Game for Intercultural Communication

The context for our work is BiLAT, a serious game for practicing the preparation, execution, and understanding of bi-lateral meetings in a cultural context. Here, we focus on face-to-face meetings between learners and virtual characters, even though BiLAT's overall scope is much broader [15]. Our focus is on basic intercultural communicative skills necessary to build trust and reach agreements.

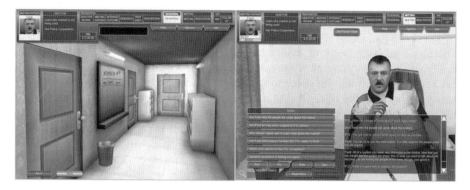

Fig. 1. Screenshots from BiLAT, a game for intercultural communication

In BiLAT, learners meet with one or more characters to achieve a set of predefined objectives. For example, the learner may need to convince a high-ranking local official to stop imposing an unjust tax on their people, or reach an agreement about who will provide security at a local marketplace. In all cases, the learner is required to adhere to Arab business cultural rules, establish a relationship, and apply integrative negotiation techniques. Specifically, BiLAT is designed as a practice environment for learning win/win negotiation techniques, which suggest learners should proactively strive to meet characters' needs as well their own [16]. To achieve these goals, learners must also apply their understanding of the character's culture to modify their communicative choices [17].

Two screenshots of the BiLAT 3D interface are shown in Figure 1. On the left is one of several navigation screens used in the game. On the right is the meeting screen, where learners spend much of their time during play. Figure 2 shows an alternative, 2D version of the BiLAT meeting screen. To take a communicative action in either, the learner selects from a menu of conversational actions. The user can engage in small talk (e.g., "talk about soccer"), ask questions (e.g., "ask who is taxing the market" and "ask if he enjoys travel"), state intentions (e.g., "say you are interested in finding a mutually beneficial agreement"), among other possibilities. Physical actions are also available (e.g., "remove sunglasses" or "give medical supplies"). There are roughly 70 actions for each character in BiLAT. In both interfaces, corresponding dialogue text is displayed in a dialogue window and available for the duration of the meeting.

Guidance is provided by an intelligent tutoring system (a "coach") that monitors the meeting and provides unsolicited help [18]. Help can come in the form of *feedback* about a previous action (e.g., explain a reaction from the character by describing an underlying cultural difference) or as a *hint* about what action is appropriate at the given time. Further, this coaching support is withdrawn gradually with time and learner success (i.e., it is "faded"). These messages appear in the dialogue window of BiLAT. After each meeting, the system also guides the learner through an interactive review that digs deeper into underlying cultural issues and decisions made by the user [15], but in the study reported below, this functionality was disabled since it is not available in the 2D interface.

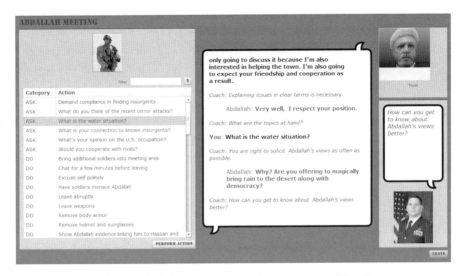

Fig. 2. A flash-based, non-immersive interface for BiLAT

BiLAT characters possess culturally-specific models of how they expect meetings to progress. This includes expectations for an opening phase, a social period, a business period, and a closing social period. These phases are derived from live role playing sessions with subject-matter experts early in the development of BiLAT [15]. An example of a knowledge component taught by BiLAT is to *follow the lead of your host*. If a learner chooses an action that is not appropriate for the current phase of a meeting, the character will respond negatively. The intelligent tutoring system provides support for phase-related problems as well as other culture-related topics [18]. Trust, which is directly affected by the ability of the learner to take appropriate and effective actions, is a major factor in whether BiLAT characters will be agreeable or difficult. It is common for learners to conduct multiple meetings with the same character to achieve objectives.

Both interfaces are controlled by the same simulation and differ only in their appearance and use of sound. Characters in the 3D version respond in a synthesized voice with physical gestures. The facial expressions, nonverbal behaviors, and speech of the characters are all synced with their utterances [15]. In the 2D interface, character images are static and only show their face. No sound is available in the 2D interface which means that learners must read character responses in the dialogue window. In both interfaces, coaching messages appear only as text and thus must also be read by the learner (if desired).

4 Method

In this section we describe an experiment intended to determine how the two interfaces differed in terms of their ability to create a sense of presence in the learner, and whether this had any impact on learning and learner behaviors.

4.1 Participants

Participants were 46 U. S. Citizens who were college students from universities in southern California. They were between 18 and 42 years of age and reported that they were able to speak English on a native level.

4.2 Design

There was a single independent variable: interface. It was manipulated between-subjects. One group of participants conducted their meetings in the 3D environment (Figure 1), which included simulated speech and animation. The other group used the less immersive—but functionally equivalent—2D interface (Figure 2).

4.3 Procedure

Pretest. After responding to fliers posted at universities in southern California, participants were emailed a link to an online pretest. The pretest had two parts. The first part was the Situational Judgment Test (SJT). The SJT presents eight scenarios, each of which is followed by three or four possible responses. Participants provided ratings (0 = "very poor action," 5 = "mixed/okay action," 10 = "very good action") for each of a total of 28 to-be-rated actions (for details on the SJT, see [15]).

The second part of the pretest comprised seven Cultural Assimilator (CA) items [19]. Each presents a scenario and four interpretations, from which the learner is asked to choose the best. Fourteen scenarios were selected using a voting process with the first two authors and a third intercultural researcher. The selected scenarios involved topics related to interpersonal situations (e.g., explaining why a waiter was confused by the behavior of an international customer) and focused on various cultural settings, including Arab, Japanese, Swedish, and more. Participants were awarded two points for selecting the best interpretation, one point for selecting a plausible but less culturally sophisticated interpretation, and zero points for selecting the weakest explanations [19]. Items were counterbalanced between pre- and posttests and the two versions were determined to be roughly equally difficult in a pilot study.

Practice with coaching. After completing the pretest and scheduling an appointment, participants arrived at our institute to interact with the BiLAT system. They were given printed orientation materials (which contained no instructional content) and were randomly assigned to encounter the 2D or 3D interface. They then spent up to 100 minutes meeting with three virtual Iraqi characters in attempts to solve a problem with a fictional U.S.-built marketplace in Iraq. All participants received hints and feedback from the coach during these meetings.

Practice without coaching. Next, participants spent up to 30 more minutes meeting with a fourth virtual Iraqi character to resolve a problem at a hospital. Participants used the same interface as they did when solving the market scenario, but the coach provided no hints or feedback during the doctor scenario.

Table 1. Summary of results between conditions (means, * = significant)

Sense of Presence (TPI, self-report)	2D	3D
Social	2.77	3.49*
Spatial	2.30	3.21*
In-game posttest (probability of errors)		
All errors	0.32	0.27
Phase-mismatch errors	0.18	0.16
Declarative knowledge (SJT correlation)		
Pretest	0.594	0.516
Posttest	0.718	0.718
Cultural knowledge (CA score)		
Pretest	10.17	9.41
Posttest	10.78	10.36

Presence. Participants then completed the social and spatial subscales of the Temple Presence Inventory (TPI), a series of self-report measures intended to capture a user's feelings of non-mediation [11]. For example, an item on the social subscale is "How often did you have the sensation that people you saw/heard could also see/hear you?" Items were rated from 1 (low) to 7 (high) and those that did not apply to both interfaces (e.g., questions about the authenticity of sound) were omitted.

Posttest. After completing the TPI, participants again completed the SJT and the counter-balanced CA (the seven previously unused questions). After completing the posttest, participants were thanked, compensated, and debriefed.

5 Results

5.1 Presence

Participants' ratings of presence are shown in Table 1. The 2D interface ($M = 2.76$, $SD = 1.04$) created less social presence than did the 3D interface ($M = 3.49$, $SD = .88$). This difference was statistically significant: $t(44) = 2.54$, $p = .02$. Similarly, the 2D interface ($M = 2.30$, $SD = .99$) created less spatial presence than did the 3D interface ($M = 3.21$, $SD = .99$): $t(44) = 3.09$, $p < .01$. These results suggest that our manipulation of presence was successful.

5.2 Learning

Declarative knowledge. The SJT required participants to rate actions based on their understanding of Iraqi cultural values. Thus, the SJT was our measure of declarative knowledge. Answers previously provided by three subject-matter experts (SMEs) were considered "correct." We defined improved declarative knowledge as an increase in participants' correlation with SMEs from pretest to posttest. Across conditions, SJT scores increased from pretest ($M = .56$, $SD = .20$) to posttest ($M = .72$, $SD = .13$), with a large effect size ($d = .92$). It appeared that participants became more correlated with SMEs—an interpretation that was supported by a repeated-measures ANOVA: $F(1, 44) = 40.04$, $p < .01$. This result suggests that BiLAT, with the assistance of the coach, is able to improve the acquisition of declarative knowledge.

Further, a median-split analysis revealed a greater improvement in SJT scores for participants with low SJT pretest scores ($M = .28$, $SD = .14$) than for those with high SJT pretest scores ($M = .04$, $SD = .12$). This difference was reliable: $t(44) = 6.27$, $p < .001$, $d = .93$, and is consistent with that the general result that lower-ability students tend to benefit most from higher levels of guidance [20]. This further suggests that the SJT taps knowledge that is reinforced by coaching.

Table 1 also suggests that participants' SJT scores increased (posttest minus pretest) more with the 3D interface ($M = .20$, $SD = .18$) than with the 2D interface ($M = .13$, $SD = .17$). However, this difference was unreliable: $t(44) = 1.52$, $p = .14$. It may appear that between-groups differences on the pretest masked this effect; participants assigned to the 2D interface ($M = .59$, $SD = .18$) seem to have scored higher than those assigned to the 3D interface ($M = .52$, $SD = .21$). However, this difference was also not reliable: $t(44) = 1.33$, $p = .19$. There was also no interaction between interface and median-split ($p = .88$). Thus, although the 3D interface created more presence, it did not produce gains in declarative knowledge.

Applied knowledge. As discussed above, the coaching system assesses all actions. We defined the learner's ability to apply knowledge as the probability that s/he would select a correct action based on this assessment. To diagnose participants' knowledge, we measured the probability that they would perform an action that was inappropriate in general or was a violation of the current meeting phase (experimenter error corrupted the data from two participants). Participants made approximately as many errors with the 2D interface ($M = .23$, $SD = .08$) as with the 3D interface ($M = .22$, $SD = .05$): $t(42) = .27$, $p = .79$. The same was true for meeting-phase errors; participants made approximately as many with the 2D interface ($M = .14$, $SD = .03$) as the 3D interface ($M = .14$, $SD = .04$): $t(42) = .09$, $p = .93$. This result suggests that there was little difference between the 2D and 3D interface in terms of errors committed.

In-game posttest. As described above, learners interacted with a fourth character with no coaching support. Although it was silent, the coaching system continued to provide records of the errors analyzed above. Table 1 shows the frequency of these errors in the doctor scenario (a software problem corrupted the data from two additional participants). As can be seen, the 2D interface ($M = .31$, $SD = .10$) led to more errors than did the 3D interface ($M = .27$, $SD = .10$). This difference, however, was not reliable: $t(40) = 1.54$, $p = .13$. Meeting-phase errors followed a similar pattern. The 2D interface ($M = .18$, $SD = .12$) led to more errors than did the 3D interface ($M = .16$, $SD = .11$), but the difference was not reliable: $t(40) = .58$, $p = .56$. These values were substantially greater than those observed during coached meetings, suggesting that coaching may have become a crutch. However, it appeared not to matter whether assistance had been delivered by the 2D or 3D interface.

Far-transfer test. The CA required participants to diagnose a short scenario based on their general understanding of intercultural interactions. It taps general intercultural skills and involves different cultural contexts than those in BiLAT. Table 1 shows participants' CA scores as a function of interface on the pretest ($M = 9.80$, $SD = 2.24$)

and posttest ($M = 10.58$, $SD = 2.10$). Although the increase appeared numerically small, a repeated-measures ANOVA revealed it to be relatively consistent: $F(1, 43) = 3.35$, $p = .07$ (one participant's data were lost due to experimenter error). This result is consistent with the SJT data; practice with coaching improves declarative knowledge and marginally improves the ability to transfer that knowledge to other situations.

A median-split analysis revealed a greater improvement in CA scores for participants with low CA pretest scores ($M = 1.96$, $SD = 2.68$) than for those with high CA pretest scores ($M = -1.00$, $SD = 2.06$). This difference was reliable: $t(43) = 3.97$, $p < .001$, $d = .27$. As with the SJT, low-performing learners enjoyed greater gains from using the system [20]. The decrease for high performers was not reliable and may be due to a ceiling effect (the top performers' average score was 12.06 out of 14 on the pretest). Thus, the increase in score for lower-performing learners (pretest score of 8.30 out of 14) shows that the CA taps knowledge relevant to BiLAT.

Table 1 also shows that participants' CA scores improved more with the 3D interface ($M = .96$, $SD = 3.28$) than with the 2D interface ($M = .61$, $SD = 2.41$). However, this difference was unreliable: $t(43) = .40$, $p = .69$. There was also no interaction between interface and median-split ($p = .70$) suggesting that the 3D interface did not promote more general cultural understanding than the 2D interface.

5.3 Interaction Patterns with Virtual Characters

We analyzed the data collected over meetings, actions, and time. Recall that multiple meetings with the same character are often necessary to succeed in BiLAT. During the training period (up to 100 minutes with three characters), participants needed more meetings in the 2D interface ($M = 13.67$, $SD = 4.15$) than they did in the 3D interface ($M = 10.30$, $SD = 2.88$): $t(42) = 3.14$, $p < .01$. Participants also performed more actions in each coached meeting in the 2D interface ($M = 17.70$, $SD = 4.12$) than they did in the 3D interface ($M = 15.09$, $SD = 2.57$): $t(42) = 2.55$, $p = .02$. With more meetings per session and more actions per meeting, participants in the 2D interface performed nearly 50% more actions than did participants in the 3D interface.

Drilling down into meeting actions, we calculated the amount of time between actions in each interface. During the training period, participants spent slightly longer deciding on their next action in the 3D interface ($M = 20.67$ sec; $SD = 8.75$) than they did in the 2D interface ($M = 17.42$, $SD = 4.92$), but this difference was not reliable: $t(42) = 1.37$, $p = .18$. During the in-game posttest (no coach), however, participants took substantially more time per action in the 3D interface ($M = 17.02$, $SD = 9.63$) than they did in the 2D interface ($M = 11.44$, $SD = 2.44$). This difference was reliable: $t(40) = 2.46$, $p = .02$. A repeated-measures ANOVA revealed a differential reduction in the interval between actions when the coach was deactivated: $F(1, 40) = 4.24$, $p = .05$. It seems that learners in the 3D system took more care in selecting actions, which, along with their higher ratings of social presence, may suggest that they may have treated it as a more authentic social interaction.

5.4 Discussion

Although learners had a greater sense of presence using the 3D version of BiLAT, we are unable to conclude from our data that presence caused any differences in learning.

Both interfaces produced similar learning gains on tests of declarative knowledge (SJT), in-game success (without coaching), and on a far-transfer test of general cultural knowledge (CA). When we combined conditions in our analysis, we found increases in learning for both the SJT (reliably) and on the CA (marginally), as well as significant gains for lower-performing learners on both measures. Since the BiLAT simulation engine drove both interfaces, we conclude that the simulated social interactions are responsible for the observed learning gains. This is consistent with well-known principles of multimedia learning [21], as well as the suggestion that sense of presence is most beneficial for learning when domain knowledge specifically demands it [14]. Our analysis of the behavioral data prevents the conclusion that the 3D interface and the 2D interface are interchangeable, however. Participants who used the 2D interface made decisions more quickly, made more decisions per meeting, and had more meetings with each character. Although the average time to take an action was not statistically different during training, we did find a significant difference in the time participants took to act when coaching was unavailable.

Why, then, were participants in the 2D interface more prone to act than participants who used the 3D interface? One hypothesis is that the 3D interface encourages participants to take meetings more seriously—a direct result of the differential presence experienced. It is also possible that the 3D interface requires more attention and cognitive resources, thereby increasing the time between actions. It took learners more actions per meeting and more meetings per character to build up relationships and successfully complete objectives in the 2D interface than in the 3D interface. If we had designed the experiment to limit the total number of actions (rather than the total amount of time at 100 minutes), then we may have observed greater, reliable differences in our learning measures.

Relatedly, these data suggest that characters' responses and coach feedback in the 3D interface were more economical in producing learning gains. With fewer actions and fewer meetings overall, participants who used the 3D interface nevertheless trended toward greater learning gains than those who used the 2D interface. One hypothesis is that learners in the 3D interface may have reflected on their actions more often than those in the 2D. As the fidelity of immersive simulations continues to increase, along with their ability to create a sense of presence, it will be worthwhile to examine whether there is a concomitant increase in learning along these lines.

Our study has a number of limitations. Perhaps most critically, we included only the meeting component of BiLAT. The full version of the game requires learners to understand a broader context, decide which characters to meet with, conduct research on characters, select an interpreter, conduct more elaborate negotiations, and review their meetings with a reflective tutoring system [15]. Because of time constraints and limitations on the flash-based, 2D interface, we were not able to incorporate these other components of the full BiLAT system, which may have further enhanced learning and presence. A second limitation is that no delayed posttest was given to participants. It is possible that a heightened sense of social presence would enhance retention of knowledge related to social communication skills (similar to [10]). Finally, we note the domain knowledge in this study focused on general communicative skills; nonverbal behaviors, tone or rate of speech, or proxemics were not involved. It is possible that social presence and 3D interaction hold greater importance for skills related to these issues.

6 Summary and Conclusion

In this paper we compared two interfaces that used the same underlying simulation engine for the practice of intercultural communication and negotiation skills in a serious game. The 3D interface used animated characters with sound while the 2D version used static images without sound. Participants reported a significantly greater sense of presence with the 3D version, but measures of learning revealed that both conditions showed significant but statistically equal gains in terms of declarative and conceptual understanding of cultural knowledge. Analysis of usage data revealed that learners using the 2D interface had significantly more interactions with characters than the 3D version. This means 3D users learned equivalently well with fewer interactions. We hypothesize that they may have been more thoughtful in their communicative choices and perhaps treated the virtual meetings as more authentic.

There are many other factors that should be considered when analyzing learning with virtual human role players. For example, it is important to consider whether learners independently establish social goals, which has been shown to be an antecedent for cultural learning with virtual humans [22]. Another important aspect is the relationship between explicit guidance and presence. In future studies, we plan to examine different feedback policies and assess their impact on users' learning and feelings of presence. The results from this study will form a baseline for comparing other feedback policies and hopefully shed light on identifying optimal levels of presence in virtual environments for learning.

Acknowledgments. The project or effort described here has been sponsored by the U.S. Army Research, Development, and Engineering Command (RDECOM). Statements and opinions expressed do not necessarily reflect the position or the policy of the United States Government, and no official endorsement should be inferred. We thank Laura Hamel and Bob Wray at SoarTech (www.soartech.com) for their generosity in sharing and repurposing the 2D interface used in this study.

References

1. Piazza, J.: Audiences experience Avatar blues. CNN (January 11, 2010),
   http://www.cnn.com/2010/SHOWBIZ/Movies/01/11/avatar.movie.blues/index.html
2. Green, M.C., Strange, J.J., Brock, T.C.: Narrative impact: social and cognitive foundations. Lawrence Erlbaum, Mahwah (2002)
3. Bruner, J.: The narrative construction of reality. Critical Inquiry 18, 1–21 (1991)
4. Ritterfeld, U., Cody, M., Vorderer, P. (eds.): Serious Games: Mechanisms and Effects. Routledge, New York (2009)
5. Vogel, J.J., Vogel, D.S., Cannon-Bowers, J., Bowers, C.A., Muse, K., Wright, M.: Computer gaming and interactive simulations for learning: A meta-analysis. J. of Ed. Computing Research 34, 229–243 (2006)
6. Wilson, K.A., Bedwell, W.L., Lazzara, E.H., Salas, E., Burke, C.S., Estock, J.L., Orvis, K.L., Conkey, C.: Relationships between game attributes and learning outcomes. Simul. Gaming 40, 217–266 (2009)

7. O'Neil, H.F., Wainess, R., Baker, E.L.: Classification of learning outcomes: Evidence from the computer games literature. The Curr. J. 16, 455–474 (2005)
8. Malone, T.W., Lepper, M.R.: Making learning fun: A taxonomy of intrinsic motivations for learning. In: Snow, R.E., Farr, M.J. (eds.) Aptitude, Learning, and Instruction, vol. 3, pp. 223–253. Erlbaum, Mahwah (1987)
9. Habgood, M.P.J.: The effective integration of digital games and learning content. University of Nottingham (2007)
10. Parker, L.E., Lepper, M.R.: Effects of fantasy contexts on children's learning and motivation: Making learning more fun. J. Pers. & Soc. Psy. 62, 625–633 (1992)
11. Lombard, M., Ditton, T.: At the Heart of It All: The Concept of Presence. Journal of Computer-Mediated Communication 3 (1997)
12. McQuiggan, S.W., Rowe, J.P., Lester, J.C.: The effects of empathetic virtual characters on presence in narrative-centered learning environments. In: Proc. 26th SIGCHI Conf. on H. Fact. in Computing Sys., pp. 1511–1520. ACM Press, New York (2008)
13. Moreno, R., Mayer, R.E.: Personalized messages that promote science learning in virtual environments. J. of Ed. Psy. 96, 165–173 (2004)
14. Winn, W., Windschitl, M., Fruland, R., Lee, Y.: When does immersion in a virtual environment help students construct understand? In: Bell, P., Stevens, R. (eds.) Int. Conf. Learning Sciences (2002)
15. Kim, J.M., Hill, R.W., Durlach, P.J., Lane, H.C., Forbell, E., Core, M., Marsella, S., Pynadath, D.V., Hart, J.: BiLAT: A Game-based Environment for Practicing Negotiation in a Cultural Context. Int. J. of Art. Int. in Ed. (in press)
16. Fisher, R., Ury, W., Patton, B.: Getting to yes: Negotiating agreement without giving in. Penguin Books, New York (1991)
17. Landis, D., Bennett, J.M., Bennett, M.J.: Handbook of intercultural training. Sage Publications, Thousand Oaks (2004)
18. Lane, H.C., Hays, M.J., Auerbach, D., Core, M., Gomboc, D., Forbell, E., Rosenberg, M.: Coaching intercultural communication in a serious game. In: Proc. 18th Int. Conf. on Computers in Education, pp. 35–42 (2008)
19. Cushner, K., Brislin, R.W.: Intercultural interactions: a practical guide. Sage, Thousand Oaks (1996)
20. Snow, R.: Aptitude-treatment interaction as a framework for research on individual differences in learning. In: Ackerman, P., Sternberg, R.J., Glaser, R. (eds.) Learning and Individual Differences, W.H. Freeman, New York (1989)
21. Mayer, R.E.: Multimedia Learning. Cambridge Univ. Press, Cambridge (2009)
22. Ogan, A.E., Kim, J., Aleven, V., Jones, C.: Explicit social goals and learning in a game for cross-cultural negotiation. In: Proc. Workshop on Ed. Games, 14th Int. Conf. on Art. Int. in Ed., pp. 51–58 (2009)

Developing Empirically Based Student Personality Profiles for Affective Feedback Models

Jennifer Robison[1], Scott McQuiggan[2], and James Lester[1]

[1] Department of Computer Science, North Carolina State University
Raleigh, North Carolina
[2] SAS Institute, Cary, North Carolina
jlrobiso@ncsu.edu, Scott.McQuiggan@sas.com, lester@ncsu.edu

Abstract. The impact of affect on learning has been the subject of increasing attention. Because of the differential effects of students' affective states on learning outcomes, there is a growing recognition of the important role that intelligent tutoring systems can play in providing affective feedback to students. Although we are only beginning to understand the complex interactions between affect, feedback, and learning, it is evident that affective interventions can both positively and negatively influence learning experiences. To investigate how student personality traits can be used to predict responses to affective feedback, this paper presents an analysis of a large student affect corpus collected from three separate studies. Student personality profiles augmented with goal orientation and empathetic tendency information were analyzed with respect to affect state transitions. The results indicate that student personality profiles can serve as a powerful tool for informing affective feedback models.

Keywords: Affect, Affective Computing, Pedagogical Agents.

1 Introduction

Affect has begun to play an increasingly important role in intelligent tutoring systems. The intelligent tutoring community has seen the emergence of work on affective student modeling [1], characterizing student emotional experiences [2,3], detecting frustration and stress [4,5], detecting student motivation [6], and diagnosing and adapting to student self-efficacy [7]. All of this work seeks to increase the fidelity with which affective and motivational processes are understood and utilized in intelligent tutoring systems in an effort to increase the effectiveness of tutorial interactions and, ultimately, learning.

This level of emphasis on affect is not surprising given the effects it has been shown to have on learning outcomes. Student affective states impact problem-solving strategies, the level of engagement exhibited by the student, and the degree to which he or she is motivated to continue with the learning process [8,9,10]. All of these factors have the potential to impact both how students learn immediately and their learning behaviors in the future. Consequently, developing techniques for keeping students in an affective state that is conducive to learning has been a focus of recent work [11,12,13,14].

However, while much work has targeted the development of optimal techniques for supporting student affect, the nature of the problem introduces a significant degree of uncertainty. In human-human social interaction it is often difficult to determine how best to respond to an individual's affective states. The problem is significantly more challenging for computational systems: they must first be able to correctly recognize student affective states and then decide how best to respond. Systems may frequently encounter situations in which they are uncertain about how to provide affective support and what the effects of a possible intervention may be.

Previous work [15] has indicated that poorly selected feedback mechanisms can have severe negative consequences for student affective states. In some cases the possibility of these negative consequences introduces such a risk that it is preferable to avoid giving any affective feedback. While this work has shed light on measures of risk and utility when considering affective intervention, systems should also be able to weigh an estimated confidence in the success of a particular feedback strategy against the risk associated with that strategy to make an informed decision on how to proceed.

In this paper we investigate the role of student personality, including goal orientation and empathetic tendencies, in estimating confidence in the benefits of an affective intervention strategy. We derive personality profiles categorizing students who tend to experience positive benefits or negative consequences of affect feedback from a corpus of student affect data spanning three user studies with a narrative-centered learning environment, CRYSTAL ISLAND. These personality profiles are then used to train machine-learned prediction models to determine confidence estimates for the expected benefit of a candidate affective intervention.

2 Background

A broad range of techniques have been developed to provide appropriate affective support. Some of these techniques are based on analyses of human-tutor responses to affect [12], while others are based on theoretical models of how to improve student performance by valuing effort over success [16]. Other work has focused on responding to specific student emotions using empathetic or task-based feedback strategies [15]. While many of these strategies have been shown to be beneficial in supporting student affect, they often do not consider specific student needs. Previous findings have suggested that a student's individual personality characteristics can strongly impact which affective states are most beneficial for the student [11] and how the student experiences and transitions from these states [17].

With these findings in mind, we seek to develop personality profiles to predict how students will respond to affective feedback and determine how this information can be utilized to better inform affective feedback models. We consider three distinct measures of student characteristics: personality, goal orientation and empathetic tendencies. These three constructs are expected to have a particular influence on the student's experience of narrative and learning emotions associated with the interactive environment as well as their ability to internalize and respond to agents' attempts to provide beneficial affective feedback.

Personality is an individual's disposition over a long duration of time, which can be distinguished from emotions or moods which are more limited in their duration

[18]. The Big 5 Personality Questionnaire [19] decomposes personality into five primary categories: openness, conscientiousness, extraversion, agreeableness and neuroticism. Of particular interest among these are openness, conscientiousness and neuroticism, as these characteristics are likely to impact emotion and learning. Additionally, because information on affective states is often obtained through self-report, we expect to find individuals who score high on openness will display genuine emotions, while others may limit themselves to what they feel comfortable reporting.

Goal orientation reflects a student's primary objective when engaged in learning activities. Students may either view learning in relation to performance or mastery [20]. A performance approach would result in a student wishing to prove her competence and achieve better results than other students. A student with a mastery approach, however, views learning as an attempt to acquire knowledge or a skill, regardless of how her ability compares to others. In addition to these categories, students may have avoidance strategies in relation to their goals. For example, students with a performance-avoidance approach would simply try to not overtly fail, rather than try to top their fellow student. We expect that these students will differ in their tendency to stay negatively or positively focused especially in response to agent feedback.

Empathetic tendencies refer to an individual's responses to the situational and affective states of others [21]. These tendencies can be measured using an interpersonal reactivity index [22], which includes four subscales: fantasy, perspective taking, empathetic concern and personal distress. Fantasy refers to the tendency to identify with fictional characters such as virtual agents, or characters in books and movies. Perspective taking is an individual's capacity to see situations from the perspective of another individual. Empathetic concern is a tendency to exhibit compassionate emotions towards those in negative situations, while personal distress refers to feelings of stress and anxiety over the misfortunes of others. These traits may directly impact the student's perception of the characters and events in a learning environment and how they respond to agents' efforts to provide affective support.

3   The CRYSTAL ISLAND Environment

The affect corpus utilized in this analysis was obtained from studies conducted in a narrative-centered inquiry-based learning environment, CRYSTAL ISLAND (Figure 1). This environment is being created in the domains of microbiology and genetics for middle school students. It features a science mystery set on a recently discovered volcanic island where a research station has been established to study the unique flora and fauna. The user plays the protagonist, Alex, who is attempting to discover the source of an unidentified infectious disease at the research station. As members of the research team fall ill, it is her task to discover the cause and the specific source of the outbreak. She is free to explore the world and interact with other characters while forming questions, generating hypothesis, collecting data, and testing her hypotheses. She can pick up and manipulate objects, and she can talk with characters to gather clues about the source of the disease. In the course of her adventure she must gather enough evidence to correctly identify the type and source of the disease that has infected the camp members.

Fig. 1. The user, Alex, with Jin, the camp nurse, on CRYSTAL ISLAND

4 Method

To empirically investigate the differential responses of students in specific affective states, we consider cumulative data from three studies of students interacting with affect-sensitive virtual agents. These agents were developed to respond to student emotion and encourage positive student affect within the learning environment through three distinct feedback strategies: (1) task-based feedback, (2) parallel empathetic statements, (3) reactive empathetic statements or by providing no feedback. Task-based feedback strategies focused on directing students towards information that would aid in improving or maintaining their emotional state (e.g.,"You may want to consider reading a book on pathogens. You can find a good book in the lab"). This strategy aims to aid both students who are struggling with environmental tasks and those lacking the necessary content knowledge without attempting to distinguish between the two. Parallel empathetic statements demonstrate an agent's understanding of the emotional situation and reflect the affective state of the student (e.g.,"I know! It's very frustrating not knowing what is causing the illness!"). In contrast, reactive empathetic statements focus on the emotional needs of the student and will try to motivate a more positive affective state (e.g.,"I know this is a tough problem, but if you keep working at it, I'm sure you'll get to an answer soon"). Each type of feedback is limited to at most three sentences and directly acknowledges the emotional state reported by the student. Additional details on response generation may be found in [14].

Affect feedback models were iteratively developed over the course of three studies to improve the ability of the virtual agents to provide beneficial affective support. An affect corpus was obtained by aggregating data collected in these three studies and includes data from a total of 115 college students who interacted with one of the three models of agent behavior within the CRYSTAL ISLAND environment. Among these students, 89 were male and 26 were female. Ages ranged from 19 to 60

(M = 24.63, SD = 4.93). Demographics included 37.4% White, 47.8% Asian or Indian, and 14.8% Other (including African American, Hispanic, Other and Non-Response).

Participants entered the experiment room where they completed informed consent documentation and were seated in front of a laptop computer. They were then given an overview of the experiment agenda, and they completed the pre-experiment questionnaires including the demographics survey, the interpersonal reactivity index survey[22], the goal orientation survey [20], and the personality questionnaire [19].

Participants were then instructed to review CRYSTAL ISLAND instruction materials. These materials consisted of the backstory and task description, character overviews and a map of the island, the control sheet, and definition sheet of the self-report emotions. Participants were then further briefed on the controls via a presentation explaining each control in detail. Participants maintained access to the materials, including the definition sheet of the self-report emotions, throughout their interaction. Participants were given thirty-five minutes to solve the mystery.

When subjects decided to interact with the agents, the following schema was used to direct subject-character interactions and virtual character feedback:

1. The agent queries the subject for a self-reported affective state ($Report_1$) by asking the question, "Hi Alex, how are you feeling?" The subject may respond by selecting one of the available emotions (*anger, anxiety, boredom, curiosity, confusion, delight, excitement, flow, frustration*).

2. The agent then responds to the subject's reported affective state with a randomized feedback response. Responses varied between parallel and reactive empathetic statements, task-based feedback or no intervention. The relative frequency of these feedback strategies varied between studies but is not the focus of this analysis.

3. If the student received a feedback response, a follow-up dialog box is then presented to the subject asking her to respond with the prompt, "… and you respond." The subject is able to choose from four Likert-scaled responses designed to evaluate the appropriateness and effectiveness of the virtual character's response. Subjects can issue responses ranging from (1) "That does not help me at all," to (4) "Thanks, that helped a lot!"

4. The agent responds with a one-word quip (e.g., "Thanks," or "Great!") directed towards the subject's evaluation response (Step 3, when executed).

5. At the conclusion of the interaction, the agent again asks the subject how she feels. The subject is presented a dialog box similar to the one described in Step 1 without the character greeting. Here, the character prompts the subject with, "How are you feeling now?" and the student selects from the same set of emotions ($Report_2$).

5 Personality-Informed Affect Feedback

It was hypothesized that individual student traits can provide insight into whether students are likely to experience positive or negative affect transitions after experiencing specific types of affective interventions. Therefore, the first step in the analysis was to classify transitions as positive or negative based on their reported affective state after receiving feedback (Report$_2$). This was accomplished by considering emotions to be positive or negative based on their valence. For instance, curiosity is a positive emotional state, while boredom is a negative state. However, this classification did not reflect findings on the sometimes positive nature of the state of confusion which was therefore considered to be a neutral state. Using this framework, transitions were labeled as positive if subjects remained in or transitioned to a more positive affective state (Report$_2$ ≥ Report$_1$). Similarly transitions were labeled as negative if subjects remained in a negative state or transitioned into a state that was more negative than they had experienced prior to the intervention. Using this framework, approximately 67.8% (n=716) transitions were labeled as positive, while the remaining 32.2% (n=340) were labeled as negative.

5.1 Personality Profiles

We first sought to examine whether or not there existed a personality profile for students who tended to experience positive or negative transitions. Exploratory t-tests compared the personality characteristics associated with positive and negative affective transitions. These tests were run on each component of the subscales for personality, empathetic tendencies and goal orientation. Results indicated that there were many student characteristics that contributed to a personality profile for positive and negative transitions (Table 1). For instance students who experience positive transitions tend to be more agreeable but also less open than students who experience negative transitions. These students also report experiencing less personal distress and greater ability to take the perspective of others. Finally, students experiencing positive transitions are more likely to have a performance avoidance approach to learning.

These results suggest interesting relationships between students' susceptibility to feedback and how they transition in response to it. For example, agreeableness and perspective taking are both associated with the ability to relate well with and consider the opinions of others. In the case of affective intervention, these students may be more willing to consider and internalize the helpful feedback of the virtual characters and consequently experience positive affective transitions. Alternatively, students who report experiencing higher personal distress may be more likely to remain in negative emotions associated with the ill characters of the island and are less likely to be consoled by the characters' interventions.

5.2 Emotion-Specific Personality Profiles

We next considered the possibility that these personality profiles may vary when transitioning from specific emotions. Therefore we conducted the same analyses on transitions from specific emotions. This analysis yielded many of the same traits reported in the overall personality profile, but also showed several emotional states that had specific personality profiles (Table 1). For instance, the trend for students experiencing positive transitions to be more agreeable was true when students reported an initial emotional state of *boredom, confusion,* or *excitement.* However, the opposite trend was found for students who reported *anger.* In this case, students who experienced negative transitions scored much higher on the agreeable subscale than students

Table 1. Trait tendencies. +/- indicate the direction of the trend, while * indicate a significance of $p < 0.05$ in exploratory t-tests

Overall			
Neuroticism	-	* Personal Distress	-
* Agreeableness	+	Perspective Taking	+
* Openness	+	* Performance Avoidance	+
* Empathetic Concern	+		

Emotion Specific			
Anger		**Anxiety**	
Mastery Approach	-	Performance Approach	+
Perspective Taking	-		
* Agreeableness	-	**Confusion**	
		Performance Avoidance	+
Boredom		Fantasy	-
* Conscientiousness	+	* Agreeableness	+
* Agreeableness	+		
		Curiosity	
Excitement		* Perspective Taking	+
* Perspective Taking	+	* Openness	-
* Agreeableness	+		
		Flow	
Frustration		* Mastery Approach	-
Performance Avoidance	+	Performance Approach	-
Fantasy	+	* Fantasy	+
* Extraversion	-	Empathetic Concern	+
Neuroticism	+	* Neuroticism	-

experiencing negative transitions. This is an interesting anomaly and one that seems to contradict the typical characteristics associated with agreeableness, suggesting that there may be something unique about the emotional state of *anger* that warrants further investigation. Alternatively, the expected trends were found for students with high perspective taking, who were likely to experience positive transitions from emotions such as *curiosity* and *excitement*.

Additional characteristics outside the general profiles were found to be indicative of differential responses in specific emotional states as well. For instance, negative transitions from *frustration* were experienced by highly extraverted students. Meanwhile, conscientious students experiencing *boredom* appeared to be more susceptible to characters' attempts to reengage them and had a stronger tendency to experience positive transitions. Additional results suggest that some students responded particularly negatively to feedback when in a positive state. For example, mastery-approach students experiencing *flow* tended to experience negative transitions as did open students experiencing *curiosity*. This result is particularly interesting since in both of these cases, the students are experiencing positive emotional states that are expected to be particularly salient for their individual traits. It may be the case that an interruption of this positive or perhaps optimal state is responsible for this negative transition.

5.3 Models of Affective Response

The ultimate goal of this line of investigation is to better inform affective feedback models by providing some measure of confidence that an affective intervention strategy will be beneficial to the student. Therefore, we explored machine learning techniques as an automatic and, perhaps, robust means of classifying candidate feedback strategies as likely to be beneficial or harmful.

To this end, naïve Bayes, decision tree, and support vector machine classification models were induced using the WEKA machine learning toolkit [23]. All models were constructed using a tenfold (within-subjects) cross-validation scheme for producing training and testing datasets, a widely used method for obtaining an acceptable estimate of error [23]. The learned naïve Bayes model performed at 69.5% predictive accuracy, which did not significantly outperform the baseline of 67.8% accuracy. However, both the decision tree (72.9%) and support vector machine (73.11%) models were able to significantly outperform the baseline at $p<0.05$. Linear regression analysis was also performed but did not yield results that outperformed the baseline model.

While these models did offer some improvement over baseline, we predicted that inclusion of the previously learned personality profiles would be able to enhance the predictive power of these models. Therefore, we created a hybrid model, in which a simple naïve Bayes model was created for each reported emotion. These models included only the personality traits that had been previously found to have a significant difference ($p<0.10$) in their prevalence with respect to the populations of students experiencing positive and negative transitions. Naïve Bayes models were specifically chosen for this hybrid as they seemed to be the natural extension from the differentiated probability distributions that make up the personality profiles. They also offer an additional benefit of producing probability distributions for each tested item, which may be used to create a numeric confidence rating to inform future models. These models were again created using ten-fold cross-validation to ensure an appropriate measure of predictive accuracy.

The results of this hybrid model indicated a statistically significant ($p<0.05$) improvement in predictive accuracy over the previously highest performing model, the support vector machine. The hybrid model achieved a predictive accuracy of 75.2%. Interestingly, the predictive accuracies for transitions from some emotional states are significantly higher than others. For instance, the highest predictive accuracy for transitions from the state of *flow* is 84.3% (baseline of 81%). This finding is particularly interesting as the state of flow has been previously identified as a state in which attempting affective intervention is particularly risky [15]. This increase in predictive accuracy for this state may play a role in mitigating the risk of intervention. In contrast, the lowest predictive accuracy (58.8%, baseline of 52%) is in response to students experiencing *frustration*. While such a low predictive accuracy is less than would desired, previous work has suggested that there is little risk in intervening during negative states such as frustration. It is unlikely that the student can experience harmful side-effects from intervention, so in this case we are less concerned about obtaining a good measure of confidence before deciding to pursue an affect intervention strategy.

5.4 Limitations

While the results of this analysis are promising, there are several limitations that must be considered. First, though the affect corpus included over one thousand affect reports from 115 subjects, some affective states are still reported in a very low frequency. In particular, the states of *anger* and *delight* were reported with very low frequencies (fewer than 30 reports each), so it is unclear how appropriate it is to draw conclusions about these states. Additionally, these analyses examined only the interactions between personality characteristics and affective states. It would be particularly interesting to understand how events and progress within the interactive environment also contributed to this complex interaction.

6 Conclusion

The ability to understand and respond to student affective states during learning has been recognized as an important goal for the ITS community. Unfortunately, intervening with student affective states is inherently risky. Therefore, developing affective support models that can consider utility, risk and confidence information is an important step in ensuring beneficial interactions with students. This paper has shown that students' personality characteristics can impact how students respond to attempts to provide affective scaffolding. The personality profiles developed through analysis of an affect corpus were able to enhance the predictive capability of models aimed at determining whether an intervention strategy was likely to have positive outcomes. Additionally, accuracy was especially high in affective states where mitigating risk is of highest importance, suggesting that incorporating these models into future affective feedback paradigms may add significant benefit.

In addition to furthering the development of effective feedback models, the analyses of the affect corpus revealed interesting relationships between certain characteristics and emotional states. For instance, we find that goal orientation traits are more closely tied with emotions associated with learning rather than other emotional states. We additionally find support for the notion that individuals with particular traits have unique "optimal" states that should not be interrupted.

The results of these analyses suggest many interesting directions for future work. For instance, certain emotions, such as *anger,* appeared to have correlations with student characteristics that were inconsistent with other emotional states and seemed to contradict expectations. Further exploration of these anomalies may reveal interesting information regarding the unique characteristics of each of these emotions. Another direction for future work is including event traces for informing models.

Detailed information about the student's progress and experience in the environment may help to better inform affective feedback models. Finally, an important next step is incorporating these findings into a comprehensive affect feedback model that is able to better gauge risk, assess confidence and provide feedback in the most appropriate and beneficial manner.

Acknowledgements

The authors would like to thank the other members of the IntelliMedia Group at North Carolina State University for useful discussions and support. This research was supported by the National Science Foundation under Grants REC-0632450, IIS-0757535, DRL-0822200, CNS-0540523 and IIS-0812291. Additional support was provided under a National Science Foundation Graduate Research Fellowship. Any opinions, findings, and conclusions or recommendations expressed in this material are those of the authors and do not necessarily reflect the views of the National Science Foundation.

References

1. Conati, C., Mclaren, H.: Data-Driven Refinement of a Probabilistic Model of User Affect. In: Ardissono, L., Brna, P., Mitrović, A. (eds.) UM 2005. LNCS (LNAI), vol. 3538, pp. 40–49. Springer, Heidelberg (2005)
2. D'Mello, S., Taylor, R.S., Graesser, A.: Monitoring Affective Trajectories during Complex Learning. In: Proceedings of the 29th Annual Meeting of the Cognitive Science Society, pp. 203–208 (2007)
3. Baker, R., Rodrigo, M., Xoloctzin, U.: The Dynamics of Affective Transitions in Simulation Problem-Solving Environments. In: Proceedings of the 2nd International Conference on Affective Computing and Intelligent Interactions, pp. 666–677 (2007)
4. Burleson, W.: Affective Learning Companions: Strategies for Empathetic Agents with Real-time Multimodal Affective Sensing to Foster Meta-Cognitive and Meta-Affective Approaches to Learning, Motivation, and Perseverance. PhD thesis, Massachusetts Institute of Technology (2006)
5. McQuiggan, S.W., Lee, S.Y., Lester, J.C.: Early prediction of student frustration. In: Paiva, A.C.R., Prada, R., Picard, R.W. (eds.) ACII 2007. LNCS, vol. 4738, pp. 698–709. Springer, Heidelberg (2007)
6. de Vicente, A., Pain, H.: Informing the Detection of the Students' Motivational State: An Empirical Study. In: Cerri, S.A., Gouardéres, G., Paraguaçu, F. (eds.) ITS 2002. LNCS, vol. 2363, pp. 933–943. Springer, Heidelberg (2002)
7. Beal, C., Lee, H.: Creating a Pedagogical Model that Uses Student Self Reports of Motivation and Mood to Adapt ITS Instruction. In: Workshop on Motivation and Affect in Educational Software, in conjunction with the 12th International Conference on Artificial Intelligence in Education (2005)
8. Kort, B., Reilly, R., Picard, R.: An Affective Model of Interplay between Emotions and Learning: Reengineering Educational Pedagogy–Building a Learning Companion. In: Proceedings IEEE International Conference on Advanced Learning Technology: Issues, Achievements and Challenges, pp. 43–48 (2001)

9. Picard, R., Papert, S., Bender, W., Blumberg, B., Breazeal, C., Cavallo, D., Machover, T., Resnick, M., Roy, D., Strohecker, C.: Affective Learning – A Manifesto. BT Technology Journal 22(4) (2004)
10. Schwarz, N.: Emotion, Cognition, and Decision Making. Journal of Cognition and Emotion 14(4), 440–443 (2000)
11. Chaffar, S., Frasson, C.: Using an Emotional Intelligent Agent to Improve the Learner's Performance. In: Woolf, B.P., Aïmeur, E., Nkambou, R., Lajoie, S. (eds.) ITS 2008. LNCS, vol. 5091, pp. 787–789. Springer, Heidelberg (2008)
12. Forbes-Riley, K., Litman, D.: Investigating Human Tutor Response to Student Uncertainty for Adaptive System Development. In: Proceedings the 2nd International Conference on Affective Computing and Intelligent Interactions (2007)
13. McQuiggan, S., Robison, J., Phillips, R., Lester, J.: Modeling Parallel and Reactive Empathy in Virtual Agents: An Inductive Approach. In: Proceedings of the 7th International Joint Conference on Autonomous Agents and Multi-Agent Systems (2008)
14. Robison, J., McQuiggan, S., Lester, J.: Modeling Task-Based vs. Affect-Based Feedback Behavior in Pedagogical Agents: An Inductive Approach. In: Proceedings of the 14th International Conference on Artificial Intelligence in Education, pp. 25–32 (2009)
15. Robison, J., McQuiggan, S., Lester, J.: Evaluating the Consequences of Affective Feedback in Intelligent Tutoring Systems. In: Proceedings of the 3rd International Conference on Affective Computing and Intelligent Interaction (2009)
16. Arroyo, I., Woolf, B., Royer, J., Tai., M.: Affective Gendered Learning Companions. In: Proceedings of the 14th International Conference on Artificial Intelligence in Education, pp. 41–48 (2009)
17. Robison, J., McQuiggan, S., Lester, J.: Differential Affective Experiences in Narrative-Centered Learning Environments. In: Proceedings of the Workshop on Emotional and Cognitive issues in ITS in conjunction with the 9th International Conference on Intelligent Tutoring Systems (2008)
18. Rusting, C.: Personality, Mood, and Cognitive Processing of Emotional Information: Three Conceptual Frameworks. Psychological Bulletin 124(2), 165–196 (1998)
19. McCrae, R., Costa, P.: Personality in Adulthood: A Five-Factor Theory Perspective, 2nd edn. Guilford Press, New York (2003)
20. Elliot, A., McGregor, H.: A 2 x 2 Achievement Goal Framework. Journal of Personality and Social Psychology 80(3), 501–519 (2001)
21. Davis, M.: Empathy: A Social Psychological Approach. Brown & Benchmark Publishers, Madison (1994)
22. Davis, M.: Measuring Individual Differences in Empathy: Evidence for a Multidimensional Approach. Journal of Personality and Social Psychology 44, 113–126 (1983)
23. Witten, I., Frank, E.: Data Mining: Practical Machine Learning Tools and Techniques, 2nd edn. Morgan Kaufman, San Francisco (2005)

Evaluating the Usability of an Augmented Reality Based Educational Application

Jorge Martín-Gutiérrez, Manuel Contero, and Mariano Alcañiz

Universidad de La Laguna. Dpto. Expresión Gráfica en Arquitectura e Ingeniería.
Avda. Astrofísico Francisco Sánchez s/n 38206 La Laguna (Spain)
Universidad Politécnica de Valencia. Instituto en Bioingeniería y Tecnología Orientada al Ser Humano (I3BH). Camino de Vera s/n. 46022 Valencia (Spain)
jmargu@ull.es,
{mcontero,malcaniz}labhuman.i3bh.es

Abstract. Technological developments and changes mean that computer-based teaching tools rapidly become obsolete or less attractive to students. In teaching, as in other fields, there is a continual need to explore new technologies that are attractive, adapted to the personal needs of students and which motivate them to learn. Students are struck by the appearance of new technology or gadgets and they show an interest in using them. This paper analyses the potential of Augmented Reality technology in university education. An AR-based application has been developed with a view to improving spatial abilities among engineering students, thus enabling them to gain a better understanding of engineering graphics subjects. We present a student satisfaction study and an evaluation of the efficiency and efficacy of the technology applied to this field of education.

Keywords: augmented reality, usability engineering, spatial ability, engineering graphics.

1 Introduction

Augmented Reality (AR) is a technology that permits one to overlay computer graphics onto the real world. Unlike immersive Virtual Reality, AR interfaces allow users to see the real world at the same time as virtual imagery attached to real locations and objects. In an AR interface, the user views the world through a handheld, monitor PC or head mounted display (HMD) that is either see-through or overlays graphics on video of the surrounding environment. AR interfaces enhance the real world experience, unlike other computer interfaces that draw users away from the real world and onto the screen. AR interface is a visualization technology that can take advantage of the limitations offered by other visual means of communication for learning. Traditional methods of learning spatially-related content by viewing 2D diagrams create a sort of resistance to learning at cognitive level. This resistance exists even when working with 3D objects on a computer screen because the manipulation of the objects in space is made through mouse clicks.

Our work is based on the educational Augmented Reality toolkit AR-Dehaes, which has been validated to see if it is an effective tool for developing spatial abilities in students and for learning the contents of engineering graphics.

2 Augmented Reality and Education

An interesting definition of AR has been described by Azuma [1], as a variation of Virtual Reality. VR technology completely immerses a user inside a synthetic environment. While immersed, the user cannot see the surrounding real world. In contrast, AR allows the user to see the real world, with virtual objects superimposed upon or composited with the real world. Therefore, AR supplements reality, rather than completely replacing it. With AR applications it is possible to show to the user a common space where virtual and real object coexists in a seamless way. From a technological point of view AR applications must fulfill the following three requirements [1]: Combination of real and virtual worlds, real time interaction and accurate 3D registration of virtual and real objects.

The versatility offered by AR technology has made it possible to develop applications in many fields of education including mathematics, mechanics, medicine, physics and planning. It is worth mentioning the application Construct 3D [2], designed for teaching geometry. This application makes it possible to create geometric scenarios that allow the student and the teacher to interact during the explanation of the geometric contents. In the field of medicine, an AR application is used in the training of future anaesthetists to simulate the equipment used in the operating theatre [3]. Also, among many others, there is an AR application used in nursery education for learning the parts of the human body [4].

As Billinghurst [5] states, although AR technology is not new, it's potential in education is just beginning to be explored. Several EU funded projects such as CONNECT [6], CREATE [7] and ARISE [8] are designing and developing AR applications in order to improve education techniques. They provide good examples of the capability of this technology to develop new tools, which based on 3D interactions with the user, will make certain concepts easy to learn for the students.

2.1 The Augmented Book Concept

One of the most known AR educational applications is the "MagicBook" [9]. The "MagicBook" interface uses normal books with AR markers as the main interface objects. People can turn the pages of the book, look at the pictures, and read the text without any additional technology. However, if they look at the pages through an AR display they see 3D virtual models appearing out of the pages, thus introducing an interesting way for smoothly transporting users between reality and virtuality using a physical object.

Tallyn et al. [10] make a comparative study of a paper book, a multimedia CDROM and an AR book, concluding that book's ergonomics provide a flexible and easily accessible interface which engenders fluid collaboration between pairs of children, and that these qualities are also observed when children work with the AR book.

The augmented book experience only requires adding a webcam to a typical PC configuration and the proper software. Using the computer screen to visualize the augmented scene is a cost-effective and eye-catching alternative in the educational context presented in this paper.

3 Description of the Learning Tool and Methodology

Although there are several public libraries with AR capabilities, we decided to develop a software library called HUMANAR in order to ensure the integration of Augmented Reality into our applications and to overcome some drawbacks present in some public libraries. HUMANAR presents several advantages over other popular AR libraries like for example ARToolKit. Among other can be cited: support for different marker types (ARToolKit markers and IDbased markers), variable pattern size at the template-based markers (e.g. 16x16, 32x32, 64x64...), adaptive threshold for avoiding illumination variations at the scene, graphical interface for camera calibration and pattern creation. The library HUMANAR uses computer vision techniques to calculate the real camera viewpoint relative to a real world marker, that it, it calculates the integration of three-dimensional objects codified by the camera and captured by the camera in real time. When the marker enters the scene picked up by the camera, the fusion of the real world with the virtual object is shown on the screen. This requires the application to relate the two worlds (real and virtual) in a single system of co-ordinates.

We have created AR-Dehaes, a toolkit that promotes active learning, and encourages discovery through interactivity and object manipulation controlled by the learner. Several researchers [11] report that learners who have active control over novel objects perform better on later tests of object recognition and mental rotation. Further evidence suggests that active exploration and control of novel objects assists the learning of 3D structures, better object recognition and improved spatial ability. The content proposed in AR-Dehaes is an effective way of improving spatial abilities due to mental visual operations students have to carry out. This set of activities contributes to the development of the spatial factor of the intelligence.

The AR-Dehaes toolkit is composed by a software application, an explanatory video, a notebook and an augmented book (Figure 1).

- The software application contains one hundred exercises with three dimensional virtual models.
- The explanatory video has duration of six minutes. It explains the theoretical contents of orthographic views and freehand sketching.
- The notebook contains one hundred exercises that have to be solved by the students.
- The augmented book that provides fiducial markers of virtual three dimensional objects.

AR-Dehaes is designed for students to work on their own, without the help of the teacher, although it can also be used in the classroom with a teacher present. The didactic material contains five levels, created according Bloom´s taxonomy [12] and they

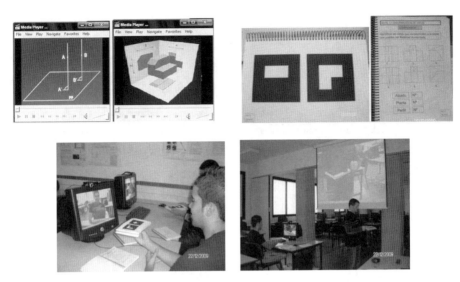

Fig. 1. Explanatory video, augmented book / notebook, students and teacher using AR-Dehaes

are organized into five sessions of training with a total duration of nine hours (four sessions of two hours and a final session that lasted one hour), see figure 2. Students can visualize the three-dimensional model in augmented reality (augmented book) and they can check if their freehand sketches correspond to the three-dimensional virtual models which they are viewing. AR-Dehaes contain one hundred 3D models to complete ones exercises.

- *Level 1 (Knowledge).* The students have to identify surfaces and vertexes on both orthographic and axonometric views of a three-dimensional virtual object, which is created on the augmented book (contain three kinds of tasks).
- *Level 2 (Comprehension).* The students have to identify orthographic views of the virtual three dimensional models from the exercise book (contain two kinds of tasks)..
- *Level 3 (Application – Analysis).* It is devoted to the identification of the spatial relationship between objects. This is carried out by means of "recount" exercises, where students are asked to identify how many object are in touch with one selected. Also there are exercises about the selection of the minimum number of views to completely define an object (contain two kinds of tasks).
- *Level 4 (Synthesis)* It has a greater difficulty than the previous levels. There are exercises where the students have to sketch a missing orthographic view, knowing two orthographic views of a model, using the virtual model as the only input, they have to sketch all the orthographic views (contain two kinds of tasks).
- *Level 5 (Evaluation).* The exercises are the most difficult ones for students, because they require a greater level of spatial ability. Students are provided with three orthographic views of each object, and they have to build in their minds the

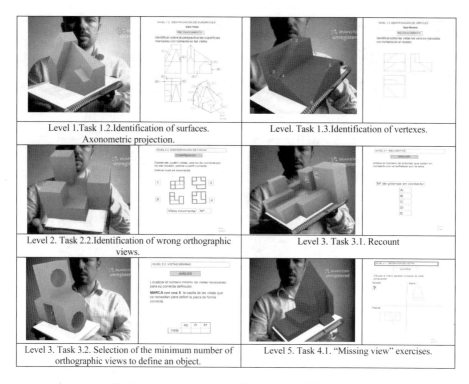

Fig. 2. Examples of several kinds tasks of AR-Dehaes

corresponding three-dimensional model and then draw a freehand perspective of it. Students have one hour to complete six exercises, without any virtual model help. This level of the course is used for evaluating the advance of students.

When they have carried out the proposed isometric drawings, they can be verified.

4 Pilot Study

4.1 Improve Spatial Ability

In order to analyse the impact of the educational content on students, a voluntary group of first year mechanical engineering students (24 participants) were called to take part in a course with AR-Dehaes for the first week of the academic year. The study also considered a control group selected randomly (25 participants), who undergo no kind of spatial skills training.

Spatial ability as one of the main components of human intelligence is a well studied topic in psychology, and according to Pellegrino et al [13] we can consider that is formed by two sub-components (Spatial Relations and Spatial Visualization). The levels of spatial ability were measured before and after the course (table 1) with with two widely used measurement tools in this field: MRT (Spatial Relations) and DAT-5:SR (Spatial Visualization) tests [14,15].

Table 1. Measure spatial ability before and after training

	Pre-test MRT	Pre-test DAT-5:SR	Post-Test MRT	Post-Test DAT-5:SR	Gain MRT	Gain DAT-5:SR
Experimental Group n = 24	19.67 (7.91)	29.17 (7.29)	27.71 (7.83)	38,46 (7.05)	8.04 (5.31)	9.29 (4.08)
Control Group n=25	17.44 (9.82)	28.40 (10.17)	22.08 (9.94)	33.52 (11.77)	4.64 (4.36)	5.12 (7.13)

An analysis of covariance (ANCOVA) was used to study it. The ANCOVA method allows eliminating the difference of pre-test scores between groups, and then the adjusted post-test scores, revealing the real effects of the experimental treatment. This statistical procedure also tested the interaction between groups (training AR and control). The dependent variables, co-variants, and independent variables were post-test measurements, pre-test measurements, and type of group, respectively. The suitability of using this analysis was tested by first conducting the analysis using a statistical model containing interaction terms between the covariants (pre-test mean scores of MRT and DAT-5:SR) and the independent variables to assess the assumption of homogeneity of gradients. The analysis of ANCOVA is summarized in tables 2 and 3.

Table 2. ANCOVA. Analysis of Covariance for Post-MRT

Source	Sum Sq Type III	Df	Mean Square	F-Ratio	P-Value
Corrected Model	(a) 3 139.087	2	1 569.543	70.259	0.000
Intercept	722.024	1	722.024	32.321	0.000
CO-VARIANTS					
Pre-MRT	2 751.191	1	2 751.191	123.155	0.000
EFFECTS					
Training Condition (AR vs Control)	166.838	1	166.838	7.468	0.009
Error	1 027.607	46	22.339		
Total	34 393.000	49			
TOTAL (CORRECTED)	4 166.694	48			

(a) R squared = 0.753 (R squared corrected = 0.743).

Table 3. ANCOVA. Analysis of Covariance for Post-DAT-5:SR

Source	Sum Sq Type III	Df	Mean Square	F-Ratio	P-Value
Corrected Model	(a) 3 208.934	2	1 604.467	47.436	0.000
Intercept	449.290	1	449.290	13.283	0.001
CO-VARIANTS					
Pre-DAT-5:SR	2 910.316	1	2 910.316	86.044	0.000
EFFECTS					
Training Condition (AR vs Control)	221.648	1	221.648	6.553	0.014
Error	1 555.882	46	33.824		
Total	68 053.000	49			
TOTAL (CORRECTED)	4 764.816	48			

(a) R squared = 0.673 (R squared corrected = 0.659).

After adjusting for covariates (pre-test scores), it is checked that there was a significant difference between control group and training AR group on the gain scores, F1,46=7.47, p=0.009 (MRT) and F1,46=6.55, p=0.014 (DAT-5:SR). The p-values are well below the 1% of statistical significance. The results of Table 4 show the correction of the mean post-test value for each kind of course. A comparison of the AR training group with the control group revealed a mean difference of 3.721 on MRT and 4.259 on DAT-5:SR.

Table 4. Multiple Range Tests for MRT gain and DAT-5:SR gain by Group

Level	Count	Mean Adjust	Std. Error			
AR	24	26.735(a)	0.969			
CONTROL	25	23.014(a)	0.949		95% Confidence Interval	
					Lower	Upper
Parameter	B	Std. Error	t	Sig	Bound	Bound
Intersection	7.141	1.645	4.341	0.000	3.830	10.452
Pre-MRT	0.857	0.077	11.098	0.000	0.701	1.012
TRAINING_AR	**3.721**	1.362	2.733	0.009	0.980	6.462
CONTROL_GR	0(a)	(a). Covariance evaluated Pre-MRT: 18.53				

Level	Count	Mean Adjust	Std. Error			
AR	24	38.112(a)	1.188			
CONTROL	25	33.853(a)	1.164		95% Confidence Interval	
					Lower	Upper
Parameter	B	Std. Error	t	Sig	Bound	Bound
Intersection	8.344	2.953	2.826	0.007	2.400	14.288
Pre-DAT-5:SR	0.886	0.096	9.276	0.000	0.694	1.079
TRAINING_AR	**4.259**	1.664	2.560	0.014	0.910	7.607
CONTROL_GR	0(a)	(a). Covariance evaluated Pre-DAT-5:SR: 28.77				

4.2 Usability Study

Defining the components of *usability* according to Bevan [16]:

— **Efectiveness:** "accuracy and completeness." Error free completion of tasks is important in both business and consumer applications. We can say that the effectiveness of a product depends on how accurately it conducts the tasks and achieves the objectives it is designed for.

— **Efficiency:** "resources expended." How quickly a user can perform work is critical for business productivity.

— **Satisfaction:** the extent to which expectations are met. Satisfaction is a success factor for any products with discretionary use; it is essential for maintaining workforce motivation.

In order to make reliable estimations of the satisfaction results, eight or ten participants are necessary and larger samples offer a more significant value of the success rate [16]. In our study, the evaluation has been done by all students who have taken the training. The effectiveness is measured as the mean value of participants' answers (using a graduated numeric scale) and that the measure of efficiency and satisfaction is a value on a qualitative scales that enables users to formulate a reflection-conclusion on the basis of how the questions are asked. The measures of usability are more reliable when psychometrically validated questionnaires are used. However, it is difficult to get hold of questionnaires of this kind that can be adapted to this experience. In our case, we designed a survey with specifically questions for our experience, based on the experience of Hornbæk [17] and studies carried out by Company et al. [18].

In the education context, another aspect of usability is considered; this is known as "Learnability", which is defined as usability measured for the task of achieving adequate performance, for example, by completing a training course or through the use of learning materials [16]. Learnability may be considered as an aspect of usability (effectiveness).

The design divides the survey into several blocks of questions that measure the component parts of usability: Effectiveness of the educational material, Efficiency of the contents and the Efficiency of the technology, Satisfaction and Opinion. Respondents used a five level Likert scale to provide their opinion.

Table 5. Results of efficiency and effectiveness measures

Effectiveness of the Educational Material	Mean Value [Std. Error]
The course material is well and carefully presented (design notebook, Augmented book, Software, WebCam)	4.83[0.08]
The structure of the course has been comfortable, working in two separate notebooks, one for the exercises and the other for the marks.	4.88[0.07]
The structure of the course regarding levels and typology of exercises is adequate.	4.63[0.10]
It is easy to locate the exercises from the Design notebook in the fiducially marks book.	4.58[0.12]
The size of the notebooks (A5) is adequate to carry out the exercises and manipulate the virtual elements.	4.67[0.12]
The formative short videos are clear, with a language and graphics easy to understand.	3.92[0.18]
The Augmented Reality application has been stable (doesn´t block).	4.25[0.17]
The formative videos are sufficient to know the theoretical contents. It isn´t necessary any other type of explanation to complete the exercises.	4.21[0.18]
In the evaluation level there are 6 exercises. How many correct answers did you obtain?	5.71[0.13]
Efficiency of the contents	
The numbers of exercises proposed are sufficient for the intended working hours.	4.58[0.15]
I felt myself capable to resolve the exercises presented.	4.75[0.11]
I have had enough time in each session to complete the exercises marked by the teacher.	4.83[0.10]
Efficiency of the technology	
The familiarization with gestures and manipulating virtual objects has been easy.	4.46[0.10]
Upon manipulating the virtual figures there is no delay in the screen, the virtual image does not produce "image leaps".	3.17[0.20]
The three-dimensional virtual figures are clear and do not present definition difficulties.	4.33[0.13]
Utilizing materials (design notebook) and Augmented Reality technology has been easy and intuitive.	4.63[0.10]

The course material and contents have been very well received, as the measure of effectiveness has obtained a good result. The students consider that the material is well structured, it is well and carefully presented, the augmented reality application is stable and the number of exercises to be done in each session is considered sufficient. They also consider that the material and the contents are efficient, because they have had time to finish the work in the time set without difficulty. To assess the learnabilty of the contents, there are 6 exercises to be done, each worth 1 point, scored as follows: 1 = exercise right and 0 = exercise wrong. The mean value of this test is 5.71,

Table 6. Question of Satisfaction

D1	Augmented Reality technology has been interesting to use in this training.
D2	Do you think the training you have completed, provided by Augmented Reality, is useful to improve spatial skills?
D3	Could you have done this course on your own?, i.e., without the need for the teacher to be there.
D4	Do you think that additional theoretical material in this course is necessary?
D5	Where would you rather do this AR training?
D6	How do you value the Augmented Reality technology working with three-dimensional models? [Excellent-Very bad]
D7	Augmented Reality technology seems…[Very Interesting-Not very interesting]
D8	Augmented Reality technology seems…[Very original-Not very original]
D9	Augmented Reality technology seems…[Very useful-Not very useful]
D10	Augmented Reality technology seems…[Satisfying – Frustrating]
D11	Augmented Reality technology seems…[Flexible – Rigid]
D12	Overall opinion of the course [Excellent - Very bad]

so we can consider learnability as effective. AR_Dehaes offers participants speed in doing tasks and in learning. AR_Dehaes is efficient. The mean score for effectiveness is 4.50 points and 4.40 for efficiency.

100% of participants believe that the course attains its purpose of improving spatial vision and that augmented reality technology is useful for improving it because they consider it to be a user-friendly technology for this kind of training. Most of the participants consider that they could do the training on their own, without the need for any support from the teacher and they believe that the course provides enough theoretical material.

After undergoing this training, the participants state that they would have preferred to have done it in a university class room and very few would have preferred to do it at home, although they do point out that they could have done it at home without any problems.

D12	70,8% Excellent	29,2% Good	
D11	41,7% Flexible	58,3% Average	
D10	83,3% Satisfying	16,7% Average	
D9	66,7% Very Useful	33,3% Useful	
D8	70,8% Very Original	29,2% Original	
D7	79,2% Very Interesting	20,8% Interesting	
D6	75 % Excellent	20,8% Good	4,2% OK
D5	45,8 (1)	41,7 (2)	12,5 (3)
D4	41,7% YES	58,3% NO	
D3	54,2% YES	45,8% NO	
D2	100,0% YES		
D1	100,0% YES		

Fig. 3. Results of Satisfaction

The participants are very positive about using augmented reality technology to work with three-dimensional models. In general, they consider augmented reality technology to be interesting, useful and original and they describe it as excellent for the kind of activities that they have done.

Table 7. Results Students opinion

	YES	NO
Do you believe that the use of three dimensional tools can improve attention and motivate you to study the contents of Graphics Engineering subjects?	100%	-
Do you believe a fast course is suitable to improve engineering student's graphic engineering knowledge?	91.7%	8,3%
Would you have preferred this course to have been based on pen a paper sketches?	-	100%

They believe that three-dimensional tools will motivate them to study the contents of Engineering Graphics and they consider that courses of this kind are right for learning basic technical drawing. In any event, they prefer tools of this kind to the traditional drawing techniques. After using AR_Dehaes, they consider this tool to be the best way for doing activities of this kind.

5 Conclusions

Learning and teaching procedures have to evolve to take into account the high technological profile that most of students show. In some cases, outdated teaching methods create a barrier for some students that are accustomed to interact with modern technological gadgets and computers. Augmented reality is a cost-effective technology to provide students with attractive contents with respect to paper books, giving new life to classical paper and pencil exercises. In educational applications, it is of utmost importance to focus students´ attention on the actual task and to reduce the cognitive overhead needed to use the application. This motivated us to design a user-friendly system and a friendly and agreeable environment. AR-Dehaes has proven to be and efficient and effective material for developing spatial abilities and for learning engineering graphics contents. In the usability assessment, AR-Dehaes was scored very positively by students with regard to both the teaching material and the technology used. The software has proven to be robust as no errors have shown up during its use.

References

1. Azuma, R.: A Survey of Augmented Reality. Presence: Teleoperators and Virtual Environments 1 (6), 355–385 (1997)
2. Kaufmann, H., Schmalstieg, D.: Mathematics and geometry education with collaborative augmented reality. Computer & Graphics 27(3), 339–345 (2003)
3. Quarles, J., Lampotang, S., Fischler, I., Fishwick, P.: Scaffolded learning with mixed reality. Computers & Graphics 33(1), 34–46 (2009)

4. Juan, M., Beatrice, F., Cano, J.: An Augmented Reality System for Learning the Interior of the Human Body. In: Proceeding of the 8th IEEE International Conference on Advanced Learning Technologies (ICALT 2008), Santander, Spain, pp. 186–188 (2008)
5. Billinghurst, M.: Augmented reality in education, new horizons for learning, http://www.newhorizons.org/strategies/technology/billinghurst.htm (accessed 03-14-2010)
6. CONNECT project, http://www.ea.gr/ep/connect/ (last accessed 03-14-2010)
7. CREATE project, http://www.cs.ucl.ac.uk/research/vr/Projects/Create/ (last accessed 03-14-2010)
8. ARiSE project, http://www.arise-project.org/ (last accessed 03-14-2010)
9. Billinghurst, M., Kato, H., Poupyrev, I.: The MagicBook–moving seamlessly between reality and virtuality. IEEE Computer Graphics and Applications 21(3), 6–8 (2001)
10. Tallyn, E., Frohlich, D., Linketscher, N., Signer, B., Adams, G.: Using paper to support collaboration in educational activities. In: Proceedings of the 2005 Conference on Computer Support For Collaborative Learning, Taipei, Taiwan, pp. 672–676 (2005)
11. James, K.H., Humphrey, G.K., Vilis, T., Corrie, B., Baddour, R., Goodale, M.A.: Active and passive learning of three-dimensional object structure within an immersive virtual reality environment. Behavior Research Methods, Instruments & Computers 34(3), 383–390 (2002)
12. Anderson, L.W., Krathwohl, D.R.: A taxonomy for learning, teaching and assessing: A revision of Bloom's Taxonomy of educational objectives, Complete edn., New York (2001)
13. Pellegrino, J., Alderton, D., Shute, V.: Understanding spatial ability. Educational Psychologist 19(3), 239–253 (1984)
14. Vandenberg, S.G., Kuse, A.R.: Mental rotations: a group test of three-dimensional spatial visualisation. Perceptual and Motor Skills 47(6), 599–604 (1978)
15. Bennett, G.K., Seashore, H.G., Wesman, A.: Differential aptitude tests. In: The Psychological Corporation, New York (1947) (Spanish official version: TEA Ediciones; Madrid, 2007)
16. Bevan, N.: Practical issues in usability measurement. Interactions 13, 42–43 (2006)
17. Hornbæk, K.: Current Practice in Measuring Usability: Challenges to Usability Studies and Research. International Journal of Human-Computer Studies 64, 79–102 (2006)
18. Company, P., Contero, M., Naya, F., Aleixos, N.: A Study of Usability of Sketching Tools Aimed at Supporting Prescriptive Sketches. In: Proceedings of Eurographics Symposium Proceedings. Sketch-Based Interfaces and Modeling (SBIM 2006), Vienna, Austria, pp. 139–146 (2006)

What Do Children Favor as Embodied Pedagogical Agents?

Sylvie Girard[*] and Hilary Johnson

HCI Research lab, Department of Computer Science, University of Bath,
BA2 7AY BATH, UK
{s.a.girard,h.johnson}@bath.ac.uk

Abstract. Embodied Pedagogical Agents (EPA) are increasingly employed in educational applications, for a variety of users and purposes. However, studies have shown that visual appearance, communicative style, and pedagogical roles of agents impact their acceptance, trust, and user interaction [1, 2, 3, 4]. In this paper, we present a study where 86 primary school children (aged 7-11) chose an EPA to 'accompany' them in their learning of multiplications in the ITS application, *Multipliotest*. The children used two versions of the software, one with an instructor EPA, and another with a learning companion EPA. Additionally, the children selected a visual appearance for each EPA: simplified or detailed, and naturalistic (humanoid-shaped) or stylized (smiley-shaped). Investigations of the possible relationships between pedagogical roles and visual appearance with respect to user preference are outlined, along with the study limitations, and considerations for future work.

Keywords: Embodied Pedagogical Agent; visual style; pedagogical role; realism; naturalism.

1 Introduction

EPAs can be found in educational software in increasing numbers, and under different visual representations, different communication styles, or adopting one or more different pedagogical roles, within the same application. EPAs are "visually represented, computer-generated characters in pedagogical roles, such as virtual instructors, mentors, or learning companions" [3], usually embedded within the software to aid social and communicative features, [5, 6]. They are used in computer-assisted learning applications for users ranging from children to elderly people, to help them in software navigation, usability, or in learning content or development of meta-cognitive skills [2, 7].

However, studies showed that visual appearance, communicative style, and pedagogical roles of agents impact their acceptance and trust, and change the way people interact with them [1, 2, 3, 4].

---

[*] Corresponding author: sylvie.girard@info.univ-lemans.fr

Consequently, there is sufficient research interest and rationale for investigating the effect of design characteristics of EPAs on users. Research on the user interface design of agents, and in the design of comics over the past twenty years, has focused on the impact of the degree of detail and naturalness of the EPA. These factors affect their processing and interpretation by users [8, 9], in addition to self-identification processes, and engagement level with the EPA [10, 11]. Other studies have investigated the impact of 'instructional roles' on learning and motivation for particular age groups [4]. A range of pedagogical roles used in EPAs worldwide, have been classified in Haake & Gulz [3] on the dimension of authority. In Haake & Gulz [3], three EPA factors were studied with children aged 12-15: visual static appearance, communicative style, and pedagogical role. Some interesting and potentially unexpected results were found, such as when female students chose 'learning companions' they preferred more stylized, visual characters. However, as children grow, their interests change. This impacts their ability [12] and willingness [13] to use intelligent environments. Therefore, there is value in investigating user's preferences according to their age and cognitive developmental stage.

In this paper, we present a study where 86 primary school children (aged 7-11) chose an EPA to 'accompany' them in their learning of multiplications in the ITS *Multipliotest*. The children used two versions of the software, one with an instructor EPA, and another with a learning companion EPA. The children selected a visual appearance for each EPA: simplified or detailed, and humanoid-shaped (naturalistic) or smiley-shaped (stylized). At the end of the session, they were asked to choose which type of EPA they preferred, and the reason why. Section 2 illustrates all aspects of the experimental study (study goal, EPA design characteristics, experimental design, participants, and research hypothesis). The results (section 3) are illustrated with their analysis (section 4) as to the possible relationship of pedagogical visual appearance with respect to user preferences. Finally, section 5 describes limitations of the study, and considerations for future work.

2 Design of the Experimental Study

2.1 Goal of the Study

In this section, the experimental study performed on June 10th 2007 with three French classes from the school 'Jean Zay' in France, is presented. The goal of the study was to investigate users' choice of EPA with respect to their visual appearance and pedagogical role. In particular, possible relationships between these variables were investigated with regards to user preferences.

2.2 Participants

86 children aged 7-11 (46 girls, 40 boys) from a French primary school participated in the study. The students came from three classes of two levels (one class of CE1, one class CE1/CE2, and one class of CE2). The majority of students had no familiarity with pedagogical agents comprised of embodied computer characters, but they were all familiar with the pictorial representation of naturalistic characters.

2.3 Characters' Visual Appearance and Pedagogical Role

In Haake & Gulz [3], a theoretical framework is defined to evaluate user's EPA choice along three design aspects: visual static appearance, communicative style, and pedagogical role. In this article, we chose to evaluate the impact of two components of visual static appearance (degree of detail, degree of naturalism) in relation to the EPA's pedagogical role and the communicative style. The results enable comparison with Haake & Gulz's study as to the user's preferences, according to the age of the child-participants.

One contribution of this paper is that our participants differ from the Haake & Gulz's study in culture, and more especially in age: they do not belong to the same Piagetan stage of cognitive development [12], nor to the same stage in Acuff and Reiher's categorization [13]. Children aged 11-15 years relate more strongly to more realistic characters, preferring realistic to fantasy worlds [13], and are able to use abstract thinking to solve problems [12]. According to Piaget [12], children aged 7-11 (within the concrete operational stage) can think logically, but not abstractly. Whilst they can distinguish between reality and fantasy, they are developing beyond a stage where perception is dominant, and thus potentially misled by what they see. According to Acuff & Reiher [13], the youngest of our age group participants are leaving the 'emerging/autonomy' stage to enter the 'rule/role' one. They are no longer dominated by a world of fantasy and magic, where there was a need of stimulation associated with comfort and love. By the age of 8, their interest shifts gradually from fantasy to reality.

For this reason, when considering the degree of naturalism, we chose to investigate the impact the level of anthropomorphism in the design versus a character based on a smiley face. This should help gauge children's interest in interacting with an EPA that is more fantasy-like (smiley-shaped), or more redolent of the real world (humanoid-shaped). The use of children and teachers as participatory-design partners in the design of the EPA's visual appearances for the study will aid in producing a sample of EPAs comprised of graphical components both familiar and appealing to children of this age.

Visual Appearance: Detailed vs. Simplified, Naturalistic vs. Stylized characters

The format of the pictorial representations to be utilized in this study arose out of a participatory design session with 2 teachers and 20 children aged 7-11, different from the child population used thereafter in the study.

During the participatory design sessions the children first perused a collection of pictures taken from Internet picture databases on learning companions and the comic literature. Each child then designed their own instructor and a learning companion. All of the children chose and drew female characters as instructors. When interviewed, they explained that the picture should be as similar to their teacher as possible. The participating school consisted entirely of female teachers, and therefore we chose to propose only one type of humanoid character for the instructor, with a female gender. However, when defining the learning companion, the children drew a mixture of female and male child characters, similar to their age. Therefore two characters will represent each naturalistic condition for learning companions, one of male and of female gender.

The expressive style for the stylized characters is based on *Peanuts* [15] characteristics: simplified, whimsy and humoristic, occupying the bottom right corner of McCloud's design space of iconography [11]. On the contrary, the naturalistic characters' expressive style is based on *'Mangas'* and French Comics: cute, emotional, friendly, which is higher up and to the left border of McCloud's diagram. A majority of French child design partners read the comics *Cédric* [16], or watch its everyday TV animated movie adaptation, and relate this to children's everyday life stories at school. Consequently, at the end of the participatory design session, the participants selected *Cédric* and his friend *Chen* for the naturalistic-styled learning companion.

Figure 1 illustrates the sets of characters the children had to choose from: the four characters grouped on the left representing the teacher/instructor characters, and the group on the right representing the learning companions.

Two approaches were taken to the design of the characters used in the study: varying the axis *'degree of naturalism'*, and the *'degree of detail'*. Characters 1, 3, 6, and 8 made use of a stylized (smiley-shaped) representational form, while the other characters (2, 4, 5, 7, 9, 10) made use of a naturalistic one (humanoid-shaped). The characters are again separated in terms of level of detail, with the top row 3D-rendered and detailed, and the bottom row 2D-rendered and simplified.

Fig. 1. The four sets of characters used in the study: each different in pedagogical goal and visual appearance

Pedagogical Role: Instructor/Teacher vs. Learning Companion

From the categorization of EPA roles in the literature [3, 17], and the studies undertaken on their impact on ITS [4], we chose to investigate two different EPA pedagogical roles:
- An EPA representing an authoritative instructor, with an instructional role of 'expert' as defined in [4], and mainly task-oriented as designed in [18].

- An EPA representing a non-authoritative, collaborative learning companion, with a 'mentor' instructional role, and a combined task-and-relation-oriented communicative style.

The two scenarios of use differed in the interaction with the EPA, but were equal in terms of pedagogical goal and activity architecture: the children could either choose one multiplication (level 1) or all multiplication tables (level 2) simultaneously to test their knowledge against. The only restriction in the game was to choose a unique activity to perform within level 1 and level 2 activities. Each visual representation of the characters was investigated in the scenarios, the interface modulated to integrate their design.

2.4 Research Hypotheses

The following hypotheses were studied in this experiment:

Table 1. Hypothesis for the research study

Hypothesis 1
Ho^1: There is no difference in the number of learning companions versus instructors, preferred as an EPA.
H1: Children will choose the learning companion more than the instructor as the software EPA.
Hypothesis 2
Ho^2: When introduced as a learning companion, there is no difference in the number of EPAs being chosen with a humanoid-shaped or smiley-shaped appearance.
H2: The learning companion version will yield a preference for a smiley-shaped EPA.
Hypothesis 3
Ho^3: When introduced as an instructor, there is no difference in the number of EPAs being chosen with a shaped-shaped or smiley-shaped appearance.
H3: The instructor version will yield a preference for a humanoid-shaped EPA.
Hypothesis 4
Ho^4: When introduced as a learning companion, there is no difference in the number of EPAs being chosen with high or low levels of detail.
H4: The learning companion version will yield a preference for an EPA with low levels of detail.
Hypothesis 5
Ho^5: When introduced as an instructor, there is no difference in the number of EPAs being chosen with high or low levels of detail.
H5: The instructor version will yield a preference for an EPA with low levels of detail.

Hypothesis 1 relates to the children's final choice, at the end of the session, after using both instructor and learning companion conditions. The hypothesis is concerned with the children's overall preference for either an instructor or learner. It is separated from the other hypotheses, and based on Acuff & Reiher's definition of a developmental stage [13], where children still need support and comfort, and respond more positively to working with a digital peer than an instructor telling them what to do.

Hypotheses 2 to 5 were drawn from theoretical work, field observations when working with our participatory-design partners in the definition of the pictorial representation, and children's reactions in usability studies with participants of the same age group in the design process of the *Multipliotest* software design. H4 and H5 follow McCloud's theoretical framework [11] where simplified characters amplify the meaning of an image, such as the character's affective components, and therefore afford more powerful social-emotional communications. This may help in the rational aspects of the EPA presented.

2.5 Experimental Design and Procedure

The participants were presented with both versions of the *Multipliotest* ITS aimed at helping children learn multiplications: one version with an instructor, and another with a learning companion. The order in which they accessed software was counterbalanced (half of them beginning with the instructor and then the companion, and vice versa). When in front of the software, the children were to choose a character as their EPA given the choices presented in Figure 1, and then performed an activity. They then followed the same procedure for the other condition. Finally, they were requested to choose the EPA they preferred, and explain why it was more appealing to them. In this experimental manipulation, the factors 'pedagogical role', 'degree of detail' and 'degree of naturalism' of the characters act as independent variables, and the user's choice acts as the dependent variable.

3 Results

3.1 Hypothesis 1: Choice of EPAs in ITS: Instructor or Learning Companion?

A Chi-square 'goodness to fit' test demonstrates that there is a significant difference (χ^2=22.512, df=1, p < 0.001) between the expected and observed frequencies, which rejects Ho[1]: children prefer EPAs in the role of learning companions when working on *Multipliotest*.

Table 2. Test data representing the final choice between instructor and learning companion

Instructor	Companion	Total
21	65	86

3.2 Hypotheses 2 to 5: Associations of Pedagogical Role and Visual Static Appearance

The test data concerning hypotheses 2 to 5 can be presented in frequencies in a three-dimensional contingency table categorized by the variables: pedagogical role (P), visual style: degree of detail (D), and visual style: naturalism (N).

Table 3. Test data categorized by the 3 variables: P, D, and N

Pedagogical Role	Detail	Naturalism Naturalistic	Stylized	Total
Instructor	*Detailed*	5	18	23
	Simplified	61	2	63
	Total	66	20	86
Learning Companion	*Detailed*	0	1	1
	Simplified	5	80	85
	Total	5	81	86
	Column Total	71	101	172

Hypotheses 2 and 3: Association of Pedagogical Role and Level of Naturalism

With the data separated into the two different pedagogical roles of instructor and companion, a Chi-square 'goodness to fit' test revealed a significant difference in the choice of humanoid-shaped/smiley-shaped visual appearance for both pedagogical roles.

We reject Ho^2 and Ho^3: The instructor version yields a preference for a humanoid-shaped agent ($\chi_2=24.605$, p <0.001), and the learning companions for a more smiley-shaped appearance ($\chi_2=67.163$, p < 0.001).

Hypotheses 4 and 5: Association of Pedagogical Role and Degree of Details

With the data separated into the two different pedagogical roles of instructor and companion, a Chi-square 'goodness to fit' test revealed a significant difference in the degree of detail chosen in the visual appearance for both pedagogical roles.

We can see in Table 3 that for the case of a learning companion, all but one child chose the simplified version of the companion, represented in Figure 1 by the characters 8, 9, and 10.

We reject Ho^4 and Ho^5: The instructor ($\chi_2=18.605$, p<0.001) and the learning companion ($\chi_2=82.046$, p< 0.001) versions yield a preference for agents with low levels of detail.

4 Analysis and Discussion

4.1 Hypothesis 1: Choice of Pedagogical Role for EPAs in ITS

At the end of the study the children were asked to provide rationales for the selection of the EPA with the pedagogical role they most preferred using within *Multipliotest*: instructor or learning companion.

The results (H1) show a statistical preference in children's choice of learning companion as EPAs. The reasons behind this choice given by the participants were that they could relate more to the learning companion, and 'trusted' the characters to help them. The instructors were seen as too formal as characters, and most children felt 'judged' by them.

Children's preference for a 'peer' feature to a more formal "instructor" one is in line with Acuff & Reiher's [13] categorization of children by developmental stage with children aged 7-11 years: they prefer to work in pairs or in groups, and this holds here even though the peer is not physically with them, but digitally represented.

Teacher's interviews on the subject revealed that the instructor figures probably represented themselves to the children, along with their style of interaction during a learning session: In their class, when children work in groups they help each other; while when interacting with their instructor, at the teacher's intervention, they only follow the teacher's instructions and advices, but are not looking for extensive and individualized help.

4.2 Hypothesis 2 and 3: Association of Pedagogical Role and Level of Naturalism

The evaluation of H2 and H3 revealed that children conveyed a preference for more naturalistic instructors (humanoid-shaped), and stylized learning companions as EPAs.

Children's preference for more stylized learning companion is coherent with the results of H2 in Haake & Gulz's study [3]. However, unlike their non-significant result when considering the instructor separately, we have here significant results: more naturalistic visual appearance is preferred. This could be related to the difference in experimental design: in this reported study, children chose the characters while distinctively knowing their role, the characters displayed were not the same in each condition, and were especially designed with this role in mind. For this reason, children may have adopted more naturalistic instructors to be closer to the more formal social role of the instructor, i.e. closer to the reality of the class teacher.

Similarly, the choice of more stylized (smiley-shaped) learning companion could be explained by children's view of the EPA in a more relational social role, like an imaginary friend that needs to be more imaginary than realistic. This corresponds with Reeves and Nass's [20] Media Equation theory of transference of real world relational strategies into a 'virtual world' – aka computerized learning environment.

The choices made could also relate to the age group of the study participants. Children of this age frequently watch animated movies or read comics, where the simplification of details emphasize the meaning or semantic association of the images [11], therefore bringing the user closer, or more associated with the learning companion, and keeping a sense of fantasy, detaching themselves from a totally realistic setting unlike older children.

4.3 Hypothesis 4 and 5: Association of Pedagogical Role and Degree of Detail

The evaluation of H4 and H5 revealed that children conveyed a preference for simplified characters for both pedagogical roles. Children's preference for more simplified agents may relate to McCloud's theory [11] that such design characteristics emphasizes social-emotional expression, and facilitate self-identification and immersion into the character of the story.

Results for H3 and H5 concerning the learning companion also correspond with the field observations of Haake & Gulz's study [3], that when the EPA is associated to a 'friend', they tend to select more simplified and cartoonish characters rather than a more detailed and naturalistic one.

5 Conclusion and Future Work

This paper reports interesting findings related to the preferences of 7 to 11 year old French children on the appearance of EPAs, according to two pedagogical roles: instructor and learning companion.

Some results in this study were similar to Haake & Gulz's study [3] on older children from a different nationality, such as the preference of more stylized EPAs as learning companion agents (H2). Other results, however, seemed specifically related to our participants' age group or cultural background (H4, H5), and school learning practices (H1).

Several potential limitations of the study relate to the scope and generality of the results. One limitation is that the children tested the interaction with the agent for a limited amount of time, and within a specific scenario. Although the study is similar in scope to other studies in this area, in advance of making claims about the generality of the results, further studies over a longer time period, and under different conditions of use are necessary. Furthermore, only two pedagogical roles have been studied here, and it would be interesting to investigate other roles used in the design of EPAs within ITS applications. Validity of the study results may also be limited to the design of EPAs for French children aged 7 to 11 years, a replication of this study with different user groups (in age and/or culture) may produce different results. It is also necessary for us to undertake further studies to identify the impacts of the different factors of visual appearance and any associated actions of the characters.

Other future work includes investigating age and gender differences in choices of EPA's appearance, actions and pedagogical roles. We believe this work in the design of EPAs for ITS may result in EPAs that are more appropriate for the children.

References

1. Nowak, K., Rauh, C.: Choose your 'buddy icon' carefully: the influence of avatar androgyny, anthropomorphism and credibility in online interactions. Computers Mediated Communication 11(1), article 8 (2008)
2. Yee, N., Bailenson, J.: The Proteus Effect: Self-transformations in virtual reality. Human Communication Research 33, 271–290 (2007)
3. Haake, M., Gulz, A.: A Look at the Roles of Look & Roles in Embodied Pedagogical Agents - A User Preference Perspective. International Journal of Artificial Intelligence in Education 19(1), 39–71 (2009)
4. Baylor, A., Kim, Y.: Simulating instructional roles through pedagogical agents. International Journal of Artificial Intelligence in Education 15(1), 95–115 (2005)
5. Johnson, L.: Interaction tactics for socially intelligent pedagogical agents. In: Johnson, L., André, E., Dominique, J. (eds.) Proceedings of the 8th International conference on Intelligent User Interfaces, pp. 251–253. ACM, New York (2003)
6. McQuiggan, S., Mott, B., Lester, J.: Modeling self-efficacy in intelligent tutoring systems: an inductive approach. User Modeling and User-Adapted Interaction 18(1-2), 81–123 (2008)
7. Baylor, A.: The impact of pedagogical agent image on affective outcomes. In: Proceedings of the Workshop of Affective Interactions: Computers in the Affective Loop. 10th International Conference on Intelligent User Interface 2005, San Diego, CA (2005)

8. Cook, M.: Perceiving others: the psychology of interpersonal perception. Methuen, London (1979)
9. Isbister, K.: Better game characters by design – a psychological approach. Morgan Kaufman, San Francisco (2006)
10. Gulz, A., Haake, M.: Design of animated pedagogical agents – a look at their look and visual form. International Journal of Human-Computer Studies 64(4), 322–339 (2006)
11. McCloud, S.: Understanding Comics: The invisible Art. Harper Perennial, New York (1993)
12. Piaget, J.: Science of Education and the psychology of the child. Orion Press, New York (1970)
13. Acuff, D.S., Reiher, R.H.: Kids' Stuff: Torys and the changing worlds of American childhood. Harvard University Press, Cambridge (1997)
14. Guha, M.L., Druin, A., Chipman, G., Fails, J.A., Simms, S., Farber, A.: Working with young children as technology design partners. Commun. ACM 48(1), 39–42 (2005)
15. Wikipedia article on the history of Peanuts comic strips, http://en.wikipedia.org/wiki/Peanuts
16. Official site of the Cédric comic strips, http://cedric.spirou.com
17. Chou, C.-Y., Chan, T.-W., Lin, C.-J.: Redefining the learning companion: the past, present, and future of educational agents. Computers and Education 40, 255–269 (2003)
18. Bickmore, T.: Relational Agents: Effecting change through Human-Computer Relationships. PhD Thesis. Media Arts & Sciences, Massachusetts Institute of Technology, Cambridge, M.A (2003)
19. Kelley, J.F.: An iterative design methodology for user-friendly natural language office information applications. ACM Transactions on Office Information Systems 2(1), 26–41 (1984)
20. Reeves, B., Nass, C.: The Media Equation: How people treat computers, televisions and new media like real people and places. Cambridge University Press, New York (1996)

Learning by Teaching SimStudent: Technical Accomplishments and an Initial Use with Students

Noboru Matsuda[1,*], Victoria Keiser[1], Rohan Raizada[1], Arthur Tu[1], Gabriel Stylianides[2], William W. Cohen[1], and Kenneth R. Koedinger[1]

[1] School of Computer Science, Carnegie Mellon University
5000 Forbes Ave. Pittsburgh PA 15213 USA
[2] School of Education, University of Pittsburgh
5517 Posvar Hall, Pittsburgh PA 15260 USA
{noboru.matsuda,keiser,atu,wcohen,koedinger}@cs.cmu.edu,
rohan@gmai.com, gstylian@pitt.edu

Abstract. The purpose of the current study is to test whether we could create a system where students can learn by teaching a live machine-learning agent, called SimStudent. SimStudent is a computer agent that interactively learns cognitive skills through its own tutored-problem solving experience. We have developed a game-like learning environment where students learn algebra equations by tutoring SimStudent. While Simulated Students, Teachable Agents and Learning Companion systems have been created, our study is unique that it genuinely learns skills from student input. This paper describes the overview of the learning environment and some results from an evaluation study. The study showed that after tutoring SimStudent, the students improved their performance on equation solving. The number of correct answers on the error detection items was also significantly improved. On average students spent 70.0 minutes on tutoring SimStudent and used an average of 15 problems for tutoring.

Keywords: SimStudent, Learning by teaching, tutor-learning effect, algebra equation solving, machine learning.

1 Introduction

There is ample evidence that students learn when they teach their peers [1]. Such an *effect of tutor learning* has been observed across different subjects, age groups, format of tutoring, and so forth. Yet, little is known about when tutors' learning would be facilitated and why. A scientific contribution of the current study is at our exploratory effort to study cognitive and social factors for tutor learning. Even when tutor

---

[*] This study is supported by National Science Foundation Award No. DRL-0910176 and by Department of Education (IES) Award No. R305A090519. This work is also supported in part by the Pittsburgh Science of Learning Center, which is funded by the National Science Foundation Award No. SBE-0836012.

learning is effective, there are practical difficulties to exercise peer tutoring in an actual classroom – not only would it be time consuming (the students must take turns) but, also, the tutees might not learn as much as tutors do. Thus, on the engineering side of our contribution, building an effective and efficient learning environment that facilitates tutor learning is one of our primary research goals.

We have developed a game-like learning environment where students learn by interactively tutoring a computer agent, called *SimStudent*. SimStudent is a machine-learning agent that learns cognitive skills from examples and through its own tutored problem-solving experiences [2]. Our long-term research goal is to investigate the effect of tutor learning with SimStudent as a teachable agent.

The aim of this paper is to provide an overview of our learning by teaching system and discuss results from an evaluation study. The primary research question in the current paper addressed whether or not the students learn by teaching SimStudent at all, and if so, how effective the system is.

2 Learning by Teaching

2.1 Type and Domain of the Proposed Learning by Teaching Environment

The *effect of tutor learning* has been studied in many different domains, across ages, and in various tutoring settings [3]. Various forms of tutoring have been observed including reciprocal teaching [4] and collaborative passage learning [5]. The effect of tutor learning has been observed for all age groups including college [6], high school [7], middle school [8], and elementary school students [9]. The tutor learning effect has been shown to be relatively more effective in math than reading [3, 10].

In the current study, we focus on one-on-one tutoring where a single student acts as a tutor and a computer agent plays the tutee's role. Although the SimStudent technology and the overall framework of the proposed learning environment are domain independent, the current learning system is built for algebraic linear equations – one of the more challenging subjects in mathematics.

2.2 Related Studies

There have been a number of simulated students (also called *teachable agents*) developed so far [11-14]. VanLehn et al. [11] developed one of the earliest simulated students and demonstrated its benefit for *teacher training* in physics. Betty's Brain [15] and its variations are the most recent examples of a teachable agent used to study the tutor learning effect. Betty's Brain learns causal relations from a conceptual map created by student by entering nodes (each representing a concept) and links (each representing a causal relation among the concepts). Students can also quiz Betty's Brain with a problem asking a causal relation (e.g., "If dead organisms increase, what happens to the animals?").

While Simulated Students, Teachable Agents and Learning Companion systems have been created, some were never used with real students and others do not genuinely learn from student input. While the VanLehn's system [11] incorporated machine learning and could be used for theory generation and to analyze instructional materials, it was not designed for use with students. On the other hand, while Betty's Brain has been used extensively by students and subject to numerous evaluations, it does not have a machine-learning component. Students teach Betty's Brain by editing a concept map, but the system does not learn from the concept map any more than making straightforward inferences from following the links in the map. This paper provides perhaps the first demonstration of a machine learning system being used as a teachable agent by real students and with significant pre-to-post learning outcomes.

3 SimStudent as a Teachable Peer Learner

3.1 Overview of SimStudent

The underlying technology for SimStudent's learning is inductive logic programming in the form of programming by demonstration [16, 17].

There are two learning strategies implemented for SimStudent so far – *learning from examples* and *learning by tutored problem solving* [18]. The learning strategy used for the current research context is learning by tutored problem solving, which requires a *tutor agent* that interactively tutors SimStudent. The tutor agent first poses a problem for SimStudent to solve. To solve the problem, SimStudent attempts to apply production rules that are already learned. When a rule is applied (i.e., a step is performed), the tutor agent provides flagged (binary) feedback that merely shows a correctness of the rule application. When the feedback is negative (*regardless of the accuracy of this tutor feedback*), SimStudent attempts to apply another rule.

When SimStudent cannot perform a step "correctly," then SimStudent asks the tutor agent for a hint about what to do next.[1] The tutor agent then *demonstrates* the step for SimStudent as a hint, which is equivalent to a so-called bottom-out hint.

SimStudent learns skills by generalizing the examples demonstrated. There are two types of examples: a *positive example* is generated either when the tutor agent provides affirmative feedback on a step that SimStudent performed, or when the tutor agent demonstrates a step as a hint. A *negative example* is generated when SimStudent receives negative feedback from the tutor agent on a step that SimStudent performed. As a result of generalization, SimStudent generates a *production rule* that covers all positive examples (i.e., an application of the rule yields the same step mentioned in a positive example) but does not cover any of the negative examples. In other words, SimStudent generates a set of production rules sufficient to solve problems that share the underlying domain principles that have been demonstrated. SimStudent is given a set of *background knowledge* that allows SimStudent to interpret the examples. See [18] for details of the SimStudent learning algorithm.

Although, the SimStudent's learning algorithm is domain independent, we use algebra equation solving for the current study. In a particular tutoring interface used in the current study (as shown in **Fig. 1**), a single *equation-solving step* is implemented with three *tutoring steps* that are modeled with two skills. For example, $3x+2=8$ is transformed into $3x=6$ by subtracting 2 from both sides, which, by definition, is a single equation-solving step. In our tutoring interface, this equation-solving step consists of (a) specifying a *transformation skill*, which in this case is "subtract 2," and (b) *typing in* a left- and a right-hand side of the transformed equation. The tutoring

---

[1] The correctness of the step, by definition, is determined by the feedback from the tutor agent. Thus, SimStudent could fail to perform a step "correctly" when the tutor agent disconfirms the step regardless of the true correctness of the rule application.

interface thus has three columns (two under "Equation" and one under "Transformation"), corresponding to these three steps.

The above-mentioned examples are accumulated for each of the skills demonstrated. In other words, when a step is demonstrated, it must be annotated with a *skill-name*. Such annotation drastically reduces the complexity of the search space when learning rules. There is another piece of information that improves the search – the *focus of attention* (FoA, for short), which is knowledge about where to pay attention when performing a step. When tutoring SimStudent, an FoA specifies the elements on the tutoring interface. In the tutoring interface shown in **Fig. 1**, FoA is a set of cells representing either the left- or right-hand side of an equation, or a transformation. Technically, the FoA composes the left-hand side of a production rule encoding a pattern matching for a rule application. Without FoA, SimStudent must search for such a pattern matching, which significantly increases the search complexity.

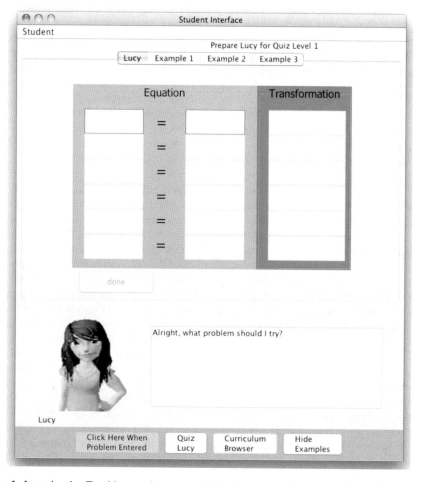

Fig. 1. Learning by Teaching environment. Worked-out examples appear in the interface by clicking the [Example 1,2, and 3] tabs at the top of the interface. SimStudent is called Lucy in this example.

An earlier pilot study showed that asking students to annotate a skill name each time they demonstrate a step is unnatural and confusing. Likewise, asking the students to specify FoA is not practical. Thus, in the current learning by teaching environment, both skill names and FoA are implicitly provided to SimStudent using domain dependent ad-hoc heuristics. When a transformation skill is performed, a skill-name is given as the same name as the transformation (e.g., "subtract"). When a type-in skill is performed following a particular transformation, a skill-name is given as a combination of the transformation and a fixed post-fix (e.g., "subtract-typein"). An FoA for a transformation skill is always the left- and right-hand sides of the equation, upon which the transformation was applied. An FoA for a type-in skill is the immediate transformation skill and the equation on which the transformation skill was applied.

3.2 Learning-by-Teaching Environment

Fig. 1 shows a screenshot of our Learning-by-Teaching learning environment (the *LBT environment*, for short). As shown in the figure, the LBT environment is composed of (1) a tutoring interface, (2) a Curriculum Browser, (3) example problems, (4) a communication window, (5) a SimStudent avatar, called Lucy in this example, and (6) the buttons to control the flow of tutoring. SimStudent and the student share the tutoring interface.

In the LBT environment, a student performs the role of the tutor agent mentioned in section 3.1. The goal of the LBT environment is to tutor SimStudent well enough to pass the quiz, which provides a bit of the flavor of an on-line game to the LBT environment.

To pose a problem for SimStudent to solve, the student simply enters an equation into the tutoring interface, and clicks the [Solve the Equation] button. The *communication window*, the box next to the SimStudent avatar, is used to display a message from SimStudent (e.g., a request for feedback on a step performed or a request for a hint). The student provides feedback by clicking on a [Yes]/[No] button that also appears in the communication window. To provide a "hint," the student simply performs a step in the tutoring interface.

One obvious question is "What if the student cannot provide a hint?" We have two supporting materials for the student to prepare for tutoring. The *Curriculum Browser* shows an overview of the curriculum to learn ("equations with variables on both sides," in the current study). It has descriptions on the goal of the subject, skills to be learned, and an example that explains how to solve a typical problem. The Curriculum Browser appears when the student clicks on the [Curriculum Browser] button. A set of examples is also available when the [Example] button is clicked. Unlike the example in the Curriculum Browser, these examples are shown inside the *tutoring interface* with the exact tutoring steps. Thus, the student can learn how to use the tutoring interface as well.

4 Evaluation Study

To evaluate the LBT environment, we have conducted a lab study. This section describes the details of the study and the results.

The goal of the study is to measure the degree of tutor learning (the effectiveness) and the efficiency and usability of the system. The effectiveness of the study was measured as learning gain using pre- and post-tests. For the efficiency and usability, we conducted a protocol analysis by video-recording the full learning sessions.

4.1 Method

The study involved 12 students ranging from 6th to 8th grade. The participants were recruited from local middle schools for monetary compensation.

All 12 participants followed the same procedure. The total of 12 study sessions were run individually. Before a study session began, an experimenter explained to a participant that for the whole study session was to think aloud. During the study session, the experimenter gave an occasional prompt to the participant to think aloud.

The participant first took an on-line pre-test (the details of the test are described in the next section). The pre-test took 46 minutes on average. The participant then watched a 10-minute video to learn how to use the LBT environment. Next, the participant was told the goal of the study session – to have Lucy (the name of SimStudent in this particular study as shown in **Fig. 1**) pass the quiz. The participant then tutored Lucy. After an hour, the experimenter told the participants that they were welcome to quit the session if they wanted even when Lucy had not passed the quiz.

Finally, the participants took a post-test. The pre- and post-tests were isomorphic, and the difference in the tests was counter-balanced across the participants. After the post-test, all of the participants completed a post-study questionnaire (due to space limitations, we will not discuss the results of the questionnaire in this paper).

All of the study sessions, including the pre- and post-tests as well as the tutoring sessions, were video recorded. The participants' activities during the tutoring session were logged into an open data repository, called DataShop, maintained by the Pittsburgh Science of Learning Center [19].

4.2 Study Materials

The pre- and post-tests were implemented as on-line tests authored using the Cognitive Tutor Authoring Tools. When taking a test, the participants were given a piece of paper to write down their work.

The on-line test consists of question items for (1) equation solving, (2) term identification, (3) what to do next, (4) equivalent expressions, and (5) error identification. The *equation solving* items are to solve equations (e.g., $-3y+6 = 8+5y$) on paper and then only enter the final answer (e.g., $y = -1/4$) into the on-line test form. The *term identification* questions are to identify variable and constant terms in a given expression (e.g., $3 = 4 - 5b$). There are six term-identification questions, which are implemented as multiple-choice questions with six or seven choices. The *what-to-do-next* questions are to identify an appropriate next step for a given equation. There are three what-to-do-next questions, are implemented as multiple-choice questions with four choices. The *equivalent expression* questions are to find an expression that is equivalent to a given expression (e.g., $4x+3$). There are two equivalent-expression questions, which are implemented as multiple-choice questions with five choices. The *error identification* questions are to identify the incorrect step in a given worked-out example of equation solving. The participants are also asked to provide a reason why the step is incorrect in a text response. An error-identification question is scored as correct when the incorrect step is correctly selected and the corresponding reason is correctly provided. There are five error-identification questions with four to six steps.

4.3 Results

This section shows the participants' learning outcomes, the analysis of the tutoring activities, and a qualitative analysis of the participants' think aloud protocols, which were recorded during the tutoring sessions.

4.3.1 Overall Learning Gain

We first compared the overall test scores, which were computed as a percent of correct answers to the total number of question items on the test. There was no main effect on the test (pre- vs. post-) for the overall test scores – average 0.58 on pre-test and 0.61 on post-test (paired-t=2.36, p=0.29). There was, however, a main effect found on the test for the equation solving (the average number of equations solved correctly increased from 1.5 out of 6 for pre-test to 2.5 for post-test; paired-t=2.36, p=0.03) and for the error identification test items (average of 1.38 out of 5 correct on pre-test and 2.63 correct on post-test; paired-t=2.36, p=0.01).

After tutoring SimStudent, the participants had improved their skills with solving equations and identifying errors in given solutions, although their conceptual understanding related to equation solving (i.e., the scores on the term identification and equivalent expressions test items) did not improve significantly.

4.3.2 Students Activities

In addition to the test scores, we have analyzed the activity logs recorded during the sessions. At the beginning of the experiment, there was a technical issue in logging and we excluded the first five participants from the activity analysis.

On average, the participants spent 70.0 minutes tutoring SimStudent. On average, the participants posed 15 problems to SimStudent. Five out of six participants reviewed examples an average of 7.8 times (counted as the number of times they switched the examples in the tutoring interface). Given that most of the participants did not actually know how to solve equations, these results show effectiveness of the LBT environment.

SimStudent requested hints 31.8 times on average during a single tutoring session. SimStudent applied rules and asked for their correctness 79.5 times on average. Finally, the participants quizzed SimStudent 4.3 times on average. In average there were 1.6 interactions per minutes during the tutoring sessions, which indicates that the participants were actively involved in the LBT environment.

4.3.3 Protocol Analysis

To see differences in tutoring activities among the students who improved their performance in equation solving and those who did not, we performed a protocol analysis with the videos taken during the tutoring sessions. We divided the students into three categories: those who showed significant improvement on the *equation solving* test-items (SI in **Table 1**), those who showed moderate improvement (not included in

Table 1), and those who showed minimal improvement (MI). The number of the equation solving test-items correctly solved by SI and MI students are shown in **Table 1**. Recall that there were six equation-solving items on each of the tests.

Table 1. Number of correctly solved equation-solving test items. There were six equation-solving questions.

	Pre-test	Post-test	Category
Student A	0	3	SI
Student B	1	3	SI
Student C	0	0	MI
Student D	1	1	MI

It turned out that the SI students used equations in the examples and quiz items for tutoring more often than the MI students. *The SI students often copied those equations to tutor SimStudent, hence more likely tutored SimStudent correctly.* On the other hand, the MI students tended to make equations by themselves and failed to solve them correctly. One particularly interesting finding is that *being able to pose equations for tutoring is one task, but being able to solve them is another.* When making a new problem, one of the MI students always started with a number in his mind and some arithmetic to make another number and then performed those operations to construct an equation. For example, he said, "*I'll start with 4, that is an x. If I multiply it with 3, I get 12. I'll add 5, which is 17. So, 3x+5 = 17. This is the equation.*" However, he could not solve equations by reverse engineering them when he did not know the "starting" place.

Another interesting comparison is that *the SI students went back and forth between examples and the Curriculum Browser contents when they got stuck more often than the MI students did.* On the other hand, the MI students did not seem to learn much from the examples and the contents of the Curriculum Browser. The SI students also tended to pose the *exact same problems* used in the Quiz and examples to tutor SimStudent, so that students could at least show SimStudent what to do next without getting stuck.

5 Discussion

5.1 Learning by Teaching SimStudent

Overall, the students in the evaluation study did improve their skills in equation solving after tutoring SimStudent for about 70 min in average. A purpose of the evaluation study was to see if the students learn by teaching SimStudent at all, and so we did not compare learning by teaching with other existing interventions. We plan to conduct a further study to compare learning by teaching with learning by being tutored, in which an existing Algebra I Cognitive Tutor will be used for the control condition.

5.2 Low Proficiency Students Do Not Learn from Examples

The protocol analysis often showed that the participants with low proficiency on equation solving often got stuck when providing a hint in response to SimStudent's request for what to do next. It is particularly interesting to see that participants could pose a problem for tutoring, but could not solve it (as mentioned in 4.3.3).

The current LBT environment is designed to encourage students to ask a classroom teacher or consult a textbook when they get stuck. The learning environment also has the Curriculum Browser and example problems. However, it turned out that these supplemental materials are not enough for some of the low proficiency participants. In particular, these participants apparently needed more direct instruction (as opposed to learning from worked-out examples) on how to solve equations.

5.3 How Would SimStudent's Prior Knowledge Affect Tutor Learning?

The current evaluation study used a version of SimStudent that starts with a "tabula rasa." Namely, it does not know anything about equation solving. Therefore, the students must start with teaching very basic equations (i.e., one-step equations), which forces more time for tutoring. It would be worth investigating how the difference in SimStudent's prior knowledge affects the tutor's learning outcome. A related issue is has to do with the *quality* of SimStudent's prior knowledge. A prior study shows that differences in the quality of the prior knowledge affects SimStudent's learning in both speed and the types of errors made on the test [20], which would also affect the tutor learning.

6 Conclusion

In this paper, we presented an on-line, game-like learning environment where students learn algebra equations by teaching a computer agent, called SimStudent. A pilot study showed that the students did improve their performance on equation solving by tutoring SimStudent.

The study did not confirm that students improved their conceptual understanding by teaching. It is an important open question how we could help students learn such conceptual knowledge by teaching. We plan to conduct a series of studies in actual classroom settings, including a self-explanation study where SimStudent will ask the student to provide justifications for the student's tutoring activities. Such self-explanation might facilitate conceptual understanding during teaching.

In the current study, we only focus of equation solving. Both the architecture of the LBT environment and the learning algorithm of SimStudent are domain generic. Thus, we can apply the proposed framework to other domains to study a generality of the tutor learning effect.

References

1. Roscoe, R.D., Chi, M.: Tutor learning: the role of explaining and responding to questions. Instructional Science 36(4), 321–350 (2008)
2. Matsuda, N., Cohen, W.W., Koedinger, K.R.: Applying Programming by Demonstration in an Intelligent Authoring Tool for Cognitive Tutors. In: AAAI Workshop on Human Comprehensible Machine Learning (Technical Report WS-05-04), pp. 1–8. AAAU Association, Menlo Park (2005)
3. Cohen, P.A., Kulik, J.A., Kulik, C.I.C.: Education outcomes of tutoring: A meta-analysis of findings. American Educational Research Journal 19(2), 237–248 (1982)

4. Palincsar, A.S., Brown, A.L.: Reciprocal teaching of comprehension-fostering and comprehension-monitoring activities. Cognition and Instruction 1(2), 117–175 (1984)
5. Bargh, J.A., Schul, Y.: On the cognitive benefits of teaching. Journal of Educational Psychology 72(5), 593–604 (1980)
6. Annis, L.F.: The processes and effects of peer tutoring. Human Learning 2(1), 39–47 (1983)
7. Morgan, R.F., Toy, T.B.: Learning by teaching: A student-to-student compensatory tutoring program in a rural school system and its relevance to the educational cooperative. Psychological Record 20(2), 159–169 (1970)
8. Jacobson, J., et al.: Cross-Age Tutoring: A Literacy Improvement Approach for Struggling Adolescent Readers. Journal of Adolescent & Adult Literacy 44(6), 528–536 (2001)
9. Fuchs, L.S., et al.: Enhancing Students' Helping Behavior during Peer-Mediated Instruction with Conceptual Mathematical Explanations. Elementary School Journal 97(3), 223–249 (1997)
10. Cook, S.B., et al.: Handicapped Students as Tutors. Journal of Special Education 19(4), 483–492 (1986)
11. VanLehn, K., Ohlsson, S., Nason, R.: Applications of simulated students: An exploration. Journal of Artificial Intelligence in Education 5(2), 135–175 (1994)
12. Chan, T.-W., Chou, C.-Y.: Exploring the Design of Computer Supports for Reciprocal Tutoring. International Journal of Artificial Intelligence in Education 8, 1–29 (1997)
13. Hietala, P., Niemirepo, T.: The competence of learning companion agents. International Journal of Artificial Intelligence in Education 9, 178–192 (1998)
14. Biswas, G., et al.: Learning by teaching: a new agent paradigm for educational software. Journal Applied Artificial Intelligence 19(3&4), 363–392 (2005)
15. Biswas, G., et al.: Incorporating self regulated learning techniques into learning by teaching environments. In: Proceedings of the 20th Annual Meeting of the Cognitive Science Society, Chicago, pp. 120–125 (2001)
16. Muggleton, S., de Raedt, L.: Inductive Logic Programming: Theory and methods. Journal of Logic Programming 19-20(Suppl. 1), 629–679 (1994)
17. Cypher, A. (ed.): Watch What I Do: Programming by Demonstration. MIT Press, Cambridge (1993)
18. Matsuda, N., et al.: Why Tutored Problem Solving may be better than Example Study: Theoretical Implications from a Simulated-Student Study. In: Woolf, B.P., Aïmeur, E., Nkambou, R., Lajoie, S. (eds.) ITS 2008. LNCS, vol. 5091, pp. 111–121. Springer, Heidelberg (2008)
19. Koedinger, K.R., et al.: An open repository and analysis tools for fine-grained, longitudinal learner data. In: Proceedings of the International Conference on Educational Data Mining (2008)
20. Matsuda, N., et al.: A Computational Model of How Learner Errors Arise from Weak Prior Knowledge. In: Taatgen, N., van Rijn, H. (eds.) Proceedings of the Annual Conference of the Cognitive Science Society, pp. 1288–1293. Cognitive Science Society, Austin (2009)

The Effect of Motivational Learning Companions on Low Achieving Students and Students with Disabilities

Beverly P. Woolf[1], Ivon Arroyo[1], Kasia Muldner[2], Winslow Burleson[2],
David G. Cooper[1], Robert Dolan[3], and Robert M. Christopherson[2]

[1] University of Massachussetts Amherst
{ivon,bev,dcooper}@cs.umass.edu
[2] Arizona State University
{winslow.burleson,Katarzyna.Muldner,
robert.christopherson}@asu.edu
[3] Pearson Education
Bob.Dolan@Pearson.com

Abstract. We report the results of a randomized controlled evaluation of the effectiveness of pedagogical agents as providers of affective feedback. These digital learning companions were embedded in an intelligent tutoring system for mathematics, and were used by approximately one hundred students in two public high schools. Students in the control group did not receive the learning companions. Results indicate that low-achieving students—one third of whom have learning disabilities—had higher affective needs than their higher-achieving peers; they initially considered math problem-solving more frustrating, less exciting, and felt more anxious when solving math problems. However, after they interacted with affective pedagogical agents, low-achieving students improved their affective outcomes, e.g., reported reduced frustration and anxiety.

Keywords: Affective feedback, pedagogical agents, special needs populations.

1 Introduction

Effective teachers regularly address students' emotional states and social backgrounds [1]. If tutoring systems are to interact naturally and supportively with students, they need to provide an environment that recognizes affect and expresses socio-emotional competence to address affective challenges and fluctuations in individual affective states. In recent years, researchers have made significant improvements in modeling students' affect [2, 3, 4, 19]. While progress has been made, very little empirical research has been conducted on how digital learning environments should respond to individual students' affect and how differences among students impact this process; yet for exceptions, see [5, 6].

Within digital learning environments, animated pedagogical characters have the potential to support students by engaging them through social interaction. Up until now, the use of pedagogical agents has mainly focused on the cognitive rather than affective aspects of learning [7]. While some effort has been made to create affective agents [8, 9], evaluation of their impact in schools is still preliminary.

Here, we report on an evaluation of pedagogical agents with about 100 students in two rural, public high schools in the northeastern U.S. We focus on the impact of affective learning companions on low achieving students (including ones with disabilities) and begin with a description of how such students need affective support when learning math. We then describe the test bed tutoring system, the learning companions, and the experiments. We present the results and conclude with a discussion of implications for intelligent tutoring systems.

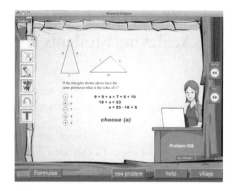

Fig. 1. The Wayang Tutor with Jane, the female affective learning companion

2 Learning Disability and Low Achieving Students: Affective Needs

Classroom interventions (e.g., providing extra time on tasks, peer tutoring) that are effective for students with learning disabilities (LD) are difficult or impossible to sustain in classrooms without additional instructional support, something that schools are increasingly unable to provide due to budgetary constraints. Currently, students with learning disabilities who require extra resources comprise 13% percent of students in USA [10]. To the extent that these students are not being educated to their full potential, there is a large negative impact not only in the lives of these students but on society at large.

The under-achievement of students with LD in math does appear to have a biological basis, and there is evidence that many of these students have difficulties with working memory, executive control and procedural knowledge [11, 12]. As a result, many students with LD may persist in using counting strategies (e.g., finger counting) long after their typically achieving peers have switched to retrieving answers from memory [13], taking longer to solve math problems and performing poorly in math class and high-stake tests [14]. Students with LD develop more negative feelings towards math, choose less advanced math classes in high school and are later under-prepared for science and math careers. LD is a complex multi-factor problem and most educational institutions do not have the tools needed to provide cost-effective instruction tailored to each individual.

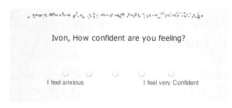

Fig. 2. Student's emotion self-reports within the tutor

Since low achieving students (both with and without disabilities) struggle with math, our conjecture was that *all* low achievers could require additional affective support. Thus, the first goal of the current study was to examine the affective needs of both low achieving and learning disability students in our data (15% of subjects). For the purpose of this paper we did not separately analyze differences between low-achieving and learning disability, because as a starting point we wanted to analyze what kind of support all low achievers require.

Table 1. Affective self-reports of high-achieving vs. low-achieving students prior to tutoring

Affective Criterion	Means, standard deviations and between-subjects test Low-achieving: N=64; High-achieving: N=43
Self-concept of math ability (in comparison to other students, other subjects, 3 items)	Low-achieving: M=3.2 SD=1.1 High-achieving: M=4.1 SD=1.0 ***$F(106,1)=18.2, p=.000$
How confident do you feel when solving math problems?	Low-achieving: M=3.1 SD=1.3 High-achieving: M=4.0 SD=1.3 ***$F(105,1)=11.5, p=.001$
How frustrating is it to solve math problems?	Low-achieving: M=3.6 SD=1.2 High-achieving: M=3.0 SD=1.1 ** $F(106,1)=7.6, p=.007$
How exciting is it to solve math problems?	Low-achieving: M=2.2 SD=1.2 High-achieving: M=2.7 SD=1.4 *$F(106,1)=3.64, p=0.05$

Data was collected and mean differences analyzed from a series of affective pretest questions given to students before tutoring, Table 1. The pretest covered general attitudes towards math and learning, such as likes/dislikes of math, how much was math valued as important, and how students felt when they solved math problems (anxiety, confidence, frustration, boredom, excitement). Low-achieving students were defined as those who scored lower than median grade on the math pretest. One third of these low-achieving students had been previously diagnosed as having a specific learning disability in math or reading and had an Individualized Education Plan (IEP), a document that identifies a student's academic, physical, social and emotional needs. Most students with IEPs (95%) are part of this low-achieving group. Table 1 shows that low-achieving students disliked math more, valued it less, had worse perception of their math ability, and reported feeling worse when solving math problems. We now present our test bed application, Wayang Outpost.

3 The Testbed Tutoring System: Wayang Outpost

Wayang Outpost ("Wayang") is an intelligent tutor that helps students prepare for standardized tests that assess general mathematic skills, see Figure 1 [16]. Problems are presented one at a time; each problem consists of the problem statement with four or five solution options directly below it. Students select an answer and the tutor provides immediate visual feedback by coloring the answer green or red, for correct or incorrect respectively. Prior to or after selecting an answer, a student may ask for a hint, which Wayang displays in progression from general suggestions to the correct answer. In addition to this domain-based help, Wayang includes a wide range of meta-cognitive and affective support, delivered by learning companions; agents designed to act like peers who care about a student's progress, and offer support and advice on how to improve student learning strategies. Wayang includes gendered and ethnically different companions allowing us to explore how the gender and the ethnicity of the companion influences outcomes (e.g., learning, attitudes) [17]. The learning companions' interventions are tailored to a given student's needs according to Wayang's affect and effort models embedded in the tutor. The *effort* model provides information on the degree of effort a student invests in generating a problem solution. A linear regression *affect* model is used to assess a student's emotional state; this model is derived from data obtained from a series of studies described in [17, 18].

4 Affective Support Delivered by Wayang's Learning Companions

Learning companions deliver approximately 50 different messages emphasizing the malleability of intelligence and the importance of effort and perseverance (Table 2). The messages also include meta-cognitive help related to effective strategies for solving math problems and effective use of Wayang's tools. Ultimately, the interventions will be tailored according to Wayang's affective student model. However, we are currently still validating the models and algorithms for deciding which intervention to provide and when, and thus relied on the effort model only to assign messages for this experiment. This section describes these interventions including *attribution* and *strategy* training, as well as *effort affirmation*.

The affective support provided by Wayang in this experiment was to train students motivationally, by emphasizing the importance of effort and perseverance and the idea that intelligence is malleable instead of a fixed trait [19]. The characters provided this support by responding to the effort exerted by students rather than to the student's emotions. Characters were either unimpressed when effort was not exerted, or simply ignored that the student solved the problem. They also offered praise to students who exerted effort while problem-solving, even if their answers were wrong, highlighting that the goal is to lessen the importance of performance in favor of learning.

The characters were highly positive, in the sense that they displayed encouraging gestures (e.g., excitement and confidence). In a separate completed study, which is beyond the scope of this paper, characters behaviorally mimicked student self-reported emotions, which is a form of a non-verbal empathetic response (e.g., learning companions appeared excited in response to student excitement, see Figure 2, right). In this experiment reported here, the companions occasionally expressed non-verbal behaviors of positive valence only, the underlying goal being to make them appear life-like and engaged, and to impart some of their enthusiasm to the students. The next three types of interventions described are verbal messages tailored according to Wayang's modeling of students' effort.

Table 2. Companions provided several responses based on student effort

Type	Sample message
Attribution (General)	I found out that people have myths about math, thinking that only some people are good in math. Truth is we can all be good in math if we try.
Attribution (Effort)	Keep in mind that when we are struggling with a new skill we are learning and becoming smarter!
Attribution (No Effort)	We will learn new skills only if we are persistent. If we are very stuck, let's call the teacher, or ask for a hint!
Attribution (Incorrect)	When we realize we don't know why the answer was wrong, it helps us understand better what we need to practice.
Effort Affirmation (Correct No-effort)	That was too easy for you. Let's hope the next one is more challenging so that we can learn something.
Effort Affirmation (Correct Effort)	Good job! See how taking your time to work through these questions can make you get the right answer?
Strategic (Incorrect)	Are we using a correct strategy to solve this? What are the different steps we have to carry out to solve this one?
Strategic (Correct)	We are making progress. Can you think of what we have learned in the last 5 problems?

Attribution Interventions. Attribution theory proposes that students' motivation to learn is directly rooted in their beliefs about why they succeed or fail at tasks [20]. If students can be taught to alter these beliefs, for instance to understand that failure is the result of a lack of effort instead of a lack of ability, then their motivation to learn and learning outcomes can be significantly improved [21]. For example:

- *General attribution* messages encourage students to reflect about myths and math learning in general;
- *Effort attribution* messages reinforce that effort is a necessary by-product of learning, and are specially tailored to situations where students are investing effort but are struggling;
- *No-effort attribution* messages are more emphatic than the ones just mentioned; they are designed to help students realize that effort is necessary to learn, and generated when students are not investing effort;
- *Incorrect attribution* interventions are generated to motivate students after they provide an incorrect response, by re-formulating how they perceive errors.

Fig. 3. Jane, the female affective learning companion, and Jake, the male affective learning companion

Effort-Affirmation Interventions. In contrast to the effort-attribution messages described above, which aim to change students' attitude towards effort during problem solving and are generated before the student actually starts problem solving, the *effort-affirmation* interventions acknowledge effort after students obtain a correct solution (see Table 2 for examples). These interventions include:

- *Correct no-effort interventions* are generated after a student invests no effort but obtains a correct solution, to make students realize that praise is not appropriate;
- *Correct-effort affirmations* are generated after a student both invests effort and obtains the correct solution, to acknowledge the student's effort.

Strategic Interventions. The final type of intervention we embedded into Wayang focuses on meta-cognitive strategies, with the goal of both making students more effective problem solvers and motivating them for learning in general.

- *Incorrect strategic* messages are generated when students are not succeeding at problem solving, to motivate them to change their general problem-solving strategy, i.e., think about why they are not succeeding
- *Correct strategic* messages are generated when students are succeeding at problem solving, to encourage them to evaluate their progress.

5 The User Study

The user study was designed to quantitatively evaluate the impact of learning companions on affective and cognitive outcomes for all students. Of the 108 ninth- and tenth-grade students, two thirds (72 students) received a learning companion of a random gender, and one third (36 students) did not receive a learning companion. We obtained complete data, surveys and posttest, for about 95 students.

At the beginning of the study, students received a math pretest and a survey that assessed general attitudes towards math, described in Section 2. The following day and for the next three days, students used Wayang instead of their regular math class. Every five minutes as well as after completing a problem, students were asked to provide information on one of the four target emotions (e.g. "How frustrated do you feel?"), see Fig. 2. At the start of each session, the learning companions introduced themselves; when students needed help during problem solving, the companions reminded students about the "help button" that provided multimedia-based support in the form of animations with sound. Characters spoke aloud the messages described in the previous section, occasionally at the beginning of a new problem and/or after the student submitted a response to a problem. Students in the control group (no-LC) had access to the same cognitive support (e.g., hints, problems read aloud), but no companions and no affective support.

After students used Wayang for three days, they took a math posttest, and answered the same questionnaire as taken prior to using the tutor. In addition, the questionnaire included five questions about student perception of the tutor (*Did you learn? Was the tutor concerned about your learning? Helpful?*). We also logged student behavior with the tutor, such as success at problem solving, gaming (abuse of hints), use of tools, and help. Students' emotions within the tutor were recorded, as well as when students muted the characters (mute button), and whether they abused help by rapidly reaching the bottom-out hint, or quick guessed (i.e., rapidly selected options until they hit the correct answer).

Table 3. General Post-Tutor Outcomes: Main and interaction effects for Affective and Cognitive Outcomes. Key: H-A — High-Achieving students; L-A – Low-Achieving students; LC — Learning Companions; ∅ — No significant difference across conditions; ∅ MathAbility — No significant MathAbility effect or MathAbilityxLC interaction effect.

	Overall Effect	**Differential Effect (High vs. Low)**
Learning	Students learned in all conditions (paired samples t-test, *t(99) = 2.4, p = .019), but no significant effect for LC	L-A students *improved* more than H-A in all conditions *F(99,1) = 5.3, p = 0.02
Perceptions of Wayang	∅	When LCs are absent, H-A students *perceive* Wayang better than L-A. LCxMathAbility **F(96,1)=6.84, p = 0.01
Liking of Mathematics	Students receiving Jane demonstrated higher math liking. *F(93,2) = 3.7, p = 0.03	∅ MathAbility
Math Ability Self-concept	Students receiving Jane showed higher posttest *self-concept*. *F(94,2) =3.6, p = 0.03	When LCs are absent, H-A students had *higher increase* in *self-concept* than L-A. LCxMathAbility: ⁺F(94,3) = 2.3, p = .08

6 Results, Discussion and Conclusion

We carried out an Analyses of Covariance (ANCOVA) for each affective and behavioral dependent variable (post-tutor and within tutor) as shown in Tables 3-4. In particular, Table 3 shows the results for general post-tutor outcomes, while Table 4 presents the results for affect-related and other variables measured within the tutor. As far as emotions, we include findings both on students' self-reported emotions within the tutor, and post test differences in survey responses (note that in Table 1, we reported how students were feeling *before* they interacted with Wayang, while Tables 3 and 4 look at how interaction with Wayang influenced these feelings). Our covariates consisted of the corresponding pretest baseline variable (e.g., we accounted for students' pretest baseline confidence when analyzing confidence while using the tutor or afterwards). Independent variables corresponded to *condition*, specifically learning companion (LC) present vs. absent and LC type (Female (Jane) vs. Male (Jake) vs. no-LC). We analyzed both main effects and interactions for achievement level (MathAbility) and conditions over all student data (see second and last columns of Tables 3 and 4). In addition, because of the special affective needs of low-achieving students, we repeated the ANCOVAs for the low-achieving student population only, for a "targeted effect," Table 4 (third column).

Results showed that all students demonstrated math learning after working with Wayang, with low-achieving students learning more than high achieving students across all conditions (Table 3). Learning companions did not affect student learning directly, but successfully induced positive student behaviors that have been correlated to learning, specifically, students spent more time on hinted problems [15] (see "Productive behavior" row, Table 4). The beneficial effect of learning companions was mainly on affective outcomes, particularly on confidence (see "Confidence" row, Table 4). Low-achieving students who received learning companions improved their confidence while using the tutor and at posttest time more than students with no learning companions, while their counterparts in the no-LC condition tended to decrease their confidence (Figure 4).

Table 4. Emotions within and after using the tutor. Key: H-A—High Achieving; L-A –Low Achieving; Ø —No significant difference across conditions; **ØMathAbilityxLC** —No significant MathAbilityxLC interaction effect/MathAbility effect; **LC**–Learning Companions.

	Overall Effect	**Targeted Effect on Low Achieving Students**	**Differential Effect (High vs. Low)**
Frustration	Less *overall frustration* self-reported with Jane **F(213,2) = 6.1, p = .003	L-A students *have lower post-tutor frustration* in the LC condition than no-LC. +F(58,1) = 3.4, p=.07	When LCs are absent, L-A students have higher post-tutor *frustration than* H-A. LC x MathAbility +F(93,3) = 2.4, p = .08
Confidence	Higher overall confidence reported in the LC condition *F(204,1)=5.3, p = .02	L-A students in the LC condition *have higher confidence.* Within Tutor LC effect: **F(108,1)= 7.3, p = .008 Post-tutor LC effect: *F(56,1)= 3.8, p = .05 and	H-A students *have higher confidence* than L-A students (but esp. when companions are absent) MathAbility effect within: *F(204,1) = 4.1, p = .05 MathAbility effect posttutor: *F(91,1) = 5.8, p = .02
Interest	Students in the *LC condition* have higher overall interest at posttest time. LC main effect: +F(94,1) = 3.4, p = .07	L-A students in the LC condition report marginally more post-tutor interest. LC main effect: +F(58,1) = 2.7, p =.1	L-A students report *more boredom* than H-A students across all conditions MathAbility effect +F(219,1) = 2.9, p = .09
Excitement	Ø	Ø	H-A students report *less excitement* when LCs are absent, no difference when LC is present. MathAbilityxLC within: *F(200,1) = 5.2, p=.02
Productive behavior: time in hint problems	Ø	L-A students spend more time in hinted problems with LCs. +F(67, 1) = 2.9, p = 0.095	Ø MathAbility
Gaming behavior: Quick–guess, help abuse	Ø	Ø	L-A students quick-guess more than do H-A students MathAbility effect: **F(109,1) = 5.9, p = 0.017 No MathAbilityxLC interaction effect

Learning companions had a positive impact for all students on some measures, e.g., all students receiving the female companion improved math liking and self-concept of their math ability. This was not the case for the male learning companion, which was muted by students twice as much as Jane, making it too similar to the control version. Some differential effects (Table 4, last column) suggest that learning comp-anions are essential for low-achieving students' affect. When LCs are present, low achieving students report positive affect

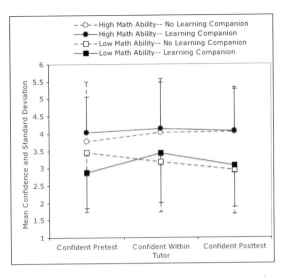

Fig. 4. Low and high achievement students' change in reported confidence during problem solving

nearly as much as do high-achieving students and it is only when learning companions are absent that a large gap exists between these student groups. This affective gap reduces when learning companions are present. This result is found for several outcome variables: self-concept, perceptions of learning, frustration, excitement.

However, learning companions did not manage to change some negative feelings and behaviors: low-achieving students did quick-guess more across all conditions than high achieving students; low achievement students reported less interest than high achieving in all conditions. We did see an increase in productive behaviors that lead to learning [16], low-achieving students spent more time in problems where help is requested (i.e. students pay more attention to hints). General implications for tutors include the possibility of defining features and tool sets that support low-achieving students differentially from the rest. In future studies we will analyze separately the impact of companions on a large population of students with learning disabilities, compared to students without learning disabilities.

Acknowledgement. This research was funded by three grants: (1) US Dept of Ed (IES) *Using Intelligent Tutoring and Universal Design To Customize The Mathematics Curriculum* to Woolf (PI), Arroyo and Maloy; (2) NSF #0734060, HRD GSE/RES, *What Kind of Math Software Works For Girls?* Arroyo (PI), Royer and Woolf; and (3) NSF #0705554, IIS/HCC *Affective Learning Companions: Modeling and Supporting Emotion During Teaching*, Woolf, Burleson (PIs) Arroyo, Barto, and Fisher. Any opinions, findings, conclusions or recommendations expressed in this material are those of the authors and do not necessarily reflect the views of the funding agencies.

References

1. Rosiek, J.: Emotional Scaffolding: An Exploration of Teacher Knowledge at the Intersection of Student Emotion and the Subject Matter. J. Teacher Education 54(5), 399–412 (2003)
2. D'Mello, S., Graesser, A.: Mind and Body: Dialogue and Posture for Affect Detection in Learning Environments. In: Frontiers in Artificial Intelligence and Applications (2007)
3. McQuiggan, S., Lester, J.: Diagnosing Self-Efficacy in Intelligent Tutoring Systems: An Empirical Study. In: Ikeda, M., Ashley, K.D., Chan, T.-W. (eds.) ITS 2006. LNCS, vol. 4053, pp. 565–574. Springer, Heidelberg (2006)
4. Graesser, A., Chipman, P., King, B., McDaniel, B., D'Mello, S.: Emotions and Learning with AutoTutor. In: Luckin, R., Koedinger, K., Greer, J. (eds.) 13th International Conference on Artificial Intelligence in Education, pp. 569–571. IOS Press, Amsterdam (2007)
5. Arroyo, I., Cooper, D.G., Burleson, W., Woolf, B.P., Muldner, K., Christopherson, R.: Emotion Sensors Go To School. In: 14th International Conference on Artificial Intelligence and Education, pp. 17–24. IOS Press, Amsterdam (2009)
6. Burleson, W.: Affective Learning Companions: Strategies for Empathetic Agents with Real-Time Multimodal Affective Sensing to Foster Meta-Cognitive Approaches to Learning, Motivation, and Perseverance. MIT PhD dissertation (2006)
7. Moreno, R., Mayer, R., Lester, J.: Life-Like Pedagogical Agents in Constructivist Multimedia Environments: Cognitive Consequences of Their Interaction. In: ED-MEDIA 2000, pp. 741–746 (2000)
8. Robison, J., McQuiggan, S., Lester, J.: Evaluating the Consequences of Affective Feedback in Intelligent Tutoring Systems. In: Proc. Inter. Conf. on Affective Computing & Intelligent Interaction, Amsterdam, pp. 37–42 (2009)
9. Lester, J.C., Towns, S.G., FitzGerald, P.: Achieving Affective Impact: Visual Emotive Communication in Lifelike Pedagogical Agents. International Journal of Artificial Intelligence in Education 10(3-4), 278–291 (1999)
10. National Center for Educational Statistics: Digest of Educational Statistics, ch. 2 (2009), http://nces.ed.gov/fastfacts/display.asp?id=64
11. Geary, D.C., Hoard, M.K., Byrd-Craven, J., Nugent, L., Numtee, C.: Cognitive Mechanisms Underlying Achievement Deficits in Children With Mathematical Learning Disability. Child Development 78(4), 1343–1359 (2007)
12. Geary, D., Hoard, M., Hamson, C.: Numerical and arithmetical cognition: Patterns of functions and deficits in children at risk for a mathematical disability. J. Experimental Child Psychology 74, 213–239 (1999)
13. Fletcher, J., Lyon, G., Fuchs, L., Barnes, M.: Learning disabilities: From identification to intervention. The Guilford Press, New York (2007)
14. Olson, L.: State Test Programs Mushroom as NCLB Mandate Kicks, Education Week (2005)
15. Arroyo, I., Woolf, B.P.: Inferring learning and attitudes from a Bayesian Network of log file data. In: AIED 2005, pp. 33–40. IOS Press, Amsterdam (2005)
16. Arroyo, I., Beal, C., Murray, T., Walles, R., Woolf, B.: Web-based Intelligent Multi-media Tutoring for High Stakes Achievement Tests. In: Lester, J.C., Vicari, R.M., Paraguaçu, F. (eds.) ITS 2004. LNCS, vol. 3220, pp. 468–477. Springer, Heidelberg (2004)

17. Arroyo, I., Woolf, B.P., Royer, J.M., Tai, M.: Affective Gendered Learning Companions. In: 14th Conference on Artificial Intelligence and Education, pp. 41–48. IOS Press, Amsterdam (2009)
18. Cooper, D., Arroyo, I., Woolf, B.P., Muldner, K., Burleson, W., Christopherson, R.: Sensors Model Student Self Concept in the Classroom. In: User Modeling and Adaptive Personalization (2009)
19. Dweck, C.: Messages that motivate: How praise molds students' beliefs, motivation, and performance (In Surprising Ways). In: Aronson, J. (ed.) Improving academic achievement. Academic Press, New York (2002)
20. Weiner, B.: Attribution Theory, Achievement Motivation, and the Educational Process. Review of Educational Research 42(2), 203–215 (1972)
21. Robertson, J.: Is Attribution Training a Worthwhile Classroom Intervention For K–12 Students with Learning Difficulties? J. Education Psychology Review 12(1), 111–134 (2000)

Use of a Medical ITS Improves Reporting Performance among Community Pathologists

Rebecca Crowley[1,2], Dana Grzybicki[3], Elizabeth Legowski[1],
Lynn Wagner[4], Melissa Castine[1], Olga Medvedeva[1],
Eugene Tseytlin[1], Drazen Jukic[2,5], and Stephen Raab[4]

[1] Department of Biomedical Informatics, University of Pittsburgh School of Medicine
[2] Department of Pathology, University of Pittsburgh School of Medicine
[3] Rocky Vista University College of Osteopathic Medicine
[4] Department of Pathology, University of Colorado at Denver
[5] Department of Dermatology, University of Pittsburgh School of Medicine

Abstract. In previous work, we have developed an advanced medical training system based on the cognitive ITS paradigm. In multiple laboratory studies, we showed a marked performance improvement among physicians in training. We now report on the evaluation of our tutoring system as a potential patient safety intervention among practicing community physicians. Fourteen community pathologists were matched for years of practice, and then randomly assigned to intervention or control groups. Participants in the intervention group used the tutoring system for a total of 4-19 (mean 11.5) hours over 1-4 (mean 3.1) sessions over a period of 37-138 (mean 86) days. Participants in the control group studied standard continuing medical education (CME) materials for a similar amount of time over a similar interval. All participants took glass slide pre-tests and post-tests, and virtual slide interval tests. Participants in the intervention group showed a significant improvement in the completeness of their surgical pathology reports when compared to the control group (p<.001, RM-ANOVA). There was no significant gain for diagnostic reasoning, likely due to the already high performance levels and small number of participants.

Keywords: Intelligent Tutoring Systems, Intelligent Medical Training Systems, Evaluation.

1 Introduction

Intelligent Tutoring Systems (ITS) have great potential in medical education [1], but there are few ITS evaluated or deployed in clinical settings. Some innovative and well known systems such as BioWorld [2] and Rashi [3] use clinical scenarios as a means of teaching scientific reasoning to high school and college students. CIRCSIM tutor [4] pioneered the combination of simulation and natural language as a means of training, teaching medical students to reason about pathophysiology. Other systems have targeted basic procedural skills such as cardiac life support [5], [6] that are typically taught to medical students and residents. Although seminal early systems such as GUIDON [7] and NEOMYCIN [8] tackled the difficult task of teaching diagnosis, there are few other systems in this area. Furthermore, ITS aimed at physicians in practice environments are essentially non-existent.

In previous work, we have developed such an advanced medical training system in Surgical Pathology [9], [10], [11] based on the Cognitive Tutor paradigm. In previous evaluations, we have shown learning gains in diagnostic accuracy [12], reporting completeness and correctness [13], and metacognition [14]. Prior studies have focused exclusively on resident and fellow physicians, who are still completing their specialty training. Furthermore, all of our previous studies have been performed in the laboratory, where we can carefully control for potentially confounding variables. The long-term goal of our research program remains the effective use of our systems to improve patient care and patient outcomes. An important first step is to show that the tutoring system can impact performance of practicing physicians in a practice environment subject to the same stressors and variability that would be encountered in the workplace.

For this evaluation, we selected an area of the domain with known clinical importance and need for patient safety interventions. Cancer of the skin is the most common of all cancers, and Melanoma accounts for about 4% of skin cancer cases but causes a large majority of skin cancer deaths. The American Cancer Society estimates that the number of new Melanomas diagnosed in the United States is increasing, and about 7,910 people were expected to die of Melanoma during 2006. Since 1973, the mortality rate for Melanoma has increased by 50% [15]. False negative diagnostic errors for Melanoma are the most frequent diagnostic errors for which patients pursue litigation against pathologists, and previous studies have estimated that approximately 10% of all pigmented lesions examined are associated with a clinically significant false negative error related to Melanoma, resulting in significant harm to patients [16].

2 System Description

The ITS used in this study was based on the Visual Classification Tutoring system that we have previously described. The system contains both a diagnostic tutoring component (Figure 1), and a reporting tutoring component (Figure 2).

Both components followed the cognitive tutor paradigm, providing immediate feedback using context-specific help and error messages on intermediate steps. In the diagnostic tutoring component, participants used a virtual microscope and provided diagnoses and histopathologic features that supported their diagnoses. Both tasks were accomplished using tree-based menu selection. In the reporting tutoring component, participants entered other key information as free text and also performed certain procedural tasks related to determining prognostic factors. These included, for example, measuring the deepest tumor to determine the Breslow depth (pictured in Fig. 2), and assessing the status of the margins. The ITS used a combination of information from the viewer and from text entered by the participant to determine the accuracy of intermediate steps. Natural language processing methods were used to identify the key variables in participant entered text, as previously described [11], [13].

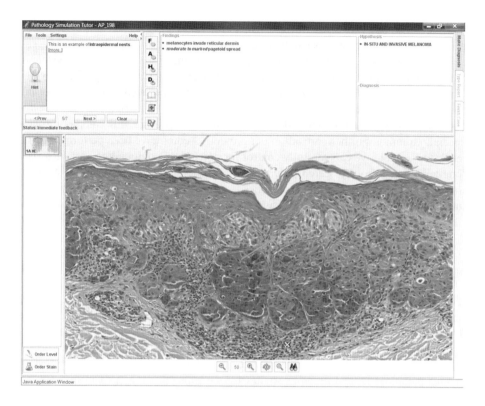

Fig. 1. Diagnostic Tutoring Component

The current ITS differed in four key ways from systems that we have previously evaluated: (1) the student model selected cases specifically for each individual based on performance across the initial case set, (2) the pedagogic model provided more leeway to these more expert participants than we typically provide to novices and intermediates. For example, the tutor allowed participants to skip intermediate steps as long as they arrived at the correct diagnosis, (3) each case could include multiple slides and multiple special stains that needed to be examined, and (4) after making a diagnosis, participants could ask for a consultation, which resulted in display of an expert consultant report on the case.

3 Methods

Institutional Review Board approval was obtained from both the University of Pittsburgh and the University of Colorado for use of human subjects. To minimize bias, the group that developed the tutoring system collaborated with an independent group of patient safety researchers (LW, SR, and DG) to carry out this summative evaluation. Both groups contributed to the overall design of the evaluation, with the tutoring system research group taking primary responsibility for the ITS intervention. The patient safety research team took primary responsibility for recruitment of subjects and informed consent, assignment of participants to intervention and control groups, study execution and monitoring of control subjects, development of a pool of cases for assessments, monitoring of the validation of assessments by an outside expert consultant, development of the continuing medical education (CME) materials that approximated the content taught by the tutoring system, and administration of the glass slide tests (GSTs). The tutoring system research group took primary responsibility for modifications to the existing ITS, development of the case set and other tutoring materials for the intervention group, assignment of the case sets for the virtual slide tests, training of the intervention groups on use of the tutor, and execution and monitoring of the intervention group. The two groups shared responsibility for scoring of assessments, data analysis and interpretation.

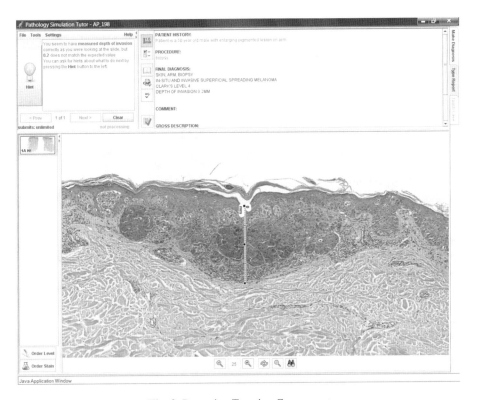

Fig. 2. Reporting Tutoring Component

3.1 Study Design

The overall design of the study is shown in Figure 3. We used a repeated measures, matched-group design. Baseline assessment included two pre-tests: (1) a glass slide test (GST), and (2) a virtual slide test (VST). Participants were given instructions to complete four learning sessions, each of which was followed by an interval VST. A VST post-test and GST post-test completed the study.

Fig. 3. Study Design

3.2 Participants

Participants were practicing community pathologists who were recruited by a combination of emails and phone calls made by the project Principal Investigator (DG). Because of the difficulty of recruiting participants (who were busy practicing physicians), the inherent variance in the population, and the small number of participants anticipated, we elected to match (yoke) participants in order to minimize any potential difference in existing expertise between the two groups. Participants were matched based on the following criteria: 1) years in post-training practice, 2) current average approximate number of surgical pathology cases examined per year, and 3) current average approximate number of pigmented lesion cases examined per year. Paired subjects were then randomly assigned to either intervention or control group.

3.3 Learning Sessions

After completing the glass and virtual pre-tests, participants were asked to self-schedule four learning sessions, followed by virtual slide tests, at a roughly one session per month interval. For each of four learning sessions, participants were asked to spend a total of 4 hours using the ITS (intervention group) or self-study learning materials (control group). It was recommended that each learning session consist of two 2-hour blocks within a day or two of each other.

3.3.1 Intervention Group
Participants in the intervention group were given a 1 hour training session on the tutoring system. Participants in this group used the tutoring system exclusively during their learning sessions.

3.3.2 Control Group
Participants in the control group used a set of pre-defined materials that included much of the information taught by the tutoring system. These materials included: (1) a textbook on diagnosis of melanocytic lesions (*Pathology of Melanocytic Nevi and Malignant Melanoma*, Barnhill, Piepform, Busam, eds. 2nd edition, Springer, 2004), (2) eleven journal articles: divided among four study sessions, and (3) a set of online case studies of melanocytic lesions (http://atlases.muni.cz/)

3.4 Assessments

Two types of assessments were used in this study. Glass slide tests were given before and after the entire set of learning sessions (GST pre and GST post), and were scored for diagnostic accuracy only. Virtual Slide tests were interval tests given before the first learning sessions (VST pre) and after each of the learning sessions (VST 1-3 and VST post). Virtual Slide Tests were scored for both diagnostic accuracy and for completeness of the written report. Glass slide tests were included in order to obtain assessments of diagnostic accuracy using a case examination method that closely mimics community pathologists' real life, day-to-day practice conditions (which primarily involves examination of glass slides by light microscopy).

3.4.1 Glass Slide Tests

Both pre-test and post-test glass slide tests consisted of 20 cases, each with one or more glass slides containing one or more melanocytic lesions of skin. Both tests contained a diagnostic spectrum of cases, but the pre-test and post-tests included different cases. For each glass slide test, the same packet of 20 cases was sequentially sent to each subject, which also contained standardized instructions for examining the cases and recording a final pathologic diagnosis for each case.

3.4.2 Virtual Slide Tests

Virtual Slide Tests were given using a web-based assessment system that provided a virtual slide viewer and text boxes for entering answers. The virtual slide viewer enabled exploration of a digitized glass slide. Each of the 4 virtual slide tests consisted of 8 cases. Each case included a virtual slide and clinical information. Participants were asked to provide a complete diagnostic report, including any relevant prognostic factors, such as status of the resection margins.

Four versions (forms) of the virtual slide test (tests A, B, C, and D) were developed. Each form contained an equivalent number of benign and malignant cases across difficulty levels. To minimize order effect, participants were given the forms in differing sequences. Virtual slide pre-tests used different forms for different participants. Whatever form a given participant took for the pretest was identical to the posttest. Thus, the four form sequences were: (1) A-B-C-D-A, (2) B-C-D-A-B, (3) C-D-A-B-C, (4) D-A-B-C-D.

3.4.3 Scoring of Glass and Virtual Slide Tests

Glass slide and virtual slide tests were both scored for diagnostic accuracy along three dimensions. Virtual slide tests were also scored for reporting completeness.

For diagnostic accuracy, all reports were scored for accuracy against a consensus reference standard developed by two expert dermatopathologists who have extensive experience with melanocytic lesions. Three levels of scoring were used, decreasing in level of specificity: (1) specific diagnosis – the answer provided by the participant was graded as correct only if it matched the exact diagnosis or a pre-determined synonym provided in the reference standard; (2) level of dysplasia – the answer provided by the participant was graded as correct if it matched the level (from a total of five levels) provided by the reference standard; (3) clinical management – the answer provided by the participant was graded as correct if it matched the clinical management guidance (from a total of four categories) provided by the reference standard. Diagnostic accuracy was recorded as a dichotomous nominal variable (correct/incorrect).

For reporting completeness, the features scored were abstracted from a widely used performance standard developed by the College of American Pathologists (CAP) protocol [17] for pathology reporting, the use of which is a requirement for accreditation of Cancer Centers by the American College of Surgeons Commission on Cancer. These features included: histological type, location, procedure, status of lateral and deep margins, ulceration, TNM stage, depth of invasion, tumor infiltrating lymphocytes, venous invasion, perineural invasion, tumor regression, mitotic index, Clark's level, growth phase, satellites, pigmentation, and solar elastosis. Greater weight was given to items that are required in the CAP protocol. The scoring rubric for each feature was developed in advance by one of the expert dermatopathologists. Points were assigned for presence of the feature (completeness) and for accuracy of the value (correctness). The final test score was calculated as the sum of all feature scores. Although we did evaluate the correctness of each feature in the report, we did not specifically probe for a value for each individual feature - participants were free to choose what to include.

3.5 Data Analysis

Diagnostic accuracy was analyzed using non-parametric tests. Report scores were analyzed by condition and test using Repeated Measures Analyses of Variance. All statistical tests were performed using SPSS v17 (SPSS, Inc., Chicago, IL).

4 Results

Because 6 of the original 15 participants dropped out, we were not able to make comparisons based on matched pairs. Instead, we compared between groups only.

4.1 Characteristics of the Participant Group

A total of 15 community pathologists were recruited to participate in the study, and 9 completed the entire set of activities. One individual took the GST pretest but completed no other activities and was replaced early on. Participants in the intervention group ranged from 1-22 years experience with a mean of 11 years, and participants in the control group ranged from 4-25 years experience, with a mean of 13 years. On average, participants in the intervention group signed out 4957 surgical specimens, of which 1370 were skin specimens. On average, participants in the control group signed out 5986 surgical specimens, of which 666 were skin specimens.

4.2 Characteristics of the Learning Sessions

The actual timing of learning sessions was highly variable. Table 1 shows mean and SD for intervals depicted in Figure 3. No systematic differences were identified between the groups.

Table 1. Intervals between VST (mean and SD in days)

Condition	Interval			
	A	B	C	D
Tutor	28.83 ± 6.79	35.80 ± 16.10	16.20 ± 10.21	16.40 ± 14.48
Control	44.83 ± 22.75	36.20 ± 16.22	36.25 ± 25.24	44.0 ± 32.07

4.3 Diagnostic Accuracy

Figure 4 shows results for diagnostic accuracy on both GST and VST using specific diagnosis (A), dysplasia level (B), and clinical management (C) rubrics. Participants in both groups start at a reasonably high level of diagnostic accuracy, and this is maintained across the learning sessions. There was no significant gain for either group, and no significant difference between groups.

4.4 Reporting Completeness

Report scores started low for both groups, and pre-test scores showed no differences between groups prior to the learning sessions. To investigate whether the data was normally distributed, we performed the Kolmogorov-Smirnov test and rejected the hypothesis of non-normality (p=.20). As seen in figure 5, pretest scores were almost identical for both groups. Report scores significantly improved over time for the tutor group. Repeated measures ANOVA results for report scores across all virtual slide tests show a significant main effect of test and condition, as well as a significant interaction between test and condition (effect of test: F=10.286, p<0.001; effect of condition: F=9.409, p=0.018, interaction: F=7.992, p<0.001). These results indicate that scores significantly improved over time for the tutor group, but not for the control group. Repeated contrasts indicate that the bulk of this effect is seen from VST Pre to VST 1 (effect of test: F=19.440, p=0.003; interaction: F=10.029, p=0.016) – other contrast results were not significant.

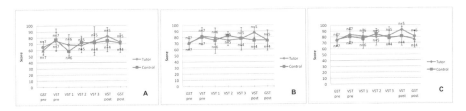

Fig. 4. Diagnostic Accuracy on glass slide tests and virtual slide tests

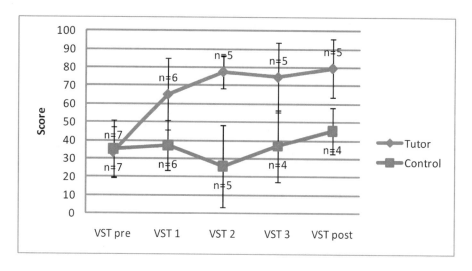

Fig. 5. Reporting completeness on virtual slide tests

5 Discussion

To our knowledge, this study represents the first summative evaluation of a medical ITS among practicing physicians, and the first study of a medical ITS outside the laboratory. Our results indicate that the ITS can move performance of practicing community pathologists closer to nationally recognized reporting standards such as those provided by the College of American Pathologists. Adherence to standard reporting schemata is an important part of ensuring the best possible patient care. Decisions on treatment and prognosis are based on these reports, and missing or incorrect elements can delay treatment or result in improper therapy.

The study did not show a significant difference in diagnostic accuracy between the intervention and control groups. Furthermore, there was no apparent learning gain for diagnostic accuracy across the learning sessions. This is quite different than several previous studies of our tutoring system among residents and fellows, who typically experience a significant gain even after 4 hours of tutoring. There are several differences between studies that could account for the absence of a learning gain for diagnostic accuracy. Most importantly, participants in this study started at a much higher level of diagnostic accuracy than participants in our other studies. Despite the fact that selected cases were considerably more difficult in this study when compared with previous studies, it appears that practicing community pathologists are already highly skilled in the diagnosis of melanocytic lesions. A second factor is that we purposely altered our tutoring system to make it much more lenient in accepting answers. We reasoned that practicing community physicians would be less accepting of the more rigid system that we have previously evaluated. However, one potential tradeoff for our feedback modifications is that it may have decreased the educational effectiveness of the intervention. Finally, the small number of participants who we recruited, the drop-out of participants from the study, and the inherent variability resulting from a field study where we cannot control other variables as we can in a laboratory, limit our ability to detect more subtle differences. Alternatively, the findings may suggest that physicians in practice are less likely to be affected by immediate feedback that focuses on specific diagnostic criteria rather than a holistic impression or pattern-matching approach. Further research is needed to determine whether diagnostic accuracy is truly resistant to criteria-based immediate feedback among practicing physicians.

This was a challenging study to carry out. The availability of participants was quite limited, resulting in a study that was clearly under-powered. The high drop-out rate in both groups limited our ability to make matched comparisons. Participants completed their learning sessions under a wide variety of conditions, and at varying intervals. Quality of access to the tutoring system differed because of many factors out of our control, such as connection speed and firewall issues. Despite these obstacles, our results are encouraging. Although further research is needed to validate these findings, the use of an ITS to bring practicing physicians closer to current practice standards provides a potential new avenue for patient safety interventions.

Acknowledgements. This work was funded by a grant from the Agency for Healthcare Research and Quality (1U18-HS016657, PI - D. Grzybicki).

References

[1] Lillehaug, S.I., Lajoie, S.P.: AI in medical education–another grand challenge for medical informatics. Artif. Intell. Med. 12(3), 197–225 (1998)
[2] Lajoie, S.P., Lavigne, N.C., Guerrera, C., Munsie, S.: Constructing knowledge in the context of BioWorld. Instructional Science 29(2), 155–186 (2001)
[3] Murray, T., Rath, K., Woolf, B.P., Marshall, D., Bruno, M., Dragon, T., Kohler, K.: Evaluating Inquiry Learning Through Recognition-Based Tasks. In: Proceedings of the 12th International Conference on AI and Education, Amsterdam (2005)
[4] Evens, M., Brandle, S., Change, R., Freedman, R., Glass, M., Lee, Y., et al.: CIRSIM-Tutor: an intelligent tutoring system using natural language dialogue. In: Proceedings of the 12th Midwest AI and cognitive science conference (MAICS), pp. 16–23 (2001)
[5] Eliot, C., Williams, K., Woolf, B.: An intelligent learning environment for advanced cardiac life support. In: AMIA Annu. Symp. Proc., pp. 7–11 (1996)
[6] Romeroa, C., Venturaa, S., Gibajaa, E.L., Hervása, C., Romerob, F.: Web-based adaptive training simulator system for cardiac life support. Artif. Intell. Med. 38(1), 67–78 (2006)
[7] Clancey, W.: Knowledge-based tutoring–the GUIDON program. MIT Press, Cambridge (1987)
[8] Clancey, W., Letsinger, R.: NEOMYCIN: reconfiguring a rulebased expert system for application to teaching. In: Proceedings of the seventh international joint conference on AI, pp. 829–835 (1981)
[9] Crowley, R.S., Medvedeva, O.: An intelligent tutoring system for visual classification problem solving. Artif. Intell. Med. 36(1), 85–117 (2006)
[10] Crowley, R.S., Medvedeva, O., Jukic, D.: SlideTutor – A model-tracing Intelligent Tutoring System for teaching microscopic diagnosis. In: 11th AIED International Conference on Artificial Intelligence in Education, Sydney, Australia, pp. 157–164. ISO Press (2003)
[11] Crowley, R.S., Tseytlin, E., Jukic, D.: ReportTutor – an intelligent tutoring system that uses a natural language interface. In: AMIA Annu. Symp. Proc., pp. 171–175 (2005)

[12] Crowley, R.S., Legowski, E., Medvedeva, O.M., Tseytlin, E., Roh, E., Jukic, D.: Evaluation of an Intelligent Tutoring System in Pathology: Effects of External Representation on Performance Gains, Metacognition, and Acceptance. JAMIA 14(2), 182–190 (2007)

[13] Saadawi, G.M., Tseytin, E., Legowski, E., Jukic, D., Castine, M., Crowley, R.S.: A natural language intelligent tutoring system for training pathologists: implementation and evaluation. Adv. in Health Sci. Educ. 13(5), 709–722 (2008)

[14] Saadawi, G.M., Azevedo, A., Castine, M., Payne, V., Medvedeva, O., Tseytlin, E., Legowski, E., Jukic, D., Crowley, R.S.: Factors Affecting Feeling-of-knowing in a Medical Intelligent Tutoring System – the role of Immediate Feedback as a Metacognitive Scaffold. Adv. Health Sci. Educ. Theory Pract. 15(1), 9–30 (2010)

[15] American Cancer Society. What are the key statistics about melanoma?, http://www.cancer.org/docroot/CRI/content/CRI_2_4_1X_What_are_the_key_statistics_for_melanoma_50.asp?sitearea (accessed: March 17, 2010)

[16] Troxel, D.B.: An insurer's perspective on error and loss in pathology. Arch. Pathol. Lab Med. 129, 1234–1236 (2005)

[17] Ruby, S.G., Henson, D.E.: Practice protocols for surgical pathology: a communication from the Cancer Committee of the College of American Pathologists. Arch. Pathol. Lab Med. 118, 120–121 (1994)

Hints: Is It Better to Give or Wait to Be Asked?

Leena Razzaq[1] and Neil T. Heffernan[2]

[1] Computer Science Department, University of Massachusetts Amherst,
Massachusetts, USA
leena@cs.umass.edu
[2] Computer Science Department, Worcester Polytechnic Institute,
Massachusetts, USA
nth@cs.wpi.edu

Abstract. Many tutoring systems allow students to ask for hints when they need help solving problems, and this has been shown to be helpful. However, many students have trouble knowing when to ask for help or they prefer to guess rather than ask for and read a hint. Is it better to give a hint when a student makes an error or wait until the student asks for a hint? This paper describes a study that compares giving hints proactively when students make errors to requiring students to ask for a hint when they want one. We found that students learned reliably more with hints-on-demand than proactive hints. This effect was especially evident for students who tend to ask for a high number of hints. There was not a significant difference between the two conditions for students who did not ask for many hints.

Keywords: intelligent tutoring systems, interactive learning environments, computer-based instruction, hints, help seeking, help design.

1 Introduction

Many tutoring systems provide hints-on-demand to support students who need help solving problems. One reason to allow the student to control when to ask for help is that it is difficult for a tutoring system to decide when to offer help or what kind of help to offer. For instance, a tutor would respond differently to an error caused by a slip (the student knows the skill but slipped up) or by a misconception or by missing background knowledge [1]. Burton and Brown [2] took a constructivist position and thought that it was best for students to discover as much of the structure of a problem as possible. "Every time the Coach tells the student something, it is robbing him of the opportunity to discover it for himself. Many human tutors interrupt far too often … and they may be preventing the development in their students of important cognitive skills – the cognitive skills that allow students to detect and use of their own errors." There are advantages to allowing the student to have more control [3, 4] in a tutoring system and studies have shown that providing hints-on-demand can improve learning [5, 6, 7, 8].

V. Aleven, J. Kay, and J. Mostow (Eds.): ITS 2010, Part I, LNCS 6094, pp. 349–358, 2010.
© Springer-Verlag Berlin Heidelberg 2010

Using hints-on-demand depends on student initiative: students are expected to ask for a hint when they want one. Students are expected to know when they need help, how to find and get help [9]. However, students sometimes don't ask for help when they should. They may try to guess or game the system [10], especially on multiple-choice questions, which can be quicker than reading and trying to understand a hint. Or students may fear that they will be penalized by the software for asking for help. Aleven and Koedinger [11] found that students frequently failed to ask for a hint after multiple errors, and Aleven et al [12] found that unproductive help-seeking behavior represented 72% of all student actions they observed.

Given that students often exhibit unproductive help-seeking behavior, perhaps tutoring systems should not wait for students to ask for a hint. Perhaps a tutoring system should give a student help when the system believes that the student needs it and before he/she asks for it. Arroyo et al. [13] reported positive learning gains when proactive help was provided to students, especially for low cognitively developed students. Murray and VanLehn [14] found that proactive help was more effective for some students and could help save time when a student is floundering and can "provide valuable information at a time when the student is prepared and motivated to learn it, and avoid the negative affective consequences of frustration and failure."

Which type of help is better? Should we wait for students to ask for help or give help when we think they need it? Is there a difference between the two types of help based on math ability? The purpose of this randomized controlled study was to compare hints-on-demand to proactive hints and to determine which was more helpful to students.

2 The Tutoring System: The ASSISTment System

The ASSISTment System [15] aims to assist students in learning the different skills needed for the Massachusetts Comprehensive Assessment System (MCAS) test or (other state tests) while at the same time assessing student knowledge to provide teachers with fine-grained assessment of their students; it assists while it assesses. The system assists students in learning different skills through the use of scaffolding questions, hints, and messages for incorrect answers (also known as buggy messages). Assessment of student performance is provided to teachers through real-time reports based on statistical analysis.

Using the web-based ASSISTment System is free and only requires registration on the website; no software need be installed. The system is primarily used by middle- and high-school teachers throughout Massachusetts who are preparing students for the MCAS tests. Currently, there are over 3000 students and 50 teachers that use the ASSISTment System as part of their regular math classes and/or for homework. Educational researchers studying the best practices for tutoring mathematics also use the system.

3 Methodology

In this study we focus on "context-sensitive" hints or hints that are pertinent to the task at hand and help the student to learn a skill by doing. Each hint is a message that provides insights and suggestions for solving a specific problem, and is part of a hint sequence of 3-5 hints. Each hint sequence ends with a *bottom-out* hint, which tells the student exactly what to do or gives the student the answer.

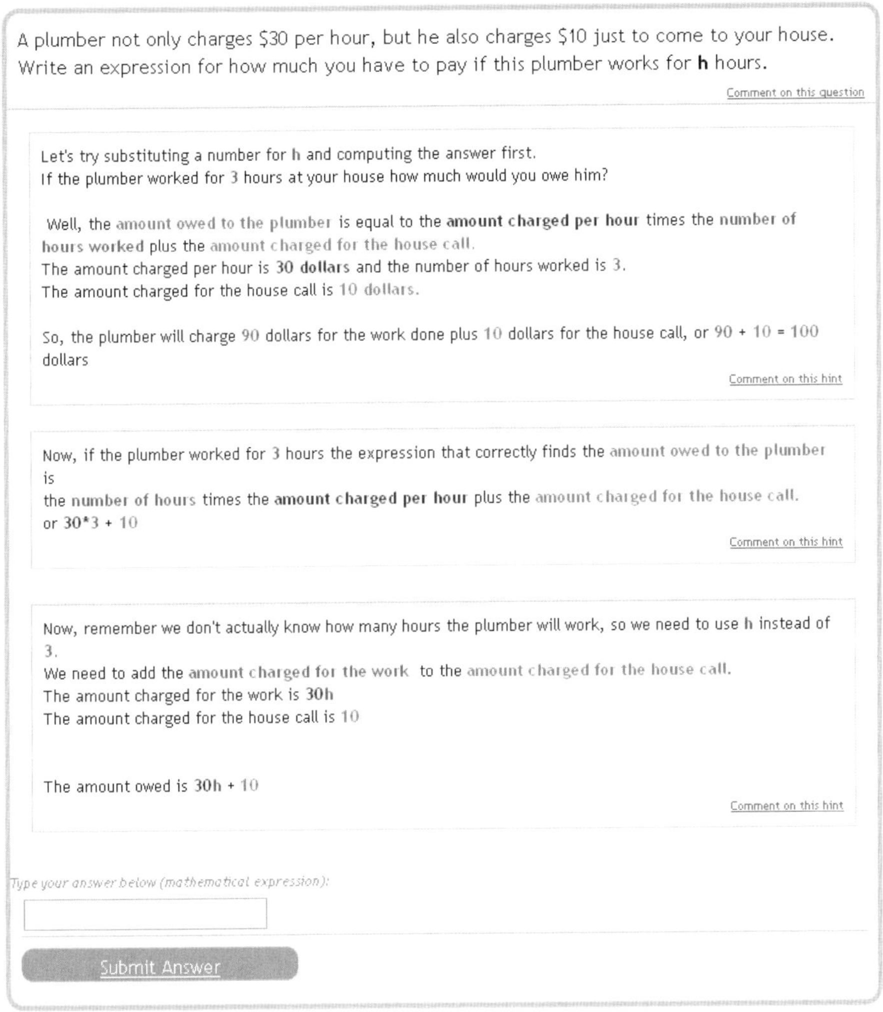

> A plumber not only charges $30 per hour, but he also charges $10 just to come to your house. Write an expression for how much you have to pay if this plumber works for **h** hours.
>
> Comment on this question
>
> ---
>
> Let's try substituting a number for h and computing the answer first.
> If the plumber worked for 3 hours at your house how much would you owe him?
>
> Well, the amount owed to the plumber is equal to the **amount charged per hour** times the number of hours worked plus the amount charged for the house call.
> The amount charged per hour is 30 dollars and the number of hours worked is 3.
> The amount charged for the house call is 10 dollars.
>
> So, the plumber will charge 90 dollars for the work done plus 10 dollars for the house call, or 90 + 10 = 100 dollars
>
> Comment on this hint
>
> ---
>
> Now, if the plumber worked for 3 hours the expression that correctly finds the amount owed to the plumber is
> the **number of hours** times the **amount charged per hour** plus the amount charged for the house call.
> or 30*3 + 10
>
> Comment on this hint
>
> ---
>
> Now, remember we don't actually know how many hours the plumber will work, so we need to use h instead of 3.
> We need to add the amount charged for the work to the amount charged for the house call.
> The amount charged for the work is 30h
> The amount charged for the house call is 10
>
> The amount owed is 30h + 10
>
> Comment on this hint
>
> ---
>
> Type your answer below (mathematical expression):
>
> [   ]
>
> Submit Answer

Fig. 1. Hints on demand, students ask for each hint by clicking on a hint button. Three hints are shown in yellow boxes.

3.1 Experiment Design

There were two conditions in this study: hints-on-demand and proactive hints. Hints-on-demand presented students with a hint only when they clicked on the hint button (see Fig. 1) and proactive hints presented students with a hint whenever they made an error (see Fig. 2). Students in the study worked on problems in two topics (symbolization and slope/intercept) and participated in both conditions in a repeated measures design. The experiment design controlled for the order of conditions, the order of topics and the order of problems and students were randomly assigned to one of four groups (see Table 1).

Table 1. Students were randomly assigned to one of four groups

	Group 1	Group 2	Group 3	Group 4
First Topic	Symbolization	Symbolization	Slope/Intercept	Slope/Intercept
First Condition	Hints on Demand	Proactive Hints	Hints on Demand	Proactive Hints
Second Topic	Slope/Intercept	Slope/Intercept	Symbolization	Symbolization
Second Condition	Proactive Hints	Hints on Demand	Proactive Hints	Hints on Demand

3.2 Participants

This study took place in a typical suburban middle school with 11.5% of students qualifying for free or reduced lunch. There were 72 eighth grade students (aged 12-14 years) who participated in the study during their math enrichment class, 32 females and 40 males.

3.3 Procedure

Students were familiar with the system and used it regularly in a math enrichment class to practice for the MCAS exam. During one class period, students worked on problems in the two topics: symbolization and slope/intercept. Students were presented with four problems in each topic that provided either hints-on-demand or proactive hints. A pretest and post-test of four problems each were given before and after each topic where students received no feedback on their answers. The pretest and post-test problems were the same.

The experiment took place towards the end of the school year and students had been introduced to both topics in their math class. Gain from pretest to post-test was used to measure learning.

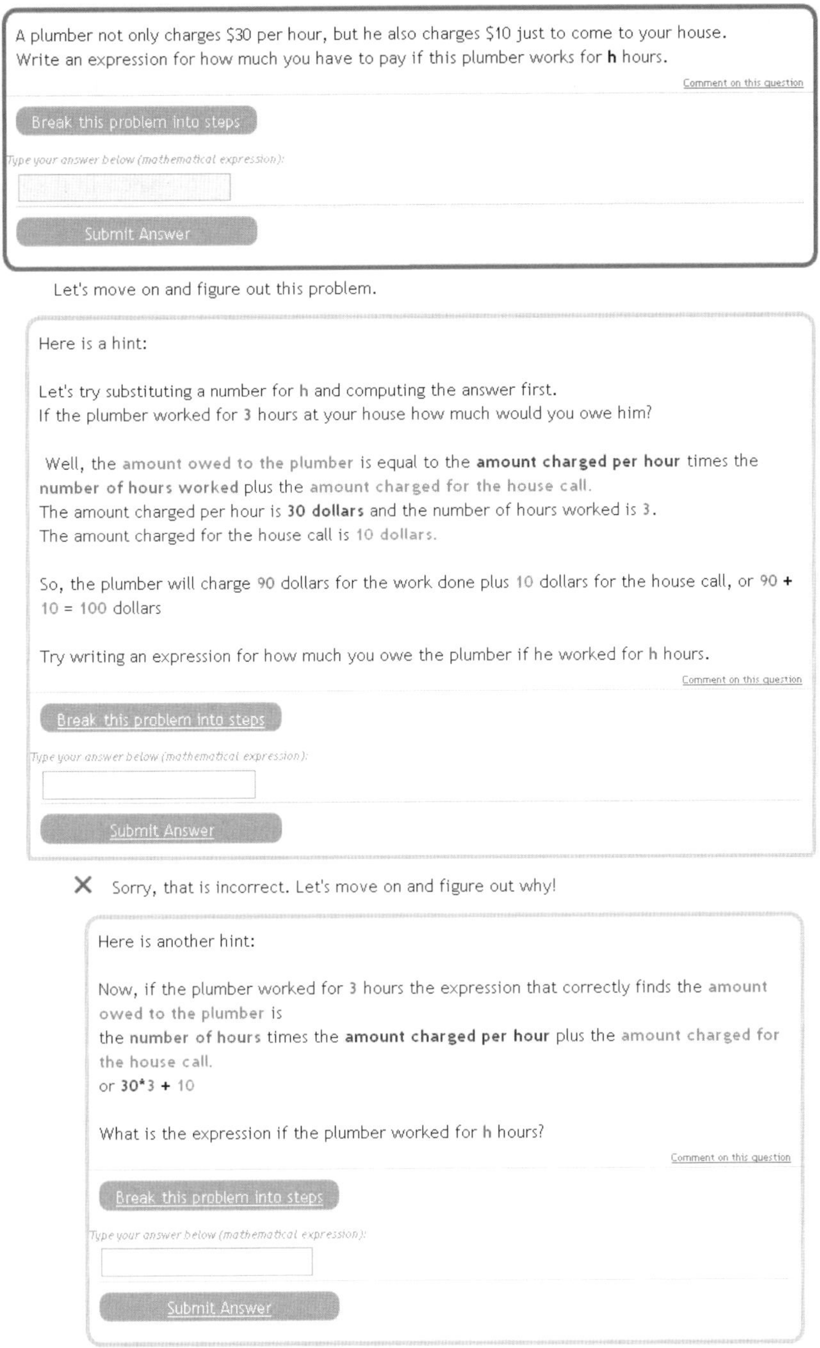

> A plumber not only charges $30 per hour, but he also charges $10 just to come to your house. Write an expression for how much you have to pay if this plumber works for **h** hours.
>
> Comment on this question
>
> Break this problem into steps
>
> Type your answer below (mathematical expression):
>
> [   ]
>
> Submit Answer

Let's move on and figure out this problem.

> Here is a hint:
>
> Let's try substituting a number for h and computing the answer first.
> If the plumber worked for 3 hours at your house how much would you owe him?
>
> Well, the amount owed to the plumber is equal to the **amount charged per hour** times the **number of hours worked** plus the amount charged for the house call.
> The amount charged per hour is **30 dollars** and the number of hours worked is 3.
> The amount charged for the house call is 10 dollars.
>
> So, the plumber will charge 90 dollars for the work done plus 10 dollars for the house call, or 90 + 10 = 100 dollars
>
> Try writing an expression for how much you owe the plumber if he worked for h hours.
>
> Comment on this question
>
> Break this problem into steps
>
> Type your answer below (mathematical expression):
>
> [   ]
>
> Submit Answer

✗ Sorry, that is incorrect. Let's move on and figure out why!

> Here is another hint:
>
> Now, if the plumber worked for 3 hours the expression that correctly finds the amount owed to the plumber is
> the **number of hours** times the **amount charged per hour** plus the amount charged for the house call.
> or 30*3 + 10
>
> What is the expression if the plumber worked for h hours?
>
> Comment on this question
>
> Break this problem into steps
>
> Type your answer below (mathematical expression):
>
> [   ]
>
> Submit Answer

Fig. 2. Proactive hints: hints are presented automatically when a student submits an incorrect answer

4 Results

Gain scores from pre- to post-test were used to measure learning. Students learned from problems in both topics. The average gain for the Symbolization problem set was 12% [t(60) = 3.7, p < 0.001] and the gain for the Slope/Intercept problem set was 4% [t(66) = 1.37, p = 0.17]. Of the 72 students who participated in the study, 61 students completed both conditions and contributed to the repeated measures analysis.

We were interested in determining if there was a difference in the effectiveness of each condition based on students' math ability. Students had completed a practice MCAS test and the median score on the test was 75%. A median split on the practice MCAS scores was used to split students into "high math ability" or "low math ability." However, there was no significant difference found based on an aptitude treatment interaction.

Table 2. Student gains in the two topics

	N	Mean	Std. Deviation	Std. Error Mean
Gain in Slope	67	.0410	.24463	.02989
Gain in Symbolization	61	.1208	.24996	.03227

The repeated measures analysis showed that students learned significantly more [F(59, 1) = 4.42, p = 0.04] from hints-on-demand and having control over when to ask for a hint (mean gain score = 0.137) compared to having the computer control when to give a hint (mean gain score = 0.04). The effect size of 0.35 has a 95% confidence interval of [0.02 - 0.74]. The results of this analysis can be found in Table 3 and Fig. 3.

Table 3. Students gained more with hints-on-demand

	Math ability	Mean	Std. Dev.	N
Gain with Proactive hints	High	.0429	.2386	35
	Low	.0385	.2201	26
	Total	.0410	.2290	61
Gain with on-demand hints	High	.1429	.2521	35
	Low	.1282	.3120	26
	Total	.1366	.2768	61

We looked at the number of hints students requested when they were in the hints-on-demand condition. Not surprisingly, students with low math ability asked for significantly more hints (mean = 11 hints) than students of high math ability (mean = 5.4 hints), [F(71, 1) = 10.85, p = 0.002]. The median number of hints requested in the

Hints: Is It Better to Give or Wait to Be Asked?   355

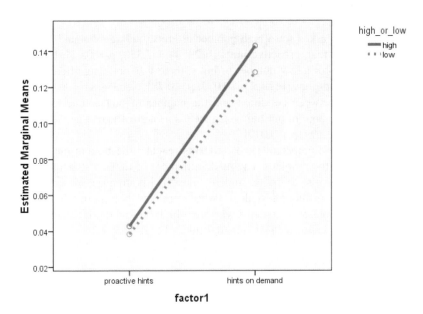

Fig. 3. Students of both low and high math ability learned more from hints on demand

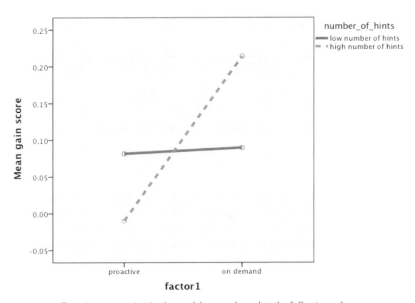

Fig. 4. Students who tend to ask for many hints do significantly better with hints-on-demand

hints-on-demand condition was seven hints and a median split on the number of hints requested was used to divide students into two groups: "high number of hints" and "low number of hints."

For students who asked for a high number of hints, hints-on-demand were significantly more helpful than proactive hints [$F(29, 1) = 7.358$, $p = 0.01$]. However, for students who asked for a low number of hints, there was not a significant difference between the two conditions [$F(28, 1) = 0.077$, $p = 0.78$], (see Fig. 4).

The interaction between condition and the number of hints requested, using the number of times the bottom-out hint was reached as a covariate, was marginally significant [$F(56, 1) = 3.199$, $p = 0.079$].

We looked at the number of times students reached the bottom-out hint, which gives the answer to the problem. The median number of times a student reached the bottom-out hint was used to divide students into "low bottom-out hinters" and "high bottom-out hinters." Although students who were low bottom-out hinters learned more in both conditions than students who were high bottom-out hinters, both groups had higher learning gains with on-demand hints [$F(59, 1) = 4.74$, $p = 0.033$]. (See Table 4.)

Table 4. Both high and low bottom-out hinters had higher learning gains with on-demand hints

	bottom_out_hint_level	Mean	Std. Deviation	N
gainProactive	low bottom-out hinters	.0833	.21348	33
	high bottom-out hinters	-.0089	.24039	28
	Total	.0410	.22904	61
gainDemand	low bottom-out hinters	.1591	.28517	33
	high bottom-out hinters	.1101	.26937	28
	Total	.1366	.27682	61

5 Conclusion

In this paper, we described a randomized controlled experiment to compare hints-on-demand to proactive hints in a tutoring system. We used a repeated measures design so all students saw both conditions. We found that middle school students working on algebra problems did significantly better with hints-on-demand and having control over when to see a hint compared to being shown a hint when they made an error, with an effect size of 0.35. We speculate that the students benefitted from having the greater learner control of hints-on-demand.

Interestingly, students who tended to ask for a high number of hints learned significantly more with hints-on-demand, but for students who asked for a low number of hints there was no significant difference between the two conditions. We do not know the reason for this result. It may be that the students who asked for a high number of hints had good help-seeking behavior and benefitted from controlling the timing of help so that they received it at the most useful moment. Proactive help may have been distracting or annoying to these students. The students who asked for a low number of hints may have been unproductive help-seekers who avoided asking for help when they needed it. These students may have benefitted from being shown a hint when they needed one.

If we had to recommend one method of providing help over another, hints-on-demand seems to be the better choice since it had better results overall, better results for high-hinters and little difference for low-hinters. However, this study did have its limitations. Students who participated in this study were more familiar with hints-on-demand as that is the norm in the ASSISTment System and students had been using the system throughout the school year. Although we explained to the students that they would see the two different types of hints, the proactive hints were unfamiliar and perhaps confusing. This study also took place over a very short period of time and students had little time to get used to the proactive hints. For future work we would like to repeat the experiment over a longer period of time with more students.

Acknowledgments. We would like to acknowledge funding for this project from the U.S. Department of Education, the National Science Foundation, the Office of Naval Research and the Spencer Foundation. This material is based upon work supported by the National Science Foundation under Grant DGE-0742503 and under Grant #0937060 to the Computing Research Association for the CIFellows Project. Any opinions, findings, and conclusions or recommendations expressed in this material are those of the author(s) and do not necessarily reflect the views of the National Science Foundation or the Computing Research Association.

References

1. Anderson, J.R.: Rules of the Mind. Erlbaum, Hillsdale (1993)
2. Burton, R.R., Brown, J.S.: An Investigation of Computer Coaching for Informal Learning Activities. In: Sleeman, D.H., Brown, J.S. (eds.) Intelligent Tutoring Systems. Academic Press, New York (1982)
3. Kay, J.: Learner Control. User Modeling and User-Adapted Interaction 11, 111–127 (2001)
4. Beck, J.: Does Learner Control Affect Learning? In: 13th International Conference on Artificial Intelligence in Education, pp. 135–142 (2007)
5. Wood, D.: Scaffolding, contingent tutoring, and computer-supported learning. International Journal of Artificial Intelligence in Education 12, 280–292 (2001)
6. Renkl, A.: Learning from worked-out examples: Instructional explanations supplement self-explanations. Learning & Instruction 12, 529–556 (2002)
7. Schworm, S., Renkl, A.: Learning by solved example problems: Instructional explanations reduce self-explanation activity. In: Gray, W.D., Schunn, C.D. (eds.) 24th Annual Conference of the Cognitive Science Society, pp. 816–821. Erlbaum, Mahwah (2002)
8. Arroyo, I., Murray, T., Woolf, B.P.: Inferring Unobservable Learning Variables From Students' Help Seeking Behavior. In: Lester, J.C., Vicari, R.M., Paraguaçu, F. (eds.) ITS 2004. LNCS, vol. 3220, pp. 782–784. Springer, Heidelberg (2004)

9. Nelson-Le Gall, S.: Help-seeking: An understudied problem-solving skill in children. Developmental Review 1, 224–246 (1981)
10. Baker, R., Walonoski, J., Heffernan, N., Roll, I., Corbett, A., Koedinger, K.: Why Students Engage in "Gaming the System" Behavior in Interactive Learning Environments. J. Interactive Learning Research 19(2), 185–224 (2008)
11. Aleven, V., Koedinger, K.: Limitations of student control: Do students know when they need help? In: Gauthier, G., VanLehn, K., Frasson, C. (eds.) ITS 2000. LNCS, vol. 1839, pp. 292–303. Springer, Heidelberg (2000)
12. Aleven, V., McLaren, B., Roll, I., Koedinger, K.: Toward tutoring help seeking: Applying cognitive modeling to meta-cognitive skills. In: Lester, J.C., Vicari, R.M., Paraguaçu, F. (eds.) ITS 2004. LNCS, vol. 3220, pp. 227–239. Springer, Heidelberg (2004)
13. Arroyo, I., Beck, J.E., Beal, C.R., Wing, R., Woolf, B.P.: Analyzing students' response to help provision in an elementary mathematics intelligent tutoring system. In: Luckin, R. (ed.) Papers of the AIED 2001 Workshop on Help Provision and Help Seeking in Interactive Learning Environments, San Antonio, Texas, pp. 34–46 (2001)
14. Murray, C., VanLehn, K.: A Comparison of Decision-Theoretic, Fixed-Policy and Random Tutorial Action Selection. In: Ikeda, M., Ashley, K.D., Chan, T.-W. (eds.) ITS 2006. LNCS, vol. 4053, pp. 114–123. Springer, Heidelberg (2006)
15. Razzaq, L., Heffernan, N.T., Koedinger, K.R., Feng, M., et al.: Blending Assessment and Instructional Assistance. In: Nedjah, N., de Macedo, M.L., Borges, M.N., Almeida, N.N. (eds.) Intelligent Educational Machines within the Intelligent Systems Engineering Book Series, pp. 23–49 (2007)

Error-Flagging Support for Testing and Its Effect on Adaptation

Amruth N. Kumar

Ramapo College of New Jersey,
Mahwah, NJ 07430, USA
amruth@ramapo.edu

Abstract. The effect of providing error-flagging support during tests was studied in spring 2009 with two tutors on `while` and `for` loops. A partial crossover design was used for the study and mixed-factor ANOVA was used to analyze the students' score per problem, number of revised problems, effect of revision on score and time spent per problem, and finally, the effect of error-flagging on adaptation and learning. Students scored better on tests with rather than without error-flagging support. This can be attributed to the fact that students revised their answers on more problems when error-flagging feedback was provided. But, they did not necessarily revise more often per problem with error-flagging feedback. Students scored the same with revisions as without revisions, whether or not error-flagging support was provided. They spent less time per problem when error-flagging support was provided, whether or not they revised their answers. One explanation for this is that error-flagging may speed up the problem-solving process. Finally, if error-flagging feedback is provided during pre-test, students solve significantly fewer problems during the subsequent practice session which uses the outcome of the pre-test as the basis for adaptation. Therefore, providing error-flagging feedback during the pre-test improves adaptation. But, it does not result in greater learning - learning was not significantly different with versus without error-flagging feedback.

Keywords: Error-flagging, Testing, Adaptation, Evaluation.

1 Introduction

One mechanism proposed to build the student model needed for adaptation in tutors is pre-testing (e.g., [1, 5]). In order to be accurate, pre-tests must avoid both false-positives, when students can solve a problem correctly without knowing the underlying concept, and false-negatives, when they end up incorrectly solving a problem in spite of knowing the underlying concept. One approach used by instructional experts to minimize false positives is to design pre-test problems that require more than recall and recognition, e.g., problems with short-entry rather than multiple-choice answers. False negatives can occur when students incorrectly solve a problem because they misunderstand the instructions or the user interface, or second-guess themselves. The hypothesis of this paper is that providing error-flagging support, i.e., error-detection, but not error-correction support during pre-test can improve student scores, possibly by minimizing false-negatives. If so, it would in turn improve adaptation that is based on the pre-test.

The effect of providing error-flagging feedback during testing has been studied with mixed results. Multiple studies of paper-and-pencil testing have reported lower performance due to increased anxiety (e.g., [3, 6]) or no difference (e.g., [12]) when feedback about the correctness of answers was provided. Studies with early Computer Assisted Instruction/Testing showed better performance with such feedback during testing than without (e.g., [2, 13]). Later studies with computer-based multiple-choice testing showed no relative advantage or performance gain from providing such feedback [11, 12]. In one of the most recent studies to our knowledge, researchers found that there was little difference among the types of feedback provided during testing with the ACT Programming Tutor [4]. In earlier preliminary studies using a tutor on arithmetic expression evaluation, we had found that error-flagging support helped students improve their test scores [8, 9].

Given the mixed nature of prior results, we revisited the issue of providing error-flagging feedback during testing. This study differs from many of the earlier studies in that the testing was done online; the problems were short-entry rather than multiple-choice in nature; and the outcome of the test was used for adaptation of problem-solving practice by a conflated software tutor.

1.1 Experimental Setup

In spring 2009, two problem-solving software tutors were used to evaluate the effect of providing error-flagging support during testing. The tutors were on two introductory programming concepts: `while` loops and `for` loops. The `while` loop tutor targeted 9 concepts and the `for` loop tutor targeted 10 concepts, such as zero-iteration execution, and dependent and independent nested loops. The tutors presented problems on these concepts, each problem containing a program whose output was to be determined by the student. The student entered the output free-hand (as opposed to selecting it from a menu of options).

Each software tutor went through the pre-test-practice-post-test protocol as follows:

- It first administered a pre-test to evaluate the prior knowledge of students and build the student model. The pre-test consisted of one problem per concept – 9 problems for the `while` loop tutor and 10 problems for the `for` loop tutor. Students were expected to attempt all the problems, although they had the option to discontinue the tutoring session at any time.
- Subsequently, it provided practice problems on only those concepts on which students had solved problems incorrectly during the pre-test [7];
- Finally, it administered post-test problems on only those concepts on which students had solved sufficient number of problems during practice as indicated by the student model.

The three stages were administered back-to-back without any break in between. The software tutors allowed 30 minutes for the three stages combined.

The evaluations conducted in spring 2009 were *in-vivo*. The software tutors were used by 365 students in the introductory programming course at 12 institutions, which were randomly assigned to one of two groups: A or B. Subjects, i.e., students accessed the tutors over the web, typically, after class. The software tutors remotely collected the data for analysis.

A partial cross-over design was used: students in group A served as control subjects on the `while` loop tutor and test subjects on the `for` loop tutor, while students in group B served as test subjects on the `while` loop tutor and control subjects on the `for` loop tutor. Both the groups worked with the `while` loop tutor before the `for` loop tutor. All else being equal, error-flagging feedback was provided during pre-test to students in the test group, but not the control group.

Error-flagging support was provided while the student was entering the answer to each problem, i.e., before the student submitted the answer. With error-flagging feedback, whenever the student entered each step in the answer to a problem, the step in the answer was displayed with red background if incorrect and green background if correct. When incorrect, no facility was provided for the student to find out why the step was incorrect, or how it could be corrected. Without error-flagging support, the steps in a student's answer were always displayed with white background. The online instructions presented to the students before using each tutor explained the significance of the background colors.

Whether or not the tutor provided error-flagging feedback, students had the option to revise their answer as often as necessary before submitting it. This included deleting or editing any step(s) in the answer. Once again, the instructions presented to the students before using each tutor explained the user interface facilities provided for revising an answer.

2 Results

For analysis, only those students were considered who had attempted most of the pre-test problems, i.e., at least 7 of the 9 problems on the `while` loop pre-test and at least 8 of the 10 problems on the `for` loop pre-test. In order to factor out the effect of the difference in the number of problems solved by students, the average score per problem was considered for analysis, which can range from 0 through 1, rather than the total score. Similarly, the average time spent per problem was considered rather than the total time spent on the pre-test.

Score Per Problem: A 2 X 2 mixed-factor ANOVA analysis of the score per problem was conducted with the topic (`while` versus `for` loop) as the repeated measure and the group (group A with error-flagging on `for` loop pre-test versus group B with error-flagging on `while` loop pre-test) as the between subjects factor.

A large significant interaction was found between topic and group [$F(1,363) = 216.563$, $p < 0.001$]. As shown in Table 1, both the groups scored better with error-flagging support than without: group A scored 0.624 on `while` loop pre-test without error-flagging support, and went on to score 0.871 on `for` loop pre-test with error-flagging support. The difference was statistically significant [$t(289) = 18.578$, p < 0.001]. Group B scored 0.842 on while loop pre-test with error-flagging support, and went on to score 0.667 on for loop pre-test without error-flagging support. The difference was statistically significant [t(74) = -7.565, p < 0.001]. *So, students scored better on tests with rather than without error-flagging support.*

Table 1. Average Pre-test Score with and Without Error-Flagging

	while loop pre-test	for loop pre-test
Without Error-Flagging	0.624	0.667
With Error-Flagging	0.842	0.871

Number of Revised Problems: Did the provision of error-flagging support result in subjects revising their answers on more problems? In order to answer this question, the pre-test problems solved by each student were grouped into those where the student revised the answer versus those where the student never revised the answer. The 2 X 2 mixed-factor ANOVA analysis was repeated on the number of problems on which subjects revised their answer, with topic as the repeated measure and group as the between subjects factor.

A significant and large interaction was observed between topic and group [F(1,369) = 399.836, p < 0.001]. Group A revised 0.990 problems on while loop pre-test when no error-flagging support was provided, and then went on to revise 5.956 problems on for loop pre-test when error-flagging support was provided, as shown in Table 2. The difference was statistically significant [t(293) = -28.686, p < 0.001]. Group B revised answers on 3.416 problems on while loop pre-test when error-flagging feedback was provided, but then, went on to revise only 1.00 problem on for loop pre-test when no error-flagging feedback was provided. The difference was statistically significant [t(76) = 8.376, p < 0.001]. *So, students revised their answers on more problems when error-flagging feedback was provided than when it was not.*

Table 2. Number of revised problems with and without Error-Flagging

	while loop pre-test	for loop pre-test
Without Error-Flagging	0.990	1.000
With Error-Flagging	3.416	5.956

Number of Revisions per Problem: Did the provision of error-flagging support result in subjects revising their answers more often per problem? A univariate analysis of the number of revisions per problem was conducted on while loop pre-test data with the problem number (1-9) and error-flagging (without versus with) as fixed factors. A significant main effect was found for problem [F(8,680) = 6.223, p < 0.001], indicating that the number of revisions per problem was not uniform across the board, but rather, depended on the problems. A significant main effect was found for error-flagging [F(1,680) = 18.98, p < 0.001]: revisions per problem was lower with error-flagging (1.566) than without (2.143). But, no significant interaction was found between problem and error-flagging [F(8,680) = 1.146, p = 0.33]. A similar analysis was conducted on `for` loop pre-test data. Once again, a significant main effect was found for problem [F(9,2096) = 2.202, p = 0.019]. But, no significant main effect was found for error-flagging [F(1,2096) = 0.137, p = 0.711]. The interaction between problem and error-flagging was marginally significant [F(9,2096) = 1.828, p = 0.059]: revisions per problem were more with error-flagging on some problems, but not others. *So, error-flagging feedback did not necessarily result in more revisions per problem.*

Effect of Revision on Score: In order to evaluate the effect of revision on pre-test score, a 2 X 2 X 2 mixed-factor ANOVA analysis was conducted of the average score per problem, with the topic (`while` versus `for`) and revision (without versus with revision) as within-subjects factors and group (group A with error-flagging on `for` loop pre-test versus group B with error-flagging on `while` loop pre-test) as between-subjects factor.

No significant main effect was found for revision [F(1,196) = 2.088, p = 0.15]. No significant interaction was found between revision and group [F(1,196) = 0.507, p = 0.477], topic and revision [F(1,196) = 0.423, p = 0.516] or topic, revision and group [F(1, 196) = 0.335, p = 0.564]. The score per problem on problems with and without revision for the two groups is listed in Table 3. None of the differences in the scores between revised and unrevised problems was statistically significant. No ceiling effect was observed in the scores either. *In other words, students scored the same with revisions as without revisions, whether or not error-flagging support was provided.*

Table 3. Score per problem with versus without revision: Group A got error-flagging feedback during `for` loop pre-test and Group B got error-flagging feedback during `while` loop pre-test

	while loop pre-test		for loop pre-test	
	No Revision	Revised	No Revision	Revised
Group A	0.606	0.667	0.865	0.883
Group B	0.878	0.892	0.672	0.684

Effect of Revision on Time Spent: In order to evaluate the effect of revisions on the time spent solving problems, a 2 X 2 X 2 mixed-factor ANOVA analysis of the average time spent per problem was conducted, with the topic (`while` versus `for`) and revision (without versus with) as within-subjects factors and group (group A with error-flagging on `for` loop pre-test versus group B with error-flagging on `while` loop pre-test) as between-subjects factor.

A significant interaction was found between topic and group [F(1,194) = 28.636, p < 0.001]. Group A spent 142.629 seconds per problem on `while` loop pre-test without error-flagging support and went on to spend 97.962 seconds per problem on `for` loop pre-test with error-flagging support, as shown in Table 4. Group B spent 99.467 seconds per problem on `while` loop pre-test with error-flagging support and went on to spend 114.915 seconds per problem on `for` loop pre-test without error-flagging support. *So, students spent less time per problem when error-flagging feedback was provided.*

Table 4. Time spent per problem with and without Error-Flagging

	`while` loop pre-test	`for` loop pre-test
Without Error-Flagging	142.629	114.915
With Error-Flagging	99.467	97.962

The interaction between topic and group was significant for both revised problems [F(1,221) = 9.848, p = 0.002] and unrevised problems [F(1,328) = 56.170, p < 0.001]. For revised problems, group A spent 172.084 seconds per problem without error-flagging feedback on `while` loop pre-test, followed by 112.781 seconds per problem with error-flagging feedback on `for` loop pre-test. Group B spent 125.168 seconds per problem with error-flagging feedback and 129.282 seconds per problem without error-flagging feedback as shown in Table 5. For unrevised problems, group A spent 109.780 seconds per problem without error-flagging support on `while` loop pre-test, followed by 82.866 seconds per problem with error-flagging support on `for` loop pre-test. Group B spent 79.063 seconds per problem with error-flagging support and 101.499 seconds per problem without error-flagging support as shown in Table 6. *So, whether or not students revised their answers, they solved problems faster with error-flagging.*

Table 5. Time spent per problem with and without Error-Flagging on revised problems

Revised Problems	`while` loop pre-test	`for` loop pre-test
Without Error-Flagging	172.084	129.282
With Error-Flagging	125.168	112.781
Significance	t(246) = -3.028, p = 0.003	t(328) = 2.125, p = 0.034

Table 6. Time spent per problem with and without Error-Flagging on unrevised problems

Unrevised Problems	`while` loop pre-test	`for` loop pre-test
Without Error-Flagging	109.780	101.499
With Error-Flagging	79.063	82.866
Significance	t(368) = -5.301, p < 0.001	t(329) = 3.945, p < 0.001

No significant interaction was observed between revision and group [F(1,194) = 0.075, p = 0.784]. No significant interaction was found between topic, revision and group [F(1,194) = 0.104, p = 0.748]. A significant main effect was found for revision [F(1,194) = 59.488, p < 0.001] – students spent an average of 94.183 seconds per problem when they did not revise their answer, and 133.304 seconds per problem when they did revise their answer. *So, students spent more time per problem when they revised their answer than when they did not.* This is to be expected since revising an answer involves undoing and redoing one or more steps in the answer.

Effect of Error-Flagging on Subsequent Adaptation: Since students score better on pre-test with error-flagging support, do they solve fewer problems during the subsequent practice that uses the results of the pre-test as the basis for adaptation? The number of problems solved during adaptive practice was analyzed using 2 X 2 mixed factor ANOVA with topic (`while` versus `for`) as within-subjects factor and group (group A with error-flagging on `for` loop pre-test versus group B with error-flagging on `while` loop pre-test) as between-subjects factor. No significant main effect was observed for topic [$F(1,279) = 0.058$, $p = 0.810$]. (The smaller N is due to the fact that some students did not solve any practice problems since they answered all the pre-test problems correctly). A significant main effect was observed for group [$F(1,279) = 5.722$, $p = 0.017$]. This is due to the fact that one group solved more problems with and without error-flagging than the other group, as shown in Table 7.

Significant interaction was observed between topic and group [$F(1,279) = 25.227$, $p < 0.001$]. As shown in Table 7, both the groups solved fewer problems during adaptive practice when error-flagging support was provided during the preceding pre-test than when it was not provided: group A solved 10.897 practice problems on `while` loop, given no error-flagging support during pre-test, and went on to solve 8.268 practice problems on `for` loop, given error-flagging support during pre-test. The difference was statistically significant [$t(223) = -5.458$, $p < 0.001$]. Group B solved 10.070 practice problems on `while` loop, given error-flagging support during pre-test, and went on to solve 12.965 practice problems on `for` loop, given no error-flagging support during pre-test. The difference was statistically significant [$t(56) = 2.674$, $p = 0.01$]. So, *students solved significantly fewer problems during adaptive practice when error-flagging support was provided during the preceding pre-test than when it was not.*

Table 7. Problems Solved During Adaptive Practice with and without Error-Flagging Feedback Provided during the Preceding Pre-test

	`while` loop practice	`for` loop practice
Pre-test without Error-Flagging	10.897	12.965
Pre-test with Error-Flagging	10.070	8.268

Learning: After the adaptive practice, students answered a post-test on only the concepts on which they had solved sufficient number of problems during practice as indicated by the student model. The learning of students was measured in terms of their pre-test and post-test scores on only those concepts (henceforth referred to as learned concepts) on which they had solved problems during all three stages: pre-test, adaptive practice and post-test. So, analysis of learning excludes the records of students who solved all the problems correctly on the pre-test, and hence, did not solve any problems during practice or post-test; and the records of students who ran out of time either during practice or post-test, since they were allowed 30 minutes for the three stages combined. In other words, only those students were considered for this analysis who learned at least one concept using the tutor, and for these students, data from only the learned concepts was used.

A 2 X 2 mixed-factor ANOVA analysis was conducted of the score per problem on the learned concepts, with pre-post as repeated measure and error-flagging (with versus without) as between-subjects factor. On the `while` loop tutor, a significant main effect was observed for pre-post [$F(1,98) = 546.021$, $p < 0.001$]: student scores improved from 0.262 on the pre-test to 0.933 on the post-test. A marginally significant main effect was observed for error-flagging [$F(1,98) = 3.800$, $p = 0.054$]: 0.630 with error-flagging and 0.565 without error-flagging. No significant interaction was observed between pre-post and error-flagging [$F(1,98) = 0.404$, $p = 0.526$]: the group that got error-flagging feedback scored slightly better than the group that did not, on both pre-test and post-test.

On the `for` loop tutor, once again, a significant main effect was observed for pre-post [$F(1,138) = 508.976$, $p < 0.001$]: student scores improved from 0.279 on the pre-test to 0.901 on the post-test. No significant main effect was observed for error-flagging [$F(1,138) = 2.731$, $p = 0.101$] and no significant interaction was observed between pre-post and error-flagging [$F(1,138) = 1.258$, $p = 0.264$]. *So, student learning was not significantly different with versus without error-flagging.*

3 Discussion

An empirically-driven study was conducted to see whether providing error-flagging support, i.e., error-detection, but not error-correction support during tests could improve student scores, possibly by minimizing false-negatives. Since error-flagging support could promote revision of incorrect answers by students, the number of problems on which students revised their answers, the number of revisions per problem, and the score and time per problem with versus without error-flagging and with versus without revisions were all studied. The results of the study could have implications for adaptation in tutors, and for online testing in general.

Students scored better on tests with rather than without error-flagging support. This can be attributed to the fact that they revised their answers on more problems when error-flagging feedback was provided. These revisions could have eliminated false negatives, resulting in higher scores. However, students did not necessarily revise more often per problem with error-flagging than without – they actually revised less often per problem with error-flagging on the `while` loop pre-test. This counter-intuitive result suggests that error-flagging does not promote indiscriminate revisions of answers by students, i.e., students do not necessarily abuse error-flagging support to guess the correct answer through trial and error. Moreover, students scored the same per problem with revisions as without revisions, whether or not error-flagging support was provided.

Students spent more time per problem when they revised their answer than when they did not. They spent less time per problem when error-flagging feedback was provided. For the `while` loop pre-test, this can be explained based on the fact that students revised their answers significantly less often per problem with error-flagging (1.566) than without (2.143) [$F(1,680) = 18.98$, $p < 0.001$]. One explanation for why students revised less often per problem with error-flagging is that given confirmation of the correctness of the answer so far, students may forgo some *false negatives*, revisions that they would have otherwise made, instances where they would have second-guessed a correct answer that they had already entered.

But, this does not explain why students spent less time per problem with error-flagging on `for` loop pre-test, wherein revisions per problem was not significantly different without (2.085) and with error-flagging (1.983) [$F(1,2096) = 0.137$, p = 0.711]. A 2 X 2 ANOVA of the time spent per problem during for loop pre-test with revision (with versus without) as within-subjects factor and error-flagging (with versus without) as between-subjects factor found a significant main effect for revision [F(1,288) = 37.792, p < 0.001] and error-flagging [F(1,288) = 9.343, p = 0.002], but no significant interaction between revision and error-flagging [F(1,288) = 0.284, p = 0.594]. So, students spent less time per problem with error-flagging (97.088 seconds) than without error-flagging (114.666 seconds); they spent less time without revision (92.921 seconds) than with revision (118.833 seconds); yet, they did not revise any significantly less per problem with error-flagging than without. This suggests that with error-flagging feedback, either students revised their answer more quickly, or saved time that was attributable to the unrevised parts of the answer, or both.

Indeed, whether or not students revised their answers, they solved problems faster with error-flagging than without. One possible explanation is that students proceed more quickly to revise their answer when it is marked incorrect, and proceed more quickly to the next step in the answer when it is marked correct by error-flagging feedback. In both cases, they save on the time they would have optionally spent reconsidering the correctness of the answer they had just entered. In other words, error-flagging feedback may have the effect of speeding up the problem-solving process. Testing this hypothesis quantitatively is part of our future work.

If error-flagging feedback is provided during pre-test, students solve significantly fewer problems during the subsequent practice session which uses the outcome of the pre-test as the basis for adaptation. Therefore, providing error-flagging feedback during the pre-test improves adaptation. Any adaptive system that uses a pre-test to build the initial student model would benefit from providing error-flagging support during the pre-test. However, error-flagging does not result in greater learning - learning was not significantly different with versus without error-flagging.

To further generalize this result, given that it is logistically easier to provide error-flagging support during online tests (as opposed to pen-and-paper tests), and such support helps students score better and answer faster even when the test items are not multiple-choice in nature, provision of error-flagging support should be considered in all online tests.

Acknowledgments. Partial support for this work was provided by the National Science Foundation under grant DUE-0817187.

References

1. Aimeur, E., Brassard, G., Dufort, H., Gambs, S.: CLARISSE: A Machine Learning Tool to Initialize Student Models. In: Cerri, S.A., Gouardéres, G., Paraguaçu, F. (eds.) ITS 2002. LNCS, vol. 2363, pp. 718–728. Springer, Heidelberg (2002)
2. Anderson, R.C., Kulhavy, R.W., Andre, T.: Feedback procedures in programmed instruction. J. Educational Psychology 62, 148–156 (1971)
3. Bierbaum, W.B.: Immediate knowledge of performance on multiple-choice tests. J. Programmed Instruction 3, 19–23 (1965)
4. Corbett, A.T., Anderson, J.R.: Locus of feedback control in computer-based tutoring: impact on learning rate, achievement and attitudes. In: Proc. SIGCHI Conference on Human Factors in Computing Systems, pp. 245–252 (2001)

5. Czarkowski, M., Kay, J.: Challenges of Scrutable Adaptivity. In: Proc. of AI-ED 2003, pp. 404–406. IOS Press, Amsterdam (2003)
6. Gilmer, J.S.: The Effects of Immediate Feedback Versus Traditional No-Feedback in a Testing Situation. In: Proc. Annual Meeting of the American Educational Research Association, April 1979, pp. 8–12 (1979)
7. Kumar, A.N.: A Scalable Solution for Adaptive Problem Sequencing and its Evaluation. In: Wade, V.P., Ashman, H., Smyth, B. (eds.) AH 2006. LNCS, vol. 4018, pp. 161–171. Springer, Heidelberg (2006)
8. Kumar, A.N.: The Effect of Providing Error-Flagging Support during Testing. In: Woolf, B.P., Aïmeur, E., Nkambou, R., Lajoie, S. (eds.) ITS 2008. LNCS, vol. 5091, pp. 799–802. Springer, Heidelberg (2008)
9. Kumar, A.N., Rutigliano, P.: The Effects of Error-Flagging in a Tutor on Expression Evaluation. In: 13th International Conference on Artificial Intelligence in Education (AI-ED 2007), pp. 599–601 (2007)
10. Montor, K.: Effect of using a self scoring answer sheet on knowledge retention. J. Educational Research 63, 435–437 (1970)
11. Plake, B.S.: Effects of Informed Item Selection on Test Performance and Anxiety for Examinees Administered a Self-Adapted Test. Educational and Psychological Measurement 55(5), 736–742 (1995)
12. Shermis, M.D., Mzumara, H.R., Bublitz, S.T.: On Test and Computer Anxiety: Test Performance Under CAT and SAT Conditions. J. Education Computing Research 24(10), 57–75 (2001)
13. Tait, K., Hartley, J.R., Anderson, R.C.: Feedback procedures in computer-assisted arithmetic instruction. British Journal of Educational Psychology 43, 161–171 (1973)

Emotions and Motivation on Performance during Multimedia Learning: How Do I Feel and Why Do I Care?

Amber Chauncey and Roger Azevedo

The University of Memphis
Department of Psychology
Institute for Intelligent Systems
400 Innovation Drive
Memphis, TN 38152, USA
dchuncey@memphis.edu

Abstract. This experiment examined the role of emotion and motivation on metacognitive judgments and learning performance during multimedia learning. A false-biofeedback paradigm was used to induce emotional states and track learners' metacognitive monitoring and control behaviors in a self-paced, linearly structured multimedia learning environment. Our results indicate that induced emotional states significantly impact these processes in college students. We will discuss the implications for these findings on the design of intelligent tutoring systems and multimedia learning environments to help learners achieve optimal self-regulation and deep learning.

Keywords: emotion, motivation, self-regulated learning, multimedia learning, metacognition.

1 Introduction

Learning about complex science topics with multimedia can be challenging and requires learners to simultaneously monitor and control cognitive, metacognitive, affective, and motivational processes in order to achieve optimal performance [2,15,16]. The cognitive and metacognitive processes used by learners have received a great deal of scientific attention and exploration [1,2,16]. However, very little research has been devoted to understanding the affective and motivational processes which occur during multimedia learning. What research does exist indicates that affective and motivational processes have the potential to impact both cognitive and metacognitive processes as well as learning outcomes [3,10,13].

It is well known that learners who are intrinsically motivated (i.e., see learning as pleasurable or as a challenge to achieve a goal) are typically expected to achieve deeper conceptual understanding of the learning material and higher performance on subsequent assessments [6,9]. However, intrinsic motivation is often impeded when negative emotions such as frustration, anger, helplessness, or boredom detract attention away from the task and onto the learner's emotional states. When this occurs, it is important for learners to have a mechanism for regulating these emotions so that motivation can stay high and optimal learning can occur [14,15]. In a culture where learners are increasingly dependent on computer-based learning both in and out of the classroom, how can intelligent tutoring systems, hypermedia and multimedia learning environments be designed to help learners effectively regulate and manage their emotional and motivational states while engaging in learning of complex science topics like biology?

This experiment used a false-biofeedback paradigm to induce emotional states in college students while they used a multimedia learning environment to learn about the human circulatory system. While there is no known method that can infallibly induce emotions in laboratory experiments, some researchers have employed a false-biofeedback paradigm [7]. This non-invasive method involves instructing participants to wear an apparatus capable of recording their heart rate and explaining that during the experiment they will hear their own heart rate through headphones while they engage in a task. However, rather than hearing their heart rate, participants are actually presented with previously recorded samples of accelerated and baseline human heart-beats. Previous empirical research has suggested that individuals often evaluate their emotional state by their perceived level of physiological arousal [4]. In false biofeedback paradigms, the goal is to induce emotions by causing individuals to believe that they are experiencing physiological arousal. The assumption is that cognitive appraisals will cause individuals to believe that the heart rate they are hearing is their own heart rate, and that this heart rate is indicative of their current physiological state (i.e., *I am anxious*, or *I am interested*). For example, when an accelerated heart rate is presented, individuals may evaluate their emotional state and conclude that they are anxious or excited. This perception may compete with other cognitive processes (such as taking attention away from the learning task and onto their emotional state) which may cause shifts in their metacognitive judgments about how well they can learn and understand the material, how much effort they exude in learning the material, and their performance on assessments related to the material.

The goal of this experiment was to determine if induced emotional states could significantly influence participants' metacognitive judgments and learning performance during multimedia learning. The following research questions were examined: (1) Can induced emotional states significantly affect participants' self-reported subjective emotional states? (2) Can induced emotional states significantly affect participants' metacognitive judgments?; and (3) Can induced emotional states significantly affect participants' learning performance? The foundations for these questions stem from the need for understanding how emotional states and motivation impact multimedia learning, and how multimedia learning environments can be improved to facilitate adaptive and effective self-regulation of these processes.

2 Method

2.1 Participants

Fifty (N=50) participants from a large public Midsouth university were recruited for this experiment. The participants' mean age was 23.3 years ($SD=7.1$), and of the entire sample there were 34 females (68%). Their mean GPA was 3.13, with a range of 2.0-4.0.

2.2 Stimuli and Software

A researcher-developed linearly-structured self-paced multimedia learning environment comprised of 24 slides about the human circulatory system was presented using Automated Testing System [8]. ATS is a computer-based testing system used for delivering learning content, presenting questions, and recording participants' metacognitive judgments, study-time allocation, and responses to multiple-choice questions about the content on each slide (see Figure 1).

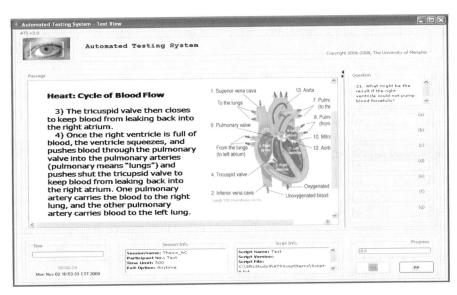

Fig. 1. Screen shot of Automated Testing System, the multimedia learning environment used in the experiment

A Reebok Fit Watch 10s strapless heart rate monitor was worn around participants' non-dominant wrist. This heart rate monitor is designed to accurately detect and display the wearer's current heart rate. However, because previously-recorded baseline and accelerated heart rates were presented to participants, this function was not used for this experiment. The purpose of the watch was simply to cause participants to believe that their heart rate was being collected, recorded, and presented back to them during the session.

The two auditory stimuli (baseline and accelerated heart rates) were presented binaurally through headphones. These stimuli intiated when participants opened a content slide and played continuously until participants exited the slide by clicking the *Next* arrow on the screen. During baseline trials, participants heard a recording of a resting human heart beat (approximately 70 BPM), and during arousal trials, they heard a recording of a human heart beat at an accelerated rate (approximately 100 BPM). During control trials, no auditory stimulus was presented. The presentation of these stimuli was counterbalanced throughout the session.

2.3 Materials and Measures

The paper and pencil materials for this experiment were a consent form, a demographic questionnaire, the Affect Grid [12], and a 3-item researcher-developed survey. The Affect Grid is a single item scale which serves as a quick means of measuring affective states along the dimensions of valence and arousal. Participants place on X somewhere on the grid, and receive one pleasure score and one arousal score. These scores are used to identify participants' emotional state along these two dimensions. For this experiment, valence was defined as pleasantness vs. unpleasantness, and arousal was defined as high motivation vs. low motivation. The researcher-developed survey was a short 3-item self-report measure which asked participants to assess their emotions and behavior during the session. The three questions asked participants to report their general emotional state when they heard an accelerated, baseline, or no heart rate (i.e., "When my heart rate was accelerated, I generally felt:_____"). Participants were asked to fill in the blank by choosing from a word bank including the following seven emotions: neutral, confused, motivated, bored, excited, anxious, and stressed.

2.4 Experimental Procedure

Participants first spent as much time as necessary to complete the informed consent and demographic questionnaire. After completing these measures, participants spent approximately five minutes receiving instructions for using the Affect Grid. They were then asked to complete one practice Affect Grid to confirm that they understood the instructions. For this task, participants were asked to indicate where the emotion *frustration* would be found on the grid by placing an X in the appropriate box. Any confusion about this task was resolved through discussion between the participant and the researcher.

All participants then watched a six minute video which provided a guided tour of the structure of ATS and instructions for the learning session. Following the video, participants were instructed to fasten the Reebok heart rate monitor around their non-dominant wrist. The researcher explained that during the learning session the monitor would record and wirelessly transmit their heart rate to a USB drive which fed this data to a software package on the computer. Participants were instructed that this software package would deliver their heart rate binaurally through headphones at various times throughout the session. The researcher explained that they would hear their heart rate when they opened a content slide, and that they would no longer hear their heart rate after navigating away from that slide. They were also instructed that during some content slides they would not hear their heart rate at all. If participants understood all of these instructions, they proceeded to the learning session.

The learning session consisted of 24 trials. For each trial, participants completed the following six steps using ATS. First, participants were presented with either a text-based or inference question and were asked to provide an *ease of learning* (EOL) judgment. Participants used a six-item signal detection scale ranging from one (*I strongly feel this question will be difficult to answer*) to six (*I strongly feel this question will be easy to answer*). Next, participants clicked a button at the bottom of the screen to navigate to a content slide. As soon as this slide was opened, participants heard either an accelerated, baseline, or no heart rate. Participants were given as much time as desired to study a content slide which contained a paragraph of text and a static diagram about the circulatory system. The text-based or inferential question remained in the top corner of the screen while participants studied the slide so that they did not have to retain the question in working memory while they studied. When participants indicated that they were finished studying the slide by clicking an arrow at the bottom of the screen, the content slide and question were removed from the screen and the auditory stimulus was no longer presented. Participants were then asked to make a *judgment of learning* (JOL) to indicate how well they understood the content they just read. Another six-item signal detection scale was used ranging from one (*I strongly believe I do not understand this content*) to six (*I strongly believe I do understand this content*). After making their selection, the text-based or inferential question was presented in a new screen along with four multiple choice foils. Participants were asked to select which of the four options was the most appropriate answer by clicking a radio button next to the item. After making their selection, participants were asked to make a *retrospective confidence judgment* (RCJ) to indicate how strongly they believed their answer was correct. This six-item signal detection scale ranged from one (*I strongly believe my answer was incorrect*) to six (*I strongly believe my answer was correct*). Finally, at the end of each trial, ATS prompted participants to report their current emotional state by placing an X in the appropriate box on an Affect Grid which was sitting on the desk beside them. Participants completed one Affect Grid for each trial in the session, yielding 24 total Affect Grid scores. After completing this process for each of the 24 trials within the experiment, participants completed a heart-rate recognition task in which they listened to ten randomly presented recordings of either an accelerated or baseline heart-rate and were asked to determine whether each recording was accelerated or baseline. The purpose of this task was to verify that participants were able to correctly discriminate these two heart-rates during the session. All 50 participants successfully completed this task. After the heart-rate discrimination task was complete, participants were thanked, compensated, and debriefed.

2.5 Coding and Scoring

ATS was designed to collect and record all participant interactions and upload these interactions to a log file which was created for each participant. Every log file was uploaded to a database for later analysis. The next section describes how this log file data was used to code and score participants' behavior and performance during the learning session.

2.5.1 Multiple Choice Questions

For the 24 multiple choice questions, participants were awarded one point for a correct answer and no points for an incorrect answer. The range of scores per participant was 0-24 since each participant answered 12 text-based and 12 inference questions during a learning session. Four mean scores were collected for each participant: the mean score for overall performance across all 24 slides, and three mean scores for each level of induced emotional state (accelerated, baseline, and no heart rate).

2.5.2 Metacognitive Judgments

For each trial within the session, participants provided a response ranging from one to six for each of the three metacognitive judgments (EOL, JOL, RCJ). Using these responses, four mean scores were calculated for each metacognitive judgment. Participants received one overall score for each metacognitive judgment across all 24 slides, and one mean score for each of the three levels of induced emotional state (accelerated, baseline, or no heart rate).

2.5.3 Affect Grid

For each of the 24 Affect Grids completed within the session, participants received a valence score and an arousal score. The valence score was taken as the number of the square selected, with squares numbered along the horizontal dimension. These numbers began at the left and counted from one to nine. The arousal score was taken as the number of the square selected, with squares numbered along the vertical dimension. These numbers began at the bottom and counted from one to nine (yielding a 9x9 grid). Participants received six mean scores: one mean valence score for each of the three levels of induced emotional state (accelerated, baseline, or no heart rate), and one mean arousal score for each of the three levels of induced emotional state.

3 Results and Discussion

3.1 Research Question 1: Can Induced Emotional States Significantly Affect Participants' Self-reported Subjective Emotional States?

For this analysis, we first conducted two separate one-way repeated measures ANOVAs to compare the effect of induced emotional states on participants' self-reported subjective emotional states (on the Affect Grid) in accelerated, baseline, and no heart rate conditions. The first ANOVA was conducted on participants' mean valance score (pleasantness vs. unpleasantness) for each of the three conditions, and the second ANOVA was conducted on participants' mean arousal score (high motivation vs. low motivation) for each of the three conditions. We found a significant main effect for valence, $F(2, 48) = 3.64$, $p < .05$, $\eta^2 = .07$. Post-hoc analyses revealed that participants reported significantly more pleasant emotions when they heard an accelerated or baseline heart rate than when they heard no heart rate (accelerated=baseline>no heart rate). We also found a significant main effect for arousal, $F(2, 48) = 11.32$, $p < .0001$, $\eta^2 = .19$. Post-hoc analyses revealed that participants reported significantly higher arousal when they heard an accelerated heart rate than when they heard an baseline or no heart rate, and reported significantly higher arousal when they heard a baseline heart rate than no heart rate (accelerated>baseline>no heart rate).

To further supplement these analyses, we conducted a frequency analysis using the mean proportion of participants' self-reported responses on the three-item researcher developed questionnaire to determine which emotional states were most frequently reported for each level of induced emotional state. We found that during accelerated trials, 45% of participants reported feeling anxious, 21% reported confusion, 10% reported excitement, 10% reported feeling motivated, 7% reported feeling frustrated, and the remaining 7% reported feeling either stressed or neutral. For baseline trials, 86% of participants reported feeling neutral, 7% reported feeling motivated, and the remaining 7% reported feeling either stressed or frustrated. For control trials, 69% reported feeling neutral, 10% reported feeling anxious, 7% reported feeling stressed, 7% reported feeling motivated, and the remaining 7% reported feeling frustrated or confused.

3.2 Research Question 2: Can Induced Emotional States Significantly Affect Participants' Metacognitive Judgments?

For this analysis, we conducted a series of one-way repeated measures ANOVAs to compare the effect of induced emotional states on metacognitive judgments in accelerated, baseline, and no heart rate conditions. First we conducted a separate ANOVA for each of the three metacognitive judgments (EOLs, JOLs, RCJs) collected from participants throughout the session. We found no significant main effect for EOL judgments, $F(2, 48) = 1.92$, $p > .05$, $\eta^2 = .04$. This is to be expected, as EOL judgments were prompted before participants received the auditory stimuli and therefore no emotion-induction had occurred. We found a significant main effect for JOLs, $F(2,48) = 4.96$, $p = .01$, $\eta^2 = .09$. Post-hoc analyses using a Bonferroni correction revealed that participants reported significantly higher JOLs when they heard an accelerated or baseline heart rate than when they heard no heart rate (accelerated=baseline>no heart rate). We also found a main effect for RCJs, $F(2,48) = 23.01$, $p < .0001$, $\eta^2 = .32$. Post-hoc analyses using a Bonferroni correction revealed that participants made significantly higher RCJs when they heard an accelerated heart rate than when they heard a baseline or no heart rate, and significantly higher RCJs when they heard a baseline than no heart rate (accelerated>baseline>control).

3.3 Research Question 3: Can Induced Emotional States Significantly Affect Participants' Learning Performance?

We conducted a one-way repeated measures ANOVA to compare the effect of induced emotional states on participants' accuracy on multiple choice questions about the science content in accelerated, baseline, and no heart rate conditions. We found a significant main effect for induced emotional state, $F(2,48) = 23.62$, $p<.0001$, $\eta^2 = .33$. Post-hoc analyses using a Bonferroni correction revealed that participants scored significantly higher when they heard an accelerated heart rate than a baseline or no heart rate, and scored significantly higher when they heard a baseline heart rate than no heart rate (accelerated>baseline>no heart rate).

3.4 Discussion

The results of this experiment offer insight into (1) the ways in which learners' emotional states impact their metacognitive monitoring and performance, and (2) which emotions may facilitate multimedia learning, and which emotions may impair learning. First, the results indicate that learners made significantly higher (i.e., more confident) metacognitive judgments when they heard an accelerated or baseline heart rate compared to no heart rate. While this finding by itself may be difficult to interpret, the results from participants' self-reported emotional states for accelerated, baseline, and no heart rate help disambiguate this potentially confusing issue. It is clear that during accelerated trials participants were more likely to feel anxious, confused, or excited. Previous research [5] indicates that emotional states like confusion can foster motivation during learning, as learners feel driven to resolve their confusion in order to overcome an impasse and more deeply process the material. Anxiety has been shown in some learners to invoke motivation to invest more effort to avoid poor performance [10], and excitement is associated with engagement and interest in the task. These emotions are assumed to translate to higher learning performance. Our results provide further evidence for this assumption, as participants achieved considerably higher scores for accelerated trials than baseline or control. Compared to accelerated trials, during baseline and control trials participants were considerably more likely to report feeling neutral. Neutrality, which can be defined as a lack of motivation or interest, would be expected to lead to decreased learning gains. However, if this is the case, then why did learners still perform significantly higher on baseline trials than control trials? By examining results from the Affect Grid, we see that participants felt significantly more motivated during baseline trials than control trials. Additionally, results from the 3-item survey revealed that participants were more likely to report feelings of motivation and frustration for baseline trials than control trials. In fact, participants were more likely to report feelings of anxiety and stress during control trials, and these emotions are presumed to lead to more shallow learning.

In sum, our results indicate that when participants heard an accelerated heart rate, they were more likely to report feelings of pleasure and motivation, to make higher metacognitive judgments, and achieve higher learning performance than when they heard a baseline or no heart rate. This highlights the importance of understanding not only learners' cognitive and metacognitive processes, but also learners' emotional and motivational processes and how these processes come together to impact learning.

These results supplant the need for intelligent tutoring systems, multimedia and hypermedia learning environments to be sensitive to these dynamic and complex processes in order to help learners achieve deep learning [1,9]. For example, intelligent tutoring systems which use pedagogical agents to scaffold learners' understanding of complex science topics might benefit from the use of physiological measures which can detect shifts in learners' emotional and motivational states on-line. If a learner shifts to a negative emotional state (i.e., stress, boredom), a system which is sensitive to these shifts could help learners transition out of these emotional states by modeling, prompting, and scaffolding appropriate self-regulatory processes. While the most optimal way to helping learners regulate their metacognitive, cognitive, emotional, and motivational processes during learning is still unclear, the results from this experiment offer a glimpse into how these processes interact to impact each other and to impact learning of complex science.

References

1. Azevedo, R.: The role of self-regulation in learning about science with hypermedia. In: Robinson, D., Schraw, G. (eds.) Recent Innovations in Educational Technology that Facilitate Student Learning, pp. 127–156. Information Age Publishing, Charlotte (2008)
2. Azevedo, R., Witherspoon, A.M.: Self-regulated learning with hypermedia. In: Graesser, A., Dunlosky, J., Hacker, D. (eds.) Handbook of Metacognition in Education, pp. 319–339. Erlbaum, Mahwah (2009)
3. Boekearts, M.: Context sensitivity: Activated motivational beliefs, current concerns and emotional arousal. In: Volet, S., Jarvela, S. (eds.) Motivation in Learning Contexts: Theoretical and Methodological Implications, pp. 17–31. Pergamon Press, Elmsford (2001)
4. Cacioppo, J.T., Bernston, G.G., Larsen, J.,T., Poehlmann, K.M., Ito, T.A.: The physiology of emotion. In: Lewis, M., Haviland-Jones, J.M. (eds.) The Handbook of Emotion. Guilford Press, New York (2000)
5. D'Mello, S.K., Taylor, R., Graesser, A.C.: Monitoring affective trajectories during complex learning. In: McNamara, D.S., Trafton, J.G. (eds.) Proceedings of the 29th Annual Meeting of the Cognitive Science Society, pp. 203–208. Cognitive Science Society, Austin (2007)
6. Hardre, P.L., Reeve, J.: A motivational model of rural students' intentions of persist in, versus drop out of, high school. J. Ed. Psych. 95, 347–356 (2003)
7. Kirsch, I., Lynn, S.J.: Automaticity in clinical psychology. The American Psychologist 54, 504–515 (1999)
8. Lehman, B., D'Mello, S.K., Person, N.: All Alone with your Emotions: An Analysis of Student Emotions during Effortful Problem Solving Activities. In: Workshop on Emotional and Cognitive issues in ITS held in Conjunction with Ninth International Conference on Intelligent Tutoring Systems (2008)
9. Moos, D.C., Azevedo, R.: Exploring the fluctuation of motivation and use of self-regulatory processes during learning with hypermedia. Instructional Science 36, 203–231 (2008)
10. Pekrun, R.: The control-value theory of achievement emotions: Assumptions, corollaries, and implications for educational research and practice. Educational Psychology Review 18, 315–341 (2006)
11. Pintrich, P.: The role of goal orientation in self-regulated learning. In: Boekaerts, M., Pintrich, P., Zeidner, M. (eds.) Handbook of Self-Regulation, pp. 451–502. Academic Press, San Diego (2000)
12. Russell, J.A., Weiss, A., Mendelsohn, G.A.: Affect grid: A single-item scale of pleasure and arousal. Journal of Personality and Social Psychology 57, 493–502 (1989)
13. Schutz, P.A., Davis, H.A.: Emotions during self regulation: The regulation of emotion during test taking. Educational Psychologist 35, 243–256 (2000)
14. Schutz, P.A., DeCuire, J.T.: Inquiry on emotions in education. Educational Psychologist 35, 243–255 (2002)

15. Tooby, J., Cosmides, L.: The evolutionary psychology of emotions and their relationship to internal regulatory variables. In: Lewis, M., Haviland-Jones, J.M., Feldman Barrett, L. (eds.) Handbook of Emotions, pp. 114–137. Guilford Press, New York (2008)
16. Winne, P., Hadwin, A.: The weave of motivation and self-regulated learning. In: Schunk, D., Zimmerman, B. (eds.) Motivation and Self-Regulated Learning: Theory, Research and Applications, pp. 297–314. Taylor & Francis, New York (2008)
17. Zimmerman, B.: Investigating self-regulation and motivation: Historical background, methodological developments, and future prospects. American Educational Research Journal 45, 166–183 (2008)

Metacognition and Learning in Spoken Dialogue Computer Tutoring

Kate Forbes-Riley and Diane Litman

Learning Research and Development Center, University of Pittsburgh, 3939 O'Hara St., Pittsburgh, PA 15260
{forbesk,litman}@cs.pitt.edu

Abstract. We investigate whether four metacognitive metrics derived from student correctness and uncertainty values are predictive of student learning in a *fully automated* spoken dialogue computer tutoring corpus. We previously showed that these metrics predicted learning in a comparable wizarded corpus, where a human wizard performed the speech recognition and correctness and uncertainty annotation. Our results show that three of the four metacognitive metrics remain predictive of learning even in the presence of noise due to automatic speech recognition and automatic correctness and uncertainty annotation. We conclude that our results can be used to inform a future enhancement of our fully automated system to track and remediate student metacognition and thereby further improve learning.

Keywords: metacognition, learning, correlations, spoken dialogue computer tutor, automatic speech recognition and correctness and uncertainty annotation, natural language processing.

1 Introduction

Metacognition is an important area of intelligent tutoring systems research, both in and of itself and with respect to its relationship to learning (e.g. [1,2]). Within tutorial dialogue, one metacognitive state that has received a lot of interest is student uncertainty. In particular, researchers have hypothesized that student uncertainty and incorrectness both signal "learning impasses", i.e. student learning opportunities [3]. In addition, multiple correlational studies have shown a link in tutorial dialogue between learning and student uncertainty or the related state of confusion [4,5,6]. Furthermore, although most computer tutors respond based only on student correctness, a number of controlled experiments have investigated the benefits of responding to student uncertainty over and above correctness during computer tutoring [7,8,9,10,11]. Some of these experiments have shown that responding to student uncertainty over and above correctness results in improved tutoring system performance, as measured by student learning, user satisfaction, and dialogue or learning efficiency.

Drawing on the metacognition literature, we are investigating relationships between the student states of uncertainty and correctness via complex metacognitive metrics that combine measures of these two states. Other researchers have previously used such metacognitive metrics to investigate multiple dimensions very similar to uncertainty and correctness, and we use and build on this literature. Our metrics include learning impasse severity [12] and knowledge monitoring accuracy [13], as well as bias (i.e., over/under confidence) and discrimination (e.g., uncertainty primarily about incorrect answers) [14]. In prior work, we investigated the relationship between these four metacognitive metrics and learning in a wizarded spoken tutoring dialogue corpus, where speech recognition and uncertainty and correctness annotation were performed in real-time by a human "wizard" [5,6]. We computed the metacognitive metrics from the wizard's annotations. We showed that although student uncertainty during the tutoring dialogues does not predict learning, average learning impasse severity, knowledge monitoring accuracy and discrimination were all predictive of learning.

In this paper, we investigate whether these metacognitive metrics remain predictive of learning in a comparable corpus that was collected using the *fully automated* version of our computer tutor. We computed two sets of metacognitive metrics: one set computed from the system's real-time automatic annotations of uncertainty and correctness, and one set computed from manual annotations of uncertainty and correctness performed after the experiment was over. Our results show that almost all of the same metacognitive metrics that predict learning during the wizarded computer tutoring also predict learning during the fully automated computer tutoring, using either the automatically-computed or manually-computed metacognitive metrics. We conclude that these metacognitive metrics are a useful construct for understanding student learning during spoken dialogue computer tutoring, even in the presence of noise introduced by fully automated student uncertainty detection and speech and natural language processing. Our results will be used to track and remediate metacognition in future system versions and thereby further improve student learning.

2 Spoken Dialogue Computer Tutoring Data

This research uses the ITSPOKE-AUTO corpus, which is a collection of dialogues between college students and our spoken dialogue computer tutor, ITSPOKE (**I**ntelligent **T**utoring **SPOKE**n dialogue system). ITSPOKE is a speech-enhanced version of the Why2-Atlas qualitative physics tutor [15].

The ITSPOKE-AUTO corpus is the second of two corpora collected over two prior controlled experiments evaluating the utility of enhancing ITSPOKE to respond to learning impasses involving student uncertainty, over and above correctness [8]. Motivated by research that views uncertainty as well as incorrectness as signals of "learning impasses" [3] (i.e., opportunities to learn), ITSPOKE was modified for use in these two experiments so that it associated one of four impasse states with every student answer, and could adapt contingently based on each answer's impasse state (in the experimental conditions), or based only on its correctness (in the control conditions). The four impasse states correspond to all possible combinations of (binary) uncertainty (uncertain (**UNC**), certain

Nominal State:	INCOR_CER	INCOR_UNC	COR_UNC	COR_CER
Severity Rank:	most (3)	less (2)	least (1)	none (0)

Fig. 1. Different Impasse State Severities

(**CER**)[1]) and correctness (incorrect (**INCOR**), correct (**COR**)), as shown in Figure 1. The incorrectness component of each state reflects the actual accuracy of the student's answer, while the uncertainty component reflects the tutor's perception of the student's awareness of this accuracy. The scalar ranking of impasse states in terms of severity combines these two components and will be discussed below. Further details of the adaptive system are discussed elsewhere [7].

For the two experiments, the experimental procedure was as follows: students (1) read a short physics text, (2) took a multiple-choice pretest, (3) worked through five problems (1 per dialogue) with a version of the system, (4) took a survey, and (5) took an isomorphic posttest.

The first corpus, called the ITSPOKE-WOZ corpus [8], contains 405 dialogues from 81 students, and was collected from the first experiment using a semi-automatic version of ITSPOKE in which speech recognition and correctness and uncertainty annotation were performed by a human "wizard", to test the upper-bound performance of adapting to uncertainty (i.e. without the noise introduced by speech and language processing). The wizard listened to the dialogues (without students' knowledge) and labeled each answer with an uncertainty (UNC, CER) and a correctness label (INCOR, COR).[2] Average pretest and posttest scores were 0.51 and 0.75, respectively.

The second corpus, called the ITSPOKE-AUTO corpus, contains 360 dialogues from 72 students, and was collected from the second experiment using a fully automated version of ITSPOKE in which all tasks were fully automated. In particular, student speech was digitized from microphone input and sent to the Sphinx2 speech recognizer whose stochastic language models were trained on the ITSPOKE-WOZ corpus and prior ITSPOKE corpora. Correctness was automatically labeled on the speech recognition output using the TuTalk semantic analyzer [16], which was trained on the ITSPOKE-WOZ corpus. Uncertainty was automatically labeled on the speech recognition output using an uncertainty model built with WEKA software from features of the student speech and dialogue context, including lexical, pitch, temporal, and energy features as well as tutor question and gender. The uncertainty model is a logistic regression equation that was trained on the ITSPOKE-WOZ corpus.

The ITSPOKE-AUTO corpus was manually transcribed after the second experiment, and the wizard from the first experiment manually labeled each student turn in the ITSPOKE-AUTO corpus for uncertainty and correctness. The system's correctness and uncertainty labels were then compared with the wizard's labels: for correctness, this comparison yielded a system accuracy of

---

[1] A 'certain' answer may actually be certain or neutral for certainty.
[2] In prior ITSPOKE corpora, this wizard displayed interannotator agreement of 0.85 and 0.62 Kappa on correctness and uncertainty, respectively [5].

ITSPOKE-AUTO$_1$: Let's begin by looking at the motion of the man and his keys while he's holding them. How does his velocity compare to that of his keys?

STUDENT-AUTO$_1$: his also the is the same as that of his keys points force **(INCOR_CER)**

STUDENT-MANU$_1$: his velocity is the same as that of his keys while he's holding them (COR_UNC)

ITSPOKE-AUTO$_2$: Actually... Their velocities must be the same, because the man's holding his keys, so they're not moving with respect to each other. [...] What are the forces exerted on the man after he releases his keys?

STUDENT-AUTO$_2$: the only force is **(INCOR_UNC)**

STUDENT-MANU$_2$: the only force is (INCOR_UNC)

ITSPOKE-AUTO$_3$: Well... Gravity is the only force acting on the man. [...] So what's the direction of the force of gravity on the man (e.g., vertically up)?

STUDENT-AUTO$_3$: vertically down **(COR_CER)**

STUDENT-MANU$_3$: vertically down (COR_CER)

Fig. 2. Annotated ITSPOKE-AUTO Corpus Excerpt

84.7%, and for uncertainty, this comparison yielded a system accuracy of 80.3% Speech recognition accuracy measured as 100% - Word Error Rate (WER) was 74.6%. WER is a standard measure for evaluating the performance of automatic speech recognition software. We compute WER using the NIST sclite program, which uses minimum edit distance to come up with a WER score by assigning penalties for word insertions, deletions, and substitutions. Average pretest and posttest scores in the ITSPOKE-AUTO corpus were 0.51 and 0.73, respectively.[3]

Figure 2 shows an annotated example of the ITSPOKE-AUTO corpus dialogues. **STUDENT-AUTO** shows the automatically recognized speech and automatic uncertainty and correctness labels for each student turn, while *STUDENT-MANU* shows the corresponding manual transcript and annotations.

3 Metacognitive Performance Metrics

In this section we introduce several ways of combining uncertainty and correctness annotations into quantitative metacognitive performance metrics. All metrics were computed on a per student basis (over all five dialogues). In addition, all metrics were computed twice: once based on the automatic correctness and uncertainty annotations (*-auto*), and once based on the corresponding manual annotations (*-manu*). Finally, note that our metrics represent inferred (or tutor-perceived) values rather than actual values, because our uncertainty labeling is done by the system or a human judge; we discuss this issue in Section 5.

---

[3] Independent repeated measures ANOVA analyses of both corpora showed significant main effects for repeated test measure, indicating that students learned a significant amount during both experiments.

Our first metric is based on a ranking of learning impasses by severity. In particular, we first associated a scalar **impasse severity** value with each student answer in the ITSPOKE-AUTO corpus, and then computed an average impasse severity. Our impasse severity values were proposed in our earlier work [12] and are shown in Figure 1. According to our ranking, the most severe type of impasse (3) occurs when a student is incorrect but not aware of it. States 2 and 1 are of increasingly lesser severity: the student is incorrect but aware that s/he might be, and the student is correct but uncertain about it, respectively. Finally, no impasse exists when a student is correct and not uncertain about it (0). These severity rankings reflect our assumption that to resolve an impasse, a student must first perceive that it exists. Incorrectness simply indicates that the student has reached an impasse, while uncertainty - in a correct or incorrect answer - indicates that the student perceives s/he has reached an impasse.

The rest of our metacognitive metrics are taken from the metacognitive performance literature. The knowledge monitoring accuracy metric that we use is the Hamann coefficient (**HC**) [13]. This metric has previously been used to measure the accuracy of one's own knowledge monitoring, called "Feeling of Knowing"(FOK) [17]. A closely related notion in the metacognition literature is "Feeling of Another's Knowing" (FOAK), which refers to monitoring the FOK of someone else [18], and is very similar to our student uncertainty labeling as performed by the system or a human judge. High and low FOK/FOAK judgments have also been associated with speaker certainty and uncertainty, respectively, in prior research [19].

HC measures absolute knowledge monitoring accuracy[4], or the accuracy with which certainty reflects correctness. HC ranges in value from -1 (no knowledge monitoring accuracy) to 1 (perfect accuracy). As shown below, the numerator subtracts cases where (un)certainty is at odds with (in)correctness from cases where they correspond, while the denominator sums over all cases.

$$\mathbf{HC} = \frac{(COR\_CER + INCOR\_UNC) - (INCOR\_CER + COR\_UNC)}{(COR\_CER + INCOR\_UNC) + (INCOR\_CER + COR\_UNC)}$$

Following [20], who investigate the role of immediate feedback and other metacognitive scaffolds in a medical tutoring system, we additionally measure metacognitive performance in terms of **bias** and **discrimination** [14]. Bias measures the overall degree to which confidence matches correctness. Bias scores greater than and less than zero indicate overconfidence and underconfidence, respectively, with zero indicating best metacognitive performance. As shown below, the first term represents the relative proportion of confidet answers (certain cases/all cases); the second represents the relative proportion of correct answers.

$$\mathbf{bias} = \frac{COR\_CER + INCOR\_CER}{COR\_CER + INCOR\_CER + COR\_UNC + INCOR\_UNC} - \frac{COR\_CER + COR\_UNC}{COR\_CER + INCOR\_CER + COR\_UNC + INCOR\_UNC}$$

---

[4] While Gamma (which measures relative monitoring accuracy) is also often used, there is a lack of consensus regarding the benefits of Gamma versus HC [13], and we found HC more predictive of learning in our ITSPOKE-WOZ corpus [6].

Table 1. Prior Correlation Results from ITSPOKE-WOZ Corpus

Measure	Mean	SD	R	p
AV Impasse Severity	.63	.24	-.56	.00
HC	.59	.16	.42	.00
Bias	-.02	.12	-.21	.06
Discrimination	.42	.19	.32	.00
%C	.79	.09	.52	.00
%U	.23	.11	-.13	.24

Discrimination measures the ability to discriminate performance in terms of (in)correctness. Discrimination scores greater than zero indicate higher metacognitive performance. As shown below, the first term represents the proportion of correct answers judged as certain, and the second term represents the proportion of incorrect answers judged as certain.

$$\textbf{discrimination} = \frac{COR\_CER}{COR\_CER+COR\_UNC} - \frac{INCOR\_CER}{INCOR\_CER+INCOR\_UNC}$$

To illustrate the computation of our four metacognitive performance metrics, suppose the annotated dialogue excerpt in Figure 2 represented our entire dataset (from a single student). Then we would have the following values for our automatically-derived (_auto) metrics for that student:

$$AVImpasseSeverity\_auto = \frac{3+2+0}{3} = \frac{5}{3}$$
$$HC\_auto = \frac{(1+1)-(1+0)}{(1+1)+(1+0)} = \frac{1}{3}$$
$$bias\_auto = \frac{1+1}{1+1+0+1} - \frac{1+0}{1+1+0+1} = \frac{2}{3} - \frac{1}{3} = \frac{1}{3}$$
$$discrimination\_auto = \frac{1}{1+0} - \frac{1}{1+1} = \frac{1}{1} - \frac{1}{2} = \frac{1}{2}$$

In prior work [5,6], we showed that these four metacognitive metrics were predictive of learning in our ITSPOKE-WOZ corpus, where speech recognition, and uncertainty and correctness annotation were performed by a wizard. We computed the partial Pearson's correlation between each metacognitive metric and posttest, after first controlling for pretest to account for learning gain. We also computed the correlation for the percentage of student turns manually annotated as correct (**%C**) and as uncertain (**%U**). Correctness and uncertainty are useful baselines since they were used to derive the four complex metrics and have previously been shown to predict learning by ourselves and others (e.g [21]). Table 1 summarizes the results of this prior work, showing the mean and standard deviation of each metric, along with its Pearson's Correlation Coefficient (R), and the significance of the correlation (p).

4 Results

Here we investigate whether our four metacognitive metrics are predictive of learning in our "noisy" ITSPOKE-AUTO corpus, where speech recognition, uncertainty and correctness annotation were fully automated.

Comparison of Table 2 and Table 1 shows that with the exception of discrimination, the two metacognitive metrics (impasse severity and knowledge monitoring accuracy) that are significantly correlated with learning in the ITSPOKE-WOZ corpus remain correlated with learning in the ITSPOKE-AUTO corpus, both when derived from the automatic (_auto) and the manual annotations (_manu). In the case of average impasse severity, both the automatically-derived and manually-derived metrics yield a negative correlation, but the manually-derived metric (R = -0.50) is closest to the result in the ITSPOKE-WOZ corpus (R = -0.56). In the case of knowledge monitoring accuracy (HC), both the automatically-derived and manually-derived metrics yield a positive correlation, but the automatically-derived metric (R = 0.35) is closest to the result in the ITSPOKE-WOZ corpus (R = 0.42). Bias is negatively correlated with learning as a trend in the ITSPOKE-WOZ corpus; in the ITSPOKE-AUTO corpus the manually-derived bias metric is nearly but not quite a trend while the automatically-derived bias metric is significant. These results suggest that less severe impasse states (i.e., impasses that include uncertainty), greater knowledge monitoring accuracy, and underconfidence about one's correctness, are all better for the student from a learning perspective during computer tutoring, even when the measurement of these metrics must take into account noise due to automatic uncertainty detection and natural language processing.

Interestingly, the simple uncertainty metric (%U) in and of itself does not show predictive utility in this data; it is not correlated with learning in the ITSPOKE-AUTO corpus, nor did it correlate with learning in the ITSPOKE-WOZ corpus. However, correctness %C does significantly correlate with learning in both corpora; the manually-derived metric is closer to the ITSPOKE-WOZ corpus (R = 0.52) than the automatically-derived metric (R = 0.39).

Although these results suggest remediating metacognition can have a positive impact on learning in both wizarded and fully automated spoken dialogue tutoring, they also raise the question of whether this will be effective over remediating correctness. We addressed this question via three further analyses. First we

Table 2. Correlation Results from ITSPOKE-AUTO Corpus

Metric	Mean	SD	R	p
AV Impasse Severity_auto	.96	.26	-.40	.00
AV Impasse Severity_manu	.82	.23	-.50	.00
HC_auto	.42	.14	.35	.00
HC_manu	.49	.13	.29	.02
Bias_auto	.21	.07	-.36	.00
Bias_manu	.06	.13	-.19	.11
Discrimination_auto	.19	.10	-.04	.77
Discrimination_manu	.30	.14	-.03	.81
%C_auto	.66	.10	.39	.00
%C_manu	.72	.09	.52	.00
%U_auto	.13	.07	-.15	.20
%U_manu	.22	.14	-.13	.28

computed bivariate Pearson's correlations between correctness and each metacognitive metric. Correctness was significantly correlated with all metacognitive metrics in both the ITSPOKE-WOZ and ITSPOKE-AUTO corpora (both manually and automatically-derived). This suggests that remediating megacognition will not add value over remediating correctness. However, we then computed partial Pearson's correlations between each metacognitive metric and posttest after controlling for pretest and correctness. In the ITSPOKE-WOZ corpus, all metrics except bias remained significantly correlated with posttest, but in the ITSPOKE-AUTO corpus, no metric remained correlated with posttest. Finally, we computed stepwise linear regressions that allowed the model to select from pretest, correctness and the metacognitive metrics. In the ITSPOKE-WOZ corpus HC was selected for inclusion in the regression model after %C and pretest [6]; this indicates that knowledge monitoring accuracy adds value over and above correctness for predicting learning. In the ITSPOKE-AUTO corpus, AV Impasse Severity_auto was selected besides pretest when using automatically-derived metrics, but %C_manu was selected besides pretest when using manually-derived metrics. These last two analyses suggest that remediating metacognition can add value over remediating correctness in the "ideal" and the "realistic" conditions of wizarded and fully automated spoken dialogue tutoring, respectively.

5 Conclusions and Future Directions

This paper investigates whether four metacognitive metrics remain predictive of student learning in a previously collected fully automated spoken dialogue computer tutoring corpus; we previously showed that these metacognitive metrics predict learning in a comparable wizarded corpus. Our purpose in this study was to determine whether our prior results could be replicated even in the presence of noise due to automatic speech recognition and automatic correctness and uncertainty annotation. Our larger goal is to use our results to track and remediate metacognition and thereby further improve student learning

Of our four metacognitive metrics, one was introduced in our prior work (impasse severity); the other three come from the metacognitive performance literature (knowledge monitoring accuracy, bias and discrimination). We computed one set of metacognitive metrics from the system's real-time automatic annotations of uncertainty and correctness, and another set from subsequent manual annotations. Our results show that average impasse severity, knowledge monitoring accuracy and bias remain predictive of learning in the fully automated corpus - both when computed from the automatic values and when computed form the manual values. We conclude that these metacognitive metrics are a useful construct for understanding student learning during spoken dialogue computer tutoring, even when their measurement includes noise introduced by fully automated uncertainty detection and natural language processing. Furthermore our analyses suggest that remediating metacognitve metrics can add value over and above remediating correctness; this result is strongest in the "ideal" conditions of wizarded tutoring, but our regression results suggest that it also holds in the "realistic" conditions of fully automated spoken dialogue tutoring.

In future work we plan to use our results to inform a modification of our system aimed at improving student metacognitive abilities and also thereby improving student learning. In particular, our results indicate that it feasible to develop enhancements for our fully automated system that target student metacognition based on the noisy version of our metacognitive metrics; if our results had not held for our automatically-derived metrics then we would have to explore system enhancements that target student metacognition using the much more time-consuming and expensive wizarded system. Note however that because uncertainty in our system is labeled by the tutor (either the system or a human wizard), our metacognitive metrics represent *inferred* or tutor-perceived values rather than actual values. It is well known in the affective tutoring literature that obtaining "actual" values for student/user affective states and attitudes is difficult; for example, student self-judgments and peer judgments have both been shown to be problematic (e.g. [22]). Nevertheless, to help measure improvements in student metacognitive abilities due to our future system modifications, we will also incorporate "Feeling of Knowing" (FOK) ratings into our testing, whereby students will provide input on their uncertainty levels. More generally, there is increasing interest in using intelligent tutoring systems to teach metacognition, and we plan to build on this literature (e.g. [1,2,20]) with future system enhancements that target student metacognitive abilities.

Acknowledgments

This work is funded by National Science Foundation (NSF) award #0914615 and #0631930. We thank Art Ward for comments.

References

1. Aleven, V., Roll, I. (eds.): AIED Workshop on Metacognition and Self-Regulated Learning in Intelligent Tutoring Systems (2007)
2. Roll, I., Aleven, V. (eds.): ITS Workshop on Meta-Cognition and Self-Regulated Learning in Educational Technologies (2008)
3. VanLehn, K., Siler, S., Murray, C.: Why do only some events cause learning during human tutoring? Cognition and Instruction 21(3) (2003)
4. Craig, S., Graesser, A., Sullins, J., Gholson, B.: Affect and learning: an exploratory look into the role of affect in learning with AutoTutor. Journal of Educational Media 29(3) (2004)
5. Litman, D., Forbes-Riley, K.: Improving (meta)cognitive tutoring by detecting and responding to uncertainty. In: Working Notes of the Cognitive and Metacognitive Educational Systems AAAI Symposium, Arlington, VA (November 2009)
6. Litman, D., Forbes-Riley, K.: Spoken tutorial dialogue and the feeling of another's knowing. In: Proceedings 10th Annual Meeting of the Special Interest Group on Discourse and Dialogue (SIGDIAL), London, UK (September 2009)

7. Forbes-Riley, K., Litman, D.: Designing and evaluating a wizarded uncertainty-adaptive spoken dialogue tutoring system. In: Computer Speech and Language, CSL (2010) (in press)
8. Forbes-Riley, K., Litman, D.: Adapting to student uncertainty improves tutoring dialogues. In: Proc. Intl. Conf. on Artificial Intelligence in Education (2009)
9. Pon-Barry, H., Schultz, K., Bratt, E.O., Clark, B., Peters, S.: Responding to student uncertainty in spoken tutorial dialogue systems. International Journal of Artificial Intelligence in Education 16, 171–194 (2006)
10. Aist, G., Kort, B., Reilly, R., Mostow, J., Picard, R.: Experimentally augmenting an intelligent tutoring system with human-supplied capabilities: Adding human-provided emotional scaffolding to an automated reading tutor that listens. In: Proc. Intelligent Tutoring Systems Workshop on Empirical Methods for Tutorial Dialogue Systems (2002)
11. Tsukahara, W., Ward, N.: Responding to subtle, fleeting changes in the user's internal state. In: Proc. SIG-CHI on Human Factors in Computing Systems (2001)
12. Forbes-Riley, K., Litman, D., Rotaru, M.: Responding to student uncertainty during computer tutoring: A preliminary evaluation. In: Woolf, B.P., Aïmeur, E., Nkambou, R., Lajoie, S. (eds.) ITS 2008. LNCS, vol. 5091, pp. 60–69. Springer, Heidelberg (2008)
13. Nietfeld, J.L., Enders, C.K., Schraw, G.: A monte carlo comparison of measures of relative and absolute monitoring accuracy. Educational and Psychological Measurement (2006)
14. Kelemen, W.L., Frost, P.J., Weaver, C.A.: Individual differences in metacognition: Evidence against a general metacognitive ability. Memory and Cognition 28, 92–107 (2000)
15. VanLehn, K., Jordan, P.W., Rosé, C., Bhembe, D., Böttner, M., Gaydos, A., Makatchev, M., Pappuswamy, U., Ringenberg, M., Roque, A., Siler, S., Srivastava, R., Wilson, R.: The architecture of Why2-Atlas: A coach for qualitative physics essay writing. In: Cerri, S.A., Gouardéres, G., Paraguaçu, F. (eds.) ITS 2002. LNCS, vol. 2363, p. 158. Springer, Heidelberg (2002)
16. Jordan, P., Hall, B., Ringenberg, M., Cui, Y., Ros, C.: Tools for authoring a dialogue agent that participates in learning studies. In: Proceedings of Artificial Intelligence in Education (AIED), Los Angeles, July 2007, pp. 43–50 (2007)
17. Smith, V.L., Clark, H.H.: On the course of answering questions. Journal of Memory and Language (1993)
18. Brennan, S.E., Williams, M.: The feeling of another's knowing: Prosody and filled pauses as cues to listeners about the metacognitive states of speakers. Journal of Memory and Language (1995)
19. Dijkstra, C., Krahmer, E., Swerts, M.: Manipulating uncertainty: The contribution of different audiovisual prosodic cues to the perception of confidence. In: Proc. Speech Prosody (2006)
20. Saadawi, G.M.E., Azevedo, R., Castine, M., Payne, V., Medvedeva, O., Tseytlin, E., Legowski, E., azen Jukic, D., Crowley, R.S.: Factors affecting feeling-of-knowing in a medical intelligent tutoring system: the role of immediate feedback as a metacognitive scaffold. Adv. in Helth Sci. Educ. (2009)
21. Litman, D., Moore, J., Dzikovska, M., Farrow, E.: Using natural language processing to analyze tutorial dialogue corpora across domains and modalities. In: Proc. Intl. Conf. on Artificial Intelligence in Education (2009)
22. D'Mello, S.K., Craig, S.D., Witherspoon, A., McDaniel, B., Graesser, A.: Automatic detection of learner's affect from conversational cues. User Modeling and User-Adapted Interaction: Journal of Personalization Research 18, 45–80 (2008)

A Self-regulator for Navigational Learning in Hyperspace

Akihiro Kashihara and Ryoya Kawai

The University of Electro-Communications,
1-5-1, Chofugaoka, Chofu, Tokyo, 182-8585, Japan
kasihara@ice.uec.ac.jp

Abstract. Self-directed learning with hypertext-based resources involves navigating the hyperspace to construct knowledge, which requires learners to self-regulate their navigational learning process. Such self-regulation also involves planning the navigation process and reflecting on the knowledge construction process. However, it is hard for them to achieve the self-regulation process since it is concurrent with the navigational learning process. The main issue addressed in this paper is how to promote the self-regulation process and to improve the coordination between navigational learning process and its self-regulation process in hyperspace, which includes coordinating two different self-regulation processes: navigation planning and reflection. Our approach to this issue is to provide learners with a cognitive tool called self-regulator with which they can reify these coordination processes with self-regulation history. The results of the case study we have conducted suggest that the self-regulator can promote learners' self-regulation process to enhance the efficiency and effectiveness of their navigational learning process.

Keywords: Self-regulation, cognitive tool, navigational learning.

1 Introduction

Self-directed learning with hypermedia/hypertext-based resources involves navigating the hyperspace to construct knowledge. Such navigation with knowledge construction is called navigational learning. Navigational learning requires learners to regulate their learning process by themselves [1], [2]. Such self-regulation process plays a crucial role in promoting efficiency and effects of the learning process [3].

On the other hand, the self-regulation process is not so easy for the learners since its target is the learning process in their mind and since it is concurrent with the learning process [2]. In fact, they often get lost in hyperspace spatially and conceptually due to the difficulty in monitoring and controlling their navigation and knowledge construction process in their mind [2], [4].

How to address such difficulty in self-regulation becomes an important issue in hypermedia/hypertext-based learning environments [5], [6]. There currently exist at least two approaches to this issue, which are adaptive hypermedia (AH) and skill development ones. The AH approach aims at facilitating navigational learning process by means of adaptive navigation and adaptive presentation support [7], which intend to decrease learners' self-regulation efforts to call their attention to understanding the contents of the hypermedia/hypertext-based resources. On the other hand, the skill development approach aims at scaffolding their self-regulation process, which encourages learners to self-regulate their navigational learning process [3], [6].

Related work on self-regulation skill development has mainly focused on instructions/prompts for learners to master strategies of self-regulation [8], [9]. However, there is little discussion about how to scaffold self-regulation with some software-based learning technology [3], [10]. Our approach to the skill development is to introduce cognitive tool, which is a computational tool for encouraging learners to externalize the process of learning or for visualizing it [11], [12]. Cognitive tool enables the learners to articulate their learning process, which could reduce difficulty of self-regulation process. We also expect that cognitive tool could allow them to reify the self-regulation process by making the learning process represented on the tool operable and controllable [13]. Such reification makes it possible to scaffold self-regulation process.

Self-regulation process in hyperspace involves planning the navigation process and reflecting on the knowledge construction process, which are viewed as representative self-regulation processes. In order to scaffold the navigation planning and reflection, we have developed cognitive tools, which are called navigation Planning Assistant PA for short and Interactive History tool IH for short [13]. PA allows learners to see through the hyperspace to plan navigation paths to be followed for achieving their learning goal. IH also allows learners to review and reconstruct their knowledge that they have constructed so far. We have also evaluated these tools [13]. The results suggest that each tool contributes to enhancing its own self-regulation process.

Although PA and IH respectively focus on scaffolding navigation planning and reflection, learners need to fundamentally coordinate these different self-regulation processes to self-regulate the navigational learning process. The learners also need to seamlessly coordinate the navigational learning process and self-regulation processes. In order to improve such coordination, we have integrated the functions provided by PA and IH to design a cognitive tool called self-regulator. This paper demonstrates the self-regulator that consists of browser and self-regulation history. This history enables learners to reify navigation planning, navigation with knowledge construction, and reflection in a seamless manner. This paper also a case study whose purpose was to ascertain the self-regulator could work well. The results suggest that it can promote self-regulation process to enhance the efficiency and effectiveness of their navigational learning process more than PA and IH.

2 Navigational Learning in Hyperspace

Before discussing the self-navigator, let us first reconsider navigational learning and its representative self-regulation process in hyperspace.

2.1 Navigation and Knowledge Construction

Hyperspace provided by a hypermedia/hypertext-based resource is generally composed of numerous pages. In the hyperspace, learners can navigate pages in a self-directed way to learn domain knowledge embedded in navigated pages. The self-directed navigation process involves making a sequence of the pages, which is called navigation path [4]. It also involves constructing knowledge, in which the learners would make semantic relationships among the contents learned at the navigated pages [2]. Such navigation with knowledge construction is called navigational learning [13]. In navigational learning, it is very important to make a navigation path since the knowledge construction process is influenced by the navigation path.

The learners generally start navigating hyperspace with a learning goal. The movement between the various pages is often driven by a local goal called navigation goal to search for the page that fulfills it. Such navigation goal is also regarded as a sub-goal of the learning goal. For instance, a learner may search for the meaning of an unknown term to supplement what he/she has learned at the current page. We refer to the process of fulfilling a navigation goal as primary navigation process [13]. This is represented as a link from the starting page where the navigation goal arises to the terminal page where it is fulfilled.

The knowledge construction process can be modeled as a number of primary navigation processes. In each primary navigation process, the learners would integrate the contents learned at the starting and terminal pages. Carrying out several primary navigation processes, they would construct knowledge from the contents they have integrated in each primary navigation process.

2.2 Self-regulation

In navigational learning process, learners need to monitor and control their learning process. In order to shape a well-balanced knowledge structure, in particular, it is necessary for the learners to decide which navigation path to follow from the current page for achieving their learning goal. It is also important for them to recollect what and why they have navigated so far, and to properly direct the subsequent navigation [2]. We call these higher-order cognitive processes self-regulation ones. Land [5] and Avezedo et al. [6] classified the self-regulation process into several sub-processes in detail. From among them, we have focused on navigation planning and reflection as representative self-regulation processes.

The purpose of the navigation planning is to decide a navigation path representing the sequence of the pages to be followed for achieving a learning goal. Navigation planning is particularly important for learners to efficiently navigate hyperspace. Navigation planning includes the following three tasks:

1. Setting up a learning goal and sub-goals,
2. Making navigation path plan for fulfilling the goals, and
3. Re-planning navigation path according to the results of carrying out the plan.

In planning a navigation path, learners first need to consider what they can learn in the resource for setting up a learning goal or its sub-goals by getting an overview of the whole structure of hyperspace. They then need to plan which navigation path to follow for achieving the goals by getting overviews of the pages. They are next expected to follow this navigation path to navigate the pages included in the path and construct knowledge in hyperspace. Afterwards, the learners would decide whether the plan needs to be modified or a new plan needs to be made according to whether the goals are achieved. In this way, navigation planning process is modeled as repeated execution of the three tasks.

On the other hand, the purposes of reflection are to monitor and control navigation with knowledge construction in hyperspace and to review/reconstruct the knowledge constructed. In particular, reflection is important for learners to make their knowledge well-structured. In this work, we model reflection as review and reconstruction of primary navigation processes carried out so far, which includes the following three tasks:

1. Reviewing and re-learning the contents learned at the navigated pages,
2. Reviewing and reconstructing primary navigation processes carried out, and
3. Reviewing and reconstructing the relationships among them.

2.3 Coordination

In navigational learning, learners usually make a navigation plan to navigate the pages according to it, and construct their knowledge to reflect on it. They then follow the findings obtained from the reflection process to re-plan or make a new plan for achieving the learning goal.

In this way, learners need to seamlessly coordinate the navigational learning process and its self-regulation process, which also includes coordinating the two self-regulation processes: navigation planning and reflection. However, it is hard for them to concurrently carry out navigation planning, navigation with knowledge construction, and reflection. In order to overcome the difficulty, we have designed and developed the self-regulator.

3 Self-regulator

3.1 Framework

The self-regulator deals with hypermedia/hypertext-based resources described with HTML to support the self-regulation process. It enables learners to reify and coordinate the three phases, which are navigation planning, navigation with knowledge construction, and reflection, with the self-regulation history. It provides them with functions for each phase shown in Table 1. The functions for navigation planning except title list correspond to the ones provided by PA. PA provides a hyperspace map instead of the title list [13]. The functions for reflection also correspond to the ones provided by IH.

The self-regulator consists of browser and self-regulation history. The self-regulation history enables learners to manipulate the pages included in it to make and execute a navigation plan, carry out and reflect on the primary navigation processes, and re-plan according to the reflection process in the same window. The self-regulation history is able to represent the sequence of the pages planned, the pages browsed/learned, and a number of primary navigation processes carried out. In this way, the self-regulator scaffolds navigation planning, navigation with knowledge construction, reflection, and these coordination processes in the same space.

Table 1. Scaffolding functions provided by self-regulator

Phase	Navigation Planning	Navigation with knowledge construction	Reflection
Shared function	Self-regulation history		
Functions	Title list	Page browsing	
	Page preview	Primary navigation process annotation	
	Link list	Note	
			Knowledge map

3.2 Scaffolding for Navigation Planning

Fig. 1 shows the user interface for supporting navigation planning, which provides title list, page preview, and link list. The title list presents a list of the titles of all pages included in a hypermedia/hypertext-based resource as an overview of the hyperspace, which is automatically generated from the resource. Clicking any title from the title list, learners can have an overview of the page corresponding to the title, which the page preview automatically generates by highlighting representative information included in the page and dimming the remaining information in the browser. The learners are allowed to use the title list and page preview to define a learning goal/sub-goal. The page preview also helps the learners to decide from which page they start planning a navigation path. In Fig. 1, their learning goal is defined as learning color tones, and the page vivid tone is previewed.

When they decide the starting point of the path, they can put the starting page in the self-regulation history window. In Fig. 1, the page vivid tone is selected as starting page. Each page put in the history window has a link list, which includes anchors of the hyperlinks the current page contains. Selecting any one from the list, they can have a preview of the page in the browser, to which the selected link points. They can then put the page previewed next to the current page, making a sequence of the pages that represents a navigation path plan. The history in Fig. 1 includes the sequence from the page vivid tone to the page deep tone.

When the learners are in navigation planning, the user interface of the self-regulator is framed with blue, which raises awareness about which phase they engage in.

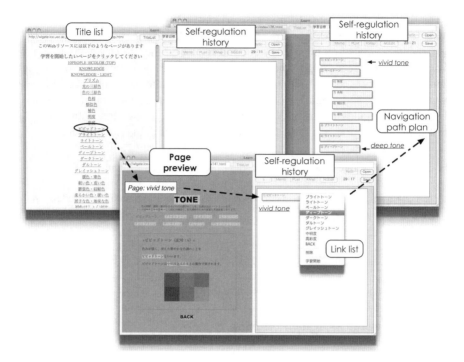

Fig. 1. User Interface in scaffolding navigation planning

3.3 Scaffolding for Navigation with Knowledge Construction

Double-clicking the starting point at the navigation path plan, the learners can start navigation and knowledge construction process. The learners are then expected to follow the plan to navigate and learn the pages with the browser. The learners can use the Next and Back buttons, which are located above the self-regulation history, to navigate the pages in the planned order. The learners can accordingly concentrate on understanding the contents of the browsed pages. In the history, the pages browsed in the browser are changed from the planned pages to the navigated ones. The planned pages are colored with blue, and the navigated ones are colored with red.

The learners can also explore pages in the browser, which are not included in the plan. The explored pages are put as navigated ones in the history. When they want to change or cancel the plan during navigation, they can return to the planning phase.

In carrying out a primary navigation process during navigating the pages with the browser, as shown in Fig. 2, the learners can take a note about the contents learned at the starting and terminal pages. They can also annotate the history with the primary navigation process, which includes annotation of the starting and terminal pages and annotation of link between these pages representing the navigation goal. Such page and link annotation is conducted with the navigation goal annotation window. In this window, they can define the starting and terminal pages and the navigation goal carried out from the list of the navigation goal classified in advance. The navigation goal list currently includes the six navigation goals: Supplement, Elaborate, Compare, Justify, Rethink, and Apply [13]. Fig. 2 shows the annotation window where the bright tone and deep tone are defined as the starting and terminal ones, and where the navigation goal is defined as supplement.

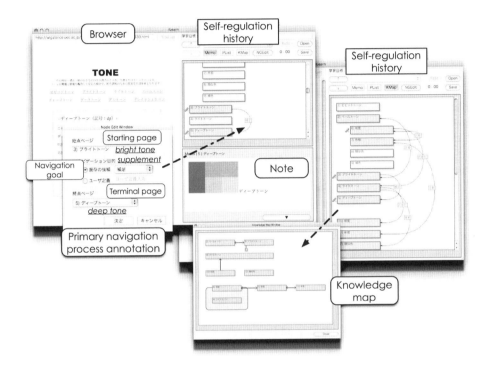

Fig. 2. User interface in scaffolding reflection

3.4 Scaffolding for Reflection

In the reflection phase, the learners can review and reconstruct their navigational learning process by adding/modifying/deleting the notes taken and the primary navigation processes carried out in the same way as the self-regulator provides in the phase of navigation with knowledge construction. The self-regulator, in addition, generates a knowledge map by transforming primary navigation processes into visual representation [13]. The nodes in the map correspond to the starting and terminal pages included in the primary navigation processes. The relationships between the nodes depend on their navigation goals. Such knowledge map allows the learners to visually grasp the structure of their knowledge constructed.

When the learners are in the phase of navigation with knowledge construction or in the reflection phase, the user interface of the tool is framed with red.

3.5 Sample Use

Let us here demonstrate a sample use of the self-regulator to present the seamless coordination between navigational learning process and its self-regulation process. First, a learner sets up a learning goal with the title list and page preview. Afterwards, he/she decides a starting page of navigation path, which is put on the self-regulation history. He/she then looks at the link list of the starting page to select one from the link list. The selected page is previewed in the browser. If he/she does not want to put it in the plan, he/she can select another one from the link list to have the page preview. If he/she wants to learn it, it is put in the history. In this manner, he/she can make a navigation path plan. It is also possible to make more than one navigation path plan.

After deciding the navigation path plan, the learner executes the plan with the browser to navigate the pages in the planned order by using the Next and Back buttons and to construct knowledge. In the knowledge construction process, he/she carries out primary navigation processes by annotating the history with them. He/she can also take notes about the starting and terminal pages. In case a lot of primary navigation processes arise, he/she would click the KMap button, which is located above the history window, to view the knowledge map. In reconstructing his/her knowledge constructed so far, he/she would delete or modify the primary navigation processes, or add new primary navigation process.

In case the reconstructed knowledge is not sufficient for achieving his/her learning goal, he/she would return to the planning phase, and make a navigation path plan that can complement the insufficiency. He/she would then carry out the plan, construct and reconstruct his/her knowledge in a spiral manner.

From the above sample use, we can say that the self-regulator has a potential for scaffolding seamless coordination between navigational learning and self-regulation, and between navigation planning and reflection via the same space provided with the self-regulation history.

4 Case Study

4.1 Preparation and Procedure

We have had a case study whose purpose was to ascertain if the self-regulator promotes self-regulation process, and enhances the efficiency and effectiveness of their navigational learning process compared to using only PA, IH, or browser.

In this study, we prepared a hypermedia-based resource described with HTML whose domain was color. The number of pages included was 70, and the average number of links per page except navigational links such as next, back, etc. was 5.1.

Subjects were 32 graduate and undergraduate students in science and technology who had more than three years experience in using Web browser. We set four conditions according to the tools to be used for learning with the resource, which were (a) learning with the self-regulator (SR-group), (b) learning with PA (PA-group), (c) learning with IH (IH-group), and (d) learning only with browser (Browser-group). We assigned 8 subjects per condition.

We also prepared pre-test and post-test before and after learning the resource with a learning goal. In the pre-test, we prepared 20 problems about color contrast to be learned from the resource, which was related to the learning goal. These included 15 problems (Concept-P) about color concepts embedded in the resource and 5 problems (Relationship-P) about the relationships between the concepts. Relationship-P requires combining the contents to be learned in the pages navigated. We prepared 30 Concept-P problems and 20 Relationship-P problems for the post-test, which in part included the problems used in the pre-test.

After conducting the pre-test, each condition group except Browser-group was first given an explanation/demonstration about how to use the assigned tool by means of another hypermedia-based resource. Each subject was afterward given the same learning goal that was to learn basic concepts related to color contrast and color contrast effects, and then was required to learn the prepared resource with the assigned tool within 30 minutes. He/she was also informed that the post-test was conducted after learning.

In the post-test, he/she was allowed to refer to his/her learning history information (self-regulation history and knowledge map for SR-group, navigation history annotated with primary navigation processes and knowledge map for IH-group, and browsing history for PA-group and Browser-group) in answering the questions. But, he/she was not allowed to refer to the notes taken during his/her learning since the contents recorded in the notes could include answers of the questions.

4.2 Results and Considerations

In order to ascertain whether the self-regulator worked well, we compared history of learning with the hypermedia-based resource and pre-test/post-test scores obtained from each group. In case coordination between navigational learning and its self-regulation process that includes coordinating navigation planning and reflection is well improved, navigational learning process is expected to become more efficient, convergent, combinative, and goal-oriented. In other words, self-regulated learners could more efficiently and precisely select the pages necessary for achieving a learning goal, and combine the contents learned at the pages. Their browsing/page visit would also converge on such pages. In addition, the pages related to the goal achievement would be revisited more.

We used the following data to analyze the efficiency, convergence, combinativeness, and goal-orientedness of navigational learning process. The convergence, combinativeness, and goal-orientedness can be viewed as indicators of effectiveness of navigational learning process.

- Number of browsing pages and number of distinct pages browsed,
- Pre-test and post test scores, and

Table 2. Average data for analyzing navigational learning process

			SR-Group	PA-Group	IH-Group	Browser-Group
		N	8	8	8	8
(a1) Browsing pages		Mean	94.0*	150.4	184.9	216.5
		S.D.	29.7	86.5	58.1	67.7
(a2) Distinct pages browsed		Mean	33.5*	39.6*	61.1	65.6
		S.D.	12.3	13.4	9.2	2.9
(b1) Pre-test	Concept-P	Mean	9.4	9.5	9.4	8.6
		S.D.	2.4	2.9	4.2	3.5
	Relationship-P	Mean	1.3	0.9	0.6	0.9
		S.D.	0.7	1.1	0.7	0.8
(b2) Post-test	Concept-P	Mean	21.5	18.5	21.4	21.0
		S.D.	2.3	1.9	2.2	3.6
	Relationship-P	Mean	9.1*	7.9	8.9*	5.6
		S.D.	3.6	2.6	1.3	2.0
(c1) Correct pages to distinct pages browsed		Mean	0.70*	0.60*	0.37	0.34
		S.D.	0.22	0.16	0.08	0.02
(c2) Correct pages to revisited pages		Mean	0.80*	0.60	0.49	0.40
		S.D.	0.17	0.21	0.12	0.07

*: p<.05

- Precision of correct pages, which we specified as pages necessary for achieving the learning goal, to distinct pages browsed and to revisited pages.

Table 2 shows the average data for analyzing the convergence (data (a1) and (a2)), combinativeness (data (b1) and (b2)), and efficiency/goal-orientedness (data (c1) and (c2)) of navigational learning process, which were obtained from histories of using the assigned tools and from the results of the pre-and post-tests.

From the ANOVA analysis with the average numbers of browsing pages (a1) and distinct pages browsed (a2) in each condition, there was significant difference between four conditions ($F(3,28)=4.72$, $p<.01$ for (a1); and $F(3,28)=16.57$, $p<.01$ for (a2)). As the results of the LSD multi-range test for (a1), the average number in SR-group was significantly lower than the ones in IH-group and Brower-group (MSe=4658.46, $p<.05$). As for (a2), the average number in SR-group was significantly lower than the ones in IH-group and Browser-group, and the average number in PA-group was also significantly lower than the ones in IH-group and Browser-group (MSe=120.37, $p<.05$). These results suggest that the self-regulator and PA make navigational learning process (page visit) more convergent, and that the convergence is supported by the tool functions for scaffolding navigation planning.

As for (b1) shown in Table 2, the results of the ANOVA analysis indicated that there was no significant difference between four conditions ($F(3,28)= 0.10$, $p>0.10$ for Concept-P; and $F(3,28)= 0.70$, $p>0.10$ for Relationship-P). This suggests that each subject seems to have similar background knowledge about the domain embedded in the hypermedia-based resource. As for (b2), there was a tendency towards significant difference between four conditions as for Relationship-P ($F(3,28)= 2.81$, $p<0.10$) although there was no significant difference as for Concept-P ($F(3,28)= 2.09$, $p>0.10$). From the results of the LSD multi-range test for Relationship-P in (b2), the scores in

SR-group and IH-group were significantly higher than the one in Browser-group (MSe=7.23, p<.05). These results suggest that the self-regulator and IH make navigational learning process more combinative, and that the combinativeness is supported by the tool functions for scaffolding reflection.

Let us next analyse the precision of the correct pages to distinct pages browsed (c1) and to revisited pages (c2). From the ANOVA analysis after angular transformation, there were significant differences between four conditions as for both (c1) and (c2) (F(3,28)=9.71, p<.01 for (c1); and F(3,28)=8.25, p<.01 for (c2))). As for the results of the LSD multi-range test for (c1), the precision in SR-group and PA-group was significantly higher than the ones in IH-group and Browser-group (MSe=107.20, p<.05). As for (c2), the precision in SR-group was significantly higher than the other groups (MSe=127.57, p<.05). The results of (c1) suggest that the self-regulator and PA make navigational learning process more efficient. Such efficiency seems to be supported by the tool functions for navigation planning. The results of (c2) also suggest that the self-regulator makes navigation process more goal-oriented, which means the revisited pages include more correct pages. Such goal-orientedness seems to be supported by the tool functions for reflection.

From the all above results, we can say that the self-regulator has a potential for scaffolding self-regulation process to make navigational learning in hyperspace more efficient and effective.

5 Conclusion

This paper has described the self-regulator for navigational learning in hyperspace whose goal is to scaffold different self-regulation processes and the coordination between the navigational learning process and its self-regulation processes. It enables learners to reify navigation planning and reflection processes by means of self-regulation history, which also enables the seamless connection between navigational learning and its self-regulation.

Some learners might feel the operations of the self-regulator complicated. But, accomplishing navigational learning in mind requires them to make cognitive efforts corresponding to the operations. It is consequently necessary to help such learners develop their skill in operating the self-regulator. We have addressed this issue with learner-adaptable scaffolding (See [10] and [14] in detail.).

This paper has also reported a case study. The results indicate the possibility that the self-regulator could scaffold the self-regulation processes in hyperspace to make navigational learning more efficient and effective.

In future, we will refine the functions and use of the self-regulation tool according to the results of more detailed evaluation. We will also seek a solution to the development of skill in operating the self-regulator.

Acknowledgments. The work is supported in part by Grant-in-Aid for Scientific Research (B) (No. 20300266) from the Ministry of Education, Science, and Culture of Japan.

References

1. Bransford, J.D., Brown, A.L., Cocking, R.R. (eds.): How People Learn – Brain, Mind, Experience, and School. National Academy Press, Washington (2000)
2. Thuering, M., Hannemann, J., Haake, J.M.: Hypermedia and cognition: Designing for comprehension. Communication of the ACM 38(8), 57–66 (1995)
3. Schunk, D.H., Zimmerman, B.J. (eds.): Self-Regulated Learning and Academic Achievement: Theoretical Perspectives, 2nd edn. Lawrence Erlaum Assoc., Mahwah (2001)
4. Hammond, N.: Learning with Hypertext: Problems, Principles and Prospects. In: McKnight, C., Dillon, A., Richardson, J. (eds.) HYPERTEXT A Psychological Perspective, pp. 51–69 (1993)
5. Land, S.M.: Cognitive Requirements for Learning Open-Ended Learning Enviroments. Educational Technology Research and Development 48(3), 61–78 (2000)
6. Azevedo, R., Cromley, J.G., Seibert, D.: Does adaptive scaffolding facilitate students' ability to regulate their learning with hypermedia? Contemporary Educational Psychology 29, 344–370 (2004)
7. Brusilovsky, P.: Adaptive Hypermedia. Journal of User Modeling and User-Adapted Interaction 11(1/2), 87–110 (2001)
8. Kayashima, M., Inaba, A.: Towards Helping Learners Master Self-Regulation Skills. In: Supplementary Proceedings of AIED 2003, pp. 602–614 (2003)
9. Narciss, S., Proske, A., Koerndle, H.: Promoting self-regulated learning in web-based learning environments. Computers in Human Behavior 23, 1126–1144 (2007)
10. Kashihara, A., Sawazaki, K., Shinya, M.: Learner-Adaptable Scaffolding with Cognitive Tool for Developing Self-Regulation Skill. In: Proceedings of the 16th International Conference on Computers in Education, pp. 133–140 (2008)
11. Jonassen, D.H.: Computers as Mindtools for Schools: Engaging Critical Thinking, 2nd edn. Prentice-Hall, Englewood Cliffs (2000)
12. Lajoie, S.P. (ed.): Computers As Cognitive Tools: No More Walls: Theory Change, Paradigm Shifts, and Their Influence on the Use of Computers for Instructional Purposes, 2nd edn. Lawrence Erlbaum Assoc Inc., Mahwah (2000)
13. Kashihara, A., Hasegawa, S.: A Model of Meta-Learning for Web-based Navigational Learning. International Journal of Advanced Technology for Learning 2(4), 198–206 (2005)
14. Kashihara, A., Taira, K.: Developing Navigation Planning Skill with Learner- Adaptable Scaffolding. In: Proceedings of AIED 2009, pp. 433–440 (2009)

How Adaptive Is an Expert Human Tutor?

Michelene T.H. Chi[1] and Marguerite Roy[2]

[1] Arizona State University
[2] Medical Council of Canada
Michelene.Chi@asu.edu

Abstract. In examine the tutoring protocols of one expert human tutor tutoring 10 students in solving physics problems, four analyses reveal that he tutored the five good learners in different ways than the five poorer learners, resulting also in greater adjusted gains for the good learners. This opens up the question of whether the tutor is non-optimally adaptive. We introduce a new conceptual framework and a new perspective in our coding analyses in order to examine how adaptive an expert tutor is.

1 Introduction

In this paper, we address a specific question, by analyzing protocol data that were collected in a 2008 study of an expert human Tutor tutoring 10 Tutees in solving physics problems [1]. Studying a single tutor tutoring 10 students allowed us to examine tutor variability as a function of the tutees. The study and its major learning results from the perspective of the bystander observers were published in [1]. Here, we report other analyses of the raw protocols to address specifically the question of whether an expert tutor is adaptive.

The common assumption among tutoring researchers is that tutoring is beneficial to all students in part because tutors are adaptive to the needs of the tutees. Adaptiveness can be defined in many ways, but the general idea is that a human tutor is adaptive in the sense that she tailors her instruction to the needs of her tutee. Tailoring can be defined in a macro way as selecting the appropriate next problem for a student to solve [2], such as a more difficult problem if a tutee successfully solved the current problem. Using this criterion, we had also examined the choice of problems our Tutor had posed to the 10 Tutees. Although the number of problems from which our Tutor could have selected were few (4 problems), they nevertheless did vary in difficulty. Overall, as we showed in our prior study [1, Pp. 334-335], there were no significant differences in whether the Tutor selected and posed the more difficult problems to the better tutees, suggesting that the Tutor was not adaptive in the macro level sense. Furthermore, the overall finding that the bystander observers could learn as well as the Tutees [1] even though the Tutor could not have tailored their instruction toward the observers, made us wonder whether tutors are in fact as adaptive as commonly believed.

From a micro perspective, tutoring adaptiveness is usually identified as choosing the appropriate next solution step for the student to work on, whether to give a proactive hint or scaffold before the step [3], or deciding on the specificity of the hint to pose [4], contingent upon the success of the student in solving the prior step. Intelligent tutoring systems generally take this finer-grained approach in defining adaptiveness. In short, whether at a more macro problem level or at a more micro solution-step level, both approaches to defining adaptiveness view it as a choice of what materials to present by the *tutor* to the tutees.

In this work, we define adaptiveness from the perspective of the *tutee*. Instead of looking at what content the tutor chose to present to a tutee, we examined instead what kind of pedagogical move the tutor made to elicit productive learning activities from the tutees. Accordingly, we also attempted to modify our coding from the perspective of the tutor to the perspective of the tutee.

Our perspective is derived from a framework we outlined in [5] to define "active learning." To improve learning, it has been widely proposed in many areas of literature that students engage in "active learning" as opposed to "passive learning." For example, in educational psychology "active learning" has been broadly defined as encouraging learners to pay "attention to relevant information, organizing it into coherent mental representations, and integrating representations with other knowledge" [6]. In engineering education, "active learning" has been defined as "engaging students in the learning process [through] activities that are introduced into the classroom" [7].

We have differentiated "active learning" into three different kinds of student activities—*active, constructive, interactive*--that can be observed overtly, and defined the cognitive processes corresponding to each kind of activities. For example, *active* activities might include copying a solution from a whiteboard, underlying a sentence in a text, or clip-and-pasting a sentence. *Constructive* activities mean producing some new knowledge that was not presented in the instructional materials, such as drawing a diagram or a concept map, comparing-and-contrasting two examples or self-explaining a worked-out example. In these cases, a student is producing something beyond what was contained in the instructional materials: such as a diagram, similarities and differences, or self-explanation inferences. Finally, *interactive* activities involve directly interacting with a peer or a tutor, such that both partners can further elaborate, elucidate, scaffold, provide feedback, and so on, to each other. Our framework explains why being "active" promotes more learning than being "passive," which was operationalized as not doing anything overtly. Moreover, we had hypothesized that participating in *interactive* activities is often (but not always) better for learning than participating in *constructive* activities, which in turn is better than participating in *active* activities, which in turn is better than being *passive* [5]. We are not saying that one must engage in a specific kind of overt activities in order to learn. Rather, we are simply proposing that in general, students are more likely to learn more by engaging in one kind of learning activities over another kind, and the ordering ranks as follows: *interactive>constructive>active>passive*.

Since tutorial dialogues involve a tutor conversing with a tutee and expects a response from a tutee, should we consider all tutorial dialogues as naturally interactive? We propose that if we examine tutorial dialogues from the perspective of a tutee's contributions, then we can clearly differentiate a tutee's contribution as either *passive, active, constructive,* or *interactive*, so that not all tutee responses should automatically be considered to be interactive. In particular, if a tutee responds to a tutor's comment with a continuer, such as "ok," or "uh-huh," then we can consider a continuer type of responses as an *active* response only. However, if the tutee responds to a tutor's comment with a content-relevant follow-up, then we can consider it a *constructive* response. We further apply the criterion that a tutee's response is *interactive* if it initiates some new topic, new direction, and so forth.

Using this operational definition of tutee's responses as a way to differentiate *active, constructive,* and *interactive,* our assumption is that some tutor moves are more likely to promote one kind of responses than another. In Fig. 1 below, we re-plotted the three largest categories of tutor moves—explaining, giving feedback, and scaffolding, averaged across 11 tutors, taken from data reported in our 2001 study [8, Fig. 3], in terms of proportion rather than frequency. Fig. 1 shows that the tutors' explanations elicited the largest proportion of continuer type of *active* responses, and a smaller proportion of shallow *constructive* type of follow-up responses. In contrast, the tutors' scaffolding moves elicited the smallest proportion continuer type of responses and the largest proportion of shallow follow-ups. Feedback moves also elicited proportionately more shallow follow-ups than continuers, but the difference was not as pronounced as for scaffolding moves. Overall, all tutor moves elicited comparable and minimal deep follow-ups. Comparing explaining and scaffolding moves only in this paper, this suggests that scaffolding was a better tutor move than explaining, because scaffolding moves often elicited some *constructive* responses from the tutees whereas explaining moves were more likely to elicit *active* responses.

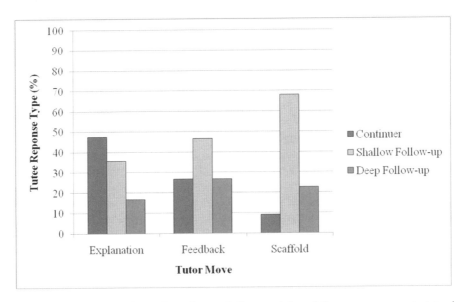

Fig. 1. The proportion of tutees' continuer, shallow, and deep follow-up responses to tutors' explanations, feedback and scaffolding moves (taken from Chi, et al. 2001 data)

2 The Data of the Current Analyses

The data analyzed for this paper consisted of an experienced teacher who had taught college physics for over 30 years. Moreover, he was in a lab that developed intelligent tutoring systems and knew that a good tutor ought to scaffold tutees, thus we consider him to be an expert tutor. In the 2008 study [1], this Tutor was asked to tutor 10 different Tutees. A pre-test was administered to the 10 Tutees after they had learned the materials in Chapter 5 of a physics text on their own, without feedback. Essentially the pre-test measured how well the students could learn the content of Chapter 5 on their own, after having learned the first four chapters to mastery. Thus, the pre-test was not a test of their prior knowledge about physics, but more of an assessment of whether a tutee is a good or a poor learner, when they had to learn unguided. After the pre-test, then these 10 students were individually tutored by the Tutor on solving four problems pertaining to Chapter 5 content.

In order to make our codings more manageable and more meaningful, we focus here on dialogue protocols segmented into episodes about "critical" nodes. Critical nodes were those nodes in a problem space that we thought were more important in terms of requiring the solver to generate a specific equation, solution step, or about main concepts and principles. The problem space of all possible nodes were identified initially by transcribing how our expert Tutor solved each of the problems that he was to tutor. All utterances pertaining to a critical node were counted in the node's episode. Thus, the tutorial dialogues of all participants have approximately the same number of episodes, because the Tutor usually made sure that all critical nodes were covered. All the analyses to be reported below used "episode" as the unit of analyses.

3 Results

Before describing four analyses to give a view of how adaptive our expert Tutor was, we first assert that although tutoring is often considered to be the best instructional technique in helping students learn, nevertheless, tutoring is not equally effective with all students. We can see tutoring's differential effectiveness easily in multiple ways. For example, the 10 Tutees in our sample varied in their pre-test scores significantly, ranging from a low score of around 30% to a high pre-test score of around 60%. And, as is the case with many other kinds of interventions, there was a significant correlation between pre-test scores and post-test scores. If we use the data of all 69 participants across all five treatment groups reported in [1], the correlation between pre-test and post-test scores were significant at the p<.0005 level (r=0.648). In focusing here on the tutoring condition only, Figure 2 below divides the Tutees into three groups (to show the incremental variability): the 3 Low Tutees obtained a pre-test scores between 30-40%, the 3 Medium Tutees obtained scores between 40-50%, and the 4 High Tutees obtained scores between 60-70% (all pre-test scores are shown in the dark bars). The results show that Tutees learned different amounts, depending on whether they had more or less knowledge coming into the tutoring situation after having learned the materials in Chapter 5 on their own.

The point of Figure 2 is simply to show that the Tutor was not equally effective with all Tutees; in fact, he was least effective with the poorest Tutees. This suggests that there is room for improvement in terms of what tutors can do to guide a poor tutee's learning. For example, was the Tutor adaptive in making the Tutees more *constructive* rather than merely *active?* The next four analyses examine the Tutor's adaptiveness from a tutee's perspective.

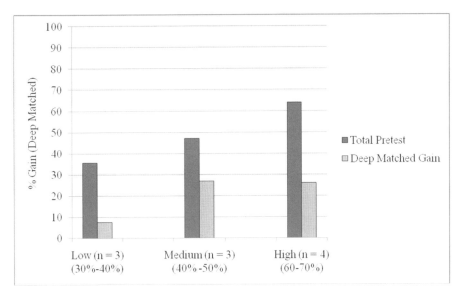

Fig. 2. Dark bars show the pre-test scores of the Tutees, divided into Low, Medium, and High, and the lighter-colored bars show how much they improved after tutoring on the same matched pre- and post-tests, scored for correct deep solution steps only

3.1 Does an Expert Tutor Jointly Explain or Take over the Coverage of a Critical Node?

Given that we only have 10 Tutees, our analyses henceforth will divide the Tutees into two groups: Good versus Poor Tutees. Good Tutees were defined as the five Tutees who gained more (on average 25% from pre- to post-test) and made fewer errors (on average 56 error steps across 4 problems); and Poor Tutees were defined as the five Tutees who gained less (16%) and made many more errors (89 error steps). Further details about the Good versus Poor Tutees split are described in [1].

Each episode comprised of either a single turn by either the Tutor or the Tutee, or multi-turns by both. When it consists of multi-turns, and if both the Tutor and the Tutee made substantive contributions, then the node is considered "jointly-covered." However, if only one person (either the Tutor or the Tutee) made substantive contributions in covering (i.e., explaining or solving) a critical node, then we consider that node to be independently covered. Thus, while tutoring, a critical node can be covered, whether successfully or unsuccessfully, either by a tutee alone, by a tutor alone, or by both of them jointly, when only substantive contributions are considered. Based on our framework described above, when the Tutor covered a node alone, then the Tutee seems *passive*. But when the Tutee covered a node alone, then the Tutee was *constructive*. However, when the Tutor-and-Tutee jointly covered a node, then the Tutee was likely *interactive*. As our *interactive>constructive>active>passive* hypothesis suggested above, *interactions* should facilitate learning more so than being *constructive*, which is better than being *passive*.

On average, the majority of the critical nodes (55) were covered by Tutor-and-Tutee jointly, whereas 32 were covered independently by the Tutor and 16 independently by the Tutees. Figure 3 shows a breakdown of how the nodes were covered for Good and Poor Tutees, and an interesting pattern of differences emerge. It is not surprising to find that Good Tutees were more able to explain/solve a node independently than Poor Tutees (F(1,8)=50.oo, p<.0005, d=4.21). However, the Tutor covered the critical nodes independently more often for the Poor Tutees than the Good Tutees (F(1,8)=98.04, p<.0005, d=5.219), whereas they covered the nodes jointly more often with the Good versus the Poor Tutees (F(1,8)=21.00, p=.002, d=2.892).

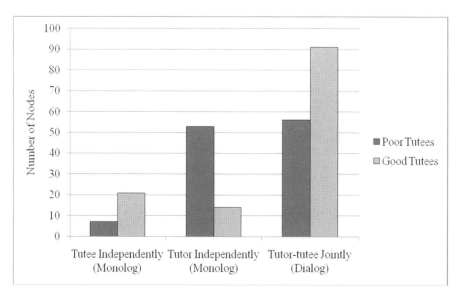

Fig. 3. The number of critical nodes covered by the Tutees alone, by the Tutor alone, or jointly by both, for Poor (dark bars) and Good (light bars) Tutees

In our framework, to maximize learning, a tutor should instead cover the nodes less frequently alone, since independent coverage by a Tutor essentially means that the Tutor explains didactically to the Tutees, allowing the Tutee to be *passive*. Moreover, the Tutor should encourage more joint coverage with Poorer Tutees than the Good Tutees, since joint coverage would encourage the tutees to be *interactive*. In short, the

Tutor was not optimizing his adaptiveness, from the perspective of differentially eliciting *active, constructive,* or *interactive* responses from the Good and the Poor Tutees.

To verify whether being *interactive* (during joint coverage) and being *constructive* (when Tutees cover a node independently) facilitated learning, there ought to be significant correlations between the frequency of joint coverage with Tutees learning (r=0.457, p=.043), and Tutees' independent coverage with Tutees' learning (r=0.640, p=.046), but not when the Tutor covered a node alone (n.s.), since the Tutees were most likely *passive*. In fact, the correlation results do support our predictions.

3.2 Could Poor Tutees Be Helped with More Tutor Scaffolding?

One could dismiss the results shown in Fig. 3 by pointing out that of course the Tutor covered more nodes independently with Poor Tutees and engaged in more joint dialogues with the Good Tutees, because the Good Tutees were more capable of independent coverage and engaging in joint dialogues with the Tutor. Our point is that to be truly adaptive, a tutor could in principle be more responsive to poorer tutees' inability to respond in joint dialogues, initiate new comments, and cover nodes by themselves. But the question is, would it help the Poor Tutees if they did receive more scaffolding?

Our argument is indirectly supported by the results from our 2001 Study 2 [8]. In Study 2 [8], tutoring in a conceptual domain (the human circulatory system), the 11 tutors were suppressed from giving explanations. In fact, they were permitted only to scaffold the tutees in a restricted content-free way, with scaffolding prompts such as "What does this mean?" The tutees in Study 2 learned just as much from the 11 tutors when they were scaffolded, as the tutees in Study 1 when the same tutors tutored more naturally. Although this is indirect evidence, it does suggest that all tutees (good and poorer ones) could learn when tutors were only permitted to scaffold them.

To address the same question here, we analyzed the proportion of tutee responses that were merely *active*, such as a continuer, versus more *constructive*, such as a shallow follow-up. Fig. 4a below shows that for the five Good Tutees, they generated proportionately more *active* continuer type of response to Tutor's explanations than to Tutor's scaffolding, whereas they generated more *constructive* follow-up responses to Tutor's scaffolding than Tutor's explanations. As before in the data collected in the 2001 study [8] and shown in Fig. 1, they did not generate many deep follow-ups.

The very same pattern of tutee responses hold for the Poor Tutees as well, as shown in Fig. 4b. They responded to explanations with more continuers than to scaffolding, whereas they responded more with shallow follow-ups to scaffolding than to explanations. This pattern of results again suggests that a tutor move such as scaffolding is advantageous to both Good and Poor Tutees. Nevertheless, the Tutor is much more likely to explain to a Poor Tutee than to scaffold a Poor Tutee, and conversely, the Tutor is more likely to scaffold a Good Tutee than explain to a Good Tutee.

Even though scaffolding is beneficial to both Good and Poor Tutees, as shown in Fig. 4a and 4b, the Tutor gave significantly more explanation statements to the Poor Tutees than the Good Tutees ($F(3,6)=8.281$, $p=.015$), but in contrast, gave predominantly more scaffolding statements to the Good Tutees than the Poor Tutees F(3,6)=7.333, p=.020). In this sense, from the tutee's perspective, the Tutor was not very adaptive.

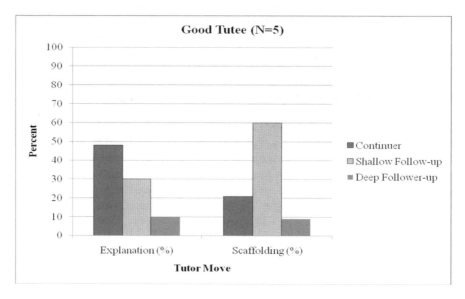

Fig. 4a. Good Tutee's responses to different types of tutor moves

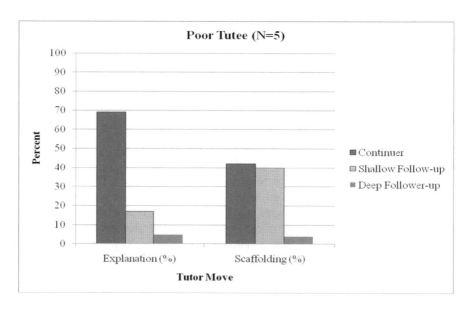

Fig. 4b. Poor Tutee's responses to different types of tutor moves

3.3 Examples of Tutor Explaining Moves versus Scaffolding Moves

In this analysis, we want to give specific contrasting examples of how explaining versus scaffolding can be coded. One way to code explaining is to determine whether the Tutor gave statements that were more telling and directing versus those that made open-ended requests. Open-ended requests are more scaffolding-like moves in that they are more likely to elicit *constructive* responses from the tutees. Figure 5 below shows that the Tutor gave didactic telling and directing statements more often to Poor Tutees than the Good Tutees, and conversely, requested fewer open-ended goals and explanations from the Poor Tutees than the Good Tutees. We recognize that the Tutor asked more open-ended requests from the Good Tutees in part because they are more able to answer such requests. So the Tutor is adapting, but not in a way that is optimal for all the Tutees' learning. That is, the Tutor should be doing the reverse, asking the Poor Tutees more open-ended questions so the Poor Tutees can be more *constructive*.

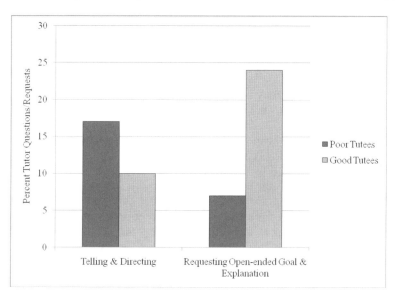

Fig. 5. Telling and directing statements versus open-ended requests made by the Tutor to Poor (dark bars) and Good (light bars) Tutees

3.4 Coding from the Tutees' Perspective: Was the Tutor Adaptive in Optimizing Tutees' Interactive Responses During Joint Dialogues?

The prior analyses, as many others have done in the literature, typically coded from the perspective of the Tutor, in terms of starting out with what the Tutor said. This is understandable given that tutors typically lead the dialogues. However, coding from a tutor's perspective cannot give us a true sense of a tutee's *interactivity*, since a tutee is obliged to give a response. Moreover, *interactivity* in the prior coverage analysis as shown in Fig. 3, was operationalized merely as both the Tutor and the Tutees having made substantive contributions. In order to operationalize *interactiveness* independent of Grice's conversational obligation and using a strict criterion, in this analysis, we coded from the Tutees' perspective, in that we coded the joint dialogues starting with what a Tutee initiated. Initiate means that the tutees commented on a new idea, a new topic, or a question that were not a follow-up, and so forth. We operationalized such tutee initiating moves as being *interactive*. Using this strict criterion and perspective, we coded four types of *interactive* dialogues, using the Tutee as the starting point.

a) Tutee initiate, Tutor revoice
b) Tutee initiate, Tutor scaffold
c) Tutee initiate with a question, Tutor answers
d) Tutee makes a meta-comment, Tutor responds.

The only tutor move that is novel in the above analysis is tutor "revoicing." In the literature, "revoicing" is defined as *a paticular kind of re-utterance of a teacher's contribution by a student* or as *a teachers' redecoration of a students response* [9]. Here, we treat revoicing as a repetition of parts of a tutee's utterances, but not necessarily verbatim. And such revoicing moves are typically undertaken by the Tutor when a Tutee makes a correct move. In essence, revoicing is a positive feedback move that is not discussed in the tutoring literature. Here are two examples:

> Tutee: First the gravity is pulling down [This is a tutee-initiated statement.]
> Tutor: Pulling it down. [Tutor revoiced.]

> Tutee: Weight is..the mass times..acceleration due to gravity and that's force.
> Tutor: Right. Right. [Tutor giving correct feedback.]
> Tutee: Ok.
> Tutor: So weight is the force. [Tutor revoiced.]

In contrast, feedback moves are typically given to errors. In the tutoring literature, feedback is identified either as a negative response ("that was incorrect" or "no"), a corrective positive response, that is giving the correct answer or equation (such as "it should be F=ma"), or it could be an elaborated corrective response (such as giving a reason for the answer) [1]. In general, about 80%-90% of both Good and Poor Tutees' errors are responded to with either a negative feedback, a corrective feedback, or an elaborated feedback. Elaborative feedback obviously is the best kind since it gives more information and justification with respect to the feedback. Here is an example of an error, followed by both a corrective and elaborative feedback:

> Tutee: FN would be…would FN be mass of A plus mass of B? Or?
> Tutor: Again you…a force cannot be mass. [Corrective feedback].
>   These are two distinct quantities. [Elaborative feedback].

In our prior analysis [1, Table 5] we found the Poor Tutees received proportionately more corrective than elaborative feedback, whereas the Good Tutees received proportionately more elaborative feedback than corrective feedback. We had interpreted this difference to suggest that the Tutor was not as adaptive as one would like, since Poorer Tutees could have benefitted more from elaborative feedback.

In the current coding from the tutee's perspective, we found a significant overall difference between the percentage of critical nodes episodes that contained Tutee initiated statements for the Good Tutees (27.5%) than the Poor Tutees (6.43%, $F(1,7)=29.851$, $p=.011$). Moreover, there was a significant overall difference between Good and Poor Tutees for the proportion of their initiatives that were revoiced (18% for Good versus 5% for Poor, $F(1,7)=11.87$, $p=.011$). Although it is not surprising that Good Tutees can initiate more (since they know more), what is surprising is that the Tutor revoiced Good Tutees' initiatives more often than the Poor Tutees' initiatives. We surmise that the Good Tutees' initiations were more correct than the Poor Tutees' initiations, therefore the Good Tutees' initiations were more likely to be revoiced. Nevertheless, this is an important feedback move that is subtle, overlooked by the tutoring literature, and could potentially be overwhelmingly beneficial to the Good (as well as the Poor) Tutees. See Fig. 6, first pair of columns.

In addition to revoicing, Good Tutees' initiations were also followed significantly more often by scaffolding moves, consistent with the results reported above for 11 tutors of the prior study [1]. There were no differences between the Good and Poor Tutees in the frequency of the Tutor's responses to Tutees' questions or meta-comments they initiated. In short, dialogues with Good Tutees were more *interactive* largely because the Good Tutees initiated more frequently, and their initiations were taken-up by the Tutor, whereas Good and Poor Tutees' questions and meta-comments were responded to equally appropriately by the Tutor. The question is how should a tutor encourage more initiations from a poor tutee.

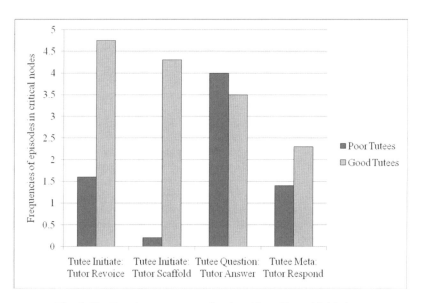

Fig. 6. The Tutor's responses to Good and Poor Tutees' initiatives

4 Discussion and Future Work

An implicit assumption among tutoring researchers and ITS developers is that tutoring is effective because in part a tutor is adaptive. Adaptiveness has been defined from the perspective of the tutor, in terms of a tutor's appropriate selection of a problem or a hint that is tailored to the tutee. We examined adaptiveness instead in terms of the kind of moves a tutor makes from the perspective of whether a move elicited *passive, active, constructive* or *interactive* responses from the tutees. We consider a tutoring move to be a "good" kind of moves if they elicit more *active, constructive* or *interactive* responses. We found that our expert Tutor tended to provide a greater number of good tutoring moves (such as scaffolding, asking open-ended questions, revoicing) to the Good Tutees than the Poor Tutees, and conversely, provided a greater number of less-effective tutoring moves (such as explaining, telling and directing) to the Poor Tutees than the Good Tutees. This pattern of tutor moves suggests that the Tutor was not optimizing the poorer tutees' learning, therefore, the Tutor was basically maladaptive. Granted that poorer tutees were incapable of offering more initiatives and responses to scaffoldings, our position is that our evidence suggests that they could if tutors gave them more guidance in doing so. We surmise that because tutors have a bias in wanting to get the correct knowledge or solutions out there, they have the inclination of telling and directing the tutees when they struggle, rather than help them get through their struggling. The results reported here suggest that future analyses may benefit from taking the perspective of the tutees, in order to understand their contributions in enhancing learning from tutoring.

Acknowledgments. The authors are grateful for funding provided by the National Science Foundation grant number 0325054.

References

1. Chi, M.T.H., Roy, M., Hausmann, R.G.: Observing tutorial dialogues collaboratively: Insights about human tutoring effectiveness from vicarious learning. Cognitive Science 32(2), 301–341 (2008)
2. Shute, V.J.: A macroadaptive approach to tutoring. Journal of Artificial Intelligence in Education 4(1), 61–93 (1993)
3. Murray, R.C., VanLehn, K., Mostow, J.: Looking ahead to select tutorial actions: A decision-theoretic approach. International Journal of Artificial Intelligence in Education 14(3/4), 235–278 (2004)
4. Wood, D.J., Wood, H., Middleton, D.: An experimental evaluation of four face-to-face teaching strategies. International Journal of Behavioral Development 1, 131–147 (1978)
5. Chi, M.T.H.: Active-constructive-interactive: A conceptual framework for differentiating learning activities. Topics in Cognitive Science 1, 73–105 (2009)
6. Mayer, R.: Learning and Instruction, p. 17. Pearson Education, Inc., New Jersey (2008)
7. Prince, M.: Does active learning work? A review of the research. Journal of Engineering Education 93(3), 223–231 (2004)
8. Chi, M.T.H., Siler, S., Jeong, Y.H., Yamauchi, T., Hausmann, R.: Learning from human tutoring. Cognitive Science 25, 363–387 (2001)
9. O'Connor, M., Michaels, S.: Shifting participant framework: orchestration thinking practices in group discussion. In: Hicks, D. (ed.) Discourse, learning, and schooliing, pp. 63–103. Cambridge University Press, Cambridge (1996)

Blocked versus Interleaved Practice with Multiple Representations in an Intelligent Tutoring System for Fractions

Martina A. Rau[1], Vincent Aleven[1], and Nikol Rummel[1,2]

[1] Human-Computer Interaction Institute, Carnegie Mellon University
[2] Institute of Psychology, University of Freiburg, Germany
{marau,aleven}@cs.cmu.edu, rummel@psychologie.uni-freiburg.de

Abstract. Previous research demonstrates that multiple representations can enhance students' learning. However, learning with multiple representations is hard. Students need to acquire representational fluency with each of the representations and they need to be able to make connections between the representations. It is yet unclear how to balance these two aspects of learning with multiple representations. In the present study, we focus on a key aspect of this question, namely the temporal sequencing of representations when students work with multiple representations one-at-a-time. Specifically, we investigated the effects of blocking versus interleaving multiple representations of fractions in an intelligent tutoring system. We conducted an *in vivo* experiment with 296 5th- and 6th-grade students. The results show an advantage for blocking representations and for moving from a blocked to an interleaved sequence. This effect is especially pronounced for students with low prior knowledge.

Keywords: Multiple representations, fractions, intelligent tutoring system, blocked vs. interleaved practice, classroom evaluation.

1 Introduction

The ultimate goal of the work presented in this paper is to generate a set of research-validated principles about how multiple representations best support robust learning in a real-world domain, and to build an intelligent tutoring system (ITS) that reflects these principles and helps students overcome their difficulties with fractions. We report on a study that is a first step in that direction.

We focus on a domain in which multiple graphical representations are often used: fractions [1]. Understanding fractions is foundational for learning algebra and more advanced mathematics [2], yet fractions pose a significant challenge for students in the elementary and middle grades, and even for college students and pre-service teachers [3]. In a recent study, we provide experimental evidence that students working with multiple graphical representations of fractions learn better than students who work with only a single graphical representation, although only when prompted to explain how the graphical representations (e.g., half a pie) of fractions relate to the symbolic representation (e.g., 1/2) [4]. The current study builds on this work; we now turn to the question of *how best to temporally sequence* multiple representations. For now, we focus on instruction that presents students with only a single graphical representation for each problem. (In future research we will include problems that involve multiple graphical representations at a time.)

Several studies in cognitive and educational psychology have demonstrated that the use of multiple representations can lead to more robust learning in complex domains [5,6]. However, providing students with multiple representations is not always beneficial [5], which has been attributed to the fact that learning with multiple representations requires several interrelated cognitive competencies [7]. Perhaps most obviously, students need to understand the format and properties of the particular representations and they need to be able to use them appropriately; that is, they need to acquire *representational fluency* with each representation [8]. In addition, students can only benefit from learning with multiple representations if they are able to make comparisons across representations and translate between them; in other words, they need to acquire *representational flexibility* [9,10].

At this point, it is an open question what the best balance is between supporting the acquisition of representational fluency and representational flexibility, and to what degree each facilitates the other. It stands to reason that representational fluency and connection making mutually influence the acquisition of one another. Fluency may facilitate the acquisition of representational flexibility. When learning to work with a new representation, it may help to connect it to one with which one is already fluent. But representational flexibility may also facilitate the development of fluency; a burgeoning understanding of one representation may help make sense of (and develop fluency with) a second, new, representation, even when that first representation is not yet fully understood. Little is known at this point about the relative strength of these mutual influences, which makes it harder to design effective instruction for learning with multiple representations.

In the study presented in this paper, we consider a key aspect of instruction with multiple representations, namely the *temporal sequencing* of representations. We ask what temporal sequence leads to more robust learning when learners work with multiple representations presented one-at-a-time: should practice with different representations be *blocked* (e.g., Pie-Pie-Pie, NL-NL-NL, Set-Set-Set) or *interleaved* (e.g., Pie-NL-Set, Pie-NL-Set, Pie-NL-Set)?

We assume that students develop fluency with a given representation as they work with that representation (e.g., during problem solving). We also assume that when representations are presented one-at-a-time, students are (somewhat) likely to spontaneously compare representations at the points where they switch from one representation to another. When practice with representations is *blocked*, students have the opportunity to build up fluency with one representation before the next one is introduced. When they (spontaneously) make connections between representations in the blocked condition, it is likely therefore that they are fluent with all of these representations except one (the one they are currently learning). In other words, this condition promotes fluency before connection making. On the other hand, when practice with different representations is *interleaved*, students build up fluency with representations in parallel; they may start making connections between representations even before they are fluent with any of them. The interleaved condition therefore facilitates connection making before fluency.

If cross-representational comparisons between different graphical representations strongly rely on students' fluency with at least one of the representations being compared, then students should learn best when practice with each of the representations is blocked – at least until they acquire sufficient representational fluency. If on the other hand, useful comparisons can be made even between representations students are not yet fluent with, then the interleaved condition should support more robust learning. Indeed, several studies have shown that interleaving practice with tasks that structurally differ from one another leads to better learning outcomes than blocked practice [11,12]. We know of no studies however that compared the blocking and interleaving of different external representations.

We investigated how multiple representations should be sequenced temporally in the context of a proven intelligent tutoring system (ITS) technology, namely, Cognitive Tutors [13]. Specifically, we developed a set of example-tracing tutors for fractions learning. Example-tracing tutors are a type of tutors that are behaviorally similar to Cognitive Tutors, but that rely on examples of correct and incorrect solution paths rather than on a cognitive model of student behavior. We created these tutors with the Cognitive Tutor Authoring Tools (CTAT [14]). We used these tutors in an *in vivo* experiment (i.e., a rigorously controlled experiment in a real educational setting).

Students in all conditions worked on the same problems, but practice with the different representations of fractions was blocked across problems to varying degrees. We used four conditions: blocked, moderate, interleaved, and increased. We hypothesize that spontaneous cross-representational comparison making builds on representational fluency, and thus predict that the increased condition will yield the best learning results. Additionally, we explore whether low and high prior knowledge students differ regarding which condition is most beneficial.

2 Methods

2.1 Material and Fractions Tutors

The tutors used in the study included three different graphical representations of fractions: pie charts (see Figure 1), numberlines (see Figure 2, top), and sets (see Figure 2, bottom). Each graphical representation emphasizes certain aspects of the different interpretations of fractions [15]. The pie chart as a part-whole representation depicts fractions as parts of an area that are partitioned into equally-sized pieces. The numberline is considered a measurement representation and thus emphasizes that fractions can be compared in terms of their magnitude, and that they fall between whole numbers. Finally, the set is a ratio representation and presents fractions in the context of discrete objects that have several features.

We employed different orders of graphical representations in addition to the blocked versus interleaved factor. Students never worked with the set representation first, because the set appears to be the representation students are least familiar with. We randomly assigned students to one of four different orders of representations: Pie chart – numberline – set, pie chart – set – numberline, numberline – pie chart – set, or numberline – set – pie chart.

The fractions tutor covered fraction identification, fractions as division, equivalent fractions, ordering fractions, and fraction addition. One graphical representation was presented at a time, but across the whole sequence of tutor problems, all graphical representations were crossed with all topics, except for obvious mismatches.

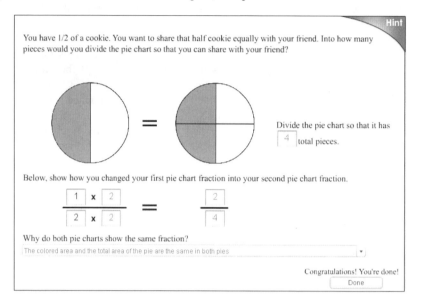

Fig. 1. Example of equivalent fractions problems with the pie chart

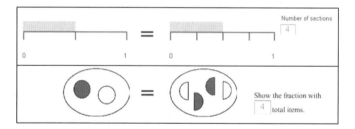

Fig. 2. Example of equivalent fractions problems with the numberline (top) and sets (bottom)

Before solving a problem symbolically, students were asked to perform the same steps by manipulating the graphical representations. For instance, students could partition them into smaller sections (for the numberline), pieces (for the pie chart), or objects (for the set). Figure 1 shows an example of equivalent fractions problems with the pie chart. Figure 2 shows corresponding problems with the numberline (top) and set representation (bottom). The tutors provided students with realistic cover stories for each problem. Students received error feedback and hints on all problem-solving steps. Error feedback messages were designed to make students reconsider their answer by either reminding them of a previously-introduced principle, or by providing them with an explanation for their error. Hint messages usually had three levels. First, students received a clarification of the goal (e.g., "You now added all pieces into the same pie chart. Before you know what fraction of the whole cake you won, you need to divide the pie chart into equally sized pieces."). They were then given conceptually oriented help, by reminding them of a specific concept (e.g., "The pieces are part of the same cake. Therefore, you keep the same denominator in the sum fraction."). Finally, students received explicit instructions regarding the next step (e.g., "Please divide the pie chart into four pieces.").

Students were prompted to self-explain their problem solution. We found this procedure to be effective in an earlier experimental study [4]. Students selected their answer from a drop-down menu, as shown in Figure 1. Previous research shows that asking students to select their answers from a menu rather than to explain in their own words, promotes a self-explanation effect [16].

2.2 Experimental Design and Procedure

A total of 269 5th- and 6th-grade students from three different schools in the United States participated in the study during their regular mathematics instruction. All students worked with a set of ITS for fractions (example-tracing tutors, as mentioned) designed and created specifically for this study. Students were randomly assigned to one of four conditions that varied regarding the degree to which practice with the representations was blocked versus interleaved: blocked, moderate, interleaved, or increased.

Students in the blocked condition encountered the representations in three blocks: They first worked through the whole sequence of topics with the first graphical representation (corresponding to 36 problems), then with a second representation, and finally with the last representation. In the moderate condition, the blocks were much smaller: students switched representations after every third problem. Students in the interleaved condition switched representations after every single problem. And finally, in the increased condition, the length of the blocks was gradually reduced from twelve problems at the beginning to a single problem at the end.

We assessed students' knowledge of fractions three times. On the first day, students completed a 30-minute pre-test. They then worked on the fractions tutor, for a total of 5 hours, spread across five to six (depending on specific school schedules) consecutive days. The day following the tutor sessions, students completed a 30-minute post-test. Seven days later, we gave students an equivalent delayed post-test.

2.3 Test Instruments

Students' understanding of fractions was assessed with respect to *representational knowledge* and *operational knowledge*. By representational knowledge, we mean the ability to interpret representations of fractions and to use them to make sense of fractions. In our specific test, we asked students to identify and order fractions using different graphical representations some of which students were not familiar with (meaning that they did not encounter them in the set of tutor problems) to assess their representational knowledge. Operational knowledge describes the ability to solve fractional tasks procedurally, by applying algorithms. The operational test items in our test assessed students' ability to convert and add fractions with and without the help of graphical representations. Test items were adapted from standardized national tests and from examples from the fractions literature. We randomly assigned students to different versions of the fractions test at the pre-test, the immediate and the delayed post-test. We validated the theoretical structure of the test with a confirmatory factor analysis using data from a large sample in a pilot study of the test instruments. The test's theoretical structure was replicated with data from the presented experiment.

3 Results

Students who stayed in their assigned condition, who were present for all test days, and who did not work on the tutoring system during the weekend were included in the analysis, yielding a total of $N = 215$. Neither the number of excluded students differed between experimental conditions, χ^2 (3, N = 269) = 1.21, $p > .10$, nor did the number of problems completed ($F < 1$), or the time spent on the tutor problems ($F < 1$).

A hierarchical linear model (HLM; [17]) with four nested levels was used to analyze the data. At level 1, we modeled performance for each of the three tests for each student. At level 2, we accounted for differences between students. At level 3, we modeled differences between classes, and at level 4 accounted for differences between schools. In addition, we used post-hoc comparisons to clarify the effect of blocking versus interleaving. The reported p-values are adjusted using the Bonferroni correction. Since there was no effect for order of representation ($F < 1$), only the results for blocked versus interleaved practice with the representations are reported.

Table 1. Rel. means and standard deviations (in brackets) for representational and operational knowledge at pre-test, immediate post-test, delayed post-test by low and high prior knowledge

		Blocked	Moderate	Interleaved	Increased
	low prior knowledge				
pre-test	representational knowledge	.39 (.12)	.38 (.17)	.35 (.15)	.42 (.13)
	operational knowledge	.22 (.15)	.28 (.14)	.26 (.16)	.27 (.14)
immediate post-test	representational knowledge	.50 (.24)	.49 (.20)	.36 (.23)	.55 (.23)
	operational knowledge	.37 (.27)	.33 (.31)	.26 (.26)	.31 (.26)
delayed post-test	representational knowledge	.51 (.25)	.27 (.30)	.29 (.27)	.50 (.26)
	operational knowledge	.29 (.27)	.27 (.28)	.26 (.20)	.36 (.27)
	high prior knowledge				
pre-test	representational knowledge	.78 (.11)	.77 (.14)	.77 (.11)	.70 (.09)
	operational knowledge	.75 (.16)	.81 (.15)	.76 (.16)	.76 (.15)
immediate post-test	representational knowledge	.78 (.21)	.70 (.22)	.72 (.17)	.67 (.16)
	operational knowledge	.84 (.22)	.73 (.33)	.68 (.34)	.75 (.23)
delayed post-test	representational knowledge	.72 (.19)	.58 (.32)	.53 (.34)	.67 (.25)
	operational knowledge	.76 (.28)	.68 (.29)	.67 (.34)	.65 (.36)

3.1 Learning Effects

First, we looked at student learning across conditions across the three test times. The tendency for the overall effect for test was in the opposite than the predicted direction, so that the overall hypothesis of a learning effect was not confirmed. Post-hoc comparisons showed a significant gain from pre-test to immediate post-test on representational knowledge for the blocked condition ($p < .01$).

To clarify this result, we split the data into groups based on median performance in the pre-test. Table 1 shows the means and standard deviations for representational and operational knowledge by test and condition for low and high prior knowledge students. For the low prior knowledge group, the results showed a significant improvement from pre-test to immediate post-test for representational knowledge in the blocked and increased conditions, which for the increased condition was also significant at the delayed post-test ($ps < .05$). No significant differences were found for operational knowledge.

3.2 Effects of Blocked versus Interleaved Representations

We had predicted an advantage for the increased condition at the immediate and the delayed post-test. The results partly support this hypothesis. We found a significant interaction effect between test time and blocked versus interleaved practice, for representational knowledge, $F(6, 422) = 5.54$, $p < .01$, and operational knowledge, $F(6, 422) = 2.19$, $p < .05$. Post-hoc comparisons showed that regarding representational knowledge, students in the blocked condition significantly outperformed students in the interleaved condition at the immediate post-test ($p < .05$). At the delayed post-test, both the blocked and the increased condition performed significantly better than the interleaved and moderate condition ($ps < .01$). As for operational knowledge, the post-hoc comparisons did not reveal statistically significant differences.

The analysis of the effects of blocked versus interleaved practice in the low and high prior knowledge groups further clarifies these results. An interaction between condition and the prior knowledge groups was significant for representational knowledge at both the immediate post-test, $F(4, 201) = 17.56$, $p < .01$, and the delayed post-test, $F(4, 202) = 6.08$, $p < .01$, as well as for operational knowledge at the immediate post-test, $F(4, 199) = 21.74$, $p < .01$, and the delayed post-test, $F(4, 198) = 17.90$, $p < .01$. Post-hoc comparisons showed that for representational knowledge at the immediate post-test, the advantage of the blocked condition and the increased condition over the interleaved condition was only significant for the low prior knowledge group ($ps < .01$), but not for the high prior knowledge group. At the delayed post-test, the advantage of the blocked condition and the increased condition over the interleaved condition, as well as the advantage of the blocked condition over the moderate condition reached the level of significance for both the low and high prior knowledge groups ($ps < .01$). The advantage of the increased condition over the moderate condition, in contrast, was significant only for the low prior knowledge group ($p < .01$). Post-hoc comparisons on operational knowledge revealed a significant advantage for the increased condition over the blocked condition in the low prior knowledge group for immediate and delayed post-test ($p < .01$). At the delayed post-test, this advantage was also significant when compared to the interleaved and moderate conditions ($ps < .01$). No further differences were found on operational knowledge.

4 Discussion and Conclusion

We found evidence that our tutoring system improves understanding of fractions for low prior knowledge students in the blocked and increased conditions. This finding in part confirms our hypothesis that the increased condition will yield the best learning results. The reason why our data does not provide evidence for learning in the high prior knowledge group may be that the fractions tutor could not add to their understanding because it provided practice on rather basic fractions concepts and procedures. In fact, the test scores in the high prior knowledge group show that students in the high prior knowledge group already had a relatively good understanding of fractions at the pre-test.

The results on blocked versus interleaved practice support our hypothesis that moving from a blocked scheme towards an interleaved scheme for learning with multiple representations yields the best learning results. The blocked and increased conditions showed more robust learning than the interleaved and moderate conditions. At the level of cognitive processes, the study thus provides some support for the notion that representational fluency facilitates the acquisition of representational flexibility more so than the other way around. While it is important to note that we did not directly support connection making between the different representations, this finding may have implications for the design of curricula that make use of multiple representations at a time. It seems reasonable to believe that instruction explicitly supports connection making between different representations will be most beneficial after students have acquired a good understanding of each individual representation's format.

The advantage of blocked and increased representations was significant for representational knowledge, but not for operational knowledge. One possible explanation is that the tutoring system supports learning of representational knowledge better than the learning of operations. Indeed, we do not find a significant learning gain on operational knowledge. We expected that a deep understanding of graphical representations of fractions would be conducive to a better conceptual understanding of operations, but our data does not support this view. Another explanation is that students are able to gain an abstract understanding of fractions operations regardless of whether a blocked or interleaved design is being used. In fact, the symbolic operations presented in the fractions tutoring system do not change depending on which graphical representation is used to illustrate it. We are currently analyzing the tutor logs to clarify whether the graphical representations in the tutoring system helped students understand fractions operations.

The fact that the interleaved condition yields the best learning results supports the interpretation that providing the opportunity for spontaneous comparison-making is beneficial to students who already acquired representational fluency. To the extent that students in the high prior knowledge group have representational fluency, should the interleaved conditions then not be most suitable for their needs? In fact, we classified students as low versus high prior knowledge students based on their performance in the pre-test, which included many representational test items, so that it seems reasonable to assume that they came in with a higher degree of representational fluency. The fact that we did not find an advantage for the interleaved condition for high prior knowledge students may be due to their performance being at ceiling for representational knowledge.

In conclusion, our study provides preliminary evidence that the acquisition of representational fluency should get higher weight in early instruction that makes use of multiple representations, compared to representational flexibility. One caveat is that the results were obtained with instructional material in which students encounter representations one-by-one, and connection making occurs only to the extent that students spontaneously engage in it. One could argue that the most extreme case of presenting multiple representations in temporal proximity is in fact presenting them simultaneously. In future studies, we will investigate whether the results generalize to situations in which students encounter multiple representations side-by-side, and in which the learning environment provides explicit support for connection making.

Our findings stand in contrast to earlier findings from a variety of domains which demonstrate an advantage for interleaved practice over blocked practice [12]. The difference between our studies and prior research is that we are investigating the effects of blocked versus interleaved practice with graphical representations as opposed to blocked versus interleaved practice of different problem types.

Our results may have implications for the design of instruction that directly supports connection making between multiple representations: It is likely that connection-making tasks will be most effective after students have had the opportunity to acquire fluency with the representations. While most studies on learning with multiple representations have emphasized the importance of helping students in making connections between the different representations [9], more attention should be paid to how to best support students' acquisition of representational fluency which appears to be an important foundation for the acquisition of representational fluency. Our findings are in line with Ainsworth's framework on learning with multiple representations [8] who points out that students often have difficulty in understanding the format of a new representation, as well as to understand how to use them appropriately in subsequent learning tasks. And while it seems logical that students have to acquire this understanding before they can relate different representations to one another, we know of no experimental evidence for this assertion, prior to this study.

Acknowledgements

This work was supported by the Pittsburgh Science of Learning Center which is funded by the National Science Foundation, award number SBE-0354420. We would like to thank Ken Koedinger, Mitchell Nathan, and Jay Raspat for their support, the students and teachers at Barrett Elementary School, Park Elementary School, and Francis McClure Intermediate School, Kyle Cunningham, Brett Leber, Jonathan Sewall, Alida Skogsholm, and Martin van Velsen for their technical support, Adriana Baker, Laura Butler, Jessica Kalka, Gail Kusbit, and Shawn Snyder for their help in implementing this study, Brian Junker, Fabian Hölzenbein, Howard Seltman, and Cassandra Studer for their support with the statistical analysis.

References

[1] Moss, J., Case, R.: Developing children's understanding of the rational numbers: A new model and an experimental curriculum. Journal for Research in Mathematics Education 30, 122–147 (1999)
[2] National Mathematics Advisory Board Panel. Foundations for Success: Report of the National Mathematics Advisory Board Panel, U.S. Government Printing Office (2008)
[3] Kaminski, E.: Promoting Mathematical Understanding: Number Sense in Action. Mathematics Education Research Journal 14, 133–149 (2002)
[4] Rau, M.A., et al.: Intelligent tutoring systems with multiple representations and selfexplanation prompts support learning of fractions. In: 14th International Conference on Artificial Intelligence in Education Brighton, UK (2009)
[5] Ainsworth, S.E., et al.: Analysing the Costs and Benefits of Multi-Representational Learning Environments. In: van Someren, M.W., et al. (eds.) Learning with Multiple Representations. Pergamon, Oxford (1998)
[6] Schnotz, W., Bannert, M.: Construction and interference in learning from multiple representation. Learning and Instruction 13, 141–156 (2003)
[7] Ainsworth, S.: Designing effective multi-representational learning environments. In: ESRC Centre for Research in Development, Instruction & Training Department of Psychology, Nottingham, vol. 58 (1999)
[8] Ainsworth, S.: DeFT: A conceptual framework for considering learning with multiple representations. Learning and Instruction 16, 183–198 (2006)
[9] de Jong, T., et al.: Acquiring knowledge in science and mathematics: The use of multiple representations in technology-based learning environments. In: Van Someren, M.W., et al. (eds.) Learning with Multiple Representations, Oxford (1998)
[10] Spiro, R.J., Jehng, J.C.: Cognitive flexibility and hypertext: Theory and technology for the nonlinear and multidimensional traversal of complex subject matter. In: Nix, D., Spiro, R.J. (eds.) Cognition, education and multimedia: Exploring ideas in high technology, pp. 163–205. Lawrence Erlbaum Associates, Hillsdale (1990)
[11] Schmidt, R.A., Bjork, R.A.: New conceptualizations of practice: Common principles in three paradigms suggest new concepts for training. Psychological Science 3, 207–217 (1992)
[12] de Croock, M.B.M., Van Merrienboer, J.J.G.: High versus low contextual interference in simulation-based training of troubleshooting skills: Effects on transfer performance and invested mental effort. Computers in Human Behavior 14, 249–267 (1998)
[13] Koedinger, K.R., Corbett, A.: Cognitive Tutors: Technology Bringing Learning Sciences to the Classroom. In: Sawyer, R.K. (ed.) The Cambridge handbook of: The learning sciences, New York, NY, US, pp. 61–77. Cambridge University Press, Cambridge (2006)
[14] Aleven, V., et al.: Example-tracing tutors: A new paradigm for intelligent tutoring systems. Document submitted for publication (under review)
[15] Charalambous, C.Y., Pitta-Pantazi, D.: Drawing on a Theoretical Model to Study Students' Understandings of Fractions. Educational Studies in Mathematics 64, 293–316 (2007)
[16] Aleven, V., Koedinger, K.R.: The need for tutor dialog to support self-explanation. In: Rose, C.P., Freedman, R. (eds.) Building Dialogue Sstems for Tutorial Applications. Papers from the 2000 AAAI Fall Symposium, pp. 65–73. AAAI Press, Menlo Park (2000)
[17] Raudenbush, S.W., Bryk, A.S.: Hierarchical Linear Models: Applications and Data Analysis Methods, 2nd edn. Sage Publications, Newbury Park (2002)

Improving Math Learning through Intelligent Tutoring and Basic Skills Training

Ivon Arroyo[1], Beverly Park Woolf[1], James M. Royer[2], Minghui Tai[3], and Sara English[3]

[1] Department of Computer Science
[2] Department of Psychology
[3] School of Education
University of Massachusetts, Amherst Mass. 01002
{bev,ivon}@cs.umass.edu, royer@psych.umass.edu,
minghui_tai@yahoo.com, senglish@educ.umass.edu

Abstract. We studied the effectiveness of a math fact fluency tool integrated with an intelligent tutor as a means to improve student performance in math standardized tests. The study evaluated the impact of Math Facts Retrieval Training (MFRT) on 250 middle school students and analyzed the main effects of the training by itself and also as a supplement to the Wayang Tutoring System on easy and hard items of the test. Efficacy data shows improved student performance on tests and positive impact on mathematics learning. We also report on interaction effects of MFRT with student gender and incoming math ability.

Keywords: Math Fluency, Intelligent Tutoring Systems, Classroom Experiments.

1 Motivation

Memory retrieval is an important skill in mathematics development since problem solving takes place in a cognitive system constrained by a limited capacity of working memory [1]. Many students have problems in mathematics in part because they are slow and/or inaccurate in retrieval of simple math facts from memory. Training the speed and accuracy of math fact retrieval (MFR) skills has been shown to be effective for students with learning disabilities, who may show number processing inefficiencies [2]. We studied how to impact students' learning through training this mathematical fluency, using software modules that supplement a traditional mathematics tutoring system.

One hypothesis is that training math facts retrieval would help female students in particular. An affective gender gap towards mathematics increases as children progress through the school system, and despite equal performance in mathematics classes and on individual mathematics projects [3][4], girls lose interest in math-related careers [4][5]. In addition, girls have consistently under-performed boys on time-based standardized tests in mathematics (e.g. SAT-M) and this underperformance has been particularly pronounced among higher-than-average-achieving girls [6].

The cognitive difference of girls' underachievement in timed tests compared to males has been mainly attributed to differences in spatial abilities [7], memory retrieval skills [8] and strategy use. Gender differences in strategy use have been found in the first grades of elementary school, suggesting that girls continue to use concrete strategies to solve arithmetic problems (finger counting) while boys move on to using retrieval from memory [10]. Continuing to use concrete strategies like these make math tougher for girls when they move on to more abstract topics and timed tests. Gender differences in mathematics performance do not appear to be biological [11], as even those basic skills can be trained and computational fluency can be enhanced with software-based interventions [12]. However, the advantages of using computer-based tools to train mathematics fact retrieval skills and their impact on mathematics achievement have not yet been fully investigated.

In addition, students with mild cognitive disabilities, and/or emotional disturbances also are under-represented in mathematics-intensive careers and fail to take additional mathematics classes. Learning disabilities (LD) do appear to have a biological basis and there is evidence that students with LD have concrete difficulties with working memory as well as executive control of math problems and procedural knowledge [1]. As a result, many students with LD may also persist in using counting strategies (e.g., finger counting)[13], take longer to solve arithmetic problems and perform poorly in classrooms and on high-stakes standards-based tests [6]. This population is poorly reached by traditional methods and has a large negative impact on society in terms of lost potential by not being educated to their maximum potential. Learning disability is a complex multi-factor problem and educational institutions do not provide potent cost-effective instruction tailored to the individual.

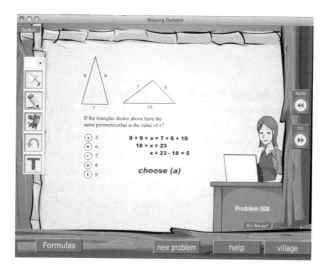

Fig. 1. The Wayang Tutoring System. Gendered affective learning companions talk to students about the need to practice and to exert effort.

2 The Math Fact Retrieval Hypothesis

The math fact retrieval (MFR) hypothesis suggests that the speed of math fact retrieval, defined as an individual's ability to "automatically retrieve correct answers to addition, subtraction, multiplication and division problems," is a source of this gap [8]. If students can quickly and automatically retrieve math facts while taking a mathematics test, for example, they will have more cognitive capacity to devote to higher-level problem-solving activities and will also be able to complete the test more quickly. This hypothesis has been explored as one source for the math performance gap for women and low performing students. The speed of math-fact retrieval is a significant predictor of middle school students' performance on mathematics tests and of college students' performance on the mathematics portion of a standardized college admissions test [8]. Males are not inherently faster than females at retrieving facts from memory, as females tend to show an advantage when retrieval speed was measured for word-naming and sentence understanding tasks (i.e., verbal processing tasks instead of mathematics tasks). In addition, the gap can be reduced, as a group of participants were allowed to practice math fact retrieval before measuring their speed, and the gap seemed to disappear among both Chinese students living in the U.S. and Chinese students living in Hong Kong, though not for a group of U.S. students [8].

We hypothesized that training students in mathematics fact retrieval (MFR) every day before using the Wayang math tutoring system would improve their learning, because it would free up cognitive resources that could be used for learning new math skills. We used a fact retrieval drill and practice system to provide interventions that emphasized fast and accurate mathematics fact retrieval along with an intelligent tutor, as described next.

3 The Wayang Tutor and MFR Training Software

The **Wayang Outpost** multimedia web-based math tutoring software is an adaptive multimedia tutoring system that teaches students how to solve geometry, statistics and algebra problems of the type that commonly appear on standardized tests [14]. To answer problems in the Wayang interface, students choose a solution from a list of multiple choice options, see Figure 1. Wayang provides immediate feedback on students' entries by coloring them red or green in the interface. As students solve a problem, they can ask the tutor for hints that are displayed in a progression from general suggestions to bottom-out solution. In addition to this domain-based help, the tutor provides a wide range of meta-cognitive and affective support, delivered by learning companions or agents designed to act like peers who care about a student's progress and offer support and advice [15,16]. The learning companions' interventions are tailored to each student's needs according to two models [16]. A simple *effort* model is used to assess the degree of effort a student invests to develop a problem solution, and is based on time per action. A linear regression *affect* model is used to assess a student's emotional state; this model is derived from data obtained from sensors, models and surveys [16][18].

General results showed that low performing students who used Wayang improved at standardized tests compared to matched groups that did not use the tutoring software. In addition, students of lower than median math ability learned more than students of high ability. Similarly positive results indicate that, while all students improve their liking of and self-concept in math when they used affective pedagogical agents in the tutor, women high school students responded to affective pedagogical agents better than did male students.

The Math Facts Retrieval Training software is commercially available based on more than 20 years of laboratory research with problem learners [17]. The software provides *training* and *assessment*. In the training phase, students study full digital pages of math facts (e.g. two operand addition/subtraction/multiplication/division of at most two digit numbers). Students click on each item to hear the answer (to learn or confirm that their guess was right). In the assessment phase, students are tested for their accuracy and speed (at the millisecond level). Students speak out the answer aloud and immediately hit the space bar, after which the correct answer is spoken back to the student. Students were instructed to code if their answers were right or wrong. Cheating was not an issue as the goal was to have students think of the answers in their head and hear the feedback. At the end of the assessment session, students saw a line chart that showed their progress (in speed and accuracy) compared to the previous assessment session, Figure 2. Students frequently became faster as they worked on more pages and progress charts showed their decline in speed, which was a motivation to "go for another round." While students generally demonstrate ceiling effects on accuracy, MFR speed predicts performance on SAT-M problems [8]. This software for *math fluency* was based on similar software for *reading fluency*, created with a similar working memory limitation hypothesis and especially used with children who had dyslexia.

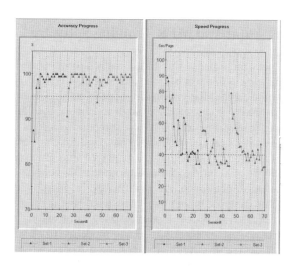

Fig. 2. Student accuracy (left) and speed (right) as displayed in progress charts in the Math Facts Retrieval Training Software

4 Empirical Studies Using the Tutor and Basic Skills Training

A Spring 2009 study evaluated the impact of using the Wayang Tutor and Math Facts Retrieval Training with 250 middle School students enrolled in a public school in Western Massachusetts, United States. The objective was to analyze the main effects of MFR by itself and as a supplement to the Wayang Math Tutoring System.

Conditions and Subjects. Middle schools students (7th and 8th graders) were randomly assigned to one of four conditions: 1) Use of Wayang Tutor after working on the MFR Training software for 15 minutes (Wayang-MFR); 2) use of Wayang Tutor alone (Wayang-noMFR); 3) Use of the MFR Training software (noWayang-MFR) and then use of other modules and web sites (e.g., National Library of Virtual Manipulatives) that did not tutor; and 4) classroom instruction instead of software instruction or use of math web sites (noWayang-noMFR). All students had similar exposure time to the software or math class. The existence of six classes of each grade created a challenge to match classes to each condition. As a result, either two 7th grade classes and one 8th grade class were assigned to the same condition, or two 8th grade classes and one 7th grade class.

Procedure. The first and last (fourth) day of the study, students completed a mathematics mock standardized test (counterbalanced, so that half of students received test A for the pretest and the other half received test B for pretest; the last day tests were reversed for the posttest). Tests A and B were similar in difficulty and consisted of a combination of easy, medium and hard items that addressed skills covered throughout the tutoring system. Students also completed a pretest of computation items (addition, subtraction, multiplication and division) online and their accuracy and speed to answer was recorded. The last day, students completed a math facts retrieval posttest within the MFR software. Speed and accuracy at individual items and averages across items were recorded. Students also completed the mock-standardized test that they had not taken the first day (A or B). Students using the MFR software used the quiz-game modules, drilling on single digit multiplication tables, single digit addition, double and single digit subtraction, and double digit by single digit division, in the fashion described in the previous section, for about 15 minutes every day. Students using the Wayang software were directed to the tutoring module (after MFR training in the case of the Wayang-MFR group), where they progressed through 9 topics, practicing in each of the problems assigned via an adaptive pedagogical module. Students were encouraged to request hints via the help button and to remember that the goal was to learn from the software. Students with learning disabilities were identified by the fact that they had Individual Educational Plans (IEP) [18].

Expected Outcomes. We expected the following outcomes: 1) improved performance on the mock-standardized posttest for the cohort who received MFR training, compared to those who did not; 2) improved performance for students in the Wayang conditions compared to the no-Wayang conditions; 3) improved performance for female students doing MFR training, compared to those females who did not train MFR; 4) improved performance for low achievement and students with LD doing MFR training, compared low achievement students who did not train MFR.

However, realistically, we were hesitant to predict that 15 minute blocks of MFR training during 2-3 days would produce improved results at retrieval. In addition, we were also concerned that taking time away from Wayang for MFR training would be detrimental to learning from Wayang.

5 Experimental Results

Despite of the limited exposure time to Wayang, the two groups that received tutoring during days 1, 2 and 3, improved in the math test by an overall 3%. This is not much compared to our past studies, but it is reasonable considering that the average student went through half of the topics in the system, and that it was the first time that Wayang was used with middle school students (7th and 8th grades). Interestingly, students in the no-Wayang groups actually decreased performance, indicating perhaps that students in general did not want to take yet another test and were less careful during the posttest than during the pretest (see Figure 3). The effect size for Wayang vs. no-Wayang groups (Cohen's d) was 0.39.

The group with highest scores at posttest time was the Wayang-MFR group, which received both Wayang and MFR training. Wayang helped students improve (or maintain, in the case of easy items) their math test performance compared to the no-Wayang control groups. An ANCOVA for posttest percent correct, with pretest score as a covariate and Wayang [yes/no] and MFR[yes/no] as fixed factors, revealed the following: a significant effect for Wayang on posttest performance ($F(222,1)=3.8$, $p=.05$), a non-significant effect on Math Fact Retrieval Training ($p=.97$), and a

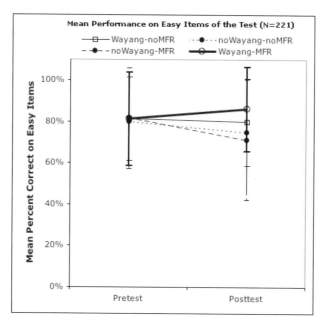

Fig. 3. Pretest and Posttest performance on easy items of the test

significant interaction effect for Wayang x MFR (F(222,1)=7.9, p=.005) suggesting a differential impact of a combination of MFR Training and Wayang on student improvement.

We analyzed the improvement of students for easy and hard items separately, in part, because, students did quite well in the pretest (the overall test was too easy for them). We generated two pretest and posttest scores for the half "easier" and "harder" items of each of the tests, depending on general performance at each item at pretest time, across the whole population of students. Items in the test were split into easy and hard items depending on pretest performance at each item, across the whole population, and scores were computed separately --as if there were two pre and post-tests, an easy and a hard one (see Figures 3 and 4). In addition, because we wanted to analyze the impact of the interventions on gender and students with learning disability, we analyzed the following fixed factors: Wayang, MFR, Gender and MathAbility [low or high achievement[1]].

For EASY items, an ANCOVA revealed a significant effect for Wayang alone (F(221,1)=10.6, p=.001); a non-significant effect for MFR alone (F(221,1)=.1, p=.7); a significant main effect for MathAbility (F(221,1)=14.7, p<.001); and a significant interaction effect for WayangxMFR (F(221,1)=5.1, p=.025). While a significant interaction effect reveals that at least two of the means are different (corresponding to the four groups defined by the combinations of MFR[yes/no] and Wayang[yes/no]), it is not clear which group(s) are better and which are worse. Bonferroni confidence intervals allow to answer specific questions such as whether one of the treatments is better than the rest, or whether two of the groups are better than the other two. For instance, Bonferroni confidence intervals revealed that the Wayang-MFR group had significantly highest improvement (higher than the other three groups), and that both

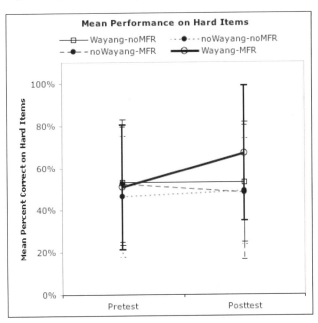

Fig. 4. Pretest and Posttest Performance on Hard items of the test

Wayang groups scored higher on easy items of the posttest than the no-Wayang groups. However, confidence intervals also revealed that the Wayang-MFR group did not do significantly better than Wayang-noMFR group, suggesting that *MFR Training does not help to significantly improve performance on easy items.* Wayang seems better at doing that.

For HARD items, the ANCOVA revealed again a significant effect for Wayang ($F(222,1)=6.8$, $p=.01$); a non-significant effect for MFR alone ($F(222,1)=.5$, $p=.5$; and a significant effect for Wayang x MFR ($F(222,1)=6.8$, $p=.009$). Confidence intervals revealed that the Wayang-MFR group had significantly highest improvement than the other three groups on hard items, and that both Wayang groups scored higher at hard items than the other two no-Wayang groups. Bonferroni confidence intervals also revealed that the Wayang-MFR group did do better than the Wayang-noMFR group, suggesting that *MFR training did help to improve performance on hard items* for students who used Wayang.

An interpretation of these results is that being more math fluent (thanks to the MFR training) frees up cognitive resources that are essential to approach hard math problems. Easy items don't require as many cognitive resources, so the math fluency training did not make a difference in performance at these easy items.

The advantage of the Wayang-MFR group can be attributed to MFR training *only if* students in the MFR groups had gotten faster at retrieving those simple math facts from memory. Thus, we analyzed the gain in MFR posttest speed and accuracy of students who received Math Facts training compared to those who did not, Figure 5. Given that pretest and posttest accuracy was at ceiling (reasonably, students were highly accurate at simple arithmetic operations), we analyzed only speed --whether students had gotten faster. We ran an ANCOVA for Math Facts Speed Posttest (a mean speed for all items in the MFR Posttest for each student) with Math Facts Speed Pretest as a covariate, and MFR[Yes/No] and Wayang[Yes/No] as fixed factors. The result was a highly significant effect for MFR ($F(197, 1)=13.9$, $p<.001$). Figure 5, shows that students who received MFR training were faster to answer those simple math facts at posttest time. A significant effect for Wayang ($F(197,1)=8.6$, $p=.023$) was unexpected, and suggests that using Wayang helps students be more math fluent, faster at retrieving simple math facts from memory.

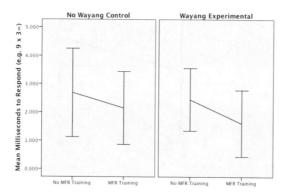

Fig. 5. Students who received MFR Training became faster at responding to simple arithmetic questions. Means and SD.

6 Discussion

Despite the limited exposure to the software (3 days), the Math Facts Retrieval Training software combined with the Wayang tutor effectively improved students performance on a standardized test and specifically improved learning on hard questions. Hard items on these tests generally involved several steps and much computation, and MFR training probably freed up memory resources that were used to think about the problem. In addition, a ceiling effect for easy items might have made that score harder to improve.

While the Wayang main effect did not surprise us, as we had evidence that Wayang can improve performance for standardized test items even with short amounts of exposure, the improvement in students' speed to retrieve simple arithmetic operation answers from memory due to Wayang was unexpected. The repeated need of computation to solve these problems may be attributed to the math facts retrieval speed improvement.

Math Facts Retrieval Training alone (without Wayang) *did not* help middle school students perform better at standardized test items, suggesting that MFR training should be supplemented with appropriate instruction on the test topics for such training to have a real impact on math standardized tests scores. Wayang tutoring seemed better than the alternative math computer activities that students used in the no-Wayang groups. The fact that the noWayang-noMFR group did somewhat better than the noWayang-MFR group can be partly attributed to classroom instruction: a large group of the students in the noWayang-noMFR group had their regular math class, and the teacher covered some of the same topics taught by the tutor during math class.

The lack of gender effects, math ability effects, or interaction effects involving gender or math ability suggest that MFR Training was highly effective for all students, not only for females or low achieving students. We conclude that MFR Training software is an invaluable supplement to traditional math intelligent tutoring software, for students of all levels, both females and males. We plan to continue to include this basic skills training within our mathematics intelligent tutoring system.

Acknowledgement. This research was funded by a NSF grant, What kind of Math Software works for Girls? Arroyo, I. (PI) with Royer, J.M. and Woolf, B.P. (#0734060, HRD GSE/RES), and a grant from the US Department of Education, Institute of Education (IES) Using Intelligent Tutoring and Universal Design To Customize The Mathematics Curriculum, to Woolf (PI) with Arroyo, Maloy co-PIs. Any opinions, findings, conclusions or recommendations expressed in this material are those of the authors and do not necessarily reflect the views of the funding agencies.

References

1. Geary, D.C., Hoard, M.K., Byrd-Craven, J., Nugent, L., Numtee, C.: Cognitive Mechanisms Underlying Achievement Deficits in Children With Mathematical Learning Disability. Child Development 78(4), 1343–1359 (2007)
2. Royer, J.M., Tronsky, L.N.: Addition practice with math disabled students improves subtraction and multiplication performance. In: Scruggs, T.E., Mastropieri, M.A. (eds.) Advances in Learning and Behavioral Disabilities, pp. 185–218. JAI Press, CT (1998)

3. Catsambis, S.: The path to math: Gender and racial-ethnic differences in mathematics participation from middle school to high school. Sociology of Educ. 67, 199–215 (1994)
4. Catsambis, S.: The gender gap in mathematics: Merely a step function? In: Gallagher, A.M., Kaufman, J.C. (eds.) Gender differences in mathematics, pp. 220–245. Cambridge University Press, Cambridge (2005)
5. Midgeley, C., Feldlaufer, H., Eccles, J.: Student/teacher relations and attitudes toward mathematics before and after the transition to junior high school. Child Development 60, 981–992 (1989)
6. Olson, L.: State Test Programs Mushroom as NCLB Mandate Kicks. In: Education Week, November 30 (2005)
7. Casey, M., Nuttall, R., Pezaris, E., Benbow, C.: The influence of spatial ability on gender differences in math college entrance test scores across diverse samples. Developmental Psychology 31, 697–705 (1995)
8. Royer, J.M., Tronsky, L.N., Chan, Y., Jackson, S.J., Marchant, H.G.: Math fact retrieval as the cognitive mechanism underlying gender differences in math test performance. Contemp. Educational Psychology 24, 181–266 (1999)
9. Eccles, J., Wigfield, A., Harold, R.D., Blumenfeld, P.: Age and gender differences in children's self and task perceptions during elementary school. Child Development 64, 830–847 (1993)
10. Carr, M., Jessup, D.: Gender Differences in First-Grade Mathematics Strategy Use: Social and Metacognitive Influences. Journal of Ed. Psychology 89(2), 318–328 (1997)
11. Beal, C.R.: Boys and girls: the development of gender roles. McGraw-Hill, New York (1993)
12. Royer, J.M., Garofoli, L.: Cognitive contributions to sex differences in math performance. In: Gallagher, A.M., Kaufman, J.C. (eds.) Gender differences in mathematics, pp. 99–120. Cambridge University Press, Cambridge (2005)
13. Fletcher, J., Lyon, G., Fuchs, L., Barnes, M.: Learning disabilities: From identification to intervention. The Guilford Press, New York (2007)
14. Arroyo, I., Beal, C.R., Bergman, A., Lindenmuth, M., Marshall, D., Woolf, B.P.: Intelligent Tutoring for high-stakes achievement tests. In: 11th International Conference on Artificial Intelligence in Education, pp. 142–169. IOS Press, Amsterdam (2003)
15. Arroyo, I., Woolf, B.P., Royer, J.M., Tai, M.: Affective Gendered Learning Companions. In: 14th International Conference on Artificial Intelligence and Education, pp. 41–48. IOS Press, Amsterdam (2009)
16. Arroyo, I., Cooper, D.G., Burleson, W., Woolf, B.P., Muldner, K., Christopherson, R.: Emotion Sensors Go To School. In: 14th International Conference on Artificial Intelligence and Education, pp. 17–24. IOS Press, Amsterdam (2009)
17. Reading Success Lab, http://ReadingSuccessLab.com
18. Arroyo, I., Woolf, B., Muldner, K., Burleson, W., Cooper, D., Razzaq, L., Dolan, R.: The Effect of Motivational Learning Companions on Low-Achieving Students and Students with Learning Disabilities. In: Aleven, V., Kay, J., Mostow, J. (eds.) ITS 2010, Part I. LNCS, vol. 6094, pp. 327–337. Springer, Heidelberg (2010)

Author Index

Aagard, Hans   II-281
Adam, Jean-Michel   II-380
Agapito, Jenilyn   II-263
Aghaei Pour, Payam   I-264
Ai, Hua   I-156, II-134
Aïmeur, Esma   II-340
Aist, Gregory   I-65, II-451
Albrechtsen, Justin S.   II-144
Alcañiz, Mariano   I-296
Aleven, Vincent   I-115, I-174, I-413, II-221, II-438
Allbritton, David   I-204
Altman, Max   II-346
AlZoubi, Omar   I-264
Anglo, Elizabeth A.   II-260
Anwar, Faisal   II-209
Arnott-Hill, Elizabeth   I-204
Arroyo, Ivon   I-327, I-423
Ashish, Naveen   II-352
Ashley, Kevin D.   I-95
Auerbach, Daniel   I-274
Azevedo, Roger   I-369

Baid, Palak   II-209
Bain, Michael   II-266
Bajanki, Sirisha   II-443
Baker, Ryan S.J.d.   I-25, II-263, II-321, II-445, II-455
Barnes, Tiffany   II-31, II-215, II-233, II-239
Beck, Joseph E.   I-35, I-194, II-254, II-321, II-399, II-439
Beek, Wouter   II-272, II-448
Ben-Naim, Dror   II-266, II-440
Bernardini, Andrea   I-125
Beuth, Jack L.   I-156
Bey, Juliet   II-451
Bieliková, Mária   II-423
Biswas, Gautam   II-405
Blanchard, Emmanuel G.   II-269
Blessing, Stephen B.   II-365
Bodnar, Stephen   II-352
Boonthum, Chutima   II-349
Bowen, Kyle   II-281

Boyer, Kristy Elizabeth   I-55
Boyle, Roger   II-443
Brandão, Leônidas O.   II-447
Bredeweg, Bert   II-272, II-448
Britt, Anne   II-327
Broisin, Julien   II-402
Brown, Christopher   II-315
Brown, Jennifer   II-178
Bühling, René   II-272, II-448
Bull, Susan   II-275
Burleson, Winslow   I-184, I-327
Butcher, Kirsten R.   II-278, II-414

Cade, Whitney   II-178
Cai, Zhiqiang   II-327
Calvo, Rafael A.   I-45, I-264
Capeli, Olimpio M.   II-92
Castine, Melissa   I-338, II-441
Cetintas, Suleyman   I-15, II-281
Chae, Hui Soo   II-209
Chaffar, Soumaya   II-285
Chakravarty, Sugato   II-281
Chalfoun, Pierre   II-288
Champaign, John   II-212
Chaouachi, Maher   II-291
Chauncey, Amber   I-369
Chen, Lin   II-315
Chen, Wei   I-65, II-451
Chi, Michelene T.H.   I-401
Chi, Min   I-224
Christopherson, Robert M.   I-327
Cocea, Mihaela   II-330
Cohen, Robin   II-212
Cohen, William W.   I-317, II-368, II-449
Combs, Rebekah   I-245
Conati, Cristina   I-125
Connelly, John   II-446, II-452, II-453
Contero, Manuel   I-296
Cooper, David G.   I-327
Corbett, Al   II-451
Core, Mark G.   I-274
Courtemanche, François   II-340
Cox, Richard   II-224
Cristea, Alexandra I.   II-82

Crowley, Rebecca   I-338, II-441
Croy, Marvin   II-31
Curran, James R.   II-303

Daigle, Rosaire   I-245
Dailey, Matthew D.   II-41
Dalmon, Danilo L.   II-447
de Albuquerque, Antonio R.P.L.   II-92
de Freitas, Sara   II-393
Delgado Kloos, Carlos   II-384
Demi, Sandy   II-455
Dempsey, Kyle   II-294
Derbali, Lotfi   II-297
Dickison, Daniel   II-300
Dietrich, Michael   II-420
Di Eugenio, Barbara   II-72, II-315
Dimitriva, Vania   II-443
D'Mello, Sidney   I-245, I-264, II-1, II-62, II-178, II-456
Dolan, Robert   I-327
Dominguez, Anna Katrina   II-303
Dragon, Toby   II-113, II-444
Drummond, Joanna   II-306
Duan, Weisi   II-451
Duke, Nell   II-451
Dunwell, Ian   II-393
Duong, Minh   II-451

Eagle, Michael   II-215
Easterday, Matthew W.   II-218
English, Sara   I-423

Feenstra, Laurens   II-221
Feng, Mingyu   II-309, II-312
Finger, Susan   II-387
Floryan, Mark   II-113, II-444
Forbes-Riley, Kate   I-379
Forbes-Summers, Elijah   I-194
Forsyth, Carol   II-327
Fortin, Mikaël   II-236
Fossati, Davide   II-315
Foss, Jonathan G.K.   II-82
Fournier-Viger, Philippe   II-318
Frasson, Claude   II-11, II-285, II-288, II-291, II-297, II-337

Garcia Garcia, Grecia   II-224
Gates, Donna   II-451
Giguere, Stephen   II-321
Gilbert, Stephen   II-365

Girard, Sylvie   I-307
Gluga, Richard   I-85, II-227
Gobert, Janice D.   II-257, II-445
Goguadze, George   II-420
Goldin, Ilya M.   I-95
Goldstein, Adam B.   I-25
Gómez Pérez, Asunción   II-272, II-448
Gong, Yue   I-35, I-194
González, José P.   II-451
Gounon, Patricia   II-324
Gracia del Río, Jorge   II-272, II-448
Graesser, Art   I-245, II-327
Gratch, Jonathan   I-165
Grzybicki, Dana   I-338
Gutierrez-Santos, Sergio   I-105, II-330
Gweon, Gahgene   II-387

Haciahmetoglu, Yonca   II-334
Haddawy, Peter   I-75
Ha, Eun Young   I-55
Halpern, Diane   II-327
Harris, Thomas K.   II-300
Hastings, Peter   I-204
Hausmann, Robert G.M.   II-300, II-446, II-452, II-453
Hays, Matthew J.   I-274
Hays, Patrick   II-178
Heffernan, Neil T.   I-25, I-35, I-194, I-349, II-41, II-254, II-309, II-312, II-399, II-439
Heraz, Alicia   II-337
Hirashima, Tsukasa   II-343
Hong, Yuan-Jin   II-269
Hord, Casey   I-15
Howley, Iris K.   II-230
Hussain, M. Sazzad   I-264

Ingram, Amy   I-55
Ishikawa, Masatoshi   I-135
Isotani, Naoko   II-92
Isotani, Sadao   II-92
Isotani, Seiji   II-92, II-346, II-447

Jackson, G. Tanner   II-294, II-349
Johan, Rasyidi   II-275
Johnson, Hilary   I-307
Johnson, Matthew   II-233, II-275
Johnson, W. Lewis   I-165, II-352, II-454
Jones, Christopher   I-174
Jordan, Pamela   II-72

Jraidi, Imène II-11
Juarez, Octavio II-451
Judd, Andrew II-21
Jukic, Drazen I-338
Jung, Sung-Young II-355

Kabanza, Froduald II-51, II-251
Kang, Jeon-Hyung II-359
Kantorzyk, Martin II-451
Kashihara, Akihiro I-389
Kato, Yukari I-135
Katz, Sandra II-72
Kawai, Ryoya I-389
Kayashima, Michiko II-362
Kay, Judy I-85
Kazi, Hameedullah I-75
Keiser, Victoria I-317, II-449
Kersey, Cynthia II-72
Kim, Jihie II-188, II-359
Kim, Julia I-174
Klahr, David II-198, II-408
Kodavali, Sateesh Kumar II-365
Koedinger, Kenneth R. I-115, I-145, I-214, I-317, II-312, II-368, II-449, II-455
Kopp, Kris II-327
Kumar, Amruth N. I-359
Kumar, Rohit I-156, II-134

Lagud, Maria Carminda V. I-255
Lajoie, Susanne P. II-242, II-269
Lane, H. Chad I-274, II-144
Lau, Lydia II-443
Lebeau, Jean-François II-236, II-248, II-450
Leber, Brett II-438, II-455
Lee, Seung Y. II-155
Lee-Shim, Kris II-275
Legowski, Elizabeth I-338
Lehman, Blair I-245, II-1
Lepp, Dmitri II-396
Leroux, Pascal II-324
Lester, James C. I-55, I-285, II-155, II-166
Lever, Tim I-85
Liem, Jochem II-272, II-448
Limongelli, Carla II-371
Li, Nan II-368
Linnebank, Floris II-272, II-448
Lipschultz, Michael II-374

Litman, Diane I-224, I-379, II-306, II-374, II-429
Liu, Liu II-451
Liu, Ming I-45
Li, Yuanpeng II-451
Lloyd, Tim II-275
Loll, Frank II-377
Looi, Chee-Kit I-1, II-426
Luengo, Vanda II-380

Mabbott, Andrew II-275
Madran, Nadine II-380
Magaro, Cressida II-198, II-408
Magoulas, George I-105, II-330
Ma, Jun II-188
Marcus, Nadine II-266
Marsella, Stacy I-2
Martín-Gutiérrez, Jorge I-296
Matsuda, Noboru I-317, II-449
Maull, Keith II-245, II-278
Mavrikis, Manolis I-105
Mayers, André II-236, II-248, II-318, II-450
McCuaig, Judi II-21
McKeown, Margaret II-451
McLaren, Bruce M. II-346, II-377, II-420
McNamara, Danielle S. II-294, II-349
McQuiggan, Scott I-285
Medvedeva, Olga I-338
Meissner, Christian A. II-144
Melis, Erica II-420
Mephu Nguifo, Engelbert II-318
Meyer, Ann-Kristin II-420
Michael, Stephen W. II-144
Michelet, Sandra II-380
Millis, Keith II-327
Mitamura, Teruko I-214
Mizoguchi, Riichiro II-92, II-362
Moguel, Patrice II-123
Montalvo, Orlando II-445
Mostafavi, Behrooz II-239
Mostow, Jack I-65, II-451
Mott, Bradford W. II-155, II-166
Mowery, Dana II-198, II-408
Mpondo Eboa, Franck Hervé II-340
Muldner, Kasia I-184, I-327
Muñoz-Merino, Pedro J. II-384
Muñoz-Organero, Mario II-384

Murray, R. Charles   II-300, II-446, II-452, II-453
Murray, Tom   II-113, II-444

Nabos, Julieta   II-263
Nagasunder, Amrut   II-134
Naismith, Laura   II-242, II-269
Natriello, Gary   II-209
Neagle, Royce   II-443
Nguyen, Dong   II-134, II-387
Nixon, Tristan   II-300
Nkambou, Roger   II-318

Oberoi, Sharad V.   II-387
Ogan, Amy   I-174
Ohlsson, Stellan   II-315
Okoye, Ifeyinwa   II-245, II-278
Olney, Andrew M.   II-178, II-390, II-456

Panzoli, David   II-393
Paquette, Luc   II-236, II-248, II-450
Pardos, Zachary A.   II-41
Pavlik Jr., Philip   II-103
Pearlstein, Mike   II-21
Perkins, Lydia   I-245
Person, Natalie   I-235, II-1
Petridis, Panagiotis   II-393
Phillips, Robert   I-55
Pinkwart, Niels   II-377
Prank, Rein   II-396

Quek, Francis   II-334
Qureshi, Adam   II-393

Raab, Stephen   I-338
Rahati, Amin   II-51, II-251
Rai, Dovan   II-254, II-399, II-439
Raizada, Rohan   I-317, II-449
Ramandalahy, Triomphe   II-402
Rankin, Jim   II-455
Rau, Martina A.   I-413
Raziuddin, Juelaila J.   II-257
Razzaq, Leena   I-349
Rebolledo-Mendez, Genaro   II-393
Renkl, Alexander   I-3
Repalam, Ma. Concepcion   II-263
Reyes Jr., Salvador S.   II-263
Ritter, Steven   I-4, II-300, II-446, II-452, II-453
Robison, Jennifer   I-285

Rodrigo, Ma. Mercedes T.   I-255, II-260, II-263
Roll, Ido   I-115
Rosé, Carolyn Penstein   I-156, II-134, II-230, II-387
Rowe, Jonathan P.   II-166
Royer, James M.   I-423
Roy, Marguerite   I-401
Rummel, Nikol   I-145, I-413, II-221
Rus, Vasile   I-45

Sagae, Alicia   II-352
Salles, Paulo   II-272
Sao Pedro, Michael A.   II-257, II-445
Saunders, Kevin   II-454
Scheuer, Oliver   II-377
Schneider, Mike   II-144
Sciarrone, Filippo   II-371
Segedy, James   II-405
Sewall, Jonathan   II-438
Shaw, Erin   II-188, II-359
Shores, Lucy R.   II-166
Siler, Stephanie   II-198, II-408
Si, Luo   I-15, II-281
Skogsholm, Alida   II-455
Sottilare, Robert A.   II-411
Stamper, John   II-31, II-455
Stylianides, Gabriel   I-317, II-449
Suebnukarn, Siriwan   I-75
Sulcer, Brian   II-405
Sullins, Jeremiah   I-245
Sumner, Tamara   II-245, II-278, II-414

Taatgen, Niels   II-221
Tai, Minghui   I-423
Tchounikine, Pierre   II-123
Temperini, Marco   II-371
Thomas, James M.   II-417
Toth, Joe   II-103
Toto, Ermal   II-445
Towle, Brendon   II-300, II-446, II-452, II-453
Tricot, André   II-123
Trotochaud, Christina   II-451
Tseytlin, Eugene   I-338, II-441
Tsovaltzi, Dimitra   II-420
Tu, Arthur   I-317
Tvarožek, Jozef   II-423

Valeri, Joe   II-451
Van de Sande, Brett   I-184

VanLehn, Kurt   I-184, I-224, II-355
Vaste, Giulia   II-371
Velan, Gary   II-266
Vidal, Philippe   II-402
Vogt, Kimberly   I-245
Volgas, Nick   I-235
Vouk, Mladen   I-55

Wagner, Lynn   I-338
Waki, Hiromi   II-343
Walker, Erin   I-145
Walker, Sean   I-145
Wallace, Patty   II-327
Wallis, Michael   I-55
Wang, Ning   I-165
Weinstein, Anders   II-451
Wetzler, Philipp   II-414
Williams, Betsy   I-235
Williams, Claire   I-235, II-62, II-178
Willows, Kevin   II-198, II-408

Wiseman, Jeffrey   II-269
Wißner, Michael   II-272, II-448
Woolf, Beverly Park   I-5, I-327, I-423, II-113, II-444
Wu, Longkai   II-426
Wylie, Ruth   I-214

Xin, Yan Ping   I-15
Xiong, Wenting   II-429

Yacef, Kalina   II-303
Yamamoto, Sho   II-343
Yen, David   II-451
Yoo, Jungsoon   II-432
Yoo, Sung   II-432
Young, R. Michael   II-417
Yuan, Brian   I-235

Zapata-Rivera, Diego   II-435

Printing: Mercedes-Druck, Berlin
Binding: Stein+Lehmann, Berlin